A Topsy-Turvy World

For a complete list of books in the series,
please see the Columbia University Press website.

A Topsy-Turvy World

SHORT PLAYS AND FARCES FROM THE MING AND QING DYNASTIES

EDITED AND INTRODUCED BY

WILT L. IDEMA,
WAI-YEE LI,
AND STEPHEN H. WEST

COLUMBIA UNIVERSITY PRESS NEW YORK

Columbia University Press wishes to express its appreciation for assistance given by the Pushkin Fund in the publication of this book.

Columbia University Press
Publishers Since 1893
New York   Chichester, West Sussex
cup.columbia.edu

Library of Congress Cataloging-in-Publication Data
Names: Idema, W. L. (Wilt L.), editor of compilation. | Li, Wai-yee, editor of compilation. | West, Stephen H., editor of compilation.
Title: A topsy-turvy world : short plays and farces from the Ming and Qing dynasties / Wilt L. Idema, Wai-yee Li, Stephen H. West.
Description: New York : Columbia University Press, 2023. | Series: Translations from the Asian classics | Includes bibliographical references.
Identifiers: LCCN 2023002097 (print) | LCCN 2023002098 (ebook) | ISBN 9780231208963 (hardback) | ISBN 9780231208970 (trade paperback) | ISBN 9780231557719 (ebook)
Subjects: LCSH: Chinese drama—Ming dynasty, 1368–1644—Translations into English. | Chinese drama—Qing dynasty, 1644–1912—Translations into English.
Classification: LCC PL2596 T67 2023 (print) | LCC PL2596 (ebook) | DDC 895.1/2008—dc23/eng/20230420
LC record available at https://lccn.loc.gov/2023002097
LC ebook record available at https://lccn.loc.gov/2023002098

Cover design: Chang Jae Lee
Cover image: Min Qiji, *The West Room*, China, Wucheng, Zhejiang Province. Museum für Ostasiatische Kunst (R 62,1, Köln). Rheinisches Bildarchiv Cologne, Walz, Sabrina, rba_d012779_19

CONTENTS

INTRODUCTION

WILT L. IDEMA

During the three centuries from roughly 1500 to 1800 (the second part of the Ming dynasty and the first half of the Manchu Qing dynasty), the fully developed form of southern drama known as *chuanqi* 傳奇 dominated the Chinese stage. While old stage favorites dating from the Yuan and early Ming continued to be performed, such as *Pipa ji* 琵琶記 (*The Lute*) by Gao Ming 高明 (fl. 1345),[1] this period witnessed the appearance of the three greatest plays in the *chuanqi* genre: *The Peony Pavilion* (*Mudan ting* 牡丹亭) by Tang Xianzu 湯顯祖 (1550–1616),[2] *Palace of Eternal Life* (*Changsheng dian* 長生殿) by Hong Sheng 洪昇 (1645–1704),[3] and *The Peach Blossom Fan* (*Taohua shan* 桃花扇) by Kong Shangren 孔尚仁 (1648–1718).[4] What strikes Western readers first, when confronted with these works in their full extent, is their exceptional length: because they often involve multistranded plots built around the meeting, separation, and eventual reunion of lovers, *chuanqi* of over forty scenes are not uncommon.[5] But in the shadow of these southern plays, these same three centuries also witnessed a flourishing dramatic literature in shorter genres. Writing for the stage or the study, the playwrights who composed these shorter plays were often quite daring in their experimentation, both in matters of content and of form, creating a large corpus of highly original works that at times not only explored the limits of Chinese performance traditions but also questioned China's social conventions and cultural values with biting wit. So far, only a few of these plays have been made available in English translations. This anthology is the first attempt to introduce a somewhat representative selection of these works to the Anglophone world. As many of the works in this anthology present a reversal of status, expectations, and values, we have called our selection *A Topsy-Turvy World*.

Playacting—the more or less stylized reenactment of a historical or imagined event by one or more persons before an audience—is a universal human characteristic and, in many cultures, this has resulted in more or less formalized traditions of theatrical performance. And such traditions, whether of simple skits or longer plays, often give rise to a dramatic literature at some stage of their development. Good actors are perfectly capable of providing an entertaining show without any written script, however, so theater might have had a tradition of many centuries before the emergence of any dramatic literature. China is one such case. We can trace the history of narrative dance and of entertainers back to the early Zhou dynasty (1045–256 BCE), and the enactment of stories to the Han (206 BCE–220 CE). But while we have a few individual short play texts from the Tang (690–906), we have to wait until the twelfth and thirteenth century before we witness the emergence of a continuous tradition of dramatic literature. When we do, we are immediately confronted with two major mature genres: *nanxi* 南戲 (southern plays, the forerunners of *chuanqi*) in China south of the Huai River, and *zaju* 雜劇 (variety plays) in the big cities of the north.[6]

Written sources (scripts, the descriptions of performances in the capitals of the Northern and Southern Song dynasties, and lists of play titles from the Song and the Jin),[7] as well as archaeological discoveries (from temple stages and inscriptions to paintings and visual materials from graves), testify to the flourishing theatrical culture of China from the eleventh century onward—a theatrical tradition that has continued to develop until the present.[8] Many areas of China throughout the last millennium knew local traditions of short saucy plays (*xiaoxi* 小戲), mostly performed by amateurs; in most cases they have been first committed to paper only in the second part of the twentieth century and tend to be made up mostly of prose. Both *nanxi* and *zaju*, however, presenting more complex stories, are forms of ballad opera musical plays in which numerous arias are performed to existing tunes.

In southern plays, as the genre developed from the twelfth century onward, these preexisting tunes were the popular tunes of southern China. As the genre continued to develop, these became a closed corpus. The Ming dynasty saw the evolution of several regional singing styles, of which Kunqu (associated with the city of Suzhou) would emerge as the most prestigious by the seventeenth century. Southern plays often were made up of tens of scenes and might take two full days to perform. In *nanxi* and its subsequent development, *chuanqi*, any player, by virtue of role type, could be assigned roles singing arias.[9] By contrast, in *zaju* as it suddenly emerged in the second part of the thirteenth century, all arias were in principle assigned to a single role (either a male or female protagonist); these arias were organized in four sets of eight to twenty songs, making for substantial but still much shorter plays.[10]

Throughout the Yuan dynasty *zaju* was the most prestigious genre. It was performed in the commercial theaters of the major cities of northern China and at the Mongol court in Dadu (present-day Beijing).[11] Following the Mongol conquest of the territory of the Southern Song dynasty in the late thirteenth century, *zaju* also was performed in some southern cities such as Hangzhou. Once the Ming dynasty was established in Nanjing, it selected *zaju* for use in court drama, despite the genre's northern origins. At the court, the conventions of *zaju* were further standardized, and the mostly anonymous plays that were composed as court entertainment came to manifest a remarkable uniformity in theme, style, and language. *Zaju* retained its position at court at least until the early seventeenth century.[12] In the south, *zaju* continued to be performed at least until the late sixteenth century in Nanjing, the original and later a secondary capital of the dynasty, by entertainers registered with the Court Entertainment Bureau (Jiaofangsi 教坊司). But when the Jiangnan area, home to such cities such as Nanjing, Suzhou, and Hangzhou, reestablished itself as the economic and cultural center of the Ming Empire in the sixteenth century, local southern plays became the most important theatrical genre there, attracting more and more elite authors during the second half of the dynasty and spreading beyond its area of origin.

As commercial theaters disappeared from big cities in the mid-fifteenth century, most of the population depended on performances during communal festivities for theatrical entertainment. But the same economic growth that supported the development of southern drama also contributed to the growth of private wealth. Increasing numbers of wealthy families began to maintain their own private acting troupes, allowing these rich patrons and their friends to enjoy drama at any time and in any shape they desired. Several owners of "family troupes" were indeed also active playwrights. The popularity of private troupes and their performances at private homes must have been a major factor in the spread of single scene performances (*zhezixi* 折子戲) of popular passages from southern plays.[13] The same popularity of private troupes among the wealthy elite from the sixteenth century onward most likely also played a major role in the emergence of original short plays; these are often set apart as "southern *zaju*" (*nan zaju* 南雜劇). Some of these so-called southern *zaju* do indeed employ southern tunes exclusively or alongside northern tunes; others stick to northern tunes only. And while some southern *zaju* abide by the convention of the four acts of regular *zaju*, others may comprise fewer or more acts that may also intermix northern and southern musical conventions. Although the court playwrights of regular *zaju* and the southern authors of southern plays were creative and experimental in their own way, it can be said that these short plays of the late Ming and early Qing present us with the most original and daring experiments in form and content of dramatic literature between the sixteenth and nineteenth centuries. Until now, translations of early Chinese drama have focused on the regular *zaju* of the Yuan and Ming and on the southern plays of the Yuan to the early Qing. This anthology of short plays cannot present a full range of these southern *zaju*, but we hope that our selection will whet the appetite for more.

Authors could also choose to write short plays in the genre known as *yuanben* 院本 (farce). This term would seem to have referred originally to a broad variety of stage routines, from little skits to more elaborate plays. But following the development of *zaju* in the Yuan dynasty, it came to refer specifically to short skits and comic routines that might be performed independently or included in larger plays. Throughout the Yuan dynasty, playwrights generally appear to have left the words of such routines to the memory and improvisatorial talents of the actors. In some early Ming editions of *zaju*, we may still encounter the stage direction *yuanben* to mark the place in the progress of the play where such a routine should be inserted.[14] The best known example is a passage in Wang Shifu's 王實甫 (ca. 1250–1300) *Xixiang ji* 西廂記 (*Story of the Western Wing*),[15] which in one moment calls for "The Skit of the Two Fighting Quacks" (*Shuangdouyi* 雙鬥醫) to be performed. During the Ming more playwrights started to write out the words of such routines, and so we find the full text for a version of "The Skit of the Two Fighting Quacks" in a court *zaju* of the Ming. This skit is an example of stichomythia, a dispute in which two characters speak in alternating single lines.

Yuanlin wumeng 園林午夢 (*A Noontime Dream in a Garden Grove*), one of two preserved stand-alone skits by Li Kaixian 李開先 (1502–1568) also uses stichomythia in an exchange between two famous female heroines, Cui Yingying 崔鶯鶯 and Li Yaxian 李亞仙, who blame each other for lack of virtue. The first play in this anthology, Li Kaixian's *Dayachan* 打啞禪 (*Cracking a Dumb Chan Riddle*), is built around a dumb show, in which the gestures of a monk, symbolizing the highest truth of Buddhism, are read by a butcher as an offer to sell the monastery's pig. We also encounter one-act plays that call themselves *yuanben* even though they include a number of arias. One example is the repeatedly translated *Zhongshan lang yuanben* 中山狼院本 (*The Skit of the Wolf of Zhongshan*), the dramatic adaptations of a fable that became quite popular in the sixteenth century: The plot involves a Mohist scholar who saves a wolf from its hunters while traveling through the mountains of Zhongshan. But the wolf wants to eat him, claiming that ingratitude is the way of the world. When the scholar protests, the wolf agrees to put their case to three judges. The first two judges, an old apricot tree and an old ox, both side with the wolf. The third judge, however, the local god of the earth, kills the ungrateful wolf. (This fable was also adapted to become a regular *zaju*, but the authorship of both plays remains in dispute).[16]

Xu Wei 徐渭 (1521–1593), the first author to establish his reputation as a dramatist of southern *zaju*, is the second author we feature in this volume. His four plays are collectively known as *Four Cries of a Gibbon* (*Sisheng yuan* 四聲猿). The four cries are represented by four separate plays, one of one act, two of two acts, and one of five acts that uses southern tunes. Once Xu Wei had set the course, others went beyond his example:

> The virtuosic experimentation of *Four Cries of a Gibbon* opened the way to even bolder tinkering with the conventions of northern drama. The northern plays that eventually emerged in the late Ming, written in many cases by southerners and often incorporating southern tunes and rhymes, had little to do with the older form. . . . The old pattern of four acts gave way to a range from one to ten; the convention of one singer per act was similarly modified.[17]

Xu Wei's *Four Cries of a Gibbon* also established the model for many later playwrights to publish their short works under a collective title. Most importantly perhaps, many of the playwrights who emerged in the wake of Xu Wei employed the genre for self-expression as he did, often combining social satire with mordant wit. But other playwrights of the last century of the Ming and beyond used this new-won freedom for the lyric adaptations of famous romantic anecdotes, and in doing so created dramatic works focused on sentiments and lyricism. And as the *zaju* of the Yuan became available in more numerous and more finely printed editions at the same time, still other playwrights reflected their influence by writing more realistic works, including love tragedies. A greater number of *zaju* have been preserved from the seventeenth and eighteenth centuries than from the Yuan and early Ming combined.

Xu Wei was the son of a Chinese official and a Miao slave who was sold off after his birth. Xu failed to carve out a bureaucratic career despite his many talents and became obsessed by issues of personal identity. Two of his plays deal with women, in male disguise, who make a career in the public world—one on the battlefield, the other in the civil bureaucracy. His best known play is probably the one-act *Yuyang sanlong* 漁陽三弄 (*Thrice-Played Yuyang*, also known as *Kuang gushi* 狂鼓史 *The Mad Drummer*), an underworld reenactment of Mi Heng's 禰衡 (173–197) tirade against Cao Cao 曹操 (155–220) when that outspoken literatus is reduced to the low status of a mere drummer. Xu Wei's *Cuixiang meng* 翠鄉夢 (*A Dream of Cuixiang*) is the only two-act play in our anthology and may well be the oddest of *The Four Cries of a Gibbon* group: it tells of a holy monk who in the first act is seduced by a courtesan at the order of an offended official and in the second act is reborn as a prostitute who eventually is enlightened by the monk Moonlight.

Whereas Xu Wei in his one-act play satirizes corruption in high places, Wang Heng 王衡 (late sixteenth century) in his one-act play *Zhen kuilei* 真傀儡 (*Real Puppets*) satirizes the common herd, whose attitude abruptly changes from high-handed arrogance to craven sycophancy as soon as a retired official is recalled to court. Similarly Shen Zizheng 沈自徵 (1591–1641), born into a family known for its expertise in southern plays, wrote a one-act *zaju* titled *Zanhua ji* 簪花髻 (*Pinning Flowers in His Coiffure*) to depict the outrageous behavior of the maverick poet Yang Shen 楊慎 (1488–1556) after his banishment to Yunnan following his principled opposition to the Jiajing emperor (r. 1522–1566). Accompanied by two courtesans, Yang Shen vents his frustration by singing the praises of wine; he adorns himself with the courtesans' ornaments, clothes, and cosmetics, writes poems on their white silk dresses, and drives away a wealthy prospective buyer of his poetry and calligraphy. The misunderstood genius behaving wildly is a common trope in the Chinese tradition, but his wildness rarely takes such outrageous forms. Like Xu Wei in some of his plays, Shen Zizheng uses inversion of gender roles and cross-dressing to project a topsy-turvy world where values are turned upside down.

During the Qing dynasty, the tradition of one-act *zaju* continued to thrive. Probably the greatest master of the form was Yang Chaoguan 楊潮觀 (1712–1791). From his collection of thirty-one plays, we translate two for this volume. In one play, we reencounter the theme of how changing societal attiudes affect a gifted man who, down and out on his luck, is suddenly recognized for his true worth. The other play addresses the overweening self-confidence of a young man who is hoping to pursue a career.

Our collection also includes several four-act *zaju* that stand out because of their daring content. Lü Tiancheng 呂天成 (1580–1618), better known as a theater critic and the author of a pornographic novel, presents an iconoclastic portrait of Shun 舜 in his *Qidong juedao* 齊東絕倒 (*Sublime Jokes from the Back of Beyond*). The mythical sage king Shun has been hailed since time immemorial as the perfect exemplar of filial piety. Lü based his plot on a hypothetical question raised in the *Mencius*: What would Shun as ruler do in case his father committed murder? When Shun's father kills a man and his arrest is ordered by Shun's minister of justice, Shun, as a filial son, abandons the throne and carries his father to the edge of the world. Following his disappearance, Yao's 堯 evil son and Shun's lascivious brother take over. Only when given assurances that his father will not be punished does Shun eventually relent and again ascend the throne at the order of his stepmother. Despite their perfect personal virtue, both Shun and the retired emperor Yao fail to transform even their closest relatives. Shun's father remains a fool, his brother is a villain, his own son a good-for-nothing, and his stepmother remains a silly creature. Such a spoof on canonical history is extremely rare in the Chinese tradition.

Ge dai xiao 歌代嘯 (*A Song for a Laugh*) is another four-act *zaju* in this volume. Its authorship is disputed: the play is often attributed to Xu Wei but it was more likely authored by Fang Ruhao 方汝浩 (first half of the seventeenth century). In this play the nonsensical action results from taking common expressions literally. Puns and other comic substitutions are the thematic heart of the play; each act absurdly literalizes a different folk saying meaning "to shift blame to the wrong target." *Ge dai xiao* is unusual in its focus on the lives of commoners, and also because the four acts connect to one another only loosely. As the author of the play concedes in his guidelines, each act could serve as a standalone play, though numerous threads also connect them. There is no record of live performance, though the guidelines' discussion of such practical considerations as the choice of role types for certain characters seems to reflect a belief that it was suitable for staging, as well as for enjoying in the study.

Our third four-act *zaju* play, *Heibaiwei* 黑白衛 (*Black and White Donkeys*) by the early Qing author You Tong 尤侗 (1618–1704), adapts the Tang-dynasty tale of the swordswoman Nie Yinniang 聶隱娘 for the stage. In a dazzling display of sword lore, the author celebrates the courage of those who redress injustice by individual acts of courage. We know that this play has been performed at least once and can only imagine what a spectacular show it must have been with its acrobatics and sword dances. It is tempting to read *Black and White Donkeys* partly as a reflection on the chaotic decades of the mid-seventeenth century when the Manchus completed their conquest of the Ming Empire.

An even more direct reaction to the collapse of the Ming is encountered in *Huarenyou ciqu* 化人游詞曲 (*Ramblings with Magicians in Lyrics and Songs*) by Ding Yaokang 丁耀亢 (1599–1671). With its ten acts, it is the longest play in this anthology. The protagonist, Mr. Who, embarks on a boat trip in the company of immortals and cultural elites from different historical eras who are meant to metonymically represent all of (Chinese) culture. During his journey, he leaves the vessel and boards a small fishing boat. Swallowed by a whale, he encounters in its belly the archetypical loyal poet Qu Yuan 屈原, the slandered Chu official who drowned himself, and discovers yet another world inside an orange. When he exits from the whale's belly, Mr. Who discovers that the ocean has turned into land. With an immortal's help he finally rejoins his illustrious company to visit the Dragon King's palace, but at the end of the play he is left boatless, just as he was at the beginning. One way to understand the constant shift of time and space in this play is through the structural convention of the deliverance play, which shows how an individual overcomes habitual perceptions and worldly attachments to achieve eventual awakening. Yet given specific references to the author's own time, the mercurial sense of time and space also invites an allegorical reading of the play as the literati's immediate response to the barbarian conquest and the imminent collapse of Chinese culture. The constant change of scenery reveals several forms in which the traumatic past (the whale's swallowing of the boat) is made present through the act of recollection and reenactment.

We conclude this anthology with a one-act play written during the High Qing, more than a century later than *Ramblings*, in fulsome praise of the Qianlong emperor as the embodiment of culture. *Longjing chage* 龍井茶歌 (*Song of Dragon Well Tea*) was one of nine one-act plays Wang Wenzhi 王文治 (1730–1802) wrote by commission on the occasion of the Qianlong emperor's visit to Hangzhou and West Lake during his fifth southern tour in 1780. The Qianlong emperor was a great lover of theater: his palaces featured three-tiered stages that allowed for the performance of spectacular pageants, and the palace repertoire was enriched by adaptations of famous story cycles in 240 acts, which took ten consecutive days to perform in full.[18] Despite its large cast of characters and elaborate pageantry, Wang's play is a quite modest affair when compared to these lavish productions.

Again and again the playwrights in this volume seem to question moral and sociopolitical order or even the boundaries of consensual reality. *Cracking a Dumb Chan Riddle* turns the notion of transcendent Buddhist understanding and communication beyond language into a farce. By reenacting the literatus Mi Heng's denunciation of the warlord Cao Cao in the underworld in *Thrice-Played Yuyang*, Xu Wei imbues the moral hierarchy pitting righteous indignation against the abuse of power with ironic melancholy. In *A Dream of Cuixiang*, although the enlightenment of the courtesan Liu Cui promises to lay to rest a cycle of vengeance and retribution, deliverance also seems to be merely schematic and boisterously carnivalesque. *Real Puppets* presents a world wherein officialdom and dignified status invite analogy with the puppet stage. *Sublime Jokes* turns canonical Confucian classics on their heads and depicts all-too-human sages, magnifying the limits of their virtue and the contradictions of their moral conundrums. To confront a world with inverted values, Yang Shen in *Pinning Flowers* finds it necessary to histrionically borrow the costume and ornaments of a courtesan. *A Song for a Laugh* foregoes the usual formula of misdeeds punished and justice restored, opting instead for a world in which greed, adultery, folly, cowardice, and malfeasance triumph as good or bad jokes. Abrupt shifts of temporal and spatial perspectives in *Rambling with Magicians* echo the political turmoil of the Ming-Qing dynastic transition. *Black and White Donkeys* celebrates the magical powers and martial prowess of the female knight-errant Nie Yinniang, as if only fantasy can rebuild order. The drastic and unpredictable reversals of fortune in *Ma Zhou Drinks Alone* and *Substitutes for a Dragon* drive home an individual's uncertainty as he negotiates the allure and perils of power. The decorous celebration of imperial authority in *Dragon Well Tea* provides an illuminating contrast and highlights the questioning or inversion of values embedded in the other plays.

Such questioning is sometimes achieved through laughter. Comic elements are especially prominent in *Cracking a Dumb Chan Riddle*, *Real Puppets*, *Sublime Jokes*, and *A Song for a Laugh*. Pantomime tests the powers and limits of language in *Cracking a Dumb Chan Riddle* and *A Dream of Cuixiang*, while *Sublime Jokes* wreaks havoc by playing with linguistic registers, and *A Song for a Laugh* wallows in the absurdities that come of literalizing common sayings. A recurrent theme is the fluid boundary between self and role. If Mi Heng denouncing Cao Cao in earlier literature presents clear-cut images of the defiant literatus and the deviant warlord, *Thrice-Played Yuyang* blurs the boundaries by mixing past and present emotions, old and new contexts, actions and their memories. In *A Dream of Cuixiang*, the monk Yutong tries to avenge the shame of being seduced by a courtesan by being reborn as a courtesan who brings disgrace to his nemesis. Does recovering one's moral nature depend on embracing and becoming the force of its corruption? The gender reversal that underwrites the structure of *A Dream of Cuixiang* speaks to a more general interest in gender boundaries and gender roles, as evinced by the figure of the female knight-errant, Nie Yinniang, in *Black and White Donkeys*. Nie Yinniang thrives on not being understood, but in other plays in this volume internal conviction is sometimes pitted against external ridicule. In *Real Puppets*, a retired minister without the paraphernalia of office suffers scorn and can only reclaim his dignity by receiving imperial summons with robes borrowed from the puppet theater. What are the parameters of self-expression when external validation is lacking or unpredictable? This problem is played out in *Real Puppets*, *Pinning Flowers*, *Ma Zhou Drinks Alone*, and *Substitutes for a Dragon*. In some ways, they revisit the theme of recognizing (or failing to recognize) worth, an abiding concern in traditional Chinese literature. *Rambling With Magicians* is an even more extreme iteration of the gap between internal and external meanings as Mr. Who traverses ever-changing vistas during his bewildering journey. The interplay between self and role underlies the notion of performance, which is especially prominent in *Thrice-Played Yuyang*, *A Dream of Cuixiang*, *Real Puppets*, and *Pinning Flowers*. In the case of the first three, the structure of a play within a play also points to a metatheatrical consciousness. The dramatic tradition is certainly ripe enough at this point for such self-conscious reflections.

Whereas most plays from the Yuan and early Ming are only preserved in heavily edited later editions, plays produced from the sixteenth century onward often have been preserved in editions put out during the author's lifetime or shortly thereafter (in our selection the only exception is *A Song for a Laugh*, which has only reached us in a nineteenth-century manuscript). This means that in general we can be fairly sure that the texts we have at our disposal are close to the texts as they were written by their authors, particularly if these texts were printed during their lifetime. In our anthology the translations are based on the earliest preserved printings, and we try to follow the conventions of each edition as much as possible.

Many of these editions were also printed with a rich body of paratextual materials. These may include prefaces that expound on the aim of the author and guidelines (*fanli* 凡例) in which the author may discuss various aspects of the construction of his play or the costuming of his characters. A number of plays come with critical comments of the playwright's friends and acquaintances or the editor of the collection in which the play was included. As a rule, our translations include these materials (even if at times these may be rather cryptic), as they illustrate how these plays were received by their first audiences. Many of these texts originally were also printed with "appreciative highlighting" of dots and circles that mark selected passages as especially important or especially fine lines. We experimented with various devices to reproduce this feature in our translations, but eventually abandoned these attempts.

Each individual translation is preceded by a short introduction that discusses the authorship, themes, and formal peculiarities of each play. The relative dearth of publications focused on these plays reflects the neglect from which these works have long suffered in scholarship, both in the Chinese speaking world and beyond. The first generation of modern scholars of *zaju* focused on the plays of the Yuan dynasty and unjustly condemned the later works in the genre as anemic and degenerate. The short plays of the Ming and Qing continued to suffer from neglect during the first five decades of the People's Republic of China despite the early publication (1958) of Zhou Yibai's 周貽白 (1900–1977) important and still useful annotated anthology *Mingren zaju xuan* 明人雜劇選 (*A Selection of Zaju by Ming-Dynasty Authors*).[19] The first major monograph on *zaju* of the Ming was the 1971 doctoral dissertation of the Taiwanese scholar Tseng Yong-yih (Zeng Yongyi) 曾永義, which was published as *Ming zaju gailun* 明雜劇概論 in 1979.[20] Only since the beginning of the twenty-first century can we speak of an upsurge in studies of Ming and Qing short plays also in the PRC with the publications of Xu Zifang 徐子方 and other scholars. This growing interest in the southern *zaju* of the Ming also has spilled over into increased curiosity regarding the Qing dynasty.[21]

Any anthology is by its very nature incomplete. We would have loved to include many more plays and other authors. The appendix to this volume lists other translations of *yuanben* and southern *zaju* (broadly defined) from the sixteenth to the early nineteenth century that are available in English.

NOTES

1. Jean Mulligan, trans. *The Lute: Kao Ming's P'i-p'a chi* (New York: Columbia University Press, 1980).
2. Tang Xianzu, *The Peony Pavilion* [*Mudan ting*], trans. Cyril Birch (Bloomington: Indiana University Press, 1980); Tang Xianzu, *The Peony Pavilion: Mudan ting*, 2nd edition, trans. Cyril Birch, intro. Catherine Swatek (Bloomington: Indiana University Press, 2002).

3. Hong Sheng, *The Palace of Eternal Youth*, trans. Yang Hsien-yi and Gladys Yang (Peking: Foreign Languages Press, 1955).
4. K'ung Shang-jen, *The Peach Blossom Fan*, trans. Chen Shih-hsiang and Harold Acton, with the collaboration of Cyril Birch (Berkeley: University of California Press, 1976).
5. Other full-length translations of southern plays of the seventeenth century include: Meng Chengshun, *Mistress and Maid* [Jiaohong ji], trans. Cyril Birch (New York: Columbia University Press, 2001); and Li Yu, *A Couple of Soles: A Comic Play from Seventeenth-Century China*, trans. Jing Shen and Robert E. Hegel (New York: Columbia University Press, 2020).
6. For general histories of Chinese theater and drama in English, see, for instance: William Dolby, *A History of Chinese Drama* (London: Paul Elek, 1976); and Colin Mackerras, *Chinese Drama: A Historical Survey* (Beijing: New World Press, 1990). For a one-chapter historical introduction see Wilt L. Idema, "Traditional Dramatic Literature," in *The Columbia History of Chinese Literature*, ed. Victor H. Mair (New York: Columbia University Press, 2001), 785–847. Also see the relevant chapters in Kang-I Sun Chang and Stephen Owen, eds., The *Cambridge History of Chinese Literature*, 2 vols. (Cambridge: Cambridge University Press, 2010).
7. Wilt Idema and Stephen H. West, *Chinese Theater from 1100–1450: A Source Book* (Wiesbaden: Franz Steiner, 1982).
8. Jeehee Hong, *Theater of the Dead: A Social Turn in Chinese Funerary Art* (Honolulu: University of Hawai'i Press, 2016); Judith T. Zeitlin and Yuhang Li, eds., *Performing Images: Opera in Chinese Visual Culture* (Chicago: Smart Museum of Art, 2014).
9. All three early *nanxi* are now available in English translation. The oldest play is *Top Graduate Zhang Xie* [*Zhang Xie zhuangyuan* 張協狀元], found in Regina S. Llamas, trans., *The Top Graduate Zhang Xie: The Earliest Extant Chinese Southern Play* (New York: Columbia University Press, 2021). The other two are *Little Butcher Sun* [*Xiao Sun tu* 小孫屠], in Stephen H. West and Wilt L. Idema, trans., *Monks, Bandits, Lovers and Immortals: Eleven Early Chinese Plays* (Indianapolis: Hackett, 2010), 389–451, and *A Playboy from a Noble House Opts for the Wrong Career* [*Huanmen zidi cuo lishen* 宦門子弟錯立身] in Idema and West, *Chinese Theater from 1100–1450*, 205–35.
10. For general introductions to Yuan *zaju*, see J. I. Crump, *Chinese Theater in the Days of Kublai Khan* (Tucson: The University of Arizona Press, 1980); Patricia Sieber, *Theaters of Desire: Authors, Readers and the Reproduction of Early Chinese Song Drama* (New York: Palgrave MacMillan, 2003); and Chung-wen Shih, The *Golden Age of Chinese Drama: Yuan Tsa-chü* (Princeton: Princeton University Press, 1976). For general anthologies of *zaju* in English translation, see C. T. Hsia, Wai-yee Li, and George Kao, eds., *The Columbia Anthology of Yuan Drama* (New York: Columbia University Press, 2014); West and Idema, *Monks, Bandits, Lovers, and Immortals*; Stephen H. West and Wilt L. Idema, *The Orphan of Zhao and Other Yuan Plays: The Earliest Known Versions* (New York: Columbia University Press, 2015).
11. To what extent *zaju* were also performed in the countryside is unclear. Especially amateur performers may have preferred simpler forms. The central government of the Yuan repeatedly issued prohibition of theatrical activities of farmers and soldiers, who based their plays on the texts of prosimetrical narratives.
12. The most comprehensive treatment of *zaju* during the first century of the Ming dynasty is still W. L. Idema, *The Dramatic Oeuvre of Chu Yu-tun (1379–1439)* (Leiden: Brill, 1985). For *zaju* as it was written by literati in northern China during the sixteenth century, see: Tian Yuan Tan, *Songs of Contentment and Transgression: Discharged Officials and Literati Communities in Sixteenth-Century North China* (Cambridge MA: Harvard University Asia Center, 2010); Wilt L. Idema and Stephen H. West, trans., *Battles, Betrayals and Brotherhood: Early Chinese Plays on the Three Kingdoms* (Indianapolis: Hackett, 2012); and Wilt L. Idema and Stephen H. West, trans., *The Generals of the Yang*

Family: Four Early Plays (Hackensack, NJ: World Century, 2013). Both contain several examples of the plays on historical themes composed at the imperial court in the early Ming.

13. For general studies of southern drama of the sixteenth and seventeenth centuries, see for instance: Grant Guangren Shen, *Elite Theatre in Ming China, 1368–1644* (London: Routledge, 2005); Jing Shen, *Playwrights and Literary Games in Seventeenth-Century China: Plays by Tang Xianzu, Mei Dingzuo, Wu Bing, Li Yu, and Kong Shangren* (Lanham, MD: Lexington Books, 2010); Sophie Volpp, *Worldly Stage: Theatricality in Seventeenth-Century China* (Cambridge, MA: Harvard University Asia Center, 2011); Guojun Wang, *Staging Personhood: Costuming in Early Qing Drama* (New York: Columbia University Press, 2020). Cyril Birch, trans., *Scenes for Mandarins: The Elite Theater of the Ming* (New York: Columbia University Press, 1995) presents selected scenes from several plays.
14. Wilt L. Idema, "Yüan-pen as a Minor Form of Dramatic Literature in the Fifteenth and Sixteenth Centuries," *CLEAR* 6 (1984): 53–75.
15. Wang Shifu's *Xixiang ji* is an anomalous *zaju* in that it is made up of a series of five four-act plays. As China's foremost love comedy it enjoyed an exceptional popularity both on stage and in print throughout the Ming and Qing dynasties. For a full translation based on the earliest preserved edition of 1498, see Wang Shifu, *The Moon and the Zither: The Story of the Western Wing*, trans. Stephen H. West and Wilt L. Idema; with a study of its woodblock illustrations by Yao Dajun (Berkeley: University of California Press, 1991); Wang Shifu, *The Story of the Western Wing*, trans. Stephen H. West and Wilt L. Idema (Berkeley: University of California Press, 1995).
16. While the one-act play is often attributed to Wang Jiusi 王九思 (1468–1551), the four-act *zaju* is often credited to his contemporary Kang Hai 康海 (1475–1540). For a detailed discussion of this controversy, see Tian Yuan Tan, "The Wolf of Zhongshan and Ingrates: Problematic Literary Contexts in Sixteenth-Century China," *Asia Major*, Third Series 20 (2007): 105–31. For a full Dutch translation of the four-act *zaju*, see Wilt L. Idema, "Ysengrimus in China: De Wolf van Zhongshan," *Tiecelijn* 32 (2019): 122–67.
17. Tina Lu, "The Literary Culture of the Late Ming (1573–1644)," in Kang-I Sun Chang, ed., *The Cambridge History of Chinese Literature Volume II: From 1375* (Cambridge: Cambridge University Press, 2010), 133.
18. Ye Xiaoqing, *Ascendant Peace in the Four Seas: Drama and the Qing Imperial Court* (Hong Kong: The Chinese University Press, 2012).
19. An extensive annotated selection of southern *zaju* of the Qing dynasty was later provided by Wang Yongkuan 王永寬, Yang Haizhong 楊海中, and Yao Shuyi 幺書儀 as *Qingdai zaju xuan* 清代雜劇選 (Zhengzhou: Zhongzhou guji chubanshe, 1991).
20. Tseng had earlier published a survey of Qing-dynasty short plays as "Qingdai zaju gailun" 清代雜劇概論 in his *Zhongguo gudian xiju lunji* 中國古典戲劇論集 of 1975. Zeng Yingjing's 曾影靖 *Qingren zaju lunlüe* 清人雜劇論略, originally presented as a master's thesis at Hong Kong University in 1970, was only published in 1995.
21. For recent surveys of studies on Ming and Qing *zaju*, see Du Guiping 杜桂萍, "Qing zaju zhi yanjiu ji qi xiqushi dingwei" 清雜劇之研究及其戲曲史定位, *Wenyi yanjiu* 4 (2003): 92–100; Xu Zifang, "Ershi shiji yilai Ming zaju yanjiu de huigu yu dianping" 20 世紀以來明雜劇研究的回顧與點評, *Yangzhou daxue xuebao* 12, no. 4 (2008): 85–91.

DYNASTIES

SHANG ca. 1300–1046 BCE
ZHOU 1046–256 BCE
  Western Zhou 1045–771 BCE
  Eastern Zhou 770–256 BCE
  Spring and Autumn 722–403 BCE
  Warring States 403–221 BCE
QIN 221–207 BCE
HAN 202 BCE–220 CE
  Western Han 202 BCE–8 CE
  Eastern Han 25–220
THREE KINGDOMS
  Wei 220–265
  Wu 222–280
  Shu-Han 221–263
WESTERN JIN 265–316
EASTERN JIN 317–420
NORTHERN AND SOUTHERN DYNASTIES 386–589
SUI 581–618
TANG 618–907
FIVE DYNASTIES 907–960
SONG 960–1279
  Northern Song 960–1127
  Southern Song 1127–1279
LIAO 916–1125

JIN 1115–1234
YUAN 1271–1368
MING 1368–1644
QING 1644–1911

1

Cracking a Dumb Chan Riddle

LI KAIXIAN (1501–1568)
TRANSLATED BY STEPHEN H. WEST

Li Kaixian 李開先, byname Bohua 伯華, sobriquet Zhonglu (Kuangren), 中麓 (狂人), was a native of Zhangqiu 章丘, Shandong, and a prominent writer and dramatist. He passed the *jinshi* examination in 1529 and rose steadily in the bureaucratic ranks, finally reaching the post of Vice Director of the Court of Imperial Sacrifices. But in 1541 the Imperial Ancestral Temples burned down, and as a normal practice all officials in the upper third of the bureaucratic ranks submitted memorials, assuming blame for the negligence that caused the fire and offering their resignations. Only twelve of these officials were cashiered, and Li was one of them. He returned to his hometown in Shandong, where he was to become a leading figure in writing *sanqu* and as the author of his own long play, the *Record of the Precious Sword* (*Baojian ji* 寶劍記), based on one of the figures from the Ming novel *The Water Margin*. He was also noted for publishing dramatic texts as well as collecting them, at one point having in his possession more than 1,500 manuscripts of *zaju* plays and *qu* lyrics. He and his students edited (and in some cases created dialogue for) early Yuan *zaju* plays that existed only as scripts of the arias. Of these *Revised Plays by Yuan Masters* (*Gaiding Yuanxian chuanqi* 改定元賢傳奇) six plays have recently been recovered.[1] His many accomplishments as a poet, critic, and dramatist are significant in the history of literature.

What we are concerned with here are the remnants of a small collection of one-act plays that he produced late in life, called *Gone with a Laugh* (*Yixiaosan* 一笑散). This term was originally a popular name of an analgesic compound for toothache that could provide immediate relief. As noted in a Ming pharmacopeia, "Make a powder of Szechuan pepper (*huajiao* Zanthoxylum bungeanum Maxim); use 600 milligrams of that powder and half of a croton seed (*croton tiglium*), crush the two together, put in a rice pellet about as large as the cavity; wrap the pellet in cotton, and place securely in the hole.

The pain will instantaneously stop, and you will be cured."[2] The relationship between his text and this prescription is explained in Li's preface to the work:

> In my leisure after working on worldly affairs and social entertainment, and in my spare time after reading and discussing ancient texts, I playfully wrote six *yuanben* plays. I entitled them *Yixiaosan* (Medical powders to bring a smile) collectively: first, *Dayachan* (Solving a dumb Chan riddle); second, *Yuanlin wumeng* 園林午夢 (A noontime dream in the garden grove); and the remaining four are *Jiaodaochang* 攪道場 (Disturbing the mass), *Qiaozuoya* 喬坐衙 (The fake court-session), *Hunsimi* 昏厮迷 (All-befuddled), and an adaptation of *Sanzhihua da'nao tuditang* 三枝花大鬧土地堂 (Three sprigs of flowers create havoc in the Temple of the Earth God). Many people borrowed the manuscript copies of the plays to read. As a result, some of the plays have been lost. Those that were lost can no longer be retrieved, and I fear it is just a matter of time that the remaining ones will also be lost in the same manner. Thus, I have had the plays carved in woodblocks and printed on paper. I have had several dozens of copies bound, and I keep them in a book box. Sometimes I take out the plays and find delight in reading them or ask my boys to perform them. They are fine substitutes for the "hundred-foot broom that sweeps away sorrow and the thousand-*zhang* hook to fish poems."[3] Furthermore, it is also because the printers were extremely poor and offered to cut their price to do the job. I think of the olden days when people, in the event of a bad harvest year, would initiate construction projects to help the poor. As the proverb says, 'Light the lamp when oil is expensive; feed the Buddhist priests when rice is dear." For this reason, I therefore gave them these two *yuanben* to print, or else my printing plans would not have included these.[4]

Since one of the oldest claimed effects of entertainments of various sorts was to "relieve anxiety and care" (*jieyou* 解憂), we can imagine that the *yuanben* farces would have the same wonderful effect on mental states as the medical analgesic did on a throbbing tooth.

Only the first two of the six plays are left, *Cracking a Dumb Chan Riddle* and *A Noontime Dream in the Garden Grove*.[5] In its earlier twelfth-century form, *yuanben* was a simple farce skit performed by a set number of actors: a female, a male, a judge, and a straight man and butt combination. The *yuanben* could contain music, narrative verse, farce skits, comic monologues, or other elements, but these texts indicate the first use of a designated troupe of actors who played specific role types. In *The Green Bower* (*Qinglou ji* 青樓集), a collection of anecdotes about actresses cum prostitutes in the Yuan dynasty, Xia Tingzhi 夏庭芝 (fl. 1300–1375) remarks:

> The Tang had its "tales of the marvelous" (*chuanqi*), which were all done by literati and were but a form of unofficial history, good only for providing some humor and laughter. The (southern style) "dramatic texts" (*xiwen*) were composed of a singing text as well as

amusing jokes. In the Jin dynasty, then, the *yuanben* was combined with "variety comedy" (*zaju*) to become one. In our dynasty (i.e., the Yuan) the *yuanben* and the variety comedy were split into two.

Yuanben are really nothing more than waves of satirical humor and teasing or poking fun at people. The variety comedy *zaju* was different. In its stories that spoke about lords and ministers . . . mothers and sons . . . husbands and wives . . . brothers . . . and friends,[6] invariably they deepened human relations and beautified the transforming power of ethical teachings. They were beyond comparison to [what came before].[7]

Li Kaixian's contribution to this iconic form of dramatic humor, on-stage slapstick, and comedy was to turn it into a vehicle to express not only humor, but to provoke complex emotions, stimulated by the subtle interplay between characters in humorous situations. In Li's "Preface to Yuan Xiye's *Lyrics on Roaming in Spring*" (Yuan Xiye *Chunyouci* xu 袁西野《春遊詞》序), he remarked, "Someone once said (about my printing of this collection), 'Lyrics are just a minor art, why have you invested so much of your effort in this?' Hmph! Is this not seeing them as overly shallow and speaking of them too flippantly? Southern lyrics have lots of music and few words; northern lyrics have a balance of each; when there are a lot of words and little music, that is *yuanben*."[8]

Li's comment does not tell us exactly what a *yuanben* is, but it does reveal that for him *yuanben* had an equal place among other texts and was a choice of one among three distinct dramatic forms to be exercised without judgments from others. Although the tradition of anthologists, bibliographers, and historians of drama has been to call the *Yixiaosan* texts *zaju*, there are several reasons we can claim them clearly to be *yuanben*. Primary among these is that *yuanben*, while using arias, does not abide by the musical rules of *zaju* that require a single rhyme be maintained throughout the entire act. All songs in *Cracking a Dumb Chan Riddle* rhyme in different rhyme categories.[9]

Li retained the comic and satirical humor of *yuanben*, what he called the "broom to sweep away sorrow," but that humor was now purposely embedded in a text meant to be savored by reading; the stage, the action, and the characters were now created primarily from the mental process of literal imagination; and when recreated in the reader's mind, they were no longer an objective physical reality that one could watch only once, but an endless subjective potential that could be realized with every reading.[10] The dense "messages" of *Cracking a Dumb Chan Riddle* would need such a rereading to appreciate its subtle social and religious criticism, qualms about the transparency of communication, and chariness about the outcomes of textual learning.

Cracking a Dumb Chan Riddle appears to be a regional form of humor, associated with Li's home province of Shandong.[11] No one, of course, can pinpoint the exact decisions that led to Li writing this short play. Dramatization of this skit was not new, appearing earlier in Chinese drama under one title as *The Monk Zhigong Opens Up a Dumb Chan Riddle* (*Zhigong heshang kai yachan* 志公和尚開啞禪), written in the late thirteenth or early fourteenth century by Gao Wenxiu 高文秀, another Shandong native.[12] Although the play is highly critical of the three protagonists, its satirical criticism of Buddhism is often seen as a projection of the author's own disappointments. As Bu Jian remarks:

> It appears that the author has no way to mask his deep disappointment at his own world through a superficial mask of laughter. He lashes out at greedy Piekong and Jia Buren, but also satirizes the abbot who so strongly desires to save the world. This abbot is perhaps an avatar of the author himself, in the sense that Li Kaixian's burning desire to save the people of the world is derided and ridiculed in the same way that the abbot is for being tricked.[13]

Xu Zifang, on the other hand, thinks that *Cracking a Dumb Chan Riddle* reveals an estrangement between the author and the true principles of Buddhism, behind which is concealed a biting sarcasm of Buddhist doctrine.[14]

There is, however, much evidence that Li Kaixian held no real antipathy to Buddhism—except, perhaps, to a single sect prevalent in the Ming, the so-called practitioners of "Wild Chan," an epithet that refers to Chan *gong'an* (cases; riddles). As early as the thirteenth century, Yelü Chucai, a more mainstream Chan Buddhist, referred to the practitioners of this form of Chan as "husk chan" (*kangchan* 糠禪), or "husk scourges (*kangnie* 糠孽), metaphors that see them as either superficial or pestilential.[15]

In the beginning Chan preached that the teachings "be transmitted outside of doctrine (*jiaowai biechuan* 教外別傳), establish no written sources (*buli wenzi* 不立文字), and point directly to the minds of men to reveal the true nature and achieve Buddhahood (*zhizhi renxin xianxing chengfo* 直指人心見性成佛)."[16] These phrases point to two things. First, both the intention at the beginning and the ultimate goal of the process of Chan learning are crystal clear: the master-teacher wants to guide his students and the disciples want to enter the realm of Buddhahood. Second, it is understood that this means an annihilation of the self. The unity in both purpose and goal, however, are disrupted by the middle, the learning process, which is complicated by the karma each person has accrued or lost. As Lin Shiying remarks:

> This part [unclarity] is a period of trying to find your way, one in which no one can replace you; life or death stem from the self alone, a person can neither be saved by all the Buddhas and bodhisattvas, nor by a lineage of patriarchs. Only the self, through actual practice and true cultivation, comes to a point where doubts arise about the concept of prior causes and everything becomes absolutely clear; then suddenly with a shout, the root of all doubt is severed; one has neither emotions nor cognition, and suddenly becomes a Buddha.[17]

These Chan elements had also become part of the "idealistic" wing of Neo-Confucianism. For instance, in a critique of Lu Xiangshan, the primary advocate of "learning of the mind," Zhu Xi was the first to suggest the major problem of "mind-enlightenment." He wrote:

> "Xiangshan's explanation of his doctrine is often crystal clear at the beginning and end but obscured in the middle." Someone asked, "What makes it obscure?" Zhu responded, "It's those places he can't explain, and the reason he can't is simply due to Chan. The lines
>
> When mandarin ducks are fully embroidered, I may let you look,
> But do not pass on the secrets of the needle to another.[18]
>
> is the self-love of the Chan adherent."[19]

The belief that enlightenment lay in an inexplicable subjectivity of experience was directly arrayed against mainstream *lixue* Neo-Confucianism, which emphasized perception of an objective set of principles that could be understood through investigation. All these tensions are implicit in what is, on the surface, simply a funny little skit about the possibilities of misinterpretation.

I am using the text as found in *The Collected Works of Li Kaixian* (*Li Kaixian wenji*),[20] which is based on a manuscript copy found in the Beijing library. My reading of the play has been guided by the notes of Tseng Yong-yih.[21] The postface, added here after the play itself, was not part of the performance but rather a dazzling and complex textual performance for the reader, challenging any attempt to simply read the play as a funny farce and prompting the reader to go back and reread the original at a deeper level.

Dramatis Personae in Order of Appearance

Role type	*Name, family, or social role*
MALE LEAD, MO, ABBOT	Zhenru
CLOWN, QIU, LITTLE MONK	Piekong
COMIC, JING, BUTCHER	Butcher Jia

CRACKING A DUMB CHAN RIDDLE: A FARCE SKIT

Weariness of the dusty world gets old,
When shall I cut off my worldly ties?
The gate to the Dharma[22] lies in wondrous enlightenment,
Our patriarchs have obtained true transmission.
The mind is only still when it is like the moon in the water,

Thoughts enter abstruseness as clouds and auras swirl;
"A golden rope opens the paths of awareness,
The precious raft crosses the stream of delusion."[23]
Close awhile your mouths' far-fetched babble,
And in stillness watch *Miming Dumb Chan*.

(MALE LEAD, *costumed as* ABBOT *enters and sings*:)

(*Chao tianzi*)
Patchwork cassock, wooden staff,
Be mindful of the power of "Bodhisattva Guanyin."
"There never was a tree—that is Bodhi,"
Thus, the Sixth Patriarch transmitted the true secret.[24]
I respect "he who faces Yang,"[25]
And embrace Maitreya.[26]
I recite the Garland Sūtra to seek penitence,[27]
But never knew that its true lesson
Would be to bear things in order "to cross to the other shore."

(*Speaks*:)

"The fundamental truth and essence of all things meld together,
The fragrant names shake us and burn us;[28]
Scrutinize things and the forms into which they separate are inexhaustible,
There is a place to enter, and the One Gate is deep."[29]
Take that medicine of Mahā-sudarśana[30]
And the many illnesses will all disappear.
Strum those lion-tendon strings on the lute:[31]
And all sounds will suddenly resolve as one.
Consider life and extinction both empty,
Only emotion and thought maintain [the illusion of existence].
Consider meaning and names both false likenesses,
Only remembrance and utterance can divide and separate [in such a way].
One finger pointing has already explained it all,
The myriad methods [used by Buddha to teach] are empty postulations.
It is easy to discern divergent paths,
But hard to find the true cave.
The miraculous peak arises from the ground of human nature,
"The more I look at it, the higher it seems."[32]
The waters of the Dharma bubble over at the true source;
Use it and it is never exhausted.
Should you wish to explain all Buddhas,
All Buddhas cease.
Should you desire to explain all laws,
All laws are extinguished.

All Buddhas and all laws,
Are then explained from what?
One lamp can light ten-thousand others,
This is the true secret [of oral transmission].

"To hear the Way: of old it was transmitted in meaning beyond language,
To forget language: it's hard to have someone right there in your eyes";[33]
"To seek religious instruction, do not discard the 'prior three.'
To give alms to the Buddha, all I can do is leave behind a six-foot statue."[34]

I am the Abbot Zhenru[35] of the Xiangguo Monastery in Bianliang. In the thirty-six years I have overseen this monastery I have seen the envy and jealousy, the covetous desire and frustrated anger of all sentient creatures who turn their backs on life and extinguish their [original Buddha] natures. I want to use the Buddha Law passed down by the lineage of our school to save them by converting them. I have a young disciple here, called Piekong,[36] who is only into gambling and cavorting, and who is always cutting down and cursing the patriarchs. I'll call him out and give him some instructions. Disciple! Where are you?

(CLOWN *costumed as a* LITTLE MONK, *enters and sings*:)

(*Zui taiping*)

Going against all the articles to break the Buddha's law,
Lying amid the willows and sleeping with the flowers,
I have filched Buddha statues, sold my begging bowl, and hocked my cassock.
I've stiffened up my head skin for a good beating,
Shiny, shiny, glossy,
Smack, smack, thwack.
"Oh, wisdom so great, so great,"
Let's have the officials on!

(*Speaks*:)

Slaying the living or taking a life,
With no thought of compassion or mercy.
Loving sex and greedy with the cups,
I abide by no regulations of purity.
At the Congregation on Miracle Peak,[37]
I annoyed the Buddha by slouching on his lotus dais,
In front of the Hall of Wonderful Dharma,[38]
I forced the Vajra to return his cudgel.[39]
Life-long, I'll never practice the pentinences of Liang Wudi[40]
And for half my life I'm too lazy to sit in "wild-fox meditation."[41]

I do not embrace Chan, I recite no scriptures,
I have long been famous in sing-song houses and liquor stalls.
Three thousand Buddhas at the Dragon-flower Tree Congregation,[42]
Over the course of the years have never uttered a sound.

I'm the major disciple of Abbot Zhenru, called Piekong. I heard him call, so I'd better go on in. Master, let's "trim out and brush away."[43]

(ABBOT *speaks*:) Disciple, what is the meaning of "trim out and brush away?"

(LITTLE MONK *speaks*:) You probably don't know, master, that when thieves meet and salute each other, that is called "trim out and brush away." It's just like when venerable monks greet each other by putting their palms together. If thieving monks like you and me don't say "trim out and brush away," what else can we use?

(ABBOT *speaks*:) I haven't seen you for the last couple of days, have you been drinking?

(LITTLE MONK *speaks*:) When have I ever?

(ABBOT *speaks*:) Been eating meat?

(LITTLE MONK *speaks*:) When have I ever?

(ABBOT *speaks*:) Keeping a woman?

(LITTLE MONK *speaks*:) When have I ever?

(ABBOT *speaks*:) Leapt over the wall?

(LITTLE MONK *speaks*:) When have I ever?

(ABBOT *speaks*:) I have a dumb Chan riddle that I've written out on this poster, and I want you to paste it on the front of the main gate. If anyone can get it, I'll give them ten ounces of leaf-gold.

(LITTLE MONK *acts out pasting up the poster*, [*sings*]:)

(*Langtaosha*)
Nothing to do, so the day is long,
Clouds chill the meditation couch.
The blessed land of the three heavenly realms conjoin my rooms,[44]
Jade trees, golden sunset rays, all appearances are just empty materiality,
A flash of sunlight, the sunlight halo of the Buddha.
(*Reprise*)
A blazing fire is hard to quell,
Who can be a *vajra*?
The Buddhist law of karma is immeasurable,
If you can see through this Chan riddle,
We'll go off to the Western paradise together.

(COMIC *costumed as a butcher, enters and sings*:)

(*Mantingfang*)
I have been a butcher for a long time.
A rope to bind their feet,
A carrying pole's baskets to cover their heads.
The fat pigs I bought are behind the fence of my house,
Where I happily laugh, singing a song,
Honing two keen blades in sequence.
I look for thick little coins, both my eyes fixed,
Cook up some fresh meat to help the wine down,

And drink dozens of flagons at a time.
(*Speaks*:)
Monks eat no meat nor strong-tasting veggies,
But I make my living rank and reeking.
Buddhists harm no life,
But I live by slaughter and butchering.
Eating three ounces of meat a day
Is better than an "eight prohibition" vegetarian feast![45]

Generation by generation my family has transmitted skill at butchery,
Others eat the meat and I smell the stink;
A filthy class who kill pigs and skin dogs indeed,
But how many heroes have hidden their names there?[46]

I am Butcher Jia, also called False Humanity Jia, and with the self-styled monicker, "Getting Inside the Skin." I haven't had much luck in the last couple of days. I'd better hit the streets to find a pig I can sell to keep the household together. Hey! Why is there a poster pasted to the gate?

(LITTLE MONK *speaks*:) It's a Chan riddle posted by my teacher. If anyone gets it, he'll give them ten ounces of leaf-gold.

(BUTCHER *speaks*:) Well, I never read any Buddhist sūtras, and I can't crack Chan riddles, but I'll rip off this poster, and if I manage to get it, I'll weasel out that ten ounces of gold. If I don't, then I shouldn't be beaten or cursed; at the most he'll be impolite to me. Let me just rip off the poster and see what happens.

(LITTLE MONK *speaks*:) Master, there is a Butcher Jia who has ripped off the poster and who wants to try and guess the riddle.

(ABBOT *speaks*:) Ask him in.

(LITTLE MONK *speaks*:) Butcher Jia, if you will.

(BUTCHER *speaks*:) Greetings to you, Abbot.

(ABBOT *speaks*:) Butcher Jia, do you know how to crack Chan riddles?

(BUTCHER *speaks*:) Well, I know a thing or two.

(ABBOT *speaks*:) Okay. I'm going to give you a riddle.

(BUTCHER *speaks*:) Bring it on!

ABBOT *extends one finger.*

BUTCHER *extends two fingers.*

ABBOT *extends three fingers.*

BUTCHER *extends five fingers.*

ABBOT *nods his head.*

BUTCHER *points once at abbot, and then to himself.*

ABBOT *blinks his eyes.*

BUTCHER *strokes his beard once.*

ABBOT *extends ten fingers and then folds back three.*

BUTCHER *does likewise.*

ABBOT *pats his hand twice on the ground.*

BUTCHER *twice points a finger toward the sky.*

ABBOT *strokes his sides twice.*

BUTCHER *wrings his hands several times.*

ABBOT *stretches out three fingers, curls one back.*

(BUTCHER, *counting on his fingers,* [*speaks*:]) Right?

ABBOT *points once at the wall, turns around and sits on the ground.*

BUTCHER *does the same.*

(ABBOT, *calling his disciple*:) Give him ten ounces of gold.

(LITTLE MONK:) Here's your gold, Butcher Jia.

(BUTCHER:) Thank you, abbot.

(BUTCHER, *having thanked him, exits.*)

(LITTLE MONK *gets angry and speaks*:) You, master, have lived in this monastery for more than a day, and you've been respectful to more than one patron, and you call yourself a living reincarnated Buddha. But if you let some guy who angles for profit in the marketplace, a butcher of the town, to win these hot little flakes of gold, what kind of an abbot are you!

(ABBOT *speaks*:) You know nothing about the affairs of this world. Right now there are worthy people living in obscurity in low positions, or talented but dying in the forests by springs, who have cut off human connections and escaped the world. They hide their names away, having assigned their traces to the muck and mud and buried themselves in the marketplace to pass their days in obscurity, and butcher as a livelihood. How could you know?

(LITTLE MONK *speaks*:) Well, I don't see any right now.

(ABBOT *speaks*:) You must have the incipient cognition of the true Dharma eye. You ordinary people with only physical eyes would not know it if this person turned a somersault and bumped into you. Is there not even half a one in all of Shanxi, Shandong, Shaanxi, Jiangxi, Fujian, and southern Zhili put together?

(LITTLE MONK *speaks*:) You have boasted that you have recited the *Sūtra of the Flower of the Law, The Pentinences of Emperor Wu of Liang, The Platform Sūtra of the Sixth Patriarch, The Garland Sūtra, The Lotus Sūtra, The History of the Buddha's Life, The Diamond Sūtra, The Sūtra of Buddha's Bequeathed Teachings*, and Qisong's *Discourse to Assist the Teachings* as well as *The Compendium of the Five Lamps*. You claim to be nothing less than Buddha preaching to the Congregation on Miracle Peak, and quite the equal of one escaping into meditation on the snowy peaks. The subjects of your lectures go beyond the three thousand Bodhisattvas and five hundred vows for saving the multitudes—and now this butcher is better than all of them? How many years did he sit facing a wall? How long did he sit in meditation? How many millions of scrolls of the Tripitaka did he read? I'm done being your disciple, I want to go off with him. Let me ask you, what was the meaning of extending one finger?

(ABBOT *speaks*:) There is but one Buddha who comes into the world.

(LITTLE MONK *speaks*:) Then why did Butcher Jia extend two fingers?

(ABBOT *speaks*:) Two Bodhisattvas returned from Nirvana.

(LITTLE MONK *speaks*:) Then why, master, did you extend three fingers?

(ABBOT *speaks*:) The three treasures of the Buddha, the Dharma, and the Sangha.

(LITTLE MONK *speaks*:) And Butcher Jia extending five fingers?

(ABBOT *speaks*:) The Dharma was passed down through Five Patriarchs, all in the West, and had yet to enter China.

(LITTLE MONK *speaks*:) And you nodded your head?

(ABBOT *speaks*:) I nodded my head because I understood why he came.

(LITTLE MONK *speaks*:) Why did Butcher Jia point once at you and once at himself?

(ABBOT *speaks*:) There are no others, there is no "I."

(LITTLE MONK *speaks*:) You then blinked your eyes?

(ABBOT *speaks*:) Maitreya, the next Buddha, will take charge of the teachings.

(LITTLE MONK *speaks*:) Then why did Butcher Jia stroke his beard?

(ABBOT *speaks*:) After Maitreya Buddha enters meditation, this heart will reach nescience, the first stage of enlightenment.

(LITTLE MONK *speaks*:) And extending ten fingers but curling back three?

(ABBOT *speaks*:) There are ten plus three living disciples.

(LITTLE MONK *speaks*:) And the same by Butcher Jia?

(ABBOT *speaks*:) There are ten plus three dead disciples.

(LITTLE MONK *speaks*:) Why did you pat your hands twice toward the ground?

(ABBOT *speaks*:) The fires of anger cannot be suppressed.

(LITTLE MONK *speaks*:) Why did Butcher Jia point a finger twice into the sky?

(ABBOT *speaks*:) Emptiness is material form and material form is emptiness.

(LITTLE MONK *speaks*:) And stroked both sides of your waist twice?

(ABBOT *speaks*:) The two prohibitions: covetous anger and love of killing.

(LITTLE MONK *speaks*:) Why did Butcher Jia keep wringing his hands?

(ABBOT *speaks*:) For those who love not killing, the eighteen arhats will pass by in sequence.

(LITTLE MONK *speaks*:) You stuck out three fingers and curled one back, Butcher Jia counted on his fingers. What was that?

(ABBOT *speaks*:) The Three Teachings are one, the school of the Buddha is the best.

(LITTLE MONK *speaks*:) You then pointed to the wall, turned around and sat down. Butcher Jia did the same. This is even harder to figure out.

(ABBOT *speaks*:) The Buddha passed through the city to practice his austere discipline, sitting completely still in the forest.[47]

(ABBOT *exits*.)

(LITTLE MONK *becomes enraged and speaks*:) I'm not going to be your disciple. I will go with him instead!

(*Acts out walking away and beating on the door.*) Butcher Jia! Open the door! Open the door!

(BUTCHER *enters and speaks*:) Ay! Who's calling me? Let me have a look through a crack in the door.

(BUTCHER *acts out looking.*) All I see is a little monk. I must have messed up the dumb Chan riddle and he's come to get the gold back. Let's just see how much power this little monk has. But can the food ever be retrieved once it's in the tiger's mouth? I'll open the door.

(LITTLE MONK *acts out entering and speaks*:) You won that yellow gold, so your teaching of Chan must be much better than my master's! With my whole heart, I want to trade the old for the new and take you as my teacher. (MONK *acts out making three obeisances.*)

(BUTCHER *speaks*:) Well, your master got an undeserved reputation because of reading a few scriptures and wriggled his way into being an abbot. Even though I work at the basest occupation, every day, after I am done killing pigs, I put away my steel knives, close my brushwood gate, finger my rosary beads, and beat on the wooden fish to accompany every little sound out of my mouth—always some passage from the Patriarch's sūtras. This is a case of having "a debased craft but an elevated heart," or "the mountain is evil, but the person is good."[48] Since you've already made me your teacher, I'll let you enjoy it to no end.

(LITTLE MONK *speaks*:) But I must ask you, when my master extended one finger, why did you extend two?

(BUTCHER *speaks*:) He extended one finger to tell me that there was one pig in the monastery he wanted to sell. I would have said, "In this monastery your daily allotment isn't very much, your disciple is lazy, and the pig isn't big or fat." So, I stretched out two fingers, and by doing so said, "No more, no less than two hundred good coins."

(LITTLE MONK *speaks*:) And what did it mean when my master extended three and you extended five?

(BUTCHER *speaks*:) Your master said, "I want to sell all three pigs I have in the stall here. Separately they are two hundred apiece, for a sum of six hundred." But to buy them all, I would need a discount, so I shot back five fingers and offered five.

(LITTLE MONK *speaks*:) What was the reason that you, after my master nodded his head, pointed at him once, and then at yourself once?

(BUTCHER *speaks*:) Pointing once at him and once at me, meant "if that's fair for you, then it's fair for me."

(LITTLE MONK *speaks*:) And when my master blinked his eyes and you stroked your beard—what did that mean?

(BUTCHER *speaks*:) When your master blinked, he said, "It won't do for those of us 'who have left the home' to trail after you to collect the money for the pig. I want it right now."[49] When I stroked my beard once, I said, "Master, it will come later."[50]

(LITTLE MONK *speaks*:) So what did it mean when my master extended ten fingers then curled back three?

(BUTCHER *speaks*:) When he first put out ten then curled three back, he was telling me, "Today is the twelfth, I need the money on the thirteenth." I did likewise, and that was to tell him, "I will give it to you on the thirteenth."

(LITTLE MONK *speaks*:) Master patted the ground twice, and you pointed a finger twice into the sky. What is the meaning of all that?

(BUTCHER *speaks*:) Your master said, "The pig has been fed here in the monastery, and it is being sold to provide people outside with food to eat. Spare him these two sledge blows." I pointed twice into the sky and made this oath to heaven, "If I hit him even once, I'm not a human anymore."

(LITTLE MONK *speaks*:) My master patted his waist twice, and you wrung your hands several times. What was that?

(BUTCHER *speaks*:) By patting his waist on two sides, your master was saying, "Send those two kidneys here to relieve the gluttony of us poor monks." By wringing my hands together several times, I was saying, "Not just the kidneys, I'll uncover all of the entrails of that pig to bring to you."

(LITTLE MONK *speaks*:) Master extended three fingers and curled one back and then you counted on your fingers, right. Tell me the whole thing!

(BUTCHER *speaks*:) In his day your master knew three women, but only one was good.

(LITTLE MONK *speaks*:) My master pointed to the wall top and then turned around and sat down. There's just this one thing left, and then you will have told me everything.

(BUTCHER *speaks*:) After he ate the pig intestines and kidneys, your master would be full, warm, and up to nothing good. He would bring that woman over the wall, sit down with her, and do whatever he felt like doing with her!

Name: A truly clever abbot chases his disciple away,
A muddleheaded butcher solves a Chan riddle.
Title: Everything is upside in the world, just like this,
The trivial stuff before our eyes is not worth observing.

POSTSCRIPT TO *CRACKING A DUMB CHAN RIDDLE*

It was once said,

When the meaningless sounds suddenly ceased,
then the correct sign of the emptiness of phenomena suddenly emerges.
And fierce fires suddenly died away,
verifying the absolute sincerity of Ling Run.[51]
The realm of the Six Dusts[52] is originally empty,
an image reflected in the mirror.

The paths of the Three Worlds[53] have no form,
sounds transmitted outside beyond the valley.
Both principle and phenomenon[54] should be embraced,
face the reality of the world but understand ultimate reality;
When the two realities perfectly mesh,
then from the ordinary mind one can see the Buddha mind.
There are no distinctions in ultimate reality,
join the three-fold nature of Buddha[55] and at once attain the Way;
Truth and emptiness are equal,
share rebirth with the ten kinds of beings and attain nirvana on the same day.
To speak of enlightenment, to speak of understanding,
turning the back on physical reality eternally condemns one to the sea of bitterness;
To not be spiritually agile and not come to realization
is to lose perfect practice and constantly blocks the gates to nothingness.[56]
True nature and conditional causation are reckoned together,
They are simultaneously incomprehensible and comprehensible;
Measurability and immeasurability circulate equally,
Reside in a world where you see and hear but negate what you see and hear as unreal."
The companions Ānanda and Śānakavāsa,
The likes of Mahākāśyapa and Manjusri
Convened at the sessions of Bodhisattvas to discourse on sūtras and Brahma,
Ascended the Diamond Throne to lecture on the Wheel of the Dharma.
The emptiness of non-emptiness,
This they called Absolute Emptiness;
Existence in non-existence
They named, "Wondrous Entities."
If strong desires are difficult to extirpate,
If learning is not banished,
Trivial dealings of mundane life do not end,
And you forget those who are closest to you,
You tread on unfathomable paths of danger,
You go along with burning desire for no reason;
Inside, you are stuck with consciousness and perception
And outside, you falsely act to make a fine reputation—
Then, even if you shave the head and don the black cassock,
Leave the home and dwell in a monastery,
You will still be a criminal in the sect of Chan
And a bold thief in the house of Buddha.
This is even worse than Chan of the Lesser Vehicle or Wild Fox Chan—
Even if you teach someone face to face,

He still wouldn't get it, he would still not get it.
How much worse then, is "Cracking a Dumb Chan Riddle?"
Being and nonbeing are the two jewels,
Anyone can take these two jewels to practice Chan,
And all will clearly attain realization—
The Chan riddle does not need to be "cracked" to hit the mark.
Jewel One is called the "Clear and Bright Pearl of As You Wish,"
It is both round and lustrous,
And can break apart all darkness, and yet nothing can stain the pearl;
Jewel Two is called the "Vajra Club that can Bring Demons to Submission,"
It is both keen and hard,
And can break apart all obstacles and yet the club is never worn down.

For anyone who sets his heart on Chan learning,
I will give him, first, the two jewels,
And follow that with the publication of this *yuanben*.

The *xinyou* year of the Jiajing reign, one day after the Duanyang Festival (fifth day of the fifth lunar month, 1561.05.18). Written by Li Kaixian of Zhonglu.

NOTES

1. These dramas are well covered in Tan (2010, 219–26), Tan (2009), and Idema (2006).
2. Xu Chunfu (1991, 107).
3. Metaphors for the power of wine.
4. Translation by Tan Tian Yuan, with some minor changes. See Tan (2010, 211–12).
5. A translation of this *yuanben* is found West and Idema (1995, 299–304).
6. The five metonymical relationships that form the foundational, hierarchically ethical interactions of family, state institutions, and general harmony in traditional China.
7. Xia Tingzhi (1990, 43).
8. Li Kaixian (2004, 494). Yuan Xiye is known by his formal name as Yuan Chongmian 崇冕 (1486–1564).
9. Lü Jingbo (2001, 140).
10. See Zhu Hongzhao (2010, 48–49) on Li's reshaping of *yuanben* into a true literati form.
11. Bu Jian (1989, 99); Liu Ming (2016, 144).
12. Xu Zheng et al. (1998, vol. 2, 1091).
13. Bu Jian (1989, 100).
14. Xu Zifang (2005, 79–80).
15. See Boretti (2004, 358–61); Lin Shirong (2010, 15).
16. From the preface to the Oral Record of Mysterious Master and Venerated Teacher Linji Huizhao (*Linji Huizhao xuangong zongshi luyu xu* 臨濟慧照玄公大宗師語錄引), see *CBT* (495).
17. Lin Shirong (2010, 18).

18. This common quote (鴛鴦繡了從君看, 莫把金針度與人) is found in a variety of Buddhist documents dating from the Tang period onward: it also exists in alternate iterations and was adopted as well into the vocabulary of Chinese poetics and poetic criticism.
19. Zhu Xi and Li Jingde (1973, 2619–20).
20. Li Kaixian (2004, 1150–56).
21. Tseng Yong-yih (1983, 433–38).
22. The teachings of the Buddha.
23. This couplet is adapted, with one character different, from Li Bai's "Sent to Meng Haoran: Returning to the Mountains on a Spring Day" (Chunri guishan ji Meng Haoran).

    金繩開覺路 The golden rope* opens the path to awareness,
    寶筏度迷川 The precious raft crosses the stream of delusion.

    *Golden rope: from the *Lotus Sūtra*, "[Kashyapa's] land will be pure and clean, / the ground of lapis lazuli. / Many jeweled trees / will line the roadsides, / with golden ropes to mark the roads, / and those who see it will rejoice." Later, this is a metaphor for binding the Buddhist sūtras with a golden string; the Sūtras. Precious raft: the dharma taught by the Buddha, a raft to bear one across "to the other side," to enlightenment. Here, "the raft" refers to the explanatory commentary of the sūtras.
24. The famous story from the *Platform Sūtra* about an exchange of poems between the disciples of the Fifth Patriarch. The head disciple wrote the following poem on the wall, "The body is the Bodhi [true awakening], / the heart like a bright mirror stand; / At all times diligently wipe it off, / do not let it stir up dust." Huineng, then working the treadle pestle to make flour, heard it and had someone write his response on a wall, "Bodhi was never a tree, / and the bright mirror has no stand; / The Buddha mind is always clean, / how could it be stained by dust?" He then, in due time, became the Sixth Patriarch of Chan (Yampolsky 1967, 130–32).
25. Perhaps the emperor, but according to Ding Fubao's dictionary, "Yang is brightness; the one who faces Yang is defined as 'one who acts while facing the brightness.'" That is, the Buddha. See *DFB*, accessed January 4, 2022.
26. Maitreya (Chinese, *mi'le*) is "the compassionate one," designated by Buddha as his successor in 5,670,000,000 years.
27. The *Garland Sūtra* (Huayan jing) is the first scripture spoken by the Buddha after his enlightenment.
28. The names of the three treasures: the Buddha, the Dharma Law, and the community of monks.
29. This is quoted from a Song dynasty work, "Annotations to the Exposition of the Heart" (Zhu Xin fu), where the lines are explained thusly: "If one observes from the basis of the phenomenal realm of things and the appearance of things, then things are made distinct and different, and the purport is lost. If one reflects upon them from a unified mind, all things are equal and return to the root (nothingness). As the Śūramgama-sūtra says, 'Simply enter deeply through the One Gate [into nirvana] and the six faculties of knowledge are cleansed simultaneously.'" *CBT* (X63n 131).
30. A previous incarnation of the Buddha, king of the ancient city of Kusāvatī on Mount Sumeru.
31. According to the commentary on the Prajñā-pāramitā Sūtra (Zhidu lun), "It is like a lion, the only four-legged beast to walk without fear; it can force everything into submission. Thus, of the Buddha: all of the ninety-six heterodox ways submit, and he is called a human lion."
32. From *Analects* 9.11 (子罕); see Confucius and Slingerland (2003, 90).
33. These lines are adapted, with a twist, from a poem, "Sent in Response to Buddhist Master Pu'an" 贈答普安師 by Yuan Haowen 元好問 (1190–1257). In the second line Li Kaixan has changed "To forget language: I now have someone right here before my eyes," a nod to Pu'an in the original, to his own rendition, which laments the difficulty Zhenru has in finding an adequate disciple. As a reader of Yuan Haowen's works, Li may also have had the comment Yuan made in his "Preface to the Taoran

Collection of Poetry": "The way in which poets differ from those outside the world (i.e., Buddhists) is that they discuss the Way as something that is not in writing, but cannot be divorced from words." See Yuan Haowen (2011, vol. 3, 1447).

34. There may be a muted gesture toward a 1037 poem by Su Shi, "For Abbot He of the Qingliang Monastery" 贈清涼寺和長老.

 代北初辭沒馬塵, 江南來見臥雲人; 問禪不契前三語, 施佛空留丈六身

 When I first left Northern Dai, I was covered in dust from the horse,
 Coming to South of the Jiang to see "the man reclining on the clouds";
 Inquiring about Zen I did not catch the "former three"
 In serving the Buddha I left only a sixteen-foot statue.

 (Su Shi 2010, 4345–4347)

 The first line refers to a story about the Tang monk Wuzhu, who visited Mt. Wutai. After the resident abbot asked Wuzhu how many were in his congregation, Wuzhu replied that there were several hundred. He then asked a abbot there how many were in his congregation, and the monk replied, "The prior three three and the latter three three [meaning, 'about the same as you']." Wuzhu did not understand this riddle and the abbot therefore refused him lodging for the night. When Wuzhu left the monastery, he turned his head, but the monastery had disappeared. The second line probably refers to the golden sixteen-foot statue of the Amituofu Buddha that Su's sons had made upon their dying mother's last wishes and which was installed in the Qingliang Monastery (Qingliang is both the name of the monastery Su visited and the name of the mountain Wuzhu went to at Mt. Wutai). The allusion is used here ironically, to upend Zhenru's authority, both as a monk who does not understand Chan riddles, but also as a person who misquotes noted writers.

35. Abbot Zhenru's name means "True Thusness," a term that in Mahayana Buddhism means "the existence of mind as true reality."

36. Literally, "to cast away nothingness."

37. Perhaps more widely known as Vulture Peak or Eagle Peak, Miracle Peak (in Bihar, India) is where the Buddha preached many of his sermons. The mountain is said to resemble a sitting vulture with its wings folded.

38. Located in the southwest corner of the thirty-three heavens where the thirty-three devas gather to discuss the good or evil of affairs of man and heaven.

39. Two *vajra*, guardians of the Law, are the fierce statues at the entrance to temples. They hold a scepter, or *vajra*, which was thought originally to have been a thunderbolt. Any being holding this scepter is considered a *jin'gang*, or "diamond hardness," a being of power and indestructibility.

40. Before Xiao Yan (464–549) became Emperor Wu of the Liang dynasty he had an extremely jealous wife who, after she died, turned into a huge snake and went into his bedchambers to communicate with him in a dream. He wrote a text on how to perform penitence at masses for compassion and mercy, through the exercise of which his wife was turned into an immortal, thanked him, and ascended to heaven.

41. To study heterodox Chan.

42. Under this tree the Maitreya Buddha gained enlightenment and there, in 5,670,000,000 years, is meant to return as the Buddha of the Future.

43. This an old term (*jianfu*) for ridding evil that was used as a greeting and written in several ways (湔/剪/翦–祓/拂). As explained in the early novel *Chronicle of the Water Margin* (*Shui hu zhuan*): "Originally, robbers did not speak the term 'to greet' because it was inauspicious in the military" (原

來強人「下拜,」不說此二字, 為軍中不利), probably because the term *xiabai* was homophonous with 下敗, "to be defeated."

44. From Daoism, the three realms refer to the realm of desire, the realm of form, the realm of formlessness; "blessed land" refers to the abode of Daoist immortals. Here, as below, Li is offering a second level of interpretation: "A paradise of lovely beauties inhabit the pleasure quarters that are next to my rooms."
45. The eight prohibitions are: (1) no taking of a life; no stealing; (2) no debauchery; (3) no lies; (4) no drinking alcohol; (5) no makeup or perfumed hair; (6) no singing, dancing, or watching of such; (7) no sitting or sleeping on a large bed; (8) no eating food out of season.
46. There is a long tradition in which heroes, swordsmen, and those avoiding revenge hide themselves among the low class of butchers and other occupations such as entertainers, prostitutes, fishermen, and woodcutters. In *zaju* drama, there are several dramas about banished transcendent beings who have been sent to base occupations on earth because of serious mistakes. After a suitable period of time, a Buddhist monk or a Daoist transcendent will visit them and guide them, after trials and tribulations, back to their heavenly abode.
47. Buddha was a prince in a city in the center of India. When he was twenty-nine, he went out of the city in his cart and, seeing many sick and dying, came to the realization of the impermanent nature of the world and at that moment decided to "leave the family." On the eighth day of the twelfth lunar month, he secretly rode out of his kingdom to the country of Rama, shaved his head, and became an ascetic. He then went into the forest, finally reaching a bodhi tree, where he sat and became enlightened.
48. That is, the environment is bad, but the person is good.
49. The word for "right now" (*yanxia* 眼下) literally means "in front of the eyes."
50. A play on the word "beard." The word for "later" is a homophone for the phrase "behind the beard."
51. Li here seems to be using a question-and-answer exchange from *The Record of the Axiom Mirror* (*Zongjing lu*) about "the authentic mind (真心)" or the "one mind (一心)" as possessed by the buddhas: a mind beyond all obstacles is "of itself (自體)" and is unexplainable through language. It is "as crystal clear as a boundless void and as translucent as the clean mirror of a full moon." Through the negation of faculties that see and obstinately hold on to the manifestations of difference, including the trap of lapsing into the mistake of seeing existence and nonexistence or oneness and difference as real, one can transcend the duality of ultimate and conventional truth. Acts of merit for the Buddha arise from the original nature of the mind and not from causal conditions, and they are infinite and universal. As such, no mind that is limited in some way can ever fully understand or express them. "Only people who fully believe are fully realized. Whether of the common world or a sage, their responses are not vacuous. They firmly believe and are unmovable, and the empty sounds of empty dharmas [i.e., all cognitive hinderance] all cease of their own accord. This clear sincerity can be verified. Ling Run's wildfires suddenly ceased. He availed himself of no supernormal powers. The demon of the mind was abruptly ceased. He relied on no other technique. He understood the fire would extinguish itself." See Yongming Yanshou (961, 2.426–27, *CBT ST* 2106). Ling Run, a Tang monk, went sightseeing with the monks and priests of his temple. They climbed a mountain when a fire broke out around them. All of them wanted to flee, except for Ling Run, who told them, "There is no fire outside of the mind, the material reality of the fire comes from the mind itself. It is said one can flee fire; but how can one escape fire?" The fire died down of its own accord when it reached Ling Run. This is a famous story found in many Buddhist sources; see, for instance, *Daoxuan* (n.d., *j.* 15.546).
52. The world of the five senses of sight, sound, smell, taste, touch as well as mental cognition.
53. The three realms of *samsāra*: realm of desire, realm of form, and the realm of formlessness. The first is occupied by desires for physical gratification. The second is release from physical gratification and the

experience of form, in the sense of something that is substantial and resistant: bodies, places, and things; a place of meditation. The third is the realm of pure spirit—the mind dwells in contemplation.

54. The enlightened mind (absolute principle) and concrete affairs (ever-changing phenomena) of daily life.
55. The Past Buddha, the Present Buddha, and the Future Buddha.
56. That is, entry into Buddhism as a whole.

2

The Mad Drummer

Thrice-Played Yuyang

XU WEI (1521–1593)

TRANSLATED BY YUMING HE AND ROBERT ASHMORE

Xu Wei 徐渭, courtesy name Wenchang 文長, one of the more striking cultural figures of the Ming, is also one of the hardest to categorize: a brilliant writer and artist who apparently suffered from at least bouts of insanity but gained lasting renown as a calligrapher, painter, poet, essayist, and military strategist. He was also deeply versed in musical and dramatic traditions, both as a historian of music and drama, and as a dramatist in his own right.

Xu Wei advanced to the status of local academy scholar, or *xiucai*, at the age of twenty, but despite eight subsequent attempts, he never advanced further in the civil examination system. He served as a secretary and aide-de-camp for Hu Zongxian 胡宗憲 (1512–1565), a prominent minister renowned for successes in campaigns against pirates during the Jiajing reign (1522–66). In the treacherous world of Ming factional politics, however, Hu's renown was to be short-lived—a series of denunciations and criminal charges led in the end to his downfall and death in prison, ostensibly by suicide. This sequence of events appears to have terrified and traumatized Xu Wei. At any rate, his later life was punctuated by shocking outbursts of violence, including self-mutilation and suicide attempts (including driving a spike into his own ear, and smashing his own testicles), as well as the murder of his wife. He had spent seven years in prison for this crime when a well-connected friend procured his release. After a few years of traveling, Xu Wei finally returned to his hometown of Shanyin (present-day Shaoxing, Zhejiang), where he remained until his death, eking out a living from his art and writing, and by selling off books from his large collection.

Xu Wei's contributions to dramatic literature include the oldest known treatise on southern drama, *A Sequential Record of Southern Lyrics* (*Nanci xu lu* 南詞敘錄), along with a set of four plays under the collective title *Four Cries of a Gibbon* (*Si sheng yuan*

四聲猿), which includes *The Mad Drummer: Thrice-Played Yuyang* (*Kuanggushi yuyang sannong* 狂鼓史漁陽三弄) presented here.

Thrice-Played Yuyang—as we refer to it in this volume—is in multiple senses a historical play: its central action derives from a renowned episode from the period of dissolution of the Eastern Han dynasty (25–220)—also the source for many of the iconic events and characters of the "Three Kingdoms" narrative cluster that had become a staple of historical drama and fiction from medieval times on. In presenting this action not as a straightforward historical vignette, but rather as a play within a play, however, *Thrice-Played Yuyang* becomes not simply a retelling of history, but also a vehicle for reflection, whether on the role of play and performance in historical events themselves or in their later reenactment and commemoration. Finally, Xu Wei's inventive mingling of antiquarian and innovative formal and musical elements in the play raises implicit questions about the relations between earlier and later dramatic traditions with histories of their own.

The central action of *Thrice-Played Yuyang* (and the source of its title) is a drumming performance by the eponymous "Mad Drummer," Mi Heng 禰衡 (173–198). Mi Heng was a brash young talent whose haughty refusal to flatter those he found unworthy offended several potential patrons, leading ultimately to his early death at twenty-six. The first of these was the warlord Cao Cao 曹操 (155–220), who at the time controlled the last Eastern Han emperor Xian as a virtual puppet. His overtures to recruit Mi Heng having been rebuffed, Cao sought revenge by conscripting Mi Heng into service as a drummer. Cao Cao arranged a grand banquet, building a large viewing stand for the purpose, and commanded the members of his drumming corps to perform one at a time. Mi Heng appeared in civilian dress; when reprimanded and commanded to change into the designated uniform of cap, smock, and trousers, he strode directly before Cao Cao and, unflustered, proceeded to strip naked. He then put on the drummer's outfit, one piece at a time—trousers last. His subsequent drumming performance was so electrifying (it became the origin story for a musical composition, also known as the *Thrice-Played Yuyang*) as to leave the entire assembly awestruck. Cao Cao is said to have commented, "I wanted to humiliate Heng, but Heng has humiliated me instead."

Thus, the historical kernel of *Thrice-Played Yuyang* is itself not simply an event but also a performance, and one that from the beginning raised problems of meaning and intention: staged with one purpose in mind, it ended up taking on an altogether different import. Xu Wei's play stages Mi Heng's performance not at Cao Cao's banquet, but rather long afterward in the office of a Judge in the administration of King Yama, the underworld divinity who judges the souls of the dead and assigns to each its proper reward or punishment. Mi Heng, now a member of the secretarial staff in King Yama's administration, is soon due to depart for an official appointment in the celestial bureaucracy of the Jade Emperor. On the eve of his departure, he agrees to the Judge's personal request to reenact his renowned drumming performance before leaving the underworld; the Judge also has the convict-soul Cao Cao brought from his cell to portray his former self.

What *Thrice-Played Yuyang* presents to its own audience is thus a reperformance of a reperformance. By framing the play's central action in this way, Xu Wei foregrounds latent ironies in the idea of historical representation itself. The Judge's initial motivation stems from his regret at not having witnessed the original drumming scene in person, but he proposes and agrees to numerous adaptations that deviate from a reenactment of "how it was" and aim instead at creating a satisfying spectacle. Mi Heng's denunciations of Cao Cao, for example, extend far past the limits of the historical Mi Heng's lifespan, to encompass the entirety of Cao Cao's own mortal existence.[1] The Judge yearns, moreover, to witness a reenactment whose authenticity is guaranteed by having the original protagonists portray themselves—but the relation between real and represented identity also proves far from simple. Cao Cao, who in the real time of the underworld performance is a prisoner abjectly under the Judge's power, for example, is warned under penalty of flogging to portray the ferocity and imperious arrogance of the prime minister Cao Cao he once was fully and "accurately."[2]

As the "play within the play" is about to commence, Mi Heng suggests that the Judge himself should not just look on, but instead should take the role of one of Cao Cao's guests—otherwise, Mi Heng says, "it wouldn't count as (a) real play (*xishua* 戲耍)." Like the English word "play," *xishua* here encompasses a narrower sense of "dramatic performance" along with the more general notion of "play" as nonpurposive action, done simply for the gratification it brings, as well as "play" as the opposite of "serious," or "real." The elusive boundary the Judge inhabits—between "watching a performance" and "playing someone watching a performance"—is one manifestation of the way in which distinctions between play and reality prove unstable in *Thrice-Played Yuyang*. The Judge's initial somewhat defensive justification for staging the spectacle was that it might serve as a lasting reminder of the moral lessons of Cao Cao and Mi Heng's stories. But after the performance is done, Mi Heng, in his final line in the play as he ascends to the celestial realm, having understood the transience and irreality of play and original alike, asks the Judge to pardon Cao Cao, and, in effect, to let the whole matter rest.

The expression "as if no one were there" (*pang ruo wu ren* 旁若無人) is often used to describe the unruffled and self-assured manner of a virtuosic performer of one sort or another—often, paradoxically, exactly the sorts of performance that exert the most powerful allure as spectacle. Some such quality is celebrated in accounts of Mi Heng's drumming performance; by the same token, his lack of regard for the actual presence in his audience of men who could objectively make or break him is what proves his undoing in the end. This alluring and risky capacity of losing oneself in play was called "mad" (*kuang* 狂) in both the historical Mi Heng, as well as in Xu Wei's Drummer. Xu Wei's play draws our attention not simply to conundrums of dramatic representation, but equally to problems of role and social performance that were inescapably real, for Mi Heng as well as for Xu Wei himself.

Formally, the play consists of a long suite of thirteen songs in the *xianlü* mode, followed by a short suite (the last five arias of the play) in the *banshe* mode; formal unity is reinforced by maintaining a single rhyme throughout.[3] The first suite, comprising the "play within a play," strictly follows the archaic (in Ming terms) *zaju* style—the *xianlü* mode is traditional for the beginning acts of *zaju*, and as in *zaju*, the arias in this portion are reserved to a single singing role, Mi Heng. In the closing section, after the conclusion of the "play within a play," the pomp of Mi Heng's celestial ascent is handled with multiple singers and stagecraft echoing the "grand reunion" scenes of the southern drama that was the more widespread and current mode of dramatic performance for Xu Wei's era. This deployment of different historical strata of dramatic tradition within a single play may have aimed at an effect of something like what Bakhtin called the "chronotope," or of the shifts between black-and-white and color to delineate the realms of the real and dream in *The Wizard of Oz*.

This translation is based on the earliest known edition of the *Thrice-Played Yuyang*, in the collection *Zaju from the Hands of Famous Authors* (*Gu mingjia zaju* 古名家雜劇) printed in 1588. The play circulated broadly in the Ming, in collections of Xu Wei's literary works, in editions of the *Gibbon of Four Cries*, as well as in general *zaju* anthologies such as *Zaju of the Prosperous Ming* (*Sheng Ming zaju* 盛明雜劇). Participants in these publishing endeavors included drama aficionados, commercial printers, and influential cultural figures of the day, such as Yuan Hongdao 袁宏道 (1568–1610). Several editions are adorned with commentary and fine illustrations (figure 2.1). The play, or selections of its arias, were also printed in the Qing with traditional musical notation for the arias. The modern Chinese typeset edition of *The Gibbon of Four Cries*, edited by Zhou Zhongming 周中明, includes a detailed commentary and supplementary materials. The present translation is greatly indebted to Zhou's work.[4]

Dramatis Personae in Order of Appearance

Role type	*Name and family or social role*
EXTRA, JUDGE, WAI	Cha You, infernal judge
GHOST, GUI	ghosts
MALE LEAD, SHENG, MI	Mi Heng, literatus
COMIC-VILLAIN, JING, CAO	Cao Cao, prime minister
MALE, MO	emissary of King Yama
YOUNG MALE, XIAOSHENG, BOY	boy emissary of God on High
FEMALE, DAN, GIRL	girl emissary of God on High
FOLLOWERS	Cao Cao's retinue
OFFICER	court lackey

THRICE-PLAYED YUYANG

(EXTRA *costumed* as JUDGE, *leading ghosts, enters and speaks:*)

The reckonings in this place of mine are exceedingly precise;
In the end, neither the good nor the bad can pull off any tricks.
Just like with debtors, they can't hide for long, even if they're good at hiding,
And in the end, no debt is left unpaid.

My family name is Cha [Scrutiny], my personal name is You [The hidden], and my courtesy name is Nengping [Able-to-set-things-right]. I'm also known as the Fireball Monk. All my life I have excelled in judgment and upheld fairness, and so I've been a good judge, clear-headed and adept, here in the administration of the Yama King of the Fifth Court.[5] Back then in the matter of Master Mi Zhengping and Cao Cao—old Aman—denouncing one another, I was in charge of the whole case file.[6] Ever since then, because Master Mi surpasses the crowd in bearing, and has splendid talent above the ordinary, our Chief has entrusted him with the drafting of all his documents, and treats him as an honored guest. During the evening court-session yesterday, our Chief told me, "All of the Gentlemen for the Cultivation of Literature that the God on High has lately employed are being transferred to other postings. He now plans to summon all those who have completed their cycles of retribution and are due for reassignment—Young Mi is among this number. Go and prepare some traveling money for him in advance, and make sure there is no delay if a summons should come." I recall it now. . . . Back then, Cao Aman had gathered guests for a banquet and ordered young Mi to play the drum for their pleasure. Yet Mi turned the tables on him—glaring angrily and stripping himself naked, he shook the drum, raised high the drumsticks, and reworked an ancient tune into the "Thrice-Played Yuyang." He feigned madness to vent his resentment; with his mimed dumbness and acted-out deafness he rebuked Cao Aman so harshly there was no place on the face of the earth for him to hide. The way he juggled heaven and earth and performed with a life-size marionette—wasn't that a wondrous spectacle? And now he is soon to ascend to heaven. I think I'll invite him here, and let out Cao Aman too, so they can both play out the way things happened on either side in that scene of the cursing at the banquet. This will leave behind an inexhaustible topic of conversation for all time down here in the Infernal Ministry—and make it clear, moreover, that, in the end, good and evil deeds are just like owing and lending money. What could be wrong with that? Underlings—go invite Master Mi on my behalf, and release Cao Cao as well, together with one or two of his former household staff, to assemble in the left gallery and await instructions. (GHOST:) I humbly receive your Honor's command.

(*Exits.*)

(GHOST, *leading* MALE LEAD *costumed as* MI; COMIC-VILLAIN *costumed as* CAO; *and two* FOLLOWERS *enter.*) (CAO *and* FOLLOWERS *stay on the left side.*) (GHOST:) I humbly report to Your Honor: Master Mi has arrived. (*They act out greeting each other.* MI *takes head position.* JUDGE, *taking an accompanying position, speaks:*) Sir, on that day, you took the opportunity of a drum performance to curse Cao Cao—that was truly one of the most wondrous events seen under heaven. Though I was able to glean the basic facts from the evidence produced in the interrogation, I have always felt it a source of regret not to have witnessed it with my own eyes.

(JUDGE *stands,*[7] *speaks:*) On a further matter—and here I congratulate you on having your merit recognized by the God on High—there are reports that you are to be summoned to the post of Gentleman for the Cultivation of Literature and will thus soon be leaving us. If this wish of mine should thus remain unfulfilled, I fear it would leave me a lifetime of lingering disappointment. That in itself is of course a trifling matter—but as material to pass down for exhortation and encouragement among the sundry officers of our Infernal Ministry and all the demonic staff, such an opportunity, I feel, really ought not to be passed up. Therefore, this lowly official, puffing up his courage, makes bold to request that you indulge us by acting out those things you did on that day in the past. I will also dress Cao Cao up in his aspect of those former days, to represent that olden scene of cursing at the banquet—and thus fulfill my long-cherished wish. What do you think, sir? (MI:) What could be wrong with that? Just one thing: when I cursed at the banquet, the evils of that Cao Aman were not yet as many as they later became. If I curse him according to that earlier list, it will be mild and bland, and won't sound satisfying. If I'm going to curse him now, it needs to hit on everything, all the way down to the Bronze Sparrow Terrace, and how he ordered the distribution of his precious incense and advised his concubines to sell shoes for a living.[8] Only in this way will it bring complete satisfaction. (JUDGE:) Even better, even better! Underlings, bring Cao Cao and his followers over here. Cao Cao, today I'm going to dress you up as prime minister like before, and together with Master Mi, have you act out that incident from the old days of beating the drum and cursing at the banquet. And if you pretend to be all timid and fearful like that and try to cover up that ferocious and evil aspect you presented then . . . Underlings! Stand on call to give him a hundred lashes with the iron whip! And then you'll act it out all over again from the beginning.

(CAO *and* ALL *act out costuming.*) (MI:) Your reverend Honor, you've always been a modest and good-hearted person—you'll surely not be willing just to sit there and look on. And if you did, it wouldn't count as a real play. Back on that day of the cursing at the banquet, there were guests in the seats. So today, just for the time being, why don't we impose on you to act as a guest of Cao Aman, who sits and views the action? Only then will it look proper. (JUDGE:) This is also a good point! (*Bows and speaks:*) Sir, with your indulgence, if I may be so bold . . .

(JUDGE *on the left and* CAO *on the right lift wine and sit.* MI, *in ordinary clothes, steps forward to pick up the drumsticks.*) (CAO *shouts:*) Savage! You are a drummer, and as such have a costume matching your position. Why are you not wearing it? Change, quickly! (OFFICER *shouts:*) You heard him—change! (MI, *taking off the old clothes, stands naked, facing* CAO.) (OFFICER *shouts*:) You animal! In the presence of our prime minister—is this a place for you to go stark naked? Don't you know "a donkey dick points east, and a horse dick points west"?[9] (MI:) Your damn prime minister's dick points south and mine points north. (OFFICER *shouts*:) Put on your clothes and stop your blabbering! (MI *acts out putting on brocade cap, embroidered gown and sash band [and sings]*:)

(*Dian jiangchun*)
In the beginning, I
Fled from violence, bade my home farewell,
And now come, a wanderer, to this region of Xu.[10]
Mounting a tower,
I turn my gaze back to the sky's edge—
Little did I suspect I'd stoop so low as to
Crawl through these men's crotches.[11]

(*Hunjiang long*)
He, over there, is
Holding a banquet, seated on his couch;
He's ordered me to take up drumsticks, and bang the drum in time with the beats.
This is just the opportunity for me
To take these drumsticks and knock him down;
This will be like
"Attacking him to the resounding of drums."[12]
My cursing,
Line after line—edges and points of flying swords and halberds;
My drumming,
Sound after sound—thunders sweeping up storms of sands.
Cao Cao! The skin of this drum is
The husk of your body,
These drumsticks are
The ribs beneath your armpits,
These nail-holes are
The pores of your breast,
These wooden planks are
The fangs in your mouth.[13]
But even if I beat right through this shameless skin
of yours
that covers the drum's two ends,
I won't be able to account for this massive wrongdoing
of yours
in this short space of time.
I'll tell it from the beginning—
So, clean out your ears and listen up![14]

(*Performs a drum solo.*) (CAO:) You madman, I commanded you to play the drum. Why are you "talking about the west while pointing east," and "likening human to animal?" Don't forget the metal rods and iron blades I've got here—they're no joke. You be careful of that tongue and teeth of yours! (JUDGE:) The guy really does lack manners! (MI [*sings*]:)

(*You hulu*)[15]

First,

You forced Emperor Xian to move the capital,

And you then had Empress Fu killed

After sending Chi Lü to find and capture her.[16]

Alas, what a pity—

The Son of Ninefold Heaven

Couldn't save his own wife?

The emperor said: "My empress,

There's no choice but for you to go ahead;

My turn to follow is just around the corner."

Still more,

Those two sons of the empress

—Flowers of no other tree;

But both true blood-stock of the Liu's

—Grown up inside the palace:[17]

How could you have them, those dragon-chicks, those phoenix-spawn, made into a vat of fish and shrimp preserve?

(*Performs a drum solo.*) (CAO:) Which deed of mine is he speaking about? (MI:)

(*Tianxia le*)[18]

Then there was Honored Consort Dong, who was

A delicate beauty, second in rank in the Han emperor's palace.

What punishment had she merited—

Are you not perverse?

In her belly

She harbored a tiny young one of two or three months' gestation.

But having killed her father,[19]

You then—fetus and all—

Had mother and child chopped into one gore-spattered toad.

(*Performs a drum solo.*) (CAO:) Madman! From of old it's been said: "the tree moves when the wind blows;" "humans kill tigers, but tigers also yearn to kill humans." Empress Fu and Dong Cheng hatched plots against me, so I did what I did. In the end, was I the one who first harbored evil intentions against them? (JUDGE:) Prime Minister, what you say is true! (MI:) But you too should think of what their reasons were, for wanting to bring harm to you. You forced the Han Son of Heaven to move to Xuchang and constrained his movements just like the ghosts around us here.

When he needed clothing, there was none; when he needed food, there was none; of all the daily necessities, there were none. When a note on a piece of paper three fingers wide had to be sent, not even a ghost would pay any attention to him. And what's more, you killed Honored Consort Dong first. They were in the direst straits—if they didn't plot against you then, what would they have been waiting for? Now you answer me this: Even supposing a Son of Heaven wants to kill his minister, does that minister get to just fucking grab him and cut him in two with one chop? Was such a thing ever heard of in this world? (JUDGE:) Now the madman is sounding reasonable again—let's raise a cup, to take the edge off this mockery. (MI:)

(*Nezha ling*)[20]
If he asked for things to eat—
You'd give him bits of stinky meat from an oxhorn;
If he asked for things to wear—
You'd give him a scrap of coarse hemp.
When at times he wanted to issue an edict,
You'd sent a ghost to deliver it.[21]
Even a rock would be stirred at heart,
Even a fool would be afraid,
Even a lamb would bite.

(*Performs a drum solo.*) (JUDGE:) Prime Minister, you won't be able to beat him in this argument. (CAO:) If I could have beaten him, I would not have come to my present plight. (MI:)

(*Que ta zhi*)
Those two houses of Duke Yuan's line—
Of them you left behind not a single plate of armor.
That holding of Liu Cong's—
You forced him to come surrender that too.
Then as for Sun Quan—ah!
How many times was he nearly done for?
And as for Xuande—ah!
Twice over, you took his women as hostages.
Place upon place—cities emptied by battle steeds;
Year upon year—corpses blanketed in cawing crows.[22]

(*Performs a drum solo.*) (CAO:) Your Honor, back at that time chaos reigned everywhere. I wasn't the only one who acted thus. (JUDGE:) As for that, the various offices of this Infernal Ministry of ours all have complete case files. (MI:)

(*Jisheng cao*)
You put on mighty airs, but all was fakery—
With all the promotions you decreed, there was nothing He could do.
A mere slip of a girl, you seated in the carriage of the Central Palace;
A mere Gentleman of Cavalry shot right up to the rank of hegemon-king;

While Bronze Sparrow Terrace soared aloft to prop up clouds and mist,
And the insolent presumption of your carriages and banners cast down the true court's pride.
Back then, you nearly stole the Jade Emperor's majesty;
To this day, you still make King Yama tremble.[23]

(*Performs a drum solo.*) (JUDGE, *in a whisper, commands the little* GHOSTS *to dress as a band of female musicians.*) (JUDGE:) So the Prime Minister married off his daughter to be an empress, and the scale of his home construction was a bit on the grand side—these seem by comparison not so big a deal. Drummer, stop your drumming for a while. I hear the Prime Minister has a fine ensemble of female musicians—let's invite them out, to trouble them for a demonstration of their skills. (CAO:) That was all in the past—where am I going to find them now? (JUDGE:) Don't you worry—if you call them, they'll be here. And make sure you give free rein to your whims in directing them! (CAO:) I obey Your Honor's command. Send word to the underlings and have them call out those female entertainers of mine. (TWO FEMALE ENTERTAINERS *enter, holding musical instruments for Wubei lyrics.*)[24] (CAO:) Today the two of you will have to make up a small song by yourself, and play and sing it as well as you can, to urge us on to drink three cups of wine. (MI *sits on the floor, facing Cao.*) (GIRL *sings:*)

( )[25]
A big pelican over there
—ya! a didu, ya! a didu—[26]
Changed into a spotted pig
—didadu, dadidu—
To sing a "Partridge" song
—ya! a didu, ya! a didu—
If she sings well that's all right
—ya! a didu, ya! a didu—
If she doesn't
—didadu, dadidu—
Call Butcher Wang
—ya! a didu, ya! a didu.

(CAO:) Why did you say, "call Butcher Wang?" (GIRL:) Butcher Wang kills pigs. (*Presents wine to* JUDGE.) (ANOTHER GIRL *sings:*)

The prime minister acts too false heartedly
—ya! a telltale, ya! a telltale—[27]
He riles up others
—tedalltale, datelltale—
To squabble and gossip
—ya! a telltale, ya! a telltale—
Snow hides the egret, you only see it when it flies

—ya! a telltale, ya! a telltale—
The willow hides the parrot
—tedalltale, datelltale—
You only know it's there when it speaks
—ya! a telltale, ya! a telltale.

(CAO:) These lines are all old news. (GIRL:) They might be old news, but they're pertinent to the topic. (CAO:) This girl is playing to the crowd! (GIRL:) Well, you've got me there—I willingly confess, and beg your pardon. (*Presents wine to* CAO.) (*One* GIRL *sings again*:)

Smear on powder, apply rouge—that pink bloom lasts but a while
—ya! a nitwit, ya! a nitwit—[28]
(*Another* GIRL *sings*:)
Repaying favors, causing grievances
—nitdawit, danitwit—
A wind that fells the flowers
—ya! a nitwit, ya! a nitwit—
(*Two* GIRLS *sing together*:)
The ten thousand things of this world don't follow human calculations
—ya! a nitwit, ya! a nitwit—
In the end it's all
—nitdawit, danitwit—
An empty stage
—ya! a nitwit, ya! a nitwit.

(*Two* GIRLS *each present wine.*) (JUDGE:) Now, *this* song is marvelous—it accords with our heavenly secrets. (CAO:) Singsong girls, withdraw. I am tired. (JUDGE *acts out laughing.* MI *stands up and says*:) You may be tired, but make no mistake, my drumming and cursing are not yet done!

(*Liuyao xu*)
With ingratiating speech your mouth is sweet as honey;
But slaughtering the good and worthy to you is like play.
You sent Yang Dezu off to summary execution by your command-post gate—
A piteous scene of splattered, trickling gore.
And Master Kong—he was the elixir-tripod's magic cinnabar,
Moon-palace's golden toad,
Immortal-belvedere's jasper-blossom;
Like the *Changes*—marvelous, yet orderly;
Like the *Odes*—correct, yet lovely.
The grounds of enmity
  Between these men and you
Were about as big as a needle's tip.
It was nothing more than some idle chatter—

What real dispute did they have with you?
The one was just too clever—
Seeing through your talk of "chicken ribs;"
With the other, it was just one thing he said that rubbed you wrong—
But both through your orders were covered beneath the yellow sands.[29]

(*Performs a drum solo.*) (JUDGE:) Prime Minister, on this charge you won't be cleared. (CAO:) I'm drunk—I'm going to sleep. (*Acts out dozing off.*) (JUDGE:) Underlings—drag him away and give him a hundred lashes with the iron whip! Then we'll act it all over again from the beginning. (CAO *acts out panic, speaks*:) I'm awake! I'm awake! (JUDGE:) So *now* you're awake. . . . (MI:)

(*Reprise*)
Ai! The roots of my own troubles are nothing too tangled—
It all started because my writing is wondrous and spirited,
My manner heroic and unrestrained.
My calling card I long clutched tight—
There was nowhere I cared to submit it to gain admission.
And as for those of embroidered gowns and ritual axes
At the Eastern Loft, the Gate of Western Splendor—
No more would I permit their names to touch my teeth.
Ai! What was that Kong Beihai thinking—
Saying there might be some viable path,
And sending me to *him*!
That well-bottom frog—
At one thing I said not to his liking,
His wrath was upon me too.
So indeed, our mutually agreeable words were few—
With intentions concealing a knife, he sent me to Huang Jiangxia.
Then came the time they stirred me up with that parrot—
By the tip of my many-colored brush, the paper filled with my heightened reputation;
They rushed to congratulate and urge me with flagons of wine,
As I tossed aside my brush in gratification, in less time than it takes to drink a cup of tea.[30]

(*Performs a drum solo.*) (JUDGE:) The misfortune will arise from this. *Hai*! Be careful, this "Rhapsody of the Parrot" is perilous! (MI:)

(*Qing ge'er*)
A sunbeam shifts across window's tracery—
It passes the window in a moment.
A rhapsody-draft, dropped to the floor, rings out like bronze—
One short metallic clang.
Huang Zu's innards were full of harsh savagery—

Once that scale of his was stirred,
He sent forth a shower of staves and forks.
Incense fears the blowing wind;
Face-powder hates being smeared on a harlot's cheek.
Men will resent a splendid talent;
Women will envy a tender beauty.
Only yesterday, a bodhisattva;
Turned in a moment into a rākshasa.
Ai!—how pitiable, this Mi Heng's head of mine!
Like a dipper-gourd at autumn's end—
Whose broken vine, with no power to grow it back,
Hangs beneath frosty eaves.[31]

(*Performs a drum solo.*) (JUDGE:) So it turns out the villain toyed as foully as *this* with the young man! (CAO:) Your Honor, you must not believe him in this! Back then, my confession to this court was given falsely under torture.[32] (JUDGE:) So according to you, then, the young man's head just fell off by itself? (CAO:) Mi, my good master, spare me already! (JUDGE:) Are you still pretending to be timid like that?—underlings, where is that iron whip? (CAO, *panicked, acts out rage.*) You madman! I did some good deeds too—I issued that order seeking worthy talents and conceded three counties from my fiefdom. Don't wipe out the credit due to me for that! (MI:)

(*Jisheng cao*)
You looked hard for worthies—
To benefit yourself.
As for yielding those three counties—
What's the big deal with that?
From a barrel you plucked a few sesame seeds, that's it.
Like a greedy cat that cries a while—your tender care was fake;
Or a hungry falcon that spares a half-length of guts to dangle from a branch;
Or a bloodthirsty butcher who grants pigs and lambs a momentary reprieve.
This late in the day, who do you think you can still fool?
Even reincarnated, you'll never lose your knack for oily scheming.

(*Performs a drum solo.*) (JUDGE:) That's the stuff! That's the stuff! Let's drink from the big cup! Master, speak on, and don't hold back! (MI:)

(*Hulu cao hun*)[33]
As for the lives you destroyed—
There were a million or so, and seventy or eighty thousand more on top of that.
As for killing court officials—
Where even to begin to take account?
It would be like taking Ao Granary's big bushel-measures to measure sesame seeds.[34]
Your evil heart—bred among knife-edges and spear-points;

Your savage countenance—uncapturable by paintings;
Your wily deceptions—the time's too rushed for me to curse them one by one.
Cao Cao,
Why do you no longer visit the East Gate leading your dog,
Or idly listen to the crane's cries at Huating?
Now look at you,
Making a shameful spectacle of yourself
In chains and cangue![35]

(*Performs a drum solo.*) (JUDGE:) Old Aman, even if you were handling this case, you wouldn't be able to spare yourself. Master, speak on, and don't hold back! (MI:) (*Zhuansha*)[36]

You built Bronze Sparrow Terrace in hopes of locking away the Qiao sisters there—
But who could have imagined—that dream of Shamanka Mountain gorges (shameful to relate!)
By Red Cliffs' fires was sent up in a blaze.
And when you were about to die,
You took a final parting in life from those slatterns of yours:
Telling them to sell shoes for a living, dividing your precious incense up among them—
What use was all of that?
Only someone as shameless as you
Could have commanded them
On each first and fifteenth day
To gaze out to your tomb there in the west,
Month after month, and wail for you.
Little did you know, those slatterns,
While still clad in hempen mourning clothes
Already clasped another in their arms.
Cao Cao, you explain it yourself—
Don't bother mentioning your lifetime tally of worth and wisdom;
Just this one charge from near your end
Would take the efforts of no few writing-brushes to account for.
Hai!—I'll let you off for now—
These drumsticks for my "Thrice-Played Yuyang" are worn out.[37]

(MALE, *dressed as* GHOST EMISSARY *of King Yama, enters*) (JUDGE:) Underlings! Quickly put Cao Cao and the others back in their cells. (GHOST:) I humbly make this report to Your Honor: the Jade Emperor has sent someone to summon master Mi. Our Venerable Chief Justice says the time limit imposed is extremely tight, and he asks Your Honor to send him off directly from here on his long journey, with suitably lavish provisions in regard to the farewell banquet and traveling expenses—you may enter these items in the Venerable Chief Justice's account book for miscellaneous expenditures. As for our Chief himself, he is extremely busy cross-checking case files, and won't be able to send master Mi off in person. He asked Your Honor to report all this to master Mi, and to assure Master Mi that when he next attends the heavenly court, he will be sure to offer his apologies in person. (JUDGE:) Understood. You may go on and report back.

(GHOST *responds affirmatively and exits.*)

(JUDGE:) Go tell the head of Accounting to put together the A-grade package of gold and silks, and farewell-banquet snacks and wine, and bring them here promptly to await my instructions. (*A voice inside responds affirmatively.*) (YOUNG MALE *costumed as* BOY, FEMALE *costumed as* GIRL, *holding the document and token of emissary, enter and speak:*)

That day, when the grasses swayed in springtime north of the Han,
The God on High himself heard the skill of your "Parrot."
Thereby we know the Jade Tower completed last night
Will not require the talents of Li Changji of Longxi.[38]

The two of us have come bearing the insignia and command of the Jade Emperor, to summon Mi Heng. Well, we'll just have to go right in and proclaim the edict. . . . Which of you here is the Judge of the Fifth Court? (JUDGE *acts out kneeling.*) The Jade Emperor has issued an edict summoning Master Mi Heng. Please invite him out, so we may proclaim the edict. (MI, *together with* JUDGE, *kneels*; TWO EMISSARIES *act out bestowing the document.*) Master Mi, God on High has an edict to summon you. You may receive and examine the tally and document yourself—you will be required to return them upon your arrival. Begin your journey immediately—you must not violate the time limit! (BOY *sings:*)

(*Shua hai'er*)[39]

Since ancient times, fine writing has indeed been beyond price:
Now it has stirred the heavenly court, so that the Jade Emperor himself
receives you.
Soaring teals and gliding cranes pace the crimson clouds—
Inviting you, master, to depart this moment on your upward journey.
It has been repaired—
That golden loft—of old adorned with heads of flying dragons;
They are laid in readiness—
White-jade serving forks—with newly minced terrine of yearling unicorn.
Jewel nectar is poured out; celestial tones are thrice performed.
A Gentleman of the Editorial Service attends
At the incense table in the immortal capital;
The Weaver-maiden leans
Beside the immortals' raft of the Milky Way.

(*Inside pipe and string music is heard.*) (GIRL *sings:*)

(*Sansha*)

Master Mi, you are

Bearer of fame unbounded, yet tardy in claiming your due—
When you wrote the "Parrot," without pausing or correcting,
Its literary radiance pierced straight up to our Three Terraces.
Though wondrous fowl and miraculous beasts are indeed fine portents,
Yet from "carving dragons" while "leaning on a horse" sprang the sprouts of your misfortunes.
Master Mi, who can compare with you in fortune first evil, then well-omened?
This pattern you've created, who can trace?
Just when
Dates fill the mouth with sweetness,
Already
Olives assault the teeth with sour.[40]

(MI:)
(*Ersha*)
We traverse upward toward heaven's gate—by degrees, no longer distant;
This parting from my chthonic host—the pain of it is ever-growing.
When shall I again accompany you in limpid chats?
Alas!—restless waves forever rock that prison where you are master.
From now on,
Whenever with fur cloak and fine steed you attend court in Heaven—my place shall be your home.
I have a word to speak to you.

(JUDGE:) I'm listening. (MI:)
Give great mercy—pardon Cao Aman.

(JUDGE:) It is not for this humble officer to do as I please in this. (MI:)
As I view it, these karmic scenes that pass before our eyes
Are all
But spring flowers emerging after rain.

(JUDGE:)
(*Yisha*)
Indeed master, you are lofty as Mount Tai—
Though lightning-keen, my eyes were as good as blind.
From now on, I
Will sweep out an austere studio
And limn a portrait of you to hang there on the wall.
Up there with you:
Troops of flying immortals to roam amid spring gardens.
Down here with me:
Throngs of captive ghosts who stir up ruckus at evening court.
When may I hope again to receive your cultured carriage?
And one more thing—if

The three *peng* spirits should make false accusations against me,
I hope
I can rely on you to cancel them with a stroke of your brush.[41]

We have arrived at the border between *yin* and *yang.* Your humble servant dares not trespass to escort you beyond this point. (MI:) Please trouble yourself no further and return home! (JUDGE:) Our Chief Justice prepared some meager parting gifts, which he commanded this lowly officer to present—I humbly hope you will indulge us by accepting them. And for my part I also hope you will demean yourself so far as to share a few cups with me, offered as a paltry token of my gratitude for your instruction throughout our time together. (MI:) I'm headed—beyond my merits—to the heavenly court. What use will I have there for such gifts? I beg of you to bear the trouble of taking those back with you, with my earnest thanks to your Chief Justice. As for your flagon of wine—that by rights I ought to accept. But I dare not further detain the heavenly emissaries. (JUDGE:) In that case, then I will bow to you in farewell here. (*Each kowtows. They sing together:*)

(*Wei*)
Since antiquity it is said: better than ten years of reading books
Is a single conversation with a cultivated man.
Enlightening instruction often comes through "pointing at donkeys in speaking of horses"[42]—
Now comes true confirmation that Manqian's jesting was no play.[43]

(MI *exits.*)

(JUDGE *speaks:*)

Watching this "Thrice-Played Yuyang" of Mi Zhengping,
I, the Scrutinizing Judge, laughed so hard my eyes narrowed to slits.
If not for fierce Yama's thousand penal statutes,
We'd all think Prime Minister Cao dwelt in the immortal grottoes.

NOTES

1. The addition of spoken/sung cursing to Mi Heng's drum performance is itself an innovation in relation to historical depictions of the event.
2. We may readily note that this compulsion under which Cao Cao plays himself is an ironic echo of (and perhaps karmic retribution for) Cao Cao's original compulsion of Mi Heng to perform as a drummer. A still more complex set of ironies surrounds the enigmatic "Wubei lyrics" inserted at the midpoint of the "play within a play": two ghosts are drafted to play the role of Cao Cao's former women musicians, and Cao Cao himself—already under a stern command to "play Cao Cao"—is further ordered by the Judge to "give free rein to [his] whims in directing them."
3. In four-act *zaju*, the *banshe* suite, if included, is usually found at the end of the third suite of songs.
4. Xu Wei and Zhou Zhongming (1984).

5. King Yama (Sanskrit, Yamaraja; in Chinese, Yanluo Wang 閻羅王 or Yan Wang 閻王) is a god who passes judgment on the dead in the underworld. Some traditions tell of ten such deities in charge of ten courts in the underworld, but typically, as here, it is the King Yama of the Fifth Court (the "Chief Justice" of this play) who figures most prominently in the popular imagination. The Judge (*panguan* 判官) serving under King Yama is a beloved and revered figure in folk belief and customs in his own right; he is frequently associated with fire.
6. Zhengping 正平 is Mi Heng's courtesy name. Cao Cao had been nicknamed Aman (written 阿瞞, meaning "Little Cheat") as a child; the derogatory use of this insultingly familiar name for him became a standard convention in popular narratives once his status as a villain had become established. Cao Cao is often referred to later in this play as Cao Man 曹瞞 (lit., Cao Cheat). The translation renders this name "Cao Aman," to avoid confusion with the English word "man."
7. While seated, the Judge spoke in his role as a private "citizen"; he now stands to indicate he is conveying official news from the celestial bureaucracy. In the following speech, he continues to weave back and forth between these two roles.
8. Cao Cao left elaborate commands regarding his posthumous commemoration, including directions that a group of female musicians should perform at fixed intervals, in perpetuity, before his spirit-tent in the renowned Bronze Sparrow Terrace. So "down to Bronze Sparrow Terrace" in effect means throughout the entirety of Cao Cao's life, and beyond. As we will see, these matters will indeed be included in Mi Heng's final aria in the "play within the play," which is about to begin.
9. A slang expression based on the idea of virility, contestation, and order in the animal kingdom, meaning, in effect, every creature has its proper rank and function. Mi Heng shows his defiance by echoing the profanity of the idiom in his response in the following line.
10. In 196, at the instigation of Cao Cao, Emperor Xian moved the Eastern Han capital to Xuchang, a region under Cao Cao's control.
11. The *zaju* form reserves the sung arias to a single role. In this play the singing role is of course Mi Heng—specifically, the "Mi Heng" played by Mi Heng himself, in the "play within the play" that has just begun. Mi Heng's song suite is in the *xianlü* mode, though unmarked here. This short opening aria takes the form of a soliloquy in which the hero introduces himself to the audience and reflects on his tribulations, similarly to the "introductory verse," a quatrain a character generally recites on first appearing on stage (compare the Judge's own "introductory verse" at the opening of the play). Since the spirit Mi Heng and spirit Cao Cao's first appearances in *Thrice-Played Yuyang* are handled naturalistically within the frame-play set in the infernal Judge's offices, they do not recite such quatrains. The biography of the renowned Han dynasty general Han Xin 韓信 (d. 196 BCE) tells how he, as a young ne'er-do-well, was once forced by a local bully to undergo the humiliation of crawling between the bully's legs.
12. In warfare, drums were traditionally used as the signal for attack, as gongs signaled retreat. To attack someone "to the resounding of drums" implied that person could be treated as an enemy with full moral justification, and that such an attack should earn the approbation of all right-thinking people. In the following lines Mi Heng continues the idea of his drumming as metaphorical warfare, attacking Cao Cao.
13. The reference of these "planks" is somewhat obscure, but may refer to the wooden drum stand, or to the staves that form the drum's body.
14. This aria marks the beginning of the "cursing and drumming" action proper, which unfolds over twelve arias (with the enigmatic interlude of the "Wubei lyrics" placed exactly in the center, between the sixth and seventh), with drum solos after each except the last.
15. This aria retells Cao Cao's killing of Empress Fu 伏 and her two sons.

16. Chi Lü 郗慮 (n.d.), an Eastern Han court official who was sent by Cao Cao to hunt down and arrest Empress Fu.
17. "Those two sons" refers to Empress Fu's sons. The imperial house of the Han dynasty was surnamed Liu 劉, thus "the Liu's" here.
18. This aria retells Cao Cao's killing of the Honored Consort Dong 董 together with her unborn child.
19. Consort Dong's father, Dong Cheng 董承 (?–200), as noted in the following dialogue, was killed by Cao Cao after a failed coup attempt.
20. This aria retells how Cao Cao mistreated Emperor Xian.
21. "Sending a ghost" idiomatically means sending no one, though here the phrase playfully hints at the site of the present performance.
22. This aria retells Cao Cao's military campaigns against rival warlords. Yuan Shao 袁紹 (?–202) and Yuan Shu 袁術 (155–199), scions of the preeminent early Eastern Han scholar-minister Yuan An 袁安 (?–92), controlled regional power bases that were among those Cao Cao liquidated in his rise. Liu Cong 劉琮 (n.d.) surrendered to Cao Cao the governorship at Jingzhou, which he had inherited from his father Liu Biao 劉表 (142–208). Sun Quan 孫權 (182–252) was founder of the southern state of Wu (222–280). Xuande 玄德 is the courtesy name of Liu Bei 劉備 (161–223) who, claiming the status of legitimate successor to the Han, established the state of Shu (221–263). The Wu and Shu kingdoms, along with the Wei (220–266), established by Cao Cao's heir Cao Pi 曹丕 (187–226), make up the "Three Kingdoms" by which the subsequent period (220–280) is commonly known.
23. This aria recounts Cao Cao's gradual usurpation of power. Cao Cao's honors and titles are called "fakery" in that they were not properly and willingly bestowed by the emperor (the "He" referred to in the aria's second line). After killing Empress Fu, Cao Cao made his own daughter empress, and also orchestrated the rapid elevation of his son and eventual heir Cao Pi to high office. At the same time as he usurped Han titles and offices to his own use and that of his family and allies, the pomp and magnificence of his own court and palaces exceeded what was proper for a subject.
24. The reference of the phrase "Wubei lyrics" (*wubei ci* 烏悲詞) is something of a mystery. It can, as here, be construed as a tune title, literally, "Songs of the crow's sadness" or "Songs of the unnamed sadness," though there is no clear evidence of the independent existence of such a tune (the lyrics Xu Wei wrote for these ghost/woman singers are themselves strikingly odd). Some scholars have suggested the phrase here is a substitute for the near homophone *huobusi* 火不思, a musical instrument resembling the Chinese lute (*pipa* 琵琶).
25. The earliest known edition of this play, on which this translation is based, leaves a spot intentionally empty (i.e., an uncarved spot on the woodblock used to print the text) at this point, where a tune title would usually be provided. This signals—intentionally or otherwise—the difficulty of assigning a musical pattern to this song. Later editions (at any rate those examined by the translators) omit this blank, removing the sign of musical difficulty at this moment in the play.
26. With their interspersed lines of nonsense syllables, these lyrics convey the sense of the singer (or the ghost playing the singer) inventing them as she goes. The pattern established in this stanza with the alliterative two syllable word (here *didu* 低都) and its scrambling with the further nonsense syllable *da* 打 later in the stanza, however, is strictly followed in the following two songs.
27. The alliterative syllables *qiaoqi* 蹺蹊 (translated as "telltale" here) are handled in the same manner as the nonsense alliterative *didu* of the first stanza—they are later scrambled with the nonsense syllable *da* to form more singsong combinations. *Qiaoqi*, however, unlike *didu*, also has a lexical meaning—it designates some odd or out of place detail (in circumstances, behavior, etc.) that arouses suspicion.
28. The rhyming syllables *donghong* 冬烘 (here rendered as "nitwit") are handled in this stanza in the same way as the alliterative syllables *didu* in the first and *qiaoqi* in the second. Like *qiaoqi*, *donghong*

has its own lexical meaning: it is a colloquial term for a slow-witted person, especially one of a pedantic bent—here, for example, it might connote a rigidly serious person who can't distinguish reality and play.

29. Dezu 德祖 is the courtesy name of Yang Xiu 楊修 (175–219); "Master Kong" is Kong Rong 孔融 (153–208). Both were renowned men of talent who fell afoul of Cao Cao and ended up as his victims. The phrases praising the classics of the *Changes* and *Odes*—drawn from a composition by the renowned Tang writer Han Yu 韓愈 (768–824)—are borrowed here for praise of Kong Rong. Likely such an association is based in part on Kong's claim to be a lineal descendant of Confucius. On a protracted military campaign against Liu Bei in Hanzhong, Cao Cao once set the phrase "chicken rib" as the night watchword. Yang Xiu correctly divined that the phrase reflected Cao Cao's disenchantment with the campaign, and predicted (again, correctly) that Cao Cao would soon abandon it—it might seem a shame to throw away a chicken rib, but the return it provides on the effort required to eat it is paltry. Enraged at having his inner thoughts "read" so transparently (and under a colorable charge of revealing military secrets and risking morale), Cao Cao had Yang Xiu executed. Kong Rong's downfall appears to have stemmed more generally from his insufficiently deferential (and occasionally sarcastic) attitude toward Cao Cao.

30. In this aria Mi Heng reflects on his own career and fate—as with the handling of Cao Cao's career in the play, the events of Mi Heng's life addressed here continue past the "drumming" encounter with Cao Cao down to his own death at the hands of Huang Zu 黃祖 (?–208). Though on intimate terms with Kong Rong and Yang Xiu (whose stories were recounted in the previous aria), Mi Heng had a low opinion of almost all the socially or politically prominent figures of his age. It was said that when he first ventured to the capital to seek advancement, he went so long without finding a patron he'd be willing to associate with that the writing on his calling card (a wooden slip with one's name and vital information one would submit when calling on a prominent social figure) became blurred beyond recognition. "Eastern Loft" and the "Gate of Western Splendor" are sites in the imperial palace—the implication of these lines is that neither in "high society" nor at court did Mi Heng find a prospective patron worthy of his notice. Kong Rong (who once served as Chancellor of Beihai) recommended Mi Heng to Cao Cao. Eventually Cao Cao, having been offended by Mi Heng on multiple occasions, yet reluctant to bear the reputational damage that would accrue to the killer of such a renowned talent, sent Mi Heng to his rival Liu Biao at Jingzhou. When a similar scenario repeated itself at Jingzhou, Liu Biao in turn sent Mi Heng to the retinue of Huang Zu, Prefect of Jiangxia, specifically because of Huang Zu's reputation for short-temperedness, with the hope and expectation that Mi Heng would not survive long in his employ. Liu Biao's role in Mi Heng's undoing is elided in this aria, as if Cao Cao orchestrated it all. During this final stint in Huang Zu's household, at a banquet held by Huang Zu's son Huang Yi 黃射 (n.d.), Mi Heng was invited to produce a rhapsody on a parrot a guest had presented to Huang Yi as a gift. Mi Heng's impromptu composition, the "Rhapsody on the Parrot," astonished all the assembled guests—and was to form the centerpiece of the scanty collection of works by Mi Heng that survived to posterity.

31. This aria recounts Mi Heng's downfall, from his brief moment of glory on composing the "Rhapsody of the Parrot" to his killing by the irascible Huang Zu. The phrase "metal and stone" refers metonymically to the bells (*zhong* 鐘) and stone chimes (*qing* 磬) of ancient ritual music; applied to latter-day writing or performance, it thus suggests the performer/author has transcended limitations of form and medium to achieve a timeless elegance and power of expression. The phrase is used in the fifth-century anecdote compilation *A New Account of the Tales of the World* (*Shi shuo xin yu* 世說新語) to describe the effect of Mi Heng's drum performance; the same compilation also records what the renowned fourth-century writer Sun Chuo 孫綽 (320–377) said proudly of his own "Rhapsody on

the Tiantai Mountains": that if the written draft were thrown to the floor, it would resound like metal and stone. Xu Wei creatively recycles both these references in applying the "ringing of metal and stone" to Mi Heng's "Rhapsody on the Parrot." Dragons are said to have a particular scale beneath their chins that, if touched, will instantly provoke them to murderous rage. In Mahāyāna Buddhist lore, a bodhisattva is a beneficent, protecting figure, and a rākshasa, a fierce demon; here the contrast depicts Huang Zu's sudden change from patron to killer.

32. There may be an implied reference here to the way in which the preceding aria left out Liu Biao's role in Mi Heng's demise, thus making Cao Cao appear more fully responsible than he perhaps really was.
33. Xu Wei here formulates his own tune *Hulu cao hun* by mixing phrases from three established tune patterns—*You hulu*, *Jisheng cao*, and *Hunjiang long*—and names his new tune by combining selected characters from the titles of the tune patterns used.
34. "Ao Granary": the state granary at Aoshan (in what is now Henan Province) in early medieval times, invoked here for its proverbial size.
35. "East Gate" and "Huating" here sarcastically invoke classical exempla of belated remorse. When Li Si 李斯 (280?–208 BCE), the former Qin prime minister, was about to be executed, he said to his son, "I want to lead the yellow dog once again with you to go out of the East Gate of Shangcai to hunt the cunning rabbit—is that possible?" When the famous literatus Lu Ji 陸機 (261–303) was about to be executed, he sighed, "The crane's crying at Huating—when can I hear it again?"
36. *Zhuansha* is the tune customarily used for the coda to a suite in the *xianlü* mode—this means that, even though the ensuing narrative suggests that Mi Heng's cursing is interrupted by the sudden arrival of King Yama's messenger, the performance is formally complete as a song suite.
37. This aria fulfills the intention announced by Mi Heng at the beginning of the "play within the play" to extend the cursing of Cao Cao all the way to the end of his mortal career; the central focus is on Cao Cao's grand "Bronze Sparrow Pavilion" and his instructions that palace women were to perform there in his memory in perpetuity after his death. The two Qiao 喬 sisters, renowned beauties, were married to leading figures of the southern state of Wu. The defeat of a large-scale invasion Cao Cao led against Wu in winter of 208 to 209 put an end to his dreams of subduing Wu and unifying the empire (and, as Mi Heng here insinuates, capturing the two Qiaos for his harem); the crucial turning point in this campaign came when Cao's enormous naval fleet was routed at "Red Cliffs" on the Yangzi River with an attack by fire-barges (assisted, it is said, by an unusual and unseasonable east wind) from the Wu side. Legend (and a series of renowned poetic works) told of an epiphanic dream in which King Huai of Chu (?–296 BCE) had an erotic tryst with the goddess of Shamanka Mountain. Here this legend is sardonically invoked to refer to Cao Cao's unfulfilled "dream" of possessing the Qiao sisters. Cao Pi took in Cao Cao's palace ladies after Cao Cao's death.
38. "North of the Han" refers to the land under the control of Huang Zu, whom Mi Heng was serving when he composed the "Rhapsody of the Parrot." The story goes that the premature death of the Tang poet Li He 李賀 (790–816, courtesy name Changji 長吉) occurred because the Jade Emperor, struck by Li's literary talent, had summoned him to heaven to compose a commemorative inscription to celebrate the completion of a White Jade Tower. Xu Wei appropriates the story here to suggest that Mi Heng's present promotion is the fulfillment of an intention the Jade Emperor had first formed at the time when Mi Heng composed his rhapsody. These four lines play the role of the "introductory verse" customary when a new character (here a pair of characters) appear on stage (see note 11 above).
39. Starting here, the remaining arias (five in all) form a small song suite of their own in the *banshe* mode, serving as an elaborate coda to the play.
40. The term "Three Terraces" refers both to sites of esoteric functions of imperial sovereignty as well as to a constellation in the sky—here both senses are combined, to refer to the precincts of the Jade

Emperor in heaven. The "wondrous fowl" refers to Mi Heng's parrot; "carving dragons" is a common expression for literary composition; "leaning on a horse" alludes to a tale of wondrously speedy composition, in which a young military attaché, while on a march with the army, composed a lengthy formal document impromptu and without any revision or retouching. Although no anecdotes with exactly these circumstances are transmitted regarding Mi Heng, his biography is filled with accounts of prodigious feats of speedy and elegant composition and faultless memory. The final image of jarringly contrasting flavors serves here to cap the point that fortune is hard to predict.

41. By legend the three *peng* 彭 spirits reside within the human body and report the person's misdeeds to God on High.
42. "Pointing at donkeys in speaking of horses" (*zhi lü shuo ma* 指驢說馬) refers to the use of rhetorical devices such as analogy and allegory. It should be noted that the phrase resembles another expression "calling a deer a horse," which means deliberately passing falsehood as truth, based on how the prime minister Zhao Gao 趙高 (258–207 BCE) of the Qin, to test his power, "called a deer a horse" to see if court officials would follow him in doing the same.
43. Manqian 曼倩 is the courtesy name of Dongfang Shuo 東方朔 (154–93 BCE), a famous jester-courtier of Emperor Wu of the Han dynasty. He was reputed in later tradition to have been an immortal in human guise.

3

Chan Master Yu Has a Dream of Cuixiang

XU WEI (1521–1593)

TRANSLATED BY SHIAMIN KWA

Xu Wei, or Xu Wenchang, was a painter, calligrapher, poet, military tactician, and dramatist whose diverse literary and artistic output is characterized by a combination of playfulness and formal clarity. *Chan Master Yu Has a Dream of Cuixiang* (*Yu chanshi cuixiang yimeng* 玉禪師翠鄉一夢) is one of a set of four celebrated plays grouped under the title *Four Cries of a Gibbon* (*Sisheng yuan* 四聲猿). The four plays are quite different from each other, particularly in terms of length, but they do share a common "cry" of indignation. In each, the main character is in one way or another bound by his or her social role. Therefore, each play offers an occasion to explore how its main character resists that situation. Because this resistance is usually conveyed by playacting in some form, this suite of plays is particularly metatheatrical in nature.

In *The Female Mulan Joins the Army in Place of Her Father* and *The Girl Graduate Rejects the Female Phoenix and Gains the Male Phoenix*, the title heroines resist the social systems of, respectively, the army and the civil service, which restrict admission to men. Both Mulan and the "girl graduate" respond to this situation by dressing up in their respective father's clothes and proceeding to perform as men. To everyone's surprise but their own, they achieve the very highest level in their respective fields. In *The Mad Drummer: Thrice-Played Yuyang* (also in this volume) and this play, *Chan Master Yu Has a Dream of Cuixiang*, the problem is the opposite. The main characters in each are male and therefore not excused from achieving on account of their gender. Instead, society expects them to achieve in a certain way, even though they would rather be left to do as they please. So it is that the "Mad Drummer," or Mi Heng, summoned to perform his famous drum song for a warlord, insulted him to such a degree that his insolence costs him his life. In Xu Wei's play, Mi Heng meets the king again in the underworld, and revisits the famous scene in which he beats the drum, playing his "three Yuyang tunes," and berates his oppressor.

Like Mi Heng, Chan Master Yu, or Yutong 玉通, wants to be left alone to meditate and direct his energies toward finishing his decades-long path and reach the goal of Chan enlightenment. The name "Cuixiang" of the title was probably a contraction from the longer expression "Cuihongxiang" 翠紅鄉, which refers to the pleasure districts: "the land of lustrous dark [hair] and rouged [cheeks]." Omitting the syllable *hong*, Xu Wei's Cuixiang can mean "the land of [Liu Cui 柳翠]" as well as "the land of the lustrous dark." The corresponding women in acts 1 and 2 of the play are associated with red (Red Lotus, in act 1) and green (Willow Green, in act 2). The Cui of her name, Liu Cui, is the lustrous green of the kingfisher feather, a color that also serves to describe lustrously black hair. Their names are also closely linked to the term *weihong yicui* 偎紅倚翠, literally "to cuddle the red rouge and lean against the black hair," that is, to have intimate relations with courtesan-entertainers.[1]

Yutong is the recipient of an unwelcome invitation: an official named Liu has been appointed as the new magistrate and, according to tradition, Yutong is expected to go to his office to pay his respects. Yutong feels that he should be exempt from such obligations and refuses to attend. Liu's response to this insult precipitates the action of reprisals and reversals that shape the plot of *Chan Master Yu*.

Yutong and his "holier than thou" attitude incites Liu to take his revenge by hiring a local prostitute, Red Lotus, to seduce Yu and thus prevent him from achieving enlightenment. She manages this by pretending to be a widow, stranded at the temple in a rainstorm, who has a chronic ailment that can only be treated by having her belly rubbed against a man's naked belly. At the end of the first act, Yu casts aside his body with a vow to be reborn in the Liu family as an act of vengeance. At the beginning of the second act, a new monk named Moonlight Monk (Yueming heshang 月明和尚, the alternate title for this play) appears. He has come to awaken Chan Master Yu, who has succeeded in being born as a girl into Liu's family but is reborn with no memory of his former identity. The Liu family has now fallen on difficult times, and their daughter Liu Cui (the unwitting reincarnation of Chan Master Yu) has become a prostitute. Out to meet a customer, she instead encounters Moonlight Monk, who proceeds to go through the arduous task of trying to communicate her previous identity to her, at first through pantomime, and then later through direct speech. In this way, Chan Master Yu is awakened to his original self, and goes off happily with Moonlight Monk.

Chan Master Yu is a remarkable play. It touches on metaphysical questions that are unresolvable: Am I what other people see, or am I what I feel myself to be? It engages these questions by taking full advantage of the theatrical form, where actors routinely tell us who they are. Xu Wei's irony is pointed: surfaces are unreliable, but surfaces are all we have. The virtuous monk can be seduced. The seemingly besotted young woman behaves like she loves her client because she expects him to be generous with his money.

In writing this play, Xu Wei drew from a long tradition of anecdotes, ballads, vernacular stories, plays, and skits—some serious, some comedic—about monks seduced by female charms and monks converting and saving courtesans. These works have been studied repeatedly, but many disagreements about causality remain in tracing the developments of the stories and the characters involved. Much depends on the dating of texts, still a thorny issue in the field of vernacular and popular literature. Moonlight Monk and Liu Cui are already featured in a deliverance play of the Yuan dynasty. A *zaju* titled *Yueming heshang du Liu Cui* 月明和尚度柳翠 (*Moonlight Monk delivers Liu Cui*) is preserved in three editions of the Wanli period (1573–1619) and beyond. This regular four-act Buddhist deliverance play is quite serious in tone and extremely allusive in its puns on "moon" and "willow." Its three printings all classify it as an anonymous work, but later critics have occasionally attributed it to Wang Shifu 王實甫 (last half of the thirteenth century), well-known as the author of *Xixiang ji* 西廂記 (*Story of the Western Wing*). Today the play is usually ascribed to his less well-known contemporary Li Shouqing 李壽卿,[2] who is credited with a play on the subject in our earliest catalogue of *zaju*. But to what extent the presently available texts reflect Li Shouqing's work (if he is indeed the original author) is also a matter of dispute.[3]

Moonlight Monk and Liu Cui also are the names usually given to the two protagonists in little skits that were performed in many places in China during the Ming and Qing (and in many places still performed), often as part of the New Year festivities and the Lantern Festival of the First Month. Such skits are often designated as *Datou heshang* 大頭和尚 (Big-headed monk), because of the large masks worn by the performers. In many places these skits go by the name of *Datou heshang xi Liu Cui* 大頭和尚戲柳翠 (The big-headed monk flirts with/importunes Liu Cui), and can be quite bawdy: many traditional observers have complained about their obscenity, while some modern scholars see the skits as an expression of a primitive fertility cult. In this connection, it should be pointed out that "monk" is a common word for penis, and that the family name Liu 柳 (meaning "willow") has close associations with female beauty and prostitution. Many scholars trace the tradition of these bawdy skits back to the Song dynasty, when in the twelfth and thirteenth centuries one of the skits performed at court as part of the New Year entertainments in Hangzhou was called *Shua heshang* 耍和尚 (Making fun of the monk). Other scholars trace *Shua heshang* back to masked entertainments of the Tang dynasty, featuring brahman priests and women (these masked entertainments of the Tang also made their way to Japan via Korea very early on, and the beautiful masks made for these skits have been preserved).

Red Lotus (Honglian 紅蓮) is already encountered in anecdotes of the tenth century as the name of the prostitute who seduces a holy monk. The choice of this name is no accident, as the expression also is used as a metaphor for the female sexual organ. Such anecdotes build on stories that were introduced by Buddhism from South Asia about ascetics whose religious exercises of many years come to naught when they end up giving in to temptation. One such ascetic, Sakyamuni, shows his superior achievements when in a final test before his definitive enlightenment, he manages to withstand the charms of Mara's three daughters as they perform their seductive dances before him; Xu Wei references this anecdote in *Chan Master Yu*. Chinese stories about seduced monks also draw on a Chinese tradition of moral exemplars who withstand female attempts to entice them. The most famous of these is Liuxia Hui 柳下惠 (ca. seventh century BCE), who was not aroused when he held a young and beautiful widowed girl close to his body through the night in order to relieve her stomach cramps. The names of the monks who are seduced by Red Lotus as well as her own status can vary in the texts where she features.

By the first half of the sixteenth century, both Red Lotus and Liu Cui were protagonists in the stories performed by blind storytellers and ballad singers in Hangzhou. The legend of Liu Cui introduced the names of Liu Xuanjiao 柳宣教 and Master Yutong.[4] We also have two vernacular stories that most likely originate from Hangzhou and were initially composed in the period between 1400 and 1550.

In probably the earliest of these two stories, Red Lotus is a foundling who is raised under a monk's patronage—albeit outside his monastery. Upon seeing her again when she has turned sixteen, he is overcome by her beauty and rapes her. He then dies from shame, and is followed in death by his best friend, a fellow monk, who is determined to save him. The two of them are then reborn as the famous Song dynasty poet Su Shi 蘇軾 (1037–1101) and his monk-friend Foyin 佛印 (1032–1098). This tale was already available in print by the middle of the sixteenth century.

The other vernacular tale has a plot even more similar to Xu Wei's play. In this tale, too, a monk (Yutong) seduced at the order of an official (Liu Xuanjiao), is reborn as the courtesan Liu Cui, who is eventually converted by Moonlight Monk. In the legend from Hangzhou as well as in the vernacular tale in the edition of Feng Menglong 馮夢龍 (1574–1646) in *Gujin xiaoshuo* 古今小說 (*Stories Old and New*, of 1620–1624), Liu Cui is, however, a pious Buddhist woman to begin with, which greatly facilitates her conversion. Patrick Hanan concludes that the plot of this tale had come together in the oral tradition by the beginning of the sixteenth century. Although Xu Wei might conceivably have known the tale in a written version, it does not appear that he based *Chan Master Yu* on this vernacular tale, which could also have been composed after his play. Even the current text of *Yueming heshang du Liu Cui* may show the influence of Xu Wei's play or one of its analogues. With its dumb show and its bawdiness, Xu Wei may well have been most influenced by the popular traditions of *Datou heshang*. This tradition has now been officially recognized in the People's Republic of China as one of its "intangible cultural assets," a designation that suggests that these performances have been considerably sanitized for contemporary audiences.

As is shown by Li Kaixian's *Da yachan,* Xu Wei was not the only sixteenth-century playwright who was intrigued by the dramatic possibilities of the dumb show and the wordless transmission of the highest truth in Buddhism on which Chan (Zen) based its authority. We may of course also compare Liu Cui's gradual enlightenment about her origins to the famous enlightenment of the orphan in Ji Junxiang's 紀軍祥 *Zhaoshi gu'er* 趙氏孤兒 (*The Orphan of Zhao*). In the latter play a young man is enlightened as to his true origins by a painting without legends: as he step by step makes sense of the painting, he comes to realize that the man he has considered his father all his life is the murderer of his whole family and that it is his duty to kill him. But even in *Zhaoshi gu'er*, it takes a follow up explanation from the orphan's foster father to make him understand that he is actually the subject of the scroll's narrative.[5] When Chan monks resort to words to explain their teaching, their message is not immediately clear. We may well wonder to what extent even well-educated contemporary audiences, even those well-read in Chan Buddhism, were able to make full sense of the long opening speeches of Master Yutong and Moonlight Monk (in acts 1 and 2, respectively) with their concatenations of learned allusions. Many audience members must have experienced these self-introductions as holy mumbo-jumbo, more intended to impress than to enlighten. Still, there is a clear difference in emphasis between the two speeches: if Master Yutong emphasizes the long struggle to achieve enlightenment, Moonlight Monk preaches that defilement is as much part of universal Buddhahood as purity, and that enlightenment is accessible to both incidental and professional sinners.

The play is extremely funny, but its humor is sourced from the dramatic potential for audiences that identify with anxieties about whether we can believe what we see. *Chan Master Yu* underscores an essential reality about theater and, specifically, serves as a reminder to the reader that what we encounter on the page represents only a few stage directions along with the spoken and sung words that make up a small portion of a dramatic performance. With its bawdiness and its ample references to physicality, both in dialogue and stage directions, it also reminds the reader how much of the performance is missing when we only engage with the words of the script. Those familiar with Richard Strauss's opera *Salome* would recognize the chords for the dance of the seven veils anywhere and look forward in great anticipation to the scene when the soprano (or her stand-in, in some cases) performs this famous dance. Yet, when we read the libretto for the opera, it mutely and simply tells us, with a few additional descriptions, "Salome dances the 'Dance of the Seven Veils'" without any commentary on the central importance of Salome's striptease to the performance. Like a recipe, the libretto assumes a player or reader will know how to fill in the blanks. When we are in an audience, we are treated to not only the sounds of the actors' voices, but the sounds of the accompanying music.

When reading *Chan Master Yu*, we must try to not only see the painted face of the actress, and the masks described in the stage directions, but the incredible feats of tumbling and acrobatics and, yes, balancing on the tips of "100-foot poles" that we commonly associate with the Chan/Zen Shaolin monks and their skills in acrobatics and the martial arts. In a short note between the two acts, Xu Wei takes pains to specify that the character Yutong should be played by someone who is capable of "playing" (*shua* 耍), to the extent that any of the troupe members capable of "playing," regardless of specialized role type, should play the part of Yutong. The term *shua* is expansive and can, just as the word "play" in English, indicate playfulness, deception, and varieties of performance. Here in *Chan Master Yu*, we can think of *shua* as including the tradition of bawdy "making fun of" the monk performances, as discussed above, in the tradition of making fun of the monk, and we can also think of the varieties of actions that may have accompanied the monks' long introductory preambles in each act, Red Lotus's seduction of Yutong in the first act, and Moonlight's pantomime efforts in the second act.

Reading a theatrical text summons our faculties to imagine an additional layer of theatrical illusion in which we are expected to participate. When watching a play, we believe that the characters are in a temple, even if we ourselves may be in a theater. When reading a play, we not only have to imagine those things about the characters, but we must remind ourselves to imagine that these are roles inhabited by real, human bodies. When the two monks walk off hand in hand together to the roar of drums, the theater audiences are asked to imagine that they walk off now as two monks, even if they see that the two walking off stage are played by a female lead and a male lead. Even this unexpected commitment to the reversals and levels of consciousness that we as readers must keep in balance helps us to understand this marvelous play. For this is a play about reaching enlightenment with or without words, and about stealing mortal lodgings to carry out its action, and about wrestling with dangers both physical and mental. In all those things can we not also read a description of the very nature of drama itself?

Xu Wei's *Chan Master Yu* consists of two acts, and each includes a regular suite of northern songs. In the first act the songs are assigned to the male lead (Yutong), but in many cases the final line(s) of his songs are performed by the additional female (Red Lotus). The clown (Yutong's servant Lazybones) is also given a song at the end of the act. The songs in the second act are assigned to the female lead (Liu Cui), but in the final two songs the lines are sung alternately by the extra (Moonlight Monk) and the female lead, or together by these two role types. When the female lead changes her dress before these final songs, we should keep in mind that the role of Liu Cui may well have been performed by a male actor who specialized in performing female roles as a *dan* 旦.

The following translation of Xu Wei's *Chan Master Yu Has a Dream of Cuixiang* is based on the earliest edition of Xu Wei's collected works of 1600 by Shang Weirui 商维濬 as *Xu Wenchang sanji* 徐文長三集 (photographic reprint in *Mingdai yishujia ji huikan* 明代藝術家集彙刊. (Taipei: Guoli zhongyang tushuguan, 1968), vol. 4, 1720–54.

Dramatis Personae in Order of Appearance

Role type	*Name, family or social role*
LEAD MALE, SHENG	The monk Yutong
CLOWN, CHOU	The acolyte Lazybones
FEMALE LEAD, DAN	Red Lotus
OLDER SECONDARY MALE LEAD, MO	Prefect Liu's servant
EXTRA MALE, WAI	Moonlight Monk
FEMALE LEAD, DAN	Liu Cui
"PAINTED FACE" MALE, JING	Feng Chaoyang's servant

CHAN MASTER YU HAS A DREAM OF CUIXIANG

ACT 1

(LEAD MALE *costumed as* YUTONG *enters and recites*:)

Against the lions of the south, one can still be prepared
But that elusive monkey is hard to subdue.
Consider how much water there is in West Lake:
Can I gulp the West River down in one mouthful?[6]

I am the monk Yutong.[7] My senior in the brotherhood, who now appears to go by the name "Moonlight Monk," and I were once a pair of revered old Buddhas of the Western Heavens together, but I had not yet cultivated myself enough to move on to the next level, and have had to remain behind, stealing a mortal lodging to travel southward.[8] Arriving in Lin'an[9] and seeing the natural beauty of its landscape, I chose to settle here to quietly practice Chan at Bamboo Forest Peak's Water and Moon Monastery. Having now lived here over twenty years, I realize I haven't much time left to reach the final level of spiritual attainment. What do I think of learning the principles of my school's teachings? I think they are rather like those climbing the steps of the civil service ranks nowadays: among those from eighth or ninth rank who manage to reach first or second rank, there are countless others who, whether deserving or not, have been promoted or demoted. It is also like the levels of a sacred stupa: even as you clamber from the first or second level up to the eighth or ninth, there are still heads banged on the way up and slip-ups on the way down. Now, think too much and feel very little, then swish-swoosh! your two feet join in flight, and you levitate up with the eighteen immortals of highest heaven in the Purple Heaven Palace. Think too little and feel very much: that's bad! You'll no doubt fall, bumpity-bump! down into that boundless and limitless Avici hell, the eighteenth layer of Black Fengdu![10] Even those highest heavenly immortals are not yet at the ultimate height: one twist or slip, and before you know it, you'll have fallen into the deepest pit of iniquity. If you've reached Avici, then you are like an eyeless needle: as much as you may fight and scoop, you will never be able to scoop yourself a path up out of those long rivers and deep seas. There are those, too, who brandish their fists, shouting at spirits and cursing at ghosts; and those who assume the lotus position, squinting down from behind lowered lids and brows. Those talking of sudden enlightenment and gradual enlightenment act like two crazed bees fighting over two kinds of honey, each one arguing over which is sweeter, which is sourer. Those promoting Confucianism and those promoting Daoism are like a lame elephant dragging a cart, neither side is ever steady. Scoff at our patriarch Bodhidharma,[11] with his way of transmitting knowledge directly from teacher to student "without words," or for facing the wall in meditation for nine years: but it is not as if, by blindly practicing the principles of cultivation in absolute silence, one will never return to the ultimate principle like leaves returning to the root of their tree. Laugh at his successor Huike's[12] singular pursuit of the Buddha mind teaching the texts to the hordes: Isn't this just spouting nonsense, mouth blabbing on and on, to stir up a deluge of heavenly flowers with one's sermon? Truth comes from attending to the sweet-smelling plum blossoms that exude all things in their fragrance alone.[13] False niceties, weeping, crying, boo-hooing—those can only fool a rat. Enlightenment that comes through speech is like, after trawling leagues below the ocean's depths, ah!, catching a flash of a golden fish scale in the net! Yet sticking to words is rather like being the man of iron balanced at the tip of a hundred-foot-long pool, rolling about as he rises in the air! So it is said: rest your feet on the bright jewel[14] though it waxes and wanes; the higher the pile of treasures you collect, the greater your debts shall be. Thus, it is that taking advantage of a flash of lightning to thread the needle is not at all a bad idea. Starving, I have chewed on wax to stave off the hunger and find that all flavors are empty. I hope that everyone can tolerate the ramblings of an old monk, oh how I always ramble! Let me bring this exposition to a close! I will now turn to a certain prefect, newly arrived in our prefecture: surnamed Liu, named Xuanjiao.[15] I have heard that he is young but very talented, and seems to have the energy to carry things through. I fear, though, that he is like yet-unfiltered gold sand, and will pollute the monastery. Traditionally we of the three teachings— Confucianists, Daoists, and Buddhists—all must follow the protocol to properly welcome a new prefect, but I have spent these last twenty years never leaving from behind closed doors, so I will neither go along with everyone to gather at his office, nor will I accept being summoned by name. Instead, it is better for me to sit here in this pure place in meditation, calming my mind. Lazybones, where are you?

(CLOWN costumed as ACOLYTE enters and acts our paying his respects to YUTONG.)

(MALE LEAD:) Lazybones, come before this Buddha's shrine and light a stick of incense, then go and shut the doors and wait while I meditate. If any temple visitors come, tell them that this little shrine is separate from the main hall, and that there's no good sightseeing here. If they want to sightsee, tell them to go to the main hall, and then you can report back to me.

(CLOWN *acts out assenting, lighting the incense and fastening the doors.*)

(MALE LEAD *acts out sitting in meditation.*)

(SUPPORTING YOUNG FEMALE *costumed as* RED LOTUS, *dressed in mourning, enters and speaks:*)

From the waist of a powdered girl hangs a soft dagger:
Before you enter the battle, your blood's running cold.[16]
Magistrate Liu, now while you're hot[17] you use this Lotus,
But after the frost I fear the Willow[18] cannot but wilt.

I am Red Lotus, a registered prostitute. Last night, His Honor the magistrate, offended that Yutong neglected to come pay him court, sought to use my body as a snare, doing "such and such." Should I manage to carry this off, then he tells me to report back to him bringing "that stuff" back with me as verification.[19] I was thinking, this Yutong is a good old fellow, so how can I carry out such a sacrilegious transgression against a Buddha or bodhisattva? Ah, the strictness of the law is unyielding as a furnace; all I can do is go along with it. As I've already arrived here, I may as well knock on the door.

(*She acts out knocking on the door.*)

(MALE LEAD *calls out to* LAZYBONES:) Lazybones, with this kind of howling wind and rain, and the sky near dark, who could be knocking at the door? If it's something you can answer to, you better do it.

(LAZYBONES *assents, acts out going to ask.*)

(LAZYBONES:) Who is knocking on the door?

(*After he asks three times,* RED LOTUS *answers and speaks:*) Open up, and then I'll tell you!

(LAZYBONES *takes on a Hangzhou dialect.*) Crikey! It's a little mama's voice!

(*He acts out opening the door.*) Here in this heavy rain . . . with the sky all dark, and you all dressed in mourning,[20] what are you doing here at this temple?

(RED LOTUS:) Today is Clear and Bright.[21] Because I wanted to make offerings and sweep the grave of my departed husband, I stopped my sedan chair inside Qingbo gate, not realizing then how long I still had to go. My feet were aching from all the walking,[22] so I sat there for a long while, until I suddenly saw that the sky was dark, and the rain began to fall. At once I sent my servant girl back inside the city gate to call for my sedan chair. Then I realized that not only were the city gates closed, but also that now even my servant would not be able to come back outside, either. Ahead of me, there was no village; behind me, there was no inn. Thank heavens for your temple! May I lodge here for the night? Tomorrow when I return home, I will send a little something to thank you.

(LAZYBONES:) I see. Wait while I go report to my master. (*Acts out reporting*)

(MALE LEAD:) Is the woman old or young?

(LAZYBONES:) She can't be more than seventeen or eighteen. And by jove is she a looker!

(YUTONG:) That is no good! I ought to tell her to leave, but there is no place for her to go. Fine, get her a bed mat and put it beneath the window on the left wall, and tell her that it will have to do.

(LAZYBONES *acts out spreading out the bed mat, then exits.*)

(RED LOTUS *acts out sitting first, then suddenly rushing forward in a beseeching manner.*)

(MALE LEAD:) Oh no don't! Oh no don't! Quick, get back out beyond the window!

(RED LOTUS *acts as if her stomach hurts and does so increasingly, and as if she is about to die.*)

(MALE LEAD *calls to* LAZYBONES:) Lazybones, quick! Warm up a bit of ginger soup and give it to the young lady to drink. I think she is suffering from a chill!

(LAZYBONES:) We haven't any ginger here, we would need to go over to the main hall and ask for some. It is the middle of the night, and pitch dark, what's the big rush?

(LAZYBONES *leaves again.*)

(RED LOTUS *acts out collapsing from pain and then regaining consciousness.*)

(MALE LEAD *calls* LAZYBONES, *and when* LAZYBONES *does not reply,* MALE LEAD *asks*:) Young lady, this affliction of yours: Is it new, or have you had it before?

(RED LOTUS:) I have had it before.

(MALE LEAD:) Since it's one you've had before, whenever it flared up, how did you remedy it?

(RED LOTUS:) I will not hide it from you, sir. In the past, when my illness flared up, I tried every kind of cure, but none worked. Saying it out loud embarrasses me, but it was only when my husband would expose his hot belly and press it against my belly, that he would, with a good rubbing, rub me back to health.

(MALE LEAD:) So it seems that the powers of all medicines cannot compare in effectiveness to that of a single person's body.

(RED LOTUS *again acts out passing out from pain.*)

(MALE LEAD *again calls out to* LAZYBONES *who again does not respond,* MALE LEAD *speaks*:) It's no good! What am I to do with this person's life in my hands? When there's an inquest about the corpse and they see that it is a woman, the officials will ask, "What were you doing harboring a woman here in the temple?" I'd have a hard time explaining. Lazybones, too, does not respond when I call him. I have no choice!

(*He acts out hoisting* RED LOTUS *on his back and carrying her inside.*)

(MALE LEAD *quickly jumps back onto the stage,* RED LOTUS *follows him on stage.* MALE LEAD *shouts loudly*:) That's it! I'm finished! I fell into this beast's snare!

(*Xinshuiling*)
On Bamboo Forest Peak I meditated for twenty years,
Passion's River was dammed up, not letting even a trickle out.
Though I lived on earth,
It was as if I were already dead, wasn't it?
This accumulated firmness,
This accumulated firmness:
Yet a puny little bug bore a leaky hole through that Yellow River embankment![23]

(RED LOTUS:) Master, if you could let a puny little bug bore a leaky hole through your Yellow River embankment, then it seems to me it was not so firm. Master, ([*sings*:])
Why couldn't you turn yourself into an impenetrable Yellow River embankment?

(MALE LEAD:) Aren't you that professional prostitute ... that "Red Lotus" who is always up to dirty tricks?

(RED LOTUS:) That's me, what's it to you?

(MALE LEAD:) You, Red Lotus, are you here by orders of a "Green Willow"?[24]

(RED LOTUS:) So I am. What's it to you? Master, how did you figure it out?

(MALE LEAD:) Under these brows are set knowing eyes of mental perception like flashing lightning. How could I not know?

(RED LOTUS:) Eyes of Perception, Eyes of Perception, what did you just moments ago let leak out?

(*Bubu jiao*) (MALE LEAD:)
To think of
That rotten Red Lotus, that cheating whore!

(RED LOTUS:) Master, lay off the insults a little, haven't you got to take half of the blame?

(MALE LEAD:)
What enmity had I with you?
On Cold Food Day, with its pear blossoms,[25]
Pretending to return from sweeping a grave and offering sacrifices,
You came in wind and rain to seek refuge in this monastery!

(RED LOTUS:) If not in this way, how could I have ensnared you?

(MALE LEAD:)
Then
You put on an act about being sick,
As if about to
Rush off to the Yellow Springs:[26]
Encircling my meditation couch,
You called on me to use expedient means![27]

(RED LOTUS:) Master, if you had not heeded my shouts, I would not have been able to do it. Had you not, I would have failed. Who told you to truly practice your "expedient means" with me?

(*Zhegui ling*) (MALE LEAD:)
She told me that her cinnabar field[28] was full of pain as if a snake was boring in,
Wanting me to bare my belly and rub it against her navel,
Lending my warmth to drive out the cold.
At the time, I was trying to save a life.
I was determined to rescue her from suffering,
I was fully devoted to saving her from her troubles,
I simply lacked the means to drive her away—
How did I ever think of sex?

(RED LOTUS:) If you didn't have those thoughts, then who did tell you to make your move once playing the game?

(MALE LEAD:)
Before I knew it, I was racing a horse, riding a boat:
Once the wind filled the sail, it was impossible to lower it;
And with rotten bridles it was impossible to rein in the horse.

(RED LOTUS [*sings*]:)

Master,
If you had not boarded the boat,
Why would you need to lower your sail?
You yourself raised the whip, and
Yet you blame the horse for being hard to rein in!

(MALE LEAD:) Alas for my twenty years of accumulated hard work: in one flash it is all cast aside. ([*sings*:])

(*Jiang'er shui*)
A few drops of Bodhi[29] water
Fell between two lotus petals.
Ah! Buddhas and bodhisattvas failed to sustain me.
Those dumb Diamond gods didn't make sure to close the temple gates,[30]
Allowing that rotten misty flower to enter this pearly palace hall.[31]
I got my precept robes hooked on a wanton's pins and bangles,
Atop a hundred-foot-long pole, it is hard to turn about.
This one Mara demon,
Smashed up my original face.
(RED LOTUS [*sings*:])
Don't you realize how much you are blessed?
A calabash like you hooking up with a peach flower face![32]

(MALE LEAD *hatefully says*:) Red Lotus, you rotten whore!

(RED LOTUS:) Master, don't curse me so!

(*De sheng ling*) (MALE LEAD:)
You are no
Miss Qincao,[33] engaging in playful meditation,
Instead, you were
A wild fox spirit full of clever tricks.
In the blink of an eye, you've turned my Bamboo Forest Hall
Into a Peach Blossom pitfall.
Red *yeme* Lotus, for whom do you toil, for whom are you sweet?[34]
For another's sake, you acted against your conscience wielding your Dragon Source:[35]
You, a powdered skeleton, a three-foot sword,
In the Western *yeme* Heavens,
Me, a flowery calabash in a single snare!
From what direction shall
The five hundred arhats be seen?
From the Southern *yeme* Springs,
What can lead away the
Twenty-year-gelded ox?[36]
(RED LOTUS:)

As for the Yellow *yeme* Heaven's
Five hundred arhats,
You should be
Ashamed before any of them.
In the Clear *yeme* Spring
There was no sign of a fisherman's hook,
You alone
Let yourself be lured away.

(YUTONG:) Matangi from the Western Heavens was a whore with magical powers who used her seductive charms to steal Ananda away in the blink of an eye, so that he nearly lost his cultivated body.[37] It was only thanks to Buddha that he was rescued and restored. Now if Ananda, a bodhisattva, could come to this, how much more so for me? ([*sings*:])

(*Jiaojiao ling*)
Matangi's turbid sea of desire
And lewd charms will always seduce Heaven.
I wanted to find the Tathagatha, but how can I find him?
I've destroyed the precept-body of this old Ananda,
Destroyed the precept-body of this old Ananda.

(RED LOTUS:) Master, I scoff at Matangi's lack of skills. If Ananda had run into me, Red Lotus, ah! ([*sings*:])

Even if he were an iron Ananda, I would have destroyed him!
An iron Ananda, I would have destroyed!
(*Shou Jiangnan*) (MALE LEAD)
Let me tell you, you'll be
Wearing a coat of fur on the "domestic animals" road to rebirth,
You'll become a grub for a hundred birds to swallow,
Your cunning cheating heart will stay until the day that sun and moon share the sky.
This situation that I've now reached,
This situation that I've now reached,
Who knows how many more cycles before I may pass through the eye of the needle,
And passing through the eye of the needle, when will the circle be done?
I've faced the wall at Shaolin's north mountain;[38]
Stopped my boat at Putuo Temple's east bank;[39]
Was reborn on the western bank of the Brocade River.[40]
But now that I am back to another karmic entanglement,
Why talk of Nirvana?
Ah!
Now my spirit will first go to the Liu family's home.

(RED LOTUS:)

Mister,

I have not sought to add to your karma,

To tell the truth: both mill stone and mill tray got polished.

Ah,

Off I go to bring these few droplets as proof to report back at Master Liu's office.

(MALE LEAD *acts out pushing* RED LOTUS *out the door.*)

(RED LOTUS:) You may try to shutter the windows to keep out the moon, but I shall be like the plum tree and make my own decisions.

(RED LOTUS *exits.*)

(MALE LEAD:) So this is my karma for refusing to pay the prefect a visit. What a pity that this should ruin twenty years of arduous work. Alas! I cannot let him get away with it! I have no choice but to turn head over heels and be reborn into the womb of Liu Xuanjiao's wife. I'll be his daughter and grow up to be a prostitute, and I will destroy the family's reputation. This is the kind of scene that should be unseen, and I should not be wasting the greater work of self-cultivation. It's just that this impudent Willow seeks to use this to insult me! He will certainly have something to say and ask for my direct response. I must therefore write a few words in response. I shall also write a few words separately to Lazybones to instruct him to prepare this and that. Then I shall sit upright[41] and send off my spirit, so it will speed off on a trip to the Liu house.

(*Acts out writing a note, then acts out reading it.*)

Since entering these Chan gates, I was without a care.
For fifty-three years, my mind was centered.
But because of this one deviating thought,
I violated the Buddha's precept against lust.
You sent Red Lotus to destroy my chastity,
And I owed Red Lotus the debt of one night.
My body's moral behavior was harmed by you,
So, your household's reputation will be ruined by me.

(MALE LEAD *again acts out writing a letter for* LAZYBONES, *and then acts out reading it.*) Left for my serving man, Lazybones: If a messenger should come to the temple from the Liu's establishment, you can tell him that there is a letter of response at the foot of the incense burner.

(*Recites a* gāthā:)

Red Lotus made a monkey out of me,
So I'll hide for a springtime in the skin of a Green Willow.
When waves beat the duckweed, not one is spared;
My only fear is that when I return you will not recognize my self of old.

(MALE LEAD acts *out leaving his body.*)

(LAZYBONES *enters and says:*) Last night I went to ask for ginger, and the master of the main temple said, "Just now there was a tiger at the foot of the hill." Knowing that,

I didn't dare to come home. I wonder how the little mama is. Oh! The little mama is gone. Oh! Master has died in seated posture! How queer! What's this all about? I've got it! She must have been a Guanyin who came to transform Master away.[42] Oh! There is a note under the incense burner.

(LAZYBONES *acts out reading*:) Oh! That little mama was actually Red Lotus, the prostitute, and it was Prefect Liu who sent her here to carry out a honeytrap. And my master walked right into that furnace. This letter is his response to Liu. Here is another letter. Ah, here are the instructions left to me.

(*Acts out reading.*) (*A* SECONDARY MALE *acting the part of Liu's* SERVANT *enters, and speaks*:)

Following Prefect Liu's instructions, I was told to present this letter to the Elder Yutong, to inquire about the Red Lotus affair, and to see if he has a response for me.

(*He greets* LAZYBONES, *who acts out replying.*)

(LAZYBONES *says*:) My master, because of this affair, has given up his life. Why are you asking for a response?

(SECONDARY MALE:) Prefect Liu wanted me to personally return with his response. Now what should I do?

(LAZYBONES *says*:) Let me look at your letter. (*Acts out reading*:)

The Water and Moon Monastery Chan Master named Yutong
For quite some time never descended Bamboo Forest's peak:
What a shame that a few drops of Bodhi water
Poured in between Red Lotus's two petals.

Well! What I said about my master having walked right into the furnace was not a bit wrong! Hey, old man, there is a response for you that was under the incense burner. You can take that back. Hold on a moment! Old Man, can I ask you, "How did this affair come about?"

(SECONDARY MALE:) How did it come about? Your master was too high and mighty and thought he was too good to go pay his respects to my master Prefect Liu. That is why he sent that whore Red Lotus to do her "such and such." Your master reached out with bare hands to put out a fire and so he got burned. There's your reason. Now I will—like a mounter of paintings redeeming an inscription—report as instructed.[43] Old monk, I shall now take my leave.

(*Exits.*)

(LAZYBONES:) So it all comes to this. I will now report this to the community in the temple. Whether they take the master's body for cremation or put his body in a shrine, I leave to them.

(*Qing jiang yin*)
In the temple I spent twenty years starving on vegetarian meals,
Long did I sneak glances at my master.
Sitting, he was a sculpted Amitabha,[44]
Standing, he was a living Arhat.

Ah!

Prefect Liu, beware! Yutong will not forget Red Lotus's scheme.

That shrew Red Lotus sold her poison as if it were honey,
Chan Master Yu was defeated on his flight to immortality.
If even a Buddha or bodhisattva seeks revenge through reincarnation,
How can people of this world avoid repaying the debts they owe?

(Explanation) Whenever the written character sheng 生 *(male lead) occurs in the stage directions, it stands for the character Yu* 玉. *Master Yutong is someone who is capable of "playing"*[45] (shua 耍*). So long as he can "play," it doesn't matter whether he is a* sheng, *a* wai 外 *(extra), or a* jing 淨 *(clown).*

ACT 2

(EXTRA MALE *playing* MOONLIGHT MONK *enters carrying a bag containing a gauze cap, a woman's face mask, a monk's hat, and a coarse robe.*)

At the tip of a hundred-foot pole, one had better not show off:
One slip and you're the neighborhood's laughingstock.
What a pity that a mouthful of West Lake's waters
Sent peach flowers afloat to entice Ruan Zhao.[46]

I am not going to speak about where I come from, but I will share a few words about my sect's teachings. What are our teachings? Like a pearl of dew on top of a lotus leaf: it wets the leaf, and yet it doesn't. Like the white root in the dirty mud beneath the lotus leaf: it does not want the filth, and yet it needs a little filth. As to the rudiments of cultivation: it is like the antelope that hangs by its horns from the precious Sala tree.[47] Though it doesn't stick, as time goes by, spots will mark the pure bamboo. As for restraints against the coarse: it is like mixing the peacock's gall[48] with fine amber wine to make a potion. Although, mixed, the gall's bitterness is suppressed by the wine's sweetness, it is still best to pour it out from your golden cup. A single loose thread becomes a mess of creeping tendrils and tangled vines. Myriad thoughts are uselessly empty; they are bound to pile up fine mountains and rivers and great worlds. I cannot clearly say how to rid oneself of the five defilements and completely divest oneself from the One Vehicle of the Lotus Sutra. I fart on the three lives and curse the four elements. One flower, five leaves:[49] they all commit the crime of hollow affection. A hundred seductions, a thousand vanities: they are our very teachings. Mix up the Milky Way with koumiss and ghee; when discussing the circle of Heaven, you can't jump outside the tiles and shards, the piss and shit. Hitting him once with your stick, kill the Buddha to feed a dog; with a laugh, put a sandal on your head to save the cat.[50] What I mean is: a stinky creature like myself, reeking of yellow leeks and rice, can still become transformed into a sweet and precious fragrance. The tiny drops distilled from filthy dog and turtle meat are like a fine jewel good enough to adorn the finest gold Buddha face. What we have just seen is like the tongs and hammer of the furnace fire; turning over all: flesh both rotten and divine. Those who don't get it treat one path as if there were two. Those who do get it kick the monkey and demons of their minds to death. Those who get it advance with blade drawn and can see the way. Those who don't get it face the mirror and then look behind them, not knowing their own face. Ah! mandarin ducks, already embroidered, are for all to see; but passing along the needle does not pass along the skill. Audience members, do you know who I am?

(*An answer from offstage*:) Who are you?

(EXTRA:) I am the senior brother of the Monk Yutong of Water Moon Monastery. I used to be a revered old Buddha from the Western Heavens, but now I have come back to earth, changing my name to Moonlight Monk,[51] all because of my junior brother, Yutong. He had not yet freed himself of the image of self and, snagged by the roots of desire, allowed Liu Xuanjiao to use Red Lotus to deceive him. Wanting revenge, he reincarnated himself as a young girl, a prostitute by the name of Liu Cui, who is now seventeen years old. Our patriarch, pitying him for still being muddled and unenlightened, has sent me specially to help turn him back around. Ah! Yet it is hard work. What is it like? It is like curing blindness by using a golden needle to carefully remove a cataract from the eye; you are fearful of pushing it over, but if you succeed in doing so, the bright vision of old will return. It is like forcing a lion on the road over Mount Taihang; some may be successful, but in doing so, how much effort will have been wasted? But this thing is not something that can be accomplished through language. We Chan practitioners have a tradition of using riddles, a marvelous doctrine of meeting one's opponent with the blade of wit. I will see this Liu Cui today, as she has a date with her frequent visitor, the Huizhou merchant Feng Chaoyang, and he is coming to take in the sights of West Lake. Liu Cui has come first to the Great Buddha Temple to wait for him, and I will wait until she comes, for I have a plan.

(EXTRA *mimes sitting in meditation.*)

(FEMALE LEAD *playing* LIU CUI *enters [and speaks]*:)

Ever since I fell from high status into prostitution,
I've lived for some years as a Little Su[52] in Qiantang.
Countless ones have I entertained upon pleasure boats;
But seeing a peach blossom breaks my heart.

I am Liu Cui. It was not long after my father's funeral that the purse of earnings from his post turned out empty. Day after day I grew poorer, until I, his very own daughter, became a whore, chasing pleasures and selling smiles. But thankfully, amid this misfortune, I've recently hooked up with a merchant from Huizhou by the name of Feng Chaoyang. He is the type who sports with the breeze and enjoys the moonlight, loves righteousness and is free with his money. Thanks to him, I can scrape by.

Today we have planned to look at the peach blossoms on the lake, and he asked me to wait for him at this Great Buddha Temple. Here I am, but where is he?

(COMIC MALE *playing a* SERVANT enters:) Sister, the boss had just reached Yongjin gate when a messenger came to report that his eldest son suddenly had taken ill. The boss had to go back to see how things are, and he will return shortly. He said that Sister should first take the boat out to the lake, or else stay at the temple and wait for the boss to go on the boat with him.

(FEMALE LEAD:) All right. Go back and let him know I got the message.

(COMIC *assents and exits.*)

(FEMALE LEAD *acts out looking around and then seeing* MONK, *and says*:) Where did you come from, old man?

(*She asks three times, and he does not reply each time.*)

(EXTRA *raises his hand and points west, then points to the sky.*)

(FEMALE LEAD) One hand points west, one hand points to heaven. You mean that you are from the Western Heavens? What nonsense! All right, so tell me, what are you up to down in the world below from the Western Heavens?

(EXTRA *hits his own head once with his hand. Then with his hands, he forms a triangle to make the* si 厶 *character, then forms a square to make the character* kou 口, *then forms a circle to make a full moon.*)

(FEMALE LEAD:) That triangle is a *si* character, the square is a *kou*, and putting them together, it makes a *tai* 台 character. The circle is a moon (*yue* 月) character, but since he first hit his head (*tou* 頭) once, it must mean that this is a way of saying "reincarnation."[53] I must ask: What does reincarnation on earth have to do with you? You have just made up this nonsense. Ah! He is a crazy monk. (*Turns and sings*:)

(*Xinshuiling*)

Just because I

Had stopped my boat awaiting a customer, and walked about these corridors,
I ran for no reason into this crazy monk.
When I asked him whence he came,
He pointed to heaven with one hand
And boasted of coming from the West.
And boasted of coming from the West.

In the end,

He formed two characters that resembled "reincarnation."

Ah! Though he is a mad monk, there's something strange about it. I don't know why, but suddenly my mind is roused. I certainly want to question him carefully. I won't go up on the lake just yet. So, master, this subject of "reincarnation" is somewhat bewildering. Could you be so kind as to explain it to me?

(EXTRA *takes out the gauze hat and puts it on his head, then acts out Prefect Liu being angry. Then he takes the hat off and puts it on a table. He then puts on the female mask and kneels down, facing the table. He kowtows, acts out a conversation, then rises.*)

(FEMALE LEAD:) This little performance fills me with even more doubt. Let me try to guess at its meaning.

(*Bubu jiao*)
Wearing the black gauze hat,
With his back to the north and facing south,
He resembles [an official] sitting in the yellow hall of a prefect's office.

Even though his countenance is not father's, these few steps he took at the end were quite like father's.

He turns his body
In a few hurried steps:
Observed closely,
That truly resembles my father's appearance.
In the end he sends off the girl wearing red:
She seems to lead her troops lying in ambush, acting the misty flowers' general.

Master, as I see it, that black gauze hat and woman's face mask must be an official who is sending that woman off on some kind of dirty business? How close is my guess? Just tell me!

(EXTRA *puts on the female mask and walks a few turns, then acts out knocking on a door. He drops on the floor and acts out a stomachache, miming rubbing himself. Then he takes off the female mask and puts it on the floor. He puts on the monk's cap and drops down next to the female mask. He loosens his clothes and acts out rubbing stomachs.*)

(FEMALE LEAD:) This demonstration seems as if the woman had some sort of trouble in her stomach, and the monk is massaging it for her. But what is all this manipulation about? This is tough to figure out.

(*Zheguiling*)
This shiny bald calabash presses on this girl in red
Like the two plates of a wooden grinder,
One grinding out the juice,
Grinding and grinding until the juice comes out.
How could one not break the gibbon reins?[54]
No way to keep the dragon from descending.[55]
Scorched, yet asking the Diamonds to add extra gunpowder to the fire,
Fasting, yet inviting the hungry ghosts to supervise the kitchen.

Master, I can't guess the better part of this; please tell me clearly.

(EXTRA *vigorously grabs* FEMALE LEAD's *earring, then acts out a finger guessing game.*)

(FEMALE LEAD:) You're asking me to guess again.[56] All right, do your gestures once more.

(EXTRA *acts out pointing in between his eyebrows.*)

(FEMALE LEAD:) Again, a head.

(EXTRA *shakes his hand, then with angry eyes acts out pointing again at the space between his eyebrows.*)

(FEMALE LEAD:) If not the head, then, it's anger.[57]

(EXTRA *puts on the female mask and points at the space between the brows.*)

(FEMALE LEAD:) Angry at this woman.

(EXTRA *takes off the female mask and exchanges it for the gauze cap. Again he acts out pointing at the space between the brows*)

(FEMALE LEAD:) Also angry at the official, but why?

(EXTRA *acts out pointing at himself, then again points to his own head.*)

(FEMALE LEAD:) Anger, again.

(MOONLIGHT MONK *acts out shaking his hand.*)

(FEMALE LEAD:) It's not anger . . . then, it's the head again?

(EXTRA *again acts out using his hands, as the first three times, to make the character* tai 胎.)

(FEMALE:) It's reincarnation again, but I just don't get it.

(*Jiang'er shui*)

He is not only angry at the black gauze official,
But he also hates the glossy-haired girl.

Angry at both, he still wants to be reincarnated; but how can a single embryo split into two bodies?

How can one slingshot's pellet split to strike a pair of crows?
To whose house did the embryo go, in the end?
Further, as the gauze official is male,
How can he be propping up a swollen belly, too?
This assumption and requital of a debt,
Must be settled in a "skirts and hairpins" ledger.

(EXTRA *takes a willow branch out of the altar vase, and again uses his hands to make the* tai 胎 [mortal frame, embryo] *character, then acts out imprinting it on the willow branch.*)

(FEMALE LEAD *acts out surprise:*) Ah! Is it that this reincarnation is in my body? I've got it: it must be that I, too, created this grievance and enmity!

(*Deshengling*)

It's not right plying my trade in green bordellos,
Where I cannot help but bury men under layers of rouge.
I remember the year, after I had earned a bit from Monk Huang,[58]
That I tore down that bridge.
Just once I let his little baldy penetrate my crotch:
Our debt on a pair was written on a paper stele,
But a blob of sticky stuff was wrapped in a lotus-leaf pouch.
The little seed of that shiny gourd will soon be nibbling on my plums' juice.
So I had better prepare some fish soup and musk deer incense.[59]

(EXTRA *laughs loudly and says:*) No good at all! A waste of energy! A waste of energy!

(*In a loud voice he reads out:*)

"Red Lotus made a monkey out of me,
So I shall hide for a springtime in the skin of a Green Willow.
When waves beat the duckweed, no one is spared;
My only fear is that when I return you will not recognize my self of old."

Ppft!

(*He acts out spitting a full mouth violently at* FEMALE LEAD.)

(FEMALE LEAD *loudly shouts*:) I get it! I get it! Had I known earlier that the lamp was a fire, the rice would have been cooked a long time ago.

(FEMALE LEAD *throws down her hair bun and acts out taking off her women's clothes*)

(EXTRA *hurriedly assists her by retrieving from his sack a monk's hat and a coarse gown and giving them to* FEMALE LEAD *to put on.* EXTRA and FEMALE LEAD *act out kowtowing to each other several dozen times.*)

(*Yuanlinhao*) (FEMALE LEAD:)
Thank you, Elder Brother, for making this trip from the Western Heavens:
You used the golden needle to remove the cataracts from both my eyes!
Only pinch the tip of the bright crystal lamp,
And a little fire cooks the Yellow Millet,
A little fire cooks the Yellow Millet.[60]

(*Shou Jiangnan*) (FEMALE LEAD)
Elder Brother,
What a hard separation of forty years it has been!
(EXTRA:)
Younger Brother,
You finished this scene in an instant.
(*Together*:)
We see stealing a dwelling for reincarnation in less time than it takes to burn an inch of incense.
(FEMALE LEAD:)
Elder Brother,
I will now move on.
(EXTRA:)
Younger Brother,
I will now not move on.
(*Together*:)
Combine moving on and not moving on to make one way.

(EXTRA:)
Little Lin'an revealed my black winds and waves.

(FEMALE LEAD:) That rotten Red Lotus revealed my powders and rouges.

(*Together*:)
The Liu family leaked out my little clot of blood.

(*From here onward,* EXTRA *and* FEMALE LEAD *sing together, alternating lines.*)

(EXTRA:)

Now I change the tune[61] and swap the costume,

(FEMALE LEAD:)

Now I trade the whore and act a girl.

(EXTRA:)

The little brother
Acted a tiger's assistant to trap a goat;

(FEMALE LEAD:)

The elder brother
By grabbing the reins, tied up the deer.

(EXTRA:)

This flavor is sugarcane juice mixed with sugar,

(FEMALE LEAD:)

That flavor is garlic shoots pounded with ginger.

(EXTRA:)

To escape the heat, chase the cool path of the early sun;

(FEMALE LEAD:)

My schemes were like measuring out the ocean spoonful by spoonful.

(EXTRA:)

Winnow and pound again the white millet and rice chaff;

(FEMALE LEAD:)

Don't scoff at the bald dancer's long sleeves.

(EXTRA:)

What a laugh: kings and emperors compete in force,

(FEMALE LEAD:)

All messed up! Ping and Liang can't be made out.[62]

(EXTRA:)

The many heroes and leaders accept submission or cede their territories;

(FEMALE LEAD:)

Lucky and unlucky affairs, one mourns the dead and celebrates a son's birth.

(EXTRA:)

Giving in to perversity: lusting for calamus,[63] eating scabs;[64]

(FEMALE LEAD:)

Gathering merits: digging embankments, rescuing the starving.

(EXTRA:)

Assisting at the palace with the three bonds and one correction;

(FEMALE LEAD:)

Illuminating a family reputation with gold tablets and jade pendants.

(EXTRA:)

False immortal in cloud villas at moonlit windows;

(FEMALE LEAD:)

Companions for life: the mandarin ducks and phoenix pairs.
(EXTRA:)
The elderly acolytes strike the gong and beat the clappers;
(FEMALE LEAD:)
The suffering ascetics chop wood and hull grain.
(EXTRA:)
All these ten thousand affairs, a hundred anxieties,
(FEMALE LEAD
Stand in for Impermanence's pasteboard robes.
(EXTRA:)
In duels of wit, swords and spears compete in sharpness,
(FEMALE LEAD:)
But dull from nature, the dung beetle tries to jump the wall.
(EXTRA:)
A fake widow with stomach pains, beautiful as a crabapple;
(FEMALE LEAD:)
A hoary one who took revenge resembled a black crane.[65]
(EXTRA:)
How many precious twigs does it take a magpie to fill a pond?
(FEMALE LEAD:)
It almost led to bustards roosting on the hall's mulberry tree.[66]
(EXTRA:)
Only when I had used all my mute and feigned miracle cures,
(FEMALE LEAD:)
Did you succeed in melting the snow and making hot tea.
(EXTRA:)
Two brothers go off together like a pair of wild geese:
(FEMALE LEAD:)
Old Bodhidharmas bundle their provisions and cross the river.
(EXTRA:)
The heels of our feet on yellow-leaved rushes and reeds,[67]
(FEMALE LEAD:)
In moments we reach our old home in the West.
(EXTRA:)
As before, we will chew the fruit before the Web-Footed King;[68]
(FEMALE LEAD:)
We see from afar the jeweled pennants, the raft of enlightenment.
(EXTRA:)
We have cast away this one skin sack full of stolen property,
(FEMALE LEAD:)
And exchanged them for washed entrails that brilliantly shine.

(*Sing together*:)

Ah!

Now we place the palms of our hands together,
And report on our mission at our Teacher's cell.

(*As a gong and drums are sounded from offstage, they quickly exit.*)

In Great Lin'an a one-third official,
Old Yutong's single thread of self-image.
Borrowing Red Lotus for a night of illicit love,
The Moonlight Monk delivers Liu Cui.

NOTES

1. See Tao Gu (2003, 31), "When Li Yu (the Southern Tang monarch 961–976) was in the capital (i.e., Nanjing), he would go incognito to the brothels, where he met a monk who was throwing a party, which Yu joined even though he had not been invited. The monk was unsurpassable at drinking games, singing and chanting, and playing wind and string instruments; noticing Li Yu's intelligence and refinement, he became his friend and held him in high regard. The drunk Li Yu inscribed these lines on the wall: 'Leisurely drinking and softly singing, cuddling red rouge and leaning against black hair, the great master is the abbot of the Love Birds Monastery, and transmits and maintains the teachings of romance.' After quite some time, the monk and prostitute retired to the inner chamber, and Li Yu quietly departed. The monk and prostitute never realized who Li Yu was. Li Yu secretly told this to Xu Xuan (916–991) in confidence." 李煜在國，微行娼家，遇一僧張席，煜遂為不速之客。僧酒令、謳吟、吹彈莫不高了，見煜明俊醞藉，契合相愛重。煜乘醉大書右壁，曰：「淺斟低唱，偎紅倚翠，大師鴛鴦寺主，傳持風流教法。」久之，僧擁妓入屏帷，煜徐步而出，僧、妓竟不知煜為誰也。煜嘗密諭徐鉉，言於所親焉.
2. Li Shouqing hailed from Taiyuan and reached the rank of assistant district magistrate. He is credited with ten plays of which two are preserved (if we accept *Yueming heshang du Liu Cui* as his work).
3. See Idema (1997, 69–71). An annotated edition of this play is included in Jing Lihu (1992, 65–151). See also Wang Zhiyong (1980).
4. See note 22 to chapter 2 in Kwa (2012, 250).
5. See West and Idema (2015, 49–56); parallel scenes can be found on 69–71 (14th c. ed.) and 99–103 (16th c. full ed.).
6. These opening lines are Buddhist allusions. The first couplet suggests that one should be prepared for both external bodily (lions') dangers as well as internal mental ones ("monkey" minds); the second couplet suggests that one cannot achieve true enlightenment all at once (in a single gulp) but must reach it through many years of study and cultivation. The West River here refers to the Yangzi, the longest river in Asia.
7. Yutong sounds like "desire for sexual liaison" (*yutong* 欲通).
8. The phrase "stealing a mortal lodging," means occupying an embryo to be born again into the world as a human.
9. Hangzhou.
10. Fengdu is one of the names of the underworld.
11. Bodhidharma (late 4th–early 5th century) was an Indian monk who came to China and in later centuries was considered the founder of Chan/Zen Buddhism.
12. Huike 慧可 (ca. 487–593) was a disciple of Bodhidharma who is counted as the second patriarch of Chan/Zen. When preaching at the capital one time, legend has it that he amassed a huge following.

13. Cf. the following quatrain on the enlightenment of a nun: "All day long I searched for spring but nowhere did I find it— / On sandals of straw I trekked through the clouds atop the hills. / When I returned, I smilingly plucked a sprig of flowering plum, / One sniff and I found that all of spring was there on this twig!" (Idema and Grant 2004, 158).
14. The highest truth.
15. Liu Xuanjiao 柳宣教 is not a historical character but a figure of legend.
16. Sex is often described in terms of battle, with the woman slaying the lust-driven man.
17. Heat is associated with power.
18. The surname Liu means "willow."
19. Red Lotus uses "such and such" and "that stuff" euphemistically to refer to having sex with Yutong and bringing the evidence in the form of semen stains back as proof.
20. Mourning dress is white in Chinese tradition.
21. Clear and Bright (Qingming) is a spring festival in early April for sweeping the graves and making offerings to the deceased.
22. In the Ming dynasty, a standard of beauty for women would be bound feet, commonly known as "golden lotuses." Therefore, any reference to a woman's feet would be highly erotic.
23. The Yellow River embankments have to be very high and sturdy because in many places the river bed is actually higher than the surrounding fields.
24. See note 18 on "Willow" and "Liu."
25. In late-imperial China "Cold Food" festival was an alternative designation of Clear and Bright (Qingming), as a significant part of the offerings made on Qingming are food offerings, cf. note 21.
26. The Yellow Springs are a common designation of the underworld of the dead.
27. "Expedient means" (*upaya*) refers to any activity that may lead to the achievement of Buddhahood.
28. In Daoist physiology man has three "Cinnabar Fields." The lowest Cinnabar Field is located three inches below the navel.
29. Highest wisdom.
30. The Diamond gods refer to the four frightening protective deities of Buddhist temples that are usually depicted in the gateway.
31. "Misty flower" is a common euphemism for a prostitute. "Pearly palace" originally referred to the splendid underwater palace of the dragons, but later also was used to refer to Buddhist monasteries and Daoist temples because of their rich decorations.
32. A calabash is a common metaphor for a monk's bald-shaven head.
33. A Song dynasty courtesan from Lin'an (Hangzhou). Su Dongpo (the literary name of Su Shi) would often have her as his companion when traveling in Hangzhou. When he introduced her to Chan Buddhism, she became a convert and later became a nun.
34. The two syllables *yeme* inserted here and in some of the following lines have no meaning but are required to maintain the melody.
35. "Dragon Source" is the name of a famous sword.
36. "Gelded ox" refers to the monk's many years of ascetic practices.
37. Ananda was a cousin of the Buddha, his long-time attendant, and one of his most loyal disciples.
38. Bodhidharma, when practicing meditation at the Shaolin Monastery, sat facing a wall for nine years.
39. Mt. Putuo (Potalaka) is a little island off the Zhejiang coast, with a temple dedicated to the worship of the bodhisattva Guanyin.
40. The best known of the rivers called "Brocade River" runs by Chengdu.
41. Holy monks may will their own death while seated in an upright position.

42. Several legends have the bodhisattva Guanyin using her physical charms to seduce mortal men as a means to enlightenment.
43. "Reporting" (*huihua* 回話) has the same pronunciation as "retrieving a painting" (*huihua* 回畫). When a mounter of paintings goes to a pawn shop to redeem pawned goods, he will likely be retrieving a painting.
44. Amitabha is a celestial Buddha, and one of the highest ranking. He is often depicted seated with hands held together in meditation (thumbs touching and fingers together), flanked by two followers. Often one of these followers is Guanyin.
45. The term *shua* 耍 can refer to playing in many different senses, including "display," or physical action, such as juggling, tumbling, and martial arts, but also playing tricks or mocking. This stage note suggests that the ability to "play" is more important than the actor's specialization in the role type for the character who plays Yutong, which may suggest a prioritization of physical abilities for Yutong in this play. See introductory text for further explanation.
46. Ruan Zhao and Liu Chen got lost in the Tiantai mountains while gathering herbs and ended up in a fairyland with two beautiful women. What feels like a short time away to them has been seven generations.
47. The antelope was believed to suspend itself from treetops with its antlers so that it would not leave any tracks behind and thus would be protected from hunters. Chan masters compared this to the notion of awakening to enlightenment, saying that chasing after enlightenment by pursuing a master's words would be like trying to follow the invisible tracks of an antelope. The "Sala tree" is a teakwood tree, under which Sakyamuni reached nirvana.
48. Peacock's gall, or bile, was believed to be a fatal poison.
49. The five sects of Chan Buddhism.
50. The Chan monk Deshan Xuanjian 德山軒鑒 (782–865) is credited with the following saying: "When Shakyamuni was born, he pointed with one hand to heaven and with the other to the earth, walked seven steps around, and looking in the four directions said, 'Up in heaven and below heaven only I am to be revered!' Now if I would have been present, I would have killed him with one hit of my staff and fed him to the dogs to ensure universal peace." The Chan master Nanquan Puyuan 南泉普願 (748–843) once tried to mediate between two groups of monks who argued over the ownership of a cat. When both sides failed to say the right thing, he cut the cat in two. When the Chan master Zhaozhou 趙州 arrived and heard about this, he took off a sandal, put it on his head and left, whereupon Nanquan Puyuan commented, "If you had been here, you would have been able to save the cat."
51. The moon reflected in all streams is a common metaphor for the one Buddha-nature that is present in all creatures.
52. A famous Hangzhou (Qiantang) courtesan.
53. The characters for reincarnation (*toutai* 投胎) are created thus by Moonlight and guessed by Liu Cui: First he acts out the second character, *tai* 胎, by breaking it down into its three component parts; he makes the triangle and square that shape the right side of the character, using his hands, and then he describes roundness with his hands to imply a moon, because the left part of *tai* is the moon radical. The first character in the compound for reincarnation, *tou* 投, is evoked by Moonlight's playing on its homophone, *tou* 頭, by striking his head. This makes Liu Cui think of the homophonous *tou* 投, and she then combines it with *tai* to come up with the compound word for reincarnation.
54. The mind is like a gibbon that needs to be reined in by religious or moral teachings.
55. Sexual desire may be described as a poisonous dragon.
56. He has used the homophones *huan* 環 for "earring" and *huan* 還 for "again." By grabbing her earring, he draws her attention to the sound *huan*, for "doing over."

57. The word for anger, *nao* 惱, is homophonous with the word *nao* 腦 meaning "brain" that could also be indicated by the monk's gestures.
58. The character for the surname Huang 黃 also has the meaning of "yellow."
59. Liu Cui believes that Moonlight is telling her that she is pregnant (craving sour things), and carrying the child of a monk, a former customer.
60. An allusion to the Yellow Millet, or Handan, dream in which a man experiences a lifetime in a dream in the time it takes to cook a yellow millet porridge.
61. *Gai qiang* 改腔 means to change the tune or to put a new face on it.
62. Chen Ping 陳平 (d. 178 BCE) and Zhang Liang 張良 (d. 186 BCE) were cunning advisors of Liu Bang 劉邦 (256–195), the founding emperor of the Han dynasty (202 BCE–220 CE). The phrase "can't be made out" is literally *ma cang* 馬藏, which refers to a stallion's retractable penis. A retractable penis is also one of the thirty-two signs of the Buddha.
63. Calamus was used to increase male potency.
64. Liu Yong 劉邕 of the Liu Song dynasty (420–479) was rumored to love eating scabs.
65. The frosty colored crane alludes to the color of monks' robes; it is another bird metaphor in keeping with the magpie/bustard couplet and the wild geese, of which Buddha leads the flock.
66. The word for "bustard" also is used to refer to a brothel procuress.
67. In one version of Bodhidharma's journey, he rides on leaves to cross the river to Luoyang.
68. The Web-Footed King is one of the designations of the Buddha because his fingers and toes were linked by skin, like the feet of a goose.

4

Real Puppets

WANG HENG (1562–1609)

TRANSLATED BY WAI-YEE LI

The author of *Real Puppets* (*Zhen kuilei* 真傀儡) is listed as "Anonymous of the Green Fields Hall" 綠野堂無名氏 in Shen Tai's 沈泰 *Short Plays* (*Sheng Ming zaju* 盛明雜劇, 1629). But there is convincing contextual evidence that the author is Wang Heng 王衡 (1562–1609), sobriquets Chenyu 辰玉, Goushan 緱山, and Master of the Green Fields Hall 綠野堂主人. For example, Shen Defu 沈德符 (1578–1642) praised Wang Heng's plays, including *Real Puppets*, for "capturing the true spirit of Jin and Yuan plays."[1] Meng Chengshun 孟稱舜 (1599–1684), who anthologized this play in *Libation at the River* (*Leijiang ji* 酹江集), also listed the author as "Anonymous," but recorded in a comment the "hearsay" that Wang Heng wrote the play to celebrate his father Wang Xijue's 王錫爵 (1534–1611) birthday.[2] Wang Xijue held high office, including stints as grand secretary. Wang Heng became the top provincial graduate (*juren*) in 1588, but accusations of nepotism, rooted in factional struggles at court, forced him to retake the examination in 1589. He did not participate in the metropolitan examinations during the years that his father served as grand secretary, and finally became a *jinshi* and a Hanlin compiler only in 1601, but he gave up office shortly thereafter.

Although Wang Heng was ultimately vindicated, his sense of grievance about the accusation in 1588 is thought to have motivated him to write *Yulun pao* 鬱輪袍 (ca. 1590). In this seven-act *zaju* play, Wang Tui 王推 impersonates the Tang poet Wang Wei 王維 (692–761) and gains the favor of royal patrons by performing the tune "Yulun pao" on the pipa. These patrons help Wang Tui secure the first place in the examination, but a more discerning examiner exposes Wang Tui's incompetence and promotes instead the real Wang Wei. Wang Tui then uses the recommendation letter he swindled from his royal patrons to accuse Wang Wei of peddling influence.[3] Although the truth is finally revealed and Wang Wei is declared the top graduate, he sees through the vanity of worldly glory, renounces officialdom, and becomes a recluse. The play ends with Wang Wei's dream of being reborn three hundred years later as the Song official Han Wei 韓維, who will enjoy great achievements without controversy.

The concern with the real and the fake, identity and impersonation, and recognition of worth are also dominant themes in *Real Puppets*, the plot of which is based on an anecdote about the Tang scholar-official Du You 杜佑 (735–812), the author of *Institutions Through the Ages* (*Tongdian* 通典):

> When the Junior Minister of State Affairs [Du You] was in Yangzhou, he once summoned his secretaries and chatted with them. "After I retire, it will suffice for me to buy a modest horse with eight or nine thousand cash, ride astride it after eating my fill, wear simple, tattered clothes, and enter the marketplace to watch puppet plays to the accompaniment of *panling* music." He also said, "When Guo Ziyi 郭子儀 (697–781) was at the height of his power, he often worried that disaster would overtake him. This is the great danger for ministers." The deep intention of the minister lies not in puppets—his goal is to besmirch himself. After he retired, he indeed fulfilled his goals. A remonstrance official submitted critiques to the throne pointing out that "high-ranking ministers should not enter the marketplace." The minister said, "He has fallen into my trap." The so-called trap is precisely what "besmirching himself" means.[4]

The historical Du Yan 杜衍 (978–1057), the protagonist in *Real Puppets*, overcame great hardships in his youth to attain exalted positions, including a ten-day tenure as prime minister. Aside from his fame as a calligrapher, he was known for his integrity and abstemiousness, dispensing with regalia and living a life of extreme simplicity after his retirement. In one story, some aristocratic young men who were offended by his failure to rise and bow, demanded of him: "What was your previous position, sir?" Du Yan replied (no doubt to the young men's dismay): "Jointly manager of affairs with the secretariat-chancellery."[5]

The wooden figures (*yong* 俑) accompanying the dead in burial in Han times and earlier might have been puppets used in funeral rites.[6] The account of a mechanical automaton that is almost human in the Daoist text *Liezi* 列子 (ca. 3rd c.)[7] offers insight into the fascination with puppets: it points to key issues about the nature of reality and the boundaries of being human.[8] The Du You anecdote cited above suggests that puppet performances existed in the Tang dynasty. Feng Yan 封演 (*jinshi* 756) described a puppet performance showing a Tang general and his Turkish adversary locked in combat, and another featuring Xiang Yu 項羽 and Liu Bang 劉邦 confronting each other at the Hongmen banquet as part of the funeral ritual for a regional military commander.[9] The Tang emperor Xuanzong 玄宗 (r. 713–756) is credited with a poem "On Puppets" (Kuilei yin 傀儡吟):

刻木牽絲作老翁	Carved wood and pulled strings turn it into an old man,
雞皮鶴髮與真同	His wrinkled skin and white hair palpably real.

須臾弄罷寂無事	In an instant, the play's done, and all reverts to stillness,
還似人生一夢中	Just like life lived in a dream.[10]

One source claims that the emperor chanted this poem to lament his irrelevance in the wake of the An Lushan rebellion (755–763). After his son (Emperor Suzong 肅宗, r. 756–762) ascended the throne, Xuanzong was increasingly marginalized as the "Senior Emperor." The silence and nothingness when the play is done—literally, "when the puppeteer is done toying with him" (*nongba* 弄罷)—reminds us that human agency is precarious and may be illusory.

The lively urban culture of the Song dynasty boasted a rich variety of puppet performances, including string puppets, stick puppets, fireworks puppets, water puppets, and flesh puppets.[11] The last category refers to humans performing as puppets, the focus of this play. The term "real puppets" is deliberately paradoxical: it means both "these are really puppets" and puppets that are "real" because they are humans acting out the movements of puppets (i.e., they can claim greater verisimilitude because they are fake puppets). Literary historians regard puppet performances as one of the precursors of Song-Yuan drama. Puppets also have a deep metaphorical connection with the theater, as *Real Puppets* implies in its metatheatrical references.

This one-act play raises fundamental questions on social reality, meaningful action, and the performance of roles. The puppeteer, who explains the historical background of the performance, makes us reflect on agency and destiny. Are the great heroes of history no more than puppets controlled by others? The puppets act out the aspirations, dilemmas, and endeavors of historical personages, but while they resonate with Du Yan, the rest of the audience misses the point. Does an action require a discerning audience to be meaningful? In any case, what does "leaving a name in history" mean when all amounts to half-forgotten or misunderstood tales? When an imperial emissary arrives on the scene, Du Yan has to borrow a court robe from a puppet to receive the imperial edict—the incognito official can reclaim his status only through theatrical costume. The villagers initially mistake the imperial summons for part of the show and ultimately conclude that it is an even more entertaining theatrical spectacle. All these prompt obvious analogies between "the stage of officialdom" (*guanchang* 官場) and the theatrical stage (*xichang* 戲場).

Comedy is never entirely divorced from political purpose, as Sima Qian 司馬遷 (ca. 145–after 91 BCE) reminds us in his biography of jesters.[12] The real drama seems to be offstage as the play ponders the meanings of a scholar-official's ambition and self-definition. Du Yan is obviously an ideal: someone uniquely suited to wielding power because he is utterly indifferent to it, or at least to its paraphernalia. He combines detachment and engagement: although he remains in retirement, he can offer crucial advice to the throne. The audience laughs with him at the pettiness and fatuous boastfulness of Zhao and Shang. The play is dated to 1607, not long after Wang Xijue was summoned to join the Grand Secretariat again but declined.[13] Some believe that Wang Heng is comparing Du Yan to his father, who also chooses to live a quiet life in retirement.[14] Yet even Du Yan's modus operandi betrays some disquiet. Is he in perfect control of the situation? Following the anecdote about Du You above, Du Yan in the play seems to imply that he is deliberately courting criticism by behaving beneath his dignity to avoid being summoned to serve again. Yet the remonstrance officials recommend his demotion and exile: Had the emperor not decided to ignore the critique, would Du Yan not have suffered?

The danger of political life was a very pressing issue for late Ming scholar-officials. We recall that the furor over the 1588 examination results was also instigated by remonstrance officials; several of them were younger officials belonging to the Donglin faction critical of Wang Xijue and his generation. Indeed, the historical examples of political success performed by the puppets also convey ambiguities: Cao Can 曹参 is always inebriated supposedly by virtue of his Daoist convictions, but his choice is also necessary self-preservation. The first Han emperor, Gaozu 高祖, ruthlessly eliminated powerful ministers who seemed to threaten him, and his de facto successor Empress Lü was similarly ruthless. Although the amity said to exist between the first Song emperor Taizu 太祖 and Zhao Pu 趙普 was celebrated in the story of Taizu's visit on a snowy night, tensions and suspicions marred their bond as well as the relationship between Zhao Pu and Taizu's younger brother and successor, Taizong 太宗, and Zhao Pu suffered major vicissitudes in his career. Zhao Pu's political survival depended among other things on dissemblance, perhaps best symbolized by the contrast between the humble bramble gates and the opulent interior of his mansion.[15] The Northern Wei official Cui Hao 崔浩, brought up in the allusion to "crystal salt," is another classic symbol of imperial recognition, but he ended up being executed along with his entire clan. Timely and resolute withdrawal to the quieter world of the country would seem to be the solution, but even the village replays power politics, albeit on a much smaller scale.

Wang Heng suffered numerous tragedies in his personal life. He married four times; three of his wives died young. When he was twenty, his older sister Wang Taozhen 王燾貞 (also called Tanyangzi 曇陽子, 1557–1580) starved herself to death but was believed to have become an immortal.[16] He lost another sister eight years later. Three of his sons died in childhood. (His only surviving son, Wang Shimin 王時敏 [1592–1680], became a famous painter.) One of his sobriquets was "Goushan," a mountain in Daoist lore upon which immortals reside. Perhaps beyond the questions on politics, officialdom, and human foibles, the puppets also promise deliverance from sufferings by urging detachment from a reality that may ultimately be illusory. This sentiment is forcefully articulated in another one-act play by Wang Heng, *Can't Be Helped* (*Mei neihe* 沒奈何). It is structured as a dialogue between Master Gourd and a man called Can't Be Helped, in which they ponder injustice and sorrows in the human world:

浪道是名千載　Why talk about everlasting fame?
不如這酒一盃　None compares to this cup of wine.

翰林院拗斷南狐筆	In the Hanlin Academy the historian's brush is bent and broken.
傀儡場搬演何場戲	Which dynasty's play is being performed on the puppet stage?

The translation is based on the version of *Real Puppets* included in Shen Tai's 沈泰 *Short Plays of the Great Ming*. The male lead sings in northern (*bei*) tunes in this one-act play. His song sequence is interspersed with the puppeteer's songs to other tunes (*Jisheng cao, Mantang hong, Qingjiang yin*). The play concludes with everyone singing an aria to the tune *Qingjiang yin*.

Dramatis Personae in Order of Appearance

Role type	*Name, family, or social role*
SHEZHANG	Village elders
COMIC, JING	Master Zhao
CLOWN, CHOU	Honorable Shang
ZHONG	Crowd
MALE LEAD, ZHENGMO, MO	Du Yan
SHUA KUILEI, SHUA	Puppeteer
EXTRA, WAI	Young officer (played by a human puppet)
OU, CHENGXIANG	Prime minister (Cao Can) (played by a human puppet)
	Prime minister (Cao Cao) (played by a human puppet)
JINÜ	Singing girls (played by human puppets)
OU, CHENGXIANG	Prime minister (Zhao Pu) (played by a human puppet)
LADY, FUREN	(Zhao Pu's wife) (played by a human puppet)
DI	Emperor (Song Taizu) (played by a human puppet)
QIANDAO	Vanguard
CHAOSHI, SHI	Court emissary
ZHONGGUI	Eunuchs

THE SONG EMPEROR SEEKS ADVICE FROM HIS FORMER COUNCILOR

DU LORD QI HIDES HIMSELF AMONG THE REAL PUPPETS[17]

Compiled by the Anonymous of Green Fields Hall
Commentary by Huang Jiahui, the Likely Daoist
Read by Huang Zhigui (sobriquet Shangda) and Wu Guohua (sobriquet Zhonghan), both from West Lake

(VILLAGE ELDER *enter* [*and recites*]:)

Beneath the Swan Lake Mountain, the grains are ripening.
Pig pens and chicken coops face each other, their gates closed.
In the mulberry's slanting shadow, the spring altar crowd disperses,
As each family supports its inebriated ones on the way home.[18]

We are two leaders in the Peach Blossom Village.[19] I am Elder Sun Third; he is Elder Zhang Third. In our village it's the custom, year after year, to pool resources, buy wine, and prepare a grand gathering for the spring and autumn altar festivals. Now it is our turn to head the celebration.[20] We heard that a troupe of puppeteers has recently arrived. It sure sounds like fun! In the past we have always had puppets pretending to be humans, but now we have humans pretending to be puppets—of course we must summon them for a performance! Even as I am speaking, people are already coming to the gathering.

(COMIC *enters*:) This is Master Zhao here. Because my father served for two terms as inspector, your humble servant followed him and studied where he was serving. By my vast knowledge about all matters, past and present, I have become a tutor at a noble house. Today I am off to Peach Blossom Village to watch a puppet show. Attendants! Take my horse! Wait for me with a sedan chair carried by four persons and equipped with a silk parasol! (*He joins the crowd.*) Greetings!

(CROWD:) Greetings!

(CLOWN *enters*:) This is the Honorable Shang here. I started out in the chicken market. Now why do we call it the chicken market? Day after day I, too, have scratched around in the sand on the street and have saved enough for a decent setup with a shop front. The neighbors think that I have what it takes to be an official and all flatter me with the name Honorable Shang.[21] Today everyone is going to Peach Blossom Village to watch the puppet show, and I too am joining the celebration. Lads! Carry my big leather casket with a pole and leave it outside the gates. For all we know I will have to distribute some coins to reward the players. (*He joins the crowd.*) Greetings!

(CROWD:) Greetings!

(ZHAO *and* SHANG:) Since we are already here, don't let in any unaccounted-for characters, for they would lack manners and embarrass us. Just set up the feast and the stage and wait for the puppets.

(MALE LEAD, *in a Daoist robe, enters astride a donkey*:) This old man is Du Yan, a native of Shanyin in Kuaiji. I served as Grand Councilor and received the title of Duke of Qi. Since I retired at seventy, twenty years have passed like a snap of the finger.[22] I am only too glad to have left behind the imperial court's magnificence and have little patience for grand country estates.[23] Day in and day out I bury my traces in town and marketplace, takings things as they come. I have borne with the scorn of nobodies, for only thus can I lower the banner of pride that sets me above others. I have made do with indifferent food and drink, for only thus can I fulfill the karmic debt that demands humble fare. Free and easy beyond the Realm of the Locust King, I smile gleefully in the midst of bamboo horses.[24] In order to refine my spirit and purge it of any hint of strife, I have to wait till none in the world knows me. People say that I please myself and gratify my whims, perversely adding excitement to an all too tame existence. Little do they know that I, having escaped from the world and eschewed fame, must preen and caper even if it means harmless offense. Now today is the birthday of the Lord of the Altar, and just the right time for me to have some wine to cure my deafness.[25] Just think of all the urgency and hubbub when I was an official—how could I be like the way I am now! (DU YAN *sings*:)

(*Xinshui ling*)

For twenty years, I have not had to brave dawn frost,
And this plain white robe of mine has remained untarnished.[26]
Cosmic principles make a ruckus in vain,
Wind and rain put the setting in disarray.[27]
What is the rush?
What is the rush?
Just let this lazy donkey bumble his way.

Ah, what is all this commotion? So this turns out to be a puppet stage. I was just in the mood for a puppet show. Let me just tie up this donkey. (*He ties the donkey [to a pole] and enters.*) Greetings, everyone!

(SHANG:) Look at you—neither towner nor villager—what sort of person are you? Why did you come here? Who invited you?

(DU YAN:) What harm is it to invite me?

(ZHAO:) What did I say? Don't let these ill-mannered types come in.

(CROWD:) Your Honor, indeed we should not have let him in.

(SHANG:) Could it be that you also want to squeeze your way in and be part of the celebration?

(DU YAN:) Just so. I too want to have a gander.

(SHANG:) Those who come late have to pay a bigger share. Hand over five strings of cash.

(DU YAN:) As for that, I do have it. In my sleeve is an ingot's worth of a Great Peace bill[28]—I don't know how many strings of cash it amounts to—just take it.

(ZHAO:) Eh? So, this old man can come up with this ingot-bill. Now how should we sit?

(CROWD:) Naturally, Your Honor should take a seat.

(ZHAO:) But on this I am absolutely not yielding to him.

(SHANG:) By the new rule of these times, position is no match for wealth. You should yield precedence to me.

(ZHAO:) Watch out or I will tell your real story!

(SHANG:) And you watch out or I will tell your real story!

(CROWD:) Please make some room for each other! Among us in the village we should just go by seniority.

(ZHAO:) What do you mean by "us in the village?" Are you saying that all of you should go by seniority with me too?

(DU YAN *sings as an aside.*)

(*Chenzui dongfeng*)

Alas!

How many bedfuls of official tablets does he have, that he should parade this official mien?[29]

How many boatloads of tea does it take to feed such smugness and swagger?[30]

(ZHAO *and* SHANG *point to the crowd.*) All of you there—go below—don't forget your manners.

(CROWD:) We do not dare. (DU YAN *sings:*)

This is but a feast for wild gulls,

Nothing comparable with the orderly rows of egrets and cranes.[31]

All this time I

Have marked how it's hard to survive the perils of officialdom,

Who could have known that the cruelty of human heart is such that wealth and power hold sway everywhere?[32]

(ZHAO *looks at* DU YAN:) Ah, I forgot about you. You have neither wealth nor position, and you are not party to the gathering. You bumbled your way in to demand a seat.

(SHANG:) Since we just took his money for joining the gathering, let us make an exception and allow him to squeeze in at the corner of the table. Old man—that's good enough for you.

(DU YAN:) Thank you! Thank you! (*Sings:*)

We'll let you hicks and yokels[33] show off your might to your heart's content,

Even if it totally breaks the rash spirit of officials like me.

(ZHAO *and* SHANG:) Those puppet players—they should be here by now.

(PUPPETEER *enters banging the cymbal, recites:*)

(*Xi jiang yue*)[34]

We got our share of half a face from the Pear Garden,[35]
And have put Old Bao in front of the revelers.[36]
A thread's beginning, a string's end, secretly pulled,
Create gracefully dancing shadows in front of our eyes,
Past and present, fair and foul in the mirror.

Coming! Coming!

(*Flute music inside, the* EXTRA *dressed as a* YOUNG OFFICER *comes on stage supporting a drunken* PRIME MINISTER. The OFFICER *kneels as he remonstrates with the* MINISTER, *who seems annoyed.*)

(CROWD:) What story is this?

(PUPPETEER:) This is the story of the Han prime minister drinking to his heart's content at the Hall of Government Affairs.[37] (*Sings:*)

(*Qingjiang yin*)
The mountains and rivers of Han
Have been secured after the turmoil of war.
The old prime minister
Worries no more.
He draws a circle of peace
And firmly adheres to Xiao He's laws.
By his side stands the wide-awake one
Urging without avail what should be done.[38]

(CROWD *asks* ZHAO:) What is the name of this prime minister?

(ZHAO:) This is Cao Wushang, Left Marshal of Lord Pei, who later became the first Han emperor. He slandered Lord Pei, but when Lord Pei became emperor, he did not hold old grudges and made him prime minister and Lord of Shifang. He was overjoyed, and that was why he was dead drunk every day.[39]

(DU YAN:) This is the prime minister Cao Can, not the Left Marshal.

(ZHAO:) Why should you of all people know anything about this? He wasn't born a prime minister—he too served as a commander at first.

(DU YAN:) Yes, yes. He served as a commander. (*Sings*:)
(*Shiba pai*)
Yet if he drove his troops on with so much valor,
Why does he fall in a heap in this wine-stricken manner?

(ZHAO *to the* CROWD:) That's just because he is a drunkard.

(DU YAN *smiles.*) Yes, he is a drunkard. (*Sings*:)
Truly this is mixing fermenting yeast, creating an excellent brew.[40]

(ZHAO *points to* DU YAN:) You of all people have much too much to say. Shut your trap! Just watch the play! (DU YAN *sings*:)
Next to my ears, a relentless clamor,
Deep in my heart, an insistent murmur.

I reckon that he who becomes prime minister sits right in the den of praise and blame and dos and don'ts. There's so much to be done for which nothing can be said. Who knows how many rounds of grinding and tempering he has borne![41]

Naught but thirty-six thousand rounds of drunken slumber
Can make him the foremost minister, twenty-four times the overseer.[42]

(PUPPETEER:) Here he comes again, here he comes again.

(*Two* SINGING GIRLS, *leading the* PRIME MINISTER *to come out, dance and seem happy.*)

(CROWD:) What story is this?

(PUPPETEER:) This is the story of Prime Minister Cao and the Bronze Bird Terrace.[43] (*Sings*:)
(*Mantang hong*)

The bronze bird comes in flight,
It comes in flight.
Twelve ladies with golden hairpins,
Golden hairpins in sight.
Terrace of songs, terrace of dance,
Terrace of chance.
The bird is buckled,
The tower has crumbled.
Where is it now?
Tiles from the terrace after a thousand years bear witness to changing names.[44]

(*The* CROWD *asks* ZHAO:) And who is this?

(ZHAO:) This is Young Cao, son of Old Cao who appeared earlier.[45]

(CROWD:) What fun! This young one has greater panache! Much better than the old one who knows no better than becoming dead drunk alone!

(DU YAN:) Alas! Cao Mengde, how foolish you are! (*Sings*:)

(*Gua yugou*)
Laughable indeed, how all your energy
You spend by the brocade zither,
Looking at these lovely souls,
Not letting them deviate in the least.[46]
You used your mental powers to the fullest, but whom can you fool?[47]
All you have earned are two ink strokes hung on the tips of your eyebrows.[48]

(CROWD:) What a handsome old prime minister! How did he come to sire such a creature with a painted face? And yet his costume and gestures really take after his father.[49]

(PUPPET:) To be honest with you—I did not have time to do a complete make-over, so I just put on a mask. (*He removes his mask.*)

(*The* CROWD *laughs.*) So this turns out to be just a play! Father and son my foot! Father and son my foot! You are just making fun of us! This is no good! Give us a new one!

(DU YAN *laughs.*) Just so! This is more like it! (*Sings*:)

One is this way,
One is that way.
Just look how the gourd is drawn, true to form.
On the pages of history books from the ages,
How many plum trees have died in place of the peach?[50]

(PUPPETEER:) For two rounds of stories from previous dynasties, you had all these arguments for what was right and what was wrong. Now let us perform a story from what is in front of our eyes. Coming! Coming!

(*The human puppets dress as a* PRIME MINISTER *and his* LADY *and come on stage. Another comes on stage as an* EMPEROR. *The* EMPEROR *braves snow and knocks on the gate.* The MINISTER *comes out, leads the emperor in, kneels and pays obeisance. The* EMPEROR *and the* MINISTER's LADY *point to each other.*)

(CROWD:) Who are these people?

(PUPPETEER:) This is the story of how the Taizu emperor of our present dynasty visited Zhao Pu on a snowy night.[51] (*Sings:*)

(*Jisheng cao*)

This is truly the heartfelt bond of ruler and minister,
So much better than soaring high on the merit of battles!
During that night, when shadows from the Nine Flicker Lamp deepened,[52]
When the fish-shaped locks of a thousand gates were mightily shaken,[53]
When the sister-in-law was from the lovebirds' dream rudely awakened,[54]
They partook of the crystal salt in the prime minister's residence—[55]
So much grander than sadly finishing a jar of pickled vegetables in the study hall!

(ZHAO:) I cannot be more familiar with this story. This emperor is your humble servant's ancestor. This Zhao Pu was the emperor's older brother. Relying on no more than half of the *Analects*, Zhao Pu helped him gain control of the entire realm under heaven.[56] Now this *Analects* can be found in my house—truly a rare book! (*Pointing to* DU YAN:) Old man—you there—you look somewhat literate. Have you seen that book?

(DU YAN:) I too have seen it. (*Sings:*)

(*Dianqian huan*)

I too have savored this taste—

As for this Zhao, the Prince of Han,

He excels in strategy, rising like the clouds with the dragon, the wind with the tiger,[57]
But this is also because his brother from humble beginnings is true and steadfast.[58]
My thoughts linger and linger:
Even if I have stern hands, do I dare leave marks on the imperial yellow paper?[59]
And this face, by now unfamiliar, can hardly make its case.

Have done! Have done! Have done! All glory can be ceded to my predecessors. But what a joke that Zhao Pu, the Prince of Han, bought a grand residence for two million and got to roam while reclining only for a day.[60] How can that compare with my twenty years (*sings:*)

Of being a companion to fishermen and woodcutters,
For with them is the minister's estate that knows no bounds!

(*A* VANGUARD *leads a* COURT EMMISSARY *and enters.*)

I am a junior officer at the Yellow Gate. Our Sage Emperor personally gave order that I should summon Lord Du. I heard that he is at Peach Blossom Village watching a puppet show, so I made my way here.

(EMMISSARY *enters:*) Which one is His Grace, Minister Du?

(DU YAN:) How did you come to be here? This old man is he.

(*The* CROWD *is shocked and asks* ZHAO:) What is meant by "His Grace?"

(ZHAO:) I suppose it means a government student.

(SHANG:) No, no. It means a *yamen* clerk.

(CROWD:) If so, why would it be worth the trouble of having an imperial emissary sent here? Depend upon it—this is part of the show.

(EMISSARY:) Your Grace, the court is sending word to summon you. (DU YAN *sings*:)

(*Yan'er luo*)

Today where on earth can I hide this body?

Who would have expected these ten rows of words?

(EMISSARY:) Your Grace, it would be best if you can get court robes to bow in thanks for imperial beneficence.

(CROWD:) How come they are asking for court robes?

(DU YAN:) How can one come by that in this kind of place? Never mind—let us just make do with the puppet's robes this once.

(*The* CROWD *is shocked*.) How come he is wearing the prime minister's headgear? We will die from shock and awe! (DU YAN *sings*:)

There is no choice but to act out court rituals on the puppet stage

And to make do, covering shabby looks with a fake robe of gold and scarlet.[61]

(*The* CROWD *looks at the robe*:) Your Grace, this doesn't fit when you put it on. It doesn't look right. (DU YAN *sings*:)

(*Desheng ling*)

Upside down I put these clothes on,

All dressed up without passing muster.

Unmistakable: this is a wooden doll coming on stage,

Showing only some slight difference in stature hard to gauge.

(DU YAN *bows*:)

I bow low again to my emperor,

Asking what is the state of affairs: Grains ripening? Silkworms suffering?

(EMISSARY:) Our sage emperor said: Your Grace has the genius to repair the firmament and bathe the sun.[62] He sent me to ask specifically: What is most important for guarding governance today? (DU YAN *sings*:)

Unused to court rhetoric,

I cannot fashion lies about holding up the firmament or bathing the sun.

(EMISSARY:) Your Grace, there's no need to be unduly modest. Please answer with a detailed list. (DU YAN *sings*:)

(*Shuixianzi*)

Grateful to the imperial kindness that seeks me out,

I am yet fearful that the old memorials have sunken into oblivion.

Although we now have peace,

"Notes of caution from quiet times serve moments of crisis," as the saying goes.

In those days when this old servant served in the government, he had three constant maxims: punishment that does not kill makes for awe-inspiring authority; troops that are not deployed build martial prowess; wealth that is not stored creates prosperity.[63] Now I heard that the imperial treasury has accumulated two million: Why not distribute it all to relieve the famished? (*Sings*:)

What a pity that the reserves from former reigns have been allowed to rot:[64]
For they suffice to feed the people, even allowing for the geese and fowls' lot![65]

I can also see that Han Qi and Fan Zhongyan are the great men of our generation; we can have them work together to assist with government. Liu Hu is the most distinguished official of his times; he should be allowed to make up for his offence through new achievements.[66]

All I wish for is that *qilins* should fall into a net tightly woven,
And that phoenix pillars should soar high.[67]
Then this humble old official's remonstrance would have its worth proven.[68]

(EXTRA *reports*:) Another palace official has come.

(EMISSARY:) I will first take these words of the old prime minister to answer the Sage Emperor.

(*exits*)

(*A* EUNUCH *of high rank comes on stage. He is followed by two persons costumed as* EMISSARIES, *one bearing a staff, another a cup. They barge in.* [*The* EUNUCH *speaks*:]) The Sage Emperor has a secret decree: Your Grace is to look at it yourself.

(DU YAN *kneels and receives the decree, declaims 'Long live the emperor!' and reads it.*)

The Official of Remonstrance and the Exhorter have made this charge at the *yamen*: "Du Yan, as a high-ranking official, enters the marketplace. This damages ministerial decorum. We beg to have him demoted and exiled in order to honor the court." This is a document of indictment.

(ZHAO *and* SHANG:) This is scary stuff! Could it be that the document includes our names? Lord Emissary: he does not belong to our gathering.

(EMISSARY:) Pschaw! (*To* DU YAN) The Imperial Advisement follows.

(DU YAN:) The Imperial Advisement says: "The remonstrance officials submitted a misleading memorial that is offensive to one who has served long years with integrity. I have already kept it in imperial precincts so that it will not go any further. But you, sir, should also be more careful about your whereabouts from now on, so as to answer the high expectations from everybody."[69] Shameful! Shameful![70] (*Sings*:)

(*Zhe gui ling*)

My hope for Your Majesty:

Do not break or blunt the sharp edge of the officials of remonstrance.[71]
They have already obtained, through the puppets, the true offending evidence.
I am indeed guilty of careless abandon in my ways,
By the side of children I play,
With rustics I forget the days.

(*Aside*:) These young ones have fallen into my trap. (*Sings*:)

Who would know that I cleverly slip through fake fame and vain renown?
And yet they try to use the aura of my former high rank to bring me down.

(EMISSARY:) The Sage Emperor wants me to personally ask Your Grace: You, sir, have been scrupulously honest as an official?[72] It has been many years since you retired. Do you have any property?

(DU YAN:) I do. I do. (*Sings*:)

These days I enjoy the common fare of tea and rice,
Relying on the light of imperial beneficence.
I also have five willows
And eight hundred withered mulberries.[73]

(EMISSARY:) The Sage Emperor also has an open decree, which I will now read to all present: "Councilor Du Yan has assisted the throne. His achievements are luminous, and many indeed are the times he closely supported us. Heaven blesses the loyal one with integrity, and he has reached an advanced age. We herewith bestow on him a white jade longevity staff and a Nine Clouds Cup made from pure gold. The officials in charge should send him grain and servants every month, attending to him in his old age on our behalf."

Thank the emperor for his beneficence.

(DU YAN:) May the emperor enjoy ten thousand years! Ten thousand years!

(SHANG *and* ZHAO:) This is good fun. His Grace Du is part of our gathering. This reward should also be shared with us.

(CROWD:) You just said that he is not part of this gathering. (DU YAN *sings*:)

(*Qiao pai'er*)

Again, I have cost the court ten thousand measures of grain,
Without offering even half a slip of paper as recompense.
What remains is my white hair, thirty-thousand feet long from worries intense.[74]

(EMISSARY:) Who but Your Grace with your great virtue can deserve such extraordinary favor? (DU YAN *sings*:)

What great virtue!

This is truly the reward gained on the puppet stage.

(The EMISSARY *exits.*)

(The CROWD *bows.*) Your Grace Du, forgive us for not recognizing you for who you are.

(ZHAO:) Your Grace, as I said earlier, you do look somewhat literate.

(DU YAN:) My friends, why say more about any of this? If I take off this robe, would you still recognize me? (*He takes off the robe. Sings*:)

(*Yuanyang shawei*)

I will return to you the tattered robe that puts up the appearance,
And go back to the narrow alley as village libationer with his pittance.

Brothers,

I advise you to banish contention
And yield to each other with affection.
Share the ride if you have a horse,

Share a sip if you have the brew.

(*To* ZHAO and SHANG:)

Don't boast about your long sleeves for dancing,[75]

For only I, Councilor Du, pass for a master of the altar with some preening.

Brothers, on this day next year, I will come here again to watch the puppet show.

(CROWD:) But now we will not dare.

(DU YAN:) What nonsense. (*Sings*:)

Let us pray that, year after year, the Lord of Spring

Always hears, among these trees, how laughter will ring.

(*Exits.*)

(CROWD:) Who would have known that this old man is such a biggie! And so easy-going! This time round is much better than watching a play! (*Sing*:)

(*Qing jiang yin*)

From what we can see, His Grace Du

Is truly adept:

He can handle all roles to good effect!

He discusses village matters with us in one moment,

And in the next is good company for His Majesty!

May our sons and grandsons, for generations to come,

Always serve you!

The ones in the play are half real and half fake.

The ones watching the play: Who's fake? Who's real?

Councilor Du is like the Zhang Guolao astride a donkey,[76]

(ZHAO, SHANG:) And will bring your humble servants on board as the eighth immortal.[77]

NOTES

1. Literally, "truly capturing the true color of garlic and cheese in Jin and Yuan plays." See Shen Defu (1997, vol. 2, 647–48). On the metaphor of "garlic and cheese," see Li (2014, 7–8).
2. See Tseng Yong-yih (1971, 16). On Wang Xijue, see *DMB* 1376–79.
3. Tui 推 and Wei 維 share a constituent component. In the Tang story on which this play is based, Wang Wei is the one who seeks the attention of royal patrons, thereby gaining success in the examination, by playing "Yulun pao" on the *pipa* 琵琶. See "Wang Wei" 王維, Xue Yongruo 薛用弱, *Jiyi ji* 集異記, included in *TPGJ j.* 197.1331–32.
4. Wei Xuan (1936, 4).
5. Zhu Yu (1989, 49).
6. See Zheng Xuan's comment: "*Yong* are puppets with faces and contraptions that allow movement like a real person" (*LJZS j.* 4.172).
7. Yang Bojun (1979, 179–80).

8. This also explains the Romantic fascination with automatons and puppets. See, e.g., the story "Der Sandmann" [The sandman] by E. T. A. Hoffmann.
9. Feng Yan (2005, 61).
10. *QTS* 1.42. According to Zheng Chuhui's 鄭處誨 *Minghuang zalu* 明皇雜錄 (855), the powerful eunuch Li Fuguo 李輔國, who had supported Emperor Suzong's ascension to the throne, moved Emperor Xuanzong to the Western Palace, where Xuanzong chanted this poem in deep melancholy. But it is not clear whether he just chanted it or composed it. The poem is also attributed to Liang Huang 梁黃 and has the alternative title "On the Wooden Old Man" 詠木老人 (Ji Yougong 2007, *j.* 29.797–98). On another version of this poem with some textual variants, see Zhang Xihou (2006, *j.* 44.2304–405).
11. Wang Guowei 1996, 30.
12. See the translation in Ssu-ma Ch'ien [Sima Qian] (2019, 149–95).
13. Xu Shuofang (1993, 355, 389–90).
14. See Huang Wenyang (1967, 326).
15. Zhang Shunmin (2012, 72).
16. Xu Shuofang (1993, 359–61); Shen Defu (1997, 593–94). Cf. Waltner (1987) and Berg (2013, chap. 1).
17. It is conventional to present a parallel couplet summarizing the play as its longer title.
18. This quatrain is variously attributed to the Tang poets Wang Jia 王駕 (under the title "Altar Day" 社日), Zhang Bin 張蠙, and Zhang Yan 張演 (for the latter two under the title "Country Life on Altar Day" 社日村居), see *QTS j.* 600.6938, *j.* 690.7918, *j.* 885.10008. On the day of spring altar (*chunshe* 春社), which usually falls in February, sacrifices are offered to the god of earth with prayers for a good harvest. Eyebrow comment: "Reading this, one feels [partial erasure]."
19. In 1382, the first Ming emperor decreed that every 110 households would put forward representatives from the ten biggest and most prosperous households to become leaders (*lizhang* 里長, *lizheng* 里正) of the group (*MS j.* 77.1878, *j.* 78.1904).
20. Eyebrow comment: "[partial erasure] retired to the woods, engaging in lectures on moral precepts and Chan conversations [partial erasure]."
21. What is translated here as "honorable" is literally "the supernumerary official" (*yuanwai* 員外): from the Song dynasty onward, this was a sinecure that could be bought. The term is also used loosely to refer to rich and powerful people in the local area.
22. The historical Du Yan died at eighty. It makes sense for Wang Heng to exaggerate his longevity, especially if this play is meant as a celebration for his father's birthday.
23. The original refers to Lüye (Green Fields) and Pingquan (Level Spring): the names of the estates of the Tang ministers Pei Du and Li Deyu. Recall that the play's author is listed as "Anonymous of Green Fields Hall" in *Sheng Ming zaju*.
24. In Li Gongzuo's 李公佐 (9th c.) "Chunyu Fen" 淳于棼 (*TPGJ j.* 475.3910–15), more commonly known as "Governor of Nanke" (Nanke taishou 南柯太守), Chunyu Fen dreams of becoming the governor of Nanke and living a life of glory and disappointment in the kingdom of Locust Peace. Upon awakening, he finds that the kingdom is an ant colony in a locust tree. Children use bamboo as horses in games of make-believe. Du Yan is claiming that he is free from the illusion of power and glory and finds pleasure in child's play.
25. According to the Daoist text *Yunji qi qian* 雲笈七籤, drinking wine on the days of altar offerings can cure deafness; cited in Gao Lian (1988, 104).
26. Court officials had to brave frost while traveling to attend the morning court audience at dawn. The "plain white robe" is literally "a white cloth robe with a band in the middle."
27. "Ruckus" (*dahong* 打哄) can also mean "mime and jest" (*dahun* 打諢), "setting" (*paichang* 排場) is also "stage setting." The metaphors are theatrical.

28. Paper money had been in use intermittently since the ninth century. However, silver pieces and copper coins remained much more common as currency. Here Du Yan produces a bill that is worth a silver ingot.
29. Officials carried tablets, usually made from ivory, at court. The Tang official Cui Lin 崔琳 (ca. 720–760) had so many office holders in his family that when his kinsmen gathered for feasts, they needed a special bed for holding the official tablets (*XTS j.* 109.4098). A similar story is told about the minister and commander Guo Ziyi 郭子儀 (697–781) in the play *A Bed Filled with Official Tablets* (*Manchuang hu* 滿床笏) by Fan Xizhe 范希哲 (17th c.).
30. Tea monopoly during the Song and Yuan dynasties created great wealth for tea merchants, who could command whole fleets for transporting tea.
31. Egrets and cranes, considered noble birds, are metaphors for officials and courtiers.
32. Literally, "everywhere [people's attitude is] warm and cold, [depending on one's wealth and power]."
33. The original has "Niu biao (literally, bovine tendon) and Sha san (Sha the Third)," common names for country bumpkins in Yuan drama, e.g., Li Shouqing's 李壽卿 drama, *Wu Yuan chuixiao* 伍員吹簫; see Jing Lihu (1992, 31).
34. The following song lyric does not follow the tune pattern of "Xi jiang yue," which has two stanzas, each following a 6/6/7/6 pattern for 50 characters total. Here we have one stanza in a 6/6/7/5/6 pattern (30 characters).
35. The Pear Garden was where the Tang emperor Xuanzong (r. 712–756) trained his musicians (*XTS j.* 22.476). The term came to refer to the arena of musical and theatrical arts. Consort Xu 徐妃 is said to have made up half of her face to mock Emperor Yuan of Liang 梁元帝 (r. 552–555), who was blind in one eye (*NS j.* 12.341). Here "half a face" may refer to the use of mask or a comical reference to puppetry as half of the theatrical arts.
36. What I translate as "revelers" is literally "the feast": the performer faces the feasting guests. Old Bao alludes to "Poem on Puppets" (Yong kuilei 詠傀儡) by Yang Yi 楊億 (974–1020): "Old Bao laughs at the Guo lad in front of the revelers, / Mocking him for his unwieldy dancing sleeves. / If Old Bao were to dance in front of the revelers, / His dancer's sleeves must be even longer" 鮑老當筵笑郭郎，笑他舞袖太郎當。若教鮑老當筵舞，轉更郎當舞袖長 (Chen Shidao 1983, 4a). Both "Old Bao" and "Guo lad" are puppets. According to Yan Zhitui's (531–591) *Family Instructions*, puppets are also called Bald Guo 郭禿, suggesting their use in comic skits (Yan Zhitui 1980, 17.453, trans. in Yan Zhitui 2021, 381). Yan mentions that the term appears in *Fengsu tongyi* (ca. 195), although no such term is found in the extant *Fengsu tongyi*.
37. The ministry *zhongshu* 中書 (translated here as "government affairs") was established in the late sixth century and is here anachronistically applied to the Han dynasty.
38. Cao Can 曹參 (d. 190 BCE) was the comrade-in-arms of Liu Bang 劉邦, the first Han emperor (r. 202–195 BCE). After the founding of Han, Cao became the Lord of Pingyang and prime minister of Qi, a fiefdom ruled by Liu Bang's son Liu Fei 劉肥. He became the prime minister of Han after Xiao He's 蕭何 (d. 193 BCE) death and is known for strictly adhering to Xiao He's laws. The "circle of peace" in line 5 suggests limits that Xiao would not exceed. Both Xiao and Cao abided by Huang-Lao teachings and believed in minimal government intervention. Cao's inebriation is thus intentional avoidance of controversial policy changes.
39. The man who served as Left Marshal was Cao Wushang 曹無傷. Liu Bang put him to death in 206 BCE for leaking his plans to Xiang Yu. Yong Chi 雍齒 (d. 192 BCE), another Liu Bang follower, was the one made Lord of Shifang. Eyebrow comment: "Such a thorough understanding of antiquity! Every line is enough to make one bend over with laughter."

40. Wine making is implicitly compared to governance. For the harmony of taste as a metaphor for government, see, e.g., *Zuo* (vol. 3, Zhao 20.8, 1586–87). "To stir and harmonize the taste in the cauldrons" (*tiaohe diangnai* 調和鼎鼐) is a common idiom describing good government.
41. Eyebrow comment: "One cannot write a single word on this subject unless one has experienced it."
42. That is, only he who knows how to sleep one hundred years (36,000 rounds of sleep) can last as prime minister. The Tang general and minister Guo Ziyi (697–781) was in power for so long that he oversaw the evaluation of officials twenty-four times ("Guo Ziyi," *TPGJ j.* 176.1311–13). Eyebrow comment: "Drinking good wine is indeed ten thousand times better than keeping the company of the powerful during their meals."
43. The warlord and poet Cao Cao 曹操 (155–220), sobriquet Mengde 孟德 (which Du Yan uses below), built the Bronze Bird Terrace at Ye as a grand venue for feasts and entertainment.
44. Tiles from the Bronze Bird Terrace were prized as ink-stones in later periods. There are numerous poems devoted to these "Bronze Bird tile ink-stones."
45. Zhao is of course wrong.
46. According to Cao Cao's "Final Decree" 遺令, his singing girls are to continue their performances on the Bronze Bird Terrace, incense is to be distributed among his ladies, and they can make shoes to pass the time (Yan Kejun 1958, *j.* 56.1068). Du Yan laments Cao Cao's fatuous hope that the women he doted on in life should remain loyal to him after his death.
47. The word "fool" or "deceive" (*man* 瞞) is a pun on Cao Cao's alias Cao Man.
48. Since Cao Cao is often represented on stage as the villainous comic, he has a face painted white with eyebrows sloping down.
49. Eyebrow comment: "[This is like] a short person watching a play, a deluded one speaking of dreams. Most marvelous! Most fantastic!"
50. In a *yuefu* ballad, worms eating the roots of a peach tree cause the death of the plum tree next to it (Ouyang Xun 1999, *j.* 86.1466). Here Du Yan is reflecting on deceptive appearance, wrongful substitution, and repetition in history. Eyebrow comment: "The twenty-one histories is but a great *chuanqi* play spanning past and present!"
51. Zhao Pu 趙普 (927–976) was the trusted advisor of Zhao Kuangyin 趙匡胤 (Taizu, the founding Song emperor, r. 960-976). The emperor's visit, which symbolizes his great respect for Zhao Pu, is told in the *Song History* (*SS j.* 256.8932): "On several occasions Taizu, in plain clothes, paid visits to his meritorious ministers [without advance notice]. [For this reason] Zhao Pu usually did not dare to be casual about his cap and gown after withdrawing from court audience. One day, heavy snow had been falling till night, and Pu reckoned that the emperor would not come out. A long while later, he heard someone knocking at the door. Pu quickly emerged. The emperor was standing in the wind and the snow, and Pu in his trepidation welcomed him with an obeisance. The emperor said, 'I already invited the Prince of Jin (Taizu's younger brother, who would succeed Taizu as the Taizong emperor).' Sometime later, Taizong arrived. Zhao Pu set out cushions and blankets in the hall and heated up charcoal to roast meat. Pu's wife served them wine, and the emperor called her 'sister-in-law.' They then conferred with Pu about the strategy to gain control of Taiyuan. Pu said, 'Taiyuan faced enemies in the west and the north. If we gain control of Taiyuan, then we would have to face those enemies alone. Why don't we wait till we have pacified the various states? By then Taiyuan would be like a mere pellet or black dot, how can it escape our control?' The emperor smiled, 'That is precisely my plan. I just want to test you.'" This scene is elaborated in drama and fiction (e.g., Luo Guanzhong 羅貫中 [attr.], *Song Taizu longhu fengyun hui* 宋太祖龍虎風雲會, act 3 in Xu Zheng et al. [1998, vol. 7, 4913–16]; *Nan Song zhizhuan* 南宋志傳, chap. 47 [Yanshi shanqiao 1985]). Cf. Idema 1974.

52. Emperor Wu of Han burned the Nine Flicker Lamp when he welcomed the Queen Mother of the West. See "Han Wu gushi" 漢武故事 (Stories about Emperor Wu of Han), in Wang Genlin et al. (1999, 173).
53. The fish-shaped lock is a common poetic image, see Ouyang Xun (1999, *j.* 32.565); Zhou Mi (1997, 219).
54. The closeness of ruler and minister is such that the Taizu emperor calls Zhao Pu's wife "sister-in-law." See note 51.
55. Taizong emperor of Northern Wei (r. 409–423) consulted Cui Hao 崔浩 (381–450) about affairs of state and was so impressed that he bestowed on him the gift of imperial wine and crystal salt, saying, "I savor your words like this salt and wine, that is why I want to share their fine taste with you" (*WS j.* 35.811).
56. Zhao Pu was not well educated and Taizu urged him to study. Whenever he returned to his private residence, Zhao Pu took a book from a casket and pored over it, relying on it to answer the emperor during court audience. After Zhao Pu died, his family discovered that the book was the *Analects* (*Song shi j.* 256.8940). In a thirteenth-century anecdote, Zhao Pu responds to the Taizong emperor's query about the *Analects* being a children's primer: "It is true that your subject's knowledge does not exceed this. Formerly I used half of it to help the Taizu emperor to gain control of the entire realm under heaven, and now I want to use half of it to help your majesty bring about peace" (Luo Dajing 1983, 128).
57. See *ZYZS j.* 1.15. Natural affinities bring together the dragon and the clouds, the tiger and the wind. Here it refers to the special bond between ruler and minister. The early Ming play, *Song Taizu longhu fengyun hui*, uses the same image to describe the bond between the Taizu emperor and his helpers.
58. That is, the emperor remains loyal to Zhao Pu.
59. Imperial decrees are written on yellow paper. Here Du Yan is rhetorically asking whether he dares to comment on or criticize imperial decrees.
60. Zhao Pu's request for retirement was repeatedly denied by the Taizong emperor. The phrase "to roam while reclining" (*woyou* 臥遊) describes the pleasure of imaginary journeys as one reads or views a painting. Zong Bing 宗炳 (375–443) first describes the concept in "Preface to Painting Landscapes" (Hua shanshui xu 畫山水序), in Wang Xun (2018, 28–30).
61. Eyebrow comment: "Is the puppet performance this time real or illusory? Is it both real and illusory? This is marvelous beyond words."
62. The goddess Nüwa repaired the firmament after a cosmic collapse (*HNZ j.* 6.206–07). Another goddess, Xihe, gave birth to ten suns and bathed them in deep waters (Yuan Ke 1980, 266, 338, 381).
63. These three lines appear with some variations in Su Shi's tomb stele for Zhao Gai ("Zhao Kangjing gong shendaobei" 趙康靖公神道碑, dated 1088): "Punishment that does not kill is efficient; troops that are not deployed are successful; wealth that is not accumulated is prosperity; people who do not make a show of their cleverness are worthy" 刑以不殺為能，兵以不用為功，財以不聚為富，人以不作聰明為賢 (Su Shi 2011, 755).
64. For "reserves from former reigns," the original has "Fengkuchun" (meaning "husked grain in sealed storehouses"), the imperial treasury established in 965.
65. Literally, "the grains that remain from feeding geese and ducks." Rulers who use grains to feed their geese or ducks (or, in the case of *Yanzi Chunqiu* 晏子春秋, some other waterfowl) are epitomes of extravagance and improvidence (*YZCQ j.* 7.450; Han Ying 1986, *j.* 7.303; Liu Xiang 1995, *j.* 8.252). Here Du Yan is saying that, even allowing for imperial extravagance, what remains can still suffice to feed the people.

66. Han Qi 韓琦 (1008–1075) and Fan Zhongyan 范仲淹 (989–1052) are both famous scholar-officials and military commanders. Liu Hu 劉滬 was imprisoned in 1044 for refusing to give up his project of building the city wall of Shuiluo 水洛 (in present day Gansu) when the directives for it had changed but was later released and regained office. (Han and Fan were on different sides of that dispute.)
67. *Qilins* (unicorns) and phoenixes, auspicious animals and birds, here refer to talented men who can serve in government. "The net of law" (*fawang* 法網), an image usually implying implacable punishment, here refers to government vigilance that will not allow worthy and able people to languish in oblivion—they will all be kept within "the net," putting their talents to good use.
68. Literally, "would emit fragrance." Fragrance is associated with virtue, worth, and a good name.
69. There is a similar episode in Wang Xijue's life, when the Wanli emperor refused to act on the recommendation of remonstrance officials against Wang (Xu Shuofang 1993, 355).
70. The tone here should be jocular rather than self-recriminatory.
71. Despite the remonstrance officials' attack against him and his father, Wang Heng made a point of empathizing with them and honoring their integrity (Xu Shuofang 1993, 386).
72. Literally, "honest (and transparent) as water."
73. Tao Yuanming 陶淵明 has five willows by his house and called himself Master of Five Willows (Tao Yuanming 1987, 175–76). Zhuge Liang 諸葛亮, in his final memorial to the Shu ruler Houzhu 後主, spoke of owning "eight hundred mulberry trees and fifteen modest acres" (*SGZ j.* 35.927).
74. Literally, "from worrying about the times, I have white hair of 3,000 *zhang* (about 30,000 feet)." See Li Bai, "Autumn Pool Song" 秋浦歌, fifteenth of seventeen quatrains: "White hair of three thousand *zhang* / that has become this long with sorrow." 白髮三千丈，緣愁似箇長。(*QTS j.* 167.1724).
75. See note 34.
76. Zhang Guolao is one of the eight immortals in Daoist lore.
77. By the sixteenth century the number of the Eight Immortals was fixed but included one woman, He Xiangu. Do Zhao and Shang hope to take her position?

5

Sublime Jokes from the Back of Beyond

LÜ TIANCHENG (1579–1617)[1]
TRANSLATED BY WAI-YEE LI

Included in Shen Tai's 沈泰 *Short Plays of the Great Ming* (*Sheng Ming zaju* 盛明雜劇), this play's author is listed under the pseudonym "Bamboo-Obsessed Layman of Moling" (Moling zhuchi jushi 秣陵竹痴居士). Qi Biaojia 祁彪佳 (1603–1645) identified the author as Lü Tiancheng 大成 when he categorized this play as "free-spirited" (*yipin* 逸品) in his *Classification of Plays from the Hall of Distant Mountains* (*Yuanshan tang jupin* 遠山堂劇品).[2] Lü Tiancheng (style name Qinzhi 勤之, sobriquets Yulansheng 鬱藍生, Jijin 棘津, Chou'an 幬庵, Aiyuan zhongzi 艾園塚子) came from a distinguished scholar-official family in Yuyao 餘姚 (Zhejiang). His great-grandfather Lü Ben 呂本 (1504–1586) was a grand councilor. His father Lü Yinchang 呂胤昌 (1560–1615) attained the *jinshi* degree the same year (1583) as his cousin and fellow drama aficionado Sun Rufa 孫如法 (1559–1615), as well as the famous playwright Tang Xianzu 湯顯祖 (1550–1616). Lü Yinchang and Tang Xianzu were good friends despite Tang's displeasure over Lü's possible role in adapting his play, *The Peony Pavilion* (*Mudan ting* 牡丹亭), for Wu-style singing. Lü Yinchang's mother, Sun Huan 孫鐶, owned a vast collection of plays that must have been available for Lü Tiancheng's perusal, and both the Lü and the Sun clans were steeped in theatrical culture.

Unlike his forbears, Lü Tiancheng did not advance beyond the lowest degree and in later life blamed his examination failures on his consuming interest in drama. He became an avid reader and collector of plays in his teens and was a prolific author by his early twenties. He is best known for his treatise on drama, *The Classification of Plays* (*Qupin* 曲品), drafted in 1602 and revised in 1610 and 1613. Although *Sublime Jokes from the Back of Beyond* (*Qidong juedao* 齊東絕倒) is his only extant play, Lü wrote at least fifteen *chuanqi* plays and eight *zaju* plays. They earned him great contemporary acclaim, as evinced by the praise from dramatists and critics such as Wang Jide 王驥德 (ca. 1542–1623), Shen Jing 沈璟 (1553–1610), and Qi Biaojia. Shen Jing, whom Lü Tiancheng honored as teacher, effusively summed up three of Lü's plays in a letter addressed to him: "And then there is *Three Stars* (*Sanxing ji* 三星記), in which you express your heroic spirit to exquisite perfection. *The Divine Mirror* (*Shenjing ji* 神鏡記), which tells Nie Yinniang's story,[3] is wondrous, surprising, and delightful. *The Four Ministers* (*Sixiang ji* 四相記) glorifies virtues that last ten thousand generations and vie with the sun and the moon for brightness."[4] Qi Biaojia reserved his highest praise for *The Divine Sword* (*Shenjian ji* 神劍記), Lü's play on the Confucian thinker and scholar-official Wang Yangming 王陽明 (1472–1529): "It allows those who scoffed at Wang to know him as if he had come alive. It can supplement what is missing in the transmitted historical records. Both arias and dialogues are beautiful; the emotions and scenes are complex and compelling."[5]

That the author of a celebrated play on Wang Yangming should also be known for his erotica testifies to a sensibility encompassing apparent opposites, at least from a modern standpoint. Lü's good friend Wang Jide described the pornographic vernacular novella, *Unofficial History of the Embroidered Couch* (*Xiuta yeshi* 繡榻野史), as the playful creation of a youthful Lü Tiancheng. Its protagonist, Dongmeng sheng 東門生, arranges for his wife's adultery with his male lover, Zhao Dali 趙大里, but the ménage à trois turns into a ménage à quatre when his wife seduces Zhao Dali's widowed mother on her husband's behalf. The idea is perhaps more interesting than its execution, for the prose of the novella is crude and repetitive. A hint of wit surfaces only when Lü reverts to classical Chinese (in the missives the characters compose), pointing to the challenge of the vernacular medium.

In some of his plays Lü's interest in erotica pushes the boundaries of decorum. *Settling Tangled Nocturnal Scores* (*Chan yezhang* 纏夜帳) seems to have been based on his experience in courtesan quarters. According to Qi Biaojia, the explicitly described sexual exploits of a handsome servant and a young maid in that play border on prurience.[6] In a letter to Lü, Shen Jing criticizes his play *The Two Licentious Ones* (*Er yin ji* 二淫記) as "a scroll of erotic painting in plain lines."[7] A year before his death (1616), Lü composed two hundred erotic quatrains (*Hong qing jueju* 紅青絕句), with titles such as "Blushing as She Looks at a Painting of Secret Games on a Spring Night" (Kan chunxiao mixi tu mian facheng 看《春宵秘戲圖》面發赬), "Buying Aphrodisiac" (Gou fangzhong dan 購房中丹), and "Spitting at the Catamite" (Tuo luantong 唾孌童).[8]

Sexual innuendoes make its way into the play translated here in references to Shun's 舜 intimacy with his wives and the voracious sexual appetite of Shun's stepmother. It is but one of the many surprising twists in this attempt to reimagine the moral choices of legendary sage kings. The play explicitly violates the interdiction of depicting rulers and ancient sages in the Ming Code. Its title means literally "jokes from Eastern Qi that make one bend over with laughter." In *Mencius* (5A.4), Xianqiu Meng 咸丘蒙 asks Mencius whether stories about Shun's father (Blind Old Man 瞽瞍) and erstwhile ruler (Yao 堯) paying obeisance to him at court are true, but Mencius dismisses them as "the words of uncouth rustics from Eastern Qi." The state of Qi (present-day Shandong), situated to the east of Mencius's native Zou, is sometimes linked to fantastic stories.[9]

"Uncouth words from Eastern Qi" (*Qidong yeyu* 齊東野語) became an idiomatic expression referring to unofficial history or freely fabricated stories.[10] What I translate as "uncouth" (*ye* 野野) also means "wild" or "backward." The connotations are usually negative, but the suspicion of over-refinement has also led to positive judgments of *ye*, as when Confucius expresses measured approval for "rustics" (*yeren* 野人) of earlier times who came to ritual and music without forgoing simplicity (*Analects* 11.1) or when he remarks: "When ritual is lost, look for it in the wilds (*ye*)" (*HS* 30.1746).

Set in high antiquity, the plot of *Sublime Jokes* unfolds around King Shun's decision to flee to the seashore with his father when the latter commits murder and Shun is forced to choose between fulfilling filial piety and honoring the law of the land. The story is derived from a hypothetical question from Mencius's disciple Taoying 桃應 (*Mencius* 7A.35):

> Taoying asked: "Shun was the Son of Heaven and Gaoyao the Minister of Justice. What should they do if the Blind Old Man commits murder?"
>
> Mencius said, "Gaoyao would arrest him—that's all."
>
> "So would Shun not forbid it?"
>
> "On what basis could Shun forbid it? For the action would be based on what is rightfully received."[11]
>
> "But then what would Shun do?"
>
> "Shun regards abandoning the entire realm under heaven as being no different from abandoning a worn-out shoe. He would secretly carry his father on his back and flee, come to the seashore, and stay there. Joyous to the end of his days, he would forget about the entire realm under heaven in his bliss."

In this conflict between private ties and public justice or political duty, Gaoyao's 皋陶 decision to implement the law is unequivocal. Shun's choice, however, is more ambiguous. As a ruler, he would not contravene his father's arrest, but as a son he would later secretly flee with him to the seashore. Mencius changes the focus to Shun's laudable indifference to power ("Shun regards abandoning the entire realm under heaven as being no different from abandoning a worn-out shoe"), but he sidesteps the question as to whether sacrificing his position earns Shun the right to break the law. The primacy of kinship here recalls this passage from the *Analects* (13.18) when the Lord of She praises a just man who exposes his father's theft of a sheep. Confucius then replies: "In our parts, a just man is different from that: when a father conceals the truth on behalf of a son, and when a son conceals the truth on behalf of a father, there is justice in it."[12]

More than any other historical figures, Shun features prominently in debates about ethical choices in *Mencius*. Shun's family is tersely described in "Yao's Canon" 堯典(Yaodian, ca. 4th–3rd century BCE) in the *Documents*: "He is the son of a blind man—his father is stubbornly errant; his mother, perfidious; Xiang 象 (his brother), arrogant."[13] Their persecution of Shun is elaborated in *Mencius* (5A.2):

> Wanzhang said, "His father and mother sent Shun to repair the barn and removed the ladder. The Blind Old Man set fire to the barn. They sent him to dig a well. He [somehow] came out, even as they piled earth in his wake. Xiang said, "The plot against Shun was fully my accomplishment. The oxen and sheep can go to father and mother, likewise the barn and granary. His shield and halberd will be mine, likewise his zither and bow. My two sisters-in-law will attend to my bed." Xiang went to Shun's abode, where Shun was playing the zither on his bed. Xiang said, "Ah, I was just longing to see you." He was ill at ease. Shun said, "I am thinking of all these subjects and people. You are to help me govern them."[14]

Shun's malevolent family highlights his virtue, since his filial and fraternal feelings do not depend on reciprocity or worthy objects. Furthermore, if Shun could influence his recalcitrant kin, it would imply his power to transform the entire polity (*Mencius* 4A.28). But execrable family members inevitably raise questions. Compromise becomes necessary: Shun has to violate ritual propriety by arranging his marriage without notifying his parents (*bugao er qu* 不告而娶) because they would have obstructed it (*Mencius* 4A.26, 5A.2).

The account of Shun's persecution is followed by a question from Mencius's disciple Wanzhang 萬章: "I don't know whether Shun understood that Xiang intended to kill him?" Mencius responds: "How can he not know? When Xiang was troubled, he was troubled. When Xiang was glad, he was glad." This provokes Wanzhang's skepticism: Is Shun genuinely glad to see Xiang? Mencius argues that Shun is truly glad and empathizes with Xiang because he sees the potential principle of fraternal devotion in Xiang's lie ("I was just longing to see you"). But the logic is labored. As the Ming iconoclastic thinker Li Zhi 李贄 (1527–1602) puts it, if Shun does not know Xiang's murderous plot, then he is not wise. If he knows it, then his gladness is insincere.[15] In *Sublime Jokes*, Xiang recapitulates this scene in his speech, adding the detail that Shun's wives were naked when Xiang barged in. What should Xiang's role be in Shun's government? For Shun to exile Xiang would violate the fraternal bond; for him to enfeoff Xiang would risk misrule. Mencius in effect equivocates, arguing that Xiang is enfeoffed at Youbi but that his power is nominal (*Mencius* 5A.3). Xiang's self-introduction in the play revisits the ambiguous implications of his position at Youbi.

As mentioned above, when Xianqiu Meng asks Mencius whether Shun's treatment of his predecessor Yao and his father as his subjects endangers the normative hierarchical order of ruler and subject, father and son, Mencius dismisses the notion as "the uncouth words of rustics from Eastern Qi." He maintains that Shun is merely "ruling on behalf of" (*she* 攝) Yao and that he is not truly the Son of Heaven during the twenty-eight years between Yao's abdication and his death (*Mencius* 5A.4). In *Shiji*, Sima Qian focuses on the twenty-eight years that Shun rules "on behalf of" Yao and implies that good governance is achieved through power sharing between a ruler retaining ultimate authority and a minister capable of governing on a ruler's behalf. In *Sublime Jokes*, however, King

Yao definitely acts like a subject. Both King Yao and the Blind Old Man pay obeisance to Shun at court, but it is only in the latter case that Shun responds with unease.

After Mencius explains Shun's "regency," Xianqiu Meng quotes an ode from the *Classic of Poetry*: "For all under heaven, / There are no lands that are not the king's lands. / Follow the land to the water's edge, / There are none who are not the king's subjects." 普天之下，莫非王土。率土之濱，莫非王臣.[16] He then asks Mencius whether this mean that Shun must treat his father as his subject. Mencius chides Xianqiu Meng for being literal minded and argues that the poetic speaker is in fact expressing longing for his parents:

> As for this poem, that is not what is meant. The poet is toiling for the king's affairs and does not get to nurture his parents. He is saying, "There's none that is not the king's affairs, how is it that I alone am worthy to bear the burden of toil?" That is why those who explain the meanings of the odes do not let embellishment go against the phrasing, nor do they let the phrasing go against the intent. Use your imagination to meet the poet's intent: that's how you get it. . . . As for the highest level of being a filial son, nothing is greater than honoring his parents; as for the highest level of honoring his parents, nothing is greater than bringing the entire realm under heaven to nurture them. Being the father of the Son of Heaven is the highest honor; bringing the entire realm to nurture one's parents is the highest form of nurturing. (*Mencius* 5A.4)

Mencius' ingenious disquisition on misunderstood poetic intention—the first of its kind in the tradition and the progenitor of a poetics of indirectness as well as allegorical interpretations—turns lines that problematize filial piety into its ultimate affirmation.

The abdication of the throne to the worthy, as practiced by the sage kings Yao and Shun, is traditionally upheld as a political ideal, the embodiment of political disinterestedness based on recognition of the polity as a common and public realm (*tianxia wei gong* 天下為公). The justification of the principle of abdication and the problem of its implementation are debated in Warring States texts.[17] Abdication upsets the hierarchical order of ruler and subject, father and son, by giving a ruler authority over his father and his erstwhile ruler. As we have seen, Mencius wrestles with this problem in many passages discussing Shun's ethical dilemmas. Abdication is justified because rulers have unworthy sons (like Yao's son Danzhu 丹朱 and Shun's son Shangjun 商君), but it begs the question of why sage kings have no moral sway over their progeny. Also, a sage king instituting perfect rule would leave no room for another would-be sage king to prove his worth and receive the mandate.[18] Some cynically imply that abdication myths mask ruthless power struggles and assert that Yao and his son are imprisoned or persecuted to make way for Shun.[19] Mencius finds it necessary to explain away the potential for creating rival loci of authority in the model of abdication. He implicitly argues, on the one hand, that expediency can be combined with filial piety and fraternal devotion (e.g., Shun can be filial without accepting absolute obedience; Xiang can earn a fiefdom without deserving it); and, on the other hand, that there is no contradiction between being simultaneously a deferential subject and a de facto ruler, between respecting paternal authority and exercising a ruler's authority. The play revels in Shun's dilemmas. It does not dwell on the potentially problematic relationship between Yao and Shun after Yao's abdication despite a passing mention that Shun is ruling on behalf of Yao, perhaps because centuries of imperial rule have rendered the notion of divided authority and power sharing quaint or politically dangerous. Instead, *Sublime Jokes* focuses on Shun's filial piety, which has received extensive treatment in multiple genres over the centuries, including primers like *Twenty-Four Stories of Filial Piety* and popular Dunhuang narratives. Our play dramatizes the tension between justice and filial piety. In upholding filial piety and the hierarchy of father and son by giving up kingship, is Shun undermining the law or "bringing the entire realm under heaven to nurture" his father?

This play has an alternative title, *Joy by the Seashore* (*Haibin le* 海濱樂). The seashore here seems to imply a space beyond political boundaries, defying the logic of the lines from the *Classic of Poetry* cited above, according to which there is no escape from "the king's land" or from being "the king's subject." Shun and his father would still be subjects of the new king even at the seashore, unless Shun's abdication is also the dissolution of the idea of kingship. Lü Tiancheng does not dwell on this paradox, however. He depicts the seashore as a beautiful place with landmarks (Mount Li 歷山, Kuaiji 會稽, Red City 赤城) connected to Zhejiang and the environs of his native Yuyao. Mount Li is also where Shun starts out as a farmer, so the journey represents a return to origins both for the protagonist and for the author. On his way to the seashore, Shun encounters recluses from *Zhuangzi* and his filial duty eventually merges with his own love of eremitic life, and when he is finally persuaded to return to court, it is not because of the Blind Old Man's pardon or the call of royal duty but because of his shrewish stepmother's emotional blackmail and her dire threats against her hen-pecked husband. While it may be possible to see the miscarriage of justice at the heart of this play as a pointed critique of late Ming society and politics, the play's irreverent energy derives from the pleasure in exploring the moral conundrums and contradictions in the exalted stories from canonical texts. Lü makes copious allusions to these texts with dexterity, and it is not clear whether such inside jokes for the literati translate into an earnest critique of political malpractice. Formally, the play mixes the conventions of Yuan *zaju* with Ming dramatic modes. The arias in each act follow the same rhyme, but the music mixes northern and southern styles. The male lead sings in northern (*bei*) tunes, while the other characters sing in southern (*nan*) tunes.

The text used for this translation is found in Shen Tai's *Short Plays of the Great Ming*, Ming Chongzhen edition (1628–1644), fascicle 30.

Dramatis Personae in Order of Appearance

Role type	*Name and family or social role*
OLDER MALE, MO	GAOYAO, Minister of Justice
SECOND MALE, XIAOSHENG	KING YAO
COMIC, JING	XIANG, Shun's younger brother
CLOWN, CHOU	SHANGJUN, Shun's son
EXTRA, WAI	BLIND OLD MAN, Shun's father
MALE LEAD, SHENG	SHUN, King Shun
FEMALE LEAD, DAN	EHUANG, Yao's daughter, Shun's consort
SECOND FEMALE LEAD, XIAODAN	NÜYING, Yao's daughter, Shun's consort
CLOWN, CHOU, BAOZI	MESSENGER
OLDER MALE, MO	ZIZHOU ZHIBO, a recluse
OLDER FEMALE, LAODAN	SHANJUAN, a recluse
SECOND COMIC, FUJING	DANZHU, Yao's son
SECOND MALE, XIAOSHENG	FARMER, Farmer of Stone Gate
SECOND CLOWN, XIAOCHOU	PERFIDIOUS MOTHER, Shun's mother

SUBLIME JOKES FROM THE BACK OF BEYOND

Author: The Bamboo-Obsessed Layman of Moling
Commentator: The Laughing Bamboo Layman of West Lake

(GAOYAO *enters* [*and recites*].)

(*Xijiang yue*)

Although the blind chap breaks the law,
The clever son knows how to hide his father.
Since ancient times we have heard rustic words from afar:
Mencius of Zou tries to fathom Yao and Shun.
The ladies turn to the couch with the zither and disrobe.
Who can find the one who has fled to the sea's edge?
Clearly old records yield their truth in songs—
Listen and take from them credible jokes.[20]

Gaoyao cannot catch the miscreant who committed murder,
Shangjun fails to make the father who bowed to his son turn around.
Arrogant Xiang cannot forgive the sovereign who yielded his throne,
The perfidious mother would not let go of the farmer fleeing to the seashore.[21]

ACT 1

(OLDER MALE *enters costumed as* GAOYAO [*and recites*]:)

There are bandits, murderers, malefactors inside and out.
Barbarians inflict disorder on the central domains.
I command you to serve as Minister of Justice,
And bring the entire realm under punishment's compass.[22]

This is Gaoyao. I have never been mute, but Liu An, King of Huinan, claims that I "was mute and served as the Great Minister of Justice."[23] When the people of the Song dynasty wrote their remarks on poetry, they also argued that the language of the "Three Counsels"[24] may well be evidence of "using the brush to take the place of the mouth."[25] It's outrageous! Outrageous! Now King Yao has abdicated the throne, and King Shun is ruling on his behalf.[26] The Four Evil Ones have been removed,[27] and the Three Miao Tribes have been brought to order.[28] The glorious clouds manifest propitious omens through their splendor; the ruler sings as I bow with my forehead touching my clasped hands.[29] This is the moment following King Shun's inspection tours,[30] and right when auspicious signs are continuously garnered. I am not like Boyi who serves as forester and oversees birds and beasts, nor am I like Boyu who manages the waters and oversees all scaly creatures. I am not like Xie, who spreads the five teachings and offers protection and help to the common people, nor am I like Ji, who sows the hundred grains and grows them for food. I am not like Kui directing music or like Long taking in the people's opinions—one serves the gods and the other remonstrates with the sovereign. I am not like Chui, taking charge of the works, or Yi, ensuring order in the ancestral temple—one manages the works and the other presides over the rites.[31] It is my responsibility to bring criminals to justice and my authority is weightier than mere debt collecting. I found out recently about the case of the Blind Old Man killing[32] an official's son because he wanted to listen to music. Come to think of it, I must apply the rule of law. I must present the case to Kui.

(SECOND MALE *enters costumed as* KING YAO *in a sovereign's clothes*:)

At fifteen I became ruler by heaven's permission,
At seventy I abdicated from that position.
Among our subjects below was one unmarried man,
My two daughters became his wives at River Gui's bend.[33]

I am King Yao. I made offerings to Heaven and sought my replacement, and had Shun receive at the Grand Ancestral Temple the position that is ending for me.[34] I had better go and pay obeisance to him at court.

(GAOYAO:) Ah, King Yao has come. Have the Chiefs of the Four Peaks, the hundred regulators, nine ministers, twelve administrators, and various lords come yet?[35]

(KING YAO:) The various lords are about to arrive. I will of course lead them in paying obeisance to King Shun.

(GAOYAO:) You, King Yao, were a ruler in the old days. Why are you paying obeisance to him at court?

(KING YAO:) Don't you know that there are no two suns in Heaven, even as there are no two rulers for the people?[36] How dare I not pay obeisance?

(GAOYAO:) The Blind Old Man is his father. How can he also pay obeisance to him at court?

(KING YAO:)

Follow the land to the water's edge—
There's none who are not the king's subjects.[37]

How dare he not pay obeisance?

(GAOYAO:) You, King Yao, married Nühuang, a daughter of the Sanyi lineage, and she gave birth to your heir, Danzhu. You created the chess game and taught him to play it, but he remained perfidious.[38] So, how could he have become King Shun's guest?[39]

(KING YAO:) King Shun has paid attention only to playing the zither and singing "Gentle Wind."[40] My second daughter gave birth to Shangjun, and Shun has let him become errant, just like my own son. Although my son is Shun's guest now, back then when Shun was in my palace, he did make life miserable for Danzhu.[41]

(GAOYAO:) King Shun is extremely filial, why would he let the Blind Old Man pay obeisance to him at court?

(KING YAO:) Back then when King Shun received the Blind Old Man, he was reverent and filled with trepidation.[42] His filial piety rose to great heights, and they reached harmony.[43] Now the Blind Old Man no longer mistreats him. In later generations there will be even those fathers who embrace the broom to welcome their sons at the gate.[44]

(GAOYAO:) When one considers genealogies, both King Yao and King Shun are descendants of the Yellow Emperor. How could you, King Yao, let your two daughters marry King Shun?

(KING YAO:) I let my daughters serve him to "observe him from within his household."[45] So what if my daughters are his great aunts? We must overlook that.[46] What's more, nowadays there is no lack of adulterous and incestuous liaisons between people from the same lineages.

(GAOYAO:) Some time ago, King Shun imprisoned you, King Yao, and blocked the way for your heir Danzhu, preventing him from seeing you, his father.[47] How does one make sense of that?

(KING YAO:) Since my virtue had already declined, one can't blame him. What's more, later eras will provide us with plenty of examples of those who murder their former rulers by poisoning them.[48]

(COMIC *enters as* XIANG *in royal costume*:)

I was given a fiefdom at Youbi,
But some said it was exile.[49]
I plotted to do him in,[50]
But my hopes were futile.

Your humble servant is the ruler of the Kingdom of Youbi. My father's first wife gave birth to Shun, and his second wife gave birth to me and my sister Keshou.[51] My sister is already married to Danzhu, and my older brother has become King Shun. He has given me a fiefdom at Youbi. Oh, such fun! The only thing is, he won't let me govern, claiming that he needs to see me often.[52] I have no choice but to come here. Ah, King Yao and the Minister of Justice are both here. (*He greets them.*)

(GAOYAO:) Let me ask you: When King Shun was city chief,[53] why did the Blind Old Man want to harm him?

(XIANG:) In the beginning it was because his stepmother loathed him—let's not go there.[54] Later I said to the Blind Old Man: "The reason why you, father, have no pupils in your eyes is because Shun has double pupils, having taken over yours as well.[55] In all likelihood, he is the one who has brought you ill luck."

(KING YAO:) Why were you so set on harming him?

(XIANG:) Because—having seen the beauty of my two sisters-in-law, I wanted to have them attend to me at my bed. Shun's shield, halberd, zither, and arrows could all serve my purpose. He had the oxen and sheep, a barn and granary that my parents lacked.[56] It did me no good at all to have this older brother; that was why I wanted to kill him.

(KING YAO:) King Shun plowed the fields and harvested grains. Why did his father send him to plaster the granary and then set it on fire? Had he not had his bamboo hats, wouldn't he have been burned to death?[57]

(XIANG:) He plowed at Mount Li, wailing and weeping all day long.[58] My mother blamed him and so had my father send him to plaster the granary. When Shun told my two sisters-in-law about this, they said: "This time they will try to burn you. Turn your clothes into bird wings and go with a bird's skill."[59] So, after he climbed up on the granary, he spread his arms like bird's wings and floated down without any harm.

(GAOYAO:) During the seventy years of King Yao's reign, a ditty from the broad avenue[60] said: "Dig a well for drinking: / What is the sovereign's power to me?"[61] Why would you perversely make King Shun dig a well?

(XIANG:) It was I who said again to my father: "At the granary he flew from above to below, the going was really easy. At the well he would have to leap from the bottom to the top, the going would be really hard." I would fain have him drown in nine years' worth of great floods.[62] Who could have known that he would again speak to my sisters-in-law? They said, "Remove your clothes and go with a dragon's skill."[63] Later he came out of another well. I figure he had created an earthen chamber in advance. After all he did make earthenware by the river and knew something about the cohesion of loess, be it loose or compact.

(GAOYAO *laughs*:) But when you entered King Shun's palace and saw him playing the zither on his couch right there and then, you must have been so ashamed.

(XIANG:) He was draped in embroidered clothes and the two ladies were naked.[64] Truly he survived by cheating death and found joy amid afflictions. My cruel cunning was wasted effort and served not the slightest purpose. How could I not be ashamed when I saw him? I was afraid that he would see through my fake mien.[65]

(GAOYAO:) Some said that you were living in King Shun's palace, and right when you were playing the zither, King Shun barged in and saw you. You were surprised and upset.[66] Is that true?

(XIANG:) This is what Sima Qian made up.[67] Nothing like that happened.

(CLOWN *enters costumed as* SHANGJUN *in a lord's clothes*:)

Sage rulers from two eras,
Spawn heirs equally worthless.
The realm ends up with others,
Is it because they are selfless?[68]

This is Shangjun here. For today's morning obeisance at court, I have to respectfully wait for my turn.

(XIANG:) My nephew Shangjun has come.

(SHANGJUN *makes a show of being wild*:) Uncle Xiang! Uncle Xiang! Ah, King Yao and the Minister of Justice have both been waiting for a long time. (*He bows.*)

(XIANG:) I have been talking with the Minister for a while. Just come and tell your story.

(GAOYAO:) Xiaoming and Zhuguang, born of your other mother[69]—to whom are those two sisters of yours given in marriage?

(SHANGJUN:) King Yao gave his two daughters in marriage to my father and then yielded his throne. Now Yu, Lord of Chong, has done great things. He married a woman of the Tushan lineage, and she became pregnant after only four days. She gave birth to a son named Boqi, who is quite wise and virtuous. It's fine if my sisters do not manage to get married.[70] If father yields the throne to Yu, Yu is not going to yield it to others.

(KING YAO:) Only those of declining virtue fail to abdicate as rulers.[71] Yu's father, Lord Gun, was struck dead by me at Feather Mountain and turned into a tawny bear.[72] Even if Yu were to become king, it would not have come cheaply.[73]

(GAOYAO:) We just kept chatting, and I forgot to mention a most important matter: the Blind Old Man committed murder, and King Shun cannot bear to put his father to death. But I too cannot bear to break the law. What is to be done?

(KING YAO:) He is the Son of Heaven. Even if his father deserves the death penalty, he should be forgiven.

(XIANG:) Back then King Shun had not taken a wife even at the age of thirty. All thanks to King Yao, he got to marry without notifying his parents. This is the kind of man who cannot be held accountable for his son's marriage,[74] how can he be held accountable for such a great crime?

(SHANGJUN:) When Boyu sees an incarcerated criminal, he alights from his carriage and weeps.[75] If grandfather gets the same treatment, he won't be put to death.

(XIANG:) You always beat the drum after the battle is over. Now just bring him here to be put to death and be done with it.

(SHANGJUN:) If he killed someone, there must have been a reason. How can we rashly apply the ultimate punishment? We must submit the case to King Shun before we act.

(GAOYAO:) Just so, just so.

(EXTRA MALE, *sightless, costumed as the* BLIND OLD MAN *in royal clothes, enters with slow steps*:)

I have a second wife at home—it's really fate,
She reduced my own son to a pitiable state.
Perfidious Mother and Errant Father had a change of heart,
But unto old age the killer from my nature does not depart.

Now why did I, the Blind Old Man, speak these lines? In the beginning I married Wodeng, who gave birth to Shun. He was really filial, but was mistreated by my second wife. Regrets are of no avail. Fortunately, he became King Shun. The other day King Shun was having a concert and I wanted to go and listen. Kui's eldest son was guarding the gate, but he would not let me in. What's more, he said: "You are a blind musician who has arrived late." I said, "Who doesn't know that I am the father of the Son of Heaven? How dare you humiliate me?" Unable to contain my anger, I grabbed that broad sword with which I cut down the rebellious captives from the Three Miao Tribes[76] and whacked him with one strike, adding several blows with my fists. He died on the spot. The various officials said: "This is a crime for which you have to pay with your life. You cannot make it go away." I am filled with remorse but there's nothing I can do. Now we are at morning court audience, and I am really upset. But I can only let them decide.

(GAOYAO:) Ah, the Blind Old Man has come.

(BLIND OLD MAN:) This sightless one will have to be remiss with ceremonies. (*He bows.*)

(ALL:) The Xiaoshao music rises from the earthen steps of the thatched hut.[77] King Shun has arrived at court. The thousand officials rise together.

(MALE LEAD *enters costumed as* KING SHUN *in a sovereign's clothes, preceded by regalia and attendants.* MISCELLANEOUS, *costumed as four officials, follow.*)

(SHUANGDIAO MODE: Northern *Xinshui ling*) (KING SHUN *sings*:)

Sudden summons for office came for one working as potter, fisherman, and farmer.
A once single man embraces two wives, each a lovely charmer.
Through the years, inspection tours have taken me to the realm within the seas,
Toiling day and night, to Heaven's work I bring light.[78]
Steadfastly I hold on to the middle way,[79]
For which graceful phoenixes in the courtyard are the auspicious omens.[80]

(KING YAO *leads* MISCELLANEOUS OFFICIALS *to pay obeisance.*)
(Southern *Bubu jiao*) (KING YAO *sings*:)
Divinely powerful, civil and military officials sing joyous praise
Of mysterious virtue that is heard and valued on high.[81]
Dignitaries, capped and gowned, bow at the sovereign's court.
Fully thriving is work of all sorts,[82]
On four sides the wind of virtue stirs the people.[83]
He embodies the order of succession ordained by heaven.[84]
His lofty achievements tribute-bearing barbarians beckon.[85]
(KING SHUN:) You various officials should stand on one side.
(Northern *Zhegui ling*) (KING SHUN *sings*:)
As always, rancor fades in the gentle wind.[86]
How can I follow the model of Chaofu and Xu You of our times,
Or that of Fuxi and Shennong in high antiquity?[87]
These days we honor the good and eradicate the wicked.
Shields and feathers are arrayed on the steps on two sides,
As pipes and bells play the six scales.
The Pole Star receives homage from surrounding stars in this perfect reign,[88]
On regular intervals the myriad states come to honor the ancestral domain.
Consider still the Heaven-bestowed tenure: it's hard to keep forever.[89]
This may not count as an example of the worthy following the sage king:
Truly the son-in-law to his father-in-law's reign continuity does bring.
(BLIND OLD MAN:) I am paying obeisance. (BLIND OLD MAN *pays obeisance to* KING SHUN, *who shows his unease. With furrowed brows he sits sideways.*)[90]
(Southern *Jiang'er shui*) (BLIND OLD MAN *sings*:)
When the ruler radiates brightness as the head of the body politic,
Good officials gladly become its arms and legs.[91]
"Aye! Verily! Alas! Nay!"[92] Offering warnings, they have their say.
Of his bright virtues and deep wisdom all sing praise.
His gentle reverence is truly pervasive: no barbs do these words raise![93]
The sea is calm, the Yellow River is clear: let the joyous cries cheer!
His virtue matches a brightness doubled[94]
And he should indeed be with King Yao coupled.
(KING SHUN:) Father, please rise for now.[95]
(KING SHUN *turns his back and sings*:)
(Northern *Yan'er luo dai Desheng ling*)
For no good reason he follows the ranks of officials with excessive reverence,
For no good reason he faces north to pay his obeisance.[96]
How this fills me with fear hard to take,
How this dooms me to a gloom hard to shake.
This time round he comes bearing guilt and secret shame.

Loathing arrest, he resorts to solemn ritual display.
But from the crowds of dignitaries it's impossible to hide.
All too easily, criticisms from the people multiply.
How can the court
Be the place for this wheeling and dealing?
In the family,
Remember to enjoy the care
That we brothers for you bear.
Remember to enjoy the care
That we brothers for you bear.[97]

(KING SHUN *turns around and sits down.*)

(XIANG *and* SHANGJUN:) Your subjects, Xiang and Shangjun, both present themselves. (*They pay obeisance.*)

(Southern *Jiaojiao ling*) (XIANG *sings*:)
The fiefdom of Youbi is close to Puban.
The sovereign's domain is expansive.
One fears that the frequent trips across the border, bringing big crowds, are overdone,
Even if a true affection of kinship is shared by the younger brother and the son.[98]

(XIANG *and* SHANGJUN *stand to one side.*)

(Northern *Wang Jiangnan*) (KING SHUN *sings*:)
Ah! Though 'a true affection of kinship is shared by the son and the younger brother,'
What is hardest to come by
Is forbearance when facing the arched bow.[99]
For my whole life we have shared joys and sorrows.[100]
Even if I sired a worthless son given to foolish deviance,
You must refrain from violence,
Refrain from violence![101]
Enjoy the sun's orb and the moon's glow,
As auspicious clouds around us flow.

(KING SHUN:) All the officials should withdraw.

(OFFICIALS *exit.*)

(KING SHUN:) Gaoyao, why did you alone not withdraw?

(GAOYAO *kneels*:) Your servant has something—

(Southern *Yuanlin hao*) (GAOYAO *sings*:)
We are considering the ultimate penalty, for he kills with no justification.
It is the Blind Old Man, who should be punished by the laws of the land.

(KING SHUN *looks shocked*:) The Blind Old Man committed murder! What is to be done?

(GAOYAO *sings*:)

I submit the case and ask Your Majesty to judge and decide:
Once we put him in prison, how can there be reprieve?
Is there ever relief
From the cangue and fetters?
Is there ever relief
From the cangue and fetters?

(KING SHUN:) It's my intention to protect my father, and it's your responsibility to execute the law. I will leave everything to you.

(GAOYAO:) I thank Your Majesty for your beneficence.

[GAOYAO *exits.*]

(KING SHUN:) My father's nature is stubbornly errant—and now he has even committed murder. What is to be done? What is to be done?

(Northern *Gu meijiu dai Taiping ling*) (KING SHUN *sings*:)
Left rudderless in my sadness,
I am overcome with unease.
Left rudderless in my sadness,
I am overcome with unease.
This is just like a wolf
Swallowing a doddering old man.

I know what to do: I will secretly flee carrying him on my back, staying somewhere by the sea.

I will act as one holding in his mouth palace flowers in the lushness of spring.[102]
He must escape fast,
But he's also blind.
Rushing to bear the burden,
The *qiongqiong* and I are two of a kind.[103]
This entire realm under heaven—what do I need it for?
I look to the mist and haze of the seashore.
Without a father, a son's life is all but a dream,
The desire to keep my position can only bring woe.
As for me,
I must head for the cloudy peaks east of the sea,
Forever taking in traces of foxes and ghostly sparks,
Chanting like rustics in the deep mountains.

(KING SHUN *exits.*)

(GAOYAO *enters again*:) Since King Shun allows me to fulfill the law, I must go and arrest him right away.

(Southern *Coda*) (GAOYAO *sings*:)
This is not a case of raging flames fanning a wrongful accusation:
I will use the stubborn criminal, who must pay with his life, to test the blade.
The four seas must tell of my merit in upholding justice in this court case.

ACT 2

(EXTRA MALE *enters costumed as* BLIND OLD MAN, *looking sad and wearing a commoner's clothes*:) I made a mistake in the beginning, and it's now too late to regret it. I, the Blind Old Man, am so upset that I killed Kui's child and can hardly escape the law of the land. But my son is extremely filial—perhaps he can devise a plan to save me. Now Gaoyao is going all out to arrest me. Let me hide in the palace and wait for my son to come out. Even if he doesn't save me, my two daughters-in-law should save me. Let me stand here for a while.

(FEMALE LEAD *costumed as* EHUANG, YOUNG FEMALE LEAD *costumed as* NÜYING, *both wearing queenly clothes, enter together.*)

(EHUANG:)

We are real sisters, not a wife and a concubine,
Together we embrace the coverlet without spewing rancor.

(NÜYING:)

In the old days we were, for a while, farmer's wives,
But now have become, in concert, ladies in the sovereign's palace.

(EHUANG:) I am Ehuang.

(NÜYING:) I am Nüying. (*They greet each other.*)

(EHUANG:) Nüying, today King Shun would not even play the zither and seems downcast. What is all this about?

(NÜYING:) I heard that the Blind Old Man committed murder, and King Shun is going to secretly flee carrying him on his back.

(EHUANG *is shocked*:) How can this be allowed? Why has our father not tried to detain him?

(NÜYING:) He would not let anyone know about it. You and I should just try to detain him.

(EHUANG *smiles*:) You are right there. I am just worried that if he should flee, the arrogant Xiang would want to become the sovereign. It will be hard to protect your body or mine from him. Even though we have Shangjun, he's useless. The daughter born of Guibi will also not be able to protect the rule of Shun's house.[104] What should we do?

(NÜYING:) If King Shun does not carry the Blind Old Man, the latter cannot make his escape. And if he does not do so secretly, others will get wind of it. We have to figure out a plan for King Shun.

(EHUANG:) The arrogant Xiang does not have much to occupy him, and all the officials resent him. Why don't we have him carry the Blind Old Man? Perhaps they can escape to Mount Sieve or the Sunlit City.[105] Who would ever find them? Even if they are caught, Xiang can be made to bear the punishment instead.

(NÜYING:) Sister, since you have this marvelous plan, please hurry up and invite King Shun to come out.

(MALE LEAD *enters costumed as* KING SHUN *in casual clothes.*)

(ZHONGLÜ MODE: Northern *Fendie'er*) (KING SHUN *sings:*)

For several years the country has prospered and the people are in harmony,
My filial wish was that there be no misfortune or calamity.
Suddenly, a shock came like an unexpected storm.

(BLIND OLD MAN *rushes out.*) (KING SHUN *greets him.*)

(BLIND OLD MAN:) Son, save me! Save me!

(EHUANG *and* NÜYING *exit discreetly.*)

(KING SHUN *sings:*)

The word has long been out for the capture of the violent offender,
They have set up the instruments for cutting you down, father.
The law is like a burning brazier.[106]
How can we brook delay?
My heart is like an arrow,
How can it bear hindrance?

(BLIND OLD MAN:) It all started with me committing murder. Now Gaoyao is going to arrest me and there's no place where I can flee. I am overcome with regret for my wrongdoing. If you had not become the sovereign, I would not have dared to commit murder.[107]

(Southern *Qi Yan Hui*) (BLIND OLD MAN *sings:*)

I drew my sword and by chance fooled around with it,
And now there's no way out.
The blows from the whip and the rod—
Pity how disaster befalls the white-haired one!
Tumbled in woe is me:
Seeing these tears stream down my withered face, falling in front of the wind,
How can you bear to have me in jail with my hands tied?
Take heed and watch out—they are going to drag me away right in front of you!

(*Sounds of the gong ring out from within.* BLIND OLD MAN *looks terrified and hides behind* KING SHUN. CLOWN, *costumed as a* MESSENGER, *enters:*) A message for Your Majesty: Gaoyao, bent on arresting the Blind Old Man, has not yet captured him. I have come especially to report this.

(KING SHUN:) Just go and arrest him. (MESSENGER *receives the decree and hurriedly exits.*)

(BLIND OLD MAN *comes out:*) What should we do?

(KING SHUN:) There's no need to worry.

(Northern *Shiliu hua*) (KING SHUN *sings:*)

Desolate and heartsick, I let tears fall with the speed of a shuttle,
How can we make use of special rules for pardon?
If captured, we cannot fly out of the cunning web of the law.

(BLIND OLD MAN:) Where can we hide?

(KING SHUN *sings*:)
There's naught to do but go into hiding—
From the shock I am already slumping.
There's no choice but to wait out the days for the Misfortune Star's passing.
Why feel any regrets for the splendid mountains and rivers of the realm?
We will escape and flee to a distant land
And let no one see through our plan.
I am all ready to carry you, father, on my back.

(*Someone calls from within.*) The queens are coming. (BLIND OLD MAN *exits discreetly.*)

(EHUANG *and* NÜYING *enter.*)

(EHUANG:) I heard that you, King Shun, are going to abandon the entire realm in order to save the Blind Old Man. How misguided it is!

(Southern *Zhuma ting*) (EHUANG *sings*:)
Grotto of jade, abode of splendor:
Fragrance lingers on hairpins as jade pendants sway with our steps.
Truly old resentments have vanished in the family,
As new auspicious signs are brewing in the state,
And waves do not roil the sea.
In vain are the deep ties between father and son magnified,
For you must know that your duty to court and country is great.

(EHUANG:) I have a plan: it would be better if Your Majesty openly declares to Gaoyao that he should pardon the Blind Old Man and not pursue the matter. [*Sings*:]
Your intention is not to pervert justice.
Hasten to have him pardoned on special grounds; it's hard to inflict punishment.

(KING SHUN:) By my power I can do this, but in fact this cannot be done.

(Northern *Hong xiuxie*) (KING SHUN *sings*:)
Even though, following me, the wind can turn the rudder around,
I must be mindful how people and officials cast blame underground.
How can I consign him to woe and turn the halberd against my own?
I cannot afford to worry about dark, distant dreams on the phoenix tower,
Nor can I regret that, barring letters, news may become rumors.[108]
For half a lifetime I have been adamant in my filial piety,
It's only in this late chapter
That it will bear fruit.

(NÜYING:) Why don't you have Xiang carry him?

(Southern *Shiliu hua*) (NÜYING *sings*:)
By the seashore, at the sky's edge,
Wind and dew lock the misty sedge.
Teardrops wane

And gather in the heart.
In vain will you discard wealth and honor as your hair almost turns white.
Clinging to their desolation
Is this pair: Nüying and Ehuang.
Feelings at parting, naturally tumultuous, find no peace.
We hold on helplessly to your robe's edge as leave-taking is nigh.
Pity the lovely maidens for whom the matchmakers their trade ply.[109]

Your Majesty, once you flee, the entire realm will be plunged into chaos.

The times are perilous.[110]
Don't you know that?

(KING SHUN:) Don't waste your words.

(*Gongs are rung backstage.* CLOWN, *costumed as the* MESSENGER, *enters again:*) I submit the message to King Shun: "The Blind Old Man is still not arrested yet. He is probably here in the sovereign's palace."

(KING SHUN:) Stop this nonsense.

(Northern *Shi'er yue*) (KING SHUN *sings:*)
Long have I known that if the law prevails,
This cangue will blot out heaven's justice.
Think of the condemned criminal's woe,
As he chants in fear of the Yellow Springs:
At this moment, facing headwinds, he must regret starting the fire.
Why must you bang the gong so urgently?
Just wait till I, as ruler, ascend my royal seat,
And then we'll let the old man confess to his crime in his own way.[111]

(MESSENGER:) Gaoyao is determined to arrest the Blind Old Man. He said that the sovereign has not set out to protect him.

(Southern *Yujia deng*) (MESSENGER [*sings*]:)
The sword of justice and bronze choppers have been put in place:[112]
How can he withstand being cut to pieces or whittled away?
With an unruly heart he was reckless back then,
And now, lily-livered, he is starved of swagger.

We have looked everywhere inside and outside the royal city.

Crisscrossing in four directions, we try to arrest him.
We fear that he may be hiding in the palace.
Unable to gauge the situation,
We ask Your Majesty to determine
Where the sightless one may be hiding.

(KING SHUN:) Just go again and try to arrest him.

(MESSENGER:) I receive the royal decree.

(*Hastily exits.*)

(EHUANG *and* NÜYING:) Now that the pursuit is urgent, one may expect escape to be difficult. Your Majesty, why must you insist on carrying him on your back?

(KING SHUN:) Don't say anything anymore. I am leaving with my father.

(Northern *Yao min ge*) (KING SHUN *sings*:)

The palaces are decked out for naught, be they as grandly imposing as they please,
My consorts I have known in vain, be their dimples as lovely as can be.
All because my aged father is to endure captivity,
This lifelong filial son must save his life.

(EHUANG *and* NÜYING *weep*:) How can you abandon us?

(KING SHUN *sings*:)

I have no choice but to let your brows furrow in sorrow.
Take good care of your mother-in-law,
And don't ask me how on my way I will stumble and fall. (*Speaks*:)

Bring me a commoner's clothes.

(EHUANG *brings the clothes and* KING SHUN *changes.*)

(BLIND OLD MAN *enters*:) Twice they have come to arrest me, and I was nearly scared to death. Now what are we to do?

(KING SHUN:) Let me carry you away.

(EHUANG *and* NÜYING:) Although he has carried off the Blind Old Man, we should send Shangjun after them and make them turn back.

[*Exit.*]

(KING SHUN:) I am mustering all the strength I had twenty years ago when I was plowing the fields and digging the well.

(KING SHUN *carries the* BLIND OLD MAN *and flees.*)

(BLIND OLD MAN:) I am much beholden to you.

(Southern *Pudeng'e*) (BLIND OLD MAN [*sings*]:)

Let's chant a song of joy,
And find the hexagram "Hiding the Light."[113]
Stealthily we leave the palace gates,
Safely preserved from the judgments of all.[114]
Faking folly and shamming a limp,
We sport bamboo hats in the sun and coir jackets in the rain.
Having earned reprieve for my head,
We make haste to flee.
Laughable indeed: the reigning Son of Heaven descends the palatial steps.

(*Coda*)

Marching at night, resting by day, we sleep among wild grass.
Laughter rings out at the expanse of clouds by the sea:
It's all because lifelong filial piety has left us no other choice.

ACT 3

(CLOWN *enters costumed as* SHANGJUN *in royal clothes*:)

The father vanished, and the son has suffered.[115]
Snatch the father-in-law away, and the daughters-in-law are flustered.
The ones who send me on the chase now,
Are neither King Shun nor King Yao.

I, Shangjun, have relied on my father my entire life. What I drink is the superb wine created by Yidi; what I wallow in is the seductive beauty of the Chen lady; what I spend is the wealth from the Six Departments of Yu; what I exert is the force whereby Gonggong smashes against the mountain.[116] And then there is this Danzhu, son of King Yao: he is my maternal uncle as well as my paternal uncle.[117] The two of us spend our days fooling around. When that Danzhu saw how the hundred beasts all danced as music rose in King Shun's court,[118] he collapsed in a heap laughing. I said, "When birds and beasts behave strangely, the Son of Heaven must suffer some sort of challenge."[119] Who could have known? The other day my father fled because my grandfather had killed someone over a row about listening to music. King Yao was so terrified that he sent Danzhu to go after them. Gaoyao put his instruments of punishment into storage and said he would not dare to put the Blind Old Man to death. The Lords of the Four Peaks said, "What matters is the realm under heaven. We can't have a day without a ruler." So they were about to recommend that Yu becomes the sovereign. Fortunately, that Yu knows something about the ways of the world. He said, "Shangjun, Shun's son, is now grown. He should inherit the throne. I will flee to the Sunlit City."[120] That Boyi said, "I am in charge of mountains and marshes. I fear he is hiding in deep mountains and great marshes. If I set a fire, he will run out for sure." That Ji Qi said, "This wouldn't do! In later times there will be someone who cannot be smoked out when the mountain is set to fire, and he will end up dying in the flames."[121] That Xihe just laughed sarcastically, and when people asked him, he said: "The realm under heaven is vast. Where are you going to look for him? I was observing the constellations at night, and saw that the sovereign's star moved from its proper place and is now between the Cowherd and Weaving Maid asterisms.[122] That spot corresponds to the eastern side of Yangzhou[123] by the seas of Yue. All of you should just take care of your own duties. All we have to do is to send Shangjun to go after them." When I heard that, although I was glad, I was deterred by the arduous journey through mountains and rivers. Let me just go to Uncle Xiang's place and discuss this with him.

(COMIC *enters costumed as* XIANG *in royal clothes*.)

Pushing aside my brother, I am ready to become sovereign,
He's stolen our father, it's bad luck ill begotten.
He leaves behind his wives—indeed they are lonesome.
Looking upon your humble servant, they may find him winsome.

(*Laughing*:) I have always been an arrogant person, and that will never change. A most curious thing happened recently: King Shun has vanished. Come to think of it, it has to be my turn to become sovereign. Who would dare to dispute it? Who is beyond my jurisdiction? My two sisters-in-law now must depend on me. That Nüying gave birth to Shangjun, who is a rather unreasonable fellow—just like me. I must not provoke him. As for the secondary consort Guibi, although she is young, she has given birth to daughters. In my entire life I have never liked women who have given birth. That leaves only Ehuang—although she is a bit older, she was never ruined by pregnancy. Furthermore, my brother was not one who set much store by sexual prowess, and her stuff is not that much worse for use. And I also don't demand virgins—I can make do. My two nieces, Xiaoming and Zhuguang, are quite beautiful. By my reckoning, we also don't have the rule that those sharing the same clan name cannot marry. Are we to let other people enjoy what we have in our family? Furthermore, my brother also took his great aunts as wives.[124] Who can criticize me? (*He laughs.*) Hehe, all these outrageous things that go against heaven—let's wait with them for now, or else I may end up having all my hopes dashed just like last time.[125] For now I will look for my nephew Shangjun and check my brother's whereabouts. Ah, my nephew is here.

(XIANG *greets* SHANGJUN.)

(SHANGJUN:) I have been waiting for you, Uncle Xiang, for quite a while.

(XIANG:) Did you hear everything I said earlier?

(SHANGJUN *laughs*:) How can I not have heard? But you are too wicked!

(XIANG:) These days the honest ones are totally useless, while the wicked ones can get their way everywhere.[126]

(SHANGJUN:) Even so, take heed and you can go anywhere under heaven; be reckless and you will be hard put to move an inch.

(XIANG:) Let me ask you: do you know where your father has gone?

(SHANGJUN:) He stole grandfather away and we don't know where he's headed.

(XIANG:) Well, well, now I really cannot forgive King Yao.

(SHANGJUN:) How so?

(XIANG:) He had possession of the entire realm under heaven and insisted on not keeping it and yielding it to others. Others didn't want it, and only then did he abdicate and give the throne to my brother. But my brother is also not one who wants to have possession of the realm under heaven.[127] For no good reason Yao gave his two daughters to Shun. And Shun cares only about father; he has abandoned the realm and fled. If from the beginning King Yao abdicated in my favor, his daughters would have had a few more children by now. Even when it comes to the Blind Old Man killing someone, I would not have allowed Gaoyao to bring him to justice, and the whole thing would blow over. And now it has come to this: the sovereign's position has long been vacated, and unrest is brewing all under heaven. It's all old man Yao's fault. I have to berate him.

(SHANGJUN:) He has nine sons, all of them fearless and strong. If you are going to go berate him, you'd better watch out.

(XIANG:) Yao's first child is Danzhu. What are the names of these other eight?[128]

(SHANGJUN *laughs*:) I did remember once, but now my memory is playing tricks on me and I have forgotten again.

(XIANG:) Never mind. Let's go together. (*They walk.*) If Yao comes out, you have to provide cover for me. Just say that I never berated him.

(SHANGJUN *laughs*:) Uncle Xiang, since you were so intent on berating him, how come you are bailing now?

(XIANG:) Nephew, haven't you figured it out yet? I can only berate someone behind his back—it's always been so. Furthermore, Yao is a great sage. I won't be able to open my mouth if I see him.

(SHANGJUN:) There is no choice but to make a show of harangue outside his gates.

(XIANG:) Just so, just so. (XIANG *faces the ghost door*[129] *and bellows out his harangue*:) Foolish old man who refused to possess the entire realm under heaven! Stupid old man who failed to recognize good men! Cruel old man who had no consideration for his own son! Sad old man who does not know how to have any fun![130]

(SHANGJUN:) Later generations will have grounds to say that you are Jie's hound barking at Yao![131] Ah, Yao has come out.

(XIANG *runs away in fear.*)

(SECOND MALE *as* KING YAO *enters costumed in a sovereign's clothes*:) Shun is filial toward his father, and secretly fled carrying him on his back. Shangjun is worthless, and Gaoyao is intent on executing the law. Ah, the two of you are here. How is King Shun?

(XIANG *and* SHANGJUN *show their obsequiousness*:) We are just waiting for you, King Yao, to seek your advice regarding our plans.

(KING YAO:) Now the three states Cong, Kuai, and Xu'ao are fomenting rebellion, and the sovereign is not here. What is to be done?[132] You must find some way to get hold of him, and, together with the hundred officials, I will welcome him back.

(XIANG *and* SHANGJUN:) We will see to it.

(*They exit together.*)

(OLDER MALE *as* ZIHOU ZHIBO *and* OLDER FEMALE *as* SHANJUAN *enter together costumed in the clothing of recluses.*)

Hearing that Xu You's ears had been sullied,
We led the calves to cross upstream.[133]
Roaming freely between heaven and earth,
We find in Fuxi and Shennong mates of worth.

I am Zizhou Zhibo. This one here is Shanjuan. When King Shun wanted to yield his throne to the two of us, I was ill with a secret sorrow, while Shanjuan's mind and spirit had found freedom.[134] We have thus become recluses together deep in the mountains. As for that northerner Wuze, who threw himself into the Deeps of Cold Purity—that was excessive.[135] What entanglements do I have with Shun? I should just carry this food and wine to the spot under the green trees by the clear stream, where I will rest awhile and eat awhile.

(SHANJUAN:) Zhibo, I am going to invite Wang Ni, Nie Que, Piyi, and Chaofu—those four—to join us in reclusion. That Xu You has become King Yao's teacher and now lives in Mount Sieve, so there is no need to invite him.[136]

(ZIFU ZHIBO:) Just so. Ah, someone carrying an old man on his back is coming from afar. Let's see what they are talking about.

(MALE LEAD *as* KING SHUN *costumed in a commoner's clothes enters carrying the* BLIND OLD MAN *and sings*:)

(HUANGZHONG MODE: Northern *Zui huayin*) [KING SHUN *sings*:]
Jade-like dew and crisp wind mark the chill of autumnal dawn,
It's hard to keep pace as we scale mountains and peaks.
Villages lie afar,
Rustic songs ring pure.
Darkly forlorn, my old father bears with the fears,
And with hunger and thirst, sadness has turned into sickness.
Let us go quietly, in fear and trembling,
Bearing a forest of shadows cast by the slanting sun.[137]

(ZIFU ZHIBO *and* SHANJUAN:) Let us take some food and wine.

(KING SHUN *listens*.)

(Southern *Huamei xu*) (ZIFU ZHIBO *and* SHANJUAN *sing*:)
Our hair let loose, we whistle into the blue yonder.
The beauty of the wilds, the light of the clouds: it's all there for the taking.[138]
What's more, we trust our traces to the woods,
Escaping fame beyond the world.
We are free to do all the clapping and carping,
Why bother to ask about bowing and scraping? (*They drink*.)
No need to ponder how woodcutting makes for a deeper quiet in the mountain,[139]
Don't leave behind any days wherein the joys have not reached their limits.

(KING SHUN *is surprised*:) Those two are Zhibo and Shanjuan. Who could have known that they are hiding as recluses here? Let me call out to them.

(KING SHUN calls out:) Zhibo! Shanjuan!

(ZIFU ZHIBO *is startled*:)

We are ashamed to have left our countenance in the world,
And it's been a long while since our names have been bandied among men.

Let's turn back.

[*Exit together*.]

(Northern *Xi qian qiao*) (KING SHUN *sings*:)
I thought they had long buried their names,
But it turns out that heaven has set them free into the woods.[140]

Lofty feelings indeed!
I could call out as much as I like, but they did not respond.
Just like crickets' chirping in an empty valley—it makes one hear the sounds of clogs beyond.[141]
I wave my hand: How can they abhor me so?
Why should I deign to hanker after glory and riches
Or to fear death and lose my way in life?

(*Cries come from backstage.*)

(KING SHUN:) Ah! The pursuing soldiers are coming. (*He hurriedly carries the* BLIND OLD MAN *and exits.*)

(SECOND COMIC *as* DANZHU *costumed in royal clothes enters leading his troops:*) I am Danzhu. Having received the order from my father, King Yao, we are here to pursue King Shun and request his return. Attendants, let's catch up with him. (*They run after* KING SHUN.)

(Southern *Diliuzi*) (DANZHU *and his* ATTENDANTS *sing:*)
Him we rush to overtake,
Rush to overtake,
A special request we make.
Impossible to make him stay,
Make him stay.
Over there they are waiting.
This journey has taken us through another landscape
Beyond myriad layers of cloudy mountains.
Like floating duckweed, their traces move evermore:
When will we find him and bring him back,
So that we can bow again to the divine sage?
We cannot catch up with him. Let's turn back.

(*All exit.*)

(KING SHUN, *carrying the* BLIND OLD MAN, *enters in haste.*)

(Northern *Chu duizi*) (KING SHUN *sings:*)
When I got wind of King Yao's order,
I fled afar, leaving the royal capital.

(BLIND OLD MAN:) Son, go back if you have to go back!

(KING SHUN *sings:*)
How can I end up letting my own father suffer a cruel punishment?
The realm under heaven is but a mere trifle, to be discarded like a worn-out shoe.[142]
Ah, let's find a house, for the sky takes on a darkened hue.

(BLIND OLD MAN:) I am hungry, let's find a place to stay the night.

(KING SHUN:) Let me go and look. (*He acts out walking.*) There is a farmer's thatched hut there. Is anyone home?

(YOUNG MALE *costumed as a* FARMER *enters*:)

A man of such vitality and strength: How can he be so deluded as ruler?
Son in hand and wife on my back, I headed for the islands of the sea.[143]

I am the farmer of Stone Gate. In the old days I plowed the fields alongside Shun and we were friends. Now he is the sovereign. He once tried to yield the throne to me, but I saw that his virtue was still not perfect, so I live in seclusion here. Who is calling outside? (*He sees* KING SHUN.) You look like that wifeless man, Shun.

(KING SHUN:) Indeed this is he. Now I have carried my father here. Please let me stay the night.

(FARMER *turns aside and speaks*:) He is one of those who burden themselves with the entire realm under heaven. How can I talk to him? (*He turns around.*) Well then, please enter. (KING SHUN *carries the* BLIND OLD MAN *on his back and enters the farmer's house.*)

(FARMER:) Coarse grains and cold leeks, straw patch and cloth cover: they are all here. The two of you can eat and sleep as you wish. I have to go.

(KING SHUN:) Where are you going?

(FARMER:)

The rustic is loath to greet and meet guests,
Old friends balk at starting a heart-to-heart chat.
(*He exits first.*)

(KING SHUN:) Ah, the farmer of Stone Gate left already. I will offer some rice and these greens to my father and let him eat something. (KING SHUN *prepares the rice and lets the* BLIND OLD MAN *eat.*)

(BLIND OLD MAN:) Sightless and hungry, I am so grateful to my filial son.

(Southern *Didi jin*) (BLIND OLD MAN *sings*:)
Fleeing afar in my declining years, it's indeed my good fortune
To steal survival at sky's edge, keeping body and soul together.
Sitting sightless, shut in an abandoned hut, I listen on alert.
Turning this way and that, we manage to hang on.
In the dusty food vessels from a farmer's house
Are chaff and coarse grains we valiantly force down.
The minced pickle is hard,
The minced pickle is hard.
I fear the taste of bitter want will not easily end.

(*Roosters crow inside.*)

(KING SHUN:) We should get going.

(KING SHUN *carries the* BLIND OLD MAN *and sings*:)

(Northern *Guadi feng*)
Alas, in a trice, roosters vie to crow under sparse stars.
Packing our things, we will soon be on our way.
My back has suffered from the affliction of toil.

Seeking and not finding my good friend from Stone Gate,
I see instead morning stars twinkling low.
If only I could gouge out my eyes to cure his blindness![144]
Unlike the eastward inspection tour of yesteryear with roadside welcome,
Splendid banners, and dragon steeds,
I can now only rely on my body to carry the load, supported by my two feet.
For all that, my goal to save my father is finally realized.

(KING SHUN:) Let's rest for a while by the road before we continue. (SHUN *puts the* BLIND OLD MAN *down and also sits down.*)

(COMIC *costumed as* XIANG *and* CLOWN *costumed as* SHANGJUN *are riding horses. They both rush onstage.*)

(XIANG:) Nephew, we have rushed all the way to Kuaiji and have searched all over Mount Li. We are not far from the seashore; let's cover one more stretch.

(SHANGJUN:) Just so.

(Southern *Bao lao cui*) (XIANG *sings*:)
In great haste we gallop—
Where at the sky's edge is the mist-shrouded boat?
My gaze breaks off, beyond wind and dust, at the thousand-mile waves.
By the stars we divined the sovereign's traces in the distant land of Yue:
A piece of good luck that gladdens the heart.

(SHANGJUN *smiles*:) Those people by the roadside look like them.

(XIANG *sings*:)
Indeed, father and son are walking side by side.
We can let them take their ease by the sea,
But they must return to court
With all the panoply of due ceremony.

(XIANG *greets* SHUN:) We are requesting that you, brother and father, go back.

(SHANGJUN:) Xihe told us you were here, and indeed we have found you.

(XIANG:) Gaoyao said that so long as you, brother, go back, he would not dare to put father to death any longer.

(KING SHUN:) We are going to end our days at the seashore. No more turning back for us. Please thank those twenty-two men on my behalf most profusely.[145]

(Northern *Simen zi*) (KING SHUN *sings*:)
Who has the patience? Who can bear roads muddy and dreary?
You, you, you,
Why oh why have you spotted us so clearly?
Having secretly fled, I would be hard put to turn back,
Beg as you must, but for us that's the wrong track.

(XIANG:) What's so good about this place?

(KING SHUN *sings*:)
We make clothes from leaves,

And soup from greens,
We lean against tall pines
To harmonize with their autumn rustling,
Just as we are awakening.
Quickly turn your carriage around,
Make haste and be homeward bound.
My other advice: pay your respects to our mother day and night.

(KING SHUN *carries the* BLIND OLD MAN *and runs for a stretch.* XIANG *and* SHANGJUN *chase them for a stretch. They stop.*)

(Southern *Shuangsheng zi*) (SHANGJUN *sings*:)
Governing at court,
Governing at court—
If he does not return,
Who holds the fort?
Consorts in the palace,
Consorts in the palace,
Pine for his return,
And fearfully the mirror spurn.
Nothing to celebrate,
Nothing to celebrate,
For the throne, no one to elevate.
No one to elevate.
We just found out his whereabouts,
But how can we report 'mission accomplished?'

(BLIND OLD MAN:) You should just go back. If I do not go back, it's hard for him to go alone.

(KING SHUN:) I do not care for the sorrows of the country, nor do I care for the resentment of my wives. I will just let the young ones do things their way. Go! Go!

(XIANG *looks at* SHANGJUN:) Let's just return for now and figure things out later.

(*They exit.*)

(KING SHUN:) They are gone already. I figure they won't come back. Install a sovereign, reward merit with fiefdoms—let them argue away. We have come to the eastern seas. What joy!

(Northern *Shuixianzi*) (KING SHUN *sings*:)
Ah, ah, ah,
The sky shines bright over the sea,
It's great, great, great
Great to watching the dragon's breath—in it terraces and towers stretch to Red City.[146]
He, he, he

Can manage the flood and settle the people.[147]

I, I, I

Will work in the fields and dig wells.

First, first, first,

First, I'll save this man on the brink of death, reviving the one who is half-alive.

Let, let, let,

Let go of "great peace under gentle rule."[148]

Bring, bring, bring,

Bring out the old commoner of those bygone days.

Done, done, done,

Done are the songs and choruses, all toil and no ease,

Thus, thus, thus,

Thus are we forever free from disturbance, able to enjoy tranquility![149]

(BLIND OLD MAN:) All thanks to you, I am in a good place now!

(KING SHUN:) Dear father!

(Northern *Coda*) (KING SHUN *sings*:)

Let's make do with this place and settle here with no further alarm.

Patiently I will while away the time, leisurely fishing, busily plowing.

Don't say that twenty years of being a ruler amount to nothing.[150]

ACT 4

(SECOND COMIC *enters costumed as* DANZHU:) I caught up with King Shun but could not get him to return, and now no one sits on the throne. I must tell my sisters about this.

(COMIC *enters costumed as* XIANG:) I never wanted my brother. But now that my brother has fled, everyone is persecuting me. My heart is sick with sorrow, how could I have any thought of stealing my sisters-in-law? If only my brother can be persuaded to come back! Ah, my brother-in-law is here. Let us go together to see my sisters-in-law.

(CLOWN *enters costumed as* SHANGJUN:) I caught up with my father but could not get him to return, and my two mothers are beside themselves with worry. King Yao also blamed me for being useless. Let me find Danzhu and seek some diversion. Ah, Uncle Xiang and Uncle Danzhu, what are you doing here?

(XIANG:) We are here to kill you.

(SHANGJUN *cries in fear and hugs his head*:) Spare me! Spare me!

(XIANG:) Have no fear! We are just teasing you for a lark! Just so that you can conjure up a living Shun!

(SHANGJUN:) For the Great Shun there is nothing to show, but it's easy to get the Little Shun!

(XIANG:) That's what we meant—the little one.

(SHANGJUN:) Can you say that I am not his flesh and blood? Let me pass for him!

(XIANG:) This is not the case of "a plowing ox's offspring that is sorrel-hued and has well-formed horns."[151] Truly, "Yao's son is totally unlike him, and Shun's son is also totally unlike him."[152] How can you take Shun's part?

(SHANGJUN:) I would just have to get my father from my two mothers.

(XIANG:) Excellent idea!

(DANZHU:) We have to go and force them to think of something. (*They walk.*)

(XIANGJUN:) Mothers, please come!

(FEMALE LEAD *costumed as* EHUANG *and* SECOND FEMALE *costumed as* NÜYING *enter together.*)

(EHUANG:)

When will the tear traces on the bamboo fade?
Dreams are lonely in autumn's deepening shade.

(NÜYING:)

With whom can we play Shun's zither strings?[153]
To slender waists ebbing strength this brings.[154]

Ah, why have our brother, along with brother-in-law Xiang and Shangjun all come? Did King Shun agree to return?

(ALL:) We are here to seek your counsel for a clever plan.

(NÜYING *deliberates*:) Let's have our father go and request his return.

(DANZHU:) No use! No use! Our father's son already made his round.

(EHUANG:) I have a plan: just ask our mother-in-law to go. King Shun is extremely filial. What's more, this is his stepmother, for whom there can only be deeper love and respect.[155] Mother-in-law should go and say: Gaoyao no longer dares to kill. If he does not come back, his aged mother will die from resentment. How would he dare not come back?

(ALL:) Clever plan! Clever plan! Hurry and bring the Perfidious Mother!

(SECOND CLOWN *enters costumed as* PERFIDIOUS MOTHER *in a queen's regalia*:)

I gave birth to a child who became the ruler of a state,[156]
And with a sage king forged a marital bond of fate.[157]
My blind man is surprisingly adept with his touch,
Intimacy with an aging wife, late to wed, is never too much.[158]

I am the Perfidious Mother, the second wife of the Blind Old Man. Back then we spent all our time trying to finish Shun off. Now that he has become the sovereign, he no longer holds it against us. Truly I was wrong to blame him. Why did you invite me to come out today? (*She greets them.*)

(ALL:) King Shun has fled to the seaside and is staying there. He refuses to come back despite repeated entreaties. We are asking you, Perfidious Mother, to personally go and put in a word.

(PERFIDIOUS MOTHER *looks scared*:) I once tried to dispatch him with the plots at the granary and the well. If I now take it upon myself to go, he could irritate all the old sores, then what would happen to me?

(EHUANG *and* NÜYING:) Mother, there's no need to be fearful. If you go, King Shun will return for sure. And Father will again take his pleasure with you, Mother. Wouldn't that be for the best?

(PERFIDIOUS MOTHER *laughs*:) This line actually tickles me where it matters. I will make this trip then.

(*All exit.*)

(MALE LEAD *enters costumed as* KING SHUN *leading the* BLIND OLD MAN.)

(KING SHUN:) For the last few days I have been staying put with my old father at the seashore. We enjoy leisure all day long. What joy!

(XIANLÜ MODE: Northern *Dian jiangchun*) (KING SHUN *sings*:)
The great sea heaves sighs with its waves.
Alone I gaze at distant mountains as the frosty dawn breaks.
Free and easy wandering
Erases memories of trivial regrets and vexations.

(BLIND OLD MAN:) My son, at the time when you ascended from being a farmer to the position of sovereign, what a great honor and exaltation it was! And now because of me you have become a farmer again.

(KING SHUN:) Although I was the sovereign, it was not as if I did not long for the life among the fields!

(Northern *Hunjiang long*) (KING SHUN *sings*:)
Vain are my regrets for being a son unlike his father,[159]
For several years at Mount Li I bewailed my fate.[160]
Living among fields and marshes,
Hiding my traces next to fishermen and woodcutters,
I remained a wifeless man at thirty but harbored no resentment:
Just then my younger brother and sister had nowhere to turn.[161]
Recommended as worthy by the Lords of the Four Peaks,
I was chosen as a match for paragons of loveliness.
Half a lifetime of dust and grime,
Graying hair on my two temples:
Endless mountains and rivers could not dispel my sorrows,
Splendid palaces could not earn my father's smile.
Dreams come back as illusions:
Who would summon them when old age comes?

(BLIND OLD MAN:) I am much beholden to you. This crime was indeed committed by me.

(Southern *Guizhi xiang*) (BLIND OLD MAN *sings*:)
The star of calamity suddenly flashed,

The demon of fury stoked mayhem.
How could I have known that my sightless eyes were beclouded?
Without meaning to, I waved my fists in frenzied rage.
Urgent as fire was the order for arrest,
Urgent as fire was the order for arrest.
It's because my son is filial
That he carried me here.
King Yao and his ministers can reset the three grand seats of power for all I care,
I will soon be watching for the first time the eighth month's tidal bore.[162]

(SECOND CLOWN *costumed as the* PERFIDIOUS MOTHER, COMIC *costumed as* XIANG, *and* CLOWN *costumed as* SHANGJUN *enter together.*) Slowly we have made our way here—this place is the seashore.

(PERFIDIOUS MOTHER *sees* KING SHUN *and cries:*) Ah, my filial son! My rich and noble son! I am sick of longing for you! Why are you here with this old good-for-nothing?[163]

(KING SHUN:) Father is guilty of a crime that deserves the ultimate punishment, and I cannot bend the law to protect him. I have no choice but to flee here so that he can live out his heaven-allotted years.

(PERFIDIOUS MOTHER:) Son, I am your stepmother, so of course you shouldn't listen to me.[164] I guess it's because your father is your biological father that you made up your mind to be with him here. How can this not crush me! (PERFIDIOUS MOTHER *faints.*)

(KING SHUN *hastens to say:*) I will just go back then. Mother, please don't be angry.

(PERFIDIOUS MOTHER:) Xiang, my own flesh and blood, is neither loyal nor filial. How can he compare to you? If you don't return, that old good-for-nothing would of course have it easy, but on whom could I rely? The good things of life would mean nothing. If I must stay with you by the seashore, how can I bear it? Son, you would do better to return. (PERFIDIOUS MOTHER *cries.*)

(KING SHUN:) I will just go back then. Mother, please don't cry.

(Northern *You hulu*) (KING SHUN *sings:*)
I cannot withstand the insistent urging of my aged mother,
As she suffers the wind and waves
At the distant edge of the sky.

(PERFIDIOUS MOTHER:) You cared only about your father when you fled. You didn't even say a word to me when you came here.

(KING SHUN *sings:*)
As for not bidding farewell and daring to abandon you,
It's all because we set out in stealth: who knew about it?
The two of us fled to the seaside: who could have guessed it?

(PERFIDIOUS MOTHER:) Son, go back. That Gaoyao said that he's not going to put your father to death.

(KING SHUN *sings*:)

Although the Minister of Justice, considering the circumstances, will not apply punishment,

For a son to steal his father is not theft.[165]

So, I can't get away after all!

Let me just roam in leisure, and let bygones be bygones,[166]

What remains are only the mountain colors so green,

And ocean clouds far in the distance.

(PERFIDIOUS MOTHER *says in aside*:) I will just have to berate the old man.

(PERFIDIOUS MOTHER *turns to* BLIND OLD MAN:) You groped your way along the walls and left! You are I are one loving couple. You made our good son leave our daughters-in-law and carry you all the way here. Why did you not care about my loneliness? You only fear death at the hands of Gaoyao? Why don't you fear death at my hands?

(BLIND OLD MAN *seems terrified*:) It was because we had no alternatives. If you do not forgive me, then truly I deserve to die!

(PERFIDIOUS MOTHER:) I am so outraged!

(Southern *Basheng Ganzhou*) (PERFIDIOUS MOTHER *sings*:)

Blind slave! Sightless old fool!

(BLIND OLD MAN *is terrified*:) Why do curses pour out whenever you open your mouth?

(PERFIDIOUS MOTHER *sings*:)

Laughable that you make do with refuge on one branch

As if you were a tiny wren.[167]

(BLIND OLD MAN:) The other day I was so rattled that I did not get to bid you farewell. It was my fault.

(PERFIDIOUS MOTHER *sings*:)

On my wrinkled skin are the comely arches of my eyebrows:

You totally forgot our shared joys of night and day.

(PERFIDIOUS MOTHER *says angrily*:) You old good-for-nothing, don't you realize?

(PERFIDIOUS MOTHER *sings*:)

For naught have you known that killing another means death for you.

Who would believe that, trying to hide your traces, no place will do?

Make a good effort to convince our son to return. If you don't convince him, I'm not going to let you live.

Old glutton,

Convince our son: How can he not come back to court?

(BLIND OLD MAN *is fearful*:) I get it, I get it.

(BLIND OLD MAN *says to* SHUN:) Son, now that Mother has come to insist that you and I must go back, let's just go back. Let them put me to death as they please. We need succor for the present crisis!

(KING SHUN:) Father, have no fear. I will figure this out.

(Northern *Tianxia le*) (KING SHUN [*sings*]:)
Ah, why did you come to bicker and make mischief?
We beg for forgiveness!
Your badgering of father is merciless!

(PERFIDIOUS MOTHER:) I just want you to go back.

(KING SHUN *sings*:)
Several times over, I tarry to no avail—
Alas! Alas! I will go back.

(PERFIDIOUS MOTHER, XIANG, SHANGJUN *are happy*.)

(KING SHUN *sings*:)
I just want us to gladly share our lot to bring joy to my parents.
The crime is unpardonable, but I can submit to the blade.[168]
Let's get our hearts ready for home and set out on the Puban Road.

(XIANG:) We came to plead with him, but he would not return. But he agreed once Mother came. Indeed, filial piety for the father and the mother is just the same.[169]

(Southern *Jie san xing*) (XIANG *and* SHANGJUN *sing*:)
So much for the leopard's splendid fur being shrouded by mist,[170]
The hidden dragon is already rising with the thunder.
In the same old way, father and mother have no quarrels.
Ply the tunes on the zither
And strike up notes of Xiaoshao.[171]

(SHANGJUN:) The carriages are here. Grandfather, please get in.

(XIANG *sings*:)
Say no more about the farmer taking to the seas because of petty family troubles,
Be mindful of how, as the sage ruler comes to court, the state's foundation is stable.

(ALL *proceed on their way*.)

(XIANG *and* SHANGJUN *sing*:)
Riding in the palanquins,
Riding in the palanquins,
We keep the lid tight on the riddle gourd,[172]
Whose mere mention is untoward.

(KING SHUN:) Back then we took this road to come here, and now we leave along the same road.

(Northern *Nezha ling*) (KING SHUN *sings*:)
This road!
Frosty wind whistled desolately all over the fields,
Frozen stiff, we passed the night.
On the misty islets waterbirds lost their way—
Going back and forth, we have covered the trip twice.
Mountain clouds blocked the broken bridge,

How many paths have we scaled?
Stumbling in haste, we came here last time.
Facing an endless expanse, regrets now overtake us.
All is abustle with fluttering banners and ringing bells.[173]

(SECOND MALE *costumed as* KING YAO *in royal clothes,* OLDER MALE *costumed as* GAOYAO *in official garb, and* MISCELLANEOUS *costumed as* VARIOUS OFFICIALS *enter*:) We hear that King Shun is coming back and we have to welcome him here. (*They greet* KING SHUN.) We have come especially to welcome Your Majesty!

(KING SHUN:) Born between heaven and earth, I could not be a ruler with bright virtue, nor could I be a filial son. Shouldn't I die of shame!

(GAOYAO:) The deaf, the blind, and the handicapped should in any case be dealt with lightly and forgiven.[174] Your humble subject deserves death!

(KING YAO:) Cong, Kuai, and Xu'ao immediately started to rebel once they heard that the sovereign had fled. Now they have already submitted to correction and transformation.

(Southern *Changpai*) (KING YAO [*sings*]:)
Great is the merit of the spirits,
Great is the merit of the spirits!
Bright is the royal decree,
And even more fulsome the glory of myriad spheres.
You have fled for no reason.
The moment you secretly carried your father marked a filial virtue as lofty as heaven.

(KING SHUN:) Now I can only offer myself to take the punishment in my father's place.

(GAOYAO:) How can this be!

(KING YAO *sings*:)
An inadvertent crime should also be forgiven.
This was not, in any case, a lawless act that violated the Way.
In this age of good governance and nonaction, the subjects dance,
Just as songs of contentment waft from alleys and byways.[175]

(KING SHUN:) Let me abdicate in favor of Yu!

(KING YAO:) It's too early for that.

(KING YAO *sings*:)
How can you yield the throne and abdicate in favor of a subject?
I fear that goes against Heaven's will
And will roil the seas and shake the mountains.

(KING SHUN:) If that's the case, let's just enter the palace. (ALL *begin to go in.*)

(KING SHUN:) All you ministers should know that the journey I undertook then—

(Northern *Jisheng cao*) (KING SHUN *sings*:)
Did not mean that I declined this exalted position,
It was all because of the law's violation.

As the minister investigating the crime, he could hardly fudge the case,
As the ruler presiding over the people, I could hardly bend the law in secret,
As the son who loves his father, I could hardly evade the issue.
That was why I resolved to sacrifice my life for the distant yonder,
But how could I withstand the ministers' urgent and relentless pleas?

(*From backstage*:) The two consorts have come!

(*The two* FEMALE LEADS *costumed as* EHUANG *and* NÜYING *in a queen's clothes enter*:)

The husband who abandoned his wives escaped and fled,
The hen-pecked father-in-law was caught and brought back.

(*They greet* KING SHUN *and cry.*) Ah, you have come back!

(Southern *Duan pai*) (EHUANG *and* NÜYING *sing*:)
Newly decked out in colorful raiment,
Newly decked out in colorful raiment,
Wreathed in resplendent jewels,
We have suffered, turning pale and haggard.
Just like the Jingwei bird trying to fill the seas,[176]
We dreaded the cuckoo's woeful cries deep into spring.[177]
Wasting away, our waists have become ever more slender.
Now what joy it is to meet as cassia wine flows in our queenly chamber.

(KING SHUN:) All you ministers should withdraw for now. Let us set forth a feast of celebration.

(*All the ministers exit first.*)

(KING SHUN:) Although I have now bent the law, father and mother get to be reunited again.

(*Zhuan sha Coda*) (KING SHUN *sings*:)
The days before—what an arduous journey!
And today—do not grieve and lament!
Speaking of it makes one faint with disquiet!
Pity the soul of the murdered one: it is nowhere to be found—
Coming and going like drifting cress, it cannot be held down.
From now on there is joy to spare,
For I have paid back their toil and care.
Hard to account for by official law is this private reprieve,
Just let them mock and censure the law-bending pardon.
When you get to the bottom of it, there's something fake
In all these clever words that the heart of great filial piety make.

(*All exit.*)

Xianqiu tells lies for a reason,
Taoying's hypothesis misses its season.
By chance is a wondrous story told,
And we could not but make it somewhat bold.

NOTES

1. The dating here is based on Li Jie (2015).
2. For a good introduction to Lü Tiancheng, see Idema (2004); Xu Shuofang (1993, 245–85); Zhang Ping (2012, 90–121); Wu Shuyin (2018); Ren Weirong (2011). See Qi Biaojia (1959, 169); cf. Pei Zhe (2015).
3. See *Black and White Donkeys* in this volume.
4. Shen Jing (1985, 899).
5. Qi Biaojia (1959, 131).
6. Qi Biaojia (1959, 169). Qi does, however, go on to justify Lü's use of detailed erotica: "Yet scenes cannot be fully realized without explicitness, lyrics lack forcefulness without explicitness. This is hard to explain to the vulgar."
7. Cited in Zhang Ping (2012, 94). Qi Biaojia calls this Lü's "playful composition" (*youxi zhi bi* 遊戲之筆) and defends its admonitory intention (Qi Biaojia 1959, 9–10). Judging from his description, the play eroticizes the story of the two Yao sisters 二姚, wives of the legendary Xia king Shaokang 少康. Like *Sublime Jokes*, it makes fun of canonical classics.
8. Xu Shuofang (1993, 282–84).
9. *ZZJS j.* 1.4.
10. It is also the title of a well-known miscellany by the Song scholar Zhou Mi 周密 (1232–ca. 1298). Zhou Mi's forbears hailed from Jinan, which would have been in the ancient state of Qi. The title indicates modest self-deprecation, although the book aspires to transmit historical information.
11. Cf. Zhao Qi's 趙岐 comment: "For the entire realm under heaven was what Shun received from Yao. He should care for the people on behalf of heaven. The king's laws cannot be bent; how can he get to forbid it?" (*MZZS* 931). In Zhu Xi's reading, what is "received" is not the highest definition of kingship but the law: "This means that Gaoyao's laws have been received from the right place. He (Gaoyao) would not dare to intervene privately, and he cannot abandon the laws even with a command from the Son of Heaven" (Zhu Xi 1983, 359).
12. In *HFZ j.* 49.1057, the story of the stolen sheep is cited as an example of how Confucian morality can undermine loyalty to the state.
13. *SSJS* 15. The same words are recurrently used to describe these characters in the play. On the definition of *yin* 嚚 ("perfidious"), see Xi 24.2 in *Zuo* (vol. 1, 382–83): "When the mouth does not speak words of loyalty and good faith, it is perfidy."
14. This passage, like some other passages about Shun quoted in *Mencius*, is couched in archaic diction, as if it is a quotation from a more ancient text.
15. Li Zhi 李贄, "Yu youren shu 與友人書," in Li Zhi (2010, vol. 1, 181–82). Li Zhi concludes that Shun's intention to be glad is genuine.
16. *Shijing* (*Classic of Poetry*), "Beishan" 北山; see Cheng Junying and Jiang Jianyuan (2017, vol. 2, 685–89). The same passage is quoted in *HFZ j.* 51.1108 to support the argument that Shun is disloyal and unfilial. "If it is as the poem says, then in public life Shun treats his ruler as subject, in personal life he treats his father as subject, his mother as serving maid, and takes his master's daughters as wives [to gain the throne]."
17. See Sarah Allan (2015); Yuri Pines (2005; 2005/2006).
18. *HFZ j.* 40.888–89.
19. According to *Bamboo Annals*, Shun imprisons Yao and blocks Danzhu from seeing his father. Cited in Zhang Shoujie's comment (*SJ* vol. 1, 31). See also Fang and Wang (1998, 65); *HFZ j.* 44.925.
20. Gaoyao's summary of the play follows the model of *fumo kaichang* 副末開場 (opening aria by the older male) in the first act of *chuanqi* drama. Eyebrow comment: "This play comes close to slandering the

sages. But Mencius already began what became the progenitor of Tang tales as well as Yuan plays. What harm is there to add these kinds of jokes that serve to wrest smiles from the Four Books?"

21. That is, Gaoyao cannot catch the Blind Old Man, Shangjun fails to make the Blind Old Man turn around, Xiang cannot forgive Shun, and Shun's mother would not allow Shun to stay at the seashore.
22. This is a paraphrase of lines from "Yao's Canon:" "The sovereign [Shun] said, 'Gaoyao! Barbarians inflict disorder on the central domains. There are bandits, murderers, miscreants, and malefactors. You are to serve as Minister of Justice. Use the five punishments to bring the criminals to justice, which will be executed in three places. Five types of banishment have their appointed places, and three locations are assigned" (*SSJS* 26–27).
23. Liu An 劉安 (179–122 BCE), uncle of Emperor Wu of Han, oversaw the compilation of *Huainanzi*, a syncretist work that combines Daoist, Confucian, and Legalist teachings. Gaoyao's accomplishment despite muteness is supposed to prove that "there is something more precious than words." See *HNZ* ("Zhushu xun," 274).
24. The "Three Counsels" 三謨 refers to "Gaoyao's Counsel" (Gaoyao mo 皋陶謨), "Yi and Ji" (Yi Ji 益稷), "Great Yu's Counsel" (Da Yu mo 大禹謨). One recension of the *Documents* takes the second half of "Gaoyao's Counsel" and names it "Yi and Ji." "Great Yu's Counsel" (Da Yu mo) is one of the allegedly archaic script chapters rediscovered (or rather forged) in the fourth century CE. On the textual history of the *Documents*, see Nylan (2001, 120–67).
25. In other words, the supposedly transcribed speeches are written compositions.
26. According to "Yao's Canon," Yao tests Shun for three years and lets him rule on his behalf for twenty-eight years. If Shun is given the responsibility in the third year of his testing period, then he rules for thirty years while Yao is still alive (*SSJS* 24, 31). Yao and Shun are also called, respectively, Tangdi 唐帝 (Sovereign Tang) and Yudi 虞帝 (Sovereign Yu) in the play, but to avoid confusion we have unified their names as King Yao and King Shun.
27. In "Yao's Canon," Shun "exiled Gonggong 共工 to Youzhou, banished Huandou 驩兜 to Mount Chong, drove the Three Miao 三苗 to the Three Perils Peaks, and put Gun 鯀 to death at Mount Feather" (*SSJS* 23). The Three Miao refers to an adversarial domain. Gonggong, Huandou, and Gun are failed ministers. Gonggong is also named as the titan that breaks the pillar supporting heaven in *Huainanzi*. In *Zuozhuan*, the "four Evil Ones" 四凶 refer to Hundun 渾沌, Qiongqi 窮奇, Taowu 檮杌, and Taotie 饕餮, the wicked descendants of ruling lineages. Yao could not remove them; but Shun did. See Wen 18.7 in *Zuo* (vol. 2, 574–75). Hundun, glossed by Du Yu 杜預 (222–285) as "blocked," may be related to Hundun or Chaos, god of the center in *Zhuangzi* (*ZZJS j.* 7.309). Qiongqi appears in several early texts as the name of a demon or a beast. Hundun, Taowu, and Taotie are also identified in some early texts as beasts or monsters, the last made most famous as the so-called monster motif in ancient bronze vessels.
28. Shun is said to have banished "Three Miao Tribes" 三苗 to the Three Perilous Mountains 三危 in the far west (*SSJS* 23). Some commentators believe that the Three Miao were natives of the area encompassing modern day western Jiangxi and eastern Hunan (i.e., south-central China).
29. According to *Shangshu dazhuan* 尚書大傳, an early Han commentary of the *Documents* (which survives only in fragments), the hundred artisans sing the song about "glorious clouds," and Shun also joins in. The first line of Shun's song is "The glorious clouds are splendid" 卿雲爛兮 (Lu Qinli 1983, 3). At the end of "Gaoyao's Counsel," Shun and Gaoyao sing about the wonderful amity between ruler and minister and their great accomplishments, and Gaoyao bows with his forehead touching his clasped hands (*SSJS* 45–46).
30. Shun is said to have made inspection tours in the four directions, see *SSJS* 19–20.

31. On the appointments and duties of these ministers in the court of Shun, see "Yao's Canon" (*SSJS* 25–30). Boyi 伯益 or Yi 益 is identified in some sources as Gaoyao's son. Boyu 伯禹 or Yu 禹 is the controller of floods who succeeds King Shun. According to Mencius, after Shun secures the livelihood of the people through Yu and Ji 稷 (Lord Millet, ancestor of Zhou), Xie 契 (ancestor of Shang) is made the minister of instruction "teaching the people normative relationships: between father and son there is affection; between ruler and subject, dutifulness; between husband and wife, distinction; between young and old, order; between friends, good faith" (*Mencius* 3A.4).
32. The character *shi* 施 here is probably a mistake for *si* 死. We will find out that the Blind Old Man had killed Kui's son.
33. The word *bin* 濱 (water's edge) in the text should have been *pin* 嬪 (to marry). See *SSJS* 15–20. River Gui is in Shanxi.
34. The wording echoes "Yao's Canon" (*SSJS* 18–19).
35. All these offices are mentioned in "Yao's Canon." The "nine ministers" refer to Boyi (Yi), Boyu (Yu), Qi 棄, Xie, Gaoyao, Chui 垂, Boyi 伯夷, Kui 夔, and Long 龍 mentioned above.
36. This saying is attributed to Confucius in *Mencius* 5A.4. Mencius cites it to prove the opposite point, namely, Yao could not have paid obeisance to Shun because Shun is only ruling on Yao's behalf.
37. See introduction to the play; cf. note 16 above.
38. Yao's invention of the chess game and Danzhu's skill with it are told in Ouyang Xun (1999, 1270), citing Zhang Hua's 張華 *Bowu zhi* 博物志, although the extant *Bowu zhi* does not include such an entry. The chess game fails to bring about the anticipated moral transformation. In "Yao's Canon," King Yao rejects the idea that Danzhu should succeed him because he is "perfidious and clamorous" (*SSJS* 13–14).
39. Commentators identify "King Shun's guest," mentioned in "Gaoyao's Counsel," as Danzhu (*SSJS* 44–45).
40. Shun is said to play a zither with five strings and compose the song "South Wind" 南風 (*LJZS j.* 38.677; *SJ j.* 14.1197–98), which links the gentle warmth of the wind to good governance and prosperity for the people (Wang Su 1991, 80).
41. This alludes to legends that the transition of power between Yao and Shun involves violence and coercion, see note 19.
42. This is quoted as a line from the *Documents* in *Mencius* 5A.4 and incorporated into the "Great Yu's Counsel" (Da Yu mo).
43. "Yao's Canon:" "They attain harmony because his [Shun's] filial piety rises to great heights" (*SSJS* 15), see also *SJ j.* 1.21.
44. When Liu Bang 劉邦 (d. 195 BCE) paid obeisance to his father after he became emperor, his father stopped him, arguing that for a ruler to bow to his subject would diminish his authority. His father thus showed his respect by embracing a broom (to clean the path) and welcoming him at the gate (*SJ j.* 8.382). Political hierarchy can thus override paternal authority.
45. The line appears in *HNZ j.* 20.672; *SJ j.* 1.33.
46. According to *Shiji* (and *Da Dai liji* 大戴禮記), both Yao and Shun are descendants of Huangdi 黄帝 (Yellow Emperor), but the genealogical chronology does not make sense. Three generations separate Huangdi and Yao, but seven generations separate Huangdi and Shun. As Ouyang Xiu 歐陽修 pointed out, this would make Yao's daughters the great grand aunts of Shun. See Ouyang Xiu (1986, vol. 1, 301, "Diwang shici tu hou xu" 帝王世次圖後序).
47. See note 19.
48. In *Mencius* and the *Documents*, Shun rules on behalf of Yao, whose virtue is not supposed to have suffered decline. Eyebrow comment: "[The author] uses Yao and Shun to speak of later eras. There are

wails and tears in the jocular talk." In other words, demystifying Yao and Shun exposes the cynicism and cruelty of the political reality in later periods.

49. After Shun ascends the throne, he sends his brother Xiang, who plotted his murder, to Youbi 有庳, either as enfeoffment or as banishment (*Mencius* 5A.3); see introduction to the play. Since Xiang's name means "elephant," and "bi" in "Youbi" is homophonous with "trunk," Wen Yiduo (1985, 75–77) believes that Xiang represents a tribe associated with the totem of elephant.
50. Reading *gai* 蓋 as *hai* 害, following Ruan Yuan 阮元, see Yang Bojun (1960, 211n.7).
51. On Shun's sister Keshou 顆手, see *HS j.* 20.878–79; Zhang Shoujie's commentary in *SJ j.* 1.34. Shun's mother in *Mencius* becomes his stepmother in *SJ*.
52. In *Mencius* 5A.3, Wanzhang asks Mencius why the evil Xiang should be allowed to govern Youbi. Mencius explains that Shun sends his officials to govern Youbi and Xiang cannot do what he wants. It is in that sense that Xiang is in Youbi as exile rather than feudal lord. Shun also wants to see Xiang often, presumably to obviate his misconduct at Youbi.
53. *SJ j.* 1.34: "In one year the place where he lived became a village; in two years, a settlement; in three years, a city." The term *dujun*, understood here as "city chief," can mean "for the chief" (reading *du* 都 as *yu* 於) in *Mencius*. "Dujun" 都君 is also said to be Shun's cognomen (*SJ j.* 1.31).
54. Shun's stepmother plays a much bigger role in slandering and persecuting Shun in some later iterations of Shun lore. See, e.g., "Shunzi bian" (Anon. 1997).
55. Shun is said to have double pupils (*SJ j.* 7.338).
56. See *Mencius* 5A.2.
57. According to *Shiji* (*j.* 1.34), Shun uses two bamboo hats to break his fall as he jumps down.
58. In *Hanfeizi*, *Guanzi*, and *Shiji*, Shun is said to be a farmer at Mount Li, situated to the northeast of Lü Tiancheng's native Yuyao. In *Mengzi* 5A.1, Mencius argues that Shun weeps and wails to mourn his parents' intransigent hostility, not to express resentment. This token of Shun's filial piety here causes a greater rift with his parents.
59. See Zhang Shoujie's comment, citing *Tongshi* 通史 (no longer extant), *SJ* 1.34–35, n. 9. Eyebrow comment: "This shows extreme dexterity in using allusions."
60. See *LZJS j.* 4.143. In that anecdote, the children's ditty is comprised of lines from two odes in *Shijing* (Cheng Junying and Jiang Jianyuan [2017, 836, 1027]).
61. This refers to a song allegedly from the era of sage kings: "I work when the sun rises, / and rest when the sun sets, / dig a well for drinking / and plow fields for food. / What is the sovereign's power to me?" Lu Qinli (1983, 1). While the song is supposed to glorify the recluse's indifference to political power, here the verbal play reframes the question: why would a future sovereign use his power to dig a well?
62. The term for "great floods" (*jiangshui* 洚水) is from *Mencius* 3B.9.
63. See Zhang Shoujie's comment (*SJ j.* 1.34).
64. *Mencius* 7B.6: "Mencius said, 'The way Shun ate dry grains and herbs—it was as if he would do it his whole life. But when he became the Son of Heaven, draped in embroidered clothes, playing the zither, and being served by two wives, it was as if it had always been so." The translation here follows Zhao Qi's interpretation that Shun does not lapse into indulgence even when his circumstances change (Jiao Xun 2015, vol. 2, 966). The playwright inserts that passage here and changes "serve" (*guo* 果 or *wo* 婐) into "naked" (*luo* 裸) to imply that Shun is in the middle of sexual intimacy with his wives.
65. On the question of whether Shun sees through Xiang, see introduction to the play.
66. These lines paraphrase *SJ j.* 1.34. In *Mencius*, Shun is sitting on the couch and playing the zither when Xiang comes into his room. In *Shiji*, Xiang is in Shun's room and playing his zither when Shun comes in.

67. Eyebrow comment: "Even histories like the one by Sima Qian are full of fabrications, let alone those by later authors. Mencius's line, 'giving full credence to the *Documents* is worse than not having the *Documents*,' is just right for mutual illumination with the passages involving Xianqiu Meng and Taoying (see introduction to the play). This is beyond the pedantic scholar's exegetical labor: one cannot speak of dreams in front of the deluded ones."
68. Alternatively, the subject of the last line can be Shangjun (speaking for himself and Danzhu): "How could we not want it for ourselves?"
69. According to *The Classic of Mountains and Seas*, Shun's third wife, neé Dengbi 登比, gives birth to Xiaoming 宵明 (bright at night) and Zhuguang 燭光 (candlelight) (Yuan Ke 1980, 320).
70. The logic here seems to be that the man who marries Xiaoming and Zhuguang may succeed Shun, just as Shun comes to the throne after marrying Yao's two daughters. However, since Yu, who will succeed Shun, is already married and has sired a son who will succeed him, it does not matter whom Xiaoming and Zhuguang marry.
71. Wanzhang asks Mencius about the saying, "When it came to Yu, his virtue declined. He did not pass on the throne to the worthy but to his son." Mencius refutes it in defense of hereditary succession: "When Heaven gives it to the worthy, then it is given to the worthy. When Heaven gives it to the son, then it is given to the son" (*Mencius* 5A.6). The recently excavated text *Tang Yu zhi dao* 唐虞之道 advocates abdication in language even stronger than what Wanzhang is quoting: "To be able to bring about the people's moral transformation without abdicating in favor of the worthy—that has never happened in human history."
72. See Zhao 7.7, in *Zuo* (vol. 3, 1422–23). Gun 鯀 is punished for failing in his mission to control the flood.
73. The playwright implies that the execution of Yu's father is somehow the price he pays for being allowed to pass on the throne to his son.
74. On Shun arranging his marriage without telling his parents, see *Mencius* 4A.26, 5A.2.
75. In a Han dynasty anecdote in *Shuoyuan* 說苑 (*Garden of Stories*), Yu (Boyu or Lord Yu), Shun's successor, comes down his carriage and weeps when he sees criminals brought to justice because he considers their crimes the result of his failed governance (Liu Xiang 1995, *j.* 1.9–10). According to this logic, crimes are not possible under sagely rule and punishment should be irrelevant.
76. For the rebellion of the three Miao tribes, see note 27. The Blind Old Man is crediting himself with military prowess even as he confesses to his crime.
77. In "Gaoyao's Counsel," "Xiaoshao" 簫韶 is Shun's music that brings auspicious phoenixes to court (*SSJS* 44–45).
78. "Gaoyao's Counsel:" "Do not let the various officials neglect their duties. The works (or accomplishments) of Heaven have to be taken up by men."
79. This is a line from the *Analects* 20.1.
80. Phoenixes dance to the music of Shun (*SJ j.* 2.81).
81. A later recension of "Yao's Canon" divides it into "Yao's Canon" and "Shun's Canon," and some lines (including this) are added to the beginning of "Shun's Canon" (*SSZS j.* 3.34).
82. This is a line from "Yao's Canon" (*SSJS I,* 9).
83. This is a line from "Great Yu's Counsel" (*SSZS j.* 4.55). The power of the king's virtue moves the people as the wind moves all things.
84. In *Analects* 20.1, Yao addresses Shun: "The heaven-ordained order of succession now rests in your person."
85. The merit of Yao and Shun is described as "lofty (like a high mountain)" (*weiwei* 巍巍) in the *Analects* (8.18, 8.19).

86. See note 39 above.
87. Chaofu 巢父 (Father Nest) and Xu You 許由 are recluses who refused when Yao tried to offer them the throne. Fuxi 伏羲 and Shennong 神農 ruled in age of great simplicity (when ritual and punishment did not yet apply).
88. *Analects* 2.1: "He who governs by virtue is like the Pole Star: it stays in its place but the multitude of stars pay homage to it." "The perfect reign" is literally "the era of effortless governance" (*wuwei shi* 無為世), alluding to the idea that Yao and Shun "just let their robes hang on them (i.e., do nothing) and all under heaven is well governed" ("Xici xia" 繫辭下, *ZYZS j.* 8.167).
89. In the *Analects* 20.1, Yao says to Shun: "If the world within the four seas should suffer hardships and impoverishment, the Heaven-bestowed tenure will be terminated forever."
90. See *Mencius* 5A.4. On whether the Blind Old Man should bow like a subject to Shun, see introduction to this play.
91. "Gaoyao's Counsel:" "The head (i.e., the ruler) radiates brightness; the arms and legs (i.e., the officials) are excellent" (*SSJS* 45).
92. These are archaic words of affirmation or negation (*du* 都, *yu* 俞, *xu* 吁, *fu* 咈) used by the ministers of Yao, Shun, and Yu in the *Documents*.
93. These contain lines from "Shun's Canon" (*SSZS j.* 3.34).
94. "Shun's Canon:" "His doubled brightness matches the sovereign's" (*SSZS j.* 3.34). Note that the Blind Old Man is speaking in a high diction incongruous with his supposed ignorance. One of Shun's names is Chonghua 重華 (Doubled Brightness).
95. The Blind Old Man is kneeling while paying obeisance.
96. A subject faces north and a ruler faces south.
97. This is of course the opposite of what transpired between Shun and his family. Shun may be implicitly urging his father to stay home to avoid the dangers and controversies of public life.
98. Xiang claims that there are affectionate ties between Shun's younger brother (Xiang) and Shun's son (Shangjun), and between them and Shun. Recall that Shun summons Xiang often to minimize the chance of misrule at Youbi (see note 52 above). Puban is identified as Shun's capital in some traditions.
99. This may refer to Shun's equanimity when Xiang persecutes him with various murderous schemes. The "arched bow" 彎弓 may also be associated with brotherhood in a story that Mencius tells in a passage that concludes with Shun: a brother drawing a bow planning to shoot someone will arouse much more desperate pleas than a mere stranger setting out to do the same thing (*Mencius* 6B.3).
100. On whether Shun can empathize with Xiang and shares his joys and sorrows, see *Mencius* 5A.2 and introduction to this play.
101. Shun may be referring to either Xiang or Shangjun, or to both.
102. There is a deliberately incongruous comparison between furtively fleeing with an old man and some vaguely romantic exploits involving palace ladies (compared to palace flowers), who also keep secrets.
103. According to *HNZ j.* 12.387, the *qiongqiong* 蛩蛩 would always carry the *jue* 蟨(another mythical animal) on its back and run away when the latter is in danger because the *jue* feeds it with sweet grass. See also Chen Qiyou (1995, vol. 1, 917).
104. Guibi 癸比 is a mistake for Dengbi (see note 69)—Ehuang 娥皇 seems to be suggesting that Guibi's daughter may be used as a ploy to buy time for Shun's return.
105. When Shun dies, Yu flees to the Sunlit City 陽城 to make way for Shun's son to become ruler, but the people insist on Yu's succession (*Mencius* 5A.6). Legend has it that Chaofu and Xu You (see note 87) lived at Mount Sieve 箕山 as recluses. When Yi on the death of Yu refuses the throne and insists that Yu's son Qi succeeds him, he also flees to Mount Sieve (*Mencius* 5A.6). The Sunlit City and Mount

Sieve are thus associated with the political disinterestedness of the virtuous, but here it is where a worthless son can flee with his criminal father.

106. This is a set expression in fiction and drama.
107. The Blind Old Man's violent act may thus be motivated in part by his certainty of impunity.
108. Shun is saying that filial duty takes precedence over his concern over his wives. He cannot afford to worry about his wives' pining for him.
109. Nüying 女英 is referring to Xiaoming and Zhuguang, Shun's daughter by his consort Dengbi. Their marriage cannot be arranged without Shun.
110. Confucius describes the situation of King Yao and the Blind Old Man becoming Shun's subjects as "perilous" (*jiji* 岌岌) (*Mencius* 5A.4).
111. Shun uses the casual and somewhat disrespectful term *laotou'er* ("old man" or "old fellow") to refer to his father.
112. *Shijian* 勢劍 ("sword of justice") is the sword empowering a minister to execute a criminal without first reporting to the emperor. Judge Bao uses "bronze choppers" to cut down criminals in stories and plays about him.
113. "Hiding the Light" (Mingyi 明夷) is hexagram no. 36 in the *Classic of Changes*. The judgment of the hexagram is that "it is fitting to firmly maintain constancy when facing adversity."
114. Literally, "safely, as no one has overturned the winnowing basket" and no chaff (i.e., rumors and judgments) would fly.
115. "The father" refers to Shun, "the son" to Shangjun.
116. Yidi 儀狄, an official in Yu's court, invents wine (Kong Yingda's comment, *SSZS j.* 14.207). Chen is Chen Yu 陳虞 in the text, so called because Chen is descended from Shun or King Yu. Here the Chen lady anachronistically refers to the Chen ruler Lord Ling's 陳靈公 consort Xia Ji 夏姬, a symbol of sexual license (*Zuo*, vol. 3, 1686–87). The Six Departments of Yu refers to resources of water, fire, metal, wood, earth, and grain ("Great Yu's Counsel," *SSZS j.* 4.53). In a mythical battle with Zhuanxu 顓頊, Gonggong 共工 butted against the mountain that served as the pillar holding up heaven, causing cosmic chaos (*HNZ j.* 3.80). Eyebrow comment: "All the jokes are canonical and accurate, while being comical and absurd."
117. Danzhu is the brother of Ehuang and Nüying and the husband of Keshou, Shun's sister.
118. The hundred beasts dance when Kui, the Director of Music, strikes the musical chime stone ("Yao's Canon," *SSJS* 28–29).
119. Danzhu and Shangjun thus turn the image of morally transformed nature (i.e., animals dancing to ritual music) into an inauspicious omen.
120. See note 105.
121. Lord Wen of Jin 晉文公 forgets to reward his loyal follower Jie Zhitui 介之推 (or Jie Zitui 介子推 in *Shiji*), who goes to the mountains and becomes a recluse (*Zuo*, vol. 1, 378–79). When Lord Wen remembers his merits and tries to convince him to come out by setting the mountain on fire, Jie Zhitui chooses to perish in the flames (*SJ*, *j.* 39.1662).
122. The Cowherd and Weaving Maid asterisms govern the area of the ancient states Wu and Yue, according to the theory of asterial-terrestrial correspondence. In other words, anachronistic cultural geography allows the audience to imagine Shun fleeing to the pleasures and prosperity of the Lower Yangzi area instead of the wilderness.
123. Yangzhou here refers not to the eponymous city but designates one of the nine regions of the realm (*jiuzhou* 九州) as described in ancient texts, notably "Tributes of Yu" (Yugong 禹貢) in the *Documents* and *Records of Ritual* (*Liji*). It is variously associated with the southeast, the area south of the Yangzi River, and the area between the Huai River and the sea.

124. See note 45 above.
125. Xiang is referring to the occasion when he goes to Shun's room after plotting his murder, fully expecting to take over his wives and property, only to find Shun alive and well. See introduction to this play.
126. Eyebrow comment: "Famous words of insight."
127. Xiang is referring to stories in *Zhuangzi*, where Yao tries to yield rulership to Xu You, and Shun tries to do the same with Zizhou Zhibo 子州支伯, Shanjuan 善卷, and the farmer of Stone Gate 石戶之農, only to have their offers rebuffed (*ZZJS j.* 1.22, *j.* 28.965–66).
128. According to *Mencius* 5A.1, Yao sends his nine sons and two daughters to serve Shun. It also says that Yao abdicates in Shun's favor because his son Danzhu is not worthy, but there is no explanation why any of the other eight sons cannot succeed Yao. Other texts mention only Danzhu as Yao's son. The playwright may be alluding to the inconsistencies in ancient texts or revisiting the hypothesis that other sons could have succeeded Yao even if Danzhu is unworthy.
129. This refers to the two sides of the stage where the actors can enter or leave.
130. Eyebrow comment: "A most accurate picture of old age."
131. The hound of the tyrant Jie 桀 (the last ruler of Xia) would bark at the sage king Yao because loyalty to its master trumps other value judgments (*SJ*, *j.* 83.2475).
132. In *Zhuangzi*, King Yao wants to attack Zong 宗, Kuai 膾, and Xu'ao 胥敖. Such a militaristic bent is cited as evidence of the sage kings' lapse from perfect virtue (*ZZJS j.* 2.89, *j.* 4.139). If Shun is only Yao's agent (as *Mencius* argues), there is no reason why Yao cannot resume the duties of the sovereign again.
133. In Huangfu Mi's 皇甫謐 "Biographies of Recluses" ("Gaoshi zhuan" 高士傳), Yao summons the recluse Xu You to be a governor, and Xu You, unwilling to listen to him, washes his ears at the banks of River Ying. Another recluse, Chaofu (Father Nest) happens to walk by and, upon being told why Xu You is washing his ears, castigates Xu You for angling for fame and polluting the water. He deems the water no longer pure enough for his calf and goes upstream (cited in Zhang Shoujie's commentary, *SJ j.* 61.2121).
134. Zizhou Zhibo declines Shun's offer because he "happened to be ill with a secret sorrow," and Shanjuan refuses it because he was "freely roaming between heaven and earth, his mind and spirit having found freedom" (*ZZJS j.* 28.966).
135. Shun's friend Wuze 無擇 is so offended by his offer to yield the throne to him that he throws himself into the Deeps of Cold Purity (*ZZJS j.* 28.984).
136. Wang Ni 王倪 and Nie Que 齧缺 appear as Daoist sages in several chapters in *Zhuangzi*, but in the chapter "Heaven and Earth," Xu You is Yao's teacher, Nie Que is Xu You's teacher, and Piyi 被衣 is Wang Ni's teacher (*ZZJS j.* 12.415–16).
137. Alternatively, "Enjoying as much as we can of a forest of shadows cast by the slanting sun."
138. The line echoes the sentiment Su Shi articulates in the first "Rhapsody on the Red Cliff" 赤壁賦.
139. This line combines imagery from lines by Wang Ji 王籍 (6th century) ("The crickets' chirping makes for a deeper quiet in the woods" 蟬噪林逾靜) (Lu Qinli 1983, 1854) and Du Fu (712–70) ("The woodcutting goes 'ding-ding' as the seclusion in the mountain deepens" 伐木丁丁山更幽) (*QTS j.* 224.2391).
140. This phrase (*tianfang* 天放, "set free by heaven") in *Zhuangzi* describes someone living a simple life and being at one with the Way (*ZZJS j.* 9.334).
141. The crickets' chirping breaks the silence and makes one anticipate footsteps.
142. This alludes to *Mencius* 7A.35. See introduction to this play.
143. In *Zhuangzi*, Shun wants to yield the realm to his friend, the farmer of Stone Gate. The latter calls Shun "a ruler of vitality" and "a gentleman of exuberant strength." Realizing that Shun's virtue does not amount to much, the farmer leaves for the sea with his wife and child (*ZZJS j.* 28.966).

144. In the Dunhuang story about Shun ("Shun zi bian" 舜子變), Shun licks his father's eyes and restores his sight.
145. In "Yao's Canon," Shun addresses twenty-two ministers, some of whom are mentioned at the beginning of the play, see note 30.
146. Mirages on the sea are supposed to be produced by the vapor from the breath of a sea dragon or a giant clam. Red City is a mountain between Mount Siming and Mount Tiantai in present day Zhejiang, thus named because its reddish slopes rise like city walls. It appears often in poetry set in the Yue area.
147. This refers to Yu the flood-controller, to whom Shun eventually yields the throne.
148. Literally, the era of great peace achieved by the ruler who does no more than holding his hands together in a gesture of respect and letting his robes drape over his body.
149. The term *yingning* 攖寧 (literally, "disturbance and tranquility") describes the attitude of total openness and acceptance in *Zhuangzi* (*ZZJS j.* 6.253). It has been glossed as "the tranquility that comes after disturbance."
150. Literally, "cakes drawn." Emperor Ming of Wei observes: "fame is like drawing cakes on the ground. They cannot be eaten" (*SGZ j.* 22.651). "Drawing cakes to satisfy hunger" (*huabing chongji* 畫餅充飢) has become a common idiom. Here "nothing" can mean "empty fame" or "wishful thinking."
151. Confucius says of his disciple Zhonggong 仲弓: "If the offspring of a plowing ox is sorrel-hued and has well-formed horns, even if one does not want to use it, would the spirits of the mountains and rivers abandon it?" (*Analects* 6.6). The bull with a sorrel hue and well-formed horns is fit for sacrifice. Zhonggong's father is wicked and lowly, but Zhonggong is virtuous and talented. Confucius is comparing Zhonggong to the ox that would surely be "used" even if its father is a common plowing ox.
152. *Mencius* 5A.6: Mencius is trying to explain why abdication takes place with Yao and Shun.
153. "Zither strings" can refer to the vagina (*Xuan[Su]nü jing*, cited in Tanbo 1996, 28.1140) or veins on the penis (*Jin Ping Mei cihua* 2007, chap. 74, 1228). David Roy (1993–2013) translated it as "frenum" in *Plum in the Golden Vase*, 5:421). Considering Lü Tiancheng's interest in pornography (see introduction to this play), one cannot rule out such associations.
154. Legend has it that the mottled bamboo came into being because the tears of Ehuang and Nüying stained the bamboo of Xiao and Xiang Rivers when they lamented Shun's death.
155. This implies that improper sexual relations between sons and stepmothers develop in some cases.
156. Here she is Shun's stepmother, following *Shiji* and other sources.
157. She is referring to the marriage of Shun's sister Keshou and Yao's son Danzhu.
158. That is, Shun's stepmother is sexually voracious.
159. "Being unlike the father" is usually meant as a negative epithet implying worthlessness. Of course, in the context here, being unlike the Blind Old Man is no cause for shame.
160. See note 54.
161. The implication is that Shun had no time to worry about his marriage when his younger brother and sister were struggling.
162. The tidal bore of the Qiantang River (Hangzhou and its environs) in midautumn (the middle of the eighth month) makes for a grand spectacle.
163. Note the contrast between the Perfidious Mother's professed affection for Shun and her abuse of her husband.
164. Of course, her professed humility is but a way to assert her claims over Shun.
165. The logic here seems to be that irrespective of Gaoyao's decision about Shun's father, Shun's act of fleeing with his father can be justified.

166. Alternatively, "bygones" can refer to Shun's escape: "My roaming in leisure, a thing of the past, is now finished for good!" If Shun is resolved to go back at this point, however, it will be harder to explain his stepmother's histrionic utterances that follow.
167. When Xu You refuses Yao's offer of kingship, he compares his modest needs with the tiny wren which needs only one branch for its nest in a big forest (*ZZJS j.* 1.24).
168. That is, Shun can take the punishment in his father's place.
169. Shun's refusal would mean that he is filial only toward his father.
170. The leopard hiding in mist and rain so that its fur can gain gloss and beauty is upheld as a model for those who manage to hide their traces and escape harm (*Lienü zhuan j.* 2.40, "Tao Dazi's wife").
171. "Xiaoshao" is the music of Shun's court, cf. note 77.
172. The riddle gourd, which probably involves a guessing game, is a toy mentioned in the Yuan play *The Moheluo Doll* (Hsia, Li, and Kao 2014, 154). The term also refers to a mystery or an insoluble puzzle.
173. Literally, the bells at the bits of horses.
174. Gaoyao is using the Blind Old Man's blindness as the excuse for leniency.
175. *Gufu* 鼓腹 (translated here as "contentment") can mean both a jutting belly satiated with food (*ZZJS j.* 9.341) or patting the belly to the beats of songs.
176. According to the *Classic of Mountains and Seas*, Jingwei 精衛 is the young daughter of Yandi 炎帝 (Sovereign of Fire). Drowned in the Eastern Sea, she turns into the *jingwei* bird trying to fill the sea with bits of wood and pebbles from the Western Mountain she carries by mouth (Yuan Ke 1980, 92, 415).
177. The original has "Wangdi (Sovereign Wang)" instead of "cuckoo"—legend has it that Duyu or Wangdi of Shu is transformed into the cuckoo bird after his death and his mournful cries lament his lost kingdom. The line here is derived from Li Shangyin's 李商隱 line: "Wangdi's spring longing has been entrusted to the cuckoo" 望帝春心托杜鵑. (*QTS j.* 539.6144).

6

Pinning Flowers in His Coiffure

SHEN ZIZHENG (1591–1641)
TRANSLATED BY WAI-YEE LI

Shen Zizheng 沈自徵 (style name Junyong 君庸) hailed from a distinguished scholar-official family in Jiangsu. His uncle Shen Jing 沈璟 (1553–1610), a famous playwright, was the acknowledged leader of the so-called Wujiang School (Wujiang pai 吳江派), known for its emphasis on musical precision.[1] His immediate and extended family boasted of many poets and dramatists, including talented women like his older sister Shen Yixiu 沈宜修 (1590–1635), his two nieces Ye Xiaowan 葉小紈 (1613–1657) and Ye Xiaoluan 葉小鸞 (1616–1632), and his two wives Zhang Qianqian 張倩倩 (1594–1627) and Li Yuzhao 李玉照 (1615–1679).[2] Shen Zizheng was a government academy student (*guozi jian sheng* 國子監生) and never held office. Like many late Ming literati, he cherished his self-image as a heroic knight-errant (*xia* 俠), but in his case the idea goes beyond extravagance, generosity, and grand gestures and is borne out by his commitment to seeking solutions to contemporary military problems. According to the 1747 *Wujiang Gazetteer* (*Wujiang xianzhi* 吳江縣志, j. 32, 12a–12b), he was interested in military strategy, traveled to the northern and western frontiers of the Ming Empire in the late 1620s to study its geography, and came back to offer military advice to officials at the capital. Among those seeking his advice was the general Yuan Chonghuan 袁崇煥 (1584–1630).[3] Shen was recommended for an official position in 1640 but declined it.

Pinning Flowers in His Coiffure is one of Shen's three extant short plays known collectively as *The Three Drum Rolls of Yuyang* (*Yuyang sannong* 漁陽三弄), a conscious allusion to Xu Wei's play *The Mad Drummer: Yuyang Thrice Played*.[4] His plays all adhere to the Yuan *zaju* rule of having only one singer and share the theme of the scholar's frustrations when confronted with persecution or the denial of recognition.[5] *Pinning Flowers* is based on an anecdote first told in Wang Shizhen's 王世貞 (1526–1590) *Balanced Words on the Garden of Letters* (*Yiyuan zhiyan* 藝苑卮言):

> When Yang Shen was in exile in Yunnan, he had a definite taste for the company of courtesans.[6] The local chieftains wanted to obtain his poetry and calligraphy but failed. They thus made clothes from fine white silk and sent courtesans wearing them to beg for Yang's work while he was drinking. Yang happily complied and took up the brush, drunkenly splashing ink over their lapels and sleeves. The chieftains rewarded the courtesans handsomely and mounted the works they brought. Yang once got drunk, painted his face with white powder, made a double-bun chignon and stuck flowers in it. His disciples lifted him [in a sedan chair] and the various courtesans held up wine cups as they wandered through the town without a trace of shame.[7]

Yang Shen 楊慎 (1488–1559), the son of Grand Secretary Yang Tinghe 楊廷和 (1459–1529), was from Sichuan.[8] A brilliant scholar and poet, he was the top candidate in the palace examination of 1511 and became a Hanlin academician. His official career came to an abrupt end in 1524, when the so-called Grand Ritual Controversy—the dispute between the Jiajing emperor (r. 1521–1567) and his officials over the elevation of his deceased father to imperial status—led to Yang Tinghe's demotion and Yang Shen's exile after being severely beaten.[9] Yang Shen was condemned to permanent military service as a common soldier at Yongchang, a guard post at the Western border of Yunnan, where he gained a local following and was treated with courtesy by some of the Yunnan governors. Aside from short trips home to Sichuan, Yang Shen spent the rest of his life in Yunnan, devoting himself to scholarship and writing extensively on many subjects, including the history and customs of Yunnan. His second wife, Huang E 黃峨 (1498–1569), was a notable poet.[10] They married in 1519 but lived apart during most of his exile. One of Huang E's most famous poems makes its way into *Pinning Flowers*.

Shen Zizheng comments on the anecdote cited above and Wang Shizhen's comment on it in the preface to the "Poem Inscribed on the Portrait of My Fifth Elder Brother After He Has Shaved His Head Following Buddhist Laws" (Ti wuxiong zhufa xiang 題五兄祝髮像詩序):

> One of the guests at Wang Shizhen's gathering commented on this: "This is his honor [Yang Shen] deliberately besmirching himself." Wang said, "It is not so. For a poor scholar wearing the red clothes of a convict, what is off limits? This is only because his heroic heart cannot bear the pointlessness of it all, and thus he has to grind himself down." Alas! Whenever I get to this in my reading, I beat my breast in extreme anguish. One would have to stop only after draining a big goblet of wine, spitting up a quantity of blood and then collapsing.[11]

Shen Zizheng obviously identified with Yang Shen: he too suffered many disappointments despite heroic aspirations. Qi Biaojia praised the play enthusiastically for its combination of comic and tragic elements: "People say that forceful expression shows through the desolation. They do not know that it is about showing tears through songs and laughter. The arias and dialogue go haphazardly this way and that, but every drop of ink is a hero's teardrop."[12]

The misunderstood genius behaving wildly is a recurrent theme in Chinese history and literature, and the late Ming is particularly rich with such examples. For a male poet to adopt a female persona or to project his perspectives through the prism of a woman's experience is also one of the oldest tropes in the Chinese tradition. Here Yang Shen refers to several common allusions along those lines in the arias—a beauty maligned by jealous women as the parallel to a loyal courtier attacked by his rivals, a bride anxious to please her in-laws as the metaphor for negotiating the dangers of public life, a palace lady sent to marry a barbarian ruler because of an appeasement policy as the icon of unjust exile. The tradition that allegorizes a woman's experience or voice is often linked to a poetics of indirectness, which may result from political discretion or point to complex and contradictory emotions. By putting on a courtesan's clothes, ornaments, and cosmetics, Yang Shen turns that poetic tradition on its head, transforming supposedly subtle and indirect expression into histrionic gestures. Writing on a courtesan's clothes turns out to be performative self-invention. Pinning flowers in his double-bun chignon comes to be a mockery of the custom of putting flowers in the headgear of top examination candidates.[13] Cross-dressing becomes a way to accuse the topsy-turvy world of inverting values. Apparent self-abasement emerges as the only means of preserving agency and self-respect when the world no longer makes sense.

The translation is based on the edition of *Pinning Flowers in His Coiffure* included in Shen Tai's *Short Plays of the Great Ming*, fascicle 14.

Dramatis Personae in Order of Appearance

Role type	*Name and family or social role*
FEMALE LEAD, ZHENGDAN	Cuiliu
ADDED FEMALE, TIEDAN	Jiaotao
MALE LEAD, MO	Yang Shen, Yang Sheng'an
CLOWNS, CHOU	Male and female villagers
COMIC, JING	Teashop waiter
SECOND COMIC, FUJING	Pawnshop hand
MISCELLANEOUS, ZA	Messenger
COMIC, JING	Curio Dealer
MISCELLANEOUS, ZA	Muslim merchant

PINNING FLOWERS IN HIS COIFFURE

Written by Shen Zizheng (sobriquet Junyong) of Songling (Suzhou)
Commentaries by Zhang Peiyu (sobriquet Junshan) of West Lake

Read by Chen Yunduan (sobriquet Yusan) and Zhu Jiong (sobriquet Menghan), both of Wulin (Hangzhou)

True Name:

Yunnan Courtesans, of Varying Merits,[14] Compete with Their White Silk Skirts
Yang Sheng'an, Drunk with Poetry and Wine, Pins Flowers in His Coiffure

(FEMALE LEAD *as* CUILIU *and* ADDED FEMALE *as* JIAOTAO, *dressed in white, enter and recite*:)

South of the bronze pillars is the white grass of spring,
How many more days before the traveler reaches Jinlin?
Jade rings pierce her ears: from what family is this girl
Embracing the *pipa* by herself to welcome the Sea God?[15]

I am Cuiliu, and this sister is called Jiaotao.[16] The two of us are top-class courtesans in Yunnan. Not long ago the court sent down a Hanlin scholar, Academician Yang Sheng'an, to join the military ranks in our Yunnan. Now he is a great talent of our times, but he loves to drink, and when he is drunk, he will chant poems and compose rhapsodies. Not caring a whit how or why, he will write these on the bodies of us courtesans. Our people here down south have heard that he is a great talent, so whatever he writes will be bought right away. That is why we Yunnan courtesans all wear white clothes. Today we heard that the Academician is having a spring outing and that we are to serve at his pleasure. Ah! The Academician has already arrived.

(MALE LEAD *as* YANG SHEN, *with a grimy face, matted hair, and a drunken mien, enters*:) This humble official is Yang Sheng'an: my given name is Shen, my sobriquet is Yongxiu, my style name is Sheng'an, and I am a native of Chengdu in Sichuan. My father Yang Tinghe, having served two emperors, was prime minister under the current reign. I have persevered in my studies and mastered great learning, and the Sage Emperor, deigning to recognize me, conferred on me the title of Top-of-the List in the palace examination, and appointed me as a Hanlin Academician. But now, because of the controversy about the Great Ritual, I remonstrated with bitter tears at court, and the Sage Emperor exiled me to Jinchi to serve in the military ranks. Everyone criticized me for my missteps. Some even suspected that I bought the title of Top-of-the-List. Having come down south, I spend my days turning poetry and wine into my proper calling. Springtime is upon us—how serene it is! (*Sings*:)

(ZHENGGONG MODE: *Duanzheng hao*)

Let's ask the spring wind:
have you also come to
the world's edge?[17]
I wake up from the wine to the oriole's cries in the banyan tree.[18]
Turning to
The wine shop, I call to rouse the mountain lad:
Can you look and see

If the bloom has come to the late rose yet?[19]

(CUILIU:) Academician, day after day you drink yourself into a stupor at home. Haven't you heard what people say these days? "Affairs require more understanding; wine requires less drinking." You really should cut down on drinking. (YANG *sings*:)

(*Gun xiuqiu*)

You would have me

Understand more of worldly affairs,

And for this

Stuff in the cup show less care.

But Cuiliu, I say that the whole world is drunk and only I, Yang Sheng'an, am sober.[20]

(CUILIU:) You are not drunk, yet you sport a drunken frenzy!

(YANG *sings*:)

The whole world sports a

Sober frenzy: they walk asleep and stand inebriated.

Cuiliu, I say, in the entire realm under heaven only Yang Sheng'an drinks wine, there is no one else drinking.

(CUILIU:) No one else? So, all those people holding wine cups are drinking vinegar?

(YANG SHEN:) What do they know about the taste of wine? (*Sings*:)

They all

Count only as dumb gourds—mere vessels for storing wine.[21]

The moment when sorrow comes to me,

I would fain

Put wine-making yeast into Lake Dongting;

The moment when frustration comes to me,

I would turn

Parrot Island into ground for fermenting.[22]

What have the sages been talking about over thousands of years? This chitter chatter is driving me out of my wits!

With wine

I want to

wash the right and wrong from the sages' chattering.[23]

You two globes of sun and moon—no one is pushing you: From east at dawn to west at dusk, what are you so busy doing?

I want

To pickle the sun and the moon that send kingdoms rising and falling.

(CUILIU:) Academician, who among the ancients did drink like you?

(YANG:) Among the ancients none but Yao and Shun did drink. (*Sings*:)

Have you not heard that

Yao and Shun bowing and yielding the throne over three cups of wine,

Actually outshone

Cheng Tang and King Wu launching wars of conquest—a mere game of *go*?[24]
Get drunk
and be done:
it's better that way.

(CUILIU:) But then you drink the whole day. What joy is there in that?

(YANG:) You don't understand. Wine has its own joys!

(*Tang xiucai*) (YANG *sings*:)

I want to pluck that
Wine star and embrace it with caresses tender and teasing.
Hit that
Pool of wine 'til waves are flying and churning.

Cuiliu, don't disdain wine. Little one, you don't understand the meaning it embodies.

(CUILIU:) I know: three measures of husks, three measures of rice, one ladle of water. Too much water turns it into drippy vinegar. What more is there to it? "When the stocking strap breaks, tie it with a straw string."[25]

(YANG:) In ancient times being wine-stricken was called being "sage-stricken."[26] (*Sings*:)

Don't take it as
Rice distillation and husk coverings,
Hidden within it are the sage's meanings.

(CUILIU:) Day after day you live and die in wine's fumes and dreams. (YANG SHEN *sings*:)

To die,
To die is to become the potter's vessel.[27]

(CUILIU:) Don't you see, even the cloth covering the wine urn is rotting. (YANG SHEN *sings*:)

To rot,
To rot is to become earth at the urn's head.[28]
This is for me
The joy of the drunken old man.[29]

Cuiliu, I have quite forgotten. Today I am going to have a spring outing. Would you lend me some clothes and ornaments?

(CUILIU:) How can you wear my clothes?

(YANG:) Never you mind, just bring them.

(CUILIU *brings the clothes and enters.* YANG *puts them on.*) (*Sings*:)

(*Gun xiuqiu*)

I will gather
The bald stork's tufts
and fashion a
double-bun coiffure.[30]

Cuiliu, break off that red flower and bring it here.

(CUILIU:) What is the meaning of this?

(YANG:) I have an idea in mind. (*Sings*:)

I fear that overnight

Wind and rain will bury again the kingdom-toppling beauty.[31]

(CUILIU:) Hair like silver strands tied to this red flower: very becoming! (YANG *sings*:)

And that is why

I have these wandering gossamer threads snag the blooming fragrance.[32]

Cuiliu, put the rouge and powder on my face.

(CUILIU *applies the rouge and powder.*) (YANG *sings*:)

I only worry

That rouge and powder, all too faint, cannot bring a blush to this cold face of mine.[33]

Help me put the clothes on. (*He puts on a red garment for women and sings*:)

The embroidered cape, all too narrow, cannot cover this wide belly of mine.[34]

(CUILIU *laughs*:) Now what do you look like? (YANG *sings*:)

Compared to

Paintings of ladies on a spring outing,

I have a few more

Spikes of curly beard.

(CUILIU:) What a plump body you have. (YANG *sings*:)

Compared to

The girls on a jade platter, singing of swirling winds,

I sort of feel

My dancing style is somewhat weighed down by a stout body.[35]

(CUILIU:) Academician, on ordinary days you would chant poems and compose rhapsodies—you do have a great reputation of talent. Why are you dressed up like this today? Academician, you should cherish your dignity. (YANG *sings*:)

I no longer want to

Leisurely chant a thousand poems on the moon at night,

And will just

Keep this spring breeze-swathed jade body closely in my sight.[36]

(CUILIU:) With your high-bridged nose and full beard, you look like a Muslim. And now this dressing up will make you even more—more like what? (YANG *sings*:)

It will make people say

This is the Bright Consort of barbarian breed.[37]

(*Speaks*:) Tie the skirt.

(CUILIU:) Even with a long skirt you need small feet.[38] (YANG *sings*:)

(*Tang xiucai*)

My

Tiny slips of lotus petal feet are a full foot long.[39]

After I have sketched my eyebrows—
As slender as willow leaves, they go just past my two cheeks.
Cuiliu, I am worried.
(CUILIU:) Worried about what? (YANG *sings*:)
Simply that now
Inside the Han palace, I fear, will be those jealous of my fair eyebrows.[40]
(YANG *pulls* CUILIU. *She laughs.*)
(CUILIU:) What are you doing that for? (YANG *sings*:)
From
The sly Cuiliu I beg to ask a favor:[41]
Look at me:
Did I paint them—faint or dark—à la mode?[42]
The dressing up is complete. Let's go on our spring outing.
(CUILIU:) This is embarrassing. How can we go?
(YANG:) There is nothing to it. Just follow me.
(YANG *and* CUILIU *walk. Two* CLOWNS, *dressed as villagers, one male and one female, enter*:) We are Wang Liu and his fat aunt. We are all coming to see the madman. (YANG *sings*:)
(*Gun xiuqiu*)
This draws that
Wang Liu'er—
With busy steps
He closely follows us.
It goads that
Fat aunt—
Who, all out of breath,
Wheezes and pants.
(CUILIU:) You who are looking—don't squeeze your way in here.[43]
(YANG *sings*:)
They are pressing me so hard that I am squeezed in front and hemmed at the back.
(MISCELLANEOUS *laughs.* YANG *sings*:)
And they are laughing so hard that they are rocking this way and that.
What place is this?
(CUILIU:) In front of us is the official hall of the prefecture on the crossroads with the four memorial archways. (YANG *sings*:)
So we have arrived at the crossroads
Where unalloyed madness is for sale.
(TEASHOP WAITER *enters and laughs*:) Well, well, well. Today is the twenty-fourth day of the last month. And here we have the wife of the Kitchen God![44] (YANG *sings*:)
That
Teashop waiter is trying his seductive wiles on me.

(PAWNSHOP HAND *enters:*) Where does this fellow come from? (YANG *sings:*)

That

Pawnshop brother is screwing up his features and getting ready for a big show.

(MISCELLANEOUS:) This is Zhong Kui marrying off his daughter or a demon taking a wife.[45] (YANG *sings:*)

One says

I'm the girl that Zhong Kui protects and sends off as bride,

One says

I'm a demon's wife at a funeral by the mourners' side.

It's all

Nonsense and fiddlesticks!

(TEASHOP WAITER:) Let's see—perhaps "he" is actually female.

(YANG:) Who is female? Let me tell you—even you may not be all that male. (*Sings:*)

(*Tang xiucai*)

As for you—

In those pants, don't bother to guess you have an extra leg!

(*Each one in the crowd touches himself.*)

I'd say that,

Holding the gates of power, you are just chicks,

and most likely

fake.[46]

(TEASHOP WAITER:) You have no idea. My head holds up heaven and I stand firm on earth—so I am a man, but you, with that red skirt tied around your waist, are the woman. (YANG *sings:*)

Not for nothing

Do you hold up and stand firm on cosmic principles—on you we rely.

But brothers, you are putting me on, for there is not a man among you.

You really shouldn't

Fool heaven and earth or cheat gods and spirits.

(TEASHOP WAITER:) That chap is stark raving mad. Who is fooling you?

(YANG:) If you are a man, it makes no odds to me, but it will be unworthy of that man of Lu. (*Sings:*)

That

Man of Lu would

secretly

be ashamed.[47]

All of you: not only am I a woman, those sages of the three teachings were all women.[48]

(TEASHOP WAITER:) How can they be women? (YANG *sings:*)

(*Gun xiuqiu*)

Those three sages

Who set up teachings
Were all
Women like any other.
What do you think they were talking about day after day?
(TEASHOP WAITER:) What they talked about must have been moral lessons. (YANG *sings*:)
You say
That they preached some moral lessons,
But it turns out
They were only talking about the inner chamber.[49]
Laozi said, "Great anxiety comes about because we have a body."
He was anxious about what was in his body, fretting about a dream of snakes.[50]
(TEASHOP WAITER:) And Buddhism?
(YANG:) He said, "Husband, sit; child, sit."[51]
(TEASHOP WAITER:) What does this mean?
(YANG:) This shows that the Buddhist sage masters ritual propriety. (*Sings*:)
He says that
Only after the husband has been most respectfully invited to eat[52]
Would it be proper
To let the beloved children take their seats.
(TEASHOP WAITER:) What about Confucius?
(YANG:) Confucius said, I am waiting to marry the bidder.[53] (*Sings*:)
He tried to arrange his marriage at seventy-two places but never stopped waiting.[54]
Didn't he say, "Red and purple are not used for intimate clothing?"[55]
(TEASHOP WAITER:) What was that about? (YANG *sings*:)
This meant
In those years he could not bring himself to use red and purple for wedding clothes.
Each one of these was
A fair lady with comely brows and lovely eyes.[56]
(MISCELLANEOUS:) Listening to his nonsense has taken us away from our proper business. Let's go!

(*Exit*.)

(YANG *walks and barks like a dog*.) (*Sings*:)
(*Daodao ling*)
The hound of the house of Jie
Should of course bark at the house of Jie.[57]
(*Someone from backstage throws bricks and tiles*:) Let's hit the madman. (YANG *sings*:)
You
Follow your rules because that is what you see.[58]

Don't shed tears at the road's end if at the road's end you must be.[59]
The one like me is always cherished by another like me.
Is it not
The scorn that would kill him?
Is it not
The curses that would kill him?

But then Yang Sheng'an is selling his one neck dripping with cold blood, though he has yet to find a buyer in the whole wide world.[60]

Those
Vendors of slaughtered animals
should
settle scores only with the slaughterhouse.

(*From backstage*:) We will die laughing! We will die laughing! (YANG *sings*:)

(*Tang xiucai*)
You laugh, but your laughter will not end
This heroic play on the puppet stage.

(*From backstage*:) What a madman! (YANG *sings*:)

You curse, but your curses will not pierce
The protective talisman, for the sages are my walls.

(CUILIU:) We were doing perfectly well at home, and now we have come out only to be the target of such contemptuous curses!

(YANG:) How can their curses touch me? Cuiliu, I have actually learned some wisdom from you. (*Sings*:)

I have learned how to be like
Willow catkins, flying with the wind, not touching mud.[61]

(CUILIU:) Such cursing and you say they are not cursing?

(YANG:) Who is cursing whom? (*Sings*:)

When we meet, it's you and me,
What we face: It's him and whom?

I have a pivot line.[62] Cuiliu, do you know it? "Even though we are living in the same house, we are still separated by layers of mountains."

He and I
Are separated by ten thousand miles.

(MESSENGER *enters*:) I have come from Chengdu. I got this letter from Lady Yang and must look for Academician Yang. (*He greets* YANG.) Are you Academician Sheng'an?

(YANG:) Indeed I am he.

(MESSENGER:) I have a letter from your lady. Look! (*He takes out the letter.*) Having delivered it, I will go now.

(*Exits.*)

(YANG *opens the letter and reads*:)

As the geese in flight do not even reach Hengyang,[63]
How can brocade words be sent to Yongchang?[64]
The flowers and willows of spring are tokens of my ill fate;
The wind and smoke of Liuzhao mark your heartache.[65]
To go back! Go back! Grieve for the year's end.[66]
O for rain! For rain! Blame the morning sun.[67]
In vain did I hear about the promise of the sword ring,[68]
When will the golden rooster go down to Yelang?[69]

(*Speaks*:) My lady, what a consummate artist you are! (*Sings*:)
(*Dai guduo*)
Now arrives
The letter sent from the desk of the pining wife,[70]
How my
Spring-lamenting girl must have stained her red clothes with tears.
Everyday,
I face miasmic rain and barbarian mist,
While you still
Hope for the jade pardon from the golden rooster.
You said, "To go back! Go back!" But I cannot get to go back.
In death, my only mourners will be blue flies,[71]
To go back is only
To go back as a barbarian ghost.
You are
The cuckoo summoning me from beyond the heavens,
But how can it help this
Francolin crying among the misty trees?[72]

(CURIO DEALER:)

Faint clouds and light breeze, it's almost midday.
By the flowers, after the willows, I pass the front bay.
People of the times do not know the joy in my heart:
For rubbings and single scrolls make a gainful start.[73]

I am called a curio dealer, one whose forte is the buying and selling of poetry and paintings. Recently there is this Academician Yang—everyone says that he is a great talent and swears by his poetry and calligraphy. I am now hauling fifty taels of silver and ten bolts of silk as a "brush-moistening fee" to request his works. I figure this round of compositions will be no dingy show. Lads! Prepare some ropes. Since I am bringing all these gifts, I will haul back a good heap of his calligraphy for sure. Ah, that Yang Sheng'an, he must have dreamed an auspicious dream last night, for today the God of Wealth is marching through his door. I must look for him. (*He greets* YANG.) Academician, your honor, I am what is called a dealer in curios. I want to ask for your poetry and calligraphy and have especially prepared fifty taels of silver and ten bolts of colorful silk as humble gifts for moistening the brush. Academician, please accept them.

(YANG:) You got it all wrong. How can my poetry and calligraphy fall into your hands? You showed up for your request out of the blue with your cash and silk as if this is child's play. (*Sings*:)

(*Gun xiuqiu*)

My poetry

Holds the secrets of heaven and earth, gods and spirits.

My calligraphy

Unfurls the energy of ten-thousand miles of rivers and mountains.

My words are hidden in the deep caves of famous mountains, where they are safeguarded at every turn by dragon spirits.

They are carefully wrapped in layers, kept in metal caskets and stone chambers.[74]

Have you not heard? White clouds surged heavenward at the place of the Feng sacrifice during the Han, so now when vermilion clouds are manifest in the sky in their wondrous strangeness, it is all because my writings have been revealed.[75] (*The* CURIO DEALER *looks at the sky*.) (YANG *sings*:)

Even now the mist moves on the hazy rainbow.

(CURIO DEALER:) Hurry up with writing. (YANG *sings*:)

How can you, a

Vegetable peddler,

manage to explore

the wonders of the cave of Yu?[76]

(CURIO DEALER:) If you have some ready made, sell them to me. (YANG *sings*:)

Just touch them once and

they will

dispel your calamities and erase your sins.

(CURIO DEALER:) Bring them out for me to see. I am not asking you to offer them for free. (YANG *sings*:)

Have one look

and it will

disperse your soul and send your spirit flying.

(CURIO DEALER:) Do hurry up with writing. (YANG *sings*:)

Where is the

Duke of Zhou, Dan, who would sell his writings to make a living?

Where is the

Confucius who would write funeral eulogies to seek prosperity?[77]

Hold your peace on the subject.

(CURIO DEALER:) In truth, I am rich. Today it's for the sake of requesting your poetry and calligraphy that I bring myself down here. (YANG *sings*:)

(*Tang xiucai*)

Nowadays,
Those who become ever poorer
surprise with
their extravagance and easy liberality,
While those who grow ever richer become meaner and more vicious in their venality.

(CURIO DEALER:) I am bringing fifty taels of silver and ten bolts of silk, I am not someone to trifle with. (YANG *sings*:)

Pecks of grain, yards of silk
are
the tears in the eyes of you rich folks.

(CURIO DEALER:) I can take your poetry and calligraphy, fast track everything, and turn them into capital and interest. Now this time round if you do well with your writing and we make a profit, I will become your main client.[78] I am rich and generous—don't miss out! (YANG *sings*:)

Even if you
Can make goods multiply and possess mounds of copper,
Who would bother
to
ask you about it?

Be off right away! Be off right away! You are spoiling my spring outing.

(CURIO DEALER *exits.*)

(YANG:) Look how beautiful the spring light is! The luminous mountains and graceful streams are shimmering and limitless. In ancient times the age of the Three Sovereigns was spring, and now I will roam with Fuxi![79] (*Sings*:)

(*Ban dushu*)
The sun glistens on shards of golden ripples,
The mountains are arrayed like a verdant screen.
Warm wind lulls the traveler into intoxication.[80]
The Yunnan River, newly swelling, rises to the sky,
Every family has warblers that with spring breath cry,
Every step is an excuse for poetry.[81]

(*Xiao heshang*)
With a chirping, chirping tune
the jade crickets have perfected the harmonic scale,[82]
A twirling, swirling swish:
the rain of red petals drifts with the loveliness of a spring couplet.
Gently stirring, stirring notes
from the willows quicken the singing voice to lingering tenderness,[83]
With velvety, velvety warmth,
soft grass cushions the ground.

With a brimming, brimming smile,
I take a cup of wine with every step.

(YANG *bows and smiles*:) So Granny Flowers and Auntie Breeze have all come. (*He pours the wine and sings.*)

The Pomegranate Sisters
have to offer libation to the flower goddesses.[84]
(*Third from coda*)
So cleansed
by this
poetry club elder's rain, my intoning mood is awakened,
The young maiden's wind teases me, urging the birth of poetic lines.
They force me
To turn expansive feelings,
The loveliness of mountains and rivers,
Grief and sorrows past and present,
Into a pile of rancor and frustration—
in a mere moment.
I want to borrow
the mountain peaks as brushes,
And use
the whole wide world as pages,
Even then I
can never fully vent
my towering passions.[85]

(*He turns to* CUILIU *and writes all over her.*) (*Sings*:)

Ciuliu, who would have known
That a hundred feet of twisty, rugged branches
Would have their shadows
stolen by you
and brought to the clear pool?[86]

(CUILIU *discreetly exits and takes off her clothes.* MISCELLANEOUS, *dressed as a Muslim merchant, grabs and buys them. He exits.* CUILIU *again puts on white clothes and enters.*) (YANG *sings*:)

(*Second from coda*)
But these
Silken clothes sport shadows moving with the grace of dragons and snakes,
how do they compare with
Bouts of the rainbow skirt dance ending with return under the moon?[87]

(*Speaks*:) Cuiliu, when I wrote on your body I had an idea in mind: (*Sings*:)

For
Beautiful lines and fair ladies make a fitting match. (*He writes again.*)

Every word
that I am writing
brings down the geese and startles the swans.[88]
(*The two* FEMALE LEADS *dance.*) (YANG *sings*:)

Every move
that you are dancing
splashes the ink and makes the brush fly.
That poem for Crimson—
Why bother to make a comparison?[89]
That song about Snow—
There is no need to copy that as a model.[90]
Cui Hui's portrait—
Don't bother to inscribe it with a poem.[91]
(YANG *looks at* CUILIU:) Cuiliu, looking at you—
You are, beyond all bounds,
Truly ravishing.
It turns out that extraordinary writing and surpassing beauty
Come together in one place to vie for wonder.
(*Backstage: wind is blowing fluttering blossoms.*)
(CUILIU:) Academician, look: the wind and the rain are spreading all over. It's again time for spring to go. We also have to go back.
(YANG:) What a pity that spring is going! (*He weeps.*)
(CUILIU:) Academician, you are not being reasonable.
(YANG:) You have no idea. Spring and I have the deepest love for each other. (*Sings*:)
(*Coda*)
Spring comes and there isn't any sliver of land without sorrow.
That's why I must face spring and bitterly weep as it passes.[92]
Think how
Making spring's first acquaintance,
Petals and pistils redden.
Spring grows old,
When rain plumps the plum blossoms.
Spring has a tiny waist
Carried by a wisp of east wind.
Spring has dark eyebrows
Like rain-washed distant mountains.
Spring has slender feet
Stirring traces in fragrant dust.
Spring has a flowing mane
As lustrous as her cloud-like hair.

Engage the crimson of spring
When peach calyxes grow long.
The money for buying spring
The elm pods will bring.[93]
Spring is asking questions
When swallows murmur.
Spring wants to sleep,
But is roused by the oriole.
Spring leaks its secrets
With wet rouge.
Spring lingers
Like clinging catkins.
Spring has tears
Like raindrops flying on the river.[94]
Spring bears children[95]
When flowers are scattered.
The moods spring is carrying
Are like days tarrying.
Spring keeps its promise to meet,
Coming in secrecy most discreet.
Embrace spring
And sleep awhile.
Spring dreams are far away
And hard to seek and find.
Take off spring's clothes,
And urge her to drink a cup.
Spring departs in haste,
Leaving no traces.
Trying to persuade spring to stay,
The weeping willows sway.
Lamenting the soul of spring
The cuckoos cry out.
On the wind-borne message for flowers,
Spring heaves a sigh.
The snipes call for rain
And spring whispers in sorrow.
We have regrets
That spring cannot appease.
Spring speaks not
But by the stealthy pull of poetry.
For dispelling spring sorrow,

There is none but wine.
Wake up from the wine,
And spring has left.
And so
The spring mountains are silent,
The spring streams limitless,
While the spring grass is lush.
But all add up
To spring rancor, ever so gentle and sweet.
I gather
A river's worth of spring
And pour it all into the wine ladle of Master Spring Intoxication.
(*All exit together*)

NOTES

1. Musical precision refers to the tonal properties of arias as set forth in music treatises (*qupu* 曲譜), which Shen Jing compiled. The dramatists identified with this group came from Kunshan, Suzhou, and other parts of Jiangsu and Zhejiang.
2. Ye Xiaoluan spent the first eleven years of her life in Shen Zizhen's household and returned to her natal family only upon Zhang Qianqian's death in 1627. Shen wrote a moving elegy for Ye Xiaoluan as well as prefaces for Shen Yixiu's collection and for Ye Xiaowan's play. See Ye Shaoyuan (2015, vol. 1, 363, 66, 17, 19).
3. See Zha Jizuo (1986, vol. 3, 2162–63).
4. See *Thrice-Played Yuyang* (*Yuyang sanlong* 漁陽三弄) in this volume.
5. For a concise introduction to Shen Zizheng's plays, see Tseng Yong-yih 1972; Wang Ayling 2005, 364–69.
6. Literally, "he definitely had a taste for the [excursions at] Eastern Mountains" (*dongshan zhi pi* 東山之癖). The Eastern Jin statesman, Xie An 謝安 (320–385), traveled in the Eastern Mountains in the company of singing girls (Liu Yiqing 1984, 7.21).
7. Wang Shizhen (1986, *j.* 149.23a–23b).
8. See the biographies of Yang Shen and his father in *DMB*, 1531–35 and 1542–46.
9. See Fisher (1990).
10. See Chang and Saussy (1999, 172–78).
11. Cited in Tseng Yong-yih (1972, 20). Wang Shizhen's comment is found in Wang Shizhen (1986, *j.* 149.23b).
12. Qi Biaojia (1959, 144).
13. In one Tang anecdote, Emperor Xuanzong puts flowers in the hair of a prince to show imperial favor ("Xuanzong" 玄宗, *TPGJ j.* 205.1560). There are many Tang poems about wearing flowers during special festivals. Even the bandits in *Water Margin* sometimes put flowers in their hair. As Zhao Yi 趙翼 pointed out in *Gaiyu congkao* 陔餘叢考, pinning flowers in the hair was a custom adopted by both men and women, see Gao Chunming (2001, 138–49). Chen Hongshou 陳洪綬 (1598–1652) painted a portrait of Yang Shen with flowers pinned in his hair (Yi 2011).
14. Literally, "Yunnan courtesans, like dragons and snakes, compete with their white silk skirts." "Dragons and snakes" here means all kinds of courtesans, of varying natures and merits.

15. See Zhang Ji, 張籍 (766–830), "Among the Barbarians" 蠻中 (*QTS j.* 386.4361). The original has "poisonous grass" 毒草 instead of "white grass" 白草. The Han general Ma Yuan 馬援 (14 BCE–49 CE) is said to have erected bronze pillars in Xianglin 象林 (in present day Vietnam) to mark the southern border of the Han Empire after successful military expeditions (41–43). Here the poet has gone past the bronze pillars but has not yet reached Jinlin 金麟 (also in present day Vietnam).
16. The names Cuiliu 翠柳 ("green willows") and Jiaotao 嬌桃 ("lovely plum blossoms") use colors ("green and red") as metaphors for the world of sensual pleasures. Eyebrow comment (partly erased): ". . . makes one believe that a talented man would, after all, not be put in the land of sorrow."
17. This alludes to Ouyang Xiu's 歐陽修 (1007–1072) "Reply to Yuanzhen in Jest" 戲答元珍: "I fear spring wind does not come to the world's edge, / In the second month there's no sign yet of flowers in this mountain town" 春風疑不到天涯，二月山城未見花 (Ouyang Xiu 1986, vol. 1, 74).
18. This alludes to Liu Zongyuan's 柳宗元 (773–819) "Chance Composition on How the Banyan Leaves Have All Fallen in Liuzhou in the Second Month" 柳州二月榕葉落盡偶題: "With the mountain town's passing rain, all the flowers are gone, / Banyan leaves fill the courtyard as orioles unevenly warble" 山城過雨百花盡，榕葉滿庭鶯亂啼 (*QTS j.* 352.3937). Liu wrote this when he was exiled to Liuzhou (in Guangxi). Banyan trees grow only in the far south.
19. Late rose (*tumi* 荼蘼) is the last flower to bloom in spring. See Wang Qi 王琪 (11th c.), "Roaming in a Small Garden in Late Spring" 暮春遊小園: "When it's the late rose's turn to bloom, the flowering's done" 開到荼蘼花事了 (*QSS j.*187.2138).
20. This paraphrases a line from "Fisherman" 漁父, where Qu Yuan 屈原 (the poetic persona) describes his alienation to the fisherman: "The multitude is drunk, I alone am sober" 眾人皆醉我獨醒 (Zhu Xi 1987, *j.* 7.116).
21. A reference to "dumb gourds" (*men hulu* 悶葫蘆) usually implies unsolved questions or puzzles.
22. Lake Dongting is associated with the goddesses of the River Xiang; they are sometimes identified with the sage king Shun's wives who died mourning for him. Mi Heng 禰衡 (173–198), the prototype of persecuted talent, wrote a rhapsody on parrots (*HHS* 26B:2657) and the warlord Huang Zu 黃祖 put him to death at Parrot Island (Li Daoyuan 1999, *j.* 35.605).
23. Eyebrow comment: "Fake pedants should get totally drunk."
24. These are based on lines attributed to Shao Yong 邵雍 (1012–1077): "Yao and Shun bowed and yielded the throne over three cups of wine, / Cheng Tang and King Wu launched wars of conquest that amounted to a mere game of *go*" 唐虞揖遜三杯酒，湯武征誅一局棋. Yao yields the throne to Shun in an idealized version of abdication to the worthy, while Cheng Tang and King Wu, founders of the Shang and Zhou dynasties respectively, launch military expeditions to gain power. Both abdication and conquest are seen as inconsequential from the perspective of philosophical detachment. Here Yang Shen is tying wine to abdication to the worthy, the highest political ideal.
25. This sounds like an idiom from that period: the idea is that one can always find an expedient solution even in case of errors.
26. Xu Miao 徐邈 (171–249) got drunk when there was an edict against drinking. He called inebriation "being sage-stricken" 中聖人 (*SGZ j.* 27.739).
27. That is, a vessel for holding wine.
28. The opening of the wine urn is sealed with mud during the process of fermentation.
29. In Ouyang Xiu's "Account of the Pavilion of the Drunken Old Man" 醉翁亭記, Ouyang Xiu (the drunken old man) is able to find joy in the beauty of nature and his good governance while he is in exile in Chuzhou (in present day Anhui) (Ouyang Xiu 1986, vol. 1, 276).
30. A man losing his hair is compared to a bald stork (Li Yanshou 1981, *j.* 5.151).
31. "Kingdom-toppling beauty" is a common idiom derived from the Han musician Li Yannian's 李延年 song: "One look at her topples the city. / Look again and the kingdom is toppled." 一顧傾人城，再顧

傾人國。(*HS j.* 97A.3951). Here it refers to fallen blossoms, alluding to Zhou Bangyan's 周邦彥 (1056–1121) "Composed After the Roses Withered, to the tune 'Liu chou'" (六醜。薔薇謝後作): "I ask: where are the blossoms? / Wind and rain that came overnight / have buried the kingdom-toppling beauty from the Chu palace" 為問花何在，夜來風雨，葬楚宮傾國 (Zhou Bangyan 1985, 202–07).

32. This alludes to Ouyang Xiu's song lyric "Yulou chun" 玉樓春: "It is right now in Luoyang the season when fragrance blooms, / when lush colors and delicate scent rise together. / Wandering gossamer threads deliberately swirl around us, not letting go, / Weeping willows, for no reason, vie to bid us farewell." 洛陽正值芳菲節，濃豔清香相間發。遊絲有意苦相縈，垂柳無端爭贈別. (Ouyang Xiu 1986, vol. 2, 1069). Yang is comparing his white hair to the "gossamer threads" of spring.
33. "Cold face" 冷面 can mean indifference and disaffection or the state before being flushed with wine, as in these lines from Su Shi's (1037–1101) poem to his friend Chen Zao 陳慥: "Where did you get this wine? / My cold face is envious of your flushed one" 何從得此酒，冷面妒君赤 ("Qiting" 岐亭, third of five poems in Su Shi 2001, vol. 2, 1151).
34. Eyebrow comment: "The frustrated man of talent has to imitate the adornment and make-up of palace ladies. This is called 'changing one's head and getting a new face.'"
35. The dancers are so light that they can dance on a jade platter, evoking the story of the light-stepped Han dynasty consort Zhao Feiyan 趙飛燕 (Flying Swallow Zhao). "Swirling wind" also describes their light and rapid movements.
36. "Spring breeze-swathed jade-like body" usually refers to a woman's body; here Yang is referring to his own. The phrase appears in Yuan plays, including *Ma Danyang Thrice Delivered Ren Fengzi* 馬丹陽三度任風子: "I am about to learn to play the three zither tunes on the moonlit night, / But who would want to look closely at this spring breeze-swathed jade body?" 我待學彈夜月琴三弄，誰待細看春風玉一團? (Ning Xiyuan 1988, 136).
37. Wang Zhaojun 王昭君 (1st c. BCE), the Han palace lady sent off to marry the Xiongnu ruler as part of a policy of appeasement, is also called the Bright Consort. In Wang Anshi's 王安石 (1021–1086) famous poem on Zhaojun ("Song of Bright Consort" 明妃曲), the poet asserts that the barbarians show her greater favor and understanding than the Han emperor and questions the notion of loyalty. The image here of a "barbarian Zhaojun" (i.e., a Zhaojun that identifies with the barbarian) is thus comically subversive.
38. A long trailing skirt can hide a woman's big feet (a supposed blemish) to a certain extent, but not totally.
39. "Foot-long lotus boats" 蓮船盈尺 is a standard term for mocking women with big feet.
40. An allusion to *Encountering Sorrow* 離騷: "The throng of women, jealous of my fair eyebrows, / Slander me with charges of licentiousness" 眾女嫉余之蛾眉兮，謠諑謂余以善淫 (Zhu Xi 1987, *j.* 1.9). Eyebrow comment: "He has joined the ranks of women, but then he fears that beauty would invite jealousy. This is extremely mischievous roguery."
41. Cuiliu is described as *qiao* 喬 (translated here as "sly"), a word that can mean "fake" or "pretentious." Yang Shen is the one taking up disguise, but Cuiliu also must enter his world of make-believe and become his instructress. The balance of power between patron and courtesan is reversed.
42. An allusion to Zhu Qingyu's 朱慶餘 (fl. 820s) "Boudoir Thoughts, Submitted to Minister of Water Management Zhang" 閨意上張水部 (*QTS j.* 515.5892): "Having finished my makeup, I ask my husband in a low voice: / The way my eyebrows are painted—dark or faint—is it à la mode or not?" 妝罷低聲問夫婿，畫眉深淺入時無? The quatrain is couched in the voice of a bride about to pay her respects to her in-laws for the first time, but the title indicates that Zhu is seeking recognition, approval, and direction from his prospective examiner Zhang Ji 張籍 (ca. 767–ca. 830).
43. The term for those who are looking is *kanguan* 看官, which is also how the audience is addressed. We can imagine Cuiliu's line as breaking the fourth wall: "Audience, don't get too close!"

44. Offerings are made to the Kitchen God (or more precisely the God of the Stove) on the 24th day (23rd or 25th in some versions) of the 12th month. He is supposed to go to heaven to report on human conduct and then return on New Year's Eve.
45. In Chinese folklore Zhong Kui 鍾馗 is an ugly scholar who becomes a demon-catching god after death. He marries off his younger sister (not daughter) with pomp and circumstance and is a popular subject in paintings and theatrical skits.
46. "Chicks" 雛兒 ("inexperienced ones") are contrasted with "holders of power" 把勢, ("the experts") in chapters 32 and 77 of *Journey to the West* (*Xiyou ji*); see Wu Cheng'en (1983, vol. 1, 391, vol. 2, 967). Here there may be associations with the penis, sometimes called "power" (*shi* 勢) or "bird" (*niao* 鳥).
47. "The man of Lu" refers to the minister Liu Xiahui 柳下惠, known for his sagacity and integrity. Mencius praises him as "the balanced among sages" (*Mencius* 6B.1).
48. The three teachings are Confucianism, Daoism, and Buddhism.
49. A Tang court jester Li Keji 李可及 (mid-9th c.) tells these jokes about the three teachings ("Jesters and Entertainers" 俳優人, *TPGJ j.* 252.1958–59). Shen Zizheng elaborates them.
50. *Youshen* 有身 ("to have a body") is homophonous with *youshen* 有娠 ("to be pregnant"). "Dreaming of snakes" is an omen for giving birth to a girl.
51. "Husband, sit; children, sit" 夫坐兒坐 (*fu zuo er zuo*) is homophonous with a line that recurs in Buddhist sutras, "He spread the seat and sat down" (*fu zuo er zuo* 敷座而坐). It appears in the *Diamond Sūtra* (Jingang jing 金剛經), for example, when the Buddha does so after begging for alms and going through rituals of purification.
52. Literally, only after the wife presents the food to the husband by kneeling and raising the tray to the level of her eyebrows (*qimei* 齊眉), an idiom derived from the story of Meng Guang 孟光 and Liang Hong 梁鴻 (Huangfu Mi 1983, 106; *HHS j.* 83.2768).
53. In the *Analects* (9.13), Zigong asks Confucius about a fine piece of jade: Should it be hidden or should one wait for a discerning merchant to offer a fair price? "The Master said, 'Sell it! Sell it! I am waiting for the merchant (or, alternatively, the fair price).'" This is taken to mean that Confucius is waiting for a ruler who can recognize his worth and put his ideas into practice. The words for "price" 價 (*jia*) and "marry" 嫁 (*jia*) are homophonous.
54. One tradition claims that Confucius had audience with seventy-two lords without being able to convince any of them to follow his teachings.
55. *Analects* 10.6.
56. Literally, "a wide forehead (like a cicada) and long, curving eyebrows (like the antennae of a moth"), see *Shijing*, "Shuoren" 碩人 (Cheng Junying and Jiang Jianyuan 2017, vol. 1, 175–82). Yang Shen concludes by restating that Laozi, Buddha, and Confucius are all fair ladies.
57. The dog of the tyrant Jie would bark at the sage king Yao because loyalty to its master trumps other value judgments (*SJ* 83.2475). Yang Shen reverses the trope to suggest that loyalty is irrelevant. Here he may also be simply implying that people or things with shared traits belong together.
58. *Bangzhou li* 傍州例 (literally "rules of the next region") is a common term in Yuan plays associated with rules and precedents.
59. Ruan Ji 阮籍 "often carelessly rode his carriage alone without following any road, and where the carriage tracks ended, he often wailed bitterly and turned back" (see Pei Songzhi's annotation in *SGZ j.* 21.604). The image thus evokes the frustrations of a talented man when the time is out of joint.
60. This is reminiscent of the Ruan brothers' words in *Water Margin* 水滸傳 (chap. 15): "The hot blood in this chest is sold only to the discerning buyer!" 這腔熱血，只要賣與識貨的。See Wang Liqi (1991, vol. 1, 218). It is not clear, however, whether Shen Zizhen knew the novel.

61. Recall that Cuiliu's name means "green willow." Yang's image reverses the logic of the well-known lines by the monk Canliao 参寥: "My Chan heart is already like willow catkins touched by mud: / It will no longer swirl up and down with the east wind" 禪心已作沾泥絮, 不逐東風上下狂 (Wu Zeng 1985, *j.* 8.188). The image of catkins in mud conveys stillness and transcendence in Canliao's lines but implies defilement for Yang.
62. A "pivot line" (*zhuanyu* 轉語) gives a drastic turn of meaning and comes up in Chan conversations.
63. Wild geese are supposed to carry letters. The Returning Geese Peak at Mount Heng marks the limit where geese would go when migrating south in fall. See Gao Shi 高適 (d. 765), "Sending Off Chamberlain Li, Exiled to Shanzhong, and Chamberlain Wang, Exiled to Changsha" 送李少府貶陝中王少府貶長沙: "How many letters do the geese returning from Hengyang carry?" 衡陽歸雁幾封書? (*QTS j.* 214.2233). Hengyang is in Hunan.
64. Dou Tao's 竇滔 (4th c.) wife Su Hui 蘇蕙 (b. 357) sent him a palindrome poem woven into brocade when he was in exile (Fang Xuanling et al. 1980, *j.* 96.2523). The brocade palindrome poem, which can be read in various directions, symbolizes artistry and ingenuity in women's writings. Yongchang is in Yunnan. One of Yang Shen's poem to Huang E echoes this line: "Easy to come by are agate trees beyond the seas, / Hard to get are the brocade words from the inner chamber" 易求海上瓊枝樹, 難得閨中錦字書 (Yang Shen 1980, *j.* 12.4b).
65. Liuzhao 六詔 (or the Six Zhao) is the name of six groups of non-Sinitic tribes in Yunnan (*XTS j.* 122A.6267). The term is used to parallel with *sanchun* 三春 (three springs, i.e., early, mid, late spring) in the preceding line.
66. "To go back! Go back!" is a line from "Picking Bracken" 采薇 in *Shijing* (Cheng Junying and Jiang Jianyuan 2017, vol. 2, 494–501). The speaker is an officer far from home.
67. "O for rain! For rain!" is a line from "Bo xi" 伯兮 in *Shijing* (Cheng Junying and Jiang Jianyuan 2017, vol. 1, 199–203). The speaker is a woman longing for her husband in military service.
68. When the Xiongnu ruler received the Han envoy and included in the meeting Li Ling 李陵, who surrendered to the Xiongnu, the Han envoy traced his fingers over his sword ring several times to convey the hint that Li Ling will be allowed to return to Han (*HS j.* 54.2458). ("Ring" 環 and "return" 還 are both pronounced *huan*.)
69. The golden rooster is used in announcement of pardon (Wei Zheng et al. 1980, *j.* 25.706). The Tang poet Li Bai 李白 was exiled to Yelang. See Li Bai, "Exiled to Yelang, I sent this to Judge Xin" 流夜郎贈辛判官: "I grieve for my exile to distant Yelang, / When will the golden rooster's pardon allow me to return?" 我愁遠謫夜郎去, 何日金雞放赦回? (*QTS j.* 170.1751).
70. For "pining wife" the text has "Zhuo shi" 卓氏, referring to Zhuo Wenjun 卓文君, wife of the Han poet Sima Xiangru 司馬相如. When late in life he thought of taking a concubine, she sent him a poem lamenting her fate (Lu Qinli 1983, 274).
71. Yu Fan 虞翻 (164–233) was exiled to the south and said about himself: "Alive, there is none with whom I can talk, and when I die blue flies will be my mourners" (see Pei Songzhi's commentary, *SGZ j.* 57.1322).
72. An ancient Shu King is transformed into a cuckoo after his death and laments his lost kingdom by weeping blood and crying mournfully. The cries of the francolin supposedly sound like "you cannot go, brother" (*xing bu de ye ge ge* 行不得也哥哥). Both are common images in Chinese poetry.
73. This is a parody of a well-known quatrain by the Confucian scholar Cheng Hao 程顥 (1032–1085), ("Casual Composition on a Spring Day" 春日偶成 (*QSS j.* 715.8229). The original fourth line is: "They will say that I steal leisure and take a youthful part" 將為偷閒學少年—that is, they will mistake his philosophical equanimity for childish playfulness.

74. Sima Qian 司馬遷 speaks of consulting historical writings in "metal caskets and stone chambers" 石室金匱 and of hiding his own work in famous mountains (*SJ j.* 130.3309, *HS* 63.2735). In Buddhist sutras, dragon spirits are said to guard the dharma.
75. Yang is implicitly comparing the supposed omen of political legitimation (the Feng sacrifice and the white smoke [*SJ j.* 28.1398]) with the power of writing.
76. Yu 禹 is said to have received magical texts from the gods that were presumably kept in the Yu Cave 禹穴 (*SJ j.* 130.3293, annotations of Zhang Shoujie).
77. Eyebrow comment: "Cai Yong 蔡邕 (132–192) said that he could not help sweating with shame when he thought about the stele inscriptions he wrote in his life. What can be a better solution than stopping to write [such things] altogether?" Laudatory tomb inscriptions and commemorative biographies constituted a significant source of income for the literati.
78. The curio dealer is in fact proposing to become his "agent" or middleman.
79. See Shao Yong's historical vision of regression in "Observing Things" 觀物: "The age of the Three Sovereigns was like spring; that of the Five Sovereigns, summer; that of the three kings, autumn; that of the five overlords, winter" (Shao Yong 1983, *j.* 12.6b). Fuxi is one of the Three Sovereigns.
80. This line is from Lin Sheng's 林升 (1123–1189) quatrain on Lin'an (Hangzhou). Lin's poem criticizes the complacency of the inhabitants of the new Song capital after the debacle of Song defeat by the Jurchens.
81. Literally, "every step is a poetic title." Eyebrow comment: "Not only poetic title—it can also serve as poetic material."
82. *Tuiqiao* 推敲 ("have perfected") means literally "push or knock" and refers to a poetic anecdote about Jia Dao 賈島 (779–843) deliberating whether he should use the word *tui* 推 (push) or *qiao* 敲 (knock) in a line about a monk at a door. It may seem odd to compare the crickets' chirping to poetic labor, unless we think of the crickets as echoing one another until they find a harmonic scale.
83. *Cuipai* 催拍 ("quicken") is a technical term in a musical sequence indicating accelerating notes. *Xu* 絮 (lingering tenderness) means both willow catkins (hence the association with willows) and something soft and continuous.
84. For "Pomegranate Sisters," the original has "Shi Cucu" 石醋醋. In a Tang tale, a Daoist meets flower spirits and protects them. Shi A-cuo 石阿措 is the pomegranate spirit ("Cui Xuanwei" 崔玄微, *TPGJ j.* 416.3392–93).
85. Cf. Li Zhi 李贄, "Agreement in Advance" 豫約 (in *Fen shu* 焚書): "Even were the whole world to turn into ink [for my brush], it would still be difficult to fully express [my sorrows] in writing." 將大地為墨，難盡寫也。(Li Zhi 2010, vol. 2, 110). Li Zhi (1527–1602) was very widely read at the time.
86. These somewhat puzzling lines probably allude to Lin Bu's 林逋 (967–1028) famous lines on plum blossoms: "Sparse shadows slant over a clear, shallow pool / As a secret scent wafts in moonlit dusk" 疏影橫斜水清淺，暗香浮動月黃昏 (*QSS j.* 106.1218). Yang is comparing himself to the rugged (in the original, dragon-like) branches of the plum tree, whose spirit is conveyed by the subtle fragrance and delicate shadows of plum blossoms, here represented by Cuiliu. The "transference" is achieved when he writes poems on her clothes.
87. The "Rainbow Skirt" 霓裳 is the dance tune that the Tang emperor Xuanzong (r. 712–756) learns during a dream journey to the moon. It is associated with courtly splendor but also excessive sensuality and decadence.
88. A beautiful woman makes the geese fall from the sky—the image is derived from a passage in *Zhuangzi*, where birds fly away from a beauty because they do not know she is beautiful (*ZZJS j.* 2.93). The startled swan (literally, *hong* 鴻 is just a bigger wild goose) describes the graceful movement of a goddess (Cao Zhi 曹植, "Goddess of the Luo" 洛神賦, see Cutter 2021, 61). Yang is deliberately using

standard idioms of feminine beauty to describe his writing. Eyebrow comment: "The entire body dances and causes the hundred flowers to move: this should be Madame Wei's 'Beauty Pinning Flowers to Her Coiffure' style." Madame Wei 衛夫人 (272–349) was a famous calligrapher.

89. Crimson 紅兒 was a Tang singing girl ("Luo Qiu" 羅虬, *TPGJ j.* 273.2156, *QTS j.* 666.7629).
90. Snowy 雪兒 was the concubine of the military leader Li Mi 李密 (582–619) ("Han Ding ci" 韓定辭, *TPGJ j.* 200.1501).
91. Cui Hui 崔徽 was a Tang courtesan who sent her portrait to her lover with these words: "The day Cui Hui no longer measures up to the person in the portrait, she will have died for you." See Yuan Zhen's 元稹 preface to "Song of Cui Hui" 崔徽歌 (*QTS j.* 423.4652).
92. Eyebrow comment: "Spring is worth a thousand pieces of gold: it is as if the author is heedlessly spending them."
93. Elm pods are called "elm coins."
94. Alternatively, "Spring has tears / When raindrops fly in Southland (Jiangnan)."
95. *Shengzi* 生子 ("bears children") also means "to set seed."

7
A Song for a Laugh

ANON. CA. 1600

TRANSLATED BY CASEY SCHOENBERGER

A Song for a Laugh (*Ge dai xiao* 歌代嘯) is a Northern-style *zaju* composed in the late sixteenth or early seventeenth century. The title refers to bawdy popular songs with lyrics (*ge*) taking the place of (*dai*) pure vocal expression beyond language (*xiao*), possibly also punning on the homophony of *xiao* with the word for "laughter."[1] Puns and other comic substitutions are the thematic heart of the play; each act absurdly literalizes a different folk saying meaning "to shift blame to the wrong target." *A Song for a Laugh* is unusual in its focus on the lives of commoners, its suggested use of clown role types as stars, and because its four acts relate only loosely to one another. As the author of its "Guidelines" concedes, each act could serve as a standalone play, though numerous threads do connect them. There is no record of live performance until recently, though the guidelines' discussion of such practical considerations as the choice of role types seems to reflect a belief that it was suitable for staging, as well as enjoying in the study.

Modern scholars do not agree on *A Song for a Laugh*'s authorship. The only extant premodern copy is a manuscript dated to 1826 held by the Nanjing Library.[2] Its cover states that it is a copy of an older edition held by the Shaoxing calligrapher and bibliophile, Shen Fucan 沈復粲 (1779–1850); its title page lists Xu Wei 徐渭 (1521–1593) of Shaoxing as author and Yuan Hongdao 袁宏道 (1568–1610) of Gong'an as editor. The edition also includes a preface attributed to Yuan and a set of guidelines (*fanli* 凡例) by the so-called Hulin Chonghe jushi 虎林沖和居士 (Hangzhou's Adept of the Primordial Energy). Those supporting the Xu Wei attribution cite the similarity of an episode in the play to a story about Xu killing his wife in a jealous rage over her suspected infidelity with a young monk. Xu was jailed for murdering his third wife, but his own account is vague and terse, citing only a fit of mental illness. The earliest version of the story to include a monk was recounted by Qian Xiyan 錢希言 (1562–1638), who reported having learned it second hand from someone in Xu's social circle after his death. This may have been the kernel of Yuan Hongdao's account, which includes an adulterous monk, and of later, more detailed retellings, like Feng Menglong's 馮夢龍 (1574–1646).

Reasons to doubt the monk story, as well as Xu Wei's authorship of *A Song for a Laugh*, include the similarity of the episode to the plot of a play confidently attributed to Xu Wei, *Yu chanshi* 玉禪師 (*Zen Monk Jade*), likely composed before the murder, if Wang Jide's 王驥德 (d. 1623) account of the order of composition is correct. Wang claims Xu, in his later years, had been his neighbor in Shaoxing, and even to have been present for composition of the last of his *Four Cries of a Gibbon* dramas, yet he never mentions *A Song for a Laugh*. Yuan Hongdao never met Xu but became the top promoter of his work soon after his death. In the preface attributed to him, Yuan states that he did not know who wrote *A Song for a Laugh*, though it was rumored to have been Xu's work.

The "Guidelines" are composed in the style of a playwright providing rules for his own play, not a later editor. Though Xu spent time in Hangzhou, "Adept of the Primordial Energy" is not one of his known sobriquets. It is, however, a name that appears in a commentarial or editorial capacity in a few early seventeenth-century works, like the novel *Chanzhen yishi* 禪真逸史 (*Lost Histories of the Chan Patriarchs*) and the drama collection, *Chantou bailian erji* 纏頭百練二集 (*One Hundred Embroidered Crowns, Volume 2*). As the latter dates to 1630, Xu Wei cannot be this same "Adept of the Primordial Energy." At the same time, assuming the Yuan preface is not a forgery, *A Song for a Laugh* must have been composed before 1610. Sun Shulei 孫書磊 suggests the Adept could be the author of the *Lost Histories* and two other fictional adaptations of stories about Buddhist monks, Fang Ruhao 方汝浩 (fl. c. 1611–1644), but this would require Fang to have assumed two separate identities in the same edition, one associated with Nanjing's Qingxi 清溪 River, and the other, in *Song for a Laugh*, with Hangzhou.[3] It is possible that Xu's uxoricide was actually motivated by jealous rage toward a handsome monk, but it could be that later anecdotalists and critics, perhaps eager to rationalize Xu's violent madness, conflated elements of his life story with a play he had written. Such possibly fictional elements may have, in turn, fueled rumors of Xu's authorship of a different fictional drama with a title reminiscent of Xu's *Four Cries of a Gibbon*. Most likely, the author of *A Song for a Laugh* was a drama connoisseur from Hangzhou, an acquaintance of Fang Ruhao's, and active from sometime before 1610 until sometime after 1630.

Related to the degree of moral outrage an audience is expected to feel about lecherous monks is the matter of *A Song for a Laugh*'s dramatic intent. A Chinese Marxist tendency to interpret all premodern depictions of corrupt officials and hypocritical religious practitioners as indictments of "feudalism" has led to similar interpretations of this play. The fact that *xiao* 嘯 can mean something like "howl," moreover, has led English-language critics to suggest translations like "singing in place of screaming."[4] I do not think this is the intended meaning of *xiao* here, nor that *Song for a Laugh* is meant to serve a strong social commentary function beyond that tendency comedy usually serves in the Aristotelian formulation: "depicting men as worse . . . than in actual life." The inclusion of a hen-pecked magistrate who takes out his frustrations on his people, a domineering magistrate's wife, a good-for-nothing son-in-law, a lecherous monk, and similar stock characters does not make *A Song for a Laugh* a serious criticism of such vices in the way that *Jin Ping Mei* 金瓶梅 (*Plum in the Golden Vase*) arguably is.

The closing poem of the play provides a clue about the meaning of the title and the dramatic intent: "Phrases from the wells and markets, told for quite some time, / It's not often such a funny thing one finds. / Sighs and songs can't tell it all, we've added lyrics of our own, / Put on a variety show, everybody all together." The literal meaning of the penultimate line is "You can't express it all through *xiao*, so we've casually added song lyrics." Such phrasing is reminiscent of a famous commentary on the *Shijing* 詩經 (*Canon of Poetry*): "Feelings stir in the heart and take form as words; when words are not enough to express them one heaves a sigh; when sighs are not enough one sings a song." Yet the rest of the poem, along with the overall tenor of the play, does not suggest a wail of sorrow, as Xu Wei's *Four Cries of a Gibbon* might.[5] In the context of vocal artistry, *xiao* refers to a medieval practice called "whistling," which may have been literally a type of whistling (perhaps with fingers in the mouth, as depicted on a famous, medieval frieze) or else simply a kind of singing with no lexical words.[6] Descriptions of *xiao* emphasize that it is refined, rarefied, and beyond language—a pure expression of the human voice. "You can't express it all through *xiao*, so we've casually added song lyrics," therefore, is an inversion of a classical hierarchy: lexical words express propositions, but singing without words (or howling, for that matter) is a more unfiltered emotional release. The implication of the final poem and the title, therefore, is something like: "Pure vocal artistry can't tell *this* story; bawdy lyrics and quips are needed to express it fully."

This translation is based on the print edition found in Xu Wei's collected works (*XWJ* vol. 4, 1232–1273), which closely adheres to the Nanjing Library manuscript; the notes to Zhou Zhongming (1984) were also consulted.

GUIDELINES

1. This play focuses on evoking comedy and satire. Any lascivious banter and base subject matter can be set to the tunes and rhymes of song.[7] Therefore, it draws nothing from refined language.
2. General prefaces that provide an outline of the story at the head of today's *chuanqi* dramas are called "stage openers." Within the acts or outside of them, Yuan drama had another small set of songs called "wedges," only stating the "full title" at the end of the play to summarize the lessons to be learned in two or four lines. This is roughly comparable to the "stage opener." In my mind, it is natural to rouse up the inherent power latent in the whole play right away, so this should not wait until the end. Therefore, I have specifically moved the full title to the beginning, where it may be considered part of the "wedge," thus preserving the old model. The full title, however, need not be sung. I have added a few optional phrases at the end of the play in the

fashion of modern "stage exiting poems"; these can be kept or dropped as desired. In keeping with the Yuan dynasty style, the individual acts do not end with poems.

3. The songs in Yuan drama are all performed by either a male lead or a female lead. All four acts come from a single throat and narrate the affairs of one character. This play tells four different stories in four different acts with no leading role. Therefore, it is okay to divide the singing parts among different actors. Nevertheless, each act focuses on a single star singer. Is not the classical model thereby upheld?
4. Since each act is sung by one voice, the other characters primarily engage in repartee. The details of their dialogue may be subject to artistic discretion so long as the meaning is communicated. The intricacy of their spoken lines should modulate on its own as they proceed, bearing in mind that it should cease when it has expressed what it should.
5. Each act uses only one rhyme scheme, following the categories set forth in *Rhymes of the Central Plain*. The "entering tone" syllables are distributed among the other three tones, so it is natural that they use a different pronunciation.[8] There are several cases where no written characters exist for a given word.[9] These should be read like the characters of similar pronunciation provided. Attempting to use Shen Yue's rhyming standards for pronunciation will result in many awkward phrases.[10]
6. The four singing characters are all suited to painted-face (clown) roles; alternatively, Wang Jidi's wife and mother-in-law may be played by female role types, with the painted-face actor taking on the part of the husband. But the wife is definitely not a refined lady.
7. Four different events are divided into four separate acts, but there are subtle threads of foreshadowing each act brings to interest. The viewer should not be lax in his attention.

—Hangzhou's Adept of the Primordial Energy

Dramatis Personae in Order of Appearance

Characters	*Full name and/or social role*
ZHANG	Monk of Three Purities Monastery, an older widower
LI	Monk of Three Purities Monastery
WORKMAN	A gardener working for Monk Zhang
WIFE	Wang Jidi's wife, Miss Wu
MOTHER-IN-LAW, CHEN	Mother of Miss Wu
SON-IN-LAW, WANG JIDI	Son-in-law of Chen
CROWD	Wang's neighbors
ZHAO	Wang's neighbor
QIAN	Wang's neighbor
SUN	Wang's neighbor
ZHOU	Wang's neighbor
ZHENG	Wang's neighbor
OFFICER	Runner for the county seat, tracks down witnesses
MAGISTRATE	The county magistrate

BAILIFF	Assistant to the magistrate in the court
CROWD	Citizens of the county
FENG	Feng Yuanjia, local scholar of the county
WEI	Wei Guanfu, local scholar of the county
LADY, WIFE	Lady of the County and wife of the magistrate
AIDES	Magistrate's personal assistants

A SONG FOR A LAUGH

WEDGE

(STAGE OPENER:)

(*Linjiang xian*)
Speak not of rectifying norms of the day,
Don't dredge up sages and saints of old.
To cry to Heaven of gain or loss, what good, in the end, can it do?
No need to polish the sword of wisdom,
Better to drink from the spring of madness.[11]

The world has always had its flaws,
Human nature's been mean and crafty from of old.
Collecting common sayings, I've cobbled together a new play.
Though it turns things upside down,
It's worth a glance in your spare time.

So, listen now to this variety play's full name:

One with no place to vent his rage:	When winter melons walk off on their own, He takes it all out on a gourd.
One shifting the blame:	A mother-in-law's toothache Burns the heel of her son-in-law.
One confusing the eyes:	Asking bald Li To wear bald Zhang's hat.
One full of his own importance:	A magistrate sets fires While forbidding commoners to light lamps.[12]

ACT 1

KIAI-LAI RHYME[13]

(*Actor playing Monk* ZHANG *enters wearing monk's garb and hat, and recites:*)
Who says a monk has no need for money?

With what will he buy his bare-shouldered shirt?
Our Buddha, born in Kingdoms to the West,
Even he needed saffron robes and that Jetavana Garden.

(*Speaks*:) I am a humble monk named Zhang of this county's Three Purities Monastery. People always say that those of us who've "left the home"[14] have fathers in the monasteries and mothers in the nunneries. But to send their kids and grandkids to live out their days in a monastery is real eternal torment! My younger comrade is called Monk Li. He's full of clever tricks but weighed down by lustful longings. It's because he left home as a child and didn't get his fill of "that flavor." But if he indulges himself, I'm afraid it will stir up a scandal. Better to lust after riches like me. I can get away with it and not break the pure laws too badly. Scrimping and saving till my clothes all hang loose, I've socked away a few private funds and bought back a vegetable garden my old master put into hock years ago. I haven't told Monk Li about this yet, though. The other day I sniffed some rouge and powder on his clothes, but I don't know where that little cat has been getting into something fishy. Come to think of it, one can't do much in this world without money, so maybe he's got a secret stash of his own. I might as well call him over and use a few clever words to entice him to invest in my garden. The only thing is, I'd rather not have to share the profits, so when the time comes, I can always fool him with a fake bill of goods and a few tricky maneuvers. With a fair and impartial mind like mine, who needs Buddha? (*Calls out*:) Little Brother, where are you?

(*Monk* LI, *wearing monk's clothes and bare-headed, enters in response*:) Here I am! Since shaving my head and entering the gate of emptiness,[15] I've slept snuggled up to a blanket all on my own. Oh, dear Buddha, you are just too cruel! If you ask me, old granddaddy Buddha, you'd better loosen these restrictions on us disciples of yours a bit, or else where will you get some new Buddha kids and grandkids?

(ZHANG, *aside, listens and laughs*:) Ah, no sooner do you open your mouth than you've touched on this topic. I knew there was something more to that rouge and powder I sniffed yesterday. (*Faces him*:) You were just talking about Buddha kids and grandkids, but since when have you ever heard of the Buddha having kids and grandkids?

(LI:) Well, if the Buddha had no kids and grandkids, then why do we call him "Grandfather Buddha" and "Patriarch Buddha?"

(ZHANG:) Oh, my little brother, you don't understand. Our great Buddhist forebears are just the patriarchs of our religion! Like how you're my "Little Brother" and I'm your "Older Brother"—we're brothers of different surnames who don't share the same blood—who ever said we all came from one ancestor? You listen to me. (*Sings*:)

(XIANLÜ MODE: *Dian jiangchun*)
Our Buddha from the west he came,
His teachings vast

And borderless.
With just his robes and begging bowl,
He founded
this
faith of personal transmission.[16]

(LI:) If Great-granddaddy Buddha didn't father us little Buddha kids and grandkids, then who did? (ZHANG *sings*:)

(*Hunjiang long*)
These
Smelly bags of skin and flesh
all start as
Fetuses grown from fathers' seed and mothers' blood.

(LI:) So how does the seed get planted to make these bodies? (ZHANG *sings*:) Through fated bonds of lust . . . (LI, *laughing*:) Marvelous! (ZHANG *sings*:) . . . the baby is created. (LI:) Fascinating! (ZHANG *sings*:)

Spending
Every day since as a Buddhist disciple,
Who remembers the
Three years it took to leave mama's breast?

(LI, *aside*:) Who doesn't know that people are born of a father and mother?! I was just trying to get those words out of him. I'll lure him in a little more. (*Faces*:) So, if we religious disciples are born of mothers and fathers, why don't we stay at home with them? (ZHANG:) You don't know (*sings*)

It's just because some are
Doomed by star-crossed fortunes of mothers and fathers,
Some are
Orphans whose parents have died.
They don't
Shave their heads and don their robes 'til then,
Hoping to
Extend their happiness and cut misfortune short.

(LI, *aside*:) That old, bald ass—he only left the home because his wife died, and he was poor. It sure wasn't because of either of those reasons he said. I'll go muddle him up one more time. (*Faces*:) Older Brother, truer words were never spoken. So, given that you and I are the sons of men, now that we are big and grown, shouldn't we become fathers to new sons in turn? (ZHANG:) Amitābha! (*Sings*:)

(*You hulu*[17])
How can you say
Such cruel and crushing words?

(LI:) Why did our parents give birth to us? (ZHANG *sings*:)

It was

Perfectly natural.

(LI:) How do you mean, natural? (ZHANG *sings*:)

Parents have

Three good reasons to hold their heads up high:

(LI:) Which three? (ZHANG *sings*:)

For one thing—having children and grandchildren carries on ancestors' blood,

For the other two—it both supports the household and is a service to the state.

(LI:) So now that you and I have left the home, how will we have kids? We're never sent out for private labor or public works. If everyone were like this wouldn't these two go left undone? (ZHANG *sings*:)

How can others compare to us,

Free from cycle of five material elements, and

Released from bonds of Heaven, Earth, and Man?

(*Speaks*:) It's the last one he keeps talking about. (*Sings*:)

He asks why

It's lucky to have a big brood,

But it's just one more

Aid to Heaven's grand design.

(LI:) He does make sense, after all. In our Buddhist community we could call it "mercy and expedient means" for all living creatures.[18] We should surely aid Heaven with acts of procreation.

(ZHANG:) But what makes monks and laypeople different? (*Sings*:)

(*Tianxia le*)

Where have you seen

An *uḍumbara* flower blooming among weeds,

Or a lotus pedestal next to King Xiang of Chu's terrace?[19]

Just like that—

A belt of conjugal bliss can't be tied 'round a monk's tattered robes.

(LI *secretly pulls out a fragrance pouch*:) Oh, but you've not yet seen this little gem of mine.

(ZHANG:) Don't say the Buddhist laws are too many, too strict, it's just that those fault-pickers would never forgive us. If they took us to court, we'd be in stockades for sure, I'm telling you! (*Sings*:)

A four-sided, square chunk of board,

With a big fat melon

growing right out of

the middle![20]

(*Speaks*:) All the great monks of old started from little monks like you and me.[21] Who knew a little monk could get a great monk caught up in such nonsense? (*Sings*:)

If that time should come, I'm afraid

This little monk would have no way to handle himself!

(LI, *aside*:) I'm sure you'll figure out something when the time comes. (*Faces*:) Though you say so, Older Brother, if you're going to call it "the Way," it should be found in all things at all times.

(ZHANG *laughs*:) There are many "Ways" one can follow in this world, why focus narrowly on just this one?

(LI:) Besides this one Way, what other way is there?

(ZHANG:) Wise Little Brother Li, have you never been all the way down it? The *Four Books* explain it well: I looked at it before me, and he presented his gift according to the Way; suddenly it was behind me, and he penetrated deeply through the Way. How could one seek and not find if he follows the Way? When he seeks consultation, he gains his heart's desire through the Way. He is not my disciple, yet he skillfully leads men on. Supplying everything from his own establishment, he proceeds smoothly with room to spare. If it seems there is not enough space, please give it a try; as you are about to enter the gate, guide him with your hand. He who advances swiftly and cannot stop with just an inch will furrow his brow and say, "Have you been pained?" Just gently, gently reply: "There's no place you can't reach," and your happy expression will say to him, "No pain!" One who is firm will consciously advance and purposefully retreat, giving it everything he can muster. It seems he will never stop. Those who lack that energy find a way to finish nicely, satisfied with good timing. If you want to enter again, you may simply ask: "I found joy within; is there anything that makes it different?" You will say, "It is a person, just the same!" (*Laughs*:) Having found the gate, you can't give it up even if you wanted to. Though some like it, none can claim to hate it. This is what is known as "the Way."[22]

(LI *laughs*:) Marvelous! Marvelous! That is one sort of "Way," indeed! (*Aside*:) Ah hah, so this villainous baldy is thinking of treading the dry path since his watery path has come to an end . . . (*Faces* ZHANG *and sighs*:) That I am unable to walk this path with you is fate. But those laymen are really too much! Besides their wives, they've also got concubines. Besides their concubines, they've also got servant girls. If they become used to this Way only, those lay wives of theirs must surely get jealous. Why, then, should we deprive them of the opportunity to use their Ways?

(ZHANG:) This is why "Each follows his own way." Some share it generously with the world, while others spend it all on themselves. This is what is meant by "Those whose ways are different cannot lay plans for one another."

(LI *laughs*:) Even more marvelous. I have heard many people speak of "the Way," but never have I heard anything this entertaining. Marvelous! Marvelous! The other day another thing happened to me in front of the local county seat, where I noticed that the clothes and cap of our district magistrate were unkempt. He was about to run outside when his old lady caught up with him and dragged him right back in by the ear. I could only hear him shout, "My Lady, let me save a little face here!" and I also heard the lady saying, "Shithead! Who told you to go filching servant girls?" Hitting and scolding him, she dragged him back inside. My brother, given that such pain is to be found on the Way, wouldn't it be better not to tread it at all? What need is there to be so serious in pursuit of the Way? Why not just watch from afar?

(ZHANG *laughs*:) This is because our district magistrate walked the wrong way. He has many underlings with him in his hall. If he were willing to follow the Way we were just talking about, how could he run into such trouble? The logic of our Way is impeccable; his certainly can't compare.

(LI:) Though he can't compare with us in pursuit of this Way (*extends arm in grasping motion*), that sword of his is far greater than yours or mine! When it comes to building a house or planting a field, such things are a lot easier for someone like him!

(ZHANG:) Who cares what kind of buildings he builds? They can't compare to our grand Buddha halls. No matter how much land he buys, it couldn't be greater than our "incense estates." (LI:) Where are these incense estates of ours? (*Sings*:)

(*Cunli yagu*)

Speaking of our
Estates back in the day:
Well, they really were a sight to see.
Field after field and row after row,
Who'd expect they'd all vanish without a trace?

(LI:) But why is that? (ZHANG *sings*:)

It's only because we
Let everything go to seed,
Courting misfortunes great and small,
That we met our deserved decay.

(LI:) I'd like to hear the details. (ZHANG *sings*:)

A long-time love for gambling games,
A greed for drink,
And a passion for chasing skirts.

(LI:) What playboys! (ZHANG *sings*:)

But how can a shiny-headed one
Have in him the bones of a playboy?

(LI:) Older Brother, our master must surely have known the Way we just spoke of, so why did he go chasing skirts?

(ZHANG:) If he didn't know, how could he have fooled around with my dear little brother?

(LI *laughs*:) I've added it to my account book. Before a little brother, the older came first.

(ZHANG:) Your older brother only left the home after the death of his wife, so don't you think I can get a free pass?

(LI, *aside*:) That bald ass let the cat out of the bag! (*Faces*:) So would you, Older Brother, like to taste that old flavor of home today? (ZHANG *sings*:)

(*Yuanhe ling*)

It's precisely because I've had my

Fill of that flavor

That I've paid it no heed ever since.

(LI:) How fortunate you've driven it from your mind! (ZHANG *sings*:)

It's not that my

Embers have cooled, or my heart grown hard as petrified wood,

It's just that

I have no such karma, no such plans.

(LI:) If embers don't cool off completely, one fears they'll light up again. If an old stump isn't petrified, there's always a chance it'll sprout once more.

(ZHANG:) I thought this way at first, but now that my pockets are empty, I don't think I could spread my love here and there like our master, even if I wanted to. Wise Little Brother, I think you're stronger and harder than most!

(LI, *aside*:) Damn, that old ass's still insinuating.

(ZHANG:) Though many fear a monk's life is hard and won't send new disciples along, I feel my spear gradually losing its thrust and my horse its speed. Even that Way of mine is feeling rather sad. (*Sings*:)

And that's why

I've carefully followed vegetarian laws,

Living a pure life these past several years.

(LI:) It sounds as if my older brother has relinquished both Ways. You may have done so, but I just can't. Perhaps I'm just lacking your spirit of the Way.

(ZHANG, *aside*:) His true intent is gradually revealed. (*Faces*:) Well, who can blame you? It's because you've never tasted this flavor that you can hardly help but indulge yourself a bit first. Because I've been through so many hardships, I've come to prefer following the rules and going into business.

(LI:) You're at it again, Older Brother. Given that we monks don't have any fields to plow nor stuff to sell, how can we go into business?

(ZHANG:) How to go into business, well (*sings*)

(*Shangma jiao*)

Fir tree planks from Sichuan and

Timber pine from up north,

They use them when they're busy,

I buy when they are idled.

I make some monk's shoes or

Even pickles when I can.

(LI:) Yes indeed, these are all ways to make money. (ZHANG *sings*:)

Ai! But now

Where will we get the capital funds?

(LI:) Well, since I don't have much capital to plant a garden, we'd better round some up too bad our garden is in hock.

(ZHANG, *aside*:) That bald ass is gradually falling into my trap. (*Faces*:) Wise Little Brother, since you've got a little capital to invest, why worry about no garden to plant? I won't keep it secret—I've already borrowed some cash from my relatives to buy back the garden. It's just the planting and the fertilizing—we need someone to do the work. If you're willing to put your trust in me, Wise Little Brother, and invest some of that capital of yours, I'll split the profits fair and square. We'll gradually build up our funds this way, and though we can't fully recuperate the glory of old, it will certainly be enough for some "expedient means." What do you think, Wise Little Brother?

(LI, *aside*:) Oh, so he's already redeemed the garden property. It's only because I've spent so much time at her place and so little time in the temple of late that I didn't look into it carefully. He shouldn't try to fool me. I've seen relatives of his come by several times. I'll have some fun at his expense. (*Faces*:) I will follow your lead and trust my fate to your hands.

(ZHANG, *aside*:) That ass's fallen right into my plan. (*Faces*:) I'm sure you'll make back the principle plus interest in no time!

(LI:) This little brother will put his trust in you, but I wonder what kind of vegetables we will plant?

(ZHANG:) Well, we need to discuss this together.

(LI:) What about swallow's nest?

(ZHANG:) That comes from the seashore. We can't plant it.

(LI:) What about chicken palm?

(ZHANG:) That's a product of Yunnan. We can't grow it here.

(LI:) What about monkey's head or lamb's belly?

(ZHANG:) Those two are also not native to the area. We won't be able to grow them.

(LI:) What about chicken's legs mushrooms or quail eggplants? (ZHANG *laughs and sings*:)

(*Sheng hulu*)

Oh, why do you only want
Plants with meat in their names?

(LI:) I was hoping to satisfy my cravings with the unsold part. (ZHANG *sings*:)

I guessed
You were hoping to quench your thirst looking at pictures of plums.[23]

(*Speaks*:) Wise Little Brother, these two are just vegetables with meat in the name, how will they satisfy your cravings?

(LI *spits*:) Oh, if they're not going to scratch my itch, what to do? Chicken legs! Quails! When will I know your flavors? Thinking about these makes me want some garlic and scallions to go with them.

(ZHANG:) Garlic and scallions are two of the five pungent flavorings. They are not appropriate for us monks to grow.[24] If you ask me, we ought to just grow some cucumbers.

(LI:) No good, their masculine energy gets spent too quickly and they grow soft.

(ZHANG *laughs*:) Hey there, as a monk you should want your cucumber to be soft.

(LI:) Don't worry about that.

(ZHANG:) What about kidney beans?

(LI:) Not as good as a budding cardamom[25] to whet the appetite. Better to be virtuous and walk the straight and narrow, planting a few scallions and garlic. If someone asks about it, I'll say I sell them but don't eat them. That way we can get away with it all day long.

(ZHANG *claps*:) Marvelous! (*Sings*:)

This

Brilliant plan of yours is truly worth applauding.

(*Speaks*:) Hearing this logical discourse of yours (*sings*)

It's like

I've been called back from a dream!

Or found a hand to scratch my itch.

As if Heaven's

Blessed this enterprise of ours.

(LI:) Older Brother, while we have a free moment, then, why don't we go survey the garden?

(ZHANG:) Certainly. (*They walk.*) We've arrived already. Please go ahead of me, Wise Little Brother.

(LI:) I wouldn't dare exceed my station.

(ZHANG:) This is just a small garden.

(LI:) If you insist. (*Aside*:) This land is fit for a feudal lord! Since you've gone to the trouble of buying it back, how can you call it a small garden? Just what Zhang family are you from? Thankfully, I haven't fallen into his trap yet. (*Walking ahead and pointing toward* ZHANG:) Aren't these garlic and scallions? (ZHANG *sings a reprise*:)

These are all things

Planted by the old owner.

(LI:) I'm not sure people will believe you. (ZHANG *sings*:)

I also feared

People would say it was our ilk.

(*Speaks*:) Who wanted to sell them at the lowest price. (*Sings*:)

Once the

Fields are empty we'll quickly change them.

(LI:) Now that we've decided we still need to plant, why bother switching things up? (*Points*:) This eggplant won't satisfy anyone's cravings, why plant it?

(ZHANG:) These were also planted by the old owner. I was planning on plucking one and splitting it with you to eat. (*Sings*:)

Even if

They can't satisfy our hunger,

The least we can do is give them to guests.

(LI:) Good enough. (*Points.*) That trellis over there—it looks like it's made for gourds.

(ZHANG:) Since people always call us monks "melon heads," would I really dare to grow gourds? It's just a few loofah gourds is all.

(LI:) If it were a grape trellis and it came crashing down on us how would we handle it?[26]

(ZHANG:) It's been a long time since my poor wife passed away, and you and I aren't walking the path of that county magistrate, so what would be the harm (*sings*) Even if it collapsed right in our faces?

(ZHANG, *aside*:) That villainous baldy's got his eye on my many trellises. Since I haven't yet borrowed his silver, how can I let him catch a glimpse of my precious winter melons? I'd better try to keep him here. (*Faces*:) That wall is the bean arbor—the cardamom buds have just begun to open. I'm worried you'll see them and get excited, so you'd better not go over there. Why don't you just take a rest here by the loofah gourds?

(LI:) Perfect. (*Points*:) Those squash blossoms are blooming quite nicely, but if there are too many, the fruits themselves won't get big. Maybe I should pick a few and give them a try to see if the water in this garden's any good.

(ZHANG:) Since you're not worried about a softening masculine principle, why don't we call the workman to pick some for you? (*Calls*:)

(*Actor dressed as* WORKMAN *enters*:) Master, what can I do for you?

(ZHANG:) Could you pluck a handful of these loofah gourd flowers and cook them for my little brother here to enjoy?

(WORKMAN *exits.*)

(LI, *aside*:) That ass, all day he's been trying to trick me, yet he's also been quite cheap. I'll trim his grass and pull him up by the root. (*Faces*:) If we eat these flowers all by themselves it seems like a bit of a waste. I've got a jar of nice, light wine that might go well with them. What do you think?

(ZHANG:) Oh, how could I let you spend the money?

(LI:) No need to spend any. Someone borrowed some money from me and gave me some wine in lieu of interest; that's where I got it from.

(ZHANG:) Oh, this foolish older brother of yours will surely pay you back with interest, whether in monthly installments or one lump sum, it will all be there. I would never stint on what's right.

(LI:) You're too kind.

(WORKMAN *returns*:) Here are the flowers.

(LI *offers wine to* ZHANG *and* ZHANG *drinks several cups*; LI, *aside*:) He can't give up a single eggplant, but now he's downed three cups of wine. This is a trap, like Empress Lü's banquet.[27] I can't swallow this.

(ZHANG:) Why aren't you drinking, Little Brother?

(LI:) I think I'd like a nice, long scallion to go with my wine, so I haven't started in yet.

(ZHANG:) What's the problem with a little, old scallion? Even three or four such stalks would be no big deal. Workman, hear my command. (*Sings*:)

(*Houting hua*)

Quickly, you

Wipe off those dipping sauce plates,

And hurry and pick a few scallions.

Wash the leaves real good,

And even

That fuzzy root, please clean it well, too.[28]

(LI *laughs*:) If it's this much work to clean, I guess we can't sell them too lightly! (ZHANG *sings*:)

Don't you

Just idly guess—

it's all a part of

My Buddhist vows,

Which say

Happiness comes to those who indulge in it rightly.

(WORKMAN *arrives with a scallion*; LI *rubs his head and shouts*:) Dammit! Dammit! Look here! (*Points to the top of his head*:) It feels like something drilled a hole through the top of my head!

(ZHANG *laughs*:) Shiny and naked with a hole in the middle, what does that remind you of?

(WORKMAN *looks*:) It's a wasp sting.

(LI:) Wasp?

(WORKMAN *points*:) It must be that one sitting over there on that seed gourd.

(LI:) That seed gourd looks like a lazy elephant's big, grey ballsack.[29] Let me go smash that wasp to let off some steam. (*Motions to move.*)

(ZHANG *looks flustered*:) Oh, what'll I do if he catches sight of my winter melons?

(LI, *aside*:) Oh, so on these trellises over here are a bunch of big winter melons. No wonder he didn't want me coming over here to look at them. Winter melons, winter melons, if not for my chasing the wasp, how would I have met thee? Soon you'll be mine! (*Faces* ZHANG:) Older Brother, those winter melons on that wall over there are growing quite well; how did you plant and water them? (ZHANG *sings*:)

I carefully spaced them, together and apart.

(LI:) Well, no wonder. (*Aside*:) The scallions and garlic are so little, but he insists the old owner planted them. Meanwhile, the winter melons are so big, but he babbles about growing them himself. He'll give himself away if I give him a start. He's been drinking, so it'll be easy for sure. (*Faces*:) Have you counted them?

(ZHANG:) How could I not? (*Sings*:)

I have the number clear in my memory.

(LI:) Why is that? (ZHANG *sings*:)

After a few days
I'll carry them to the roadside
And trade for rice and kindling.
You and I'll
Close up the gates nice and tight,
Strain some wine real well,
And
Drink till our hats hang crooked,
Drink till our hats hang crooked!

(LI:) Older Brother, it's easy for you to talk about drinking your hat crooked while a bare-headed one like myself suffers angry stings!

(ZHANG:) What happened to your hat?

(LI, *aside*:) Feh! I've spoken too quickly. I left my hat as a pledge with her, but how to explain? I'll make up a story to scare him off the trail. (*Faces*:) Oh, don't bring it up again—that day I passed by the county seat and witnessed the squabble between the magistrate and his old lady—I could hardly count how many people came gathering round to gawk. In the confusion somebody made off with my hat. I've been so angry about it these past two days I've shut myself in at home drinking.

(ZHANG *laughs*:) Though the top of your head is lacking a little something, you've added quite a lot to your belly. You must really have it made to drink such fine wine day in and day out!

(LI:) The wine I've been drinking isn't what I'd call "fine." That wine I got as interest on a loan you asked about was several times better to be sure. That stuff was good for drinking hot or cold. This wine can't beat that one for drinking cold, but if you heat it up it's even better.

(ZHANG:) Well why didn't you say so! Let's heat some up and give it a try.

(LI, *aside*:) He's fallen into my trap! I've got a knockout drug right here. (*Pours it into wine; turns to face* ZHANG:) I've got the wine warmed up now. Please quickly give it a taste.

(ZHANG *drinks*:) You're right. This wine is delicious warm—spicy and flavorful! Wonderful! Wonderful!

(LI *offers wine to* WORKMAN:) You should also have a cup of this fragrant brew. (WORKMAN *drinks.*) (LI *pours himself a bowl, drinks, spits it out, and pretends to fall to the ground in a drunken stupor.*) (WORKMAN *tries to support* LI, *but the two collapse together.*) (LI *rises and points at* ZHANG, *laughing*:) Bald ass! Are you still going to tease me for being austere? Or tell how our master diddled me? Do you still think my words are crushing and cruel? I'm going to pick all your melons and hide them at my gal's place. What will you barter for your rice and kindling then? You can't even spare half an eggplant; scallions you only call for two or three. How will you like it when you wake up and find your melon trellis empty? I'll make sure that if you stick out that money-grubbing head of yours it ends up in a copper cangue![30] (*Leaves and then rushes back on stage.*) The melons are all picked and stored up for safekeeping. And those two fools are sleeping! But if they get up too late, they might get suspicious. I'd better wake them with a splash of water. (*Splashes water.*) (LI *resumes his fake drunken sleep as the two gradually wake up.*)

(ZHANG:) Little Brother, what great wine this is! Oh, he's still out like a light. Ah, laying on the ground, look how he's messed up his clothing. Workman, help me wake him up (*calls to* LI.)

(LI *pretends to talk in his sleep*:) Lady, let me off the hook! (LI *rouses, eyes closed*:) Oh Reverend Lady, I dare not do it again! (*Blinking eyes, pretends to be embarrassed; bows to* ZHANG:) Oh, thank you, Older Brother, for saving me!

(ZHANG:) Wise Little Brother, it sounds like you were just getting into it with a lady when we tactlessly disturbed you. Why do you thank us?

(LI:) What lady?

(ZHANG:) The workman here heard it all too. Why deny? Could it be that you met our old master's mistress in a dream?

(LI:) I've never met her in real life, so how could I meet her in a dream?

(ZHANG:) Maybe it was that lady who was beating on the county magistrate?

(LI *shakes his head*:) No, that lady wasn't as cruel as this one. If you hadn't woken me, Older Brother, I would have continued to suffer.

(ZHANG:) Suffer what?

(LI *sighs*:) Here's how it went: when I fell asleep in my drunkenness, I saw an old man with white whiskers, white hair, and a cane. He said something I couldn't hear and a big, tall lady in clothes not quite black and not quite white came walking out of the garden. Behind her were several young beauties in greenish yellow dresses, followed by a throng of young boys and girls of about seven or eight years, some in blue and some in green, each a slightly different color. Each of them took turns kowtowing to that old man. The ancient one said, "You are all going to suffer the disaster of being killed within the next few days." Everyone burst out crying, pleading with the ancient one to save them.

(ZHANG:) Save them, but how could he save them?

(LI:) That group of beautiful ladies all cried in a very charming and elegant way, so much so that they moved me to tears myself. The old man just shook his head, though, and said, "Their minds are made up and it's been planned for quite some time. Soon they'll take you to market to trade for rice and kindling before locking themselves up at home to drink; what can I do to save you?" Then the whole group began crying again and the big lady took the old man by the shoulders, angrily shouting, "Being traded for rice in the market is our proper destiny, but locking oneself up indoors and drinking, how is that appropriate behavior for monks? If you, our great holy master, do not save us, then these bald asses will just keep defiling the sacred precepts more and more." The old man nodded his head, saying, "You speak the truth, but how do you expect me to save you?" The big lady said, "Better to have them make their way to a different garden; though they will not escape the coming disaster, at least it will foil the rotten plans of those corrupt monks." The ancient one happily said, "Alright, as you say, as you say. You and these beauties may go." The big lady then said, "Your Holiness, please show your compassion to this whole group." The old man said, "That monk still understands the need to 'indulge rightly.' They can't all go—you just worry about yourself." So saying, he got up and swaggered off.

(ZHANG:) And what about the rest of the group?

(LI:) The group of beauties all bowed to the big lady and said, "Thank you, Auntie, for your efforts on our behalf. Please allow us to go on ahead." The big lady angrily exclaimed, "You can go, but I'm staying." The beauties said, "You have spoken expedient means for us, so how can you stay to suffer baldy's anger?" The lady said, "You think he'd dare lose his temper with me? The sage spoke rightly. Am I a bitter gourd to be hung up out of the way of being eaten?[31] He won't eat me, anyway, because I've got little ones in my belly. Would he dare cut off the sprout of his own seed? That bald ass, he's waking from his drunkenness—quickly, all of you get out of here!" Hearing this, that group of beauties all scattered to the four corners, but this little monk caught sight of one of the most beautiful of the group and tried to give her a hug. She called out for help and that big lady came running over and grabbed my hair. With those fourteen-inch golden lotuses[32] of hers she kicked and kicked. I said, "I've got no quarrel with you, Auntie!" She said, "You say you have no quarrel, but didn't you just call me an elephant's ballsack to that workman? How about I give those balls of yours a few good kicks!" (LI *cries*:) Look and tell me: Are there no new bruises on my body? Is there still hair on my head?

(ZHANG:) Your head looks even shinier than before, though there is still a little hole in it. It sounds like that lady got mad at you for comparing her to an elephant's ballsack. She must have been a gourd fairy.

(LI *pretends to be shocked*:) Gourds can become fairies?

(WORKMAN:) I suspected earlier that you shouldn't have made such a crude comparison. Who was the ancient one?

(ZHANG:) It must have been the earth god of the garden.

(WORKMAN:) Why do you say that?

(ZHANG:) White hair and a cane and everyone calling him "Your Holiness"—what could he be but the earth god himself?

(LI:) You're right. His clothing and head wrap sure had that look. But what about those beauties? (ZHANG:) Hmm, I can't think of a good answer right now. (LI *pretends to think*:) What if they were the spirits of the winter melons?

(ZHANG:) What makes you think that?

(LI:) What beauty in this world doesn't powder her face like a white winter melon? For a winter melon to become a beauty, then, is not so strange.

(WORKMAN:) Indeed! This interpretation is quite logical. Their clothing was not quite yellow, not quite green—sounds like the color of a winter melon to me! When we think of it this way, those other boys and girls must have been the spirits of the eggplants and beans.

(ZHANG *looks flustered*:) Since the beauties dispersed, that makes me worry about my winter melons. Let's go have a look. (*Runs and looks surprised*:) Oh no! They really have gone and left me! What about the eggplants, the loofah gourds, the beans, the scallions, and the garlic? Quick, workman, go take a look!

(WORKMAN *turns around*:) They are all still in their places, and I found this one melon by the side of the field ridge.

(LI, *aside*:) I do recall dropping one of them. Since I was in a hurry, I didn't go back to pick it up. I almost let them catch sight of the horse tracks. (*Faces*:) Looks like this melon was leaving by this path—good thing I decided to hug one of those beauties, pinning down its material form and preventing it from leaving. (*Moving to embrace the melon*:) Oh, my beauty, who told you to cry out so? (ZHANG *points at melon and sings*:)

(*Liuye'er*)

Oh, melons!
I treated you as precious treasures,
Fixed you high on trellises, supporting you with care,
Watered in the morning and tended in the evening,
I worked so hard, I hoped to fill up a whole cart—
You'd be stacked so high!
Who knew you'd
Cruelly disappear into the dust?

(ZHANG *speaks*:) This is the fault of that old earth spirit. Knowing I was grasping after happiness, he couldn't help but ask them to go away to teach me about wrongful clinging.

(LI:) It's a good thing that ancient one had his head on straight. If he had listened to that gourd fairy, even the eggplants and beans would have left too. (ZHANG:) You're right. (*Sings*:)

(*Qingge'er*)

Oh, you
Naughty Gourd Fairy, Gourd Fairy,
Who sent my melons off
Beyond Ninth Heaven's ninth cloud,
What grudge did I
Ever give you cause to bear?

(*Speaks*:) It's one thing not to persuade my melons to stay, but you incited them to leave and even urged them on! I'm suffering so badly while you're perfectly contented. Oh, you rotten gourd fairy! (*sings*)

Why
Won't you explain?
You're making me
Pull at my ears and claw my face.
(*Starts plucking*:) I'll pluck up all your roots!
(LI:) You're going to hurt your hands.
(ZHANG *hits and sings*:) I'll smash your mortal frames!
(LI:) How sad their seed will not pass on. (ZHANG *sings*:)
But
Even if I scattered each seed 'til green moss dotted over,
It would not be enough to
Relieve my frustration.
(ZHANG, *crying, sings*:)
(*Jisheng cao*)
How the times are unlucky,
My fate so perverse!
Oh, melons,
You were hanging so beautifully arranged just this morning,
But in the blink of an eye
You mysteriously dissolve.
Oh, Gourd Fairy, your unexpected
Slander's just too cold and cruel.
(LI:) I've still got my capital funds; maybe you should plant again in the future, Older Brother? (ZHANG *sings*:)
Even if
New roots and sprouts began today,
How long before I
Carry my pole to market for sale?
(LI:) The wine's still not finished, why don't I pour you another cup and we can drown our sorrows? (ZHANG *sings a medley cadence*:)
Even were it
Liquid jade, my mouth would find it hard to open.
(LI:) In that case, I think you should return to your meditation chambers. (ZHANG *sings*:)
On this
Ruined garden my feet are too tired to tread.
(LI:) You shouldn't have exerted yourself so attacking that seed gourd—you've worn yourself out. (ZHANG *sings*:)
It's not that
I wanted to exhaust my energy,
But how could
I help but curse these things to hell!

(LI:) The two of us will help take you home. (ZHANG *sings*:)

Even if you support me,

My footsteps are pained.

(*Speaks*:) But stop, Workman, pick up that spade for me and strike another thousand blows on those damned gourd roots!

(LI:) Older Brother, why do you want to molest it so?

(ZHANG:) There are many good reasons to be angry. It encouraged my melons to run off; that would have been enough. But it just lazily stuck around. It's clearly trying to bully me. I'll cut off its line of descent—why not? I'd be better off wandering around beating a drum, clanging some cymbals, and singing about the theory of karma; it couldn't be worse than planting a garden. (*Sings*:)

You

Caused my melons to run away,

Playing tricks to get the best of me,

While you yourself

Stand tall and proud to bully me.

About the ones that are gone

there's

nothing to be done,

Go ahead and sue if you dare!

We'll see

If any court would convict!

(*Throws his hat down in anger.*) (LI *secretly picks up hat and hides it in his sleeve as he and* WORKMAN *support* ZHANG *and exit.*)

ACT 2

KIAŊ-IAŊ RHYME

(LI, *carrying a monk's hat, enters, laughing*:) When a man has a good intention, Heaven will surely support him. Ever since my dearest took possession of my hat, my head's been suffering for lack of an outdoor covering. Lucky for me, I played such a trick on Monk Zhang yesterday that he collapsed in a rage and dropped his hat. I secretly picked it up. (*Puts it on.*) Now this hat's got Li's name on it, I'd say![33] Last night I was planning to go out, but Zhang started talking crazy and desperate, so I could only stick around and try to calm him down. He's relaxed a bit now and is lying down in his room. I'll take the opportunity to go out and see my dearest. For one, it'll be a bit of fun, for two, I can unload some of those melons I got yesterday. This part may be risky, so I'll bring along some paper talismans to burn and attain my aim. Third, I can get back my old hat (*points at his head*)—this is all thanks to you.

(*Exits.*)

(*Actress playing Wang Jidi's* WIFE *enters and recites*:)

A form like a flower and a figure like jade,
I am driven to secret delight by making love in the night.
Though Ānanda resisted temptation and entered emptiness at last,
I only laugh that Mātaṅgī's daughter lacked the proper skills.[34]

I am the wife of Wang Jidi, Madame Wu. Looking over the face in the mirror, I see I can compare with the best of them. I never expected when I married Wang Jidi that he would turn out so sly and ugly, such an extraordinary good-for-nothing. What a shame for a juicy lamb's meat morsel to fall in the mouth of a dog. This is really all my parents' fault. From ancient times it's been said: "Match the wife to the husband." But even if you didn't see your future son-in-law's adult actions the least you could have done was to take a closer look at your daughter's inborn talents—just who do they think I am? (*Sings*:)

(ZHONGLÜ MODE: *Fen die'er*)

Oh, I am the
Devil Queen[35] of the flower troupe,
Showing my romantic charm, the first one into battle.
I've always been elegant from the time I was little,
Even better now that
I'm adept with brush and makeup.
For my skills in teasing banter
The possibilities are endless!
I can't help but
Resent
that
foolish mom and dad of mine,
For not
Finding me a better match.

(*Zui chunfeng*)

Leaving me to
Stare at my reflection alone in self pity;
If you ask me to
Tie up the monkey of my mind, he only grows the stronger.[36]
Idly, I drop hints
to
several passionate lads,
I can't help but think . . .

(*speaks*) how hard it is to find someone whose insides match the out. (*Sings*:)

The elegant ones lack the talent,
Those with a strong arm have a limp wrist,
Still others talk a good game but never back it up.

(*Speaks:*) I guess none of them can compare to Monk Li, after all. People say there are three advantages to living with a monk: One, they don't blab; two, they won't leave you; three, they don't tire out. I never used to believe it, but now I know it really hits the nail on the head. (*Sings:*)

(*Tuo bushan*)
He's outwardly fun and carefree,
But inwardly
still
tough and firm.
When I'm hungry for it he gets it on,
A handsome figure with tricks up his sleeve.

(*Speaks:*) The other day I was worried he'd miss our appointment, so I took hold of his hat as a guarantee. And glimpsed (*Sings:*)

(*Xiao Liangzhou*)
The blackish blue of that shiny, newly shaved head,
Dabbed with
Pine seed ointment, fragrant and fresh.

(*Speaks:*) No good for him to leave his hat, and he wouldn't dare ask for it back, so he'll just have to go bare-headed! (*Sings:*)

One can see his
Warm, romantic bearing is common,
But I gaze at him with mercy,
And call him my
Hairless King Xiang of Chu.

(*Speaks:*) Yesterday he came by and left a bunch of melons here in a rush. He spoke only a few words and ran off. He didn't come back that night, and I don't know what he's after. He's got me worried, indeed. (*Sings reprise:*)

In matters of love there should be no distance,
But the way things are now sure puts me ill at ease.
He left me to
Keep these safe and hidden,
Idly worrying on my own,
Yet lets slip a little lack of concern.
Would he dare scatter our brocade mandarin ducks?[37]

(*Speaks:*) When he shows up, I'll ask a few more questions. I'm sure he'll come by soon.

(LI *knocks on the door, bows, and enters.*) (WIFE *remains silent.*) (LI *acts flustered:*) I guess you're upset with me for running off yesterday without spending time with you. It's perfectly understandable. (*Kneels.*) (WIFE *sings:*)

(*Shang xiaolou*)
What's all this prancing in front of my face,

There
Must be someone else at your side!

(LI:) Since when did I ever have anyone else? Only Heaven can attest to the purity of my heart. (WIFE *sings*:)

For your sake
I've bitten my lip,
Cut a lock of blue-black hair,[38]
And bestowed on you a fragrant sachet.

(LI, *aside*:) Yet you've not yet burned your incense marks.[39] (*Faces her and takes out the fragrant sachet.*) And I've got your black locks stored up safely with the sutras, and your fragrant sachet on my person at all times. (WIFE *sings*:)

You look
At just this one,
And think
Of these other two.
Yet still
You plan to toss me aside?
Ai!
Truly there are no merciful monks in this world.

(LI:) If I, a humble monk, should forsake my passionate love, may hungry demons torment me for all eternity.

(WIFE:) Since you're willing to offer these big-time vows, I guess you're being straight with me. (LI *rises to thank her.*) (WIFE:) But I've got to ask you, why didn't you come yesterday morning?

(LI:) Because I didn't have my hat.

(WIFE:) Since you left the other evening with your head bare and shiny, why couldn't you come back yesterday morning?

(LI:) The other evening was simple; yesterday morning was hard. If my shiny head could go back and forth at will, what would be the point of your hanging on to my hat, babe?

(WIFE:) When you brought over those melons yesterday, I didn't see you wearing a hat.

(LI:) That time my mind was on melons, so I forgot to cover up my gourd. But today I've specially got hold of this one to hurry over and see you.

(WIFE *laughs*:) Where did you get this other hat? (LI:) It's my older brother's. The melons are his too.

(WIFE:) Since you've stolen his things, you better think of a way to get rid of them and scat. It's a good thing that bastard of mine didn't come home last night—if he had seen them, what would I have done?

(LI:) I was hoping, my dear, that you could help me unload these. (WIFE *sings reprise*:)

This fellow's not so clever,
He offers not to share the bounty,

While asking me
To handle it for him.
How can I keep a secret?
How'll I keep it under wraps?
You're
Too hot-headed,
Too much in a hurry.
With no wisdom in your head,
You push all your problems onto me to unload.

(*Inspects* LI*'s hat*:) This hat is unattractive. Not as nice as your own.

(LI:) They're not very different.

(WIFE:) Oh, maybe you're just wearing it wrong. Come over here and I'll straighten it out for you.

(LI:) "Messy clothing is the fault of one's lover"—truer words were never spoken! (*Walks forward.*) (WIFE *steals the hat and hides it in her sleeves.*)

(LI *pleads for it back*:) Okay, then, I'll leave this hat with you, my dear, if you give me back the old one from the other day.

(WIFE:) Oh, that one—I just happen to have it stowed away right over there.

(LI:) Why don't you take it out and show it to me, then? (WIFE:) What's the rush? I'll give it to you when you leave.

(MOTHER-IN-LAW *enters, covering her mouth and moaning*:) Oh, my toothache is acting up again; when it does this, I've no place to run. I'll just go on over to my daughter's house and look for her there. Here we are already. (*Knocks on gate.*) (LI *looks frightened.*)

(WIFE:) That way of knocking didn't sound like him. What are you afraid of? Just hide over here and listen.

(*Opens gate,* MOTHER-IN-LAW *enters.*) (WIFE, *speaking loudly*:) Oh, it IS you, mother! (LI:) Oh, no worries in that case. (*Comes out and greets her.*)

(MOTHER-IN-LAW:) Who's this young man?

(LI:) I'm a preceptor from Mandarin Duck Temple.

(WIFE:) He came here to sell winter melons.

(MOTHER-IN-LAW:) If you're selling winter melons, don't scoop the beans out of my daughter's pod to take care of your own gourd sprouts.

(WIFE:) Your words are too serious, mother. This young master here is quite skilled in the medical arts. He is good at treating toothaches. I was just about to set out a vegetarian meal to treat him in return for a prescription for your pain.

(MOTHER-IN-LAW *looks happy*:) Oh, it's a good thing I came over, then. This little dodge of mine has brought me right to a young master of dentistry. What luck! (WIFE *sings*:)
(*Manting fang*)
This young man's

Knowledge is wide and deep,
He just has to work a little magic
To stimulate the hardest-to-reach places.

(WIFE *eyes* LI.)

(LI:) I can't fool you. This young monk is quite good at treating ailments of the mouth and teeth. I'm also an expert gynecologist. Whether a cloistered young lady deep in a boudoir or an elderly white-haired matron, my hands always get to the root of the problem. (WIFE, *facing* LI, *sings*:)

But once
You've plucked that root,
Just a smile and everything's better.
I'll expend my utmost on your vegetarian provisions.

(LI:) Herbs cure nonfatal illness; Buddha transforms those whose time has come—how could I accept payment? (WIFE *sings*:)

Though it's not a deadly disease,
The pain—it
Can last for days.
Now that fate's brought you here
how dare I not
open my purse?

(LI:) No need for thanks. Just tell your friends. (WIFE *sings*:)

As I take a closer look, yours is truly the face of Buddha.
I'll surely
Spread your name far and wide.

(MOTHER-IN-LAW:) Truly, Young Master, it's my daughter's filial heart, your compassionate mercy, and my fortunate karma that have brought you here today. Please, tell me your prescription.

(LI, *aside*:) I know fuck-all about fixing teeth! I only remember my master saying that for all types of tooth pain one should burn moxa on the *lüxu* bone. What is a *lüxu* anyway? I guess he must have meant *nüxu* [son-in-law].[40] If I tell her about this, it would be an act of secret merit. (*Whispers to himself*:) Wait a minute; this is no good. Her son-in-law has bones all over his body. How will I find the right bone for burning? I know! I'll just burn any fucking nonlethal spot. (*Turns to face* MOTHER-IN-LAW:) Old bodhisattva, this prescription is one that others don't know—it's very special, but suitable for use on an old Buddha like yourself. (WIFE *sings*:)

(*Kuaihuo san*)
Oh, rare and miraculous prescription from far away,
You reveal yourself in this humble abode,
Right in front of our eyes.
Just this one young lady
faced with her

poor old mum.

(*Speaks*:) Where is the medicine? (*Sings*:)

And so on and so forth,

that's all I can

come up with right now.

(LI:) No need for anything special, just something on the person of your fine son-in-law.

(MOTHER-IN-LAW:) Could it be ox's knee?[41]

(LI:) No.

(WIFE:) Could it be tortoise shell?

(LI:) It's not that either. All we need is for your gracious son-in-law to extend his foot for us.

(WIFE:) Why would you want a stinky old thing like that?

(LI:) We need only apply heat three times to his heel. And then, my old bodhisattva, your venerable tooth will feel the fire subside and all the pain will stop!

(WIFE *laughs*:) Burn which leg?

(LI:) When a man is sick, we use the left side; when a lady, the right.

(WIFE:) Have you tried this prescription before?

(LI:) This little monk has burned for both wife and mother before—it's really quite miraculous.

(MOTHER-IN-LAW:) Oh, so you only left the home later in life?

(LI, *aside*:) Oops, I've spoken too quickly and almost . . . (*Faces and laughs*:) My older brother was so, but not me. You must have misheard. Years ago, I had a neighbor called Mother Qi, and she suffered from tooth pain even greater than that of your worthy self. It was this little monk who taught her this method. With just a little bit of heat on her nephew-in-law, Little Zeng, we cured her fiery tooth pain for many years to this day.[42]

(WIFE *laughs*:) What about her son-in-law?

(LI:) If it was so successful with him, it will be even more so with a son-in-law. But with the correct prescription one must know the right method for moxibustion.

(WIFE:) What is that method?

(LI:) Though this method of mine uses incense to burn, what I'm burning's not moxa, but paper talismans.[43]

(WIFE:) Why talismans?

(LI:) These are talismans I've empowered with my mantras. But they lose their power overnight and are rendered ineffective if the one receiving treatment moves even an inch.

(WIFE:) Have you got these talismans with you?

(LI:) "Medicine monk, medicine monk, carries medicine everywhere he goes!" Naturally I keep such items on my person.

(MOTHER-IN-LAW:) Oh, I'm in luck. Please let me have one right away!

(LI:) Let me get them out. (*Aside*:) I originally brought these talismans for you-know-what. I never expected this old lady to butt in. If I can't have my way today, then I might as well shift the blame onto him. I don't even know if he'll show up today. Even if he does, he's not likely to politely hold out his leg to get burned. If he moves even a little, the blame will be on him, because his mother-in-law will say it's his fault for not holding still. She'll never fault my prescription. What a brilliant trick! (*Pulls out paper slips.*) The talismans are right here. Please carefully accept them. We'll use them at the right time and must not expose them to the winds.

(WIFE:) Why so many restrictions?

(LI:) The old prescriptions have always been so. It's not that I'm bragging, but not only can this prescription cure people, it can even cure trees. There was once a great peach tree half rotted out and dying, but seeing that the owner hated to see it go, I gave him one of these and had him burn it on a plum tree. As it turned out, that plum tree had just been grafted onto the peach tree, just like how your daughter here has been grafted onto the family of your son-in-law. But with this little burn, the peach tree revived to its former glory, while the plum tree dried right up.

(WIFE, *aside*:) Could this really be true? I wouldn't mind if it sucked all the life out of that bastard. (*Faces* LI:) Oh, to think it is truly so efficacious!

(LI:) This is a special kind of mantra-enchanted talisman that takes the life from one and gives it to another. The plum may harden in place of the peach, just like hiring someone else to do your public service for you.

(MOTHER-IN-LAW:) Oh, my son-in-law, when will you return? Don't leave me in pain too long!

(SON-IN-LAW *enters*:) Since my wife is such a pain, I've been running around town all day. (*Sneezes several times.*) Sneezing several times must mean someone is thinking about me. (*Knocks on the door.*)

(WIFE:) This is him—you two please sit down.

(MOTHER-IN-LAW:) Oh, he's arrived. I'll soon be better!

(LI:) Now that he's here, I'd better leave soon.

(SON-IN-LAW *enters and sees everyone*:) Greetings, dear Mother-in-Law.

(LI *bows*:) Oh, so here's that son-in-law. Your medicine has arrived, so I'll just be on my way now.

(WIFE:) But we haven't given you a reward yet.

(LI:) I have an appointment with another client in the village ahead, so I don't dare tarry. I'll collect my thanks on the day of my follow-up visit. (LI *exits temporarily.*)

(SON-IN-LAW:) What was that monk here for?

(WIFE:) He happened to pass by the gate, so we invited him here to treat my mother.

(SON-IN-LAW:) What's wrong with my mother-in-law?

(WIFE:) Some son-in-law you are—you don't even know about your mother-in-law's toothache!

(SON-IN-LAW:) Oh, this is a pain she's had for a while. How could I not know about it?

(WIFE *sings*:)

(*Chao tianzi*)

Though it is a chronic pain,
It has lately changed its character.
Pain is quite hard to bear
When you're too lazy to drink medicinal tea
And too antsy to lie in bed.
All you can do is pray for a spirit to come and save you.

(SON-IN-LAW:) Oh, so that's what's up. I'm sorry I did not enquire.

(WIFE:) You're always running around outside all day, but you never bother to ask after your mother-in-law. (*Sings*:)

It's a good thing I ran into a man of purity,
Who gave us a miracle cure.

(SON-IN-LAW:) You always run into a good doctor after the illness is gone. (WIFE *sings*:)

Truly, "When the illness is cured,
You bump into a good doctor."

(SON-IN-LAW:) So what type of prescription is it? (WIFE *sings*:)

My sick mother—
She cannot return to health
Without help from you and your mercy.

(SON-IN-LAW:) By "me providing mercy" you mean lending you to the doctor as thanks?

(WIFE *laughs*:) Heh! Wide of the mark, you are. Crazy talk. I mean we need something of yours.

(SON-IN-LAW:) What thing of mine do you need? (WIFE *sings*:)

(*Sibian jing*)

We need you to
Endure a bit of pain.

(SON-IN-LAW:) I hope you're not asking me to feed her my flesh?[44]

(WIFE:) Well, it's close to your thigh, but we don't need to cut it.

(SON-IN-LAW:) I hope you're not asking me to burn incense?

(WIFE:) Well, you're getting close, but it's not incense. (*Sings*:)

Near your thigh, but not cutting,
Burning, but not incense.

(*Speaks*:) We just need you to extend that long-unwashed right foot of yours.

(SON-IN-LAW:) What do you need it for? (WIFE *sings*:)

It's just that
Near your ankle and on the heel,
We need to burn talismans—just seven or eight.

(SON-IN-LAW:) Burn these? (WIFE *laughs*:) Hah. Scared, are you? You didn't eat cooked turtle feet, so no need for so many—just let us burn you a measly three times.[45]

(SON-IN-LAW:) Still no good. (WIFE *sings*:)

If it treats my mother's illness,

then

Our mandarin duck quilt sharing won't have been in vain.

(SON-IN-LAW:) You're going to cook my flesh and roast my skin. I'm afraid I can't take the pain.

(WIFE *whispers*:) Heh! When they sent me to live in your house years ago, don't you think it hurt when your father defiled me? I've endured pain for your father, but you won't endure pain for my mother?

(SON-IN-LAW:) That was a long time ago. So, you want the son to repay a debt of pain for the father? I don't want to go limping down the road.

(WIFE:) This miraculous prescription should cure your senseless wanderings.

(SON-IN-LAW:) Forget it! If what's hurting is my mother-in-law's tooth, what's that got to do with her son-in-law's leg?

(WIFE:) How could it not connect to you? I came out of her belly, and your little thing has been up inside mine. How could pathways of energy not be linked?

(SON-IN-LAW:) Well, if that's the way you want to look at it, we should pick an auspicious day as well. A good day for scorching my spirits!

(WIFE:) That young master said he enchanted the talismans with mantras before the Buddha. If allowed to sit overnight they will lose their efficacy.

(SON-IN-LAW:) Let me see those. (*Aside*:) I'll just have to throw away those stupid things.

(WIFE:) I can't let you look at them. They'll get exposed to the wind.

(SON-IN-LAW:) Alright, then let me get in a place where I'm protected from the wind, and I'll burn them myself.

(WIFE:) Since when did you become so obedient? You weren't willing to do it in front of everyone but now you're willing to do it in secret?

(SON-IN-LAW:) Actually, I was a little scared. (WIFE *sings*:)

(PANSHEDIAO MODE: *Shua hai'er*)

You've

Always been healthy and tough,

Why, today, are you suddenly a wimp?

(MOTHER-IN-LAW *bows*:) Son-in-Law, you should accrue some hidden merit—just get it over with! (WIFE *sings*:)

Just look at

This white-haired matron taking steps so tiny,

Why should she kowtow to her son-in-law?

(SON-IN-LAW:) She just doesn't like the pain. (WIFE:) At it again. (SON-IN-LAW:) If she doesn't like pain, then what's wrong with me not liking pain? (WIFE *sings*:)

You're

Young and fit and can endure;

She's

Old and frail—how can she stand it?

You should

Give up your own comfort—why be so stiff-necked?

If you feel no mercy nor compassion,

You'll leave me no choice but brute force.

(WIFE *pushes* SON-IN-LAW *over,* SON-IN-LAW *yells.*) (LI *enters and listens in secret, laughing*:) What a trick I've played on them! While they push and pull, I'll get another look at my hat.

(MOTHER-IN-LAW:) Who's there?

(LI:) It's your humble monk.

(MOTHER-IN-LAW:) What are you doing back so soon?

(LI:) I've come to receive my reward.

(MOTHER-IN-LAW:) I thought you said you'd come back later. Why so soon?

(LI:) I haven't come just to receive a reward. I came for your sake, my dearest old bodhisattva. An old saying goes: "Free medicine is worth what you pay for it." Having not yet received my emolument, I was afraid it might delay your recovery. Though I've still got plenty of medicine and talismans, I was worried your son-in-law might endure but one burning and not be willing to take another. If this is an inconvenient time for you, then two old monk's hats would be sufficient reward for now.

(MOTHER-IN-LAW:) I'm sorry, we don't have something like that on hand.

(LI, *aside*:) She doesn't know, but watch me get them out of her. (*Calls out loudly*:) If you haven't got two, just one will be fine.

(WIFE *lets go of* SON-IN-LAW, *aside*:) He must be back for his hat; I'll have to get rid of him.

(A CROWD, *dressed as neighborhood men and women, enters.*)

(LI:) Sounds like a bunch of busybodies hungry for a scoop! (*Leaves in surprise.*)

(WIFE *opens door and crowd enters.*)

(MOTHER-IN-LAW:) Who are all these people? (WIFE *points and sings*:)

(*Fifth from Coda*)

This here's Grampa Zhao, nicknamed "Little Bridge."

(ZHAO:) My deceased father was nicknamed Eastern Bridge. (WIFE *sings*:)

This is Uncle Qian, also called Second Dyke.

(QIAN:) My brother is called Little Dyke, and we all started with my father, Willow Dyke. (WIFE *sings*:)

This is our neighbor from across the way, a tailor named Leatherworker Sun.

(SUN:) I mostly work on leather jackets. (WIFE *sings*:)

This one with the clean-shaven chin is called Zhou the Beard.

(ZHOU:) It was ripped off by my wife. (WIFE *sings*:)

This is Mrs. Zheng, whose belly's big right now.

(ZHENG:) It's just that I'm expecting soon. (WIFE *sings*:)

Why have you all come to call?

(CROWD:) We heard shouts coming from your honored household and came to check on you.

(WIFE:) Sorry to trouble you. (*Sings*:)

All for the sake of

My heartless husband,

And poor old, sick mother.

(*Fourth from Coda*)

If you want to sit, I'm afraid we've no benches or stools to spare.

(ZHAO:) I feel better standing anyway. (WIFE *sings*:)

If you want to stay for tea, I'm afraid I'm too busy to prepare it.

(QIAN:) What with?

(WIFE:) My mother's tooth is hurting her.

(SUN:) Oh, that is the worst sort of ailment. An old saying goes: "A toothache is not a disease, because when a disease kills no one hears it." Oh, it's bad! (WIFE *sings*:)

If you don't mind me rambling on, then please let me explain.

(ZHOU:) I'm willing to hear you out. (WIFE *sings*:)

From times of old a woman's husband

is like

a real son,

Who doesn't treat his mother-in-law

as well

as his own mother?

(ZHENG:) How could it be otherwise? My own little son-in-law now calls me "mum." (WIFE *points at husband and sings*:)

But he doesn't take this to heart!

(*Speaks*:) I asked him to burn a charm on his heel for the sake of curing my mother's tooth pain. How can that not be important? But he's too pigheaded to help no matter how I thrash him! (*Sings*:)

He only makes sure

That he himself is alright

And completely ignores my suffering mother.

(ZHAO:) Sounds like Mr. Wang Jidi doesn't want to help out. (*Turns to face* SON-IN-LAW:) Brother, it's only right that you force yourself to follow her directions. (WIFE *sings*:)

(*Third from Coda*)

All because his heart is unfeeling,

It's not that I want to use force.

(QIAN *faces* SON-IN-LAW:) Brother Wang, have you no reply? (WIFE *sings*:)

He's so
Stubborn he won't let us get at his toothache burning point.
(*Points at* MOTHER-IN-LAW *and sings*:)
Look at how much pain she's in,
Eyes closed and furrowed brow, hoping to die.
(*Points to self*:)
Crying so
That my guts are wrenching and tears streaming down.
(*Points to* SON-IN-LAW:)
He doesn't call on his conscience to reconsider,
what kind of
Compassionate fellow doesn't
Have a care for his own flesh and blood?

(SUN:) Where is this prescription from? (WIFE *sings a penultimate cadence*:)
It's troubled her for many years
With no medicine to treat it,
Fortunately, a holy monk
Bestowed this great prescription.

(ZHOU:) Where's this prescription from? (WIFE *sings*:)
He says it comes from the dragon palace.

(ZHENG:) So, it's a miracle drug.

(WIFE:) He's got many miraculous methods, this monk! (*Sings*:)
Beans can be made to grow from a wet lotus pod . . .

(ZHAO:) Very true, what bean doesn't grow out of the dirt? (WIFE *sings*:)
Tender ginger sprouts can bloom on a willow tree.

(QIAN:) Very true, fragrant fungus can grow on a dead tree—even more so with a live one.

(WIFE *sings*:)
And a noodle-rolling stick
can
grow yellow flowers.

(SUN:) I've seen it happen in the three months of winter. (WIFE *sings*:)
There are even sticky-cooked jujubes
that
still have leaves on them.

(ZHOU:) Why don't you give me one, and I'll give it to my child to play with. (WIFE *sings*:)
And sugar as spicy as horseradish.

(ZHENG:) Oh, my old man needs some of that for his cold bean noodles—I'll have to remember to pick some up.

(ZHAO:) Since you've got this miraculous prescription on hand, why don't you stir up your sympathies, Brother Wang?

(SON-IN-LAW:) Sympathy, sympathy, the problem is the pain of being burned, I'm telling you.

(WIFE:) It's not like my mother's asking you to burn for nothing.

(QIAN:) Not for nothing? Could it be you also need to make a payment for this treatment that you can't afford? (WIFE *points at mother and sings final cadence*:)

Though ours is a small household, she's got some assets of her own;

We've got some things we can use to pay him later.

(SUN:) What have you got? (WIFE *sings*:)

In that old, broken box we've got several Buddhist vajras.

(ZHOU:) Oh, but you shouldn't give up something like that! You should just give him several catties of grain and be done with it.

(SUN:) How about some millet? (WIFE *sings*:)

Like big pearls stored in half-broken pots,

(ZHENG:) I have some at my place, but they don't have eyes.[46]

(QIAN:) I think you must mean peas. What about string beans?

(WIFE *points at* SON-IN-LAW *and sings*:)

Your unwillingness to share with us

Is because

You were born a scabby dog.

How dare you, then,

Climb over that east wall?[47]

(ZHAO *faces* SON-IN-LAW:) See, it's not like you don't get anything out of the deal. Too bad I'm not your in-law; if I were, I'd make you do it for sure. Enough! We'll leave this kind of thing to you. We're off. (*Exeunt.*)

(WIFE *faces* SON-IN-LAW:) Did you hear? (*Sings coda*:)

An old saying goes: "the locals are magistrates of morals."

(SON-IN-LAW:) Even if a magistrate were here right now, I still wouldn't do it. (WIFE *sings*:)

So, you'd rather be bullied than a hero. (*Takes off clothes.*)

(WIFE *speaks*:) Mother! (*Sings*:)

Close the door,

And take off your robes,

We'll go at him together and the deed will be done.

We've got no time to sit around cajoling him all day.

(SON-IN-LAW *grabs* WIFE'*s clothes and runs off.*) (MOTHER-IN-LAW:) Now that he's gone, we'll never get him back, and as the night passes on, the medicine's strength will wear off. Heh! Too bad we've wasted this miracle prescription. Oh, when will my tooth pain ever get better?

(*Exits.*)

(WIFE:) He's run off with my clothes, but at least I've still got all these melons. If I sell them, I can buy material for any number of robes. But Monk Li's hat was still in the sleeve—what to do? Eh, I'm not afraid of him—we'll see if he can out-cheat me.

(*Exits.*)

ACT 3

KI-UUI RHYME

(*Monk* LI *enters, bare-headed*:) A vulgar woman you can't push away, while the one in your heart won't come when you call. A moment ago, I had just teased my darling to the point where the fun was about to begin when I got cornered by that old lady. And just when I was yelling for my hat, I got pushed aside by that big crowd. Even if my darling could get away, I couldn't meet up with her. Joyfully I went along and return disappointed. Now's not a good time to go back again, but to stay away is hard to bear. I'm really at a loss! It's all because of that inauspicious talk Monk Zhang spouted the other day. All about beatings, stockades, and blackmail—what a buzzkill! That damned fool. What does he know about such joy? (*Sings*:)

(YUEDIAO MODE: *Dou anchun*)

One

like me who

breaks vows for pleasure

Can still have

Pure intentions and destined bond.

She loves me as

A diamond-forged vajra,

I love her

Like a fresh bud in spring.

One like

A slender vine winding round a gourd,

The other like

A lively loach sporting in the wet,

We monopolized

The realms of lusty form,

And enjoyed

A mandarin duck meeting.

All because of

My destined darling,

I've become

A romantic hungry ghost.[48]

(*Speaks*:) Oh Older Brother, oh Older Brother, all that fine talk of yours, though it sounds good on the surface, it lacks humanity. Just look at how we dress, live, and eat. (*Sings*:)

(*Zihua'er xu*)

What we enjoy are fine clothes and good food,

Where we live are sacred temples and monasteries,

What we keep are

those

chilly curtains and lonely screens.

(*Speaks*:) I want to stop doing just this one thing, but (*sings*:)

I fear

Passionate regret can burn down a temple,[49]

While a single act brings

A springtime of wisdom.

Thinking it over,

This must be

Karma from a past life:

Who has time to

Worry about punishment in the next?

I've got a good plan,

In secret

I'll polish the spear and sharpen the sword,

And borrow another's doleful face to put on an act.

Older Brother, you went on and on about how your garden was well planted, but now all your melons and gourds are gone—what good did it do you? Though you planted them well, in the end you were nothing but a manure-covered monk, baking in the sun and stinking to high heaven. (*Sings*:)

(*Jin jiaoye*)

To the point your

Hands and feet grew calluses grasping vines.

How can that compare to me,

Snuggling up to that tender beauty?

(*Speaks*:) Let alone (*sings*:)

My one

Glorious moment of wind and rain,[50]

Or your

Half a lifetime's companion—a wife who shared tough husks and rough grain!

(*Speaks*:) Oh, that queen of my heart, I was really scared when the old lady showed up, but that, "Oh, it *IS* you, mother!" line of hers set my mind at ease. Then she threw me a meaningful glance, saying she'd invited me to fix her mother's tooth pain and

I played along to stir up some trouble—what a sight it was! What perfection! We really are a great secret love match, masters of lies and deceit—a rare pair, indeed! (*Sings*:)

(*Tiaoxiao ling*[51])

When it comes to poking fun,
I sure am the best.
  She
Saw the situation and played along to perfection.
  If it hadn't been for
That meaningful glance,
That smooth talk,
If not for quick thinking,
I might have given myself away.
  But for me
Swinging my hands going home bare-headed,
  I really
Pulled one over in every single way!

(*Speaks*:) I guess that big crowd has already dispersed, and old Wang Jidi should also be out of commission—either he's nursing his pain from the burns, or he's run off to escape them. I'll go check it out again.

(*Exits temporarily.*)

(WANG JIDI *enters in a rush*:) Oh creator! Oh creator! My mother-in-law's tooth was hurting her; and for some strange reason, they tried to nab me for a burn cure. I had to escape after snatching some clothes—I ran three or four miles at a go. You, mother and daughter, think you can still burn me now? Let me just fold up this robe neatly and take it to the pawn shop. That'll be enough for me to live on my own for ten days or two weeks. Then I can take my time getting back home. (*Folds robe.*) Oh, what's this here in the sleeve? So, it's a monk's hat. I wonder how this hat got in this sleeve. Could it be that monk didn't come to cure my mum's tooth pain, but the wind in my wife's belly?[52] (*Looks at hat.*) Oh, there's a name in the hat. It says "Zhang. Three Purities Monastery." So, it's Monk Zhang, is it? The other day I was walking home drunk, and I saw someone jump out the window, leaving a shoe behind. I took it for a pillow and fell asleep, waiting to get back at him the next day. What a surprise when I woke up to find my head resting on my own shoe! She insisted it was me who came through the window that night, and since the shoe was my own, I had nothing to say. Now, with this hat in hand, they can hardly claim it was me who came to treat my mother-in-law! With the name and address in this hat, I can find someone to write up a complaint and take that son-of-a-bitch to court. For the crime of trying to burn my foot alone I shouldn't let him off the hook.

(*Exits temporarily.*)

(LI, *bare-headed, enters with* WIFE.) (WIFE:) Why did you go so soon? It was never like this before. Could it be you've forsaken your devotion, and, in the next town, you've got someone on the side? (LI *sings*:)

(*Gui santai*)

How could I ever give up my devotion?

I'd sooner shatter my very own skull.

(WIFE:) Then why'd you run off so soon? (LI:) I guess I must own up. Yesterday your husband ran off with your clothes and shook a hat out of the sleeve. Now he's gone and had a formal complaint written up and is taking it to the county seat today. Fortunately, the one who wrote up the complaint is an acquaintance of mine. Yesterday I happened to run into him, and he said the court order was for Baldy Zhang, but being as it was for my older brother, he tipped me off. (WIFE:) Why didn't you say this last night? (LI:) I was afraid I'd spoil your romantic mood. (WIFE *looks sad*.) (LI, *aside*:) This little cry of hers makes her even more lovable. (*Sings*:)

Her tears like

A crabapple, with rain drip-dripping,

That crying voice like an

Oriole beyond the willows, warbling in the wind.

(WIFE:) This is all my fault for keeping that hat. (LI:) Dearest, don't say that. When you first kept the hat, it was out of love. (*Sings*:)

Don't think your good intentions an error.

(WIFE:) Don't you think after this we'll be torn apart? (LI *sings*:)

Our joy may yet not turn to sadness,

The fates of Heaven are made by man,

Let's consider very carefully, my dear.

(WIFE:) Well then hurry up and consider! (LI:) If the magistrate only interrogates Monk Zhang, then everything will be fine. But if they point out that the face of Monk Zhang doesn't match the one seen treating your mother, then they'll have to call on you and me. At that point (*Sings*:)

(*Tusi'er*)

Just say this

Monk used force and bullied you,

You never willingly went along,

So you

Grabbed his hat and were about to go sue.

(*Speaks*:) Just because of your mother's illness, things got confused, (*sings*)

And that's why you

Hadn't yet reported it all.

(WIFE *cries*:) But in that case, you'll be in trouble. How can I stand it? (LI *sings*:)

(*Sheng Yaowang*)

Even if

I must suffer,
And my body burn to ash,
I'd not allow
A single harm to befall your perfect jade person.

(WIFE:) Is there no better plan than this? (LI *sings*:)

If you want to be bold,
And never look back,
I can guarantee we'll
Be husband and wife, joined forever,
With a
Judge and a bailiff our matchmakers.

(WIFE *laughs*:) So what's this plan of yours? (LI:) Since you, my dearest, care about me deeply, you shouldn't mind harming that Monk Zhang a bit—I want you to memorize the scar on his hand and the eight characters governing his birth.[53] When the time comes you can shape your testimony accordingly, and that information will come in handy. If the judgement is divorce, I'll return to lay life and marry you. Then we'll be husband and wife, together forever. (*Looks sad.*) My only fear is that you may suffer a little in facing the magistrate—how will I bear it? (WIFE:) That is no problem—if not for one bone-chilling frost, how could the plum blossoms' fragrance emerge from the snow? This is your old hat—I'll return it to you now. (LI:) Now this is important. (*Puts it on.*) (WIFE:) Leave now—I'm going to my mother's place.

(*Exit.*)

(WANG JIDI *enters with* OFFICER *of the Court and Monk* ZHANG.)

(ZHANG:) Close the gates and disaster rains down from Heaven! (*Points at* WANG.) I don't know why this man has sued me and had me brought to court in chains. The other day my melons walked out on me, and now I'm caught up in a legal dispute. It's true what they say: when it rains, it pours.

(LI *enters and sees him, attempts to avoid being seen.*) (ZHANG *calls out loudly*:) Monk Li, come save me! (LI *sighs*:) You said the Buddha's laws were strict and many and the courts were harsh besides. Why, then, have you contravened them? (*Sings*:)

(*Malang'er*)

You've
Always been timid and afraid of trouble,
Who knew your heart just didn't match your words?
It seems
In a split second, your horse of desire got away,
As you hungered for a taste
of that
old home cooking.

(*Speaks*:) You've brought this upon yourself. Trouble never comes calling on those, like me, who uphold the pure laws. I can't help you. (*Tries to leave.*) (WANG *grabs him*:)

Hey, where are you going? You look a bit familiar. I think I saw you the other day too. (LI:) Why are you grabbing at me now? (WANG:) It was a Buddhist monk who was at my place the other day. (LI *points at* ZHANG:) And is he a Daoist priest? (WANG:) Though you make a good point, that one-armed robe of yours looks familiar. (LI:) What about what was on his head? (WANG:) He had no hat. (LI *points to his head*:) And what about me? (WANG:) You've got one on. (LI:) Of course. I'd never go out with my head bare. (OFFICER:) So only people with bare heads are monks? You all will have to work it out in front of the judge! (LI *points to* WANG:) Whom is he suing? What name is it on your bill there? (OFFICER:) It says Monk Zhang. (LI:) At it again. (*Sings reprise*:)

My
Name is Li,
Stop confusing the two.
If a name's not on the bill, how dare you weave it in?

(OFFICER:) The plaintiff says you were involved. (LI:) Well if that's the case, why is he suing him? (*Sings*:)

You believe his empty bluffs,
Without a shred of proof.

(LI *pulls the* OFFICER *aside*:) C'mon brother, let me off the hook and I'll give you a few nice melons. (OFFICER:) What would I want with something like that? I'm taking you to the magistrate for sure. I'd rather bring in an innocent man than have the magistrate say I've let a guilty one go.

(*Exits temporarily.*)

(*County* MAGISTRATE *enters with* BAILIFF:) As magistrate I've never asked for a bribe, yet the silver keeps pouring into my pocket. Commoners' grateful tears alone can't support one in old age. I am the upright official magistrate of this county. This morning I received a complaint from one Wang Jidi, and I have already sent someone out to apprehend the offenders. Why haven't they come back yet?

(OFFICER *enters, pushing* ZHANG *and* LI *ahead of him*:) The criminals have arrived.

(MAGISTRATE *reads out names*:) Monk Zhang. (ZHANG:) Here I am. (MAGISTRATE:) So you're Monk Zhang. What a fashionable old Buddha. A lecherous *sangha* indeed! Miss Wu. (OFFICER:) She's not here yet. (MAGISTRATE:) The mother-in-law? (OFFICER:) Also not yet arrived. (MAGISTRATE:) I hope they didn't bribe you to let them go? (OFFICER:) I wouldn't dare. It's just that we ran into a monk on the street and the plaintiff said he looked familiar, so we brought him in as well. We'll go get the two ladies next. (MAGISTRATE:) You will indeed! You've brought one more than asked for and not brought two you were asked for! Get out of here and get them for me! If you don't, you'll have to answer to me. (OFFICER *obeys and leaves.*) (LI:) Oh, truly you are just as pure as the blue sky above, my lord. (*Sings*:)

(*Luosi niang*)

This guy grabbed a Li for a Zhang,

Seeing clear as the sun on a cloudy day.

But my lord, with

Your honorable reputation, pure as water, white as flour,[54]

I know

You'll find the truth straight away.

(MAGISTRATE:) In this world there's nothing purer than water or whiter than flour—you speak well. (*Asks*:) So what does the plaintiff have to say? (WANG:) The other day I returned home to find my mother-in-law, wife, and a monk all sitting together. The monk only spoke a few words before departing. Afterward, my wife took off her clothes and drove me out of the house. I grabbed the clothes and later found someone's hat in the sleeve. That's why I reported impropriety. (MAGISTRATE:) From the sounds of it, this must be a false accusation. You say the monk left, and only afterward did your wife take off her clothes—so why do you accuse them of adultery? (WANG:) She committed adultery before and took off her outer garment to burn me after. (MAGISTRATE:) More nonsense. She wanted to burn you, but took off her own clothes instead of yours? It wasn't you trying to burn her? (WANG:) It was because I wouldn't let her burn me that she took off her robe and tried to force me. (MAGISTRATE:) Who is she? (WANG:) She's my wife. (MAGISTRATE:) So, it was your wife who wanted to burn you—but why? (WANG:) To cure her mother's tooth pain. (MAGISTRATE:) You harebrained bastard, you must be mistaken! Given that he came to treat tooth pain, he must have been a dentist. So why are you suing a monk? (LI *and* ZHANG:) You are truly just, my lord. (WANG:) The burning was a prescription ordered by the monk. (MAGISTRATE:) So, he is a medical monk. Which of the two was it you invited to treat her? (WANG:) I never invited them. (MAGISTRATE:) Are you saying he just showed up at your door selling medical services? (WANG:) That's why I was suspicious.

(MAGISTRATE:) Even I am a little suspicious now. (*Points to* ZHANG.) Plaintiff, is he the one you intended to sue? (WANG:) It doesn't look like him, though the hat is his. (MAGISTRATE *points at* LI.) What about him? (WANG:) He looks familiar, but the hat didn't have Li's name in it. (MAGISTRATE:) Indeed. I wonder if Monk Li borrowed Monk Zhang's hat. (LI:) I've got my own hat right here, so why would I set it aside to borrow someone else's? (MAGISTRATE:) In that case, maybe Monk Zhang borrowed your face? (LI:) Why would I lend him my face to go commit such an evil deed? (MAGISTRATE, *aside*:) Since the hat and the face do not match, what more can I learn? In that case I'll have to figure out which of the two practiced physicking. Monk Zhang, you look like you know medicine. (ZHANG:) I don't have that ability. (MAGISTRATE:) What can you do, then? (ZHANG:) I'm only good at gardening. (MAGISTRATE:) This monk doesn't study medicine but studies the fields. Monk Li, what about you? (LI:) I'm even less able. (MAGISTRATE:) Don't be so humble. How could it be that neither of you knows anything about medicine? (LI:) I can't even plant a garden, much less practice medicine. (MAGISTRATE:) Since both of you are unable, I'm guessing it was his wife treating your teeth? (LI, ZHANG:) We two aren't suffering from tooth pain, so why would we seek treatment? (MAGISTRATE:) Exactly! Plaintiff, please step forward. Perhaps your wife can make monks' hats and so went out, door-to-door, taking this as a sample? (WANG:) Why keep a sample in a sleeve? (MAGISTRATE:) This son-of-a-bitch is getting even stupider. If you don't stow things away, how can you keep from losing them? (WANG:) My wife can't sew. (MAGISTRATE, *angry*:) You're too suspicious! And this monk is too tight-lipped. Nobody recognizes this stupid hat—did it just walk in here on its own? Put the finger clamps on all of them! (LI *cries out*:) No need to clamp! I admit it! (MAGISTRATE, *aside*:) I knew threatening torture was the best route. If I'd relied on my questions alone, by this time next year I'd still have no answers. (*Faces* LI.) Confess! (LI *sings*:)

(*Xiaotao hong*)

The other day
I was still blissfully asleep.
First tread as carefully
as a
fox upon ice.

(MAGISTRATE:) What do you mean by "a fox upon ice?" (LI:) My lord, when a fox crosses ice, he's afraid it may not be hard enough, so he always pricks up an ear and proceeds slowly. (MAGISTRATE *acts out listening*:) I'm waiting to hear the rest of the story. (LI:) Let me deliver my sentiments personally. (*He does so and sings*:)

When a cicada first emerges from its shell, it carefully hides itself,
When a heron surveys its pond,
Or a *yakṣa* plumbs the ocean, they do it circumspectly.
One of them
Pretends to be Boya, slowly plucking his zither,
One of them
Pretends to be dumb, hoping to stall his foe.
At such a time
To name a name
Who'd dare even utter a peep?[55]

(MAGISTRATE *looks surprised*:) Oh, this is a reference to my tryst with the maid the other day—how could he know so much detail? There must be something more to this guy. I shouldn't provoke him. Let's just question Monk Zhang then. (*Faces*.) Li turned out to be a real green one—I just said the word "squeeze" and he admitted everything. That Monk Zhang is a bit more venerable—he looks more like old "Master Rice."[56] Let's put the squeeze on him first. (*Applies finger presses*.)

(OFFICER, *bringing in* MOTHER-IN-LAW *and* WIFE, *who witness this*:) Your Honor, we've brought the two women.

(MAGISTRATE *points to* MOTHER-IN-LAW.) (MOTHER-IN-LAW:) Oh, I dare not approach, Your Honor. (MAGISTRATE:) Get out of here, I wasn't calling you. (MOTHER-IN-LAW:) Whom were you calling, then? (MAGISTRATE *laughs*:) Miss Wu. (WIFE:) Here I am. (MAGISTRATE *sees her*:) Come up here! A little further! Oh boy, come on up! (BAILIFF:) Your old lady's coming out of the back hall. (MAGISTRATE:) Well, let her, then. If I hadn't set up that back-door hall with a fence the other day I'd be afraid of her, but now I'm not. (*Laughs.*) (MOTHER-IN-LAW *faces* ZHANG:) Master Zhang, why don't you just answer the questions? Why are you enduring these finger clamps? (MAGISTRATE:) Who's chattering down there? (LI:) The old lady was calling to Master Zhang. (MAGISTRATE:) Okay, let's have that old lady come up here. So, how do you recognize him as Monk Zhang? (MOTHER-IN-LAW:) He gave me a prescription and sat with me for some time. How could I not recognize him? (MAGISTRATE:) But your son-in-law just said his appearance is not the same as the monk he saw. Sounds like your old eyes aren't seeing clearly. (MOTHER-IN-LAW:) Although my eyes may be old and my vision blurry, I certainly remember that when he was giving me the medicine his palm had a scar on it. (MAGISTRATE:) Officer, let's have a look. (BAILIFF *looks at* LI:) None here. (*Looks at* ZHANG:) One mark here on the right hand. (MAGISTRATE:) Monk Zhang, how'd you get this scar? (ZHANG:) I got it digging up gourd roots. (MAGISTRATE:) The scar's on your palm, but when you were getting your fingers squeezed you kept your palms pressed together. The old lady couldn't have seen it just now. As I thought, a few words spoken in parting can't compare to a long sit with someone. Step down! (LI *looks pleased, aside*:) See, my plan's coming to fruition already. (MAGISTRATE:) Young lady, your husband claims to have pulled a hat from your sleeve. That's why he's suing you for cavorting with a monk. (WIFE:) Your Honor, truly there was a hat in my sleeve, but truly there was no impropriety. (ZHANG:) Given that it is a monk's hat, we still need to figure out the truth of the matter, Your Honor! (MAGISTRATE:) Bring the hat up for me to see. (*Looks at it.*) Plaintiff, you're mistaken! This hat is yours—isn't the first character in it "Wang?" (WANG:) Your Honor has inserted an extra vertical line. The four characters read: "Zhang of the Three Purities Temple."[57] (MAGISTRATE:) Indeed. So, this Wang Jidi can read. (*Tosses hat.*) Monk Zhang—recognize it! (ZHANG *looks*:) This hat is truly my own, but I don't know how it ended up in his hands. (MAGISTRATE:) Could the wind have blown it away or a cat carried it off? Even then, how could it fly right up into her sleeve? (ZHANG *thinks*:) I know—it was the day my melons went and left me. I was lying in bed sick with anger and from that point on I haven't worn it. If it wasn't Monk Li who picked it up and walked off with it, then he must have stolen it to try to frame this poor monk! (LI:) Your Honor! This is surely a lie. If inanimate melons could walk, then us lively gourd-heads should be able to fly. (MAGISTRATE:) Precisely. (*Points to his head*:) If that were true, I could use the little wings on my hat here to fly away as well.[58] This monk's speaking a load of nonsense. This reveals the impropriety! (ZHANG:) As for the melons, Your Honor, please just call my workman and ask him about it. He'll tell you the truth. (LI:) The workman is his workman—how could he not defend him? If this mother-in-law here were my mother-in-law, for example, she would surely protect me. (ZHANG:) This was all your dream the other day—how can you deny it today? (LI:) Did you see my dream the other day? It sounds like you're the one who's dreaming. Why else do you sound like you're talking in your sleep? (MAGISTRATE:) Then I'll ask the young lady. Take the finger squeezers off the monk and put them on the lady! (*Takes them off.*) (WIFE:) No need to squeeze me, I know I can't take it. (MAGISTRATE:) I knew those tender little fingers of yours couldn't endure this, so hurry up and confess to avoid the pain. (WIFE:) The other day Monk Zhang brought a big bunch of melons over to my house and left them there. (MAGISTRATE:) You shouldn't have let him. (WIFE:) I only left my door open a crack, but he came charging right in. How could I stop him? (MAGISTRATE *laughs*:) I guess you couldn't! Well then what happened next? (WIFE:) The next day Monk Zhang came looking for the money from the sale of the melons. I said, "I never agreed to buy the melons, so why are you asking me for money?" He laughed and said, "I didn't come to sell melons. I don't want you, Lady Bodhisattva, to spend money to buy them. I was just hoping you'd take pity on me and fulfill my heart's desire." He got down on his knees pleading for favors. (MAGISTRATE, *imitating the motion*:) He got down on his knees like this? (BAILIFF:) Your Honor, please maintain your dignity. (MAGISTRATE *gets up*:) Nonsense! Are you saying I'm not allowed to interrogate in detail? (WIFE:) So, I grabbed his hat off his head and put it in my sleeve, saying I'd wait for my husband to come back and show it to him and take him to court with Your Honor. (MAGISTRATE *gets angry*:) Dammit, what kind of person asks for favors and then dares sue me? (WIFE:) I meant, we would sue him and take the case to you. (MAGISTRATE:) How important is that word "take" in this case! Why didn't you say so in the first place? (WIFE:) Monk Zhang got scared and held me tightly with his two hands—I didn't know if he was still looking for fun or just trying to get his hat back. Just as I was in such a fix, my old mother walked in. (MAGISTRATE:) So, she just walked in on you two with no respect for privacy? (WIFE:) She came because of her tooth pain. Monk Zhang, seeing my mother covering her mouth and moaning in pain, said he could treat my mother's tooth pain to make up for his crime. I was suspicious he was just looking for a chance to escape, but he got down on his knees and made a vow to Heaven, including his eight astrological birth characters, so after all that I decided to trust him and seek his prescription, hoping to cure my mother. I never expected my husband would refuse to submit to the treatment, so I never found out whether the prescription was effective and so didn't know whether to forgive Monk Zhang or not. I'll leave the rest for Your Honor to decide. (MAGISTRATE, *aside*:) The eight astrological birth characters—that's something you can't fake. (*Faces* WIFE.) Come up here and whisper the characters for me. (WIFE *whispers and* MAGISTRATE *listens with his ear cupped.*) (MAGISTRATE:) Step down! Monk Li, please speak your eight birth characters and I'll be the judge of the truth. (LI *speaks his birth characters.*) (MAGISTRATE:) That's not right! Now Monk Zhang, step up. (ZHANG *speaks his own birth characters.*) (MAGISTRATE:) Exactly the same. Good thing that young lady has a good memory. (LI *smiles to himself:*) How about that? They've fallen into another of my traps. (MAGISTRATE:) Monk Zhang, what are you at? Originally you said your melons just walked off on their own, but they all walked over to the Wang's house? I ask you: did you push them there or carry them on a pole? (WANG:) Yeah, I was wondering why all those melons were piled up in our house. Your Honor, it must have been his bait on a hook—now I've finally seen the truth. (MAGISTRATE:) So why did you say again that he looked like Monk Li? (WANG:) I've just got these two little eyes: how can they compare to the four eyes of wife and mother-in-law? (LI:) It's really hard to allay this suspicion. Your Honor, there's something else. (*Points at* ZHANG *and sings:*)

(*Xiaotao hong*)

He was a

Commoner first and only later an *ācārya*,[59]
Full of the flavor of worldly desire.

(MAGISTRATE:) Well, that settles that, then. What about you? (LI *sings:*)

I've been

Wearing this monk's robe since I left mother's breast,
Chanting Amitābha's name,

And searching for

Enlightenment in form of emptiness and emptiness of form.

(MAGISTRATE:) Oh Reverend Monk, you don't happen to have a prescription for jealousy, do you? (LI *sings:*)

The verdict of this hat's hard to question.

(*Speaks:*) If he hadn't admitted it himself, (*sings*)

Those melons wouldn't have found their owner,

As expected,

The word *pardon*'s always on the lips of a scoundrel.

(MAGISTRATE:) Everyone, listen to the decision. (*Reads.*) The truth will out; there's no ambiguity in the facts. How could it be that A's hat should be worn on B's head? Given that the Pilgrim of the family from Qinghe lost his hat, how could it be the Master of the family from Longxi who was pursuing pleasures below the belt?[60] Though Miss Wu did not allow the impropriety, she did entice impropriety through her appearance—therefore, it's hard to let her off entirely. Monk Zhang, since the garden will be left unattended with you in the cangue, it should be turned over to the magistrate's office. For arresting the monk and not the offender, the officer shall be fined three catties of rice, but no more. The plaintiff refused to help his mother-in-law when she was in pain, so the melons will be taken from him as a penalty.

Monk Li, alone, is an innocent abbot, his clothes and his hat caught up in a legal brief. The mother-in-law is free to go, but she is not to bother her son-in-law again about her tooth pain. (OFFICER, *aside*:) I knew it. Even if I didn't want the melons, I should have just let him go. (LI:) Today I finally see the sun. (*Bows and sings*:) (*Dongyuan le*)

Thanks be to you, oh beneficent one, for upholding justice
In a case of family squabble, so difficult to decide.

(MAGISTRATE:) This upright official is a specialist at handling family squabbles. (LI *sings*:)

You truly are a
Rescriptor Bao,[61] studying cases by day
and
night,
Reincarnated right here.
Oh master, if I
Encountered a wrongful suit in the world below,
I'd call on you
Again to solve it.

(MAGISTRATE:) So why has that Monk Zhang not spoken a word—is he perhaps unwilling to accept the sentence? Tie him up for me and put him in chains. After he serves his sentence, he'll have to return to secular life. (LI:) Your Honor, in deference to our spiritual kinship, I would like to help my older brother in this one matter—I will return to secular life in his stead. (MAGISTRATE:) Who knew there were such virtuous monks in the monastery! But you've not yet trod the path of politics we spoke of. Wait until your brother completes his sentence and we'll revisit the issue. (LI *faces* ZHANG:) Brother, your words were portentous, after all. (*Sings coda*:)

A big, round melon growing in a square, square box.

(*Speaks*:) It's been years since you left the home, (*sings*)

Now you'll perform your Buddhist *mudrās* standing in chains.
I ask you,
Who'll be the subject
of everyone's
gossip then?
This is all
Because you were too stern in following the rules.

(*Speaks*:) I'm going off to pick some eggplants and eat some beans with my nuptial wine.

(*Exits.*)

(ZHANG *pulling at the* MAGISTRATE *refuses to leave.*)

(CROWD *of citizens enters and reports*:) The back apartments are on fire!

(MAGISTRATE *looks frightened*:) Quick somebody help put it out!

(*All exit in a panic.*)

ACT 4

KIA-MUA RHYME

(MAGISTRATE*'s wife*, LADY *of the County, enters*:)

It's not that I was born jealous,
It's that the watery nature of men shifts their affections this way and that.
If you don't take good care of your wife,
It's only natural she should take matters into her own hands.

I'm the lady of this old county, the magistrate's wife. That shithead didn't ask for my permission before going off to cavort with a maid. Only after I'd noisily driven him out of the county office did he start to regret it. The other day I went up to the hall to listen in, afraid that shithead was making eyes at that pretty, little wife who came forward to testify. I was quite concerned she'd lead him astray. So, I went up to the back screen for a look. But to my surprise, someone had added a new fence to the hallway. I pushed on it but couldn't budge it an inch. Ugh, this was surely the doing of that shithead of mine. So, he thinks he's got a plan to keep me out of the main hall—doesn't he know I have ways of making him come down to the back hall? I threw a torch onto the reed roof of a shed in the back. In no time flat, it burst into flames and black smoke poured over the ground. There's no way he wouldn't come back here and fess up to his crimes. Once he returned, I got him to call someone to put out the fire, then took a rest. Now the danger's already past, so I'm going to call that shithead over and teach him a lesson. At least that'll cure my boredom for a bit. (*Calls out*:) Shithead, where are you?

(MAGISTRATE *enters in casual clothing*:) Here I am, here I am. I've been waiting around here patiently for some time, not daring to take a step out on my own. (LADY:) Shithead! You love cavorting with maids and yet dare to complain it was your first time? I no sooner established the new rules than you were craftily manipulating them! A brazen "Blue Sky Bao," you'll send me to my grave with your wanton disregard! If I didn't lay down some rules for you, you'd never see reason. (MAGISTRATE:) Sweetie, I've been following the new rules—when haven't I? (*Sings*:)

(SHUANGDIAO MODE: *Xin shuiling*)

Never in my life have I dared cheat on my wife,
  Just one
Look at your lovely face haunts me
  even in
    my dreams.
  Though your
New rules are fair indeed,
  My
Old ailment just relapsed.
Since I've already been punished,

Can't you let me off the hook for a first-time offence?

(LADY:) "Punished?" "Punished," you say, while not mending your ways! For your next five-hundred deaths and rebirths you'll be mine. (MAGISTRATE *sings*:)

(*Zhuma ting*)

What

Tricks could you mean?

You

Could always send me reeling with a glance of those starry eyes.

(LADY *berates him loudly*:) Day after day you compound your crimes—what a coward! (MAGISTRATE *sings*:)

What need is there to scold

With those sandalwood lips of yours?

When you're happy you're a living bodhisattva,

But when you get angry

you become

a real *rākṣasa*.[62]

(LADY:) Who said you could raise your voice? (MAGISTRATE:) Dare I raise my voice?[63] (*Sings*:)

I measure my voice carefully,

All to make sure

You don't explode on me!

(LADY:) You say you haven't been sneaky, but when did you build that fence in the hall to the back apartments? (MAGISTRATE *shudders*:) I only had it built just yesterday. It was an order sent down from a higher-up; how dare I disobey? (LADY:) Even an order sent down from a higher-up should be reported to my jurisdiction. (MAGISTRATE:) My Lady is quite right, indeed. I was momentarily drowned in work and didn't have time to explain it properly. Please forgive me. (*Sings*:)

(*Chenzui dongfeng*)

The crime of acting on my own,

For now, please forgive.

Before establishing a new law,

I should think of my wife first of all.

(LADY:) I only started this ruckus the other day, and just yesterday you receive this order from a higher-up? Are you telling me that was all a coincidence? (MAGISTRATE *sings*:)

For a long time now

It's been universally in force,

But I only

Just recently complied with this command.

(LADY:) What higher-up!? Are you afraid of him or me? Hurry up and tear this thing down! (MAGISTRATE *sings*:)

Though he holds not the emperor's license to kill,
To put it up or pull it down requires committee decision,
So, please, let's leave it up just a little longer.

(LADY:) So, you're afraid of this higher-up but not me? I guess the higher-ups are the only ones you care about? (MAGISTRATE *looks afraid*:) You're right, I'm a damn coward—though I do fear the higher-ups, they're nothing compared to you, my dear. They only pay lip service to punishment and reward; how can that compare to you, who straight away takes up cane and sword? I've only ever heard about their diligence in rooting out corruption; how can that compare to the way you scratch the skin and bite the flesh? (LADY:) How can you say something like that? Why don't you talk about some of my good qualities? (MAGISTRATE:) How could I ever forget them? Let me just take my time to list them. Though higher-ups may flatter me with kind phrases, how can that compare to your words of clouds and rain on the pillow? Though he may have vulgar serving girls at his knees, how can they compare with my service to you? My Lady, surely you can see (*sings*)

(*Yan'er luo*)

Though
I might toady up to him,
For you I
Tremble so much I don't dare turn around.
His
Awful form astride a steed,
How can it
Compare to a tigress like you?

(LADY:) Who'd believe such empty flattery? (MAGISTRATE:) Would I dare flatter you with empty words? After all, he's just a big boss, whereas you are a big wife—the character for "wife" has one more line than "boss," so surely a "wife" is even bigger than a "boss"![64] (LADY *looks slightly mollified*.) (MAGISTRATE:) It's not just me who says this, even Confucius agrees. He says, "When in public, serve your lord; when in private, serve your fearsome wife!"[65] And Mencius said to respect ferocity all the time, but your higher-ups only some of the time.[66] How could I not respect the words of Confucius and Mencius? (LADY *laughs*:) So today you finally get it. If only you government types would actually follow all the lessons in your books, you wouldn't mess up so much. (MAGISTRATE:) Please instruct me. (*Looks afar in surprise*.) Since I've already admitted to my crime, why did you have someone set fire to the office again? (LADY:) You're imagining things! (MAGISTRATE *points*.) How could the fire of a torch not light up the night? (*Sings*:)

(*Desheng ling*)

Why did the
Front hall catch fire again,
Such that you've

Scared me half to death?
My teeth are all a-chatter,
And my face's as white as wax.

(*Calls* AIDES *and speaks*:) Quick, call everyone from the officers to the townspeople—we've got to put out the fire! (*Sings*:)

Send out the message,
If we
Put it out quick,
I'll send a
Report to the higher ups
And
Make a record
of the
deed.

(AIDES:) Your Honor, fire has not broken out; it's just that people have brought lamps with them to help put out the fire. (LADY:) I told you there was light but no smoke. (MAGISTRATE:) The lamps are so bright? (AIDES:) There are many lamps held by many people. (MAGISTRATE *looks pleased*:) Oh, I see. You had me scared there for a moment. (*Gives orders*:) Good thing those commoners have a spirit of public duty. Tell them all to go home and take a rest, and I'll give them a reward tomorrow. (*Aside*:) I've still got some farm almanacs left over from last year. One for every three of them out to be enough! (LADY, *aside*:) He's so happy about these guys coming to put out a fire; he must secretly hate me for starting a fire. I can't forgive him for this. (*Faces*:) You scoundrel, whom are you going to reward? (MAGISTRATE:) I'm going to reward the commoners. (LADY:) Why are you going to reward them? (MAGISTRATE:) Because they came to help put out the fire. (LADY:) Why did they want to put out the fire? What fire are you talking about? (MAGISTRATE:) The fire that came from the back apartments. (LADY:) How did a fire come from the back apartments? (MAGISTRATE *remains silent.*) (LADY:) You rascal! Cat got your tongue? I'll say it for you then. You scabby dog, you're bound to say it was me who set the fire! If your higher-ups find out and ask why I set the fire, I'll say it was because you built a fence without consulting me. If they ask why you built the fence, I'll say it was because you were afraid of the ruckus caused by your fooling around with serving girls. (MAGISTRATE *clasps* LADY*'s mouth*:) My good little Lady, you're going to be the death of me for sure. (*Sings*:)

(*Qiaopai'er*)
My wife,
please
stop playing around,
In this case
I think no one's at fault.

(*Speaks*:) When I get up to the hall tomorrow, I'll have my own way to settle it. (LADY:) Since you are willing to reward them, how do you plan to do so? (MAGISTRATE:) No need for you to worry about that. (*Sings*:)

I happen to be

Noted for my ability to shift with prevailing winds,

I don't want to be subject of everyone's gossip.

(LADY:) If you don't handle things according to the law, then I'm going to set fire to something again. I can do it any time I want. Your handling of cases can't beat my handling of torches! (MAGISTRATE:) Please, do instruct me! But since day has now dawned, first rest for a while. I'll go up to the hall to attend to matters. (LADY:) You're not allowed to lock that new gate! (MAGISTRATE:) I know, I know!

(LADY *exits.*)

(MAGISTRATE *changes clothes*:) What a hazard, what a mess! It's a good thing I got her to say that idea herself, otherwise I might have rewarded the wrong person by mistake, and she would have suspected me of blaming her for setting the fire. Morning and night stirring up a ruckus—it would have been too late to regret it then. Enough! Enough! I need to set aside my suspicions and worries for now. If I don't pay attention to what's going on in the front hall, a new fire may erupt in the back. (*Ascends to the main hall, calls to* AIDES:) Have those people who came to help with the fire last night arrived yet? (AIDES:) They never dared disperse. (MAGISTRATE:) They did not disperse? How many of them are there? (AIDES:) Several hundred at least. (MAGISTRATE:) Let me see that register of names. (*They give it to him, and he looks.*) Let's see: County Graduate Wei Guanfu and forty-seven others, commoner from the old quarter, Feng Yuanjia and five hundred twenty others, Monk Li and sixty-three other monks and priests, and Mama Chen, along with thirty-five others. (*Asks*:) Is this Monk Li the same Monk Li from yesterday? (AIDES:) It is. (MAGISTRATE, *aside*:) That bald bastard! Yesterday in court I didn't press him hard at all. He didn't say anything about money then; he just flattered me. Could it be that he was hinting at money somewhere in there? Who knew he'd come back to see me again? Since he's not treading the path of politics like me, I've got ways of dealing with him. Aides! Take the record book outside and just call in the people whose names have red dots next to them.

(CROWD *of citizens enters, dressed as graduates and commoners, along with Monk* LI *and* CHEN.)

(MAGISTRATE *sings*:)

(*Tianshui ling*)

I just see

Men,

And women,

And monks,

And laypeople,
with no
rhyme nor reason,
All of you beating down my precinct trap-door.

(*Speaks*:) Look how happy he looks; they're all lusting after rewards. (*Sings*:)

I'll make you
Happy enough when you come,
Oh,
But sighing of injustice as you go.

(WEI:) Graduate humbly reporting. (MAGISTRATE:) No need for formalities. (WEI:) That tone of voice doesn't sound good. (*Everyone kowtows.*) (MAGISTRATE:) Besides the graduate, everyone else listen up! Feng Yuanjia! (FENG:) Here! (MAGISTRATE:) Monk Li! (LI:) Here! (MAGISTRATE:) Mama Chen! (CHEN:) Here. (MAGISTRATE:) Okay, everyone's here. Hold on. You're the mother-in-law from the other day. Why are you called Mama Chen now? Is it not a crime to use a fake name? (CHEN:) Your Honor, I was originally surnamed Chen, but only because my son-in-law decided to file a complaint did I enter my name as "Mother-in-Law." The other day you sent down your heavenly decision that I should not bother my son-in-law anymore. Thus, my old son-in-law does not recognize me anymore, and my new son-in-law is still "one who left the home," so who is there to claim me as "Mother-in-Law" now? (LI, *aside, looks frightened.*) (MAGISTRATE:) I see. I did decide that, so you are allowed a change of name. But, since your daughter enticed one monk before and is now marrying another, it sounds like she's gotten one too many blessings from monks. I think I better ask a few more questions about this inappropriate behavior. (LI:) Your Honor, I'm afraid that elderly person did not give a clear account. The new son-in-law that she summoned has not yet moved in. Since he's not yet in her home, she therefore referred to him as "one outside the home." She didn't mean there's another monk. (MAGISTRATE:) Whether a monk or not is no business of mine. I guess I won't pursue it. But you, monk, why are you testifying on another's behalf? It seems like you are quite fond of court cases? (LI:) Oh no, I have no fondness for entering and exiting the public gate.[67] (MAGISTRATE:) You say you don't enter and exit the public gate, but (*sings*)

(*Zhegui ling*)

In just
These past two days,
You've twice raised a ruckus at the county seat,
Through the
Side gate, it seems,
You
Slide very smoothly.

(*Speaks*:) Come up here. (*Asks in a low voice*:) So, are you looking for a government job? (LI:) How could I not want one? But I don't know how far the trip might be. (MAGISTRATE:) It's a mere two or three hundred miles.[68] (LI:) That's too far. I don't think I have enough travel money. (MAGISTRATE:) Get out of here, you bald ass! I'm not just asking you about one crime! (*Sings*:)

The first of the crimes is ingratitude.

(LI:) But I came forward to help put out the fire—wasn't that showing my gratitude? (MAGISTRATE:) Nonsense! Are you saying all these people here have come to repay a debt? If there weren't a fire for one hundred years in my district, I'd never repay such a debt in a hundred years! (*Sings*:)

The second is going off on your own at night.

(LI:) But I came here with everyone else. I wasn't on my own. (MAGISTRATE:) Nonsense! If it wasn't on your own, then who exactly called you over? (*Sings*:)

The third is gathering crowds to cause a disturbance.

(LI:) Our arrival together was unplanned. I didn't intentionally get everyone together. (MAGISTRATE:) Nonsense! If you were really coming to put out a fire, then you would have brought water with you. Why, instead, did you bring lamps? Were you trying to extinguish fire with fire? Were you trying to take hostages? Maybe you were hoping to kidnap one of the beautiful young ladies who came running out? (CROWD:) Originally, we weren't planning to bring lamps, but because it was late at night, we could not do without them. If we hadn't lit lamps, we wouldn't have been able to make it here. (MAGISTRATE:) More nonsense! Even if one needs a lamp to go out at night, there's something strange about coming to put out a fire with lamp in hand. You could have roasted our county seat to the ground by morning! (WEI:) My lord, they are mistaken. When a fire has first broken out, the key is to smother it. Everyone brought hooks, ladders, blankets, buckets, and other tools for putting out fires. (MAGISTRATE:) If that were the case, they should have donated such items to the county seat for preventing future fires. (WEI:) Because people were waiting in the dark after the fire was put out, they sent those items back and called for torches to stay on the lookout. People were afraid someone might steal from the storehouse. (MAGISTRATE:) More nonsense! The grain and beans in the storehouse (*points to own sleeve*) I've got them all stored up right here. Nothing to worry about. Even in our prison, everyone is generous and full of filial sentiment. Feeling so grateful to me for my lenience, they can't even bear to leave. As for stingy and cruel people like that Monk Zhang, well he's out in the stockades right now. Even if he wanted to get out and steal something, he couldn't. Nothing to worry about. (*Points to* WEI:) What is your name? (WEI:) This graduate's name is Wei Guanfu. (MAGISTRATE *sings*:)

No one needs you to do a government job![69]

(*Points to* FENG:) What's your name? (FENG:) I'm Feng Yuanjia. (MAGISTRATE *sings*:)

Today you've met your match![70]

(CROWD:) Your Honor, you're too touchy! (MAGISTRATE *sings*:)

It's not that

I mean to be so tough,

But you

Don't understand what punishment's all about.

(*Speaks*:) If I were to be really tough, I'd question you all under suspicion of openly carrying fire and cudgels.[71] (CROWD:) What fire? What cudgels? (MAGISTRATE:) If I give you a torch set on fire, then you'll have nothing more to say? (*Sings*:)

The fire was in the lanterns, the conspiracy was in the cudgels.

(CROWD:) Carrying flaming torches to do what? (MAGISTRATE:) Though you've not yet carried out your heist, you had all the tools to do it. Listen to my judgment! (*Pronounces judgment*:) Since you had the tools all ready for a heist, you can't deny it. But since you are such a large number, it's inconvenient to punish you all, so I'm inclined to leniency. From the followers I'll accept a minor fee; from the leaders I want a big donation. (WEI:) How unfair! If the county seat hadn't caught fire, we wouldn't have come here in the first place. Your Excellency and Your Ladyship have schemed together to entrap us! (MAGISTRATE:) If someone else were to speak to me like this it would be okay, but as a graduate you should know better! How can you be so lacking in your mastery of language and logic? (WEI:) How do you mean? (MAGISTRATE:) As for the word "fire:" if someone accidentally lets a fire get out of control, we call it a "break out," but we say someone "sets" a fire if he does it on purpose. If a fire were to rage out of control, it could "raze" the whole county seat. If a fire is "set," then its creation and extinguishing are under my control. These two words make a big difference! (WEI:) So Your Excellencies' fire was "set?" (MAGISTRATE:) What if it was? (WEI:) Why did you set it? (MAGISTRATE:) If I don't explain it, I guess a scholar of your caliber will never figure it out. It was like how, if you keep something wrapped in a package for years, it keeps its shape even if you take the thing out, or how characters get rubbed off papers if you carry them around for a long time. As for the original items and writing, through moving and rubbing, they end up going to Master Improbable. It was like a public statement or testimony for which one secretly hires a ghostwriter. In the end you should commit them to Lord No-Such.[72] A fire can burn a path if no one lets it get out of control. It was like secretly feeling your wallet to make sure it hasn't fallen out. Forgive the confusion: this is what I meant by "set." (WEI:) If one can set a fire, can one kill a man? (MAGISTRATE:) I didn't ask you to confess to a real crime. Who said anything about killing? It's not that we couldn't do it if we wanted to, though. You should not look lightly on our local county's power. (*Sings*:)

(*Jinshang hua*)

My

Five-horsed chariot—people look up to it.

A magistrate can turn bad omens to good,
How can
those
commoners compare with me?
A sub-county that can pass a death sentence
Still must yield to me.
I'm
Practically a grand protector,
Who can wipe out a whole clan.

(*Speaks*:) This is a matter of respect for my authority. If we want to talk about logic, then not only should you people not have brought lanterns here, you shouldn't even be burning them at your houses! (WEI:) Why not? (MAGISTRATE:) There are three advantages to not lighting lanterns and three ways in which lighting them is harmful. (WEI:) I would like to hear them. (MAGISTRATE:) If you go to bed late, then you wake up late—to waste the day is one harm. When you light a lantern, you expend oil. That's two. Lastly, it causes people to get up to no good. That's three. The first advantage to not lighting them is that it makes your sleeping and waking natural. It also saves oil, and third, there's no worry it will get out of control—aren't those three advantages? There's no need to say more, these virtues alone are enough! (*Sings*:)

See how
I don't promote anything useless,
Yet root out any harm.

(WEI:) You truly are supporting the good and eliminating the bad. Please allow us to erect a stone tablet in your honor. (MAGISTRATE:) Indeed, indeed. (*Sings*:)

Truly, we must spread word of good governance,
And not neglect proper donations in our turn.

(*Speaks*:) Oh Master of Ceremony Wei, you were once a good man and today you've become a criminal, so I'll forgive you half. (WEI:) Thank you, my lord. However, I'd ask that you please loosen your restrictions on lanterns a bit. After all, as a scholar, I must read both day and night. (MAGISTRATE:) You're being foolish again. (*Sings*:)

Why don't you
Catch a few fireflies to read by?

(WEI:) That may be okay for summer nights, but what about winter? (MAGISTRATE *sings*:)

The reflection of the moon on the snow.

(WEI:) Spring and Autumn? (MAGISTRATE *sings*:)

You can read by the light of the moon.

(WEI:) What about on cloudy nights? (MAGISTRATE:) You can't have to read on every single night of the year. Take advantage of the sun! (*Sings*:)

Draw on what's in excess to supplement what's lacking.

(FENG:) If his reading is like this, then what should we businessmen do? (MAGISTRATE:) Why do you need to light lanterns to do business? From times of old the market has been held in the daytime, not at night. (*Sings*:)

(*Biyu xiao*)
Why don't you live your life in the sun,
Instead of by light of a bonfire?

(LI:) It may be okay for buying and selling, but surely we need to be able to offer some candles to the Buddha? (MAGISTRATE:) The fire of the stars can light up the fields. (*Sings*:)

With lanterns burning bright,
It's a recipe for disaster.
I urge you to
Count on your rosary beads
To illuminate your ignorance.

(CHEN:) Your Honor, it is appropriate for those who have left the home to assiduously train in darkness, but what about us small households, which need to get some chores done at night? (MAGISTRATE:) This is even less of a problem. The night time's for fun—just ask your daughter over there. She certainly needs to start going to bed earlier! (*Sings*:)

You
Old woman, you
Need to
Patch up the holes in your own pants,
Rather than
Using a lantern to sew cloth at night,
Why don't you
Lessen the gossip you stir up by day?

(*Speaks*:) Listen, all of you, at the noon court I will issue a proclamation prohibiting the use of lanterns. Those ignoring it will be subject to three kinds of punishment. At home they should be ridiculed, in the street punished, and more severely punished if near the town hall. Don't forget it! (CROWD:) On a dark night like tonight how will we manage? (MAGISTRATE:) Don't blind people manage all the time? (*Sings*:)

(*Liting yan* with *Rhythm-end Coda*)
Though you open your two eyes wide,
it will be
just like you're blind.

(CROWD:) Ancient people had to read by borrowed light, but you won't be burning any in your own home either, Your Honor? (MAGISTRATE *sings*:)

As for
Borrowing light
The punishment

Should be for digging holes in walls.

(WEI:) Your lordships, there's one other prohibition you've not yet mentioned. (MAGISTRATE:) What prohibition? (WEI:) Prohibiting moonlight. (MAGISTRATE:) Very true. (*Sings*:)

How dare that moon

Come barging into people's homes late at night?

(WEI:) In that case, I'm afraid I won't be able to read by moonlight, since I will commit the same offence. (MAGISTRATE:) There's another way of looking at it. Since the moonlight enters people's homes without permission, we should allow people to use it without asking too many questions. (*Points to* WEI *and sings*:)

Starting now you must

Put away torches and timbers; burn oil to stretch out sunlight.

(*Points to* FENG *and* CHEN:)

Cite no more the precedent of tying ropes at night.[73]

(*Points to* LI:)

And no more talk of eternal lamps to Buddha.

I'm even going to

Send a memorial to our wise sovereign,

Explaining how we do things here, and

Asking to

Remove the line from the *Book of Rites* about traveling with lantern by night.

To Xiao He's strict legal canon

We will add a prohibition on burning lanterns on Lantern Festival.

You commoners

can just treat

every night like Cold Food Festival![74]

(CROWD:) What will you do if your lady lights a lantern? (MAGISTRATE:) My wife is setting fires all day; what need has she to light a lantern? (*Sings*:)

My

Dignity's maintained in the court-room hall,

But I must defer to my wife in the home.

(CROWD:) What of the three swords and five horses?[75] (MAGISTRATE *sings*:)

Even one who's above ten thousand

May himself be below one other.

(*Speaks*:) Don't you worry about me. I've got another bit of good advice. (CROWD:) Please speak. (*As the* MAGISTRATE *lowers his head to whisper*, LI *begins to sneak away behind him.*) (MAGISTRATE:) Everyone go home and buy a gourd. Put the money you save on oil in it and at the end of each year open it up. (*Sings*:)

If you can send me a bit of what you save up

On oil each day

And at the end of each year

Offer a little to show your devotion,
It would not be out of place.

(WEI, FENG, *and* CHEN *exit.*)

(MAGISTRATE:) Aides, please leave us. I want to go to the back apartments for a conversation.

(AIDES *exit.*)

(MAGISTRATE *laughs*:) Those silly commoners waited all night and I've found a way to get money out of them instead of giving rewards. Just as they say, talking is hard work (*extends hand*) but it can make you a bundle! (*He turns around and* LI *looks to the side, embarrassed,* MAGISTRATE *yells to go after him.*) (LI *runs away.*)

(MAGISTRATE *exits.*)

Phrases from the wells and markets, told for quite some time,
It's not often such a funny thing one finds.
Sighs and songs can't tell it all, we've added lyrics of our own,
Put on a variety show, everybody all together.

NOTES

1. For more on "laughter" and its appearance in titles of late imperial plays and miscellanies, see He (2013). Drawing on Bakhtin, Shang (2003) analyzes the newspaper-like layout of such works as they appeared in woodblock print, often with multiple registers on a single page excerpting and juxtaposing a wide range of popular songs, dramatic scenes, quotations, and jokes. *A Song for a Laugh*'s variegated, episodic nature arguably suggests this milieu. See also Schoenberger (2019).
2. For more details on this edition, see Sun Shulei (2011).
3. For more on the authorship question, see Zhang Zhengxue (2019).
4. See, for example, Besio (2009).
5. Gibbon cries, along with tiger roars and other natural sounds, are sometimes described as *xiao*. This similarity might have inspired rumors of a connection with the author of the *Four Cries of a Gibbon*. Paired with *ge*, however, *xiao* generally refers to human vocal artistry, referencing singing with and without lexical words, respectively.
6. For more on medieval "whistling" and the associated Daoistic privileging of the human voice over pure tones of the zither, see Zeitlin (2019).
7. Traditional Chinese opera includes segments of vocal music composed to fit preexisting musical-poetic patterns. The playwright here emphasizes that, while the song lyrics in this play use more vulgar, colloquial language than typical, they nevertheless fit traditional prescriptions.
8. "Entering tone" refers to words that ended in -p, -t, or -k in Middle Chinese. These endings are absent in *Putonghua*, as they were from northern Mandarin of the Yuan dynasty. Thus, the proper performance of a northern style drama should not include these endings.
9. Refers to dialect and slang words with no standard form in written Chinese. One example may be the word 台垓 in act 1, also appearing as 台孩 or 胎孩 in Jin and Yuan dynasty storytelling and drama scripts, and here translated as "hold one's head up high" (be proud). It may be a way of writing a phrase properly written with the characters *taike* 擡頦 (literally "raise the chin") but pronounced differently in colloquial language. In performance it should likely be pronounced *taihai*.

10. Shen Yue's 沈約 (441–513) rhyming standards refers to the Middle Chinese language system encoded in such works as Lu Fayan's 陸法言 *Qieyun* 切韻 (*Initials and Rhymes*) of 601. Many poets continued to use these for composition in a classic style.
11. Story from an official history of the Song dynasty about a king whose subjects all drank from a spring that made them go mad. His subjects then viewed the king, the last sane person in the kingdom, to be suffering from insanity and attempted to treat him with medicine. The king finally drank from the spring to become insane himself. This phrase contrasts with the preceding Buddhist metaphor about a sword cutting through illusion, implying it is better to be immersed in the same illusions as others than to be alone in clarity.
12. Each act of this play is a literal enactment of a folk idiom. Act 1: "when winter melons are gone, take out your anger on the gourds" (走了冬瓜，拿瓠子出氣). Act 2: "burning the son-in-law's heel to cure the mother-in-law's toothache" (丈母娘牙疼，灸女壻的腳跟). Act 3: "Li wears Zhang's hat" (張冠李戴). Act 4: "government officials set fires while forbidding commoners to light lanterns" (只許州官放火，不許百姓點燈). Each saying means "to shift blame to the wrong target."
13. Each act uses characters belonging to one traditional phonetic category in places where the prosody requires end rhyme. As the guidelines stipulate the usual standard for northern-style arias, Zhou Deqing's 周德清 (1277–1365) *Zhongyuan yinyun* 中原音韻 (*Rhymes of the Central Plain*), I here transliterate 皆來 and other rhyme schemes following the IPA renderings in Li Huei-mian's 2016 edition.
14. Monks and nuns were called "those who have left the home" (出家人).
15. "The gate of emptiness": the study of Buddhism.
16. Chan Buddhism, attributed to patriarch Bodhidharma.
17. The word *hulu*, used in two common song titles in this act (*You hulu* and *Sheng hulu*), literally means "gourd," likely punning on the theme. *You hulu* is also a word for a field cricket.
18. "Expedient means" (Sanskrit *upāya*, Ch. *fangbian* 方便): a Buddhist term indicating the permissibility of using half-truths and tricks to help someone see a deeper truth. Here used euphemistically to mean taking liberties.
19. The flower of the *uḍumbara* fig, which blooms inside its fruit and is therefore not seen, is an image of something delicate and rare, like Buddhist enlightenment, here juxtaposed with common weeds. King Xiang of Chu's terrace on Mount Wu is an erotic image of the site of a romantic meeting between a king and a goddess, here juxtaposed with the image of a lotus pedestal, on which a Buddha would sit alone.
20. The image of a bald head imprisoned in a cangue.
21. "Little monk" is a slang term for penis.
22. This passage jokingly weaves together quotations from the Confucian *Four Books*, a primary focus of the late imperial civil service examination, in such a way as to hint at anal sex. Turning classical quotations into jokes through recontextualization was a common late-imperial pastime. The "Way" is a philosophical concept associated especially with Daoism and Neo-Confucianism.
23. An idiom meaning to uselessly fantasize.
24. In addition to meat, Buddhist monks were expected to abstain from eating strongly flavored roots, like garlic and onion.
25. Slang for female sex organs.
26. The image of sour grapes, like the idiom "eat vinegar," implies jealousy in Chinese.
27. Dowager empress Lü (d. 180 BCE) of the Han dynasty famously entrapped and attempted to poison guests at a banquet.
28. The root is not cut off; they are cleaned well so they can also be consumed.

29. "Like a lazy elephant chewing melon seeds" is a folk saying (*xiehouyu* 歇後語 or "anapodoton") implying the rejoinder "though his eyes get their fill, his belly never will."
30. Play on the image of a Chinese copper coin with a hole in the middle and a phrase meaning "money grubbing."
31. A metaphorical quotation from the *Analects*, here used literally.
32. Women's tiny bound feet were called "golden lotuses."
33. Originally a reference to Empress Wu Zetian (d. 705), whose husband belonged to the imperial Li family of the Tang dynasty, but whose lovers were surnamed Zhang. The phrases "Zhang drinks but Li gets drunk" and "Li wearing Zhang's crown" came to refer to misattribution or shifting blame to the wrong target.
34. The daughter of Mātaṅgī attempted to seduce Ānanda, a cousin and disciple of Śākyamuni (Gautama) Buddha, but Śākyamuni broke the spell of seduction by reciting a mantra before Ānanda could break the precepts.
35. A play on the Buddhist "Devil Prince," who keeps good deeds from happening.
36. Daoist metaphor comparing the mind to a wild horse or monkey: difficult to control.
37. Mandarin ducks: a symbol of conjugal bliss. To scatter the mandarin ducks would imply ending the affair.
38. Cutting off a lock of blue-black hair (*qingsi* 青絲) is a pun for cutting off thoughts of other lovers (情思).
39. A woman would allow her lover to burn small scars on her body as a mark of devotion. There are numerous references to the practice in the sixteenth-century novel *The Plum in the Golden Vase* (*Jin Ping Mei*).
40. The word for an acupuncture point, *lüxu*, sounds like the word for son-in-law, *nüxu*.
41. An herb used in Chinese medicine.
42. Monk Li invents fake names to account for his slip of the tongue: "Mother Qi" (齊母) sounds like "wife and mother" (妻母); Little Zeng (小曾) sounds like "little monk" (小僧).
43. Moxibustion: similar to acupuncture, a traditional Chinese medical treatment involving burning herbs, usually mugwort (moxa, Ch. *ai* 艾), to heat up points thought to affect the body's energies.
44. Thought to be one of the highest forms of filial piety, *gegu* 割股, literally "cutting the thigh," was a possibly apocryphal practice of cutting a piece of a child's flesh to feed in a soup to a sick parent.
45. Reference to a magical creature called a three-legged softshell turtle.
46. "Pearls without eyes" is the first half of an idiom, the second being "blind baby/treasure." It means something one thinks important which is actually worthless.
47. The phrase "climb over (a neighbor's) east wall to steal his daughter," taken from the *Mencius*, means to commit (sexual) impropriety.
48. Hungry ghosts: beings trapped in a Buddhist hell of unfulfilled desire. Loach: a type of catfish; its cylindrical body here suggests a penis.
49. Reference to story of a princess who agreed to meet her lover in a Zoroastrian temple but found him there asleep and left a token. Awakening to realize he had missed their liaison, his rage transformed into a fire that burned the whole temple.
50. Euphemism for sexual intercourse related to the previously cited King Xiang of Chu legend.
51. The title of this song means "teasing for a laugh."
52. Literally, "intestinal wind," a condition believed to result from excessive "damp heat" in the lower body. Here implies sexual urges.
53. Numbers of significance in astrology, such as date and time of birth.
54. Though clear and white, water and flour together make a mess.

55. *Yakṣa*: a Buddhist demon. Boya: a famous zither player, the deep meaning of whose performances only one, perceptive friend could understand. The image of plucking a zither slowly could also hint at manual stimulation of female sex organs. "Facing the foe": sex was frequently compared to battle. Here, Li suggests the magistrate tread carefully, since the former knows details of the latter's embarrassing love affair.
56. Comparison of Monk Zhang to Zhang Ling, an ancient Daoist master.
57. The Magistrate mistakes the character "three" (三) for the character for surname Wang (王).
58. A traditional Chinese judge's hat had two "wings" extending from either side.
59. *Ācārya*: Sanskrit term for a Buddhist teacher.
60. Qinghe: ancestral home of the Zhang clan. Longxi: ancestral home of the Li clan.
61. Rescriptor-in-Waiting Bao Zheng (999–1062): legendary judge with reputation for brilliance and incorruptibility. Star of many, more serious legal dramas, he was nicknamed "Blue Sky Bao" 包青天, a reference to his clear insight.
62. *Rākṣasa*: a Buddhist demon.
63. Possible metatheatrical reference to the fact he had just begun singing.
64. The first Chinese character in the word for "wife," 夫人, has one more horizontal stroke than the first character in the word for "boss," 大人, which literally means "big."
65. A pun substituting the phrase "fearsome wife" for the homophonous "fathers and older brothers" (父兄).
66. A pun substituting "fearsome" for "older brother" and "higher-ups" (上人) for "villager" (鄉人). See *Mencius*, "Master Gao, Part One."
67. Here, "public gate" (公門) is a pun on the word "anus" (肛門).
68. The magistrate solicits a bribe in coded language.
69. The name Wei Guanfu 衛官甫 is a pun for the phrase "doing a government job" (為官府).
70. The name Feng Yuanjia 馮願嘉 is a pun for the phrase "encounter an enemy" (逢冤家).
71. The phrase "carry fire and sticks" means to openly commit evil.
72. "Master Improbable" and "Lord No-Such" are two fictional characters from Sima Xiangru's 司馬相如 (179–117 BCE) famous poem "Zixu fu" 子虛賦 (Rhapsody of Sir Vacuous). Here the magistrate urges the crowd to forget the question of who started the fire.
73. Reference to lines from the *Canon of Poetry* about collecting grasses by day and twisting them into ropes by night.
74. A festival for cleaning out the hearth at the end of winter. Cold food is consumed, as no fires should be lit.
75. "Three swords" (三刀) here references the character for county magistrate, *zhou* 州.

8

Ramblings with Magicians in Lyrics and Songs

The Secret Copy of the Play from the Wild Crane Studio Newly Intoned on the Terrace for Whistling

DING YAOKANG (1599–1669)

TRANSLATED BY XIAOQIAO LING

Ding Yaokang's 丁耀亢 (1599–1669) ten-act southern *zaju* play *Ramblings with Magicians* 化人遊 (hereafter *Ramblings*) presents a most intriguing story. The hero He Sheng 何生 (literally meaning Student Who), a Chinese Everyman who is also the author's alter ego, boards a large boat on which he has gathered a galaxy of exceptional persons from across space and time—illustrious poets and legendary beauties from antiquity to medieval periods, Daoist magicians, and other cultural luminaries such as a knight-errant, a court jester, a cook, and a tea master. In the midst of his carefree roaming with this distinguished company, Student Who leaves the vessel and boards a skiff to go fishing, to end up being swallowed by a whale. In the whale's belly, he encounters Qu Yuan 屈原 (ca. 340–ca. 278 BCE), China's archetypical poet. Qu Yuan had been a minister of the ancient state of Chu, who had warned its ruler of its impending doom, and when alienated from the king and banished from court because of slander, had voiced his frustration in long laments. In a final gesture of desperation Qu Yuan had drowned himself, unable to reconcile himself to a corrupt world. Qu Yuan quotes his own poetry and then treats Student Who to an orange, but upon cutting it open, they find another world inside inhabited by two old men playing a game of *go*. After the two old men mysteriously disappear, Mr. Who gets out of the whale's belly only to discover to his dismay that the ocean has turned into a field of mulberry trees. Only after he encounters a Tibetan monk at the Temple of Whale Bones does he learn the whereabouts of the large vessel. After Student He reunites with his fellow travelers, the group visits the palace of the dragon king before it disperses: the poets and beautiful women all depart resuming their old destinies, leaving Student Who alone and without a boat just as he was at the beginning of the play.

Ramblings is essentially a deliverance play, a subgenre of the northern *zaju* play from the fourteenth century. Deliverance plays typically feature a spiritual journey of a protagonist through a period of crisis that so fundamentally destabilizes and endangers his perception of self and the world that he becomes enlightened to the futility of all attachments. Student Who's encounter with the leviathan poses the same kind of crisis: it both challenges his sense of being and offers a chance for spiritual cultivation. Yet *Ramblings* departs from earlier deliverance plays by staging a distinctive group of immortals: these are not deities from the popular Daoist pantheon (such as the Eight Immortals), but historical figures who have not transcended their own memories of the past. Since their senses of the self are still circumscribed by time and place, they share Student Who's limitations of understanding. The structure of the deliverance play therefore seems to have offered a rhetorical device through which the author contemplates the meaning of transcendence in what appear to be carefree ramblings.

There is a strong historical urgency in this authorial contemplation. Ding Yaokang has told us that he composed the play to commemorate the bitter displacement of a close friend as it was conveyed in a long poem titled "Ballad on *Ramblings with Magicians* for Master Li Xiaoyou. Worn Out by Traveling, the Master Lodged His Words in Poetry Collections Such as *Driven by Hunger* and *The Bright Moon*. I Have Therefore Composed *Ramblings with Magicians* for His Consolation" 化人遊歌寄李小有先生，先生困於遊，寓言〈飢驅〉、〈明月〉諸篇，因作〈化遊〉以廣之. Ding Yaokang met Li Xiaoyou 李小有 (Li Changke 李長科, fl. 1571–1647) in 1647 during his visit of Taizhou in an attempt to find a livable place in the south. Their shared experience of displacement must have played a role in forging friendship: Ding Yaokang took to hiding along the coastal islands in Shandong in 1642 when the Manchu army sacked his hometown and in 1644 when the Ming dynasty fell to peasant rebels. The sea voyage featured in *Ramblings* may therefore have been derived from his personal experience as well.

Failing to settle down in the south, Ding Yaokang went to Beijing in 1648 and started his decade-long service under the Manchu regime first as an instructor in Manchu banner schools and later in a local Confucian academy. He made a name for himself in the capital area as a playwright. Three of his southern *chuanqi* plays that survive from this period (two historical plays and one romantic play) all deal with various ways of perceiving the self in relation to Manchu authority—such persistent concerns were emblematic of pervasive inner struggles shared among many of Ding's acquaintances in the capital area who had chosen to serve the new political order. Ding Yaokang himself also vacillated in his positions. He made his way toward the south to assume an administrative post as magistrate in Fujian after his tenure as Confucian Instructor but never assumed office. Instead, he submitted his resignation en route and spent a good part of 1660 at the West Lake in Hangzhou before he headed back to Shandong, where he spent the rest of his years in retirement. During his stay at the West Lake, Ding completed a vernacular novel that was a sequel to *The Plum in the Golden Vase* 金瓶梅, an erotic novel well circulated among the cultural elite. In this sequel he uses the fictional world to present a veiled comment on his own time as an apocalyptic present in which personal survivals are contingent upon one's commitment to, rather than repudiation of, one's flawed past. This is a drastically different message from the reconciliatory attempts made in his *chuanqi* plays with regard to the Manchu authority.

Fiction and plays as marginal modes of literary production therefore provide the necessary sense of distance that allows Ding Yaokang and his fellow literary men to contemplate their memories of the traumatic past and to explore various options of coming to terms with the new political order. *Ramblings* repeatedly refers to the shift of mountains and rivers and the ocean transforming into mulberry fields, which are stock references to the dynastic transition. Such an elegiac tone suggests that the "carefree ramblings" evoke actual experiences of displacement or escape at a time of crisis. Ding Yaokang has clearly conceived of *Ramblings* as a community-building experience: he enlists his close friends to contribute their own comments on the play after the end of each act, in effect staging the reading of the play as a group activity. In this communal reading, Ding Yaokang's friends are not so much vicariously joining the playwright's alter ego, Student Who, in an allegorically significant free rambling as they are pondering multiple ways of coming to terms with the past following a literal representation of "ferrying to the other shore" across the traumatic divide of the Manchu conquest of China in 1645.

By Ding Yaokang's time, the northern *zaju* play, which typically features four acts with only the male or female lead singing, had largely receded from the stage and been replaced by southern *chuanqi* theater in which all role types participate in singing. Writers nevertheless continued to compose *zaju* plays as a reading practice, though they often mixed northern tunes with southern tunes and attributed singing to all role types just like southern theater. The length of a play also ranges from one to ten acts. *Ramblings* markets itself as a southern *zaju* play, as it includes in its title references to both southern lyrics (*ci*) and northern songs (*qu*). Ding Yaokang pushes the potential of this form to an extreme by evoking musicality to represent multiple perspectives and voices within the play. He has made his characters sing to the same tune to bring out their contrastive perspectives, such as Qu Yuan and Student Who's different responses to the chess-playing old men found within the orange. Ding has also explored divisions between northern and southern tunes to represent gender-specific perspectives of the famous poets as opposed to the legendary beauties. Tunes from different modes are also juxtaposed within a single act to organize multiple modes of reading. In act 9, for example, three different sets of northern and southern modes are employed to prescribe three levels of meaning: elegy and romantic longing designated by melancholic southern tunes on the one hand, and vigorous vitality and comic relief indexed by robust northern tunes on the other.

Ramblings therefore makes a good example for us to come to understand how a traditional man of letters might have made use of dramatic and musical innovations in a performance tradition to explore the full potential of fiction and theater. Student Who's blatantly fictional nature resists definitive attributes of subject identity, thus accommodating multiple possibilities in the shuffling of time and space for the imagination to probe the conquest experience in a malleable but ultimately resilient way. After the initial shock of finding himself in the whale's belly, Student Who vacillates between identifying his personhood with the small fishing skiff that remains intact (a symbol of preserving individual integrity) and the large vessel that epitomizes a collective social body (characterized by a cultural space inhabited by iconic figures). Such a dilemma mirrors the existential choices Chinese men of letters had to face when the Qing regime mandated that all nonclerical male subjects adhere to Manchu hairstyles. Whether to avoid the shame of shaving one's hair by committing suicide or taking the Buddhist tonsure for self-exile in the mountains, or whether to compromise one's individual integrity to build the cultural continuity of the Chinese civilization were crucial questions that helped define the seventeenth-century Chinese experience of trauma.

Ramblings also provides meaningful commentaries on the traumatic experience itself by revisiting the cataclysmic event of the leviathan's swallowing of the boat and by inviting different interpretations of this event. There are two reenactments of the whale's action after its initial introduction. The first, captured in the form of self-recollection in a song suite sung by Student Who, shows the disruptive power of trauma on our psyches—how confrontation with our immediate past is emotionally taxing and capable of changing our perceptions of the self and surroundings. The second, delivered in a slapstick fashion by the whale in the dragon king's palace, suggests ways of containing trauma through comic relief and self-empowerment. In addition, the author accentuates the malleability of this event in post-traumatic recollections by attaching comments from his coterie of friends. In this virtual gathering on the book page, the author himself participates in a discussion of the possible ramifications of the event, his own opinion being but one of the many possible understandings. Some of these comments focus on religious cultivation by noting the pitfalls of Student Who, such as a unilinear understanding of past and present and opting for expediency and profit. Others highlight the emotional contour of Student Who: his sense of betrayal and reflections on true friendship, as well as his resolve to overcome fear.

In addition, *Ramblings* invites comparative perspectives since it addresses fundamental questions about human experience in times of catastrophe. Since literature, as Aristotle pointed out, deals with universals and possibilities rather than the particularity of history, *Ramblings* may also shed light on human society's collective quest for amnesia, as well as how memories are formed and remain in the minds of post-trauma generations. The oceanic imagination that structures the play, especially the disaster related to shipwreck, is also a topic of universal appeal, one that invites comparison with issues of identity and self-transformation in such seminal Western works as Homer's *Odyssey*, Shakespeare's *Tempest*, or Defoe's *Robinson Crusoe*.

This translation follows the original woodblock edition of this play that is extant and has been reproduced in a modern facsimile edition.

THE SECRET COPY OF THE PLAY FROM THE WILD CRANE STUDIO

RAMBLINGS WITH MAGICIANS IN LYRICS AND SONGS

NEWLY INTONED ON THE TERRACE FOR WHISTLING

PREFACE TO THE PLAY *RAMBLINGS WITH MAGICIANS*

The summer heat is stifling like steam, but a sudden thought of rubbing one's bare feet against ice will cool one off. A traveler's situation is bleak like autumn, yet an immediate reading of *Ramblings with Magicians* will fire him up.[1] With such transformative power at my disposal, even if I were Tao Yuanming begging for food,[2] Yan Zhenqing pleading for rice,[3] or Du Shaoling on the way to Pengya Road, unable to get a plate of food[4]—such poverty cannot keep my roaming from being free-spirited.

The play's composition and language are marvelous and fantastic; the selection of beauties and recruitment of heroes startle the mind and stir the spirit. As a result, those wearing plain dark shoes and socks[5] get to share eternal fame with those from the Ten Isles.[6] It is a long time since Daoist Master Mei's "Biography of Young Master Li" that we see ingenuity like this.[7] Old Zhuowu said: "Those who composed *The Western Wing* and *The Hidden Boudoir*[8] must have had significant pent-up frustration over matters concerning the ruler and subject, peers and friends."[9] This remark perfectly describes the situation. It is probably the case that, since the author was not able to find those who understood, he came up with these roaming magicians—we therefore know that this is no casual composition.

Summer of the *dinghai* year (1647), Master Zhilu from the Huainan Poetry Society, Gong Dingzi, at the Yu Garden in Hailing.[10]

GENERAL COMMENTS

Ramblings with Magicians is not just a play with lyrics and songs. It is an allegory of my friend So-and-so about ferrying across the people of this world that is put into lyrics. Since one cannot address the present world in solemn words,[11] he cast his intent in chanting and singing; yet neither chanting nor singing can address the world in a solemn manner, so he cast it into a *chuanqi* play.

My friend believed because all *chuanqi* plays today are about romantic affairs between scholars and ladies, the usual manifestations of sorrow and joy, and do not suffice to expound his hidden thoughts and fantastic imagination. Therefore, he cast them all in the marvelous transformations of boundless, fantastic, and unbridled wanderings; yet in fact these are *not* marvelous transformations of boundless, fantastic, and unbridled wanderings.

Those who understand take them to be akin to words of the Lacquer Garden official Zhuangzi, to Qu Yuan's "Encountering Sorrow," to recorded conversations of Chan Buddhism or the Daoist Canon, or to the self-account of the Grand Historian[12]—only these are worthy to roam with the magicians.

Wuzi year (1648) of the Shunzhi Reign (1644–1661), inscribed by Song Wan (Yushu) from Laiyang.[13]

MAKEUP AND COSTUMES FOR THE CHARACTERS IN *RAMBLINGS WITH MAGICIANS*

CHENG LIAN:	From the Spring and Autumn period (770–421 BCE). After enlightening Music Master Xiang with his instructions on zither-playing, he entered the sea to become an immortal. He should wear a Daoist gown, yellow cap, and hold a sambar-tail chowry.[14] Played by EXTRA.[15]
STUDENT WHO:[16]	He should wear a free-roaming cap[17] and a long gown. Played by MALE LEAD.
ZUO CI:	From the Three Kingdoms period (220–280). He was famous for his skills at conjuring up illusions. He should wear a Daoist gown adorned with sashes, his hair in a two-pronged bundled tuft.[18] His face is painted red, and he brandishes a sambar-tail chowry. Played by MAIN VILLAIN.[19]
WANG YANG:	From the Han dynasty (202 BCE–220 CE). He was famous for his ability to turn objects into gold. He should wear a small square cap and a Daoist gown. He is hunchbacked and carries a medicine gourd, wearing painted-face makeup. Played by SECOND VILLAIN.[20]
QU YUAN:	From the Warring States period (480–221 BCE). Minister of the Chu Kingdom. He should wear an official's cap, a dark blue gown, and a silver belt. Played by OLD MALE.
LI TAIBAI (LI BAI):	From the Tang dynasty (618–907). Scholar at the Hanlin Academy, renowned for poetry. He has a white face with long mustache. He should wear a headscarf for a Tang *jinshi* examination candidate and an embroidered palace robe. Played by SECOND MALE LEAD.

DU ZIMEI (DU FU):	From the Tang dynasty. Renowned for his poetry. His official position reached that of a Reminder. He should wear a square turban and plain attire. Played by OLD MALE.
CAO ZIJIAN (CAO ZHI):	A son of Lord Wu of Wei (Cao Cao). Famed for his talents at poetry. He should wear a hair-collecting golden cap and green brocade robe. Played by SECOND MALE LEAD.
LIU GONGGAN (LIU ZHEN):	From the Three Kingdoms period (220–280) . Poet of the Jian'an era (196–220) whose fame rivaled that of Cao Zijian in his time. He should wear a square turban and plain attire. Played by SECOND MALE LEAD.
DONGFANG SHUO:	From the Western Han (202 BCE–9 CE). Renowned jester. He should wear a Daoist's cap, a recluse's robe with sashes, and a white mustache. Played by EXTRA.
LU YU:	From the Tang dynasty. Excelled in brewing tea. An idle visitor from Suzhou. He should wear plain attire. Played by SECOND OLD MALE.
KUNLUN SLAVE:	From the Tang dynasty. Swordsman. He should wear military garb armed with a sword. His face is painted red and he sports a curly beard. Played by MAIN VILLAIN.
YI YA:	From the Spring and Autumn period. Well versed in preparing food and drink. Renowned for his discerning tastes. He should wear a short beard, a painted face makeup, a low headscarf and a short shirt. Played by CLOWN.
XI SHI:	From the Kingdom of Yue during the Spring and Autumn period. Consort of the King of Wu. She should wear light makeup in Suzhou style and a palace robe with plain flower patterns. Played by FEMALE LEAD.
ZHAO FEIYAN:	Consort of Emperor Cheng of the Han (r. 33–7 BCE). She should wear heavy makeup and an embroidered palace robe. Played by SECOND FEMALE.
ZHANG LIHUA:	Consort of the Last Ruler of Chen (r. 582–589). She should wear heavy makeup and an embroidered palace robe. Played by SECOND FEMALE.

LU MOCHOU:	Courtesan from Hangzhou who lived at the West Lake. Excelled at singing and dancing. She should wear courtesan makeup and a dress for dancing. Played by SECOND FEMALE LEAD.
XUE TAO:	Courtesan from Chengdu who was well versed in songs lyrics and rhapsodies. She should wear courtesan make-up and a blouse for dancing. Played by SECOND FEMALE LEAD.
TAOYE:	A maid of Wang Xianzhi (344–381) from the Jin Dynasty. Well versed in poetry. Played by SECOND FEMALE LEAD.
LINGBO:	blank.[21]
THE DRAGON KING:	He should wear a golden gauze cap, a python robe, and a red moustache. Played by OLD MALE.
THE WHALE DEMON:	He has a black face and red beard. He should wear military garb, a gold kerchief, a gold headpiece and sports pheasant feathers. Played by SECOND VILLAIN.
OLD LADY SHRIMP:	She should wear painted face makeup, a high bun, and be lavishly adorned. Played by CLOWN.
OLD MEN IN THE ORANGE:	They should wear yellow caps and yellow Daoist gowns.

RAMBLINGS WITH MAGICIANS IN LYRICS AND SONGS, TABLE OF CONTENTS

RAMBLINGS WITH MAGICIANS IN LYRICS AND SONGS

CASUALLY COMPOSED BY THE LAYMAN WHO TRAVELS THROUGH THE WILDERNESS

PRELUDE: OPENING LYRIC

(*Manting* fang) (SECOND OLD MALE *enters wearing a Daoist cap and a colored robe*:)
Flower petals drop, so spring departs;
Orioles twitter as the moon is waning.
Wasted and worn is the "white hair, three thousand yards long."[22]
At the Qin palace and the terrace of the Han,
Tomb mounds are enveloped by desolate mist.
In days of iron horses and metal spears[23]
The hero is entrapped at the prime of his merry-making years.
Astride a donkey,
He buys wine at the West Lake,
Where he inquires into the boat for deliverance.

Master Void must have a rhapsody to write[24]
About Student Who: he asks about being ferried across,[25]
And gets to encounter Cheng Lian,
Together with immortals, knights-errant, renowned friends,
As well as beauties beyond the mundane realm.
They perform sounds and sights unprecedented for a thousand years:
Between ocean and sky, they in vain stir up the slumbering dragon.
Inside the belly of the whale, the boat returns to the Peng Island: [26]
Deeply intoxicated, they let the ocean turn into mulberry fields.[27]

(*Recites*:)
He Who Travels through Wilderness gives himself over to the rivers and oceans;
Seeking jade flowers, he assembles distinguished figures from all over.
Going beyond creative transformation, the cinnabar pill forms inside the fish belly,
Returning to Peng Island, the Dragon King encounters the transcendent craft.

ACT 1

PURCHASING THE SKIFF AND ENCOUNTERING ILLUSION

([XIANLÜ MODE:] Northern *Dian jiangchun*) (VILLAIN *in Daoist attire enters playing* CHENG LIAN *brandishing a sambar-tail chowry*:)
On the transcendent waves of the illusory seas,
Clouds are sorrowful while the sky smiles.

(CLOWN *enters playing* FISHERMAN, *sings*:)

It is good to be a fisherman,
On a single skiff, free-spirited,
watching
Flowers fill the Peach Spring boat.[28]

(CHENG LIAN:)

Ying Ocean and the Peng Island cannot be found.
Against the floating clouds, the setting sun sinks oh-so casually.

(FISHERMAN:)

Ever since I, an old fisherman, left Peach Blossom Spring,
My single skiff has sailed from past to present.

(CHENG LIAN:) I am Cheng Lian, transcendent zither master from the Eastern Ocean. At the end of the Zhou and the beginning of the Qin I went out on the ocean holding my zither. I spent a long time on Peng Island and achieved the Way of transcendence. When I observed that my disciple Music Master Xiang's[29] mortal bones had yet to transform—since the piping of Heaven is hard to transmit—I turned to a breathing technique that can summon wind and rain to sublimate his emotions and disposition. Thus I was able to enlighten and transform his mundane build, such that he was able to enter the realm of the immortals. It is now more than two thousand years since the Spring and Autumn period, and all this time I have lived in reclusion without revealing myself. I want to take my zither into the human realm to bring universal deliverance to mundane beings. But, alas, worldly beings are deeply enmeshed in their hindrance and troubles. The disaster for this kalpa has yet to be fully realized.[30] This makes me truly miserable! Now, at this mountain peak, I see in a good distance a shaft of blue light. This is because an extraordinary being, Student Who, is here to rent a boat so he may visit immortals out on the sea. I shall summon the fisherman from Wuling, Master Mysterious Perfection, to come out, dressed up as a boatman who rents boats. He is to show Student Who the way to deliverance by letting him experience all the beauties from the past to the present and to enjoy to the full the pleasures of sound and sight, so that later he can put to rest his wild nature and return to the state of transcendent perfection. What could be wrong with that? Fisherman, where are you?

(FISHERMAN:)

The skiff, riding the spring tide, divides the present and the past;
If humans ask about the peach blossoms, they will lose the Qin and Han.[31]

I bow to you, Transcendent Master. What instructions do you have for me? (CHENG LIAN:) You shall dress up as a fisherman and guide this transcendent boat, mooring it at the seashore. Now there is this traveler Student Who—he is truly destined to attain immortality. You must do your best to show him the way to deliverance. If he has any wishes, see to it that they are fulfilled to his heart's content. You must not use the eyes of vulgar kinds to belittle a lofty being. Ah, before I finish speaking, I see there, far away, that Student Who has already arrived.

(*Exits.*)

(*Reprise*) (MALE LEAD *enters playing* STUDENT WHO *in the robe of a recluse*:)
Across the four seas I have roamed,
With wind on my cape and rain on my hat.
Those who truly know me are few—
Carrying my short sword, I am solitary and lonesome.
I can only give it a laugh, as
My waxed clogs have worn out all the blue seas and mulberry fields.

(STUDENT WHO:)

A short coat, a wide-brimmed bamboo hat, and a Daoist robe;
Clouds and water, mists and a rosy haze—all in a single bag.
Without pursuing immortality, I yet encountered a maid collecting transcendent herbs—
How did it come about that, in seeking refuge, I find a fisherman?
The Way, through delusion, is comprehended and there is enlightenment;
As my bones have a marvelous karma, for I am, after all, wild.
If the Grand Creator allows me to bring it all together,
I should combine past and present into one happy scene.

My family name is He and given name Gao, and my courtesy name is Yehang (traveling through the wilderness). My ancestors were from the Wushan area in Zhejiang. From the time I was born I've always had a goal in mind, my spirit unrivaled in this world. For ten years my multicolored brush made me dream of Jiang Yan,[32] yet I have only made a humble name at the village banquet.[33] I traveled for a thousand miles in hempen sandals seeking the Grand Historian Sima Qian, only to realize that I must entrust my traces to a pact with sea gulls.[34] I have inquired into confidential instructions at Yellow Rock, yet I missed my appointment with the immortal.[35] Expounding military tactics in the camp of a general wielding Qingping, I am ashamed to seek reclusion in a low rank. But the people of the world have a range of vison that is equally clouded, so it is in vain that I have sought all over for lofty men. All under Heaven is nothing but a chaotic and bustling show, so what good is there in searching for the land of joy all by myself? It is only that I hold deep feelings for the ancient past, and I resent that I cannot rouse heroes from the pages of my books. As a result, I am burning with indignation, and it is impossible to tolerate the filth of this human realm. Student Who, Student Who, what an idiot you are! It's just that my heroic heart is still alive. Even when the greatest warrior of the state seeks patronage, his unbridled spirits are hard to repress. The famed flowers have caught my fancy, so I desire to roam wildly all over the rivers and oceans bringing together the heroic kind. My only worry is that cash kept on my rope-tied bed is running out, so I do not have the means by which to make friends. My earthenware cup is empty of wine, so the songs that I solicit are out of tune. Now that I have arrived here at the Eastern Ocean, I must first secure a boat and find a few companions. Oh, good, over there I can see a fisherman coming.

([SHUANGDIAO MODE:] *Xinshui ling*) (STUDENT WHO:)

Watery mists and showers of flowers ruffle this traveling gown,[36]
As I gaze at the Fusang tree, beyond the reach of wind and clouds.[37]
The red dust is like illusory ants,[38]
Historical records resemble unprovable dreams.[39]
I fix my intent on free rambling,
To turn events from the past to the present into a good laugh. [*Speaks*]:

I, forlorn with a solitary sword, on this never-ending road, have two eyes to capture the spirit of the wind and a liver and gall to share life and death with a soul-mate—Could it be that I will never meet another extraordinary being? This makes me heave a heavy sigh.

(*Zhuma ting*) (STUDENT WHO:)
People of my kind, lonesome and forlorn,
Drift to south and north, the hair at our temples thinning away.
Woefully I let out a long whistle,
As I wander by rivers and seas to find the fisherman and the woodcutter.[40]
I shall take
Grass huts merely as a single goose feather;[41]
Since that road to Handan was no longer the one of the past,[42]
I gaze into the floating clouds where far my old home lies.
I figure that in Wuling,
There may be no fisherman's craft.[43]

(CLOWN *playing* FISHERMAN *enters rowing the boat*:)

My home is by the side of Wuling,
To and from Wuling the travelers go.
We are both men of the Qin-era source,
So how come we do not know each other?

(STUDENT WHO:) Fisherman, let me ask you. Is this boat for yourself or for ferrying people?

(FISHERMAN:) My friend, what do you mean by "for yourself" and "for ferrying people?"

(STUDENT WHO:) If it's for yourself, then you will just be fishing at the shore, frolicking with egrets, minding your own business. You are not setting out for anywhere. If it's for ferrying people across, then you cannot be bogged down in your own family situations, nor can you set your own port. You welcome the like-minded and generously practice expedient means.[44] Once we settle on a fee, we shall roam at will across the three rivers and five lakes, where we'll share no end of bright moon and pure breeze.[45]

(FISHERMAN:) Then I'm for ferrying people. Only, there have been too many travelers recently, and they have really messed up my business. Even my original investment is all gone! Now, there is something great about this boat. Let me tell you:

([XIANLÜ MODE:] *Hunjiang long*) (FISHERMAN:)

Look,
The wind churns up high waves:
In a darkness a thousand feet high, one lonely little skiff.
The Wind God churns the dancing waves,[46]
The River Count roars fiercely,
Toward the end of the night, the sun of a thousand ages emerges red;
From time immemorial a million-layered flood-crest weighs down like snow.
Don't talk about
Baleful goblins and demonic pythons,
Venomous toads and savage dragons—
I have my own
Iron rudder to bore through the wave,
Bronze punt to reach the shore.
As my scull divides them, mountains revolve on their own,
When my sail is steadied, the waves cannot shake it.
When the wind rises, immortals play the iron flute,
When the moon is bright, dragon maidens deliver merfolk's silk.
Still, can't it be the case that—
No matter if
The wind blows from the eight directions,
You are still free to
Find your way to the immortal land of three Mao brothers?[47]

(STUDENT WHO:) Pretty boastful! A boatman like you can get that far? Here is another thing. I will need a few good mates before I go, but in this world, one cannot find men like me. Do you know of dwelling places of extraordinary beings beside the sea?

(*You hulu*) (FISHERMAN:)
You reckon that
In the field of wealth and fame, the powerful and the bullying
Are not worth inviting;
So, you want instead a group of
Wind-summoning and moon-chanting
People who are already
Half transcendent—
Mists and rosy clouds their breaths; an integrity like ice and frost.
You want all of them to
Wield their brushes and indulge in wine, their primal dragons filled with pride?[48]
Well, then even if you asked me to
Send a letter or pass along a note, I would not be able to find them,
Because to the Lotus City[49]
The road is far;

At Mount Haoli,[50]
Souls drift in nothingness.
But if you are not afraid of
Falling for the talent and beauty of immortals of poetry,
I shall get you to
Share a tent with people from antiquity.

(STUDENT WHO:) My passion for poetry and wine is unchecked and I think of rivers and lakes with great zeal. But if we do not carry with us beautiful ladies, line up tripods of food, and summon the best female performers, then it will just be us intoning poetry about poverty and sorrow, lamenting the wind, and mourning the moon—that would dampen the pleasure of roaming. Furthermore, these jovial fellows were all born to wealth and high position and have refined their craft through music and songs. So, we do need a bevy of stunning ladies to top off our joy. Can you find them?

(*Tianxia le*) (FISHERMAN:)
There's no need for
The blue bird messenger or a Feiqiong to summon the Queen Mother of the West—[51]
Every single one of them
Holds the banners in Her Highness' retinue, their skirts of rosy clouds rippling in the wind.
Since you cannot correct the ways of your greedy eyes and the lust for beauty of your mortal body,
I have it here—
Xu Hongke's phoenix glue to fix snapped strings[52]
And the medicine to summon back Lady Li's soul.[53]
I will not leave you in dismal solitude, chanting the "Sorrows of Chu."[54]

(*Speaks*:) Before I'm done talking, two more are in line to get on board.

(SOUTHERN XIANLÜ MODE: *Fanbusuan*) (VILLAIN *enters playing* ZUO CI:)
Throughout the world a black vapor floats,
But one beam of numinous light shines through.
(CLOWN *playing* WANG YANG *enters hunchbacked and carrying a gourd*:)
In the human realm I've produced thousands of magical transformations,
We'll buddy up to kick over the furnace of the magic elixir!

(ZUO CI:)

With one breath I inhale the grand chaos;
This grand illusion originally had no illusion.

(WANG YANG:)

There is no need to refine mercury or lead,
True lead does not call for refining.[55]

(ZUO CI:) Master Wang, you and I are under Supreme Lord's decree to guide Student Who so he may exit from this world. Now we can see from afar someone talking to a fisherman. That must be him. Let's get ourselves on board, so we may find a chance to deliver him. Excuse me, old chap, do you take passengers on your boat? We are here for the ride. (STUDENT WHO:) May I ask with due respect you two gentlemen's names? (ZUO CI:) This humble Daoist practitioner's surname is Zuo, given name Ci. Among the four oceans I have no home and I lack any knowledge of my ancestral place. (WANG YANG:) My surname is Wang and given name Yang. I know the way of the magic elixir and can go back and forth between fire and water.[56] (STUDENT WHO:) So between the two of you, we have one itinerant Daoist who drifts like clouds and streams, and one man of the rivers and lakes.[57] Either you sell medicine in Chengdu, or you set up a furnace for alchemy—I have no use for your kind on my boat. We are a bunch crazy for travel, so we take only those with no strings attached to join us on board. Be it the three rivers or four oceans, the five peaks or ten isles, we shall spend a good three to five years and we'll definitely have marvelous encounters. You two each have urgent business, so please attend to it as you like. I dare not delay you. (ZUO CI:) Ridiculous! You can go and I can't? Most likely, I'm afraid, I can set foot where you cannot. (STUDENT WHO:) What do you mean? (ZUO CI:) First, let me tell you where you cannot go.

(ZUO CI:)

Within your purview are Heaven's wind and black waves,
And the gushing Weak Stream that knows no bounds.[58]
Giant turtles with huge bellies will swallow your boat—
Where will you flee?
When blown off to another place or a foreign country.
You have no grain or silver left on board.
How can a divine craft carry mundane beings?
No doubt you, Sir, will end up among ghosts.[59]

(STUDENT WHO:) Please continue. How is it that you can go?

(ZUO CI:)

One mouthful of my breath levels and stills the grand ocean,
My two feet kick over Mt. Kunlun.
I gallop across the Nine Continents before the day's over,
And carry along flying talismans to expel ghosts.

(WANG YANG:)

I pinch a single cinnabar pill,
And turn it into a mountain of gold.
You are free to divide it among thousands as you see fit,
So you can travel to the edge of Heaven without any hardships.

(STUDENT WHO:) Now it is clear to me that both of you are extraordinary beings. It is my luck to have met you. Please get on board, and we will talk about recruiting travelers and soliciting songs later. (ZUO CI:) No worries, sir. The two of us will take care of this. (STUDENT WHO, ZUO CI, *and* WANG YANG *act out getting on the boat.*)

([XIANLÜ MODE] *Jisheng cao*) (ZUO CI:)

A baleful wind darkens the wilds as it roars,
Kalpic fire burns until mountains collapse.

Student Who, Look! Heaven and earth reside within the Mysterious Sea,[60] and the Ying Sea lies between heaven and earth. Even the Four Grand Continents[61] are but single grains of rice in the ocean. How laughable are worldly beings—aren't they simply ants the size of mustard seeds drifting along on wine dregs?[62]

We shall take the human realm as a mayfly hanging from a thread,
The ravages of war as a blanket of mist and clouds,
And Heaven and Earth as floating water bubbles.
Let
The six giant turtles roll their eyes to move the constellations.
To me it's only
Floating sea gulls starting to flap their wings or Qiaoqing's laughter.[63]

(ZUO CI:) About recruiting travelers and seeking singers, let us set a date and each makes a set of invitations. This will help make sure we set off on schedule. (STUDENT WHO:) I was just about to trouble you with this. (ZUO CI:) The way I see it, the boatman and Master Wang will go and meet the travelers. But as for the immortal ladies from earlier eras, they are privileged in position and noble in rank. You and I will have to greet them ourselves.

(*Coda*) (STUDENT WHO *and* ZUO CI *sing together*:)

Our spirits will commune across the distance of a hundred generations,
There will be beauties that put to shame flowers and the moon for a thousand years.
They all have
The trick for escaping from cycles of rebirth and returning to immortality—
A lifetime of chastity and righteousness; perfected loyalty and filial piety.
They are sparkling stars just like those banished immortals returning to the celestial court,
Standing in seeming obscurity among brilliant constellations.
All alike can
Ride the wind and drive the clouds, led on by circling simurghs.
We will knock discreetly on their bejeweled chambers,
To extend night invitations to those holding jade musical pipes.
What need is there to build a golden chamber to impress one's love?[64]

(WANG YANG:)

Once one encounters the authentic boat, one may set sail,

(STUDENT WHO:)

The enormous waves on the Grand River are quieted in a moment.

(ZUO CI:)

With my perch stew, why should I envy Emperor Wu?[65]

(WANG YANG:)

A swath of rosy cloud draws near the crimson city.[66]

(*Exit.*)

End-of-Act Comment

Student Who said: "In this world one cannot find men like me." This remark truly brings out profuse tears, and there is no need to compose "The Treatise on Severing Friendship."[67]

Comment by Lu Xuansheng from Wuling.

ACT 2

RECRUITING FRIENDS AND PURSUING BEAUTIES

([SOUTHERN XIANLÜ MODE:] *Yeyou gong*) (SECOND FEMALE *and* SECOND FEMALE LEAD *playing* TAOYE *and* LINGBO *enter.* TAOYE:)

Silver ocean dark, frosted moon cold.
The chill of the Icy Pot[68]
Seeps through purple chambers and mica screens.

(LINGBO:)

The azure lad is late with his crane message.
Rosy clouds are distant, the waves are clear.
I wipe the crystal curtain,
Burn cassia chips,
At the Palace of Stamen Gem.[69]

(TAOYE:)

My celestial cap is cold under the pale moon.
The silver pheasant starts to dance but remains alone.
The dark sky, the blue sea—all provoke deep thoughts.[70]

(LINGBO:)

If there is no rendezvous in Heaven, then no star would cross the River of Heaven.[71]
To the human realm there is a road, but even in dreams it is long.
Why did the peach blossoms bewitch Young Master Ruan?[72]

We are the transcendent ladies Taoye and Lingbo. We have shed our worldly ties, and our souls have returned to the cinnabar office. Even though we fail to take central positions at the Simurgh Palace,[73] we are often granted permission to accompany the phoenix chariot. The White Lady decreed:[74] "Those banished to the common world from the Registry of Transcendents are incapable of stopping their 'true lead' from leaking away.[75] But the consorts of previous dynasties were all originally transcendent beauties in Heaven. After their kalpic cycle has come to an end, they are to take up their original positions as before." After we ascended to Heaven, only one sixty-day cycle has passed, but in the lower realm it has been many thousands of years. Now, the Queen Mother of the West issued an edict that immortal ladies should gather at the transcendent boat to deliver perfected beings—this feat will count toward one full cycle of our merit-accumulation. But who in the lower realm is worth delivering? Well, before I have finished speaking, Lady Zhao and Exalted Consort from the Chen have arrived.[76]

([NANLÜ MODE:] *Lan huamei*) (SECOND FEMALE LEAD *playing* ZHAO FEIYAN *enters*:)

Rays from the azure sky scatter over light little ripples,
Simurgh pendants sway in the wind to the sound of the pacing of Yu.[77]
I still recall that
Autumn scenery in the palaces of Han was like that in the Jade Capital.

(SECOND FEMALE LEAD *playing* ZHANG LIHUA *enters*:)

So clearly are the jade trees paired up before the wind.[78]
There, in the moonlight are the Jieqi and Linchun Towers.[79]

Greetings, my lady. (ZHAO FEIYAN:) Here you are, Exalted Lady. Today we are under the divine edict to head eastward with Lady Xi Shi.[80] It's been a while but she's not here yet. Look, the colored clouds open up, and from there we can hear the cries of flying simurghs and cranes. It must mean that the creature who bewitched the King of Wu is coming.

(*Reprise*) (FEMALE LEAD *playing* XI SHI *enters*.)

A slash into the icy silk, the Jade Heaven is empty,[81]
Over the white crystalline reflection my sandals make no sound.[82]
The radiance from a lake: am I passing on a boat?

(ZHAO FEIYAN *sings*:)

You,
From the Zhuluo Mountains, are far from the flower-covered paths;[83]
Yet you left
The crying cuckoos of Wu and Yue filled with an unending resentment.

(XI SHI *acts out being enraged. Speaks*:) How do you, Missy Zhao, dare get off making fun of me? Although I lowered myself in the palace of Wu, I did not violate my initial oath to make the state of Yue rise again. Declining a noble title, I retreated to the lakes. My virtue as a woman may be scant, but scholars appreciate me highly. No way am I like you and your unscrupulous younger sister Hede![84] Your blade fell on the fetus of the heir, and because of this the imperial lineage of the Han did not extend beyond the Emperors Ai and Yuan. Are you alone not ashamed to hear the ballad, "A swallow pecks on the imperial descendants?"[85] You have not shed your mundane attachments and here you are flashing your arrogance. Where is the sense in that?

(ZHAO FEIYAN:) I was just teasing but now I realize that was a violation of our compassion as immortals. I sincerely beg you to forgive me. (ZHANG LIHUA:) Prior transgressions and old burdens are a thousand years removed from us. To get wrapped up in them again is something that immortals should avoid. Not to mention that we have received the order to head east. We must pay due respect to each other. There are still two more transcendent ladies who are not yet here, Xue Tao and Lu Mochou.[86] Let us get a crane to send words so we can go as a group. Look, the vapor sealing the lower realm just gave way to one shaft of golden light. Must be some extraordinary person taking the lead. Let us get out of the way.

(*Exit.*)

(*Reprise*) (ZUO CI *enters*:)

A whole heaven of dewy ethers conceals Lotus City.

All I see

In this misty vapor, dim and hazy, are the stars of the lower realm.

(STUDENT WHO:)

Suddenly I hear,

Deep inside the cassia fragrance, a jade flute being played.

Master Zuo, why is it that on our way here, clouds are misty, stars twinkling, flowers sweet, and the wind carries transcendent music? What world is this? (ZUO CI:) Heaven's designs should be secret and not lightly spilled. (ZUO CI *sings*:)

I shall

Lift the golden ring to tap, like the blue phoenix pecking away,

yet, I am afraid

I will startle the noisy mastiff[87] by pulling those bells under the flowers.[88]

(ZUO CI *acts out knocking on the door.*) This is Zuo Ci, official holding a sinecure at Penglai. I have come a long way to pay my respects. May I trouble you to announce us? (*Response from backstage*:) We already received the order three days ago about the trip. Since you have in your company a lofty one who is still weighed down by mortal ethers, we dare not entertain you. Please go back. (STUDENT WHO:) In that case we have to turn back. (ZUO CI:) There are still the divine officials overseeing the thirty-six palaces,[89] Lu Mochou and Xue Tao, residing in the eastern wing. Let's go there instead to extend our personal invitations. Please be prudent and cautious.

(*Exit.*)

(*Reprise*) (SECOND FEMALE *playing* XUE TAO *enters with* SECOND FEMALE LEAD *playing* LU MOCHOU. XUE TAO *sings*:)

On the jade tower, amidst the redolence of flowers, my jet-black chignon loosens,

As I cut the Shu damask into stationery for jade-pure scripts.[90]

I am Xue Tao, a humble immortal. (LU MOCHOU:) I am Mochou from the Lu family, also a humble immortal.

The romantic scenery on the Six Bridges only chills the Qin zither.[91]

(LU MOCHOU *acts out listening.* ZUO CI *enters.*) This is Zuo Ci, official holding a sinecure. I have come a long way to pay my respects. (XUE TAO *and* LU MOCHOU *sing together*:)

Who

Has floated his raft to intrude upon the dream of roaming immortals?

You say we

Will soon ride the simurgh to descend on a jade chariot.

(XUE TAO *and* LU MOCHOU *exit.*)

(CLOWN *playing* WANG YANG *enters holding a bag*:)

With gold one can purchase life back for a talented person,

Without a cinnabar pill it's impossible to cure ordinary men of poverty.

Why did I speak those two lines? Since surviving the treacherous Taihang Mountains, I, Wang Yang, have awakened to my errant ways. I left my official's cap at the Han court and went roaming, free as a bird. Later I met an extraordinary being who taught me the techniques of gold and silver transformation, as well as inner and outer cultivation.[92] I was thus able to live forever. This old geek, Emperor Wu of the Han, was after some marvelous pills. So he kept me in prison trying to get to the True Elixir, but I ran off, using the Escape Method for sneaking away. Now I have received the order to go and greet lofty beings from the Han and the Tang for an assembly with roaming immortals. The usual suspects—Cao Zhi, Liu Zhen, Li Bai, Du Fu[93]—the same bunch long dominating the drinking and poetry societies. These people should not have been allowed to die in the first place. Have you ever met anyone who, having seen my feat of turning things into gold with bare hands, does not lighten up? Now that Li Taibai has always boasted of his talents and big name. Even he bought his wine by handing over his precious fur coat worth a thousand pieces of gold.[94] Du Zimei was a sourpuss who'd keep one coin in his purse just to look at—here is one who can't avoid being cheap.[95] Dongfang Shuo fought with those dwarfs over grain;[96] Yiya served people by pleasing their palates;[97] and that Lu Yu may have served some good tea, but he was actually a Suzhou con artist, full of tricks.[98] I wouldn't worry about them not showing me any respect. (WANG YANG *acts out producing the gold.*) They will see how I, with this ingot of pure gold and this ladle of cinnabar, can instantly turn a rock mountain into a gold lair. This is why these travelers will come when they catch wind of me—they are all after my bounties. I can see them coming from afar. (SECOND MALE LEADS *playing* CAO ZHI, LIU ZHEN, LI BAI, *and* DU FU; OLD MALES *playing* DONGFANG SHUO *and* LU YU; VILLAIN *playing* YI YA *enter.*) We are immortals under the order to deliver the one on the transcendent craft. We shall have to make this trip.

([XIANLÜ MODE *entering into* SHUANGDIAO MODE:] *Second Variation of Jiangershui*) (LI BAI *sings*:)

The offerings to the Heavenly Gate;

Scarce are the offerings to the Heavenly Gate.

In the divine breeze, waist pendants are cold.

(LIU ZHEN:)

Truly

We were flickering flames in the human realm;

Stars that have fallen from Heaven.

Heavy hang the ashes of kalpa,

And tall rise the grave mounds.

(CAO ZHI:)

I rhapsodized about "The Goddess of the Luo" in vain;

(DONGFANG SHUO:)

Heavy frost covers the bell at the Changle Palace.[99]

(LI BAI:) In my opinion, the gentlemen from the Han and the Tang were either struck by misfortunes of factional strife or succumbed to the calamities of war. They cannot compare to you and me, whose bodies and reputation are still intact. I thought such things were merely floating clouds, water bubbles, and shadows that would wind up dissolving into naught. Who would have known that our karma of talent found its place in Heaven, such that we are still here today?

(DU FU:)

Yelang, in the barbarian land;[100]

(MALE LEAD:)

Cancong, and the road to Shu;[101]

(LI BAI:)

Deeply intoxicated, I asked, "Who'll hold the imperial palace inkstone for me?"[102]

(DONGFANG SHUO:)

The old palace of Boliang,[103]

Where is

The old palace of Boliang?

(LI BAI:)

The new tomb of Zhaoling,[104]

Where is

The new tomb of Zhaoling?

(*Chorus*)

How lamentable is this floating life.

We entreat the golden immortal to hold the plate for sweet dew.[105]

(*Exit.*)

(*Reprise*) (FEMALE LEAD *playing* XI SHI; SECOND FEMALE LEADS *playing* ZHAO FEIYAN *and* ZHANG LIHUA; SECOND FEMALES *playing* LU MOCHOU, XUE TAO, TAOYE *and* LINGBO *enter.*) (XI SHI:)

Attendant at the jade terrace—

In vain I speak of being an

Attendant at the jade terrace.

At the Zhaoyang Palace, my spring dream had ended.

I recall

The brocade sails and verdant grass,

The golden chamber full of blooming flowers,

The corridor resounding with my footsteps,

And onto the mosses, the spurting spring.

(ZHAO FEIYAN:)

My charming dances, light enough to bear in the hand;

(ZHANG LIHUA:)

The Jingyang palace, deserted after war.[106]

I have been thinking, from the past to present, the fall of cities and the destruction of states were all due to beguiling women like us. And later, when disasters befell the state, jade was smashed and fragrance dissipated—then our lot was the first to suffer misfortune. It's just that, when vying to be the most charming in the struggle for imperial favor, the outcome did not depend upon us. How bitter it was! (*Sings:*)

The silver vase had fallen to the bottom of the well,[107]

(ZHAO FEIYAN:)

Lavish feasts are gone with the wind.[108]

The mist of the Six Dynasties—

What can I say—

Had dulled gold and kingfisher ornaments.

(XUE TAO:)

Palace-style damask and colored brocade—

No use thinking about

The palace-style damask and colored brocade.

(LU MOCHOU:)

The road to the Zhang Terrace—[109]

Not to mention

The road to the Zhang Terrace.

(*Chorus*)

Crossing the Silver River,

We laugh at

The Herd Boy—for how many times has he come to greet the Weaving Lady?

(SECOND FEMALE:) My lady, we have left the Heavenly realm and are approaching the mundane dust. Since our bodies have already transformed into an immortal state, it is not advisable for us to re-enter the human world. We shall have to use a transcendent craft to reach the opposite shore.

(FEMALES *exit.*)

([SOUTHERN XIANLÜ MODE:] *Busuanzi*) (VILLAIN *playing* KUNLUN SLAVE *enters in military garb carrying a sword.*)

One single sword, its tip radiating rainbows,

A thousand miles, reached within moments.
In the human world, how many faithless ones—
There is no end to venting a hero's resentment.
Penetrating iron barriers and bronze walls is the aura of my sword,
Coming with no traces, gone like a gale.
Though there is no sight of a head falling,
A glittering dot of red remains in my hand.

I am the Swordsman Kunlun Slave.[110] At Guo Fenyang's mansion, I killed the divine hound to save the student and his lady and then concealed my body to flee. I saw that the Altar of Grain had changed for the Tang house after the havoc wrought by Huang Chao.[111] So I retired to the Eastern Ocean where I stilled my heroic aspirations before achieving Grand Perfection. Now this Student Who has invited a group of immortals for free-spirited roaming. Student Who! You do not know that in this world, it is precisely pure joy that is hard to enjoy, and marvelous wanderings easily fall apart. Now that you have gathered several thousand years' share of talented men and famed ladies in one group, surely there will be trials and tribulations. I, Kunlun Slave, have in my hands this precious sword that can behead dragons in the water and slay goblins on the land. Here I am offering protection to help you make this delightful accomplishment. What can be wrong with that? I can see from afar Student Who coming.

(*Yexing chuan*) (MALE LEAD *playing* STUDENT WHO, VILLAIN *playing* ZUO CI *and* CLOWN *playing* WANG YANG *enter.* STUDENT WHO:)

A free-spirited roaming since antiquity, now fulfilled;
Like the numinous raft, passing floating constellations and the drifting stone.[112]

(ZUO CI *and* WANG YANG:)

In dreams, friendship strong enough to split gold and fragrant like orchid;[113]
From paintings, flower-shaming and moon-paling charms—
How fortunate it is that they now share the same ferrying boat.

(STUDENT WHO:) Master Zuo, look. I can see reeds and rushes everywhere, as well as gulls and egrets surfing the wave. The sky and the water share one color, and not the slightest breeze is stirring. What a serene scene! Only, the fair ladies and magnificent guests are not here yet. Could it be that the dream to roam with immortals is just a fantasy? (ZUO CI:) What nonsense! At the edge of the sky one lotus boat and one painted boat are approaching. They must be arriving.

(*Exit.*)

([ZHONGLÜ MODE:] *Putian le*) (MALE LEAD, SECOND MALE LEADS, EXTRA, OLD MALE, *and* MISCELLANEOUS *enter with* BOATMAN.) (MALE LEAD:)

Wisps of evening clouds, red as a rose,
Mountain peaks, emerald.
Light from the water, white as silk
Rippling between Heaven and Earth.

Beyond the Penghu Island—
Beyond the Penghu Island vaguely appears the cinnabar ladder.
We gaze at the land of Qi, the nine dots behind mist.[114]

(*Chorus*)

Yah,
Look at the water and the sky, merged in a single color,
Verging on the void, a thin watery mist.
Imagine, at the side of the sea, the lonesome sail barely visible.
So barely visible that we gaze in vain anticipating its return.

(ALL *speak*:) Master Who, accept our greetings. (*From backstage*:) The banquet for the travelers is not ready yet. We do not dare to receive you lightly. Please stop the boat for the moment.

(*Exit*.)

(*Reprise*) (FEMALE LEAD, SECOND FEMALES, SECOND FEMALE LEADS *together with* MISCELLANEOUS *playing* BOATMAN *enter*. FEMALE LEAD:)

Sweet fragrance, oh so fresh,
Pitch-black chignons, oh so dainty.
Light are the jade pendants,
Our cloud-patterned handkerchiefs waving.
A gale of wind rises—
A gale of wind rises, and we dread its startling breath,
Our wave-crossing steps disturbed, our ethereal shoes misaligned.[115]

(*Chorus*)

Yah,
Look at water and sky merged as a single color,
Verging on the void, a thin watery mist.
Imagine, at the side of the sea, the lonesome sail barely visible.
So barely visible that we gaze in vain anticipating its return.

(SECOND FEMALE:) The immortal ladies have arrived. Please accept our greetings (*Response from backstage*:) The banquet for the ladies is not ready yet. We do not dare to receive you lightly. Please stop the boat for the moment.

(ALL *exit*.)

End-of-Act Comments

One must keep in mind that the part on pursuing the beauties is all poetry of roaming into the world of immortals.[116] There must not be any hint of unctuous flippancy. The bickering among the ladies is excellent.

The guests all introduce themselves in a fresh way. A single line captures their histories to be passed down for generations. This is truly well-crafted writing from a deliberate mind. Wang Yang with his abundant gold plays his part with a painted face. For him to belittle Li Bai and Du Fu with a vicious tongue naturally accords with the ways of the world. He further opines: "People like Li Bai and Du Fu should not have been allowed to die in the first place." This is a most penetrating remark.

ACT 3

UNTRAMMELED SAILING ON THE TRANSCENDENT CRAFT

(CLOWN *playing* BOATMAN *enters.*)

A grand ship one thousand feet tall, its canopy a hundred meters wide.
Its single sail hangs high, between the empty sea and sky.
In intoxicated slumber, we entrust ourselves fully to the wind,
Around us, nothing but cinnabar mountains and emerald waters.

I, this old fisherman, am here to sail the boat for Student Who, who has invited a company of lofty figures and unparalleled beauties for a wild roaming across the sea. Now all the guests are here, and we have set off riding the wind. I shall have to give you all the details about the ocean scenery and the banquet onboard. Behold:

Glittering in kingfisher shades, ten thousand acres of limpid waves;
Deep, shimmering green, the sky is like plain silk.
From the Fusang tree, the blazing mirror rises either in the third or the fourth watch, and this golden basin flares like a myriad of scarlet hibiscus flowers.[117]
In the Bo Ocean, the icy wheel bathes whether waxing or waning, and from beneath this kingfisher quilt escape one thousand rays of gold-emerald light.[118]
At the edge of sky, the blue mountains are half concealed, in three or two spots, like gems clearly reflected in a mirror;
Surfing the waves, white egrets flutter, in flocks of ten or five, like gold millets bouncing on a plate.
When the giant turtle turns over, in an instant the waves churn and the sea boils until Mount Sumeru emerges—which turns out to be one dorsal vertebra.
When the *peng* bird stretches its neck all of a sudden the sun dims, the sky darkens, the grand ocean of the nine constellations is blocked—but it is only two feathers.[119]

Enough about the ocean's transformations. Now let me move on to the scenery onboard:

Why talk about paddles of cassia and sweeps of magnolia?
No need to envy a stern painted with fish hawk patterns or the magpie-shaped helm.
With triple towers and terraces,
With encircling corridors on the four sides,
This clearly is Emperor Yang of Sui's dragon-phoenix craft of a hundred feet,
Only missing the rowing ladies who sing about the moon and intone about the breeze.[120]

Its elegance yields nothing to Mi Yuanzhang's Calligraphy-and-Painting Boat,[121]
With no need for bare-headed slaves to boil tea and rinse ink-stones.
The inner decor and the cuisine of the banquet—
These also have no parallel in the present or the past, hard to find in the celestial or worldly realms:
Around the brocade performance rug, sitting mats are neatly arranged,
All over the cabin, incense repelling worldly dust burns.
Crystal curtains, on all sides, hang before patterned windows;
Stretched on the tables is gossamer woven from icy silkworm cocoons.[122]
One set of tunes from the Pear Garden, accompanied by ivory flutes and sandalwood clappers—one cannot hear enough of such beautiful voices;[123]
Eight female entertainers from the Imperial Music Academy, playing zither, harp, and *konghou*—their lowered eyebrows exude charm beyond description.[124]
The wine, with dregs floating,
Glistens at the bottom of the goblet like amber.
The tea is ground and compacted into dragon-cakes,
Water boils in the kettle, like wind rustling through pines and churning white snow.
We partake of:
Dried unicorn meat and fried phoenix, bear palms and leopard fetus
Prepared by Yi Ya's own hands, eclipsing steamed suckling pigs from Shi Chong's kitchen.[125]
We use as ingredients:
The *zhuan*-weed from the river and jujube from the sea, auspicious oranges and perch from the Song River, conjured from Zuo Yuanfang's (Zuo Ci) sleeves—why trouble riders on horseback to transport lychees?[126]
We shall freely chant about pure breezes and intone about the snow,
Why fret over the mountain path running out or the river coming to its end?
Before I'm done talking, here comes Student Who.

([SOUTHERN XIANLÜ MODE:] *Busuanzi*) (SECOND MALE LEAD, EXTRA, OLD MALE *enter followed by* MISCELLANEOUS. ALL *sing*:)
As if in a dream, we recall having roamed together,
Across generations, we meet again.
(FEMALE LEAD, SECOND FEMALE LEADS, SECOND FEMALES *enter.* ALL *sing*:)
Transcendents suddenly meeting mundane beings, we are still bashful and hesitant,
Our handkerchiefs and sleeves moistened by misty rosy clouds.

(SECOND MALE LEAD:) When extraordinary beings meet, there's no need for worldly protocols. Just one deep bow and then we shall sit down in groups. (STUDENT WHO:) I am much obliged. (MALE LEAD *and* SECOND MALE LEADS *together bow to* FEMALE LEAD *and* SECOND FEMALE LEADS. MALE LEAD *and* SECOND MALE

LEADS, EXTRA, OLD MALE, VILLAIN *all act out bowing to one another.*) (STUDENT WHO:) I have met you through bound books and in my dreams have looked up to you. Heaven has granted me this marvelous occasion. How else could I have imagined seeing your faces! (SECOND MALE LEAD:) You, Master, have rare talents from your previous lives, and we have retained high spirits from our prime—even though we are far apart across lives, we may still bond at the same banquet. (STUDENT WHO:) I do not dare to be so presumptuous. (STUDENT WHO *turns around to bow to* FEMALES:) In my dream I have longed for Goddess Elü and I have occupied myself with thoughts of the Luofu Mountain.[127] Do I dare join you on the River of Heaven to enjoy the sight of carnelian blossoms? I am overwhelmed with longing and appreciation. (FEMALE LEAD *and* SECOND FEMALE LEAD:) We are those who in the past untied pendants at the side of the Xiang River and left orchids in garden tracts.[128] We have long severed our ties to the mundane world, yet now we find ourselves among the lofty and refined. We are just worried that the officials' caps and ladies' shoes are all mixed,[129] violating the principles of propriety. (STUDENT WHO:) Why would you say this? My nature may be uninhibited, but I am ever diligent about observing the rites. Since we have entered into an alliance like the States of the Spring and Autumn period, "The Han imperial lineage has its own rules."[130] Please ascend the boat, and I see no danger in us conversing with our knees pressed together. (*Music is played backstage.*) (BOATMAN *puts out the gangway.* ALL *act out going up the boat.*)

(VILLAIN *playing* KUNLUN SLAVE *enters.*) You people can't make it without me. Look at the rolling dark waves and the roaring gusts of wind. If you do not have a mighty warrior guarding the boat, you will certainly suffer the disaster of landing in a fish belly.

(VILLAIN *playing* ZUO CI *enters.*) Good point! Good point! Since you are the swordsman Kunlun Slave, that renowned knight errant, please join us onboard. (STUDENT WHO *acts out inviting* KUNLUN SLAVE *to get on board.*) We shall set off right away. (MALES *and* FEMALES *divide into two groups facing each other. Music is played backstage.* ALL *act out moving.*)

(MALE LEAD:) We take as water the ice-holding pot and as our craft the moon.[131]
(LI BAI:) Famed flowers, drinking guests, and immortals of poetry.
(XI SHI:) On the Five Lakes there is no need to seek the original appointment,[132]
(DU FU:) Only at the Three Islands do we know of past ties.
(ZHAO FEIYAN:) The purple swallow with a secret formula cleanses away the liquid of the mundane.
(LU MOCHOU *and* XUE TAO:) The blue simurgh's beak fetches stationery from Chengdu the Brocade City.
(EXTRA:) After years of amusing myself I have achieved *Samādhi*,[133]
(WANG YANG *and* ZUO CI:) In our bags, the blue mountain warrants its own wealth.

(ZUO CI:) This is a good one—"In our bags, the blue mountain warrants its own wealth"—but not as good as untethering the boat to ride the wind. Let's start.

(BOATMAN *sings a boatman's ballad. Acts out setting off the boat.*)

([SOUTHERN NANLÜ MODE:] *Liangzhouxu*) (MALE LEAD:)

Jade ropes woven by the constellations demarcate the azure,
Icy ripples ruffle the emerald sea.
Waves tumble in the wind, splashing onto our sleeves;
The tides rock the moon,
Startling a skyful of egrets and gulls.

(SECOND MALE LEAD:)

I watch the shadow of the Fusang Tree grow dim,
From the Sunrise Valley, light emerges,[134]
Encompassing the entire human world.

(EXTRA:)

I
Desire to go, astride a whale,[135]
Back to the old Jade Pond.
I shall not inquire after the fishing rock in Kunming.[136]

(*Chorus*)

The present and the past, all those changes,
Are as different as daily tides.
In a snap, mulberry fields can transform into boundless ocean.
So, we shall drink,
Don't refuse to drink for fear of inebriation.

(*Music is played and wine served from backstage.*) (MALE LEAD:) I would like to ask Master Zuo whether he could provide Song River perches and fresh oranges from Jiangnan to accompany our drinking? (*Response from backstage*:) Here they come.

(*Reprise*) (FEMALE LEAD:)

On gauze robes fragrance lingers faintly,
Inlaid with hair ornaments, raven chignons rise like clouds.
As the air is saturated with moisture, a chill creeps over our bracelet-adorned arms.
Ice-pure skin and snow-like bones,[137]
And reflections of our jade hairpins stir in the crystalline surface.

Xue Tao and Lu Mochou, you two sing us a song and make a toast to the master. (SECOND FEMALE *and* SECOND FEMALE LEAD:)

We recall our spring laments at the West Lake,
And autumn sorrows in the Southland,
The flowers and grasses sealed in the Wu Palace.

(FEMALE LEAD:) Lingbo and Taoye, you may dance and make a toast to the masters.

(SECOND FEMALES *act out dancing.*)

Mermaid silk, light, teasing,

When blown in the palms,
Transforms into transcendent rosy clouds, every piece bewitching.

(*Chorus as earlier.*)

(MALE LEAD:) We've had a few rounds of drinks, but we are yet to exhaust our joy on the boat. We shall have Master Lu Yu boil the water from the Spring Number One of Jiangnan for the tea that was pressed into small dragon cakes. We will then play the game of linked verse. For any blunder there is a penalty set by Master of the Gold Valley Villa.[138] (SECOND MALE LEAD:) I'd be happy to follow your instructions. The form of five-syllable verse started in the Jian'an period, so Cao Zijian (Cao Zhi) shall take the lead. The other gentlemen may follow him.

(CAO ZHI:)

I moor the boat beside the cassia islet,
And slowly so slowly, a mist arises.[139]

(DU FU:)

A heavenly wind generates the night's chill,
On lotus clothes,[140] clear dew drips down.

(LI BAI:)

In intoxication, I clutch the White Lady's garments
And I am left with two white deer.[141]

(XI SHI:)

Lush and dazzling are the carnelian branches,
No more regards for the flower of the ephemeral hedge-tree.[142]

(TAOYE:)

In the gold chamber, remnant rays of light linger,

(LINGBO:)

The jade terrace is open for leisurely walks.

(LU MOCHOU:)

Clouds cling to the sky where the seagulls seem pasted,

(XUE TAO:)

From the swirling waves, one knows the fish's paths.

(LIU ZHEN:)

Holding the plate to collect dew, Wengzhong remained doubtful,[143]

(DONGFANG SHUO:)

Peaches stolen, the Queen Mother of the West was enraged.[144]

(ZUO CI:)

The cup transformed into two white doves.[145]

(WANG YANG:)

The furnace roasted one yellow hare.

(STUDENT WHO:)

In inebriation we gaze at the Three Mountains,
The divine bridge is ready for crossing.

(*Speaks*:)

Now fetch the wine! Master Lu was boiling tea; Yi Ya was attending to the cooking, and Kunlun Slave was monitoring the game. They all failed to participate in the composition, so they each will compensate for that by drinking three full goblets. Li Taibai could not stop himself from being insolent. How can it be acceptable to clutch the White Lady's robe? He was somewhat guilty of disrespect, so he has to drink according to the Master of the Gold Valley Villa's rule. We shall now steer our boat toward the Three Islands.

(*Reprise*) (LI BAI:)
We are to collect the corals, but cannot locate the iron net;[146]
When we try to steal the bright pearl, the black dragon refuses to sleep.[147]
So let's for the moment exchange poems and pass around drinks,
Waving our sleeves in intoxication.

(LI BAI *acts out being drunk and trying to hold onto* SECOND FEMALE.)

Don't talk about
Me having my boots removed at the court,
Or me receiving brocade at the pool—[148]
The rams-hide drum is not the same today.[149]

(DU FU *acts out pointing at* LI BAI.)

How ridiculous is this wild one—there's none like him.
Even when the jade hill is collapsing,[150]
Don't engage in the suspect behavior of the dream on the sunlit terrace in the Shamanka Gorges.[151]

(*Chorus as earlier.*)

(STUDENT WHO:) I heard that Master Dongfang Manqian is good at blind guessing of covered items. Let us divide into two groups and each hide one item.[152] Those who guess the object correctly will drink. Lady Xi Shi, please cover your item first. (XI SHI *acts out removing a hairpin to hide under a cover.*) (DONGFANG SHUO *acts out divining*:) It is gentle yet hard, not round but can be an ornament, not piercing but sharp—a jade hairpin it is. (DONGFANG SHUO *acts out revealing the covered item and laughing heartily*:) Guests, let's drink. (STUDENT WHO:) Master Cao, please cover your item. (CLOWN *playing* WANG YANG *acts out passing him the cinnabar pill.*) (DONGFANG SHUO *acts out divining*:) It is one yet also two, residing in its form; round and glittering, liked by all. That which is one yet also two are the hexagrams *li* and *dui*.[153] To be round and glittering is the form of gold. This is a golden cinnabar pill. (DONGFANG SHUO *acts out retrieving the covered item and laughing heartily*:) Immortal ladies, your turn to drink. (WANG YANG *acts out looking for the cinnabar pill but failing to find it*:) The golden cinnabar pill was right here. Who took it away? I must do a thorough search. (WANG YANG *acts out searching both sides*:) These ladies have used gold before. They will certainly not hide the pill.[154] As for these talented men of letters, the Academy Scholar Li Bai once said that gold used up will come again—he too is extremely liberal with gold and would not care.[155] Only Du Shaoling (Du Fu) dwells on being poor and bitter. So please open up and allow me to search you. (WANG YANG *acts out searching without finding*:) Then, Master Dongfang, please divine who has it. (DONGFANG SHUO *acts out divining*:) Curling and thumbing; flying and entering. It was Master Zuo who had transported it. (ZUO CI:) How do you explain this? (DONGFANG SHUO:) Master Zuo has a thick and curly beard. It is therefore certainly hiding under his left thumb. (ZUO CI *acts out producing the pill with a guffaw.*) (ALL *act out laughing loudly.*) (VILLAIN *playing* KUNLUN SLAVE *acts out being exasperated*:) Today's roaming is supposed to be a refined gathering. Without anyone monitoring the games, then in this mixed company of gentlemen and ladies, we can indulge in wild behavior and bring Heaven's punishment upon ourselves. Allow me to oversee the drinking game holding my sword following Liu Zhang's example.[156] (STUDENT WHO:) You are right. We shall obey immediately.

(*Reprise*) (ZHANG LIHUA *and* ZHAO FEIYAN *sing together*:)

We laugh at the brilliant literary men, whose sleeves entangle in their drunken stupor,
The dances are buoyant, our slender waists aslant.
Over time hairpins become askew and coiffures disarrayed,
Skirts and boots pressing against one another.[157]

(LU MOCHOU *and* XUE TAO *turn around and sing*:)

We gaze at the distant Silver River that's like a thread,
The emerald ocean in its thousand layers.
Locked behind the clouds, the Xiang River Goddess weeps.
On the jade terrace, spring has come to an end.
The fallen petals are scanty,
As Xiao Shi's rendezvous on the Qin Tower does not come to pass.[158]

(*Chorus as earlier.*)

(CLOWN *playing* BOATMAN *enters*:) I am here to report that this grand ocean does not have a port where we can moor. A northern wind will send us to Ryukyu and Japan; a southern one will blow us to the Blue Ocean or the Black Ocean.[159] This is no joking matter. Only the Eastern Ocean surrounds mountains for immortals, but the Weak Stream[160] makes it hard to reach—even a goose feather would sink on it; venomous pythons and baneful dragons encircle the mountains from a hundred miles around. Therefore no one dares head that way. We'd better stop and wait for the gale to subside. (ZUO CI:) Boatman, just go with the wind. There will be some place where we can stop. (BOATMAN:) Then we shall not drop the sail. Let us turn around the boat to go along with the wind, enjoying ourselves in a foreign kingdom. (ALL *act out moving.*)

(*Jiejie gao*) (ZUO CI:)

You just

Leave it to the wind to carry us.
Holding the sail,
We cross the void and, within one breath, travel a thousand miles.
Tail of the mother kraken,
Whiskers of the master shrimp,
Backs of steeds that descend from dragons—
Inside the crystal palace we shall frolic with these merfolk,
Tipsy among clams' reed pipes and shrimps' drums.

(*Chorus*)
We drew all the water from the Eastern Ocean to fill a goblet:
Such a group of travelers, truly amazing.
(*Reprise*) (STUDENT WHO:)
The tide has subsided, the water is smooth like silk,
An expansive crystalline surface.
The sound of the flute startles the black dragon from its slumber.
The Yanyu Rock,
The Jutang Gorge,[161]
The narrow Dragon Gate—
Such are the likes of trials and tribulations in the human realm.
Riding the wind and braving the waves; we've nothing to worry about.

(*Chorus*)
We drew all the water from the Eastern Ocean to fill a goblet,
Such a group of travelers, truly amazing.

(STUDENT WHO:) We will stay at Yuntai for now.[162] Tomorrow we will follow the wind heading east, all the way in search of the Weak Stream.

(*Coda*) (STUDENT WHO:)
The wide ocean has already fulfilled the travelers' wishes!
How rare it is to find such
Extraordinary friends and famed ladies who follow me with every step.
I am only afraid that you, "my immortal company sharing my boat, will move further at night."[163]

(MALE LEAD:)
Oars of magnolia and a boat of *shatang* wood,

(VILLAIN:)
Jade flutes and golden pipes sit on the two ends.

(FEMALE LEAD:)
The immortals are waiting to mount the yellow cranes,

(EXTRA:)
The travelers on the ocean have no heart to frolic with white gulls.[164]

(*Exit.*)

End-of-Act Comment

The launch of the boat is the cardinal act of this play. It exudes such free spirits and exhilaration that it makes one break into dance. An unbridled travel like this must bring in its wake the kalpa of the leviathan's swallowing the boat. Regarding the successive compositions of couplets and objects covered for the guessing game, they can supplement the biographies of the Han and Tang—and no one would be able to distinguish the original text from the additions.
Comment by Zhang Cichen

ACT 4

SWALLOWING THE BOAT INTO THE BELLY OF THE FISH

(VILLAIN *playing* TURTLE DEMON[165] *and* CLOWNS *playing* SHRIMPS *and* LOBSTERS *enter.* TURTLE DEMON:)

Inhaling fog and swallowing waves, it's been tens of thousands of years,
Inside the dragon palace, I spit out the old kraken's saliva.
From the time I was born I've had this boat-swallowing prowess,
Not falling for a fisherman's fragrant bait.

I am the Turtle Demon from the Eastern Ocean. Long have I inhaled the light of the sun and the moon; coiled up I reside at my mansion in the Blue Ocean. When I spit out foam, the tide boils and the sea overflows; when I stir my fins, the waves soar high to reach the sky. Because I inhale and exhale the primal ether as I preside over the Eastern Drain, the Supreme Lord ordered me to guard the Weak Stream and monitor access to Penglai. This Mt. Penglai reaches up all the way to the Supreme Lord's throne and down to the Gate of Mystery. It is the Caudal Funnel of Heaven and Earth,[166] the control channel of *yin* and *yang.*[167] Thus, all waters from the myriad directions flow together here to be completely drained just to rise again to the surface a thousand miles away. Worldly beings, being ignorant, call it the Weak Stream, but it is in fact the mysterious female.[168] Above it you have the immortal mansions, and below it you find the dragon king's palace. It has ten thousand apertures and a thousand gates, it embraces the sun and moon, its springs are fragrant as brew, and its air is warm as spring. How laughable were those two vulgar louts, the First Emperor of the Qin and that Emperor Wu of the Han! They wasted all that money and still dared not approach the mountain by a single step! Recently I heard of this Student Who who has the audacity to roam freely and to intrude on my borders. There are in addition some kingdom-toppling shrews and meddlesome men of letters creating a ruckus. This is all driving me crazy. Generals, you wait till they are about to arrive and work up some gusts of wind and fierce waves to smash the boat and let them drown and be buried inside fish bellies. Wouldn't that be the best? (SHRIMP:) My lord. I heard that Student Who's boat is full of extraordinary men. If some of them happen to possess the magic of reversing wind or dodging water, they will cause great inconvenience. Now we have General Whale who is an expert in swallowing boats. Just wait till Student Who is here and then have him take a big mouthful and suck the whole thing into his belly, where the vessel and passengers will all be digested. Wouldn't that be wonderful? (TURTLE DEMON:) Good thinking! Truly:

With a sleight of hand covering the sky and tumbling the clouds,
I'll capture the man who startles Heaven and stirs Earth.

(ALL *exit.*)

(CLOWN *enters playing* BOATMAN:) What a strong wind! Look! The waves are churned into ten thousand silver mountains; the tides roar like there were a thousand streaks of ferocious tigers. The mast and the helm are completely out of control, and the flagpole is dancing wildly. How can this craft make it? Even with our transcendent power it is hard to make way, not to mention we still have with us a mortal who has yet to be transformed. Master, master! Please stop and moor the boat at the base of the East Mountains. We shall continue our journey tomorrow. (*Response from backstage*:) As you wish.

([SHUANGDIAO MODE:] *Yexing chuan*) (MALE LEAD *enters playing* STUDENT WHO *with* VILLAIN *playing* KUNLUN SLAVE. STUDENT WHO:)

The solitary craft floats up and down with the sea gulls,
Toward the edge of Heaven, the end of our wandering life.

(KUNLUN SLAVE:)

The Weak Stream is boundless,
The Oyster Palace unfathomable.[169]
Reaching this point, the transcendent and mundane alike are taken aback.

Master, so far we have been moving fast in our boat riding a steady breeze, which was quite delightful. But today a wild storm is whipping up the waves, and the churning water is engulfing the sky. In the distance we can see mountain ranges stretching without a break. This must be the Weak Stream. Master, use caution. (STUDENT WHO:) What kind of talk is this? I have heard that "The perfected person does not die;" and that "The Great Way is hard to learn." Today this wind and tide may exactly be a test from the Supreme Immortals—you never know. Let the two of us disembark to take a leisurely walk. Look, at the foot of the cliff there is a terrace for fishing. With the moon so bright, it is the right time to toss the fishhook. So I shall get a fishing pole and sit here by myself. Truly:

Before encountering the True Immortal who will grant us the grand potion,
I'll first with fragrant bait catch a divine fish.

(*Exits.*)

(VILLAIN *plays* WHALE DEMON *and acts out peeking surreptitiously.*)

([NANLÜ MODE:] *Southern and Northern Yizhi hua*) [170] (MALE LEAD *enters playing* STUDENT WHO *holding a fishing pole.*)

I thought I would rise aloft and seek that Han-time raft.[171]

Who could have known that

I would only be a loose sprig adrift in the wilderness?

I just wanted to follow my fancy to mount a crane and fly away,

Yet I end up playing with the pearls at Dark Waters.

I am thinking, talented men act on the spur of the moment, just like Liezi riding the wind and Lu Lian marching to the sea's edge—all for nothing.[172] How can one in fact instantly ascend above the clouds?

Say nothing about

Jujubes the size of melons;

These are all

Master Anqi's concocted tales of the immortals.[173]

I lament that this fetus is still a mortal frame that is hard to transform.

I have under my nose guests from the cinnabar hill and transcendent ladies,

Yet I am still afraid that

This is all a dream that stretched far, in which I will end up visiting the Jade Pond with Heavenly steeds.[174]

Here the torrent is quick and the pond deep, so there are not necessarily any fish. Beside the rock is a little skiff. There the water must be shallow. Let me board that boat for fishing. (STUDENT WHO *acts out stepping into the skiff.*) (WHALE *acts out being pleased on observing this.*)

(*Liangzhou diqi*) (STUDENT WHO:)

All I see is waves surging to the sky, thunder roaring and lightning flashing,

What's to be done as

Those angrily roiling whitecaps are about to destroy my raft?

(STUDENT WHO *acts out moving the boat following* WHALE, *now moving forward, then backward.*)

Yah yah yah! Could I have hooked a divine fish and thus pulled my leviathan vehicle?[175]

(*Speaks:*) Slowly I am getting further away from the large boat.

I no longer see the brocade sail hanging aslant,

Nor do I hear strings or pipes making music.

Instead I have become the one burning a rhinoceros horn in the dragon's grove;[176]

The one who taps on the orange tree to inquire about the dragon king's mansion.[177]

(*Speaks:*) Why is this skiff moving by itself, as if someone was pulling it along?

This boat—

Before I got on it, I took it to be an empty boat or a flying tile.[178]
After I got on board, it has transformed into a poisonous *yu* creature holding sand.[179]

(WHALE *uses its mouth to suck in the boat.* STUDENT WHO *again acts out going forward even as he tries to pull back.*) (STUDENT WHO *acts out shouting*:) My friend, Kunlun Slave, also abandoned me. (STUDENT WHO:)

Yah yah yah! When I am about to get on the shore, this skiff turns into iron chains and a bronze cangue.
It is fine for this skiff to be
Empty and light, pressed by a thousand meters of grand waves.
But could it be that
My hot body has turned into wisps of bubbles or floating foam?

(WHALE *uses its mouth to suck in the boat.* STUDENT WHO *again acts out going forward even as he tries to pull back.*) (STUDENT WHO:) I have shared the boat with fellow guests and enjoyed myself with immortal ladies for more than a day. Now my leisurely walk has taken me here, yet not a single true friend comes looking for me, leaving me adrift without a place to return to. My fellow travelers, you are so lacking in feelings!

Say, what about
Our pact with gulls or affinity with egrets?[180]
(*Repeat*)
I will do away with *belle-lettres*, poetry, and wine,
So that I might chill my hot heart.

(*Speaks*:) My transcendent ladies!

You never consider where Song Yu and King Xiang of Chu make their home—[181]
One little leaf at Heaven's edge.

(WHALE *sucks in the boat again.* STUDENT WHO *is being gulped down into its belly and exits.*) (WHALE:)

Do not say that my mouth brings no good fortune;
Know that my belly houses a transcendent craft.
(*Exits.*)

(STUDENT WHO *enters, shouting loudly*:) It is so dark! So dark! I just saw a cloud floating by and then dark waves dimmed the sky and extinguished the stars. Before I knew it I was stranded here. Not only did I lose my transcendent vessel, but I have also fallen into this dark disastrous place. I have no idea when I will be able to get out to see the sky and the sun again. How miserable I am!

(*Muyang guan*) (STUDENT WHO:)

Here
Everything is pitch-black with no trace of the sun,
Gloomy darkness extends without end.

Look at these towering white bones chaotically intermeshed.
How can I
Break through this murky dusk and come out into the radiant light?
I do not see
Ropes binding or locks confining.
Only
This flesh bag of mine, already entrapped below Mt. Fengdu.[182]
This truly resembles "concentration of primal energies into cinnabar pills, reaching nirvana at Mount Lanka."[183]
At the Gate of Ghosts I've made a vain divination.
(*Speaks*:) Suddenly there is a breeze.
I can hear the blaring of blowing and a strident drumming:
Seems to me the breathing and inhaling here is as vast as Heaven,
This may well be the top place between Heaven and Earth.

By chance I took a skiff to go fishing and drifted to this land, but I have no idea where. The mist of wilderness is thick and heavy, and I see no trace of human habitation. It is dark and windy, and I see no sun or moon at all. I wonder if my little fishing skiff is still here? (STUDENT WHO *acts out reaching for the boat and finding it.*)

(*Ma yulang*) (STUDENT WHO:)
I see that the orchid oar and cassia sweeps are undamaged:
Stretched across a village ford,
With little impairment.
I shall mend the cabin and wield the rudder again.
Say nothing about
The waves not rippling,
The sky having its bounds.
Yah yah yah, no need to talk about the boat fee.

Now that the boat is here, I cannot but trace the way back to the ocean, looking for my old acquaintances. Even if I cannot forge ahead to mountains for the immortals, I can still avoid getting lost in my old way. (STUDENT WHO *acts out rowing the boat and then halting.*)

(*Ku huangtian*)
I cannot go against the floating light like the craft at the Red Cliff,[184]
Nor can I row in a boat through white snow to Shanyin.[185]
Instead, I am going to chisel a hole through Chaos,
Rise above the hills and valleys,
Shut off the sun and the moon,
And cultivate the magic elixir.
Yah yah yah! By that time, I won't fear seeing the boat or its passengers.
I shall seek the old path
And my face will show no change from before.

One day when the whale flies and the *peng* bird transforms,
I will be able, all on my own, to manipulate "fire to produce the sprouts."[186]
Of my tossing the bait and the fishing pole,
One by one, I shall tell them.
This is indeed the dragon king's palace, bright and spacious,
Absolutely not just fish bones, dry and bleak.

(STUDENT WHO *acts out lying down on the side.*) (VILLAINS *playing* ZUO CI *and* KUNLUN SLAVE *enter.*) Student Who has already achieved the Great Way. Why is he not asserting his presence? What is he waiting for?

(*Exit.*)

(STUDENT WHO:) When I first entered here, the boat was narrow and the place wide. Now suddenly the boat is wide and the place narrow. What is all this pipe music and hints of white light filtering through? I will have to run off, carrying the boat on my back.[187]

(*Coda*)

Coming to the end of waterways and mountains, my boat is still fake;
Those with fish scales are still living a borrowed existence in the Dharma realm.
Just the right time for me to carry the solitary boat and go out into the sea.
Alone I took a long pole to fish for the gigantic turtle,
And inside the belly of the boat-swallowing whale I took to free roaming.
I had no clue that the cosmos inside the belly was so big
That the *kun* fish and the *peng* bird could soar a hundred thousand feet high.

End-of-Act Comments

One cannot rely on Kunlun Slave and the guests. Only when the waves are about to turn heaven upside down does one discern whether they are "pine or cypress."[188] This is also faulting Student Who for relying on his guests without truly knowing them.[189]

Student Who deserted the large vessel to board the small one. This betrays his thoughts of opting for profit and chasing after expediency. Here comes General Whale!

When Student Who bewailed the darkness of the sky, it was like the thirtieth night of the last month at the end of the year—a time that scares one to death.[190] Yet upon hearing musical instruments being blown and struck in the belly, he was not as fearful as before. The old saying "to let go your hold when hanging from a sheer precipice" can be comprehended as solid Dharma. Old Man Crane has the compassionate heart of an old lady.[191] Fearing that worldly beings are such recalcitrant and obtuse listeners, he finds it necessary to blow it all out of proportion and put on a show like this. If everyone puts down that boat hidden in a ravine in the middle of the night, it cannot be carried away.[192]

Comments by Qiu Haishi

ACT 5

VISITING ILLUSION WITHIN ILLUSION

(VILLAIN *in golden armor and dark red robe playing* FISH DEITY *enters*:)

Opening the whale's spine I can see the pass to Heaven,
The myriads of crevices and thousands of gates just a foot away.
As up in Heaven the ocean of constellations is accessible,
How could we lack a Mt. Sumeru inside this belly?

I am King Fish Bone inside the whale's belly. This is a separate kingdom here with its own human and celestial realms. Moving the *kan* trigram to fill the *li* trigram, summoning wind and calling forth fire,[193] we surpass the mapped extent of the Four Grand Continents[194] and are connected to the dark palaces of the thirty-three gods in Trayastriṃśa Heaven. The wheel of rebirth spanning six realms of existence does not stray from its original position; the sun and the moon from nine palaces create their own *yin* and *yang*.[195] Ever since "Heaven, Number One of the universe, produced water,"[196] I have established my kingdom here, producing life from moisture,[197] swallowing and spitting out the ten thousand creatures. Now there is this Student Who here who is close to success in cultivating the Way. This is too much of an inconvenience for us. I shall send Fish Intestine Swordsman[198] to kill him, so the student will not harm my heaven endowed primal energy. Where is the swordsman? (CLOWN *playing* SWORDSMAN *enters*:)

People all know that swords are like intestines,[199]
But they don't know that bowels are like swords.[200]
Only if you were as pliable as water,
Could you ever be cut into two.

My lord, Swordsman Fish Intestine at your service. (FISH DEITY:) This Student Who has been staying in our land for a long time without being fully alive or dead. You may carry three thousand fish intestine swords to pierce his bones and turn him into worldly dust. You must obey me. (SWORDSMAN:) Yes, my lord.

(*Exit.*)

([SHANGDIAO MODE:] *Ji xianbin*) (MALE LEAD *enters playing* STUDENT WHO:)
Golden waves, under the gleaming moonlight, rock the Purple Palace;
By my solitary sail I sit alone among the clouds.
Morning and evening, the tides follow surging waves,
As I listen to pendants tinkling in the Heavenly breeze.
My cleansed mind aloft and reflective,
Extending to where rosy clouds vaguely reel.

(*Speaks*:) Since I am here, I have lost count of years and months. It is so peaceful here.
My soul awakens all on its own,
From where comes the wind to take me to the Tower of Prince Teng?[201]

Now that I have stilled my breath, let me sit down in meditation. (STUDENT WHO *acts out sitting and falling asleep.*)

(CLOWN *playing* SWORDSMAN *enters*:) Under the order of King Fish Bone I have come to assassinate Student Who. There he is, circled by a golden light and guarded by a white halo. Where can I hit him? Let me pierce his bones with my sword to test his Dharma power. (SWORDSMAN *acts out stabbing* STUDENT WHO *all over with sword.*) Alas, my Fish Intestine precious sword has broken into pieces that turn into lotus blossoms. This person has truly achieved the Way. I will have to kowtow to him. (SWORDSMAN *acts out kneeling.*) (STUDENT WHO *acts out waking up*:) What kind of demon are you to disturb my power of the Way? Let me ask you: What is the name of this land? Are there any other human beings? Tell me the truth and I will spare your life. (SWORDSMAN:) Transcendent Master, this is the Kingdom of Fish Belly. Its vast void stretches a myriad *li* and its empty vacuity is beyond measure. There is only that former minister of Chu, Qu Yuan,[202] who has been living here for more than a thousand years. After him there have been no others inquiring after the ford.[203] If you, Transcendent Master, desire to meet this person, I will gladly be your guide. (STUDENT WHO:) Fantastic! Fantastic! Ever since I have been living here, I suffer most from the lack of friends. If we could go together, please lead the way, so we can intone "Encountering Sorrow" together to appease my loneliness.[204] Truly:

The wind is not yet strong enough for the *peng* bird to soar ninety thousand miles,
But the waves are deep, and I should just mourn the Lord of the Three Wards.[205]

(*Exits.*)

(*Reprise*) (OLD MALE *playing* QU YUAN *enters.*)
How I resent that the Xiang orchids are distant—the misty stream empty.
The Fair One, her beauty fading, cannot find accommodation.
Flowering ivy and mantles of foliage, their fragrance remote:
Across the river, on the bank, who is there to pluck the lotus flowers?
To summon my soul, the labor fell to Song Yu—
I left the fisherman alone to wallow in sorrow.[206]

I am a high dignitary of Chu, Qu Ping. After I was slandered by Shangguan and then estranged from King Huai, I did not forget about my old home.[207] I expressed my intent in "Encountering Sorrow" and drowned myself in a river to be buried inside the belly of this fish. Who would have known that the world inside is so much superior to the human realm? In vain did Song Yu summon my soul, and Jia Yi compose an elegiac rhapsody.[208] How could they have known that my supreme joy rests here? I cannot but sing a *sao* song in memory of my hometown far away. It goes:

High Heaven is not constant in its dispensations,
See how the country is moved to unrest and error!
The people are scattered, and men cut off from their fellows.
In the middle of spring the move to the east began.
I turned my back on Xiapu, and my thoughts went speeding westward,
As I grieved that the Old City grew daily farther from me.
I climbed a steep islet's height to look into the distance,

Thinking to ease the sorrow in my heart.[209]
I voiced my laments for old Ying,
As leaves were shed, and the waves of the Dongting Lake came clear.

(MALE LEAD *playing* STUDENT WHO *enters together with* CLOWN *playing* SWORDSMAN. STUDENT WHO:)

The giant turtle, black as the sky, connects to the Deepest Dark Mystery,
The eyes of fish, red like the waves, open the way to the Crimson Tower.[210]

I have come to visit Master Qu, and here is a Daoist compound, quiet and peaceful.

Let me knock. (STUDENT WHO *acts out knocking on the door.*)

([SOUTHERN NANLÜ MODE:] *Yijiangfeng*) (STUDENT WHO:)
Which mountain peak is this?
Tranquil, the misty clouds are unmoving—
Green trees against vermilion gates.
Across the waves
Are a stretch of Oyster Buildings.[211]
I pass through the meandering paths beside the stream
Where the peach blossoms are damp with rain.[212]
In addition,
"The man of whom I think is right there."[213]
Just at a time when clusters of cassia on the hill
Cast shades resplendent with fragrance.[214]

(OLD MALE *enters playing* QU YUAN.) Who can be visiting? Must be someone extraordinary. (QU YUAN *acts out responding*:) I'm coming.

(*Reprise*) (QU YUAN *sings*:)
I have rhapsodized about the goddess of the Xiang River.
Striking the zither, I recalled the Master of Fate:
His lotus robe with handsome melilotus girdle.
Riding on the whirlwind,
Cloud-banners flying,
He dried his hair on the Bank of Sunlight.
Deer weeds covered the kingfisher banner,
Yet,
As he rode the clouds, he grasped the Broom Star.[215]
I remember the Holy One who'd untied her pendant.[216]
Who was there for her to give it as a gift?

(*Speaks*:) As the song has it,

"I plucked pollia in the scent-laden islet,
To give to the one who is remote.
Time once gone cannot be recovered:
Let me roam freely at my ease."[217]

Where are you from, my guest? Please ascend to the hall. (QU YUAN *acts out bowing to* STUDENT WHO:) I, Qu Ping, have long withdrawn from the human realm and found my abode here in the fish kingdom. I see that you are not of mortal make. How did you get stranded here? (STUDENT WHO:) Please let me tell my story.

(*Hong na'ao*) (STUDENT WHO:)

I am not here to rhapsodize about soaring beyond the clouds to pay tribute to the Heaven of Primal Clarity,[218]

Nor did I come to mourn you in Changsha for seeking refuge in this desolate pit.[219]

I am here only because I was tossed on the River of Heaven like tumbleweed.

So, I have

Entrusted myself to the floating waves, sailing on a square ark.

I have visited the Cinnabar Mound to fulfill in person the jade-pestle pact,[220]

Also seeking the fair Weaving Lady's loom stone to share her company.

(*Speaks*:) I have given free rein to my heart on the rivers and at the sea, where I met many extraordinary beings. When by chance I went angling, I fell into this place. It is my good fortune to have found you here as a longtime resident. I have come specially to seek your advice.

Please point me the way to the ford so I can make it back to the numinous raft.

Do not leave me

Loose on the rivers and lakes as a guest star.

(*Repeat*)

(*Reprise*) (QU YUAN:)

I thought I was plucking fragrant orchids but got lost among cassia clusters.

Who would have known,

When I crossed the bank of the river I would be blocked by others from the moon's realm?

I was unable to

Climb up to Kunlun to consume the flower of jade,

But wound up, instead, intoning an elegy for the mountain ghost and chanting "Summoning the Soul."

Day in and day out,

I was stranded in the deep woods in twilight gloom,

In vain

Fancying myself driving dragons and krakens to turn around the Heavenly Dipper's handle.

(*Speaks*:) Sir, you have long stayed in the human realm. My "Encountering Sorrow" and *Nine Pieces* carried the significant message of transcending the world. Yet those who study Classics do not understand this. They took them to be merely works of literature.

You and I

should

lift our lower garments, wet our feet, and intone "Embracing Sand."[221]
What's the need of *zongzi*[222] and dragon boat racing to mourn Qu Ping?
(*Repeat*)

We have been sitting here talking for a while, but I have no wine to treat you. Let me ask Fish Intestine Swordsman. What kind of exotic object do you have in your kingdom to entertain my guest? (SWORDSMAN:) Our kingdom is empty, devoid of objects and long cut off from worldly fire and smoke. There is only an orange the size of a *yojana*, a tribute from the South Sea.[223] No one has opened it so far, and there is no use keeping it for long. I shall have it fetched for you, Master, to cut it open. Perhaps you will find something inside. (QU YUAN:) Fetch it.

(CLOWN *and* VILLAIN *enter carrying the orange. A piece of yellow cloth covers it, and two old men are hidden inside.*) (QU YUAN:) A wonderful orange indeed! Let me chant "In Praise of the Orange Tree":

Fairest of all God's trees, the orange came and settled here,
Green ones with yellow intermingling to make a pattern of gleaming brightness,
Commanded not to move, but only grow in the south land.[224]

Master, let us slice it open together. (STUDENT WHO *and* QU YUAN *cut open the orange*, removing the yellow cloth to reveal two old men sitting still, face to face, playing *go*.) (STUDENT WHO *and* QU YUAN *act out being greatly startled.*)
(*Xiangliuniang*) (STUDENT WHO:)
Yah! Who are these inside the orange—
So
Solid, substantial, and seamless?
Chiseled from the primal chaos, an empty nature.
These two are deeply immersed in a game of *go*.
But
What are their stakes whether they lose or win?
Within moments the axe handle will rot away.[225]
I can see that the horizontal and vertical paths are clear;
In addition
The decisive attacking move is not yet delivered,
So, the outcome of the game is hard to decide.

(TWO OLD MEN *laugh heartily as they address each other.*) (FIRST OLD MAN:) You have lost to me one Penglai Island and three mountains at the Lang Palace. You must get them to me in three thousand years. (SECOND OLD MAN:) Ack! You owe me ten ladles of fiery jujubes and ten thousand ladles of divine brew.[226] Wait until dust arises from the Eastern Sea[227] and then pay them off! (EXTRA *hits the gongs*, TWO OLD MEN *jump off the stage and out of sight.*) [228] (QU YUAN:) They have left all these *go* stones. Let me look:
(*Reprise*) (QU YUAN:)
I think the yellow at the center is secretly accessible,[229]

just like

The pierced grain of the Ganges River.

The Chou Pond also has nine Lotus Blossom Caves[230]

For admiring Nüwa's merit in smelting stones.

In addition

The stars and constellations, projected in disarray on the *go*-board;

The orthodox and the heretical again divide what was united.

I lament that vanity exists within vanity,

And

That the hero is completely cornered.

This is a winning game.

(QU YUAN:) Pining away at the riverbanks, I am utterly at a loss,[231]

(STUDENT WHO:) Upon meeting, men of letters lament their being stranded.

(QU YUAN:) I already knew that within the illusion hid more illusions,

(STUDENT WHO:) Who would believe that inside the vessel was yet another craft?

(QU YUAN *exits.*)

(STUDENT WHO *ends the scene*:) How strange! So there turns out to be quite a spectacle here. I cannot but return to my old path and seek some way out. Alas, as I move along, I see a pile of fish bones transmogrified into a large temple. Here is my little skiff, tethered to the ground. The waves have subsided, and there are signs of human habitation all around. It is just the time to leave.

(*Coda*)

To hide my body in the method of six breaths is a difficult maneuver;[232]

Much easier it is to rise straight up to connect with the aiding wind.

Only now do I know that the boat's journey at sea amidst the waves and clouds has not come to an end.

In the fish belly I came to seek the Minister of Chu—

What to make of winning and losing inside the orange?

They clearly have pointed out to me the authentic form

Of the *kun* fish transforming and the *peng* bird flying, of being and nonbeing.

End-of-Act Comments

It is quite adequate for Student Who to take the fish belly to be the land of Huaxu.[233] What, then, is the need to seek Master Qu and have him express his sorrow? It is quite appropriate that the old men in the orange sneered at him.

In this act there is [the line] "After him there have been no others who inquired after the ford." The author involuntarily reveals his impassioned intention to deliver worldly beings here. The fantastic nature of the play makes Master Zhuang cede first place.

Comment by Ding the Wild Crane

How abominable it is for this old whale to gulp down an entire boatload of people and send them into a dark sea! What kind of creature is this Qu Yuan that he really wants to wind up buried in this belly?
Comment by Qiu Chaicun

ACT 6

SEEKING THE BOAT OUTSIDE THE BOAT

(MALE LEAD *enters playing* STUDENT WHO *carrying the boat*:)

When you look for the donkey while on its back,
Those on the side will laugh on seeing you.
The boat was swallowed yet I found it,
As I resumed the path I took when I came.

I, Student Who, was roaming on the sea pursuing immortality with a group of extraordinary beings, and I remember clearly having moored the boat and boarded a small vessel to go fishing. Without knowing how it happened I suddenly fell into a land of darkness where I almost suffocated. Then, again not knowing how, seeing a bright beam of light I edged my way out. Fortunately the solitary boat has not been damaged and my old self still remains. I have no option but to carry this skiff to seek the old path looking for the large boat, so I may fulfill my appointment of rambling with the immortals. What could be wrong with that?

([BANSHE MODE:] *Shua haier*) (STUDENT WHO *sings*:)
Floating around on a giant gourd, with no bank in sight,[234]
I am like that single-sandal Bodhidharma who snapped a reed leaf to return.[235]
My mind determined, I am not afraid of fish and dragon wreaking havoc.
This paper skiff may well cross water of a thousand layers.
Who cares if the iron waves rock Nine Mile Mountain?
I am truly a man as firm as a diamond.
Let the torrents topple the sky and churn the sea,
For I am here sitting secure in my fishing skiff.

(*Speaks*:) I recall fishing on a small skiff and then landing in a dark hole. How miserable I was!

(*Fifth from coda*)
It was so steaming hot that it seemed miasmic;
It was so pitch black I lost count of the years.
In a flash, it seemed, I was nothing like I was when coming here.
It was like the Kingdoms of Maul and Buffet, hidden on the contracted horns of a snail,[236]
Or the crowded courtroom and market bustle in the dream of ants.[237]

How could I distinguish Qin and Han?
Clearly it seemed I had ended up in a deserted lair of ghosts,
That I took to be the transcendent Spring to escape from the world.

Come to think of it, how stupid I am. There was clearly this large vessel that I had rented after a far-off journey when coming to the Eastern Ocean. On board were many extraordinary men and immortal ladies, bejeweled *se*-zithers, jade flutes and gold pipes; limitless delights that I could never exhaust. Why did I abandon the large vessel and take the skiff on the bank to be mine? Of what use could it be to me? I should just cast it aside and go seek the original boat. (STUDENT WHO *acts out deserting the skiff.*)

(*Fourth from coda*)
I clearly had this large vessel,
Sailing across the Eastern Ocean for thousands of miles.
Unexchangeable even if one tried with gold and pearls, damask and brocade.
The bronze mast and iron rudder were commanded by a transcendent elder,
Brocade cables and ivory mast were pulled by jade maidens.[238]
What use do I have for this skimpy sliver of gourd?
Only when I desert the teachings of the Small Vehicle,[239]
Can I encounter the karmic connection to the Great Way.

How strange! How strange! I remember the other day, when I left the ship and took a walk with Kunlun Slave; we walked for no more than half a mile. How come that after all this long trek, I see only a wild desert and limitless mulberry fields? The wide ocean and layering mountains have all disappeared. Good Heavens! Good Heavens! Where could my large vessel be?

(*Third from coda*)
I had tied mast and stern tight to this shore, and
To dodge the wind, we kept close to the mountains.
I still remember
Grasping the vines and clinging to the creepers to get up the bank.
How come these expansive deserted fields have no streams
But the weeds are so lush that all I see is a hovering mist?
Where can I summon the boatman?

(*Speaks:*) Could it be that the Dragon King is also a drifter constantly on the move?

I feel like the one misled by banana leaves, losing the deer,[240]
Like a cicada startled by a falling leaf.[241]

And even all that reed and pipe music, all those immortal travelers and famed beauties—they could not have been unreal. How come they have all disappeared?

(*Second from coda*)
I recall the swaying pendants of the immortal maidens,
And the linking of couplets by famous poetic luminaries:

Amidst clusters of blossoms and piles of brocade, reed organ music was played.
Could it be that the fish swam in water when there was no water at all?
And birds flew in the sky before there was a sky?
How could these actual forms ever be illusory?
It was clearly
Penglai in the orange.
How could it be
Handan in a dream?
(*First from coda*)
I sigh that I am all by myself with only my two fists,
As I think about the former and the latter vessels—
When the ocean dries up and the boats are lost, there are no more strings attached.
The lord of Chu, away from home, sorely missed his lost shoe;[242]
The monarch of Shu entrusted his spring thoughts to the cuckoo.[243]
The Way and the Law are truly hard to see!
I will
Seek being from the midst of non-being,
So why search for perfection in lack?

The large vessel is nowhere to be found, and I have deserted the small one. Now even the sea is not visible anymore. Completely empty-handed with fistfuls of nothing, it's hard to return to the old home, but I have no option but to go on looking.

(*Coda*)
Like being in a drunken stupor,
As if I have lost my mind,
I will
Search throughout the Sacred Land, the Entire Realm,[244]
I'm only afraid that, having lost a sheep at the forking paths, I may take the wrong turn.[245]

I have worn out my straw sandals in search of the floating raft,
Who would believe that I have yet another home at Mt. Penglai?
All say that the yellow millet can be turned into a meal,
Do they also know that the iron tree indeed can bloom?[246]

End-of-Act Comment

To chase after exotic tastes on the sea only to have the boat disappear into the fish belly shows the natural difference between matters of sorrow and joy. Yet as soon as he leaves the fish belly, Student Who can sing a suite to the tune of *Shuahaier.* This act indeed shows his naturally endowed capacity to transcend the ordinary.
Comment by Qiu Haishi

ACT 7

ONCE AGAIN ENCOUNTERING THE LAND OF IMMORTALS

([SOUTHERN XIANLÜ MODE entering into SHUANGDIAO MODE:] *Puxian ge*)
(VILLAIN *enters playing* TIBETAN MONK:)
Heaven opens to reveal the Spirit Vulture overseeing the plain by the river,
From Earth emerges the golden turtle penetrating the vermilion sky.
Banners flap beyond the clouds,
Fish and dragon surge inside the gate.
Such a Jetavana is rare in this world.[247]
(*Recites*:)
When the moon rises above the forest of Meditation, mountains and rivers turn white;
After the floodtide of the ocean recedes, heaven and earth are dark.[248]

I am an old Tibetan monk from the Western Ocean, Chan Master Huiguang. When I came to the Central Land and reached Chaozhou, I saw a big temple beside the sea composed of whale bones, its height reaching dozens of meters, its width enough to accommodate a thousand people. How big could this fish have been? According to tales of the elders, during the Kaiyuan reign of the Tang [713–741], the passing tide lowered to reveal this fish, its length extending several miles and its height equal to that of a hill. Later, when the tide receded, the fish dried out leaving its skeleton here, which was constructed into a grand temple with a statue of Fish-basket Guanyin inside.[249] Scholars and ladies gathered for worship giving bountiful donations. Now it is the fifteenth day of the seventh month.[250] We shall see if any visitor will be here.

(*Manjiang hong*) (MALE LEAD *enters playing* STUDENT WHO:)
Hills and valleys have shifted,[251]
It is like waking from a dream; all whom one encounters invite elegies.
On the square pillow of blue porcelain,
I come seeking my old path.[252]
The crane from Liao has returned but the city walls have changed,[253]
In the woods crows vainly circle the southern branches.[254]
Trekking in straw sandals, I have come a thousand miles in search of a solitary boat
Lost in misty waves.

On my way here the ocean has dried up and the sky came to an end, yet I did not find any news about the large vessel. Here I am at the Southern Sea. There is an old temple in the distance. I shall pay a visit and perhaps ask about the vessel. (STUDENT WHO *acts out bowing to the monk*:) May I ask you, Chan Master, what is the name of this temple? I would like to stay here for a short while. Ah! It's clearly written on the front plaque "Temple of Whale Bones." Indeed:

The wind blows high, and the *peng* bird, not yet transformed, soars to no avail,
The bones, transmogrified, in vain transmit the story of the *kun* fish.

(STUDENT WHO *acts out being startled and sighing.*) (TIBETAN MONK:) May I ask, Master, why did you come in with a sigh? There must be a reason. I would beg to learn.

(*Guizhi xiang*) (STUDENT WHO:)
The Eastern Ocean is just a tiny pit,
The Southern Darkness a mere inch-deep swamp.
Changing winds and clouds—that skinny divine *kun* fish,
Blocking the sun and the moon, that minuscule little *peng* bird!
I lament the dried-out fish, so pitiable!
In addition
Its gills and skull all exposed.
Tall as a hill, its bones have aged,
Why in the waves,
Did its scales persist?
For all vanished in an instant in the wind and thunder.

(*Speaks*:) I wonder how much wind and how many waves this fish stirred up, only to come to this.

(*Reprise*) (TIBETAN MONK:)
Roaming the sky it shone like the sun,
Heedlessly charging, it made mountains collapse.
It roused wind and waves, so rivers churned and peaks leapt;
It stirred its scales and fins, and *qian* and *kun* easily flipped.
Stranded in mud and sand, it remained proud.
Still
Ants now deride it.
None of its towering glory was sustained
When the tidal bore of the river fell.
It truly is
White bones embodying a thousand years of resentment,
And limpid waves stretching for ten thousand miles.

(STUDENT WHO:) Let me ask you, Chan Master. Here at the Southern Sea, have you ever seen a large boat carrying several lofty men and beautiful ladies? Is this craft still around? (TIBETAN MONK *acts out leaving a gatha on the wall and exits.*) (STUDENT WHO:) Look, this old monk left a gatha on the wall and took off just like that. (STUDENT WHO *acts out reading the gatha*:)

To where does the grand ocean return?
The divine whale's belly is already empty.
If you desire a message of Truth,
Search further at the Iron Boat Peak.

I have no clue where this Iron Boat Peak may be. I see an itinerant Daoist nun in the distance. Let me ask her.

(*Bubu jiao*) (FEMALE LEAD *playing* DAOIST NUN *enters and sings*:)

A roseate road through the clouds
To the Island of Cinnabar Mountains:
My lotus steps rippling the delicate waves, and
My cloudy skirt and feathery robe swaying.
Between Heaven and the human realm,
Each place illuminates the root of emotions.
The blue bird finds its road blocked by layered heavens: [255]
When will the transcendent raft return to Wuling?

(*Recites*:) The blue ox has long shaken off its yoke,
The white crane, from time to time, visits its descendants.

I am Xi Shi. Dressed up as an itinerant nun, I have come a long way to greet Student Who. Fortunately, we encounter each other today. (STUDENT WHO *acts out stepping forward to bow and speaks*:) Nun, where are you coming from? (XI SHI:) I am a Daoist nun at the Iron Boat Nunnery.[256] May I ask where you are heading? (STUDENT WHO:) Yah, may I ask you, Daoist nun, where is the Iron Boat Peak?

(*Zuifugui*) (XI SHI:)

You thought it was
Far, far away, and the road blocked beyond the edge of Jade Heaven,
But didn't know that I
Gazed hopefully, leaning against the bridge with red railing.[257]
To the Iron Boat Peak, no oars of cassia and orchid are tied.
The pines between tangled clouds should have been fishing line and hook: [258]
No need to mention
The old roots and sprouts on the stone of three incarnations,[259]
In faint shadows,
Under the bright moon, you've trekked a thousand miles to share my tune.

(XI SHI *speaks*:) This is where the Cangwu realm comes to its end.[260] An iron boat has been floating at the shore among the empty mountains. To this day the rudder is still intact, but there has long been no trace of a visitor. In fine nights under a bright moon, from time to time, the tremolo of transcendent music can be heard. The story goes that when a person with a kindred spirit arrives, the iron boat will move on its own. May I inquire why you gentleman asked about this? The boat is not far from here.

(*Zaoluo pao*) (STUDENT WHO:)

So, it turns out boat and valley have secretly moved to Mt. Yuanqiao.[261]
I had wanted to hide my boat on the emerald ocean,
But have trouble finding the tide to take me back.

In the carnelian palace, where are the dancing slender waists?
How many brocade bags are buried under fragrant grass?[262]
Cloud-woven envelopes and roseate scripts,
Military strategies hidden in famed mountains,
The rainbow skirts and wine vessels—
All guarded securely halfway up the cliff.

(*Speaks*:) Those talented men and beautiful ladies who were with me, where are they now, I wonder?

What a shame about
All that poetry of a thousand years
And those
City-toppling glamorous looks.
(*Hao jiejie*) (XI SHI:)
The verdant mountains on all sides roll on like emerald waves;
Beyond the solitary craft, lush duckweed.
Even though the hills and mountains have shifted,
The divine sail flutters just like before.

(*Speaks*:) The mountain is not far, it's right under the bright moon. Let's go there together.

(STUDENT WHO *and* XI SHI *act out walking together*.) (STUDENT WHO:) Look, the iron boat is half-revealed. A breeze is rising from all directions, so it seems that the boat is going to soar into the Void riding the wind. I believe it won't be long before this boat heads back. (*Together*:)

Leisurely we gaze into the distance,
Brimming and full, the Weak Stream is bright but remote.
As we flee from the Qin, the Spring is close enough for beckoning.
(*Hupo maoer zhui*) (STUDENT WHO:)
The mountains hold back the slanting sunshine;
Where the clouds end is the distant sky of Chu.
Misidentifying the gate to immortality, I knocked on the rock,[263]
A fisherman vainly drifting amidst peach blossoms on Wuling's creek.
Alas!
I fear the flowers will conceal the transcendent spring,
Blocking this world from the fisherman and the woodcutter.

(*Reprise*) (XI SHI:)

The phoenix has left Gou Mountain;[264]
Under the bright moon, subdued is the sound of flute.
Verdant bamboos were watered by the ladies of the Xiang with tears,[265]
Moss flowers completely eroded kingfisher hair ornaments.[266]
Wasted.
I observed

Dancing coming to an end and songs trailing off,
The green dimming and the red dissipating.

(*Speaks*:) Why don't you take a rest here and set off early tomorrow morning? You will surely find something.

(XI SHI *exits*.)

(*Coda*) (STUDENT WHO:)
In an empty mountain it is impossible to call up a fisherman.
All I see are
Gibbons crying and tigers whistling.
So, I fear that at the deserted ferry site the boat will age on its own.[267]
Visiting the Eastern Ocean in the morning and the Cangwu Mountain in the evening,
I trek to the edge of the world seeking the jade pot.
Just look for the transcendent craft outside the cave,
There's no need to step on Qin Gao's old carp.[268]

End-of-Act Comment

The whale has morphed into an old monastery; the solitary vessel into cloudy mountain peaks; and Xi Shi into an itinerant nun wearing a Daoist cap. All at once, Student Who's deluded attachments to sound and sight dissolve into naught.
Comment by Song Yushu

ACT 8

KNOWING THE FORD AND GETTING TO CROSS

(VILLAIN *playing* ZUO CI *enters with* KUNLUN SLAVE:)
Mulberry fields change into oceans, oceans change into fields:
Before one game of *go* ends, several shifts have taken place.
If one wants an iron craft to cross the ocean,
Seek a dried ocean first before seeking the boat.

(*Speaks*:) Student Who, time for you to wake up from your dream. (MALE LEAD *enters playing* STUDENT WHO *and exclaims*:)

The grand ocean never dried up,
The old craft stopped by itself.
If I had not met the boat-swallowing fish,
How would I know about such illusions?

(ZUO CI:) Let me ask you. After you fell into the fish belly, how were you able to get out? (STUDENT WHO:) If I could get in, I could also get out. (ZUO CI:) If you had the strength to carry the little skiff, why did you put it down? (STUDENT WHO:) If I could pick it up, then I could also put it down.[269] (ZUO CI *and* STUDENT WHO *act out laughing heartily.*)

([SOUTHERN ZHONGLÜ MODE:] *Qi Yan Hui*) (ZUO CI:)

Looking back, I laugh out loud:
Seek an empty boat on the ocean and you will find few,
For they are anchored by the root of emotions.
When encountering the boat-swallower sucking in all mountains and rivers,
You followed the wind and floated on the waves.
With the old scourging iron pick and hammer you smashed the fish's gills.

(*Together*)

What is the need to ask again about the transcendent craft?
Within an instant you broke the stoneware pot.[270]

(*Reprise*) (STUDENT WHO:)

The stone statue nods its head greeting the Pengpo rock in the east.[271]
On the bronze bridge we crossed the ocean,
Where iron trees swayed elegantly.
Our boat lay across the Weak Stream,
So whatever havoc fish and dragon wreaked
Had no effect on us.
We easily crossed the Eastern Ocean with a single leap, so so easily!

(*Together*)

Not only did my dogged efforts miss the mark because they were premeditated,
But I also, identifying the empty and void, fell prey to the demon of dried-wood meditation.[272]

(*Speaking from backstage*:) The big boat has returned to the ocean, and it is approaching Mt. Penglai. Immortal gentlemen and ladies, please prepare to ascend the boat. (STUDENT WHO *and* ZUOCI:) Coming!

(ZUO CI:)

When two blind men are fighting in a fury,

(KUNLUN SLAVE:)

It greatly amuses a couple of mountain wrens.

(STUDENT WHO:)

With one hit of my fist I smashed the void and emptiness,[273]

(ZUO CI:)

And the monkey has thrust itself into the ox horn.[274]

End-of-Act Comment

Simple and marvelous!

ACT 9

A TRANSCENDENT BANQUET AT THE DRAGON KING'S PALACE

(VILLAIN *enters dancing, playing* WHALE DEMON:)

One, oh, so short and bald tail,
Two, oh, such thick long sideburns,
My nickname is Old Whale,
An under-water sponger who knows how to have fun.
At leisure, I bicker with Old Lady Shrimp,
When bored I exchange poems with Gentleman Squid.
I once followed a water demon to wreak havoc at the Celestial Boulevard,
A veteran I am at the feat of swallowing boats.

(CLOWN *playing* OLD LADY SHRIMP *enters dancing*:)

Don't boast about how terrifying you are in swallowing boats,
Let me first ask who was the one that was swallowed?
Fish stinks and shrimps smell—one cannot stand the stench.
Swallowed, they are only good for piling shit.
If the Eight Immortals happened to be crossing the ocean,[275]
And you would suddenly open your mouth like a basin,
What you swallowed would pierce through your spine,
And the food would clean out your guts, bowels, and kidneys.

No more babbling. Brother Whale, let me ask you. About ten years ago I remember you swallowed a boat along with its passengers. Did they turn into a pile of shit? Or did it become a bladder full of piss? (WHALE:) Say no more of this! In my life-long career of swallowing boats, this topped the list of bad luck.

The vessel was neither big nor small,
The person neither skinny nor fat,
In one mouthful I swallowed the whole thing,
And the lump stuck in my bowels.

(WHALE *acts out hitting his stomach*:)

The person first pounded frantically with his fists,
As if hurried on by the sound of a drum.
My entire body burned with pain, it was almost pummeled into ashes,
My bowels were ripped apart and my lungs scraped.
I tried to use brine to induce vomiting,
But that person was indeed quite capable.
He urinated all over the bottom of my throat,
Adding quite a rank smell.[276]

(SHRIMP:) Brother Whale, so you still have not digested the boat? Wouldn't you be so distended that you'd split open? (WHALE *mimes poling a boat.*)

He took after Ao, commanding the boat inside my belly,[277]

Poling this way and that,
And used my rib bones as flag poles,
And composed a boat song for fun.

(WHALE *sings a Suzhou ditty and acts out poling the boat*:) He said:

"I was born to love fiddling with the boat,
Wielding a pole, I find myself beside the big river.
When I hook one, I'll eat the whale bladder,[278]
Just like all my sisters at the Yangzhou customs port.
I do not know whether they are glued on the bed,
Or are glued below the bed."

That guy stayed in my belly for a few years and then disappeared, even taking the boat away. How could something like this come to pass! (*Speaking from backstage*:) General Whale and General Shrimp, heed your orders. Have the water creatures put together a crew to clean out the Ocean Treasury in Dragon King's palace in order to greet a group of immortals who will be paying a visit. Quickly go meet them and do not violate your order. (WHALE:) What are the immortals' names? Where are they now? (*Speaking from backstage*:) It is in fact the Student Who you swallowed a year or so earlier. He has moored the boat below Mt. Penglai. You have your orders, so move. (WHALE *acts out being astonished*:) Blimey. How can there be such a thing! So, he is a divine immortal! No wonder he wouldn't die. How can I bring myself to face him? I have no choice but to go.

(*Exits.*)

(MALE LEAD *playing* STUDENT WHO *enters with* VILLAIN, CLOWN, SECOND MALE LEADS, FEMALE LEAD, SECOND FEMALE LEADS, SECOND FEMALES, *and* MISCELLANEOUS.) (VILLAIN:) We've got an invitation from the palace of the dragon king of the Eastern Ocean. We shall all go and pay a visit. (STUDENT WHO:) I'd be happy to follow you. (*Music played from backstage.* ALL *act out walking.*)

(OLD MALES *play* DRAGON DEITY *and* DRAGON LADY. MISCELLANEOUS *enter playing* WHALE *and* SHRIMP.) (ALL *act out greeting*:) We did not know that you, supreme transcendents, had come all the way here, so we have been remiss in welcoming you. We have respectfully swept the water abode for your transcendent chariot to land for the moment. (ZUO CI:) This poor Daoist practitioner is just roaming about on his own whim, while the transcendents, compassionately leading all to deliverance, guide the lofty ones. We have invited ourselves to your precious mansion and are uneasy about our intrusion. (ALL *act out bowing to one another.*) (DRAGON DEITY:) So this is the crystal palace. (ZUO CI:) Behold!

Inlaid mica screens are unfolded,
Shrimp-whisker curtains rolled up.[279]
On all four corners of the bejeweled towers hang bright pearls,
On both sides of jade beds, icy mats are spread out.

Indeed, this is most extravagant. (DRAGON DEITY:) General Whale and General Shrimp, please serve wine. (EXTRA *plays music while backstage wine is served.*)

([SOUTHERN HUANGZHONG MODE:] *Huamei xu*) (ZUO CI:)

The palace's reflection dips in pellucid waves,

The purple pavilion is tall and imposing, locked by frost.

(STUDENT WHO:)

I see

Dragons wrapped around icy columns,

Cranes dancing on jade coral branches.

(SECOND MALE LEAD:)

Dust-repelling incense

Wafts on cloud-like garments of silk.

Goblets of emerald snail-shell

Shimmer with a sugar-cane brew.

(*Chorus*)

There clearly is joy on the jade terrace,

How would those in the human realm know of this?

(*Reprise*) (FEMALE LEAD:)

The white moon is reflected in ripples alongside immortal ladies,

On icy mats and cloudy pools the flowers are bedewed.

We see coral growing into trees,

And satin damask shuttling with the flow.

The air so chilly, like snow generating cold,

A fragrance so sweet, like a springtime that does not fade.

(*Chorus as before*)

(*Speaks*:) We shall summon a group of female entertainers to play music and serve wine. (*Backstage music is played.* DRAGON LADIES *act out dancing.*)

(*Reprise*) (STUDENT WHO:)

Shrimps and perches are playing pipe music.

Just like before:

Roseate capes and immortal makeup amid the cloudy smoke of incense burners.

I see

Tall and towering beings with fish scales,

Impressive clusters of turtles and alligators.

I recall how you swallowed the boat and roamed with a bloated belly,

How could I play the puny fish in a dried-up pond raising my cup for a toast?[280]

(STUDENT WHO *acts out eyeing* WHALE DEMON:) You—aren't you the old friend who swallowed my boat? (WHALE *acts out evading him, muttering "How dare I."*)

(*Chorus as before*)

(*Reprise*) (DRAGON DEITY:)

The water mansion, connected to the Silver River,
Guards Mt. Penghu, serving as its key.
Even if
Wild tides have crashed,
Eventually no waves are disturbed.

(*Speaks*:) Generals, let's move the banquet to the Pavilion of Dark Silk, where dragon maidens will accompany the immortal ladies as they watch mermaids weave icy silk. We shall also set up a vegetarian banquet at the Hall of Golden Rays. There the transcendent guests will read the Buddhist sutras in the Ocean's Tripitaka and the divine books on cinnabar techniques.

They are free to browse the thousand volumes of the dragon's Tripitaka,
And they will be at liberty to pick a few bright pearls.

(*Chorus as before*)

([SOUTHERN XIANLÜ MODE:] *Zhao jiaoer*) (FEMALE LEAD *and* FEMALES *act out walking and singing together*:)

We admire the icy silk,
Soaked with the mermaids' copious tears,
As they lightly weave a fabric gleaming with dazzling colors of clouds.
They weep over the ladies of the Xiang—Nüying and Ehuang—whose tears stained bamboo,
Their tears spraying the Oxherd crossing the bridge of dark magpies.[281]

(*Speaks*:) How many causes for heartbreak are there for these mermaids, such that their tears never stop falling?

And
It is precisely for the sake of Heaven,
For the sake of earth,
For the sake of you,
And for the sake of me,
That these tears fall fast like a shuttle thrown.

(*Chorus*)

Pearls of tears pile up,
Teardrops turn into a river.
And they are indeed
Seeds of resentment for the whole world,
All the lovers within the seas.

(*Exit.*)

(*Reprise*) (STUDENT WHO:)

Tying together books in silken blue-and-yellow covers, ancient red scripts pile up;
Opening jade volumes, a golden light gleams and glistens.
Alas, in the human realm it's hard to see such marvelous books;
Only on entering the dragon king's collection do I know that great joy.

What is the need
To inquire about Xuanyuan,[282]
To draw Fu Xi's hexagrams;[283]
To read Nine Plan's categories,[284]
To consult the Diagram from the Yellow River and Writings from the River Luo—[285]
Just a sputtering flame.

(*Chorus*)
The Qin ashes were easy to ignite,[286]
Bookworms have turned into demons.
How can one
Store books underneath the sea,
Or form a club at Mt. Penglai?

(DRAGON DEITY *turns toward* LI BAI:)[287] Master Li, you enjoy a literary fame that has lasted a thousand years. Today our gathering cannot do without poetry. Please bestow on us a poem as an heirloom of our water mansion. (WHALE:) Ever since I, this old whale, have shed my old shell and transformed my bones,[288] I have swallowed quite a few pedants and learned a couple of lines of doggerel. May I have the audacity to get your comments? Please do not laugh at me. How does this sound? (LI BAI:) Please go ahead.[289] (WHALE *acts out chanting poetry*:)

A deep pool of a hundred feet, ten thousand yards the dragon!

(LI BAI:) How can a small pond of a hundred feet deep accommodate a dragon ten thousand yards long? This does not make much sense. (WHALE:) In the current world where can one find a roomy place? Master Li, in your poem you wrote "White hair three thousand yards long." Now where can one find hair like that? Furthermore, the dragon can transform, and perhaps the nine-thousand-nine-hundred-and-ninety yards remain in the air—this can also explain it. (LI BAI:) Please chant the next line. (WHALE *acts out chanting*:)

With thunder and lightning he descends from Heaven's Palace.

(LI BAI:) This is excessively heroic. (WHALE:) This is Li Cangming's style, which emphasizes exclusively the matter of air and register.[290] Now let me finish the poem imitating the Jingling style.[291]

But as the dark-blue sea has turned into brown dust,[292]
I'll turn myself into a loach and find my joy in mud.

(LI BAI:) Why did you suddenly reduce your scale, so the beginning does not match the end? (WHALE:) Master, you may not know, but nowadays in the world everything is great at the beginning but small in the end. This is surviving by adapting oneself to the circumstances and by mingling water with mud.[293] Now we shall learn from you. (LI BAI:) What should be the topic of my poem? (DRAGON DEITY:) Please use the bright moon as topic. (LI BAI *acts out chanting*:)

The full moon—for how long has it existed?

I raise my wine and ask the sky this question.
I do not know for the moon
What year it may be tonight?
I rise and dance and play with my shadow:
Quite different from the world of mortal man.

(DRAGON DEITY:) Good poem! What a shame Su Dongpo copied this as his own.[294] General Whale and General Shrimp, prepare one hundred coral trees, one peck of bright pearls, one thousand bolts of icy silk damask woven by dragon ladies for our immortal guests as their bounty[295]—these hardly add up to a proper gift. (CLOWN *playing* WANG YANG:) I have no use for this golden cinnabar pill anymore. Let me respectfully give it to Old Dragon in return. (DRAGON DEITY:) The cinnabar pill has to belong to the proper person, so how can I take it? The feeling of sufficiency without seeking anything is called "the true cinnabar pill." Since this is the authentic elixir, there is no division between water and fire.[296] (ALL *act out expressing gratitude.*) (STUDENT WHO:) Many thanks.

([SOUTHERN SHANG MODE:] *Huangying er*) (STUDENT WHO:)
Laughing merrily at a dance of Mara's daughters,[297]
Drunk at the dragon king's palace, nestled amidst damask and brocade.
The pupils of the impoverished scholar are always ravenous:
How many pearls bright as moonlight,
And how many coral trees?
The bounty has never been so abundant as today.

(*Chorus*)
Our eyes cast furtive sidelong glances at the enchanting dragon ladies,
Whom we refuse to exchange for our village hags.
(*Coda*) (STUDENT WHO:)
The bright moon in the water shows not a ruffle,

(DRAGON DEITY:)
One new poem served as a joke.

(*Chorus*)
Let the boundless ocean turn into mulberry fields,
We would just sing our carefree songs.

(STUDENT WHO:)
Tipsy, I ask the old dragon about arcane knowledge,

(DRAGON DEITY:)
Numinous mushrooms and vermilion grasses are exuberant and dark.

(ZUO CI:)
Know that among the full assembly of guests of mist and rosy clouds,

(STUDENT WHO:)
There is a crane from Liaoyang with the surname Ding.

End-of-Act Comments

Student Who's feat inside the fish belly was enacted by the old whale in a slapstick fashion. The poem on the bright moon chanted by Li Taibai also received its embellishment from the old whale. Thus do we know that the business of swallowing the boat is truly a compassionate deliverance. The whale is indeed worthy of providing the ride for Taibai to roam in Heaven. A good friend indeed!
Comment by Zhong Yishi

The guests have had their fill of the pearls and the treasure in the dragon king's palace, yet they further contemplate the dragon ladies to be included in their bounty. What kind of creature is this Student Who—how audacious is he to trouble the dragon king with the request to join the court as his protégé? Patronage-seeking guests like these are plenty.
Comment by Zhang Cichen

ACT 10

THE BOAT RETURNS TO PENGLAI OCEAN

(CLOWN *enters playing* BOATMAN:)

Seen horizontally it becomes an ocean, seen vertically it becomes a peak:
Near, far, afloat, and sinking—all depends on the wind.
If I do not know Mt. Penglai's true face,
It's because my own body is on this boat.[298]

Under the order of the divine master Cheng Lian, I had rented out this ocean-crossing iron boat to Student Who for him to roam far and wide. Now the fruit of the Dao is completed, we are about to return to the immortal island. It is just about time to return the original boat, and to let him take flight to the void. Masters, what a convenient wind! What a convenient wind! We shall return to the Eastern Ocean today. ([SOUTHERN ZHENGGONG MODE:] *Po zhenzi*) (MALE LEAD *enters playing* STUDENT WHO:)

The river with nine curves is about to turn,
The two disks of sun and moon resemble balls.

(CLOWN *and* VILLAIN:)

Happily, the boat is light, so a return journey is easy,
One speck of floating duckweed between Heaven and Earth.

(ALL *enter.*)

Between Peach Blossoms we lose count of the years.

(MALE LEAD *recites:*) A single reed crosses the Weak Stream's one thousand miles,[299]

When the moon is bright, I rise leisurely to fix my fisherman's cape.
(VILLAIN:) At the time we believed Mt. Penglai was far away,
(CLOWN:) Yet when we reached it, the road turned out not to be far.[300]

(STUDENT WHO:) Ever since I, Student Who, roamed far with you gentlemen, we have visited the dragon palace, the shell terrace, Mt. Yuanqiao and Fanghu Island. I have exhausted my passion for roaming and so let this empty boat return on its own. Boatman, you can release the boat toward the east and find the old path. I shall bid farewell with my fellow travelers. (SECOND MALE LEAD, EXTRA, FEMALE LEAD, SECOND FEMALE LEADS ALL *enter.*)

([NORTHERN SHUANGDIAO MODE:] *Xinshui ling*) (STUDENT WHO:)
This piece of sail, this single reed, returns with the clouds,
And for the eyes—sunset clouds and returning geese beyond count.
The tide is calm, and further, there is the moon,
The wind subsided, and the mountain is gone.
Having crossed all those flowing waters,
Yet
We gaze again at the Eastern Ocean, still the other shore.[301]

([SOUTHERN XIANLÜ MODE ENTERING INTO SHUANGDIAO MODE:] *Bubu jiao*) (FEMALES:)
Ferried across Penglai, as if we were flying; the waves are clear and shallow,
The edge of the sky is like a thread.
The transcendent sail was drawn by a rope of ten-thousand yards.
As if in a mirror, Fanghu Island
Vaguely appeared amidst the waves.
The back of the crane is cold in the jade Heaven.
And we fear
That cassia flowers will fall upon the Palace of Pure Void.

([NORTHERN SHUANGDIAO MODE:] *Zheguiling*) (MALES:)
Gazing at the expansive vastness, we ride the clouds aloft the mist,
Having gone through winds, tides, tides and winds,
Twisting and turning, turning and twisting.
Now, at this moment, the ten thousand acres stretch in front of us,
The waves tranquil without a stir,
The sail's shade hanging high.
Oblivious—peach blossoms on warm waves,
Desolate—knotweed leaves covered by frost.
The moon sinks in the western sky,
Tired birds return to the east.
What is the need to
Accompany gliding seagulls floating on a thousand folds of waves?
I am already

That divine fish, transformed to vault across the Three Mountains.
([SOUTHERN XIANLÜ MODE ENTERING INTO SHUANGDIAO MODE:] *Jianger shui*) (FEMALES:)
The Weak Stream gleams like a bolt of silk,
Floating mountains emerge like lotus flowers.
Airy and light, we entrust ourselves to the whirling winds and waves;
Churning and turning, the transformations of the *kun* fish and the grand sea turtle fill our vision.
Filled with joy, we have walked all around the Penghu Island—
Just like the golden cinnabar pill that has gone through nine transformations.[302]
When the *peng* bird spreads its two wings,
It is still as before one sliver of a gourd.
([NORTHERN SHUANGDIAO MODE:] *Yaner luo* continued with *Desheng ling*) (MALES:)
I will never again dream in a thatched hut of a butterfly flitting and fluttering its wings,[303]
I will never again work up my gills to touch the dragon gate with my forehead;
I will never again search for the Dark Pearl in the sand of the Red Water;[304]
I will never again cast an iron net for coral embankments.[305]
When the boat was swallowed, I had passed thousands of mountains.
Others' trials and tribulations I shall carry for them,
Having cut off the tether of attachments,
Having opened the pass of Non-Image.[306]
Launch the boat!
Sitting astride a whale I will fly across half of Heaven,
Insouciant and leisurely—
Let me lean against my simple window and fall deeply asleep.

(ALL *act out moving.*)

([SOUTHERN SHUANGDIAO MODE:] *Jiaojiao ling*) (FEMALES:)
Rosy clouds are remote at the edge of Heaven,
The emerald ocean, has it ever dried out?
Sharing a merry banquet in jade buildings and alabaster towers,
Inevitably
We will have to bid farewell within moments.

(CLOWN *enters playing* BOATMAN:) The boat is already approaching the shore, and Mt. Penglai is not far away. These gentlemen and young ladies will have to disembark first. The big boat was originally rented by Master Who, so he'll have to settle the bill once on land. The owner will be waiting there for his money. (ZUO CI:) The immortals originally came riding their own painted boat, and the transcendent ladies had a lotus boat. Both are moored at the bank. Please go separately back to your own boats, and the boats will sail side by side, so each will return by its own way.

(SECOND MALE LEADS *act out bowing to* STUDENT WHO *and then ascending the craft to leave.*) (STUDENT WHO *acts out bowing to* FEMALES, *who then ascend the craft to leave.*)

([NORTHERN SHUANGDIAO MODE:] *Shou jiangnan*) (ALL:)

Yah! We had always known that we were to part ways at Tuṣita Heaven,
Descending thousands of miles en route to Penglai and Yingzhou.
For nothing you asked our jade maiden Shuangcheng to deliver the roseate letter,
And the transcendent guests on Gou Mountain to send back the blue phoenix:[307]
It must be that our fated love karma is still tugging at us.

Again and again it is said:

Even when dreaming a Daoist enjoys no leisure.

([SOUTHERN XIANLÜ MODE ENTERING INTO SHUANGDIAO MODE:] *Yuanlin hao*) (STUDENT WHO:)

I gaze at the mountains from the past, clouded by mist and covered with greens,
As I navigate the empty boat, breaking through rocks and crashing waves.
In the distance I see wind and waves splashing on the bank:
Ascending the path to enlightenment, I will emerge from the perilous currents.

(*Reprise*)

([NORTHERN SHUANGDIAO MODE:] *Gu meijiu* connected to *Taiping ling*) (ALL *act out moving.*)

We gaze at Penglai in the distance—resembling a single fist;
The road to the Eastern Ocean is like a cup suspended in the air,[308]
Only the original scenery falls within our sight.
Poetry and wine: what is the need to indulge till tipsy?
Gems and jade must eventually all be cast aside.
Inhaling the West River, I turn the Silver River around;[309]
Scattering ghee, I hold the grand ocean upside down.[310]

As for me,

I do not fear heaven crumbling, earth crumbling,
Mountains or rivers being destroyed.
Yah! Even when the kalpa turns to ashes, the iron vessel will not decay.

(ALL *act out disembarking from the boat.*)

(SECOND MALES *and* CHORUS:) The Heavenly Gate is hacked open, and waves are surging,

(SECOND FEMALES:) While the guests disperse, leaving by the ways they came.

(ALL *exit.*)

(STUDENT WHO:) Were it not for a poetic exposition on the bright moon,

(BOATMAN:) Could we have returned with a boat fully loaded with treasure?

(CLOWN *playing* BOATMAN:) Sir, your body has gone up the shore. You no longer have any need for the boat. (*Acts out pointing*:) Look! Over there the master is coming.

(STUDENT WHO *acts out mounting the shore and turning around to look.*[311] BOATMAN *exits beyond sight.*)

(STUDENT WHO:) Yah! Why has the boat disappeared too?

(*Qingjiang yin*) (STUDENT WHO:)

In this world the sea of bitterness sweeps you, it seems, away with its waves,
The myriad things disperse like floating water bubbles.
Whence came the divine craft,
Where immortal guests kept me company?
A whole sky's worth of autumn I'll entrust to the care of the bright moon.[312]

I once visited Cheng Lian in a boat out on the sea,
In my dreams I have often roamed with magicians.
Only figures from the Han and the Tang could become my friends,
As songs of an age of decline bring too much sorrow.
Underneath the tongue, the blue lotus rivaled the brocade zither,[313]
In front of the banquet, "White Snow" conjured up the Cinnabar Hill.[314]
From these years of idle amusement, I have attained *Samādhi*,
Wondering in vain whether my name will remain on the ornamental pillar.[315]

End-of-Act Comment

The return of the boat to its immortal origin is just like coming back to the hot liveliness before.[316] This is the Bodhi of afflictions. Plucking the finest figures from thousands of years and having them meet one another in the same hall—for such a fine history of the Traveler through the Wilderness a marionette show is perfect.[317] To maintain, at all times, one's mind as pure as ice in a pot while carrying a wooden pole—only then do we see the author's profound power of the Way.[318]
[Comment by] Hai'an

NOTES

1. Heat and coldness are stock references to high and low points in one's life.
2. See Tao Qian's 陶潛 (365–427) poem "Begging for Food" (Qi shi 乞食) that starts with the line "Hunger came to drive me ahead." For an English translation and discussion of the poem, see Tian 2005, 127–31.
3. Yan Zhenqing 顏真卿 (709–785) had famously written a note "On Pleading for Rice" (Qimi tie 乞米帖) addressed to Li Guangjin (751–815), whose official rank reached that of Grand Guardian for the Heir Apparent.
4. Du Fu's 杜甫 (712–770) wrote "Pengya: A Ballad" (Pengya xing 彭衙行), in which he recounts his flight from the rebels during the An Lushan 安祿山 rebellion (755–763) before he reached home on the Pengya road. English translation in Owen 2016, vol. 1, 349.

5. Literally, shoes and socks made from dark cloth for common men and women.
6. Mythical land out in the sea inhabited by immortals.
7. In his "Biography of Young Master Li" (Li gongzi zhuan 李公子傳) Chen Jiru 陳繼儒 (1558–1639) gives a fantastic account on Young Master Li's gatherings with immortals.
8. The thirteenth-century writer Wang Shifu's 王實甫 northern drama *The Story of the Western Wing* (*Xixiang ji* 西廂記) was one of the most frequently reprinted plays throughout late imperial China. See West and Idema (1995) for a complete English translation. *The Story of the Hidden Boudoir* (*Yougui ji* 幽閨記) is a popular southern theater's rendition of the northern drama *Praying to the Moon* (*Baiyue ting* 拜月亭) attributed to Guan Hanqing 關漢卿 (c. 1245–1322). An English translation of the latter is included in West and Idema (2010, 77–104).
9. This citation comes from an iconoclast thinker Li Zhi's 李贄 (Zhuowu 卓吾, 1527–1602) "Miscellaneous Discourses" (Zashuo 雜說) in his controversial title *A Book to Burn* (*Fenshu* 焚書). See Handler-Spitz, Lee, and Saussy (2016) for English translations of selected writings.
10. Gong Dingzi 龔鼎孳 (1615–1673) was an important cultural figure from the Ming-Qing transitional period in the second half of the seventeenth century. The signature is followed by two personal seals of Gong Dingzi.
11. A phrase from "The World" (Tianxia 天下) of *Zhuangzi* 莊子: "He believed that the world was drowned in turbidness and that it was impossible to address it in sober language." Translation from Watson (1968, 373).
12. Sima Qian 司馬遷 (ca. 145–87 BCE), author of the first individually compiled history in traditional China, *Records of the Grand Historian* (*Shiji* 史記).
13. Yushu is the courtesy name of Song Wan 宋琬 (1614–1674), an influential literary and political figure from Laiyang of Shandong.
14. A common stage prop for Daoist adepts to indicate the purity of their mind beyond worldly dust.
15. The play actually presents Cheng Lian 成連 as played by VILLAIN (JING) 淨.
16. Literally Student He. In addition to being a surname, *he* is also a question word. Student He as a phrase can therefore become a question: Who is this student? In this translation I use Student Who to be consistent with the intended pun.
17. This is a kind of soft fabric cap worn for informal occasions.
18. In addition to Daoist practitioners, it was also common for young servant boys and maidens to wear their hair in this style.
19. The role type VILLAIN wears a painted-face makeup and originally appears in northern theater as a jester or a villain. In this play, several dramatic characters played by this role type are not comic figures or villains. They are rather Daoist magicians and heroic figures such as Kunlun Slave, a fictional knight-errant.
20. The play actually presents Wang Yang 王陽 as played by CLOWN (CHOU) 丑.
21. The printed edition has a black spot here that indicates that the block had been changed, but no new characters had been inscribed. *Lingbo* 凌波 appears in Cao Zhi's 曹植 (192–232) "Fu on the Goddess of the Luo River" (Luoshen fu 洛神賦) as a phrase to describe her dainty steps. See Knechtges (2006, 355–65) for an English translation.
22. See Li Bai's 李白 (701–762) well-known line in one of the seventeen quatrains titled "Songs on Qiupu" (Qiupu ge 秋浦歌): "My white hair extends for three thousand yards; / This is because my sorrow drags just as long" 白髮三千丈，緣愁似箇長.
23. Metonyms for weapons of war.
24. Master Void is a fictional character in Sima Xiangru's 司馬相如 (ca. 179–117 BCE) eponymous rhapsody. See Xiao Tong and Knechtges (1987, 53–72) for an English translation.

25. The word "to ferry" (*du* 渡) here puns on "to deliver."
26. The Peng Island, also known as Penglai or the Penghu Island, is a place for immortals.
27. A stock image for great changes over a long span of time that first appears in the goddess Magu's 麻姑 self-introduction from Wang Yuan's 王遠 story in *Biographies of Immortals* (*Shenxian zhuan* 神仙傳) by Ge Hong 葛洪 (283–343).
28. In "Peach Blossom Spring" (Taohua yuan ji 桃花源記) attributed to Tao Qian, a fisherman stumbles upon a land blissfully removed from war. Once he has left the place, the fisherman can no longer find his way back. For an English translation, see Owen (1996, 309–10).
29. Music Master Xiang 師襄, with whom Confucius supposedly studied, was from Wei.
30. *Kalpa* is a Buddhist term for a very long period of time that ends in complete destruction.
31. A direct reference to the "Peach Blossom Spring" as a timeless utopia. Its residents, who had fled from the tyranny of the Qin 秦 dynasty (221–207 BCE), were so blissfully unaware of worldly turmoil that they did not even know that Qin had been replaced by the Han 漢 (202 BCE–220 CE), or that the Han, in turn, had been replaced by Wei 魏 and Jin 晉 (220–420).
32. Jiang Yan 江淹 (444–505), a famed writer, owned a writing brush of many colors. Upon surrendering the brush in a dream, Jiang Yan woke up to find himself bereft of his literary talent. The multicolored brush thus came to stand for literary creativity and authorial ingenuity. For details, see Swartz et al. (2014, 390).
33. A reference to Student Who's failure at passing the civil service examination.
34. In the "Yellow Emperor" (Huangdi 黃帝) chapter of *Liezi* 列子 is a story of a man who enjoys the company of hundreds of sea gulls so long as he does not harbor any specific intentions in his mind. The phrase "pact with sea gulls" (*oumeng* 鷗盟) in later poetry comes to refer to the lofty mind of a recluse. Student Who sought Sima Qian likely because he saw a kindred spirit in the Grand Historian, who preceded his own time by almost two thousand years.
35. According to Zhang Liang's 張良 (?–ca. 186 BCE) biography in Sima Qian's *Records of the Grand Historian*, Zhang Liang missed his appointment with an immortal who identified himself to be Yellow Rock twice before he was finally able to show up ahead of the immortal. As a reward, Liang was left with a volume on military strategies that helped him cement his career as a brilliant military strategist aiding the founding emperor of the Han to attain the throne.
36. Buddhist teachings are typically compared to showers of flower petals.
37. In Chinese mythology, the Fusang 扶桑 tree is located where the sun rises.
38. The ant kingdom in Li Gongzuo's 李公佐 (770?–850?) tale "The Prefect of Nanke" (Nanke taishou zhuan 南柯太守傳). In a dream, Chunyu Fen marries the princess of the Huai'an Kingdom and becomes a distinguished official. He loses an important battle and then his wife succumbs to disease. Chunyu Fen leaves the kingdom only to find out that what he has experienced took place in a dream and that the Huai'an Kingdom is but a pit full of ants. For an English translation, see Nienhauser (2010, 131–88).
39. In "King Mu of Zhou" (Mu tianzi 穆天子) chapter of the *Liezi* is a story about a man who, upon failing to locate a deer he hid under banana leaves, believes that the act of hiding took place in a dream. Overhearing him, his neighbor manages to retrieve the deer. It then becomes not clear whether the man dreamed of his neighbor finding the deer or whether he had a dream of hiding the deer that came true.
40. The fisherman and the woodcutter are both established cultural figures removed from the hustle and bustle of the worldly realm. They are therefore unbiased judges of human affairs.
41. A phrase from "The Turning of Heaven" (Tianyun 天運) of *Zhuangzi*: "Benevolence and righteousness are the grass huts of the former kings; you may stop in them for one night but you mustn't tarry there for long" 仁義，先王之蘧廬也，止可以一宿而不可以久處. Translation from Watson (1968, 162).

42. A reference to Shen Jiji's 沈既濟 (ca. 750–ca. 797) *chuanqi* tale "Record Within a Pillow" (Zhenzhong ji 枕中記), which recounts the story of a Daoist adept Old Man Lü who, en route to Handan, stops at an inn and provides a pillow for a frustrated young man surnamed Lu to take a nap. In a dream Lu lives through an entire life of ups and down as a prominent official only to wake up finding that the millet is yet to finish cooking. Realizing that worldly pursuits are as illusory as a dream, Lu embraces the Daoist way of self-cultivation instead. For an English translation, see Nienhauser (2010, 73–130).
43. The fisherman's craft to Peach Blossom Spring, a place of timeless bliss irretrievably lost to the fisherman once he left.
44. The phrase "practice expedient means" 方便 (Skt. *upāya*) is a prominent concept in Mahayana Buddhism that refers to teaching according to the capacity of the hearer.
45. Likely an echo to the first of Su Shi's 蘇軾 (1037–1101) well-known rhapsodies on the "Red Cliff" (Chibi fu 赤壁賦): "A light wind wafted by, and not a ripple was stirred. I poured wine for my guests as we chanted the poem about the bright moon and sang the song about the graceful maiden" 清風徐來,水波不興,舉酒屬客,誦明月之詩,歌窈窕之章. Translation from Strassberg (1994, 185–86).
46. Feng Yi 馮夷 is the god of wind that appears in "The Great and Venerable Teacher" (Da zongshi 大宗師) of *Zhuangzi*.
47. In Daoist lore, the Three Mao Brothers attained immortality at a mountain that came to be named after them. This is the Mt. Mao 茅山 located in the Gourong County in modern-day Jiangsu Province.
48. "Primal dragon" (*yuanlong* 元龍) is a Daoist term that refers to the ultimate *yang* energy and the achievement of the Way.
49. Ouyang Xiu 歐陽修 (1007–1072) writes that his friend Shi Yannian 石延年 (994–1041), upon death, was placed in charge of the Lotus City.
50. Mt. Haoli 蒿里 (next to Mt. Tai) is a place for the dead.
51. Xu Feiqiong 許飛瓊 is an attendant to Queen Mother of the West and the blue bird is a messenger of the deity. In *Past Anecdotes on the Emperor Wu of the Han* (*Han Wu gushi* 漢武故事), the Queen Mother of the West manifested herself flanked by two blue birds when she paid a visit to the emperor.
52. Daoist legend has it that a special glue made of a phoenix's beak and a unicorn's horn can fix any snapped strings with maximum strength. The term later comes to refer to fixing ruptures in conjugal relationships, in particular a man's remarriage after losing his wife.
53. Emperor Wu of the Han 漢武帝 (r. 141–87 BCE), was given a pill that could summon the soul of his beloved late consort, Lady Li 李夫人.
54. The long poem "Encountering Sorrow" (Lisao 離騷) attributed to Qu Yuan, in which the Chu minister laments being at odds with the corrupt world before proclaiming the wish to drown himself. The poem came to represent the Chu songs (Chuci 楚辭) as a distinctive poetic tradition.
55. According to the Shangqing 上清 (Highest Clarity) Daoist doctrines, the two main emblems at the basis of its discourse are Real Mercury and Real Lead, corresponding to Original Yin and Original Yang, respectively. This view of the alchemical process paved the way for the development of both outer and inner alchemy in the Daoist tradition (*EOT* 1003).
56. In the Daoist rite of Salvation through Refinement, the central element is the refinement of the "spiritual body" through the power of water and fire (*EOT* 647).
57. Student Who dismisses these two as an itinerant Daoist looking for charity and a charlatan peddling some "magic pills" as panacea.
58. The Weak Stream 弱水 is a mythical locale that is mostly associated with the myth of the Kunlun Mountain. The phrase literally means waters that do not carry enough force to keep things afloat.

59. Another meaning of the expression, "hanging out with ghosts" (*guihun* 鬼混) means just fooling around.
60. The Mysterious Sea is located in the north where the *yin* and *yang* forces converge.
61. In the Buddhist worldview the Four Grand Continents make up the world in which humans exist: The Southern Continent of Jambudvīpa, the Eastern Continent of Pūrva-videha, the Western Continent of Avara-godānīya, and the Northern Continent of Uttarakuru (see *DEB*).
62. The term *xiji* 醯雞 refers to flotsam on top of a wine cup.
63. Zhang Zhihe 張志和, a literatus-turned Daoist practitioner from the Tang, received as a gift a servant lad and a maid from the emperor. He made them husband and wife, and Qiaoqing 樵青 is the wife's name.
64. Emperor Wu of the Han, when still a child, promises a chamber of gold for his queen.
65. Zhang Han 張翰 (3rd c.) resigned from office in order to enjoy perch stew back at his hometown. The phrase "the 'Autumn Wind' wayfarer" 秋風客 as a reference to Emperor Wu derives from Li He's 李賀 (790–816) opening line in "Bronze Immortals Take Leave of Han" (Jintong xianren ci Han ge 金銅仙人辭漢歌): "Master Liu of Maoling, the 'Autumn Wind' wayfarer" 茂陵劉郎秋風客. Emperor Wu was credited to have composed the "Song on the Autumn Wind" (Qiufeng ge 秋風歌). Translation from Robert Ashmore in Cai (2018, 386).
66. The realm of the immortals.
67. It is recorded in *History of the Latter Han Dynasty* (*Hou Han shu* 後漢書, *j.* 43) that Zhu Mu 祝穆 had a composition with this title, but it did not survive. The well-known letter on severing ties of friendship that did survive is Ji Kang's 嵇康 (ca. 223–ca. 262) letter addressed to Shan Tao 山濤 (205–283) collected in *Anthology of Literature* (*Wenxuan* 文選) compiled at the court of Xiao Tong 蕭統 (501–531). See Jansen (2006) for a study of this topic.
68. The moon.
69. The Palace of Stamen Gem is one of the legendary celestial palaces in Daoist lore.
70. A reference to Li Shangyin's 李商隱 (813?–858) poem, "Chang'e" 嫦娥 on what the goddess might have felt about her theft of the magical pill that sent her to the moon: "Chang-e must regret stealing the elixir— / Over blue sea, in dark sky, thinking night after night" 嫦娥應悔偷靈藥，碧海青天夜夜心. Translation from Charles Egan in Cai (2008, 219).
71. Oxherd crossing the Milky Way (River of Heaven 天河 or Silver River 銀河) to meet the Weaving Lady.
72. Ruan Zhao's 阮肇 encounter with goddesses in deep mountains.
73. The central position in the Simurgh Palace is occupied by the empress who presides over the imperial harem.
74. The White Lady 素娥 is the moon goddess more commonly known as Chang'e.
75. In the Daoist teachings of outer alchemy, Perfected Lead corresponds to the Original *Yang*, while Perfected Mercury corresponds to the Original *Yin*. Since the elixir (Pure Yang) is obtained through combining the two refined essences, a process that draws an analogy to sextual intercourse, the White Lady's remark also refers to these banished goddesses' failure to escape sexual entanglement.
76. Lady Zhao is Zhao Feiyan 趙飛燕 (45–1 BCE), known for her superb dancing skill—she could dance on a palm-sized plate like a flying swallow. Zhao dominated the imperial harem as the favored consort of Emperor Cheng of the Western Han. She was remembered as a femme fatale who presided over schemes against her rivals that resulted in Emperor Cheng's lack of imperial heir. Zhang Lihua 張麗華 (559–589) was a favored consort of the Last Ruler of Chen at the end of the Six Dynasties (Chen Shubao 陳叔寶, 553–604), who had extravagant palaces built on her behalf. Historical records have it

that, when the Sui army sacked the Chen capital, the emperor Chen Shubao was found hiding in a well together with Zhang Lihua and another consort, Lady Kong.

77. The Yu steps are standard components of Daoist rituals.
78. The song "Jade Tree and Rear Courtyard Flowers" (Yushu houting hua 玉樹後庭花) was performed at the court of Chen Shubao.
79. Luxurious mansions constructed for Chen Shubao and his beloved consort Zhang Lihua.
80. Xi Shi 西施 was a legendary beauty from Yue who was sent by Goujian 勾踐 (ca. 520–465 BCE), King of Yue, to bewitch King of Wu, Fuchai 夫差, the most menacing foe of Yue. Smitten with her beauty, Fuchai became negligent of state affairs. After the Yue army conquered Wu, Xi Shi disappeared. There were anecdotes of her having left with her lover Fan Li 范蠡, Goujian's prized adviser, to roam freely among the five lakes.
81. The image evokes a sailboat piercing the water as if slashing a deep cut through a stretch of plain silk. This line refers to the story that Xi Shi ended her days roaming among the lakes with her lover.
82. The sound of Xi Shi's footsteps as she walked in the Wu palace, where a corridor was named accordingly as Corridor Resounding with Clog-Clicking 響屧廊.
83. According to *Annals of Wu and Yue* (Wu Yue chunqiu 吳越春秋), Xi Shi was daughter of a woodcutter in the Zhuluo Mountains. This line is derived from Li Bai's "Climbing Phoenix Terrace in Jinling" (Deng Jinling Fenghuang tai 登金陵鳳凰臺): "Flowering plants of the palace of Wu bury secluded paths" 吳宮花草埋幽徑. Translation from Owen (2006a, 196).
84. The phrase *juyou* 聚麀 here literally means incestuous sexual activities. It is used in a more general sense to refer to Zhao Feiyan and her younger sister Hede's 合德 ruthless efforts at seduction that left Emperor Cheng heirless.
85. Zhao Feiyan's name literally means "flying swallow." The ballad comes from "Discourse on the Five Phases" (Wuxing zhi 五行志) in *History of the Han* (*Han shu* 漢書). It voices a popular belief that Zhao Feiyan actively kept the emperor from getting a male heir in order to secure her own position as a favored consort.
86. Xue Tao 薛濤 (768–831) was a courtesan who spent all her life in the city of Chengdu. She was a talented poet and was best remembered for the lavish stationery that she used for her writings. Lu Mochou 盧莫愁 was a beautiful girl from Luoyang who was married into the Lu household, according to a song attributed to Xiao Yan 蕭衍, Emperor Wu of Liang 梁武帝 (464–549). In this play, she is identified as a courtesan from Hangzhou, even though her name is typically associated with a lake in Nanjing instead.
87. From "Shao Nan" 召南 (Ode no. 23) of *The Book of Poetry* (*Shijing* 詩經): "Softly now, and gently, gently, / do not touch my apron, sir, / and don't set the cur to barking" 舒而脫脫兮、無感我帨兮、無使尨也吠. It is typically understood that these lines depict an illicit love scene. Legge (1991, 34).
88. These are golden bells attached to flowers to guard them from birds; from *Forgotten Stories from the Tianbao Era* (*Tianbao yishi* 天寶遺事).
89. The thirty-six lesser Grotto-Heavens in the Daoist tradition.
90. The Shu damask refers to a special artistic stationery named after Xue Tao. The phrase "jade pure" (*yuqing* 玉清) evokes the Daoist teaching on Clarity. It may therefore be a reference to Xue Tao's later years as a Daoist priestess.
91. The Six Bridges are on the Su Dike in West Lake, constructed under Su Shi's jurisdiction. The *zheng* zither with thirteen strings was allegedly created by the Qin general Meng Tian 蒙恬 (d. 210 BCE).
92. This is a fictional rendition of the phrase "Wang Yang can forge gold" in Ying Shao's 應劭 (ca. 153–196) *Comprehensive Discussion of Customs* (*Fengsu tongyi* 風俗通義). Wang Yang is Wang Ji 王吉, style name Ziyang 子陽. Ying Shao's phrase introduces a critical discussion in response to Ban Gu's 班固

(32–92) comment in *History of the Han* on Wang Ji being able to maintain a sense of affluence without resorting to resources as an official (in other words, he could create wealth on his own terms as a private person).

93. Cao Zhi was one of the three Caos—the other two being his father Cao Cao 曹操 (155–220) and his older brother Cao Pi 曹丕 (187–226)—whose patronage of literature shaped the literary landscape of the Jian'an era. Cao Zhi's literary achievement was considered the highest among the three. Liu Zhen 劉禎 (?–217) was one of the seven prominent literary figures of this period who were identified by Cao Pi as one of the Seven Masters of the Jian'an Era. Li Bai and Du Fu are hailed as the best poets of the Tang dynasty; Li Bai is known as the Immortal of Poetry and Du Fu as the Historian of Poetry.
94. Li Bai's *yuefu* song "Bring on the Ale" (Jiangjinjiu 將進酒) reads: "Take the dapple horse, / take the furs worth a fortune, / just call for the boy to take them to pawn for fine ale, / and here together we'll melt away the sorrows of eternity," 五花馬，千金裘，呼兒將出換美酒，與爾同銷萬古愁. Translation from Chang and Owen (2010, 308).
95. Du Fu's poem "Empty Purse" (Kong nang 空囊) ends with this couplet: "Fearing shamefaced awkwardness if my purse were empty, / I hold on to one copper cash" 囊空恐羞澀，留得一錢看. Translation from Owen (2016, vol. 2, 183).
96. Dongfang Shuo 東方朔 (154–93 BCE) was a renowned jester at the court of Emperor Wu of the Han. This a reference to an anecdote in Dongfang Shuo's biography in *the History of the Han*, in which Shuo makes a subtle reference to how his meager income was incommensurate with his talent by complaining that he was starving on the same amount of grain that was instead stuffing dwarfs to death.
97. Yi Ya 易牙 (ca. seventh century BCE) was a legendary connoisseur of culinary art who served at Duke Huan of Qi's 齊桓公 (?–643 BCE) court from the Spring and Autumn period.
98. Lu Yu 陸羽 (733–804) was a master of tea known for having authored *Classics of Tea* (*Cha jing* 茶經).
99. The Palace of Eternal Joy was constructed on the basis of an old Qin palace at the court of the founding emperor of the Han.
100. Yelang 夜郎 was an ancient state in modern Guizhou that was wiped out at the end of the Western Han dynasty (206 BCE–9 CE). Following the defeat of the rebellion of the prince of Yong in which Li Bai had participated, he was banished to this area.
101. See Li Bai's well-known ballad, "The Road to Shu is Difficult" (Shudao nan 蜀道難). English translation in Minford and Lau (2000, 723–25). Li Bai in this scene is played by SECOND MALE LEAD, but the stage direction instead designates MALE LEAD for singing.
102. According to a popular anecdote, Li Bai once had the Exalted Consort Yang hold the inkstone and the favored eunuch Gao Lishi 高力士 take off his boots as he was making an impromptu poetic composition at the behest of Emperor Xuanzong of the Tang 唐玄宗 (r. 712–756).
103. The Boliang Terrace was constructed at the court of the Emperor Wu of the Western Han.
104. Zhaoling is the mausoleum built for Emperor Taizong of the Tang 唐太宗 (r. 626–649).
105. Emperor Wu of the Han had a bronze statue of an immortal holding a plate erected to collect heavenly dew.
106. Chen Shubao, the last ruler of the Chen, had the Jingyang Palace built for Zhang Lihua. Traditional historiography considered Chen Shubao's extravagant spending to be the reason for the fall of his state.
107. The image of the sinking water vessel in a well has been well established as a metaphor of romantic affairs gone awry or a lady dying. Bai Juyi 白居易 (772–846) had a *yuefu* poem titled "Pulling up a Silver Vase from the Bottom of the Well" (Jingdi yin yinping 井底引銀瓶) to caution against elopement.

108. Literally, feasts set on tortoiseshell mats.
109. The Zhang Terrace 章臺 road is a euphemism for the courtesans' quarters.
110. Kunlun Slave 崑崙奴 is a fictional knight-errant from the eponymous tale in Pei Xing's 裴鉶 (fl. 860) story collection *Tales That Transmit the Strange* (*Chuanqi* 傳奇).
111. Huang Chao's 黃巢 (835–884) rebellion and its aftermath precipitated the fall of the Tang.
112. Zhang Qian 張騫 (164–114 BCE) encountered a herd boy when he traveled on a raft along the River of Heaven. The herd boy gave Zhang Qian a stone, and Zhang found out later that the stone belonged to the Weaving Lady.
113. From "Commentary on the Appended Phrases, Part One" (Xici zhuan 繫辭傳上) of *The Book of Changes* (*Yi jing* 易經): "But for two people to share mind and heart, / Such sharpness severs metal, / And the words of those sharing mind and heart, / Such fragrance is like orchids" 二人同心，其利斷金；同心之言，其臭如蘭. Translation from Lynn (1994, 58).
114. This line derives from a couplet in Li He's "Dream of Heaven" (Mengtian 夢天) "Gaze far off on the middle continent, those nine spots of smoke: / a single stream of ocean water poured into a cup" 遙望齊州九點菸，一泓海水杯中瀉. Translation from Robert Ashmore (2008, 188).
115. Literally "shoes conjured from water birds." From the story of Wang Qiao 王喬 traveling on shoes that are turned into ducks in *History of the Latter Han*.
116. The Jian'an poets were credited for having established subgenres of classical poetry on a range of topics, including those of feasts, sightseeing, roaming into the world of immortals, and abandoned women. Poetry on roaming into immortality remained a broadly practiced poetic tradition throughout early medieval China (3rd to 6th centuries).
117. The Fusang tree in Chinese mythology marks the place where the sun rises.
118. According to the "Treatise on the Feng and Shan Sacrifices" (Fengshan shu 封禪書) of Sima Qian's *Records of the Grand Historian*, the Bo Ocean is where the three immortal mountains are located.
119. The *peng* bird, transformed from the *kun* fish, is a mythical creature from "Free and Easy Wandering" (Xiaoyao you 逍遙遊) in *Zhuangzi*. The *kun* fish covers a distance of several thousand miles, and the *peng* bird has wings that stretch like clouds covering the entire sky.
120. Emperor Yang of the Sui 隋煬帝 (r. 604–618) had an extravagant pleasure fleet that took him from Luoyang to Yangzhou by way of the Grand Canal. For the task of rowing he had one thousand tall and fair ladies selected for each vessel equipped with carved oars laced with gold.
121. Mi Yuanzhang is Mi Fu 米芾 (1051–1107), a famed northern Song artist.
122. Legend has it that silk produced from icy silkworms is water-and-fire resistant.
123. The Pear Garden 梨園 is a synonym for theater.
124. The *konghou* 箜篌 is a small harp-like instrument, of Central Asian origin, with seven strings.
125. Shi Chong's 石崇 (249–300) wealth and extravagance are well documented in early medieval Chinese sources.
126. Exalted Consort Yang's extravagance exemplified by the galloping steeds transporting lychees is documented in the first of Du Mu's 杜牧 (803–852) three quatrains titled "On Passing by Huaqing Palace" (Guo Huaqing gong 過華清宮). Translation in Owen (1996, 452–53).
127. Elü 萼綠, or Elühua 萼綠華, is a goddess whose manifestation is recorded in *Declarations of the Perfected* (Zhen'gao 真誥) in the Daoist Canon. The Luofu 羅浮 Mountain is one of the ten major Grotto-Heavens in Daoist lore.
128. A reference to the story of Zheng Jiaofu 鄭交甫 encountering two goddesses who gifted Zheng with their pendants only to disappear together with the pendants. Orchid is known for its fragrance. It is part of the trope of "the beauty and fragrant plants" of the Chuci tradition as a symbol of virtue and purity.

129. A reference to a banquet scene of abandon that, as the jester Chunyu Kun 淳于髡 claims, can prompt him to consume one hundred liters of wine. See Sima Qian's biographies of jesters in *Records of the Grand Historian.*
130. This phrase originally comes from the Emperor Xuan of the Western Han (r. 74–49 BCE) in Ban Gu's *History of the Han*. It was part of reference to the Founding Emperor of Han's installment of military rule following the examples of past hegemons as opposed to Confucian teachings that were part of the status quo. Later this phrase typically refers to a distinctive rectifying mechanism following its own pedigree.
131. Probably a combination of the image of the magical gourds in Daoist teaching and the moral meaning of an ice-holding pot (ice standing for the integrity and purity of one's interior world).
132. Xi Shi's appointment with Fan Li to roam on the Five Lakes.
133. *Samādhi* (*sanmei* 三昧) is Sanskrit for Wisdom, or Enlightenment in Buddhism.
134. It is recorded in *Master Huainan* that the sun rises from a valley called Yanggu and bathes itself at the Pond of Xian.
135. The image of Li Bai riding a whale after drowning is captured in Du Fu's influential poem in memory of Li Bai titled "Seeing Off Kong Chaofu, Who Has Resigned on Account of Illness and Will Go Back to Visit East of the Yangzi; Also for Li Bai" 送孔巢父謝病歸遊江東兼呈李白. English translation in Owen (2016, vol. 1, 34–35).
136. The fishing rock is often associated with the story of Yan Guang (39 BCE–41 CE), a well-known recluse who ended his days fishing and farming at the Fuchun mountain in modern Hangzhou.
137. A reference to Su Shi's "Song on the Immortal in a Grotto" (Dongxian ge 洞仙歌) on Lady Huarui 花蕊夫人, a consort of the last ruler of one of the Ten Kingdoms, the Later Shu (934–965). It starts with these lines: "Ice-pure skin and jade-like bones, / Naturally free of perspiration" 冰肌玉骨, 自清涼無汗.
138. Shi Chong's preface to a collection of poetry composed at a banquet on his grand estate, the Gold Valley Villa 金谷園. Those who fail to come up with the right line would drain three goblets of wine. For an annotated translation of Shi Chong's biography, see Wilhelm (1959, 315–27).
139. This line derives from Cao Zhi's poem "At the Imperial Command" (Yingzhao shi 應詔詩).
140. A reference to the line "I made a coat of lotus and water-chestnut leaves" 製芰荷以為衣兮 in "Encountering Sorrow." Translation from Hawkes (1985, 71).
141. A humorous rendition of Li Bai's old-style poem "In Response to Yin Mingzuo's Gift of his 'Song on the Fur of Five Clouds'" 酬殷明佐見贈五雲裘歌. The poem celebrates an ethereal fur coat patterned with five-colored clouds made by the Moon Goddess (the White Lady). The coat has even attracted attentions from immortals astride white deer. These lines, instead, invite the reading of a mortal Li Bai clutching the robe of the Moon Goddess as she ascends to Heaven only to be left behind with two white deer.
142. The "flower of the ephemeral hedge-tree" comes from "Airs of Zheng" 鄭風 (Ode no. 83) of *The Book of Poetry*: "There is the lady in the carriage, / With a countenance like the flower of the ephemeral hedge-tree" 有女同車, 顏如舜華. Legge (1991, 136).
143. Wengzhong is the name of the statue of the immortal holding the tray to collect dew.
144. In *Past Anecdotes on the Emperor Wu of the Han,* Dongfang Shuo was a banished immortal who had stolen peaches from the Queen Mother of the West.
145. A story about Zuo Ci in Ge Hong's *Biographies of Immortals.* Zuo Ci incurred mistrust from Cao Cao with his uncanny magical power. During a drinking banquet with Cao, Zuo Ci sends his wine cup flying in the air like a bird, catching everyone's attention so that he is able to slip away unnoticed.

146. Derived from the Li Shangyin's "Jasper City" (Bi cheng 碧城), the last of his three poems so-titled: "The rabbit is being conceived in the jade cakra, / The coral behind iron nets are yet to have branches" 玉輪顧兔初生魄，鐵網珊瑚未有枝.
147. The "Lie Yukou" 列禦寇 chapter of *Zhuangzi* tells of a pearl worth a thousand pieces of gold which the Black Dragon had tucked under his chin.
148. See note 102 for the story of Li Bai having his boots removed at the imperial palace. Li Bai also received brocade as a reward for his lyrics to the newly composed song "The Qingping Tune" (Qingping diao 清平調) at a pool-side banquet.
149. Emperor Xuanzong was known to have played the rams-hide drum, a leisurely activity interpreted to be an omen of dynastic crisis as a result of the An Lushan rebellion in 755, which significantly weakened the Tang imperial house.
150. Derived from Shan Tao's comment on Ji Kang in "Appearance and Manner" (Rongzhi 容止) of *A New Account of Tales of the World* (*Shishuo xinyu* 世說新語): "As a person Ji Kang is majestically towering, like a solitary pine tree standing alone. But when he's drunk he leans crazily like a jade mountain about to collapse" 嵇叔夜之為人也，巖巖若孤松之獨立；其醉也，傀俄若玉山之將崩. Translation in Liu Yiqing and Mather (2002, 331).
151. King Xiang of Chu had sexual intercourse with a goddess in a dream, who identified herself to be the clouds at the sunlit terrace of the Shamanka Gorges.
152. A reference to Dongfang Shuo's biography in the *History of the Han*.
153. *Li* is hexagram no. 30, and *dui* is hexagram no. 58. These are two opposing hexagrams.
154. A reference to the wealth and prestige these legendary beauties had enjoyed as favored consorts.
155. A reference to the following line in Li Bai's *yuefu* song "Bring on the Ale:" "I toss away a thousand in gold, it comes right back to me" 千金散盡還復來. Translation from Chang and Owen (2010, 308).
156. Liu Zhang 劉章 imposed capital punishment as military discipline during an imperial banquet in Sima Qian's *Records of the Grand Historian*.
157. A reference to Chunyu Kun's story in Sima Qian's *Records of the Grand Historian*. See note 129 for details.
158. Xiao Shi was a master flute player whose music could bring visits of the phoenix. Lord Mu of the Qin wedded his daughter Nongyu to Xiao Shi and also had a tower built for the couple, which was called the Phoenix Tower.
159. The Blue Ocean is a mythical place where *yin* and *yang* forces merge. The Black Ocean refers to the world of darkness in the netherworld.
160. See note 58 for details on the Weak Stream.
161. The Yanyu Rock in Jutang Gorge is well known for its torrents that pose a fatal threat to travelers. See Li Bai's "Ballad on the Changgan Neighborhood" (Changgan xing 長干行). For a translation see Hinton (1996, 12–13).
162. The Yuntai Mountain as a particular locale seems to be an autobiographical reference to Ding Yaokang's own experiences during his sea travels to the islands between 1639 and 1645.
163. This line comes from the last of Du Fu's eight "Autumn Stirrings" (Qiuxing 秋興): "sharing a boat, undying companions moved further on that evening" 仙侶同舟晚更移. Translation from Owen (2016, vol. 4, 361).
164. These four lines come from Li Bai's "Song on the River" (Jiangshang yin 江上吟). See Minford and Lau (2000, 756–57) for two versions of English translation.
165. The Chinese phrase here means "turtle essence" 鱉精, implying that the turtle had cultivated its primal energy to have attained transcendental power.
166. A mythical place mentioned in "Autumn Floods" (Qiushui 秋水) of *Zhuangzi* that is an orifice in the ocean where water endlessly leaks away without ever being exhausted. This is also the first of

the three stages of inner alchemy in Daoist teaching at the level of the coccyx in the human body. *EOT* 835.

167. In traditional Chinese medicine, the control channel refers to a conduit that runs along the spine. In *The Yellow Emperor's Classic of Medicine*, it is the conduit that forms an assembly with the last of twelve conduits in the body, thus crucial for regulating the overall flow of beath and blood. *EOT* 389–90.
168. The term Mysterious Female comes from the sixth chapter of Laozi's *Scripture of the Dao and the Virtue* (*Daodejing* 道德經): "The spirit of the valley does not die. / It is called the mysterious female. / The gate of the mysterious female, / is called the root of Heaven and Earth" 谷神不死, 是謂玄牝. 玄牝之門, 是謂天地根. From de Bary (1999, vol. 1, 82).
169. The mythical oyster whose breath creates mirages of mansions and towns is one kind of dragon, according to *Compendium of Materia Medica* (*Bencao gangmu* 本草綱目) compiled by Li Shizhen 李時珍 (1518–1593).
170. Here the author has mixed both northern and southern conventions in filling the tune to "Yizhihua" of the Nanlü mode.
171. Zhang Qian's celestial encounter. See note 112 for details.
172. Liezi riding the wind appears in "Free and Easy Wandering" in *Zhuangzi*. Lu Zhonglian 魯仲連 (ca. 305–245 BCE), also known as Lu Lian 魯連, was a strategist from the Qi who sought reclusion on oceanic islands in Sima Qian's *Records of the Grand Historian*.
173. In Sima Qian's *Records of the Grand Historian*, Master Anqi 安期生 is spotted consuming gigantic jujubes on a coastal island where immortals reside.
174. King Mu of Zhou 周穆王 visited the Jade Pond in a chariot pulled by eight heavenly steeds.
175. Literally, "my Kun-Peng carriage" 鯤鵬駕. See note 119 on details about the *kun* fish and the *peng* bird.
176. Wen Qiao 溫嶠 (288–329) burned a rhinoceros horn to light up the bottom of a pond, where he spotted all kinds of exotic water creatures.
177. Liu Yi 柳毅 tapped on an orange tree to deliver a letter to the dragon king on behalf of his daughter. See Hung (1994, 61–69) for a discussion of this story.
178. These are both phrases from *Zhuangzi* to refer to gratuitous happenings with consequences to which one cannot respond with anger, as there is no one to be held accountable.
179. The *yu* 蜮 creature poses a lethal threat by spitting sand on its victims.
180. Lofty mind of a recluse. See note 34 for details.
181. Reference to the divine goddess who manifests herself to King Xiang of Chu in Song Yu's "Rhapsody on the Gaotang Shrine" and "Rhapsody on the Goddess." Also see note 151.
182. There was supposed to be an entrance to Hell at Mt. Fengdu 酆都.
183. A combined reference to the practice of cultivating Golden Elixir in the inner alchemical practice in Daoist teaching and the Buddhist teaching of attaining nirvana (full awakening).
184. This line derives from Su Shi's "Rhapsody on Red Cliff."
185. The tune "White Snow" is typically associated with refined music beyond the ken of common folks.
186. Part of the vocabulary of self-cultivation in the Daoist teaching of inner alchemy: to move the energy of fire to help the sprout of the inner cinnabar pill.
187. Reference to a story of one hiding a boat in a ravine in the middle of the night only to have it carried away by a mighty person in "The Great and Venerable Teacher" of *Zhuangzi*. The story challenges the assumption that things in this world are static and thus can remain securely hidden.
188. A reference to Confucius's remark in the *Analects* (*Lunyu* 論語): "Only after winter comes do we know that the pine and cypress are the last to fade" 歲寒然後知松柏之後彫也. Translation from Confucius and Slingerland (2003, 96).

189. Wang Jian 王建, King of Qi, lost his kingdom to the Qin on account of misplaced trust on strategists who counseled Wang against rallying troops. See "Biography of Hereditary Family of Tian Wan" (Tian Wan shijia 田完世家) in Sima Qian's *Records of the Grand Historian*.
190. The night of the last day of the year in Chinese lunar calendar is when the monster Xi 夕 wanders around seeking its prey.
191. The author of the play, Ding Yaokang, often adopts the literary name Wild Crane 野鶴. As the cover page shows, the play was a secret copy from the Wild Crane Studio.
192. Reference to "The Great and Venerable Teacher" of *Zhuangzi*. See note 187 for details.
193. The practice of inner alchemy in order to restore pristine Oneness.
194. The Buddhist conceptualization of the cosmos locates Mt. Sumeru at the center and the rest of the world divided into four main continents: Pūrvideha, Jambudvipa, Apara-godāniya, and Uttara-Kuru.
195. One way of understanding "nine palaces" is the eight directions represented by the eight trigrams plus the central position, hence the term "nine palaces and eight trigrams" in traditional Chinese cosmology.
196. From the discourse on the Five Phases from *the Book of Documents* (*Shangshu* 尚書).
197. One of the four ways of birth in the Buddhist discourse: creatures born from eggs, from the womb, from moisture, and from transformations.
198. It is recorded in *Annals of the Wu and Yue* that Zhuanzhu 專諸 assassinated the King of Wu by hiding a dagger inside a roasted fish. The dagger came to be known as the Fish Intestine Sword.
199. Li He, in the twentieth of his twenty-three poems on horses, has the following line: "The precious sword is like fish intestines" 寶劍似魚腸. Based on this image, the dagger known to be Fish Intestine Sword 魚腸劍 may be curved. Alternatively, the simile may refer to decorative patterns on the dagger that helped with its concealment.
200. A satirical comment on malicious minds and intentions.
201. Zeng Zao 曾慥 (?–1155 or 1164) in *Categorized Stories* (*Leishuo* 類說) records an anecdote of a water god aiding Wang Bo 王勃 (ca. 650–ca. 676) with a timely breeze so he can reach the Tower of Prince Teng 滕王閣 in time to compose the poem that will win him literary immortality.
202. Qu Yuan was a minister of Chu. He was credited as the poet who wrote "Encountering Sorrow" in the Chuci tradition to vent his frustration after he was scandalized and alienated from King Huai of Chu. Hailed as a paragon of loyalty and moral integrity, he was believed to have drowned himself in the Miluo River.
203. The phrase "inquiring after the ford" 問津 appears in book 18 ("Master Wei" 微子) of the *Analects*. Later it is associated with a worthy man's pursuit of learning. A similar line—"Since then there has been no one interested in trying to find such a place" 後遂無問津者—appears at the end of Tao Qian's "Peach Blossom Spring," which refers to the elusive nature of the timeless utopia. Translation from James Hightower in Minford and Lau (2000, vol. 1, 516).
204. "Encountering Sorrow" is the longest poem in the Chuci tradition attributed to Qu Yuan, who is accordingly hailed to be the first poet in the Chinese poetic tradition.
205. Qu Yuan's official title, according to "the fisherman" (Yufu 漁父) was Lord of the Three Wards 三閭大夫. My translation takes the word *ri* (day) to be possibly *zi* (just, on my own).
206. A combination of phrases from "Encountering Sorrow." The last two lines refer to two poems in the Chuci tradition, "Summoning the Soul" (Zhaohun 招魂) attributed to Song Yu, and "Fisherman," as direct responses to Qu Yuan's suicide.
207. In the biography of Qu Yuan in Sima Qian's *Records of the Grand Historian*, the Shangguan minister Jin Shang 靳尚 was jealous of Qu Yuan and slandered him in front of the King Huai of Chu 楚懷王.

208. Jia Yi 賈誼 (200–168 BCE) composed "Rhapsody on Mourning Qu Yuan" (Diao Qu Yuan fu 弔屈原賦) after he was banished to Changsha as Grand Tutor to the King of Changsha.
209. From "A Lament for Ying" (Ai Ying 哀郢) of *The Nine Pieces* (*Jiuzhang* 九章) in the Chuci tradition. The first four lines are separated from the last four by lines on the poet's journey in the original piece. Translation from Hawkes (1985, 164–65).
210. These two lines derive from Wang Wei's 王維 (701–761) poem "Seeing off Secretary Chao Jian back to Japan" 送秘書晁監還日本國. Chao Jian is the Chinese name of Abe no Nakamaro 阿倍仲麿 (698 or 701–770).
211. Buildings conjured by the breaths of giant oysters at the bottom of the ocean. See note 169 for details.
212. This line comes from Li Bai's poem "Visiting the Daoist Master on Daitian Mountain and Not Finding Him" 訪戴天山道士不遇.
213. From "The Reeds" 蒹葭 in "Airs of Qin" 秦風 (Ode no. 129) of *The Book of Poetry*.
214. These two lines derive from "Summons for a Recluse" (Zhao yinshi 招隱士) in the Chuci tradition.
215. The above six lines derive from "The Lesser Master of Fate" (Shao siming 少司命) of *Nine Songs* (*Jiuge* 九歌) in the Chuci tradition.
216. "Holy One" is traditionally taken as a figure for King Huai of Chu in Qu Yuan's "Encountering Sorrow."
217. These lines are based on the last four lines from "The Goddess of the Xiang" (Xiangjun 湘君) of *Nine Songs*. Translation adapted from Hawkes (1985, 107).
218. Scene of a celestial journey derived from "Far Roaming" (Yuanyou 遠遊) in the Chuci tradition.
219. Jia Yi's "Rhapsody to Mourn Qu Yuan." See note 208 for details.
220. Pei Hang 裴航 manages to secure a conjugal pact by preparing medicine with a jade pestle for a hundred days in the palace of the moon.
221. The first half of the line comes from "Thinking of a Fair One" of the *Nine Pieces* in the Chuci tradition. "Embracing Sand" is the fifth poem from that same work.
222. Triangular cakes of sticky rice, bound with a flat leaf and steamed. Eaten on the fifth day of the fifth month (an inauspicious day), at the Duanwu festival, in celebration of Qu Yuan's death. When he drowned himself, people rushed in their boats to save him, the origin of the Dragon Boat Race, and when they could not find him, they threw these large dumplings into the water so that the fish would eat them, and not the body of Qu Yuan.
223. *Yojana* is the Sanskrit word for a space equivalent to between twelve and twenty-four miles.
224. "In Praise of the Orange-Tree" (Ju song 橘頌) is the eighth poem of *Nine Pieces* in the Chuci tradition. Translation adapted from Hawkes (1985, 178).
225. A woodcutter Wang Zhi 王質 watches a game of *go* among immortals. When the game ends, the handle of his axe has already rotted. Wang returns home to find people contemporary to him are no longer around.
226. Fiery jujubes, together with jade brew, are potions that can allow one to fly.
227. Magu's self-introduction as a deity who had witnessed three full cycles of such great changes. See note 27 for details.
228. The stage instruction has "ONE OLD MAN *jumps off the stage and out of sight*" here, which may have been a mistake.
229. The term "the yellow at the center" 黃中 appears in the appended judgments to the fifth line of the second hexagram *kun* in *The Book of Changes*. In the context of this aria, the phrase can also refer to the monarch who resides at the center of the five phases.
230. The Chou Pond 仇池 (modern Gansu Province) is the birthplace of Fu Xi 伏羲, the progenitor of Chinese civilization, according to "Chart to Open the Mountains by Use of the Technique of the

Wondrous Gate and Hidden Shield" (Dunjia kaishan tu 遁甲開山圖) cited by *Imperial Digest of the Taiping Reign Period* (*Taiping yulan* 太平御覽). Nüwa's 女媧 merit of smelting stones at this place seems to derive from a tradition of poetic imagination that started with Su Shi's citation of Du Fu's miscellaneous poems on Qinzhou in his own poem "Two Rocks" (Shuang shi 雙石). According to Su Shi's preface, he named one of his treasured stones after the Chou Pond. The connection between Nüwa and the Chou Pond is further reinforced in Qin Guan's 秦觀 (1049–1100) poem in response to Su Shi's "Two Rocks."

231. Image of Qu Yuan in "The Fisherman:" "After Qu Yuan was banished, he wandered, sometimes along the river's banks, sometimes along the marsh's edge, singing as he went. His expression was dejected and his features were emaciated" 屈原既放，遊於江潭，行吟澤畔，顏色憔悴，形容枯槁. Hawkes (1985, 206).
232. The method of the six breaths in the Daoist tradition consists of inhaling through the nose and exhaling in six ways through the mouth.
233. Huaxu 華胥 is a kingdom that the Yellow Emperor visits in a dream in *Liezi*. The utopic land eludes language and is only accessible through spiritual wanderings.
234. The image of the gigantic gourd floating comes from "Free and Easy Wandering" in *Zhuangzi*.
235. This line alludes to two famous stories of Bodhidharma 達摩 (?–ca. 532) in the Chan Buddhist tradition. In the first story, Bodhidharma snaps off a reed leaf to cross the river after Emperor Wu of the Liang 梁武帝 (r. 502–549) failed to understand his teaching. In the second story, Bodhidharma, after passing away, was spotted heading to the west holding a single sandal.
236. The tiny kingdoms of Maul 蠻 and Buffet 觸 on the two antennae of a snail fought a fierce war against each other that resulted in severe casualties. This parable comes from the chapter "Zeyang" 則陽 of *Zhuangzi* and came to refer to the triviality of things and tensions therein.
237. The ant kingdom in "Prefect of Nanke." Also see note 38.
238. Derived from a line in the sixth of Du Fu's eight poems titled "Stirred by Autumn" "From brocade cables and ivory mast rose a white gull" 錦纜牙檣起白鷗. Owen (2016, vol. 4, 359).
239. The teachings of the Small Vehicle is a derogatory reference to Hinayana Buddhist teachings in India, which emphasized the arhat's pursuit for individual Enlightenment. The Grand Vehicle promoted by Mahayana Buddhism, by contrast, promotes universal deliverance of sentient beings from the bitter cycles of *samsara*.
240. The story from *Liezi* on the illusory nature of dreams. See note 39 for details.
241. The cicada startled by falling leaves suggests impending death for the summer insect.
242. King Zhao of Chu 楚昭王, defeated in a battle with the Wu, lost a shoe when fleeing. The missing shoe becomes a symbol of the lost state.
243. Lord Wangdi of Shu 蜀望帝 who, after a forced abdication, turns into a cuckoo that cries sorrowfully in the spring until it coughs blood. This line derives directly from Li Shangyin's "Brocade Zither" (Jinse 錦瑟): "Emperor Wang's springtime heart is entrusted to the cuckoo" 望帝春心托杜鵑. Translation from Ashmore (2008, 195).
244. This is Mencius's view of the Central Region in his biography in Sima Qian's *Records of the Grand Historian*.
245. This refers to the story of Yang Zhu in *Liezi*. Upon learning that his neighbor lost a sheep because he had taken wrong turns where the paths forked, Yang Zhu is sorrow-stricken for days. This also recalls another story of Yang Zhu weeping profusely on a forking road, overwhelmed by the weightiness that comes with either of the choices.
246. Since an iron tree rarely blooms, once it does it marks a rare and cherished occasion.
247. Jetavana is a park near Śrāvastī, a favorite resort of the historical Buddha Śākyamuni.

248. Derived from Wang Wei's poem "Seeing off Military Commander of Guizhou Xing Ji" (Song Xing Guizhou 送邢桂州): "When the sun sets, mountains and rivers turn white, / Upon the arrival of floodtides, heaven and earth are dark" 日落江湖白, 潮來天地青.
249. The Fish-basket Guanyin is a feminine image of Bodhisattva Guanyin (Skr. Avalokitêśvara) that had a significant impact on popular imagination. A well-known *baojuan* 寶卷 (precious scroll) tells the story of Guanyin adopting the guise of a beautiful fish-monger to convert sentient beings by promising to marry whoever can chant the *Lotus Sutra* and observe Buddhist precepts.
250. The day to appease hungry ghosts in traditional Chinese calendar.
251. A stock phrase that typically refers to the shift in dynastic rule.
252. Reference to Shen Jiji's tale "Record Within a Pillow." See note 42 for details.
253. Ding Lingwei 丁令威, who practiced Daoism on a mountain, transformed into a crane and flew back to his hometown on the Liao, perched on an ornamental pillar. Speaking as a crane, he left the following remark: "The city walls are the same, but the people have all changed" 城郭如故人民非.
254. Allusion to Cao Cao's "Short Song" (Duange xing 短歌行): "Crows and magpies are flying south. / They circle the tree three times around, / on what branch can they find a roost" 烏鵲南飛, 繞樹三匝, 何枝可依. Owen (2006b, 198).
255. Blue birds are messengers of Queen Mother of the West. See note 51 for details.
256. In Buddhism, to become enlightened is called "being ferried across." In order to be ferried across, one needs a boat, so the teachings of the Buddha may be compared to a boat that will be discarded when one reaches the other shore. An "iron boat" was traditionally considered an impossibility (whereas wood floats on water, iron will sink). To call Buddhism an iron boat stressed its contradictory nature.
257. The bridge with red railing is a common poetic trope of romantic engagements.
258. To fish on a skiff at the five lakes is an image associated with both the reclusive ideal and the Chan concept of enlightenment.
259. Reference to a Tang tale of Li Yuan's 李源 rendezvous with a Buddhist monk Yuanguan 圓觀 in the monk's next reincarnation. When Li and Yuanguan in his incarnation as a herd boy reencounter each other, the herd boy sings a song that begins with the line "The old spirits and souls on the stone of three incarnations" 三生石上舊精魂. See *Rumors of the Sweet Water Pond* (*Ganze yao* 甘澤謠) attributed to Yuan Jiao 袁郊 (late ninth c).
260. The Cangwu 蒼梧 mountain was where the sagely king Shun 舜 lay buried. It marks the southern boundary of Chinese civilization.
261. Yuanqiao 圓嶠 is the name of a mountain for immortals. This is another reference to the folly of hiding a boat in a ravine from *Zhuangzi*. See note 187 for details.
262. The brocade bag originally comes from the story of Li He, who carries it with him to hold new poetic compositions.
263. The line derives from a poem by Qingxia 青霞, a mysterious Daoist immortal with whom Ding Yaokang developed a friendship between 1632 and 1633, when he was living in the mountains.
264. Where one may attain immortality.
265. The two daughters of Yao 堯, who are consorts of Shun, wept after Shun's death beside the Xiang River, their tears staining the bamboo. Both Yao and Shun are legendary sagely kings.
266. Moss flowers typically appear beside a spring or a well. This line therefore most likely refers to the story of Zhang Lihua, whose fallen hair ornaments are left to rust after she was seized by the Sui army from within the well.
267. Derived from Wei Yingwu's 韋應物 (731–791) "West Stream in Chuzhou" (Chuzhou xijian 滁州西澗): "At the deserted ferry site a boat drifts sideways all by itself" 野渡無人舟自橫.

268. In Ge Hong's *Biographies of Immortals*, Qin Gao 琴高 is a zither master who disappears into the Zhuo River and reemerges as an immortal on the back of a red carp.
269. These are exchanges typical of Chan Buddhist teachings that strive to go beyond any specific reasonings as doctrinal truism in order to comprehend the Buddha Nature as a constant truth that transcends duality.
270. A Chan Buddhist phrase that refers to achieving instant Enlightenment.
271. A possible reference to the oceanic voyage launched by the First Emperor of the Qin seeking the elixir for immortality.
272. These two lines refer to two kinds of pitfalls in attaining instant Enlightenment: the fault of volition in the first line, and self-confinement within abstraction in the second line.
273. A common expression on attaining Buddhist Enlightenment and the Perfected state of being in Daoist teachings.
274. An expression on excessive fixation of the mind in Chan meditation.
275. The Eight Immortals each have their own trick to pass the ocean.
276. This description evokes the image of the Monkey King in *The Journey to the West* (*Xiyou ji* 西遊記). It is one of Sun Wukong's 孫悟空 usual tricks to get inside an adversary's belly. He has also urinated on Tathagata Buddha's palm under the false impression that he had reached the end of the world.
277. Ao 奡 was a powerful naval commander mentioned in "Xianwen" 憲問 of the *Analects* along with the master archer Yi 羿. Both were well-known for their military prowess yet met their demise prematurely. The implied message is that those who cultivate virtue rather than military prowess are better equipped to rule the state.
278. The word for bladder is also a pun on copulating with a prostitute. The shape of a fish bladder resembles that of the male organ, and since the bladder is a kind of gelatin, the glue mentioned in the following lines likely suggests the prostitute's performing fellatio on her male client.
279. Dainty, finely woven curtains are often called shrimp-whisker curtains in song lyrics and northern songs.
280. In the chapter "External Things" 外物 in *Zhuangzi* a perch stranded in the carriage rut seeks a dipperful of water so it can stay alive. When given a vain offer of changing the course of the West River toward its direction, the perch is flushed with anger and replies: "If you give me an answer like that, then you'd best look for me in the dried fish store" 君乃言此，曾不如早索我於枯魚之肆. Watson (1968, 295).
281. According to legend, Oxherd and Weaving Lady meet once a year over the Silver River on a bridge put together by magpies on the seventh day of the seventh month.
282. Xuanyuan 軒轅 is the name of the hill where the Yellow Emperor had resided. The Yellow Emperor is generally considered the founder of Chinese civilization.
283. Fu Xi 伏羲 is supposed to be the inventor of the eight trigrams that form the basis of the sixty-four hexagrams in *The Book of Changes*.
284. "Hongfan" 洪範 is a chapter in *The Book of Documents* that contains knowledge on flood control divided into nine categories, it is allegedly bequeathed to Yu, the flood-taming sage king.
285. Seminal texts recorded in the "Grand Commentary" of *The Books of Changes* that mark the beginning of Chinese civilization.
286. This refers to the book burning allegedly decreed by the First Emperor of the Qin.
287. The original stage direction here, "OLD MALE *turns to* MALE LEAD *and exits*," which I replaced, was probably a mistake.
288. A humorous rendition of Huang Tingjian's 黃庭堅 (1045–1105) technique of internalizing models of Tang poetry known to be "seizing the embryo and replacing the bones" (*duotai huangu* 奪胎換骨).

289. Although the woodblock edition designates the role type to be MALE LEAD, it is Li Bai's character speaking in this conversation. So the role type should be SECOND MALE LEAD.
290. Cangming 滄溟 is the literary name of Li Panlong 李攀龍 (1514–1570), who was the head of the second generation of the Revivalist moments called "Seven Late Masters" 後七子. Li Panlong's poetry is known for its grandiose imagery. Whale is specifically mimicking the hyperbolic phrases often found in Li's compositions.
291. The Jingling 竟陵 school was named after Zhong Xing 鐘惺 (1574–1624) and Tan Yuanchun's 譚元春 (1586–1637) native town in Huguang Province. The Jingling School's poetics "expressed themselves in practice as a propensity for the difficult and the obscure." Chang and Owen (2010, 90).
292. Whale's attempt at the drab and obscure imagery known to be the Jingling style.
293. Parody of the well-known formulation in Laozi's *Scripture of the Dao and the Virtue*: "We should temper our brightness, and bring ourselves into agreement with the obscurity of others" 和其光, 同其塵. Translation from Legge (1962, 50).
294. Dongpo is the literary name of Su Shi. The poem cited by SECOND MALE LEAD (Li Bai) is Su Shi's song lyric to the tune "Shuidiao getou" 水調歌頭.
295. Guests who invite themselves to houses of wealthy figures would typically seek monetary gifts from their host as patrons. Such fund-raising attempts are known as "seeking bounties" (*choufeng* 抽豐).
296. Wang Yang's gold-transforming cinnabar pill belongs to both the Daoist furnace and the dragon king's palace.
297. In Buddhist lore, Mara's daughters attempted to seduce the historical Buddha to no avail.
298. An adaptation of Su Shi's "Inscribed on the Wall of West Forest Monastery" 題西林壁: "From the side it's a mountain wall, from the end a single peak, / Near, far, high, low—each view is different. / I do not know Lu Mountain's true face, / Because I find myself in the mountain's midst" 橫看成嶺側成峰, 遠近高低各不同. 不識廬山真面目, 只緣身在此山中. Translation from Egan (1994, 185).
299. See the first story of Bodhidharma in note 235.
300. Derived from Li Shangyin's poem "Untitled" 無題: "Young Liu despised the distance to Peng Mountain, / Yet on the far side of Peng Mountain, ten thousand iterations more" 劉郎已恨蓬山遠, 更隔蓬山一萬重. Translation from Roberts (2018, 23).
301. A Buddhist reference to ferrying sentient beings across the shore for Enlightenment. The Eastern Ocean as a place for immortals is designated as "still the other shore" to echo the Buddhist teaching against attachment to linear progression in one's self-cultivation.
302. The golden elixir that goes through nine transformations come from *The Master who Embraces Simplicity* (*Baopu zi* 抱朴子), an important treatise on alchemy in the Daoist canon.
303. This refers to Zhuang Zhou's dreaming of a butterfly in "Discussion on Making All Things Equal" from *Zhuangzi*. In this story, Zhuang Zhou dreams of himself being a butterfly flitting and fluttering around. When he wakes up, he does not know if he is Zhuang Zhou who had a dream in which he was a butterfly, or a butterfly dreaming he was Zhuang Zhou.
304. The story of the Yellow Emperor losing his Dark Pearl when he went wandering north of the Red Water and ascended the slopes of Kunlun. From "Heaven and Earth" ("Tiandi" 天地) of *Zhuangzi*.
305. See note 146 for details on the coral behind an iron net.
306. Wangxiang 罔象 (Non-Image) is a water demon mentioned in "Mastering Life" (Dasheng 達生) in *Zhuangzi*.
307. See note 145 for Zuo Ci's story.
308. Dong Shuangcheng 董雙成 is a maid in attendance of the Queen Mother of the West, and the blue phoenix is also a messenger for the Queen Mother. See also note 51.

309. Reference to a Chan Buddhist *gong'an* 公案 (koan) story from *Records of the Transmission of the Lamp* (*Jingde chuandeng lu* 景德傳燈錄). When Pang Yun raises a question toward the Chan master Mazu Daoyi 馬祖道一 (709–788), the latter replied that he would withhold the answer till Pang "inhaled the West River with one breath" 一口吸盡西江水.
310. The term ghee (clarified butter) is a metaphor for the highest level of Buddhist teachings.
311. The gesture of looking back after crossing over is another reference to the Buddhist idea of deliverance to the other shore.
312. *Qiu* 秋 (autumn) is a sorrowful time because the vegetation is dying and also because of its orthographic connection with *chou* 愁 (sorrow).
313. A common metaphor for eloquent speech is to spell out words that turn into lotus blossoms on the tip of one's tongue. The "brocade zithers" probably refers to Li Shangyin's famous poem "The Brocade Zither" (Jinse 錦瑟) which is a powerful poetic rendition of the feeling of loss.
314. A reference to the evocative power of elegant tunes (White Snow) in conjuring up a virtual space that transcends the realm of worldly worries.
315. For details of Ding Lingwei's story see note 253.
316. The line in the modern edition, *The Complete Work of Ding Yaokang* (*Ding Yaokang quanji* 丁耀亢全集), departs significantly from what is in the woodblock edition and reads instead: "When the boat returns to its immortal origin, discontent arises because of the idle melancholy of earlier times" 舟返仙源, 怨起從前閑愁. Ding Yaokang (1999, vol. 1, 737).
317. Images of marionette shows feature prominently in Buddhist scriptures as a metaphor for the illusory nature of the myriad things. The intrinsically pure mind is compared to the craftsman who pulls the strings of the puppets to give performances that are ultimately illusory. It is also a stock metaphor for human life in drama.
318. The phrase "carrying a long wooden pole" 竿木隨身 comes from a Chan Buddhist *gong'an* story involving a conversation between Mazu Daoyi and Deng Yinfeng 鄧隱峰. The phrase refers to a Buddhist master's readiness to stage a show when needed as an expedient means of deliverance.

9
Black and White Donkeys

YOU TONG (1618–1704)
TRANSLATED BY S. E. KILE

Black and White Donkeys (*Heibai wei* 黑白衛), a 1664 *zaju* play by the renowned literatus You Tong 尤侗, reworks and expands the story of the archetypal female assassin, Nie Yinniang 聶隱娘. The earliest extant version of the classical tale to tell Nie Yinniang's story is found in the Song dynasty anthology *Broadly Gathered Stories from an Era of Great Peace* (*Taiping guangji* 太平廣記), with a note that it was originally included in Pei Xing's 裴鉶 (825–880) earlier collection, *Transmitting the Strange* (*Chuanqi* 傳奇).[1] The story explains how Nie Yinniang is abducted by a Buddhist nun at age ten and subjected to intense physical and mental training in mysterious sword techniques. After five years, she is returned to her family, although she frequently undertakes secret nocturnal missions. A few years later, she selects a mirror polisher to be her husband and with him serves as a protector to two rival military governors (*jiedushi*) in turn, Tian Ji'an 田季安 of Weibo 魏博 and Liu Changyi 劉昌裔 of Chenxu 陳許—both historical figures who wielded substantial power in the early ninth century. The tale is replete with vivid and memorable details: Yinniang liquefies the heads of evildoers, stores a dagger in her skull, transforms paper into donkeys, and even becomes a midge to hide in her patron's intestines. The most recent adaptation of her story is Hou Hsiao-hsien's 侯孝賢 2015 film, *The Assassin* (*Cike Nie Yinniang* 刺客聶隱娘).[2]

Black and White Donkeys, like the classical tale on which it is based, is set in the tumultuous period that began around the middle of the Tang dynasty (618–907), when military governors like Tian Ji'an and Liu Changyi gained increased control over various regions under their command. Following the An Lushan rebellion (755–763), during which one of these military governors led an uprising against the Tang dynasty, the provinces were restructured. Many regional military governors thus attained autonomous authority over the regions in their control, marking a dramatic decentralization of power. Weibo Circuit (in modern-day Hebei) was the strongest of these, and it successfully defended itself against a coalition attack from the central government and other provincial forces in 775. After nearly a decade of intermittent rebellion, a new military governor of Weibo, Tian Xu (764–796), agreed to renew formal relations with the court, but the provinces in the northeast maintained their autonomous status. Tian Xu was the father of Tian Ji'an, the villain in this play who serves as military governor of Weibo (see act 3).[3]

The playwright You Tong hailed from Changzhou 長洲, Jiangsu Province, and was among the generation who had come of age during the final years of the Ming dynasty. As a consequence, he faced both corruption in the Ming civil service examination system and complex loyalties in the new Qing dynasty. Although he was employed at the prestigious Hanlin Academy in the Qing capital of Beijing after passing the special palace examinations (*boxue hongru* 博學鴻儒) in 1679, he retired after just three years.[4] You Tong is perhaps best remembered as a dramatist who wrote five *zaju* plays and one longer *chuanqi* play, *Celestial Court Music* (*Juntian yue* 鈞天樂). His *zaju* plays are generally interpreted as his attempt to vent his frustrated ambition, renewing old stories with new twists and fresh language.

Black and White Donkeys, You Tong's fourth *zaju* play, develops Nie Yinniang's story in several ways. He provides rationales for many confusing elements of the classical tale. For instance, in the tale we do not learn why Nie Yinniang chooses the lowly mirror polisher for a husband. Neither do we see the promised return twenty years later of the nun who trained her, nor do we discover the purpose of the sword instruction. You Tong introduces the plot device of a four-line *gāthā* given to Yinniang by the nun who trains her: "Meet Mirror, Then Unite / Meet Magpie, Then Stay / Meet Void, Then Hide / Meet Gibbon, Then Gather."[5] You Tong then has Yinniang recall these lines to guide her decisions at the following crucial moments: when she decides to marry the mirror polisher, when she decides to stay in Chenxu (in modern-day Henan) to serve Liu Changyi, when she successfully defends Liu against several assassination attempts, and when she makes her way back to Zhongnan Mountains to be reunited with her teacher. The addition of these riddles, given for her guidance by the nun, lends her choices a supernatural justification.

Through densely allusive language, You Tong also adds backstories adapted from the narrative tradition to flesh out the otherworldly figures who appear in the story. He makes the nun the Maiden of Zhao, who had lived in the tumultuous fifth century BCE, and he adapts her backstory almost verbatim from a brief classical anecdote of an old man turning into a gibbon ("The Old Man Turns Into a Gibbon" [Laoren hua yuan 老人化猿]), which is the first story included in Wang Shizhen's 王世貞 (1526–1590) compilation *Tales of Knights-Errant* (*Jianxia zhuan* 劍俠傳).[6] He makes the mirror polisher the immortal Wang Ziqiao 王子喬, who has taken on human form. He also elevates the mirror itself to the level of a symbol on a par with the sword: "As I see it, of all the marvelous things in this world, only the sword can wipe out depravity, and only the mirror can ward off evil. That is why the fairies in the world above have carried these two treasures." Mirrors were believed to unmask demons that had taken on human shape by reflecting their true form, and by showing this true form they were believed to undo the magical powers of these demons.

You Tong weaves Nie Yinniang's story together with existing accounts of assassins and knights-errant, including Jing Ke 荊軻, Zhang Liang 張良, and Red Thread (Hongxian 紅線), thereby providing a synthesis of that narrative tradition. By introducing the complex history of sword lore into Nie Yinniang's story, he makes the play a repository of sorts for a range of historical accounts of justified righteous killing. You Tong's version of the story also elaborates its plot by adding historically and geographically specific allusions: Nie Yinniang travels a very specific route along the Zhang River that layers dense historical allusions related to righteous conflict, one on top of the other. Perhaps the most noteworthy change of all occurs in You Tong's characterization of Nie Yinniang; she begins in the tale as fierce and inscrutable and goes on in the play to become a thoughtful and principled person carrying out righteous and justified killing on behalf of heaven. Fitting then, that she is summoned to see the Jade Emperor in the play's final lines.

Black and White Donkeys is a regular four-act *zaju*. In the first act, the songs are assigned to the female lead, who plays the part of the Old Nun of Zhongnan Mountains. In the second and third acts, the songs are again assigned to the female lead, who now plays the part of the grown-up Nie Yinniang. The fourth act divides the arias between the female lead playing the part of Nie Yinniang and a few other famous women sword fighters from history.

Zaju plays in this period are often assumed to have been written only for reading, but there is evidence that *Black and White Donkeys* was performed in the early Qing. In the preface to You Tong's *Xitang quye* 西堂曲腋, for instance, he notes that the official and poet Wang Shizhen 王士禛 (1634–1711) loved *Black and White Donkeys* and took the play to Rugao 如皋 (Jiangsu) to have it performed by Mao Xiang's 冒襄 (1611–1693) household troupe.[7] One of the attractions of the play in performance would certainly have been its many sword dances. There is also evidence that another of You Tong's *zaju* plays, *Du* Lisao 讀離騷 [*Reading* Encountering Sorrow], was performed in the palace for the Shunzhi emperor.[8]

This translation is based on the earliest extant edition of *Heibai wei,* which is included in You Tong's collected works, *Xitang quanji* 西堂全集 (ten fascicles, published in the Kangxi period, ca. 1684), in a supplemental six-*juan* section titled *Xitang yuefu* 西堂樂府 (the first thirty *juan* are *Xitang shiji* 西堂詩集). This original edition is reproduced in the first collection of Zheng Zhenduo's 鄭振鐸 Zaju *of the Qing dynasty* (*Qingren zaju* 清人雜劇) of 1931.

A foreword by Peng Sunyu 彭孫遹 (1631–1700) precedes the first edition. Peng was a scholar, calligrapher, and poet, who took first honors in the special examinations of 1679 and enjoyed a successful career afterward. The main text of the play is accompanied by *pingdian* commentary and the "eyebrow" comments, printed in the upper margins, are translated in the notes.

BLACK AND WHITE DONKEYS: FOREWORD

Sima Qian's "The Biographies of the Assassin-Retainers" is so uninhibited and so perfect that a thousand years later, his words still seem to be alive.[9] At the end of his biographies, he wrote, "What a pity that he [Jing Ke] was not better schooled in swordsmanship." This statement did not refer only to Qingqing [i.e., Jing Ke]; he seems to have felt a deep pity for the likes of Yao Li and Nie Zheng, who "smashed their own heads and the jade disk at once."[10] Looking for meaning in this, one finds that it imperceptibly hints at the likes of Yinniang and Red Thread, making them appear now and again to delight our spirit.[11]

Hui'an [You Tong] relies on a peerless talent, and he writes many compositions that vent his frustration. His play, *Black and White Donkeys,* is marvelous and unrestrained, and better than reading the "The Biographies [of the Assassin-Retainers]" of that man from Longmen [i.e., Sima Qian]. Although it was written as a lodge for his feelings, it also serves to strike fear in the hearts of men of the world who lack a sense of righteousness.

I have often said to myself privately that the unjust affairs of this world are like dust that accumulates until it forms mounds, never easy to eliminate. Only two things can eradicate them: wine and daggers. Floating around in a sea of wine, unrestrained in our stupor, our pent-up indignation can be tempered somewhat, but it cannot help us act on our aspirations. It is no match for a "three-inch lotus"[12] in bringing a person satisfaction.

I will buy a Ruoye sword,
And go tomorrow to study with Mr. Gibbon.[13]

I sent word to Hui'an, "From now on he can look for me amidst the treetops and the sheer cliffs."

Written on the tenth day of the sixth month of the year Jiachen (1664) by Peng Sunyu from Haiyan.

Dramatis Personae in Order of Appearance

Role Type	*Name, family role, or social role*
OLD NUN	Maiden of Zhao, now an old Chan Master
GIRL ONE	Li the Twelfth of Linying
GIRL TWO	Jing the Thirteenth of Suzhou
FEMALE LEAD	Nie Yinniang
VARIOUS ROLES	Several vile men
EXTRA	Nie Feng, Yinniang's father
OLD WOMAN	Yinniang's mother
MALE LEAD	Mirror Polisher, Yinniang's husband
OFFICIAL	Liu Changyi, Military Governor of Chenxu

OFFICER	Officer under Liu Changyi
[FEMALE]	Jingjing'er
[FEMALE]	Kongkong'er
COMIC	Mr. Yuan
FEMALE	The Woman in the Carriage
[UNSPECIFIED]	White Gibbon
FEMALE	Red Thread

BLACK AND WHITE DONKEYS

WRITTEN BY YOU TONG, STYLED HUI'AN, OF CHANGZHOU

TITLE:

THE OLD NUN EXPLAINS SWORD FIGHTING IN THE ZHONGNAN REGION;

THE MIRROR POLISHER PLAYS THE PART OF A WORTHY SON-IN-LAW.

VICE DIRECTOR LIU FIERCELY COMPETES WITH WHITE AND RED BANNERS;

NIE YINNIANG PLAYFULLY RIDES ASTRIDE BLACK AND WHITE DONKEYS.

ACT 1

(OLD NUN *enters carrying a whisk, with* TWO GIRLS *who hold a sword and a medicine box*:)

When I was young, flying swiftly through the air, I was called "Sword Immortal,"
Of late with my penetrating insight, I'm an old lady Chan Master.
So many unjust affairs before our eyes,
Are cleared up on their own once told to the Green Duckweed.[14]

Long ago when I was the maiden of Zhao, I excelled at the art of sword fighting.[15] Goujian, the King of Yue, heard about my skill and summoned me to his throne.[16] Along the way, I came upon an old man who called himself "Mr. Yuan" and asked to pit his skill against mine. He then plucked a stalk of bamboo from the forest's edge. I took up the tip, and he grasped the base of the stem to try and stab me. I then struck him with my staff. He flew up into the tree and changed into a white gibbon, then fled.[17] From that time onward, I was enlightened and then went on to live as a recluse; I've been here in the Zhongnan Mountains[18] for round about a thousand years. Now, I'm already shorn of hair as a nun, and I've already gone through the rituals of initiation into pure karma. Why is it then that I still pass on this art of sword fighting that I practice to later generations? It is simply because this world continues to abound with disloyal ministers and thieving sons, wild husbands and unfaithful wives. Not only is it difficult to rein them in with the laws of the state, but even Buddha coming to the world can't save them. I simply need this dagger in my sack, and the deed is done in a split second—this is for the great use of putting the Way into action on behalf of Heaven and protecting the people on behalf of the state. Over the years, I've instructed no fewer than one hundred disciples. At present I have two girl disciples. One is Li the Twelfth of Linying, and the other is Jing the Thirteenth of Suzhou.[19] Both are ten years old.[20] They have mastered the art of breath control and no longer need to eat. They can run along cliffs just like flying birds. Yesterday, when I was in Weibo Circuit, I happened to see the daughter of the great General Nie Feng whose childhood name is Yinniang. She is also about ten years old, and quick with a gentle grace to her, so I asked the general whether I could take her along with me. He flew into a rage and berated me, but I just smiled and said, "Even if you lock her inside an iron box, I will surely still take her away." And that night, I did indeed take her away and brought her to this place. This girl has immortal bones in her body and was not frightened in the least. Why don't I call her to come out and teach her some tricks with the sword? Yinniang, where are you?

(FEMALE LEAD *costumed as* YINNIANG *enters and acts out greeting*:) Master, I bow before you.

(NUN:) Yinniang, I am the old nun of the Zhongnan Mountains and the progenitor of the knights-errant. Because of your extraordinary features and because we have a predestined relationship I will teach you the art of the sword, so you must set your heart on it. (NIE YINNIANG:) I would like to hear about it.

(XIANLÜ MODE: *Dian jiangchun*) (NUN:)

Originally, I
Wanted to study the Way in the Zhongnan Mountains,
Intoning scriptures and practicing repentances,
With a thousand Oms,[21]
When, all of a sudden,
A beam of light shot through my thatched hermitage
And left a Sky-Soaring Sword.[22]

Yinniang, I have a cinnabar pellet for you. Swallow it to steel your courage. And one precious sword just over a foot long keen enough to sever a hair blown across its edge. I now bestow it upon you to wield. This is no trifling matter.

(ONE GIRL brings out the cinnabar) (NIE YINNIANG bows in thanks and acts out swallowing it. THE OTHER GIRL presents the sword. The OLD NUN takes it and sings:)

(*Hunjiang long*)

Ah, this sword:

Formed from smelting together Li and Kan,[23]
Like a lotus in first bloom, or the flashing of the seven stars.[24]
You must remember:
The furnace was opened by the Great Unity,[25]
And the coals were fanned by Feilian.[26]
The metal ore was drawn from Mt. Chijin:[27]
Tempered and honed in the waters of the Ruoye pool.[28]

(NIE YINNIANG) Master, how many names of fine swords have been passed down from ancient times? (NUN:)
Let us speak not of
Zhanlu of Wu,[29]
Juque of Yue,[30]
Feiying of Wei,[31] or[32]
Longyuan of Chu.[33]
There is the one with which old Liu Bang
Climbed a mountain to chase and behead the long serpent.[34]
There is the one with which young Ci Fei
Crossed the river and angrily slashed the flood dragon.[35]
There is the one with which that rash King Zhuang of Chu
Climbed the wall, ordering his men to take enemies' heads.[36]
There is the one with which the fierce Zhuan Zhu
From his hiding spot ripped out the barbarian king's gall.[37]

(NIE YINNIANG:) Master, what is the name of *this* sword?[38] (NUN:)
This sword
Needs have no name at all.
Ask no more!
In brief,
Pure integrity is its edge,
Loyal sagacity is its pommel.
Proud heroism is its hilt, and
Wisdom and courage are its scabbard.

(*She acts out drawing the sword.*)
Held aloft,
An impressive sight:
Frost patterns sparkle, and
Rhinoceros horn speckles shimmer.

(*She produces the howling of a sword.*) (NIE YINNIANG:) Master, the sword just howled!
(NUN:)
A single howl,
Resounds far and wide:
A thunderclap startles and rouses

Fishes and dragons to fury.

(*Acts out dancing a sword dance.*)

One turn of a dance, and
All of a sudden, with a crash,
A flash of lightning
Reveals a rainbow blaze.
Recoiling at the attack,
Mountain spirits and tree imps howl all at once;
Overturned by its jab,
Heaven and earth suddenly quake.[39]
On careful inspection,
Her metal heart is steady;
I can commit into her
Jade-like hands this sword to wield.

(*Hands the sword over to* NIE YINNIANG, [*speaks*]:) Li, Jing, come over here. You two teach Yinniang how to climb trees and fly along the walls. Make her body as light as the wind so it will be easy for her to complete her tasks. She must master these skills. (TWO GIRLS:) As you command.

(*They act out teaching* NIE YINNIANG *to climb trees and scale walls.*)[40]

(*You hulu*) (NUN:)

Look at the delicate grace of Twelve and Thirteen:[41]
Going so wispily,
Returning so softly.
Flying from tree to tree,
Running from cliff to cliff.
Upside down on walls, their phoenix boots alight;
Up and down tree branches, they explore turtledoves' nests.
Like gibbons, they make hundreds of leaps,
Like ravens, they turn a somersault.
Of such a little play
The craft is not lightly achieved.
So go ahead
And pick up the pole on the stage![42]

(*Backstage, the sound of wind howling.*) Yinniang, your sword training is now complete. A great wind has arisen, and soon that fierce tiger of the Southern Mountain will arrive. You can chop off its head and bring it back. (NIE YINNIANG:) As you command. (*A tiger leaps onto the stage.* NIE YINNIANG *takes up the sword.*) (*Acts out stabbing it to death.*)

(*Tianxia le*) (NUN:)

Suddenly one sees
The white-browed lord of the mountains dancing on a stony peak.[43]

Eyes fixed in a deadly stare,
Murderous air severe.
Who could have guessed that
It would meet a Yang Xiang, seeking danger right at the tiger's lair?[44]
Someone who surpassed General Li who slept on a pile of bones?[45]
Someone who scoffed at Dou Wutu who suckled at a tiger's teat![46]
This has proven your first daring feat beyond this nunnery.[47]

Yinniang, running beasts are easy to slay, but birds of the air are more difficult to fell. Do you see that that falcon flying by? Leap up and stab it. (NIE YINNIANG:) As you command. (*Acts out killing a falcon, which falls down.*)

(*Zui zhong tian*)[48] (NUN:)
Don't take up the "Crow's Call" Bow,[49]
But take the "Pulley-hilt Sword" to strike.[50]
Eagles and ospreys circling in the clouds are like sparrows caught on birdlime:
Look how it rains down blood, feathers gusting in the wind.[51]
Don't say that these jade talons and golden pupils are truly extraordinary.
I want you to cross the heavens and go beyond the moon,
Determined to nab that rabbit and grab that toad![52]

Yinniang, you have pursued flying fowl and chased roaming beasts, never failing to hit your mark. The skills of the ancients—making apes wail and felling geese—need not even be mentioned![53] But in this world there remain a good number of beasts among men. If you do not wipe some of them out, how will you demonstrate the way of the "Sword of Righteousness Punishing Evildoers?" I will now leave the two girls here to look after the lair for the time being, and I will take you into the city to show you. (TWO GIRLS *exit.* NUN *and* NIE YINNIANG *climb to a height.* [EXTRAS] *dressed as* VARIOUS SORTS OF PEOPLE *enter.* NUN *points at them,* [*sings*]:)

(*Nezha ling*[54])
This man, oh!
He's like a jackal or a wolf—
Most gluttonous and corrupt.
This man, oh!
He's like an eagle or a hawk—
Too cunning to bear.
This man, oh!
He's like a boar or a goat—
Most shameless and filthy.

[*Speaks*:] Yinniang, now you go cut of their heads and bring them back, without letting them take notice of you. (NIE YINNIANG:) As you command. (*Acts out assassinating and bagging the heads.*)

In a single swipe, you'll cut off their heads.
With a single bite, I'll devour their hearts and livers.

[NUN *speaks*:] Yinniang, now pour some medicine on those things in your sack to transform them into liquid.[55] [*Sings*:]

In a split second, blue blood will turn to red dust.

Yinniang, when it comes to dealing with such petty men, there are too many to execute them all. Have you not heard that "if you want to shoot a man, first shoot his horse" or "if you want to capture bandits, first capture their leader?" There is a certain important official who, for no reason at all, has destroyed a number of people. His evil deeds have reached their limits. Go tonight into his home and cut off his head, and then bring it back with you. (NIE YINNIANG:) Might I inquire, Master, as to the nature of this man's crimes?

(*Que ta zhi*) (NUN:)

This man, oh!

He's full of greed, and vile too.

Relying on his rat's altar or fox's city wall,[56]

He sets out Ji's net and Luo's pincers.[57]

He tricks people with his honeyed lips and concealed sword.[58]

But the tip of my sword does not recognize the newly appointed.

(NIE YINNIANG:) As you command. (*Exits.*) (NUN:) Yinniang has been gone for a while. I wonder why she's not back yet.

(*Jisheng cao*)

Quick in the going—

She went out the gates with alacrity and resolve;

Slow in the return—

Could she have stopped to help someone out?[59]

Could it be that

The court physician raised the medicine bag and, defying all odds, struck Jing Ke?[60]

Or could it be that

Chu Ni felt remorse on seeing his intended victim in court dress?[61]

Or, if that's not it, did

The Kunlun Slave look on as the trousseau was transported?[62]

How strange that

A guest who has entered the innermost sanctum should fail to recognize the master!

Come to think of it,

Increasing the number of stoves and troops may not be of help to the main army.[63]

(NIE YINNIANG *enters, carrying a head.* NUN *speaks angrily*:) What took you so long? Why would you keep an old woman waiting? (NIE YINNIANG *bows and apologizes, saying*:)

When I went, I surmised that since the door was ajar, there was nothing to get in the way of our plan. But when I looked down from the rafters, I saw that man playing with a child. It was so precious a sight that I could not bear to attack. I waited until dusk before I could finally get his head. That's why I was slow in returning. I hope that you might forgive my offense, Master. (NUN:) In the future, when you meet people of this sort, you must first cut down that which they love and then kill them.[64] Don't be a weakling without follow-through!

(*Reprise*)

Why get so attached?
You asked permission nicely!
Faking the yellow robes, he privately imitates the imperial carriage to scurry about;
Banishing them to Vermillion Cliffs,[65] he makes a habit of framing the "pure sort";
Wresting away the Green Pearls, he abducts women of good families.[66]
You say that plucking a gourd, you can't bear to cut a side branch.
I say that in paying back, he still has not made up for all he owed.

(NIE YINNIANG:) Your disciple understands. (NUN:) I have a ram's horn dagger with a blade three inches wide. I will open up the back of your head for you and store it there. It won't harm you. When you want to use it, just pull it out. Your art is now realized, so you may go back home for the time being. We'll see each other again only after twenty years. There is a four-line *gāthā* that you must keep firmly in mind:

Meet Mirror, Then Unite
Meet Magpie, Then Stay
Meet Void, Then Hide
Meet Gibbon, Then Gather

(NIE YINNIANG *bows in thanks.* NUN *acts out concealing the dagger*:)

(*Zhuansha*)

The ram's horn is honed,
The dragon design is dim.
Paying attention to the sparkles of divine light at the back of your head,
Through ten thousand miles of gusting wind, you need fear no danger.
Who would know that this weak girl is not a boy?
You wear a red embroidered shirt,
And coil up your locks into a high chignon with a rhinoceros horn hairpin.[67]
Just like a swallow returning to a tortoise shell curtain.
On this departure
The precious mirror of your happy match,
Will reveal your awesome power at the altars of covenants,
Wait until twenty years have passed,
And I will tap out a sword song with you,
And speak of a pearled shrine.

(*Exit.*)

ACT 2

(EXTRA *costumed as* NIE FENG *enters together with* OLD WOMAN:)

Back then I slew the Krorän in service to my country,[68]
Old now, I have returned to retire in Weinan Village.
It breaks my heart that my sweet little girl has become a drifter,
The pair of us—hair turned white—lean against the door and weep.

I am Nie Feng. I used to be a high-ranking general in Weibo Circuit. Now I've retired as I'm getting along in years. My wife, Lady Ding, and I had just one daughter, who was called Yinniang. When she was just ten years old, a nun begging for food used sorcery to steal her away. We searched everywhere but there was no trace of her. The two of us weep day in and day out. Already five years have flown by. Lads, look out the front door—is someone coming by? (*Acts out weeping.*) Oh, my beloved daughter! My Yinniang!

(OLD NUN *enters with* NIE YINNIANG:)

Ten thousand miles back home in a little alizarin-red skirt,
Rough-hewn gate half closed, sun sinking toward dusk.
That old general of the northern parts must be graying by now,
And will struggle to measure up to the raven bun of a lady soldier.

Yin'er, this is your home. You may go inside. (*Acts out entering and greeting.*) (NUN:) General, the instruction of the daughter whom I begged from you is now done. You may take her back. (*Both act out crying.*)

(NUN *exits.*)

(NIE FENG:) Oh my! That old nun is suddenly nowhere to be seen—she is most certainly an immortal. Yin'er, where have you been these past five years? You've had me worried sick!

(ZHENGGONG: *Duanzheng hao*) (NIE YINNIANG:)

Five years I've been away from Ma and Pa,
Over ten thousand miles I followed my teacher:
At the farthest reaches of the sky, I had no goose to carry a letter home.
But this morning sudden joy! I return to my hometown.
I cannot express all the thoughts on my mind.[69]

(NIE FENG:) Yin'er, in what line of study did your teacher instruct you? Could you describe it to us?

(*Gun xiuqiu*) (NIE YINNIANG:)

It was nothing more than
A string of prayer beads,
The beats of a wooden fish.[70]
All day long we would burn incense and light candles.
Join our palms, recite "Namo," or[71]
Hold a scroll

Of the Prajñāpāramitā Sūtra
And bow to a painting
Of Sea and Land.[72]
I was never able to
Dispatch the Six Ding Deities or do the Paces of Yu with quickening voice,
I was never able to
Harness the Five Sacred Peaks with water mantras or written charms.[73]
She's turned out to be
A servant of Guanyin who moves with the clouds and looks after the moon,
Don't take her for
A venerable holy mother who commands the winds and rains.[74]

(NIE FENG:) My child, this is nonsense. (NIE YINNIANG:)
I am telling the truth. This is no lie![75]

(NIE FENG *acts out considering her statement*:) If the old nun doesn't possess any magic arts, then how was she able to snatch you away? And since you have been gone for five years, how could she not have taught you those magic arts? Today your parents stand before you. You must not prevaricate or cover up the truth. (NIE YINNIANG:) I fear that if I were to tell the truth, you wouldn't believe it. Oh! What should I do? (NIE FENG:) Just speak freely. (NIE YINNIANG:) When I first arrived there,
(Tang xiucai)
I traveled to the end of a winding, craggy mountain path,
Counted all the gnarled old trees:
In all those innumerable mountains and streams, there was no trace of human life.
I saw only
Gibbons and monkeys dancing in the treetops,
Birds and squirrels calling around the forest.
It was just there that I lived in a hollow with a stone door.

(NIE FENG:) Who else was in that lair?
(Gun xiuqiu) (NIE YINNIANG:)[76]
Come there first
Were two young girls
Of just about the same age: ten-odd years.
So clever: their speech like parrots;
So agile: their bodies like swallows.
In a moment
They could leap onto high cliffs as if they were low roofs;
And climb up steep walls like they were level roads.
Those maidens were quick as escaping hares;[77]
You'd think beautiful girls had turned into flying foxes.[78]
They taught me to
Run like the wind or a lightning bolt, this way and that;

I learned how to
Follow quickly in their steps, over mountains and streams:
It was as if I had sprouted wings to soar through the air.

(NIE FENG:) What other magic arts did that old nun teach you?

(*Zui taiping*) (NIE YINNIANG:)
She gave me
A pellet of powdered stalactite,[79]
And, as well,
A precious sword, three feet long.
With that green snake in my hands,[80] my courage grew bolder,
Letting me
Slash sidewise, then jab straight ahead.
There were times that I
Pursued and felled a gray-coated deer in the Western Garden;
There were times that I
Dragged out and killed a yellow-whiskered tiger on the Southern Mountain;
There were times that I
Cut down a white-crested crow in the Northern Forest:
To me, these were all like
Abandoned chicks or rotting rats.

(NIE FENG:) My child, you haven't harmed any *people*, have you?

(*Dai guduo*) (NIE YINNIANG:)[81]
I have also once
Raised a severed head and harangued the offender,
Drenched with blood from his spouting neck:
For that crime he deserved death,
For that evil deed his clan should be exterminated.
Quick!
Stab Dong Zhuo![82]
Chop up Wang Mang![83]
Decapitate Cao Cao![84]
Attack Linfu![85]

(NIE FENG:) Dreadful! How dreadful this is! But if you killed a man, where did you leave the body? (NIE YINNIANG:)
I rely on
A single flash of my inch of iron,
To shrivel up his brains and liver.
A single daub of my medicine,
To turn bones and flesh into thin air![86]

(NIE FENG:) If you, my little girl, do such terrible things, how could I not be implicated?

(*Tuo bu shan*) (NIE YINNIANG:)
This is
A secret magic bestowed upon me by Old Heaven himself.
It is not a matter of
A mere girl ranting and raging.[87]
As for you—
There's no need, old general, to fear:
Our whole family
Is protected by divine troops.[88]

(NIE FENG:) That's even worse! These days the imperial law is very strict. What if someone outside were to hear about this? They might say that I have not properly managed my household, and that I have led the people astray with false doctrines. The punishment would not be mild! What would you have me do then? (OLD WOMAN:) My husband, stop worrying. At present our daughter is already grown up. We can soon find an appropriate family and give her away in marriage, and this problem will disappear on its own. (NIE FENG:) That makes sense. (NIE YINNIANG:) Ma, Pa—please don't bring that up.

(*Xiao Liangzhou*)
No need to speak
Of the "charm of fifteen" or the "immaculate nutmeg fruit";[89]
Or of the prospective groom stopping his carriage in the next alley, eager to urge the bride to complete her adornment.[90]
Don't you know that the Mysterious Woman of the Nine Heavens never had a husband?[91]
Even if you were to leaf through the entire Marriage Register,
How could you
Pair a tiger cub with a mere house cat?

(NIE FENG:) Child, have you not heard that, "The birth of a son occasions the wish that he should have a wife; the birth of a daughter occasions the wish that she should have a marital home?" This is "the orders of your parents," so stop your obstinacy.[92] (NIE YINNIANG:) If you, my parents, have commanded so, how dare your child refuse? But I must select a match myself, and this precious sword will serve as my matchmaker!

(*Reprise*)
Gan Jiang was the husband, Mo Ye the wife.[93]
To distinguish male and female, I stroke my sword and hesitate.[94]

(NIE FENG:) My child, what sort of person do you fancy? (NIE YINNIANG:)
I don't want
A Gentleman of the Palace Guard,
Nor do I want
A merchant from Xiangyang,

Nor do I want

An Imperial Guard or a Myriarch.[95]

It occurs to me that my master gave me a four-line *gāthā*. The first went, "Meet Mirror, Then Unite." Might that not mean that my marriage destiny is with the person in the mirror?

I will search and wait for

Half a mirror to match with Luofu's.[96]

(MALE LEAD *costumed as* MIRROR POLISHER *enters*:)

I was originally the pipe-playing immortal Wang Zi[qiao],[97]

Now turned mirror-polishing youth for a time.

I wish to reflect the faces of fair maidens

For as long as the bright moon is in the sky.

As I see it, of all the marvelous things in this world, only the sword can wipe out depravity, and only the mirror can ward off evil. That's why the fairies in the immortal realm have carried these two treasures. Now, the swordswoman Nie Yinniang has received the art of the sword from the old matron of the Zhongnan Mountains, and by the karma of this life, she is destined to become my wife. I think I'll just take up the profession of mirror polisher and go on over to her house. When sword and mirror meet, there will be a natural reaction between them. Let's see whether she can see through things—I'll just call out "Polish your mirrors, polish your mirrors!" ([OLD WOMAN] *acts out listening.*) Just as our daughter is saying "Meet Mirror Then Unite," here comes a mirror polisher. (NIE FENG:) Let's call him in. (OLD WOMAN *calls,* MALE LEAD *acts out coming in and meeting.*)[98](NIE YINNIANG *acts out looking at him and says to* NIE FENG *and* OLD WOMAN:) I beg to report to father and mother that this man will be my husband. (NIE FENG:) My child, make no mistake—this man is a humble mirror polisher, how could he be joined in matrimony to a prominent family like ours? (NIE YINNIANG:) Papa, you don't understand. This mirror polisher,

(*Daodao ling*)

Is like

Wu Gang playfully wielding his axe in the Lunar Palace.[99]

His encountering Yinniang today

Is like

Secretly accepting Pei Hang's pestle at Indigo Bridge.[100]

(MIRROR POLISHER:) My only fear is that your humble servant may not have the good fortune to serve you, young maiden.

(NIE YINNIANG:)

You—

A true romantic suited to be the lotus master.

I—

Of one heart ready to find a match like the dogwood girl.

(NIE FENG:) My child, you must think this over carefully, so you don't come to regret your decision. (NIE YINNIANG:)

Papa,
Now you stop being so obstinate,
Stop being so obstinate!
At this very moment,
In the reflection of the mirror, a pair of phoenixes dance.[101]

(NIE FENG:) Since you insist on this, my daughter, I suppose we have no choice but to allow it. Young man, come here, and be joined with her in matrimony, as husband and wife, this very day. (MIRROR POLISHER *bows in thanks*:) As you command, father. Although I am a mirror polisher by trade, my household is actually quite well off. From now on, I vow to provide you with food and clothing and never leave your side. (NIE YINNIANG:) You need not hide the truth from me.

(*Shawei*)[102]
I—
In highest heaven, I loved you from a distance;
You—
Must have furtively taken note of me in Paradise.
Oh, happy event, that we are paired this very day:
Like harmonizing zithers, we will be,
Delighting in each other, like fish in water;
Two lotus flowers on a single stalk,
Calamus flowers knotted together;
Side by side, we'll drive a decorated carriage,
Together, we'll share dreams behind gauze netting;
Close the tasseled canopy,
Roll up the shrimp-whisker curtain;
We'll trim incense in golden ducks,[103]
Sculpted jade and bronze crow.
Lifting a wine pot among the flowers,
Playing the mouth reed-organ under the moon;
Gambling and playing at dice,
Dancing drunk on a red rug;[104]
Crystal hairpin stuck in askance,
I will softly sway my rosy skirts;
Open up that secret black book,
Small seal-script stamped in red;
And pointing to the far-off Heavenly Palace,[105]
Inquire after my crazy fool with a smile.
Then I will ride with you upon this heavenly wind,
Off to make clouds and rain.[106]

(*Exits*)

ACT 3

(OFFICIAL *enters, leading his retinue*:)

By birth a military man, offspring of noble Han family.
At thirty, I mounted the altar and made ministers bow to me.
Last night the vanguard reported back with enemy heads;
On west wind, drums and trumpets filled the yamen gate.

I am Liu Changyi, and I hold the position of Military Governor of Chenxu.[107] I'm glad to say it's quiet at court, and the border is calm. It is unfortunate that I do not get along with the Commander of Wei, Tian Ji'an,[108] and my heart is filled with anxiety and suspicion. This morning I made a prognostication, and the omen said that he would be sending a husband and wife to assassinate me. I have already arranged to thwart this plan and put them in my service instead. Is that not an excellent strategy? Now where's that officer? (OFFICER *enters*:) Yes, my Lord, what is your command? (LIU CHANGYI:) Go right away north of the city wall and wait. A man and a woman astride black and white donkeys will arrive at the gate, where they will encounter a magpie chattering. The man will shoot at it with his bow, but he will miss. The wife will then take her husband's bow, and with a single pellet will kill the magpie. Greet them, saying that I would like to meet them and thus have sent you to welcome them. Don't mess this up! (OFFICER:) Yes, sir.

(*Exit together.*)

(MIRROR POLISHER *and* NIE YINNIANG *enter riding on donkeys.* [NIE YINNIANG *speaks*]:)

Off on a mission through this land under arms:
Who says young lovers can't be heroes too?
The river Zhang rushes eastward as we cover a thousand miles:[109]
A single sword pierces the void as we pass through the morning breeze.

I am Nie Yinniang. After I returned from the Zhongnan Mountains, both my parents passed away, and my husband and I were recruited with gifts of gold and silk by Commander Tian of Wei to be his personal aides. We have already served him for several years. Unexpectedly, Commander Tian had a falling out with Commander Liu of Xu, so he has sent me to come and cut off his head. To my mind, the art of the sword my immortal master taught me was meant to take the heads of traitors and execute the cruel, so how can I use it unscrupulously to harm an innocent person? However, since I have already benefited from the grace of Commander Tian, I am not in a position to disobey his command. So, I decided to come over to this Circuit to size up Commander Liu's movements and come up with a suitable plan. I thought I might as well turn these two paper bills in my sack into a black and a white donkey and head that way with my husband.[110]

(SHUANGDIAO MODE: *Xinshui ling*)

We are just like

The flautists soaring off from the painted tower—
A lovely couple of matching leaves and blossoms.[111]
My husband,
You carry a purple magpie in your mirror case;
And as for me,
My sword box spits out a rainbow.
Not for us
To ride together on painted phoenix,
We just ride these black and white donkeys.[112]

While I've been talking, I have just caught sight of the city of Daliang in the distance.[113]

(*Zhuma ting*)
I see:
Bronze Sparrow Terrace rising up to the clouds;[114]
In Emerald Hall, on autumn's breeze I hear drums and horns.[115]
Else, all I see is
Rain falling freely on the Golden Dike;
And spring waters of the Yellow River raising banners and flags.

I have heard that this place is where Zhu Hai struck Jin Bi[116] in the Wei army and Zhang Liang hammered Zulong in the state of Qin.[117] They were all men of my kind, yet where are they today?

I think of that
Assault on the palace carriage when he roused himself at Bolangsha to strike,[118]
Or the theft of the military tally—who held the reins at Yimen?[119]

Ruan Ji once climbed up Mt. Guangwu and said with a sigh: "In an era without heroes, weaklings will attain fame."[120]

Now they are all gone.
I reckon that heroes and weaklings alike have turned to mere traces in the dust.

(*[Backstage] Act out magpie chattering.*) (NIE YINNIANG:) Ach, that magpie is making such a baleful noise!

(*Chenzui dongfeng*)
All aflutter, the magpie flies up into the air,
Squawking so much it startles these "long ears,"
Nearly makes one
Lose these jade stirrups,
Drop this pearl-studded whip.
Husband, take your pliant bow, and do your best to shoot it down.

(MIRROR POLISHER *acts out shooting and missing.*) (NIE YINNIANG:) What a good-for-nothing this man is. Well, then, let your old lady do it herself. (*Acts out killing the magpie with a single shot and laughing.*)

Look:

As soon as my hand touches the golden pellet it fells that green-cloaked bird.
Better even than that
High officer of Gu who shot a pheasant at Rugao.[121]

(OFFICER *rushes in*:) Miss, are you not the one sent by Military Governor Tian? My master, Vice Director Liu has been waiting for you for some time now. He sent me with special orders to welcome you. (NIE YINNIANG *acts out being surprised*:) This Vice Director Liu is truly a person with supernatural prescience. Otherwise, how could he have known in advance that I was coming?

(*Qiaopai'er*)
Could it be that he
Heard the magpie's good omen in advance,
And divined ahead of time that travelers would arrive?
It seems that this General's
Courtesy in receiving guests is swift!
And meeting him on a narrow road,
It's impossible to avoid him.[122]

I've got it! My Master gave me a four-line *gāthā*, which said, "Meet Magpie, Then Stay." Could it be that I am meant to "stay" in this place? (*Says to* MIRROR POLISHER:) Since Vice Director Liu knows about the two of us, let's go and meet him before we take care of our business. (MIRROR POLISHER:) Yes, let's do as you say. (OFFICER *reports them and acts out admitting them to an audience*) (OFFICIAL:) You are Nie Yinniang, are you not? I, Liu Changyi, have admired you for quite some time now. (MIRROR POLISHER *and* NIE YINNIANG *act out making obeisance*:) For our offense against Your Honor, we should die ten thousand deaths! (OFFICIAL:) Not at all! Each person serves their own master—such is the way of the world. Now that we have met, please don't harbor misgivings. (NIE YINNIANG:) From what I can see, the Vice Director is the only hero in the entire realm under heaven!

(*Zhegui ling*)
I have admired your honor—a reputation that echoes like thunder.
A courage enough to slay dragons,
He's brilliant as a flaming rhinoceros horn:[123]
Magnanimous and lenient.
He regards me as his closest ally,
Putting an end to all suspicions.

(OFFICIAL:) What kind of a person is Tian Ji'an? (NIE YINNIANG:)
Considering that rat—a corpse about to breathe its last;[124]
How can he compare with your magnificent might extending in all directions?
This time, oh,
He sent me in vain on a perilous mission;
Unjustly showed me false regard.
It is such good fortune to have encountered you today, Vice Director!

This was a close call—if you had not shown benevolence,
You would have lost your head.[125]

(OFFICIAL:) What's the difference between Wei and Xu? If you would not abandon me, then why not stay here? (NIE YINNIANG *acts out bowing*:) The Vice Director has no able person by his side. The pair of us are willing to abandon our former lord and serve you from today forward.

(*Shuixianzi*)
Whip in hand, drum in arms, we'll traverse the palace steps;
Behind the horse, before the carriage, we'll heed every command.

(OFFICIAL:) How much remuneration do the two of you require? (NIE YINNIANG:)
Back in Weibo, we received a hundred cash per day.
One hundred cash: please follow this precedent.

(OFFICIAL:) Even so, as you stay here, might you not think back on your former master? (NIE YINNIANG:) I have heard that "A good bird chooses a fine branch and perches there; a good minister chooses a sovereign to serve," how could I be swayed by trivial sentiments?

It's not that I
On finding a new town would leave the old place,
But that I've learned to follow the example of
The good bird who chooses a fine branch and perches there.[126]

There's just one thing: when Tian doesn't receive a report, he'll surely send someone after me. Allow me to take a lock of my hair tied with raw red silk and deliver it tonight to the Commander of Wei's pillow to convey to him that I will not be returning.

This strand of plain hair
Makes clear our strong bond;
Half a length of raw silk
Conveys that I won't be back.

(OFFICIAL:) Once Commander Tian finds out, he'll surely send someone after you—what will you do then? (NIE YINNIANG:)
I'm afraid that
Even a team of four steeds could not overtake me![127]

(*Acts out cutting her hair and tying it with a strand of silk. She tosses it into the air and circles the stage once*:) In faith, I have delivered it. Tonight, he will surely send Jingjing'er to kill me and take your head.[128] I will come up with ten thousand schemes to kill her—don't worry! (OFFICIAL:) My lot is with Heaven. What need have I to fear rats like him? (NIE YINNIANG:) Vice Director, please hold a candle, sit up straight, and observe my technique. Husband, let's retire for the time being.

(NIE YINNIANG *and* MIRROR POLISHER *exit.*)

(*Onstage, two banners are arranged, one red and the other white. They act out fighting for a long while, after which a human head falls out of the air, and* NIE YINNIANG *hurries on stage*:) I report to the Vice Director that Jingjing'er has been slain. I dragged her out of the hall and used a potion to transform her into liquid—not a single hair remains. (OFFICIAL:) Marvelous! Marvelous! What magic art is that? (*Yan'er luo*) (NIE YINNIANG:)

All you saw
Was a pair of banners fluttering in the lamplight.
You never heard
Two blades ringing as they stabbed beside the bed.
All I could do
Was float through the air as I flipped that red skirt upside down in the dark.
And as for her, well,
Her white bones fell from midair with a solid thud.[129]
(*Desheng ling*)
I made her
Hair scatter into ashes,
Flesh turn to paste.
Her resentful soul be scattered by the wind,
Her floating phosphorescence carried back with the rain.
With marvelous skill, I played three performances on this stage,
Winning and losing are determined by a single move on this *go* board.[130]

(OFFICIAL:) You've worked so hard, ma'am. Now you may rest. (NIE YINNIANG:) Not just yet. Tonight, he will surely send the supremely skilled Kongkong'er to follow up.[131] Kongkong'er's wondrous arts are such that humans cannot spy out her means, nor can spirits grasp her traces. She can follow the void and enter the netherworld, and she excels at formlessness, able to conceal even her shadow. My skills do not even amount to one ten-thousandth of hers. All will depend on the Vice Director's luck. (OFFICIAL:) In that case, what can we do? (NIE YINNIANG:) Fear not! You need only to wear this Khotan jade around your neck and wrap yourself in a thick quilt. I will transform myself into a midge and slip into your intestines to wait. There is no other place to hide from her. (OFFICIAL:) Lady, why would we wish to hide from her? (NIE YINNIANG:) I recall that one line of the *gāthā* my Master gave me was, "Meet Void, Then Hide." This is fated to be and cannot be avoided. Vice Director, please rest easy. (OFFICIAL *acts out lying down.* NIE YINNIANG *places jade around his neck and covers him with a blanket. She acts out hiding herself under the bed.* SOMEONE *dressed as* KONGKONG'ER *flies on carrying a dagger and stabs his neck. Above she flies off with a sound and exits.* NIE YINNIANG *acts out leaping out*:) Congratulations, Vice Director, you have come to no harm! (OFFICIAL:) How is that? (NIE YINNIANG:) After the third watch, Kongkong'er stabbed your neck, then there was a clanging sound. Now, she is like a skilled falcon—if she does not hit her mark on the first try, she will fly far off out of shame that she did not succeed. Within one watch she will already be a thousand miles away. (OFFICIAL *removes the jade and acts out looking at it*:) How strange! Look—indeed the jade has marks on it from the dagger, exceeding several inches in length. Kongkong'er is truly a marvelous creature. (NIE YINNIANG:) Oh, that Kongkong'er,

(*Gu meijiu*)
"Listened to but never heard, it takes the name *ethereal*."
"Looked at but never seen, it takes the name *invisible*."
Without shadow and without form, "it takes the name *gossamer*."[132]
This magical marvel sure knew how to
Interfere with a good night's sleep!

(*Taiping ling*)
Suddenly arriving—shocking the heavens and shaking the earth;
Leaving just as quickly—at lightning speed, as swift as the wind.

Vice Director, today you have reason to rejoice!

Who dares chop off such a fine head as yours?
The person in your belly shouted, "A shame!"
I congratulate you—on whom did this depend?
It's all thanks to:
A single piece of jade that took your place by lying over you.[133]

(OFFICIAL *acts out thanking him*:) On this day, I have been given a new life, and it is all thanks to your favor. I swear to provide for you; I will not forget this as long as I live. When I go to the capital for an audience with the emperor next year, in the eighth year of the Yuanhe reign-period, I shall invite you to join me as my bodyguard so that I am sure to be protected.[134] (NIE YINNIANG:) I dare offend your dignity: for such magnanimous treatment as I have received, I have rendered such a minor service in return. There is no need to mention it. Your future prospects are bright and filled with auspicious signs. I will have my husband stay to serve you as an attendant. I, however, must now head for the mountains and streams to visit enlightened beings there. A few years from now, I'll return to see you off. (OFFICIAL:) Lady, how could you say this out of the blue? If you're not willing to stay on as my retainer, at least let me expend a thousand taels of silver to make a mountain dwelling for you. (NIE YINNIANG:) The clouds and waters have no fixed abode: how can such things be planned in advance? (OFFICIAL:) Lady, since you are determined to go, tomorrow we should have a great banquet at which guests can compose poetry to bid you farewell to express my deep gratitude. (NIE YINNIANG:) Thanks to you, esteemed Sir. Let us call my husband and inform him. (MIRROR POLISHER *enters*.) (NIE YINNIANG:) Husband, serve the Vice Director well, take care in everything, and be attentive. I must go to the Zhongnan Mountains for a while to see my Master. I will be back before long. And now I bid you farewell! (*They act out exchanging bows*.)

(*Yuanyang sha*) (NIE YINNIANG:)
The sword bids a temporary farewell to the minister's mansion,

In the past, I came riding astride black and white donkeys. Today, I will leave them in my sack, and not take anything with me.

Instead I will hand this cloth sack to my coiled-dragon groom.[135]

As I go this time,

Let me go
With deer steps or in unicorn chariot,
To Penglai Isle or the Peach Spring.
With jade sisters and orchid aunts,
I'll imbibe cinnabar and collect kingfisher feathers.
My only resentment is the water-caltrop song on seeing off guests.
The water flows on forever, the sky has no edge:
Where would I ask after
The Goddess of the River Luo, who rides the mists?[136]
I suppose in the white clouds of the Zhongnan Mountains.[137]

(*They exit together.*)

ACT 4

(COMIC *costumed as* MR. YUAN, *enters*:)

Long ago, this noble man transformed into a Lord of the Mountains[138]
Who could draw the general's ten-thousand-stone weight bow.[139]
Old now, I've heart no more for grappling fights,
Alone, I lean on an old tree and howl in the autumn winds.

Back in the Spring and Autumn period, I was a white gibbon. I attained the Way after a thousand years and transformed into an old man. I competed in the art of the sword with a maiden of the state of Zhao, and I lost and fled. The maiden became an old nun, and I followed her to practice the Daoist arts. At present, she has attained the completion of her merit, and she is going to ascend to the Heavens. Her disciple Nie Yinniang is returning to the mountains from the human world. My master was worried that she might get lost, so she commanded me to come and guide her. I'll just transform myself into my original form with a somersault.

(*Exits*)

(NIE YINNIANG *enters, bearing a sword on her back*:)

Since I went off to the dusty world, twenty years have passed;
On these empty mountains, my destiny shared with gibbons and cranes.
Here I am at the "rock of three incarnations," but where is she?[140]
I only fear now that I'm here again, we can speak only of loss and confusion.

Since I, Nie Yinniang, left Vice Director Liu and my husband, I came to the Zhongnan Mountains to look for my master. I need no carriage or horse, just my body hurrying along.

(ZHONGLÜ MODE: *Fendie'er*)
I've just left
Jade curtains and golden marten furs.
I've shed my military outfit, brocaded coat, and patterned hat,
For a nun's headdress, linen stockings, and silk waistband.
Forfeiting a thousand gold pieces,
And retaining only this single sword,
I let a long cry to the heavens.[141]
When I
Turn back and gaze at the clouds,
I still hear
The plaintive notes of the horn that saw this traveler off.[142]

Since I left Daliang City, it's been scenic sights without end.

(*Zui chunfeng*)
The morning moon: blue just beginning to gather;
The distant mountains: green expanse without end.
These Zhongnan Mountains, a speck between presence and absence,[143]
Appear in the distance when I gaze afar:
They connect to
The Three Peaks of Mount Hua,[144]
The Five Rods of the Wugong,[145]
And the single current of the River Wei.[146]

Just think—when I was in these Zhongnan Mountains, I was just ten years old. Now, without my even realizing it, twenty years have passed. How quickly time flies!

(*Yingxian ke*)
I recall when I was young
And lived in the Zhongtiao Mountains
Playfully grabbing at Magu's fingers.[147]
Amid my busy life,
I leapt out of the red dust,
To perch on white grasses.
While I did quick somersaults,
Across the wide seas and high heavens,
Unknown to me
The green mountains of days gone by have aged.

Making my way along this winding path, I've already reached the Zhongnan Mountains.

(*Hongxiu xie*)
All I see are
Fairy-expecting steps encircled by rosy clouds;

A resting-in-mist courtyard, where orchids and angelica sway:
With jade pool and emerald curtain, the thatched cottage remains.

The brooks and mountains are as they were; the stone cave just the same. But where could my Master be? And where are the two girls?

Why don't I see
Blue Zither arrive at Jade Stream,[148]
Or Yellow Rock invite me to Gu City?[149]
Oh my!
Why is the Wuling source closed off?[150]

(WHITE GIBBON *leaps onto the stage*) (NIE YINNIANG:) Oh! That's right, the final line of the four-line *gāthā* my master bestowed upon me was, "Meet Gibbon, Then Gather." I will go along with this white gibbon now, and I'm sure to find the meeting place. (*Acts out walking quickly.*) (WHITE GIBBON *leaps offstage. The sound of drums from offstage.*)

(*Shiliu hua*) (NIE YINNIANG:)
Suddenly, I hear the cloud gongs echoing in the sky—
A white crane carries Wang Qiao.[151]

(*Backstage, a cave door opens. Sundry* [FEMALE ROLES] *costumed as* LI THE TWELFTH, JING THE THIRTEENTH, THE WOMAN IN THE CARRIAGE, and RED THREAD, *each carrying a sword and crowding around* OLD NUN, *enter.*) (NIE YINNIANG:)

Look at the rainbow banners and crimson insignia as hundreds of spirits come to pay homage.

(*Acts out entering the door*:)
I entreat the servant to announce,
Announce the triple-eared one.[152]

(*Acts out bowing.*) Esteemed Master, I, Nie Yinniang, kowtow before you. (NUN:) Dear Yinniang, it's been twenty years since you left. (NIE YINNIANG:)

Speak not of matters twenty years now past—
Let us rejoice in our reunion, and converse once more as fishers and woodcutters.
Long-lost dear ones are safe and sound, so let's laugh in the lamplight,
While we wipe our swords and patterned hilts.[153]

[(NUN:)] Yinniang, your achievements while traveling in Wei and Xu are many indeed. If the Mirror Polisher is well, why did he not accompany you?

(*Dou anchun*) (NIE YINNIANG:)
Do not mention again
Tian Dan of Jimo, or
Liu Biao of Jingzhou.[154]
They are nothing more than
Snake's legs added after some wine, or[155]
Goose tracks in the snow.[156]
What I have is—

The old magpie's nest that was there before the Jade Mirror Stand.[157]
Could it be
That this conjugal union cannot be undone?
At present, I am ready to follow my master in committing to the Buddhist dharma.
Let me attain quickly
This White Altar's censing training!
Just as if
Awakening from a Yellow Millet Dream.[158]

(NUN:) Yin'er, you have already left the Sea of Bitterness to travel westward—is that not marvelous?[159] But our art of the sword is not of the ordinary kind: Above, it can exact retribution from the enemies of fathers or lords; below, it can punish the wrongs of sons or subordinates. In the world of light, it can avenge the indignation of the people; in the world of darkness, it can exorcise the evil of demons and ghosts. Although a sovereign may mete out rewards and punishments, it cannot surpass this. The compassion of our Buddha knows no greater expression than this.[160] Today, all of my disciples have gathered here in a large assembly. Why doesn't each offer an account of her karmic causes and conditions, as well as of the merit she has accumulated, so we can register their names with the Celestial Lord as testament to their attainment of enlightenment—would that not be wonderful? (*Sundry* [FEMALE ROLES]:) As you command. (NUN:) Yinniang, come over here, and recount your experience for us first. (NIE YINNIANG *performs a sword dance and sings*:) I, Nie Yinniang—
(BANSHE DIAO MODE: *Shua hai'er*)
A young girl behind vermilion gates, my crow-black bun was small.
But taking up a hooked sword, I was as ferocious as a panther.
Above I pursued hawks and falcons, below monkeys and gibbons.
I also
Wiped out ruthless and callous officials.
That Jingjing'er—oh!
After one bout, slain like a chicken!
That Kongkong'er—oh!
Was fended off and fled like a sparrow!
My fighting skills are ingenious!
If you don't believe, just watch:
My soul-snatching ram's horn dagger
Will prove it
By fetching a robe stained orangutan red.[161]

(NUN:) Li the Twelfth, come over here. You were originally Mistress Gongsun's pupil,[162] and you excelled in sword-dancing. The Old Man of Shaoling presented you with a song that said, "The beauty of Linying is here at Baidi City, / The song of her marvelous dance stirs the heart."[163] That was supreme praise indeed. Try to recount your experience for us. (LI *performs a sword dance and sings*:) I, Li the Twelfth,

(*Wusha*)
I passed on the Lady's fragrant fame;
I marveled at the pathos of Old Du's fluid recital.
Brocade garments and face of jade—a natural wonder.
At the Courtyard Fit for Spring, waves roiled the pleasure lanes;
Near Baidi City, thunder and lightning cracked.[164]
Who knew that
I had also
Slain a white tiger on land, and
Cut down a black dragon at sea?[165]

(NUN:) Jing the Thirteenth, come over here. You were originally a merchant woman who married the scholar Zhao Zhongli. His friend, Li Zhenglang, had a beloved courtesan whose parents tried to marry her to Zhuge Yin.[166] You got the three heads, put them in a sack, and gave it to Li.[167] How can the assassin Jing Ke compare with such a chivalric act as this? Please recount your feats for us. (JING *performs a sword dance and sings*:) I, Jing the Thirteenth,

(*Sisha*)
Purer than the widow of Baling,[168]
Braver than the merchant of Wujiang.
A beauty by chance married to Lord Pingyuan of Zhao.[169]
For her betrayal I beheaded that whorehouse courtesan;
Yanking out its tongue, I drove away the white horse demon.[170]
Rowing back together,
I will long accompany Fan Li on the five lakes,[171]
Far surpass Wen Xiao in his opulent tent.[172]

(NUN:) Woman in the Carriage, come over here.[173] You lived incognito in Chang'an's alleyways, and the young men under your command possessed superb skills. Because the scholar from Wu Commandery could walk several paces on the wall in his boots, you invited him and observed his skill. You borrowed his mount and stole things from the forbidden palace, causing him to be imprisoned. You flew down into the prison through a hole, tied some silk around his arm, and then leapt out and over the palace wall. This marvelous skill is unlike anything seen before, so please describe it for us. (WOMAN *performs a sword dance and sings*:) I, The Woman in the Carriage,

(*Sansha*)
Hair done up in a full bun,
White silks all aflutter,
I rode my ornamented carriage for pleasure—I have no name.
In my youth, I taught young men to show off their flying skills like birds
And I lifted the scholar out of that tigers' den.

But I'm no thief!
I can scoff at that
Penglang and the jade pillow,[174]
That Mo'le and Hong Xiao.[175]

(NUN:) Red Thread, come over here. You "took the golden casket from Tian Chengsi's bed" for [Military Governor] Xue Song. "For six hours in the middle of the night, you went back and forth over seven hundred miles," in order to ensure that "both places preserved their walls and moats, and ten thousand people preserved their lives."[176] There is no accomplishment greater than this. I have admired you for a long time. Please recount it for us. (RED THREAD *performs a sword dance and sings*:) I, Red Thread,

(*Ersha*)
A servant girl in black who played the lute,
A secretary in white who presented reports,
In a westerly wind at midnight on the road to Hanling.
From under the pillow decorated with rhinoceros horn, I carried away the golden casket;
To a painted bugle's sound, I returned in a purple robe.
And left as if nothing
The smallness of the "magnolia wood boat"
And the loftiness of the "hundred-foot tower."[177]

(*SUNDRY* [FEMALE ROLES]:) We disciples have all presented our stories. We dare entreat our master to instruct us with a thing or two. (NUN *laughs and says*:) When it comes to this old nun's previous deeds,

(*Shawei*)
Long since cast aside, so long since cast aside—
Bring them up no more, no, bring them up no more.[178]

(*Backstage announces*:) The Lord on High has a decree: The old nun of Zhongnan Mountains, along with her disciples Nie Yinniang and the rest are to report immediately to the Heavenly Court to discuss the arts of the sword.

(NUN:) We are coming
All of a sudden, we heard that the Jade Emperor loves swords.
By Heavenly Writ summoned,
All of you and I
Must now mount the horse o' winds and the chariot o' clouds and be on our way.[179]

(*They perform a sword dance together and exit.*)

In the hustle and bustle of the sixth month, daily troubles mount up,
No plans to achieve my lofty ambition, I'm worn down instead.
I sometimes think of knights-errant and read of their marvelous feats,
And I happened to think of following a long song with a short one.[180]

When you take a wife, she should be like Nie Yinniang;
Be willing to be the Mirror Polisher, and aid in her make-up.
In this human world, chop off the heads of all evil-doers,
Fall off your ass and have a good laugh.[181]

NOTES

1. Altenburger (2009, 58).
2. See Liu and Peng (2019).
3. See Peterson (1979).
4. For more information, see Cuadrado (1986).
5. The vernacular story "Daoist Li Enters the Cloud Gate Cave Alone" includes a similar quatrain riddle: "Go when you see a rock; / Ask when you hear clappers. / Live next to where you see Jin; / Flee upon the advent of a Pei" (Yang and Yang 2009, 895). *Shuihu zhuan* likewise features a similar *gāthā* as a plot device in chapter 5: "When you find a forest, you will rise. / When you find a mountain, you will prosper. / When you find water, you will grow. / When you find a river, you will cease" (Dent-Young and Dent-Young 1994, 111).
6. The earliest instance of this anecdote is in the *Annals of Wu and Yue* (*Wu Yue chunqiu* 吳越春秋), an account of legends and events in the states of Wu and Yue during the Spring and Autumn period (Zhou Shengchun 1997, 151–52; Van Gulik 1967, 40). Compilation of these classical tales of knights errant is usually attributed to Wang Shizhen, though the stories date to the Song dynasty and earlier, and there are a number of versions in circulation. One version credits Ming dynasty scholar Wu Guan 吳棺 (active 16th c.) as editor. See Anon. (1936).
7. "Wang (Shizhen) Ruanting 王士禎阮亭 liked *Black and White Donkeys* very much, so he took it with him to Rugao and gave it to Mao Bijiang's household troupe so that he could appraise it himself." Preface to *Xitang quye* 西堂曲腋 cited in Zeng Yingjing (1995, 180).
8. "My *Reading* Li Sao was submitted for the emperor's viewing, and he commanded that the actors in the Imperial Arts Academy (*jiaofang* 教坊) perform it for him." Preface to *Xitang quye* cited in Zeng Yingjing (1995, 167).
9. Sima Qian 司馬遷 (145–86 BCE), a historian of the Han dynasty (206 BCE–220), was the first to write a comprehensive history of the known world, the *Records of the Grand Historian* (*Shiji* 史記). His *Records* included biographies of assassins, the most famous of whom is Jing Ke (d. 227 BCE). Jing Ke was sent by Prince Dan of the state of Yan to assassinate King Zheng of the state of Qin. Jing Ke hid a dagger in a map and attempted to kill King Zheng. He was unsuccessful, and King Zheng eventually was able to stab him with his sword. Had he succeeded, King Zheng would not have been able to unite all the states under the Qin, marking reunification and the beginning of dynastic rule. See *SJ j.* 86.2515–2538; "The Biographies of the Assassin-Retainers" translated in Watson (1969, 45–67).
10. Yao Li 要離 (d. 513 BCE) was an assassin from the state of Wu. His mission was to kill Prince Qingji 慶忌 (d. 513 BCE). To quell any suspicion about his motive, Yao Li killed his own wife and children, and had his hand cut off as evidence that he had been punished by King Helü 闔閭 of Wu (547–496 BCE). The plan worked, and Yao Li was able to get close to Prince Qingji and kill him. Nie Zheng 聶政 (d. 397 BCE) assassinated the prime minister of the state of Han to avenge a friend, after which he disfigured his face before killing himself to protect his family from punishment. Yao Li's biography is included in the *Wu Yue chunqiu* (see Zhou Shengchun 1997), while Nie Zheng's is in Sima Qian's

Records of the Grand Historian. "Smashing the jade disk and one's head at once" is a reference to Lin Xiangru 藺相如 (ca. 3rd c. BCE), a minister in the state of Zhao. When the powerful Qin state requested that Zhao exchange a renowned jade disk known as "Mr. He's Jade" for fifteen cities, the king of Zhao could not decline, and Lin Xiangru was entrusted with negotiating the exchange and delivering the jade disk. When Lin Xiangru suspected that the king of Qin was not going to keep his word, he threatened to "smash the jade disk and his head at once" against a pillar.

11. The term "imperceptibly" here translates *yinyin* 隱隱, which is the first character in our heroine's name—Yinniang—redoubled. As the following sentence introduces her, we can assume that this is intentional foreshadowing. Red Thread is another renowned female assassin who appears as a minor character here. See Yee's (1985) English translation of the story of Red Thread ("Hung-hsien" 紅線, by Yüan Chiao).

12. The "three-inch lotus" here is a metaphor for the dagger mentioned above. The lotus referenced is the bud just before it has bloomed, when it has the shape of a dagger. For an early reference to a sword as a lotus ("like a lotus when it first emerges"), see "Waizhuan ji baojian" 外傳記 寶劍 in *Yuejue shu* 越絕書 (Li Bujia 2013, 301). This text has been translated in Milburn (2010, 281), but she translates *furong* 芙蓉 as "peony."

13. These are the final two lines of a quatrain by Li He 李賀 (790–816), "Southern Garden no. 7," the first two lines of which read,

    Sima Xiangru, dejected, grieves in the empty room,
    Dongfang Shuo, with facetious humor, makes himself desirable.

    The two choices of the talented: sitting alone after having been rejected by the court or hiding your talent behind humor to make the court recognize you. The Ruoye 若耶 sword refers to Fan Li 范蠡 of the state of Yue who was determined to give up civil pursuits for the swordsmanship of the military; the last line refers to when the king of the state of Yue, Goujian, once invited a gifted swordswoman to the capital. She met an old man there who called himself Mr. Yuan (a homophone for "gibbon") who fought the swordswoman with his bamboo staff. He then changed into a gibbon and fled to the treetops. Peng himself has evidently been inspired by the play to become a knight-errant.

14. "Green Duckweed" (Qingping 青萍) is the name of a famous sword associated with Emperor Guangwu (5 BCE–57 CE) of the Han, a descendant of the Han dynasty royal family celebrated for reclaiming the throne after Wang Mang's usurpation. See Chen Lin's (160–217) "Da Dong'a Wang qianjian 答東阿王鉛牋" (Letter in reply to the Prince of Dong'a), that is, Cao Zhi (192–232), in the *Wen xuan* (*Selections of Refined Literature*) (Xiao Tong (2008 [1977], 565). The term "green duckweed" later came to refer to swords in general.

15. The maiden of Zhao is a historical swordswoman who is supposed to have lived during the Spring and Autumn period. She is sometimes conflated with the maiden of Yue, and elsewhere called Aqing. She is supposed to have used a bamboo pole to fight with a white gibbon, just as recounted here. Her story is recorded in *Annals of Wu and Yue*, see Zhou Shengchun (1997, 151–52); Van Gulik (1967, 40). For another traditional account of the maiden of Zhao meeting Mr. Yuan, see *Laoren hua yuan* in Anon. (1936, 1).

16. King Goujian (r. 496–465 BCE) ruled the state of Yue near the end of the Spring and Autumn period.

17. "Yuan" has a double meaning here. The Yuan 袁 of Mr. Yuan is a common surname that the gibbon cleverly took as a homophone of his name, a "gibbon" 猿, written with the quadruped radical on the left.

18. Mountain range in Shaanxi, south of Xi'an, famous for attracting recluses.

19. Li the Twelfth 李十二 (late eighth c.) was a female disciple of Mistress Gongsun 公孫大娘 who excelled in the performance of the sword dance. Linying is located in present-day Henan. Du Fu's poem about Li the Twelfth, "Guan Gongsun Daniang dizi wu jianqi xing" 觀公孫大娘弟子武劍器行 can be found

in *QTS* 2361. An account of Jing the Thirteenth 荊十三 was included in the collection of classical tales *Beimeng suoyan* by Sun Guangxian (ca. 901–968) of the Five Dynasties period. Jing rescues a courtesan for Li Thirty-nine 李三十九郎, a friend of her friend Zhao Zhongxing 趙中行. See Sun Guangxian (2002, 181–82).

20. Their ages are given in *sui* 歲, in which a person is one *sui* at birth. In Western reckoning, they would be nine years old.
21. "Om" is a transliterated syllable of a Sanskrit mantra.
22. "Sky-Soaring Sword" (Tengkongjian 騰空劍) is the name of the famous sword associated with Zhuan Xu, grandson of the Yellow Emperor and one of the Five Thearchs. The sword is supposed to have come from the sky to defend him against enemies. When it was stored in a box and needed to be used, it would roar like a dragon or tiger.
23. Li and Kan are the names of two of the eight trigrams found in the *Yijing* (*Book of Changes*). The former is represented by a broken center line and two solid lines, indicating fire, and the latter a solid center line with two broken lines, indicating water. Together, as here, they denote the foundational elements of the universe. See *ZY* 258–270.
24. "Seven Stars" (Qixing 七星) is another name for the Longyuan 龍淵 "Dragon Abyss" sword from the late Spring and Autumn period. On the Longyuan sword, see "Waizhuan ji baojian" in *Yuejue shu* 越絕書 (Li Bujia 2013, 301; Milburn 2010, 285).
25. The "Great Unity" (Taiyi 太一) was another name for the Dao (Way), the unified origin of all things. As described in the *Nine Songs* (*Jiuge* 九歌) of the *Chuci* 楚辭 (*The Songs of Chu* [Sukhu 2017, 5–6], where Sukhu renders *taiyi* "Great Unique"), it also came to name a god that was worshipped during the Warring States period in the state of Chu. See also Milburn (2010, 282, n. 32).
26. Feilian 飛廉 is the god of wind.
27. The Chijin mountains, in Zhejiang near Shaoxing, were an important source of metal ore.
28. Ruoye (near Shaoxing), where the renowned beauty Xishi 西施 is said to have washed silk, is a source of copper used in swords: "The stream at Ruoye dried up and brought forth copper" (Milburn 2010, 281).
29. The sword Zhanlu 湛盧 apparently left King Helü of Wu (r. 514–496 BCE) because he was not possessed of the Way and went to offer itself to the worthier King of Chu. See the third year of the "Helü neizhuan" 闔閭內傳 in the *Wuyue chunqiu* (Zhou Shengchun 1997, 55–56; Milburn 2010, 282–83).
30. Juque 巨闕 was one of King Goujian's (r. 496–465 BCE) swords, known for its ability to cut stone and iron without breaking. On this sword, see "Waizhuan ji baojian" in *Yuejue shu* (Li Bujia 2013, 301; Milburn 2010, 280). Milburn notes that the Juque was mentioned in the *Xinxu* 新序 (New accounts), a collection compiled by Liu Xiang 劉向 (77-6 BCE), where it was said that the sword could cut through stone, citing Zhao Zhongyi 1997, 175 ["Zashi 雜事5"] (Milburn 2010, 280, n. 22). I follow Graham Sanders in translating *Xinxu* as "New Accounts" rather than "New Prefaces" as Milburn does (Sanders 2014, 101).
31. Feiying 飛影 (Flying Flash), likely refers to Feijing 飛景 (Flying Flash), the sword of Cao Pi 曹丕 (187–226), the first emperor of the state of Wei (220–266). An early account of its forging seems to have been included in *Dianlun* 典論 ("Normative disquisitions" in Knechtges's rendering), which has been lost. There is a reference to this sword in a comment in the "Jian" (Swords) section of the *Beitang shuchao* 北堂書鈔 included in the *Siku quanshu* (*juan* 122, 3b). See Cutter 2012, 537.
32. Eyebrow comment: Cao Gu'an 曹顧菴 [Cao Erkan 曹爾堪 (1617–1679)] says, "From inside the sword case comes a roar of thunder."
33. On the Longyuan ("Dragon Abyss") sword, see "Waizhuan ji baojian" in *Yuejue shu*. It is described as distinctive for its form, which is like climbing a mountain and looking into a deep abyss (Li Bujia 2013, 303; Milburn 2010, 285).

34. Liu Bang (256–195 BCE) was the first emperor of the Han dynasty. According to historical accounts, he slew a large snake, which was later identified as a "White Emperor" to him by a mysterious woman. He took this as a sign that he would eventually become emperor, which he did. See "Gaozu benji," *SJ j.* 8.350; Watson 1971, 80–81.
35. Ci Fei 佽飛, a man from the state of Chu, had recently acquired a sword, when he was confronted by two dragons while crossing the Yangzi River. He jumped into the river and beheaded both. See the translation of an early account of Ci Fei in the *Huainanzi* (Major 2010, 476). See also: Lü Buwei (2002, *j.* 20.1354–55); Knoblock and Riegel (2000, 518–19). On Ci Fei's slaughtering of dragons, see Milburn (2008, 425).
36. King Zhuang of Chu reigned from 613 to 592 BCE and is usually included in lists of the Five Hegemons of this period. See Blakely (1999, 62–64). This incident may refer to an account included in the "Renjian xun" (Among others) chapter of the *Huainanzi* in which King Zhuang of Chu attacked Song after all able-bodied men had perished, so children and elderly people had to climb the city walls to defend it. King Zhuang had all of them killed. The story is included to illustrate the way in which blindness exempted a father and son from participating, and thereby from death. See Major (2010, *j.* 18.7, 728). In the earlier version of the Chu siege of Song in the *Zuo Tradition*, King Zhuang behaves humanely. See *ZZ*, Xuan 15.2; *Zuo* 675–79.
37. Zhuan Zhu 專諸, from the state of Chu, was hired by the future King Helü to assassinate the latter's cousin, King Liao of Wu (r. 526–515 BCE). Zhuan Zhu posed as a servant at a banquet and killed the king with a dagger he had hidden inside a fish to be served. The account is included in the "The Biographies of the Assassin-Retainers" (*SJ j.* 86.2517–18) and multiple other early sources.
38. Eyebrow comment: Wang Ruanting (Wang Shizhen [1634–1711]) says, "Even Zhuangzi's 'Discourse on Swords' does not have such sound reasoning."
39. Eyebrow comment: Peng Xianmen 彭羨門 [Peng Sunyu, see introduction] says, "Like horse's tracks or strands of a spider's web, the lines of text wind round so naturally."
40. Eyebrow comment: Wang says, "Where they ascend and descend, even a startled goose or soaring dragon fail to offer an adequate analogy."
41. These lines allude to a famous poem by Du Mu 杜牧 (803–852) on the beautiful courtesans of Yangzhou, adroitly shifting the meaning of the earlier lines: "Graceful, swaying, she was all of thirteen, / Like a cardamon pod at the beginning of March." Translated in Li and Zimmerman (2014, 522); original in Du Mu (1984, vol. 4.82, 321).
42. The pole here refers to a long pole that acrobats would anchor at the base, and then climb up to perform handstands and other acts on the top. These four lines are self-referential—they describe stage directions, but also suggest that the playwright is congratulating himself on his achievement.
43. Refers to a tiger.
44. Yang Xiang 楊香 (Jin dynasty, 266–420) is remembered as a filial daughter. When her father was attacked by a tiger, she grabbed the tiger by the neck until it let her father go. The anecdote is included in the *zhiguai* collection *Yiyuan* 異苑 (Liu Song dynasty, 420–479), and is widely cited in later collections of accounts of filial actions. See Liu Jingshu (1996, 97).
45. It is possible that this is a reference to the Western Han official Li Guang 李廣 (d. 119 BCE), known for fighting the Xiongnu. He is supposed to have mistaken a rock for a crouching tiger and shot at it with such force that his arrow became embedded in the rock. In the account in *Shiji,* however, there is no reference to him sleeping on a pile of bones. See *SJ j.* 109.2865–78); Watson (1993, 117–28).
46. The person nursed by a tiger was Dou Gouwutu 鬭穀於菟, also known as Dou Ziwen 子文, Chancellor of Chu. See *ZZ*, Xuan 4: "Lady Yun had [Dou Gouwutu] abandoned at Meng Marsh. A tiger suckled him. When the master of Yun went hunting, he saw this and returned in fear. His wife told

him what had happened, and he thus had the child brought back. The Chu people called suckling *gou*, and tigers *wutu*. That was why the child was named Dou Gouwutu [Dou suckled by the tigress]" (*Zuo* 613).

47. Eyebrow comment: "Wang says, "The word 'gan' 敢 is a tricky one to rhyme!"
48. Eyebrow comment: "Peng says, "A marvelous line!"
49. The "Crow's Call" Bow is a reference to a bow used by the Yellow Emperor. "Crow's Call," or "Wuhao" 烏號, is the name of a tree related to the mulberry, identified by the translators of the *Huainanzi*, Harold D. Roth and Andrew Meyer, as *Cudrania tricuspidate,* or the melon berry tree. Gao You's traditional commentary on the *Huainanzi* suggests that it was so called because its branches were so sturdy that when a crow would land on a branch, the branch would bend and snap back, sending the bird and its nest flying. Since the bird did not wish to fly away, it would caw. See the comment to "Yuandao" [Originating in the Way] in Liu An and Liu Wendian 1989, 5b.
50. "Pulley-hilt Sword" (Lulu 鹿盧) is the name of the sword of Qin Shihuangdi (259–210 BCE), the first Qin emperor. Its hilt was made of jade fashioned in the shape of a well pulley.
51. This line originates in the "Western Capital Rhapsody" by Ban Gu 班固 (32–92), where it describes a hunting scene. See Knechtges (1982, 137).
52. Legend has it that a rabbit and a toad live on the moon.
53. These are references to Yang Youji 養由基 (d. ca. 559 BCE) causing apes to huddle under a tree and wail for fear of his arrows and the instant felling of a goose by the beautiful woman, Wang Zhaojun 王昭君 (b. ca. 50 BCE). For an account of the former, see *Huainanzi*: "The king of Chu had a white ape. When the king himself shot at it, the ape grabbed his arrows to show off. He ordered Yang Youji to shoot it. When [Yang] began to draw the bow and aim the arrow, [even] before he shot, the ape hugged a tree and shrieked" (Major 2010, 648). For the Chinese text, see Lü Buwei (2002, *j.* 25.1628); for another English translation Knoblock and Riegel (2000). For a comparative discussion of different versions of the story, see Van Gulik (1967, 41–42). Wang Zhaojun, who was sent to marry the leader of the northern Xiongnu group during the former Han dynasty, is said to have been so beautiful that passing geese forgot to flap their wings and fell to their deaths.
54. Nezha 那吒 is a Chinese transliteration of Nalakūvara or Nalakūbala, a fierce and powerful protector deity in Hindu and Buddhist scriptures. In the late-Ming novel *Fengshen yanyi* 封神演義, he is depicted as having been born as a ball of flesh, emerging as a child after his father attacks the ball, and he goes on to perform many miracles on behalf of the people. This aria is distinctive for the correspondence between the tune title and its content, which is appropriately fierce, and which associates Nie Yinniang with the role of Nezha.
55. Eyebrow comment: Wang says, "These daring words destroy ghosts' gall and turn it into extreme beauty."
56. A rat living in an altar or a fox in a city wall are used as examples of animals taking advantage of that which does not belong to them. There is an account of the altar rat in the *Yanzi chunqiu* 晏子春秋 (The Spring and Autumn Annals of Master Yan), Inner Chapters, Questions, Part One: "Lord Jing asked Master Yan: 'What should I beware of when governing the country?' Master Yan replied: 'You should beware of rats at the state altars.' His lordship said: 'What do you mean?' [Master Yan] replied: 'The state altars are constructed of lengths of wood tied together, bedaubed with mud. For that reason rats go and make their nests in them. If you try and smoke them out, I am afraid that you may set fire to the timbers; if you try and drown them, I am afraid that you will wash away the earth. The reason why these rats cannot be killed is because of the state altars. The state also has these creatures; they are your lordship's entourage. Within the palace, they conceal all rights and wrongs from your lordship. Outside the court, they sell their power and influence to the common people. If you do not

execute them, they will cause chaos; if you do try and execute them, then you discover that they are protected by the ruler who treats them as his trusted advisors" (Milburn 2015, 252). As for the fox in the city wall, in historian Xie Kun's 謝鯤 biography in the *Jinshu,* there is an account of how the general Wang Dun 王敦 (266–324) asked him to get rid of a corrupt official, Liu Kui 劉隗. Xie refuses on the grounds that he is a "fox in the city wall" or a "rat in an altar"—if one were to dig up the fox hole, the city wall would come down with it. See "Xie Kun zhuan" in "Liezhuan 19" in Fang Xuanling (1974, 1378).

57. During the Tianbao reign period (754–756) of Emperor Xuanzong of the Tang, Li Linfu 李林甫 (d. 753) was the prime minister. Li promoted the corrupt judge Luo Xishi 羅希奭 to the rank of imperial censor, and had Ji Wen 吉溫 manage the prison. The two worked together to frame and imprison many officials who opposed them. See Luo's biography in the "Biographies of Oppressive Officials, Part Two" 酷吏傳下 of the *Jiu Tang shu* 舊唐書 (*juan* 192). Liu Xu (1975, 4858–59).
58. Eyebrow comment: Wang says, "This could cure Cao Cao's headache!"
59. This allusion refers to the story that Confucius instructed his disciple Zigong to give away his horses to cover funeral costs. Here it refers to the possibility that Yinniang has given away her horse to help someone in need. See "Tangong" 檀弓, *Book of Rites* [*Liji* 禮記], translated in Legge (1885, 136–37).
60. On the assassin Jing Ke, see note 9. Jing Ke's attempted assassination of the future First Emperor is supposed to have been thwarted when a royal physician threw his medicine bag at Jing Ke. This line asks whether Yinniang has been attacked before carrying out her mission.
61. Chu Ni 鉏麑 (d. 607 BCE) was an official in the state of Jin during the Spring and Autumn period. Duke Ling of Jin commanded him to assassinate Zhao Dun 趙盾. He went to carry out the command, but when he saw Zhao Dun carefully arranging his official dress, he was impressed by his behavior and could not bear to go through with his plan, so he killed himself by dashing his head against a pagoda tree. See *ZZ*, Xuan 2.3 and *Zuo* 595. This line suggests that Yinniang might have had a change of heart.
62. The Tang tale "The Slave of Kunlun" (Kunlun nu 崑崙奴) by Pei Xing tells of a dark-skinned servant with magical abilities who aids his master in obtaining a woman the latter fell in love with while visiting a high-ranking minister (she was the minister's concubine). The servant makes several trips to secretly transport all of the woman's belongings out of the minister's mansion while she and his master wait. Although he uses magic, it still takes some time, thus its use here to mark the delay in Yinniang's return. This story was included in the collection *Chuanqi.* See Wang Pijiang (1971, 267–70) and Kao (1985, 351–56). This line asks whether Yinniang's mission had been delayed.
63. Eyebrow comment: Cao says, "This picks up the essence and spirit of Guan Hanqing and Ma Zhiyuan." (Guan Hanqing 關漢卿 [ca. 1225–1302] and Ma Zhiyuan 馬致遠 [ca. 1250–1321] were celebrated Yuan-period playwrights of the *zaju* dramatic form.)
64. Eyebrow comment: Peng says, "The entire range of actions of sages and the virtuous, immortals and buddhas, extraordinary heroes and treacherous conspirators is covered with these few words."
65. Vermillion Cliffs is one of the designations of Hainan, the southernmost point of the empire, well-known as a place of banishment.
66. Green Pearl (Lüzhu 綠珠), known for her exceptional beauty, was the favorite concubine of Shi Chong 石崇 (249–300). The emperor's brother-in-law became infatuated with her and tried to force her to marry him. She leapt to her death, and fifteen members of Shi Chong's family were later executed. See Shi Bao's 石苞 biography in *juan* 33 of Fang Xuanling (1974, 1008).
67. Specifically, a "Man" chignon. "Man" is an abbreviation for "Wuman," and it indicates here a hairstyle associated with the ethnic group of the same name from southwest China. The story of Red

Thread remarks that she wore this hairstyle, so it has an established association with female knights-errant by this time.

68. Kroran (*pinyin*: Loulan 樓蘭) refers to an ancient kingdom in the Tarim Basin in modern-day Xinjiang, whose inhabitants nowadays are thought to have been related to the Indo-European Tocharians. In the Chinese historical record, Kroran was contemporaneous with the Han dynasty, and its status vacillated between independent, tributary, and Han-controlled. Mummies from the area have been dated to nearly 2000 BCE. See Mallory and Mair (2000). This line alludes to a Tang poem by Zhang Zhongsu 張仲素 (769–819), "Saixia qu wushou" 塞下曲五首.
69. Eyebrow comment: Peng says, "Not too much and not too little: this sentence renders her stance perfectly."
70. The "wooden fish" is a hollowed woodblock shaped like a fish that is beaten with a mallet in Mahāyāna Buddhist rituals.
71. Eyebrow comment: Cao says, "The hand of a genius, the spirit of a master of elegy, the courage of a soaring immortal or knight-errant."
72. These are common Mahāyāna Buddhist practices. "Namo" means "to pay homage to" and is chanted with the name of the Buddha as a devotional practice.
73. The Six Ding 丁 deities are *yin* deities of the void, complementing the Six Jia 甲 generals, which are *yang* deities. Both were derived from the heavenly stems and earthly branches (*tiangan dizhi*). See Schipper (1993, 143). The "Paces of Yu" is a ritual sequence of steps based on the limping dance of the ancient Yu after he controlled the floods. See Schipper (1993, 173). All these magical skills are associated with Daoist martial techniques such as invisibility and impermeability. They are described in detail in Ge Hong's (283–after 343) *Baopuzi* (The master who embraces simplicity). See Campany 2002.
74. These lines again distinguish between Mahāyāna Buddhist practices, represented by the bodhisattva Guanyin (Avalokiteśvara) and deemed acceptable in this play, and esoteric Daoist practices, represented by power over nature and deemed as posing a threat in this play.
75. Eyebrow comment: Peng says, "Of course a skilled writer would write like this."
76. Eyebrow comment: Peng says, "Is it a beautiful woman or an immortal knight-errant, or are they one and the same?"
77. In Sunzi's *Art of War,* the stillness of serene maidens is contrasted with the swiftness of hares, and maidens and hares are used as metaphors to describe warfare strategies: "For this reason, at the beginning be as still as a virgin, but when the enemy relaxes his guard, spring forth like a rabbit that has escaped from its cage" (Mair 2007, 124). From the *jiudi* chapter in Sunzi 1987, 30. In *Black and White Donkeys,* the female disciples defy expectations for young girls in their swiftness, and by alluding to these terms in the *Art of War,* You Tong draws attention to that defiance.
78. Eyebrow comment: Wang says, "They are described in such a hazy and barely discernable way that I waver between belief and doubt."
79. Intended for the treatment of *yang* deficiency. See "Stalactite [*Shi zhong ru*]" in the "Metals and Rocks [*Jinshi*]" section of *Bencao gangmu* by Li Shizhen. In Zhang Zhibin et al. (2001, 553–55).
80. "Green snake" (*qingshe* 青蛇) refers to a sword. In Bai Juyi's 白居易 (772–846) rhapsody on Liu Bang's slaying a white snake, the sword with which he does so is a "green snake." See *Han Gao huangdi qin zhan baishe fu* 漢高皇帝親斬白蛇賦 in Bai Juyi (1999, 592).
81. Eyebrow comment: Wang says, "One can put an end to tyranny with Zizhang's skull." (Duan Zizhang 段子璋 [ca. 761] was a prefect in the Sichuan region during the Tang dynasty. He rebelled and was able to gain control over the region for about a month before he was captured and beheaded. His story is recorded in the *Suzong benji* 肅宗本紀 [*juan* 10] of the *JTS* (261.)

82. Dong Zhuo 董卓 (d. 192) was a military general who attempted to usurp the throne at the end of the Han dynasty.
83. Wang Mang 王莽 (45 BCE–23CE) was a Han dynasty official who overthrew the ruling family and founded the Xin dynasty in 9 CE.
84. Cao Cao 曹操 (155–220) was a chancellor at the end of the Han dynasty who controlled the emperor without officially overthrowing the dynasty.
85. See note 57 above. Li Linfu (d. 753) was chief minister during the Tang dynasty from 734 to 752 who was blamed for weakening the court leading up to the An Lushan rebellion. Among the men listed in this and the previous three lines of the play (and identified in notes 82 to 85), he is the only one who is historically close to the events described in the play.
86. Eyebrow comment: Peng says, "The words of an expert!"
87. The "ranting and raging" here likens Nie Yinniang to Xiang Yu 項羽 (232–202 BCE), the hegemon-king of Chu who battled Liu Bang for the right to rule all of China after the dissolution of the Qin. See the biography of "Marquis of Huai-yin" (Han Hsin) 淮陰侯列傳 in Watson (1993, 211): "When Xiang Yu rages and bellows it is enough to make a thousand men fall down in terror."
88. Eyebrow comment: Cao says, "The writing flashes like lightning, striking suddenly. One cannot look too closely!"
89. Both refer to a young woman who has reached marriageable age.
90. This line is likely a reference to Chen Ziliang's 陳子良 (575–632) poem, "Seeing the Bride Stopped in a Carriage Across the Way On the Double Seventh" 七夕看新婦隔巷停車." *QTS* (vol. 1, 502, *j.* 39).
91. The Mysterious Woman of the Nine Heavens, first mentioned in Han-period texts, was a goddess of war, sex, and eternal life who was eventually incorporated into the pantheon of Daoist deities. See Cahill (1992).
92. This line is from the "Tengwen Gong" *xia* (3b) chapter of the *Mencius*. See Bloom and Ivanhoe (2009, 63–64).
93. Gan Jiang 干將 (*yang*) and Mo Ye 莫邪 (*yin*) are the names of "husband" and "wife" swords. They were made in the state of Wu by a husband and wife for King Helü of Wu. After the swordsmith Gan Jiang had worked for three months without producing a sword, his wife suggested that they first required human elements to transform the metal, so she cut her hair and nails and added them to the fire. The metal finally melted, and two swords, one *yin* and the other *yang*, were formed. See the "Helü neizhuan" 闔閭內傳 in the *Wuyue chunqiu*, Zhou Shengchun (1997, 40).
94. Eyebrow comment: Peng says, "Such deft flair as this!"
95. "Myriarch" is a Jin-Yuan term for a military leader who was head of ten thousand households.
96. Luofu 羅敷 was known as a stunning beauty. An anonymous song about her was included in the 6th c. collection of love poetry, *New Songs from a Jade Terrace* (*Yutai xinyong* 玉臺新詠). See Birrell (1982, 33–34). "Half a mirror" alludes to a story about a Princess Lechang 樂昌公主, who lived during the Chen dynasty (557–589). During a period of unrest, when she and her husband were separated, each took half a mirror as a token of their love in the hope that they would be reunited and the mirror made whole again. For this anecdote, which was preserved in Meng Qi's 孟棨 *Benshi shi* 本事詩, and its translation, see Sanders (2006, 262–64). Afterward, "half a mirror" became a common reference to a token of devotion promising reunion.

    Eyebrow comment: Cao says, "The way in which these heroic words are bundled into delicate sentences is just like 'autumn ripples turned back on parting'—very nearly sublime." The backward glance on parting is a well-known line in the popular play *The Story of the Western Wing*, "How can I withstand her, who turned her autumn ripples on me as she left?" West and Idema (1995, 123). Here, it may refer to a playful eight-legged essay that You Tong wrote, "A Turn of Autumn's Ripples" 怎當他

臨去秋波那一轉. See Stephen H. West's unpublished translation, "1499 Edition of *Xixiang ji* Essay 'On Autumn's ripples'; You Tong's Eight-legged Essay on 'A Turn of Autumns' Ripples,'" https://www.academia.edu/2265426/1499_Edition_of_Xixiang_ji_Essay_On_Autumns_ripples_You_Tongs_Eight_legged_Essay_on_A_Turn_of_Autumns_Ripples_Translation. Presented at the Association for Asian Studies annual conference, Toronto, 2012. For a discussion of this and other playful eight-legged essays, see Wu (2016.)

97. The instrument mentioned here is the *sheng* 笙, a free-reed woodwind instrument that consists of many vertical bamboo pipes of varying lengths fitted into a bowl. Wang Ziqiao was the son of King Ling of Zhou (r. 571–545 BCE), and he played the *sheng* in the manner of a phoenix's call. He learned the art of Daoist cultivation from a Daoist, and one day rode away on a crane. See Wang Shumin (1995, 65–68).
98. Eyebrow comment: Wang says, "A needle that hits the right place—there is no room for a Chan turning phrase." According to Dōgen (1200–1253) "a pivot word or turning phrase [. . .] manifests the 'great function of the buddha-dharma' and says it should immediately awaken those who hear it" Maraldo (2009, 205).
99. Legend has it that Wu Gang 吳剛 was charged to cut down an endlessly regenerating cassia tree on the moon as punishment for a crime. The specific nature of the crime ranges from laziness to murder in various accounts.
100. Pei Hang 裴航 is from a Tang *chuanqi* tale, "The Tale of Pei Hang," in Pei Xing's collection *Transmitting the Strange* [*Chuanqi*]. Pei Hang is a scholar who wishes to marry a beautiful woman. To win her hand, he must grind cinnabar into a powder with mortar and pestle for one hundred days. Wang Pijiang (1971, 272–75).
101. Eyebrow comment: Peng says, "In this small painting the dragon turning to face its ancestors appears once again."
102. Eyebrow comment: Cao says, "Startling intellect and matchless beauty!"
103. The ducks are duck-shaped incense burners.
104. A red rug would traditionally indicate a stage for theatrical performance.
105. Eyebrow comment: Peng says, "Lines that would please even Tang Xianzu." Among the most celebrated playwrights in Chinese history, Tang Xianzu (1550–1616) is best known for his play *The Peony Pavilion*.
106. Eyebrow comment: Wang says, "Having read this far, one cannot help but slap the table and shout 'Bravo!'"
107. Liu Changyi 劉昌裔 (752–813) is a historical figure from the Tang period. He held the position of military governor of the Chenxu Circuit, also known as the Zhongwu 忠武 Circuit, in modern-day Xuchang (Xu) and Huaiyang (Chen) in Henan Province. See "Liezhuan 101" *JTS* 4056–57.
108. Tian Ji'an 田季安 (781–812) is a historical figure from the Tang period. Tian Ji'an's father, Tian Xu, assassinated Tian Yue, military governor of Weibo Circuit, and took his position. Tian Xu married a daughter of Tang emperor Dezong, and she adopted Ji'an as her own son. Upon Tian Xu's death in 796, Ji'an succeeded him as military governor of Weibo. An introduction to the Tian clan's rule is found in Peterson (1979, 464–560, especially 493–548); Tian Ji'an is mentioned in passing on p. 540.
109. The Zhang River runs through the ancient city of Ye, north of the Yellow River, in modern day Hebei Province. It has an association with female knights-errant, as Red Thread also observes the eastward flow of the river Zhang in the account of her life. See Yee (1985).
110. The reference here is to sacrificial paper money, not actual money.
111. Nongyu 弄玉 was the daughter of Duke Mu of Qin during Spring and Autumn period. She fell in love with a flute master Xiao Shi 簫史, who was living in a cave. He taught her to play the flute like a

phoenix call, which attracted phoenixes, and one day they flew away riding astride the phoenixes. Recorded as "Xiao Shi" in the *Liexian zhuan*. See Wang Shumin (1995, 80–84).

112. Eyebrow comment: Peng says, "From the pedestal of the Yuan masters!"
113. Daliang (modern Kaifeng in Henan Province) was the capital of Wei during the Warring States period.
114. The Bronze Sparrow Terrace at Ye (not Daliang [modern Kaifeng]) was initially associated with Cao Cao, but over time grew to be associated more strongly with the female performers who had offered ritual performances after his death. See Tsao (2017).
115. Eyebrow comment: Cao says, "A most melodious musical composition!"
116. This is a reference to the Battle of Handan during the Warring States period. The state of Qin had invaded the state of Zhao, and the latter sought help from the state of Wei. Lord Xinling 信陵君, a noble scion of Wei, was related to Lord Pingyuan 平原君, the brother of the Zhao king. Initially, the king of Wei was willing to aid Zhao, and sent his general Jin Bi 晉鄙 with 100,000 troops, but after Qin threatened to attack any state that aided Zhao, the king ordered his troops to desist. Lord Xinling wished to circumvent the king's orders and carry out the military aid. The queen agreed to help by sneaking a military tally out of the king's private quarters. Jin Bi was not convinced by the ruse, so Lord Xinling had his butcher friend, Zhu Hai 朱亥, kill Jin Bi and take over command of the Wei army himself. See "Wei gongzi liezhuan" in *SJj.* 77.2377–81); Nienhauser (1994, vol. 7.216–18).
117. Zhang Liang 張良 (250–186 BCE) was born into the state of Hán 韓 during the Warring States period. After Qin conquered Hán, he tried to assassinate Qin Shihuang, but failed. He then became an advisor to Liu Bang, and helped found the Hàn 漢 dynasty. See "Liu Hou shijia" ("The Hereditary House of the Marquis of Liu [Zhang Liang]") in *SJj.* 55.2033–49 and Watson (1971, 134–35). Zulong 祖龍 is another name for Qin Shihuang.
118. "He" refers to the henchman Zhang Liang, just mentioned, had hired. Bolangsha is the name of a place in modern Henan Province.
119. Yimen is the Yi gate of Daliang. See note 113 above. Using the military tally was Hou Ying's 侯嬴 idea. He had previously been criticized for not showing proper deference to the Royal Scion Lord Xinling, but Lord Xinling recognized his hidden talent.
Eyebrow comment: Peng says, "Genius! Genius!"
120. Ruan Ji 阮籍 (210–263) was a talented and eccentric poet who lived during the upheaval of the Three Kingdoms period. See Owen and Swartz (2017, 3–25). Mt. Guangwu was the site of a decisive battle between Chu and Han in 204 BCE, as Xiang Yu and Liu Bang each sought to unite China under their rule. Ruan Ji could be referring to either or both of them.
121. To make his beautiful wife smile. The lesson conveyed by the anecdote is that good speech is like shooting: if he does not speak up, a talented man may be overlooked. See *ZZ* 28, *Zuo* vol. 3, 1690–93.
Eyebrow comment: Wang says, "I happened to read this today en route to Rugao, and I laughed in spite of myself!"
122. Eyebrow comment: Wang says, "Every word is so natural—I suspect the gods have lent him a hand."
123. This is a reference to Wen Jiao 溫嶠 (288–339) lighting a rhinoceros horn in order to reveal the forms of creatures beneath the water's surface. Later the expression comes to mean an ability to discern the depths of things.
Eyebrow comment: Wang says, "When heroes converse, naturally it is remarkable."
124. This idiom eventually came to describe an inept official, but it originally indicated a person who was literally on the verge of death.
125. Eyebrow comment: Cao says, "Rustic, and yet also refined: he is a virtuoso of playwriting."

126. The metaphor of a bird choosing a tree alludes to Confucius's refusal to advise on matters he did not consider in keeping with ritual propriety. As recorded in the *Zuozhuan,* refusing to advise Kong Wenzi, an official from the state of Wei, on warfare, Confucius stated, "A bird chooses its tree, but how can a tree choose a bird?" See *Zuo* vol 3, 1905.
127. Eyebrow comment: Wang says, "Unmatched excellence!"
128. "Jing" 精 means "essence," and this name might be translated as "Aetherea."
129. Eyebrow comment: Cao says, "These words are like Li [Bai] and Du [Fu] among poets and Ni [Zan] and Huang [Gongwang] among painters." Li Bai 李白 and Du Fu 杜甫 are the best-known poets of the Tang dynasty, while Ni Zan 倪瓚 and Huang Gongwang 黃公望 are two of the Four Masters of Yuan-dynasty painting.
130. Eyebrow comment: Wang says, "This is just like the record in *The Glory of Yue* of King Fuchai of Wu's cursing of his vassal Gongsun Sheng." For a translation and interpretation, see "The Record of the Divination of the King of Wu's Dream" in Milburn (2010, 257–72). It includes such lines as, "The king ordered Shi Fan, a very strong man, to beat Sheng with an iron bar, and he hit him until the bar broke into two pieces" (264), and "May tigers and wolves eat your flesh, may the wildfires roast your bones, so that when the east wind arrives it can stir your ashes" (265).
131. "Kong" 空 means "emptiness," and this name might be translated as "Void o' Voids."
132. Quoted text from book 14 of the *Daode jing.* This translation is from Hinton (2015, 46). The final line is a variant, reading in the standard *Daode jing* as, in Hinton's translation, "Held tight but never felt, it takes the name *gossamer*" (46).
133. Eyebrow comment: Wang says, "Between ethereal and earthly, she travels without hindrance."
134. That is, 813 CE.
135. "Coiled dragon" here may refer to her husband's hidden identity as the immortal Wang Ziqiao, as a synonym for the "hidden dragon" of the idiom "hidden dragon, crouching tiger." The term could also indicate Yinniang's husband's occupation as a mirror polisher through reference to the common "coiled-dragon" design featured on mirrors.
136. The Goddess of River Luo is a mythical deity, supposed to have been supremely beautiful. In the best-known literary treatment of her, she is invisible to all but the poet Cao Zhi. His "Rhapsody on the Goddess of the River Luo [Luoshen fu 洛神賦]," describes her this way: "Her body soars lightly like a startled swan, / Gracefully, like a dragon in flight." See Watson (2000, 314–18, quoted text 315). For the original poem, see Zhao Youwen (2016, 419–37).

    These lines rework the closing lines of the "Tale of Red Thread," which in turn is citing a quatrain written by Xue Song's 薛嵩 retainer Leng Chaoyang 冷朝陽 at the parting banquet for Red Thread. For the original poem, see *QTS* 3473. The lines here include many of the same images as the quatrain and establish their status as a standard parting song for a woman knight-errant:

    Singing "Plucking Water Caltrops," we lamented in the magnolia boat;
    When we parted, our spirits melted away in the hundred-foot tower.
    She returns like the Goddess of the L[u]o River, riding the morning mist;
    Beneath the boundless turquoise sky, the river flows on forever.

    Translated in Yee (1985, 369–70).
137. Eyebrow comment: Wang says, "One sees the magic dragon's head, but not its tail—the charm lies in its unpredictability."
138. Both "noble man" and "Lord of the Mountains" are common references to gibbons. See Zhao Lin (1939, 11) and Van Gulik (1967). On Mr. Yuan and the Maiden of Zhao, see note 15.
139. "Ten-thousand stone" here is a measure of the strength of the bow. Gibbons were thought to be far more adept with the bow than humans because of their longer arms. Guo Pu wrote an encomium to

an illustration in the *Shanhai jing* 山海經 (*Classic of Mountains and Seas*) that praises the gibbon's skill with the bow and arrow:

The White-Gibbon's skill is without doubt.
Like Yang Youji it can draw a bow.
Casting but a glance, it lets out a shout
Instinctively hitting the mark just so.
Time after time, it never gives out.
Its marvelous talent presents an endless show.

Translated in Strassberg (2002, 85). For the original, see Hao Yixing (1900, 1b).

140. The "rock of three incarnations" is featured in the story of the friendship between lay Buddhist Li Yuan 李源 and the monk Yuanguan 圓觀. In the story, Yuanguan predicts that he will die and then be reincarnated as a particular child, and he instructs his friend Li Yuan to meet him in thirteen years at the "rock of three incarnations." Thus, the rock serves as a meeting place for those separated by life and death. For this account, see "Yuanguan" in *TPGJ j.* 387, 3089–90.

141. This line quotes the lyric "Man jiang hong" 滿江紅 attributed to the Song general Yue Fei 岳飛 (1101–1141). That fiercely loyalist poem opens like this:

My hair bristles in my helmet.
Standing by the balcony as the rain shower stops,
I look up to the sky and loudly let Heaven know
The strength of my passions.

Translated in Ebrey (1993, 169). The allusion to Yue Fei's poem here would intensify the sense of loyalty to the lost Ming dynasty.

142. Eyebrow comments: Peng says, "Genius! Genius!" Wang says, "[The ability to write the poems] 'Traveling beyond the Borders' [and] 'Roaming with Immortals' are combined in one hand. How many Tang poets does he topple?"

143. This line borrows from Wang Wei's 王維 (d. 761) description of a mountain scene in the poem "Floating on the Han River" (Hanjiang linfan 漢江臨汎). See *QTS j.* 126, 1279.

144. The three peaks are Lotus (*furong* 芙蓉), Jade Maiden (*yunü* 玉女), and Bright Star (*mingxing* 明星).

145. Wugong is another mountain range in Hunan.

146. Eyebrow comment: Wang says, "'The Bronze Tower rising high and the Zhang River flowing eastward:' Looking at this, it seems as though [the earlier account] is lacking in skill." (This comment quotes a line from the Tang *chuanqi*, "The Tale of Red Thread." In Anon. (1936, 38) and trans. in Yee (1985, 367).

147. The Zhongtiao Mountains in Shanxi Province are associated with Daoism, and Magu 麻姑 is a Daoist immortal. See Campany (2002, 259–70).

148. "Blue Zither" (Qingqin 青琴) is a fairy who drowned in Luo River. "Jade Stream" is the residence of the Queen Mother of the West.

149. Master Yellow Rock (Huangshigong 黃石公) was Zhang Liang's teacher. Gu City (in modern-day Hubei) was where he lived. See note 117.

150. Eyebrow comment: Cao says, "In a guesthouse on a scorching day, I happened to hear some music from my neighbor to the west while I read this through a few times, and I sighed, feeling that something had shifted in me, as if I had immersed my body in a cold kettle and forgotten that it was on a cooking steamer."

151. That is, the immortal Wang Ziqiao. See note 97.

152. Yinniang's family name, Nie 聶, is written with three ear components 耳.

153. Eyebrow comment: Wang says, "So the canniness of his writing goes so far as this!"

154. Tian Dan 田單 was made general in the state of Qi during the Warring States period, when Qi had been overrun by its northern neighbor Yan. He successfully defended Jimo when it was one of Qi's last remaining cities, and helped Qi regain its lost territories. Biography in *SJ* 82. See "Tian Dan liezhuan" in *SJ j.* 82.453–57. Liu Biao 劉表 (144–208) was governor of Jingzhou, and a warlord at the end of the Han dynasty. He successfully defended Jingzhou against an attack by Yuan Shu 袁術 (155-199). See Mansvelt Beck (1986). Both Tian Dan and Liu Biao were canny strategists, committed to defending their territory. Yinniang's reference to them here serves to minimize the importance of such loyalty in worldly affairs, to Liu Changyi, and even to her husband.
155. "To draw a snake and add legs" is an idiom from the *Zhanguo ce* 戰國策 (*Strategies of the Warring States*). A group of men hold a snake-drawing competition to determine who will win the small amount of wine available. After the first finishes, he adds legs to his drawing, allowing another man to finish first and win the wine. The expression refers to something superfluous. See "Zhaoyang wei Chu fa Wei" in "Qice er," Liu Xiang (1995, vol.1.355–56).
156. The expression "Goose tracks in the snow" is credited to the poetic genius Su Shi 蘇軾 (1037–1101), who compared human life to the fleeting tracks of wild geese left on snow in the poem, "He Ziyou Mianchi huaijiu" 和子由澠池懷舊. See Su Shi (1968, 12).
157. "Old magpie's nest" refers to her life before she returns to the human world.
158. "Yellow Millet Dream" (*huangliang meng* 黃粱夢) refers to the Tang tale, "Record from Inside a Pillow" (Zhenzhong ji 枕中記), by Shen Jiji 沈既濟 (late 8th c.), in which a young man dreams that he lives a full life, only to awaken and discover that the millet his companion, a Daoist immortal, was cooking on the stove was not yet done. Thus, he learned that "life is but a dream." See Knickerbocker (2010).

     Eyebrow comment: Peng says, "Masterful! Matchless!"
159. Traveling westward here indicates India, and, by extension, Buddhism.
160. Eyebrow comment: Wang says, "In the end, all is revealed: Fenggan blathers on and the granny's compassion is fervent." Fenggan 豐干, known for his nonsensical responses to questions, was a Chan monk who lived during the early Tang dynasty. "Granny's compassion" refers to "Chan masters who had a deep enough love and compassion for their students to make use of seemingly ruthless, even violent, devices to awaken their minds." See Grant (2009, 32). Both expressions imply that at this point in the play, enlightenment is imminent.
161. Eyebrow comment: Wang says, "'When drunk, I open my marten-fur coat, and count the arrow scars': the mood of that like is just like this."
162. Mistress Gongsun 公孫大娘 was a historical dancer from the Tang who lived in the early eighth century. Altenburger documents how she went from being known as a dancer to being associated with the Nie Yinniang–type of swordswoman. See Altenburger (2009, 208), citing Peterson (2016, 209–11).
163. "The Old Man of Shaoling" refers to the great Tang poet Du Fu. For the poem, see note 19.
164. These two lines refer to the disruptions of the An Lushan rebellion (755–763), which would have brought the bustling pleasure quarters to an abrupt end. Baidi City (Kuizhou, in modern Sichuan Province) is the place where the poet Du Fu stayed for some years during the rebellion. The translation "Courtyard Fit for Spring" is borrowed from Li (2020, 68).
165. Eyebrow comment: Peng says, "The technique of supplementing."
166. Zhao Zhongli 趙中立 should be Zhao Zhongxing. Li Zhenglang is Li Thirty-nine. See note 19 above.
167. In the original version of the story, Jing the Thirteenth delivers the courtesan in a sack to Li (so he can marry her), along with the heads of her parents.
168. This widow is discussed in "*SJ j.* 129: The Biographies of the Money-Makers" (Watson 1993, 440): "There was also the case of a widow named Qing 清 of the region of Ba and Shu. Her ancestors got possession of some cinnabar caves and were able to monopolize the profits from them for several

generations until they had acquired an inestimable amount of wealth. Qing, although only a widow, was able to carry on the business and used her wealth to buy protection for herself so that others could not mistreat or impose upon her. The First Emperor of the Qin, considering her a virtuous woman, treated her as a guest and built the Nühuaiqing Terrace in her honour."

169. Zhao Sheng (308–251 BCE). See *SJ j*.7.2365–66.
170. Possibly a reference to the girl's madam.
171. Fan Li was an advisor to King Goujian of the state of Yue during the Spring and Autumn period. In his retirement, he is said to have drifted about on Lake Tai with the renowned beauty Xi Shi.
172. "Wen Xiao" 文簫 is another Tang *chuanqi* tale by Pei Xing, included in his collection *Chuanqi*. Wen Xiao, a poor scholar, falls in love with a beautiful woman, Wu Cailuan 吳彩鸞. It turns out that she is an immortal, and she gets into trouble with her heavenly superiors for her close relationship with a mortal. She marries Wen Xiao and supports him, first by selling manuscripts rendered in her excellent calligraphy and later by teaching. Finally, they drift away into the mountains, and were spotted riding tigers in the wilderness. The *chuanqi* version of the story has not been preserved, but several other versions exist, including one from the 13th century titled "Entering the Divine Altar" (*Ru xiantan* 入仙壇) included in *juan* 33 of *Suishi guangji* 歲時廣記 by Chen Yuanjing 陳元靚 (1939, 371–72).
173. For a translation of this tale, see Feng (2017).
174. References the Tang *chuanqi* "Tian Penglang" 田膨郎. This story takes place during the reign of Emperor Wenzong of the Tang (r. 827–840). Someone steals the emperor's white jade pillow, and a servant helps discover the thief, who turns out to be a man named Tian Penglang. This story is included in Anon. (1936, 41–45).
175. References the Tang *chuanqi* "Kunlun nu," by Pei Xing. See note 62. Mo'le 磨勒 is the name of the dark-skinned servant and Hongxiao 紅綃 that of the woman he abducts for his master.
Eyebrow comment: Peng says, "How exceedingly well they enhance one another!"
176. See note 11. The lines in quotation marks are taken verbatim from the *Tale of Red Thread*. See Yee (1985).
177. The lines in quotation marks are adapted from the poem by Leng Chaoyang, "Seeing off Red Thread," which was included in the *Tale of Red Thread*. For a translation of the poem, see note 136.
Eyebrow comment: Peng says, "It is just perfect that he has used this line from Leng Chaoyang's poem here."
178. Eyebrow comment: Peng says, "If anything further were said, it would be a sign of an inferior brush."
179. Eyebrow comments: Peng says, "You Tong is a true genius." Wang says, "Reaching this point, I've grown overwhelmed for some time now without realizing it. I also say that You Tong is a genius."
180. This line is taken from Fu Xuan's 傅玄 (217–278) poem, "Yange xing" 艷歌行. See Guo Maoqian (1989, vol. 2, 442).
181. This line alludes to an anecdote about a man named Chen Tuan 陳摶 who lived in reclusion just before the Song dynasty was established (in 960). He is supposed to have fallen off his donkey and laughed when he heard the news that Zhao Kuangyin had succeeded in founding the Song dynasty. Later the expression came to indicate peace following a period of chaos. Here it means that since the evil people will have been killed, the world will be at peace. See Chen Tuan's biography in "Biographies of recluses" (Yinyi zhuan 隱逸傳) in Wang (1795, vol. 12, *j*. 118, 1b).
Eyebrow comment: Wang says, "A most superb and excellent poem!"

10

Zaju from the Studio of Singing on the Wind

YANG CHAOGUAN (1710–1789)
TRANSLATED BY STEPHEN H. WEST

Yang Chaoguan 楊潮觀 (1710–1789) was born into an impoverished but well-educated family; his father and grandfather had both been students in the county schools, as was Yang Chaoguan himself. He was raised as a foster son in the household of his father's elder brother; unfortunately, his uncle died early and the household was plunged into dire poverty, leaving Yang Chaoguan as the sole responsible male. He was a gifted calligrapher and writer, however, and brilliant enough at age fifteen to be invited to a gathering of the literary elite in Suzhou that was held under the auspices of the eminent Manchu official Örtai (1677–1745). At age seventeen, he supposedly compiled a large work, *The Combined Essentials of Good Governance from Past to Present* (*Gujin zhiping huiyao* 古今治平彙要), a fourteen-volume text that laid out practical advice for would-be officials.[1]

Despite his literary gifts, he never succeeded in the Advanced Scholar examinations and spent most of his career as a local official in Shanxi, Henan, Yunnan, and Sichuan. During his thirty-odd year career he was a prolific writer and, in addition to poetry and prose, he also compiled his collection of one-act plays, *Thirty-Two Plays from the Studio of Singing on the Wind*. From the time that the famous literatus Yuan Mei 袁枚 (1716–1798) wrote his biography of Yang, it has been assumed that the name of his studio, "Singing on the Wind," derived from a construction of a detached two-story studio on the supposed site of Zhuo Wenjun's toilette loft:

> He [Yang] had no strong desires by nature, just abandoning himself to the composition of musical lyrics and loving flowers and bamboo. When he was in Qiong Prefecture in Sichuan, he obtained the old site of Zhuo Wenjun's makeup loft and constructed a Studio of Singing on the Wind in several rooms. When the clerks and people of the area came to offer birthday wishes they all brought flowers and trees to

> plant. They selected dozens of plays from past and present that could affect the world and turned them over to actors to perform in order to celebrate the studio's completion.[2]

But, as the modern scholar Du Guiping has pointed out,[3] he had consistently used this name for his literary studio wherever he was stationed; the Sichuan construction was simply the first building he designed for that purpose. Yang was by all accounts a caring magistrate. He saved the lives of many by opening the public granaries at appropriate times and he spared the lives of invalids and the disabled by exempting them from corvée labor tax. As Yuan Mei remarked in his biography of Yang:

> The gentleman was an official for more than thirty years, and he held sixteen different offices. He worked tirelessly guided by the single principle of perfecting himself by enriching the lives of others. When he was in Wenshui County [in Shanxi] he arrived at the five-year review of the population and tax registers. For several years the corvée tax had been unequally applied and the gentleman himself made fine distinctions in the register. He exempted about a thousand of the widowed, widowers, orphaned, and solitary. Once he passed Qi County [in Henan] and there were more than a hundred men and women, decrepit and disabled, who were burning incense at the side of the road. The head of the local neighborhood unit head pointed to them and said, "These are people you have saved." The gentleman was amazed, and the unit head said, "Don't you remember, sir, in such-and-such a year the case where you came back from a trip providing relief? Your superiors would not allow you to claim reimbursement? These were the people saved by you having to take it from your own salary."[4]

This is one of several anecdotes in the biography that show Yang's compassion for those he ministered as well as the practical bent to his mode of governing. He retired in his seventies with a near unblemished record of achievement. On his seventieth birthday, Yang held a renewal of his marriage vows with his wife of many years, a gathering attended by his sons and grandsons.

The picture that this kind of evidence gives is of a committed Confucian scholar, engaged in the quotidian chores of administering local populations at the lowest level of government, where he concentrated on the practical implementation of activities of direct benefit to the local populace. Yang was not stodgy, however, and we see in his plays a lively and somewhat sardonic view of officialdom, of family behavior, and of relations with the unseen. His plays are noted for their didactic nature, but as several other readers have remarked, he carried this off with a literary aesthetic and an open mind that enlivens the action and brings the protagonists closer to real life than to models of stereotypical didactic behavior. There is humor and compassion mixed in with a tendency toward moral education. We can get a sense of these paradoxical strands in his short preface to his collection:

The musical lyrics of "On the Wind" are what I wrote from inspiration in idle times during my past public service. Are they the pipes of heaven?[5] Or are they the pipes of men? I clearly do not know myself. As the years passed, I began to deliberate on [the plays] one by one with close friends, and set them to wind and string instruments, but it is only when I reached this point in my life that I can begin to give them their final, error-free, form.

Now, grief and happiness mutually affect other—in their sounds, there is poetry. They are a forest of human success and failure. It has been a long time now that men of learning and position have made poetry—but without singing it. The wind and moon are borderless, the mountains and rivers like a painting—can I not be stirred emotionally by them?

Bai Juyi 白居易 (772–846) simply hoped that all old crones would understand his verse; Xie An 謝安 (320–385) could not avoid the fact that the younger generation would also become aware of [his feelings about old age].[6] The time: Autumn of the *jiawu* year of Qianlong [late 1774].[7]

Yang begins the preface by asking a question about whether what he had learned during his idle time was an inspiration that arose from the subjective consciousness of his own being, or whether it came from his observation of human activity. That is, how much was imagination and how much was reality? The lack of clarity becomes moot as he commits the stories to music as drama, which of course relies on both sources of inspiration. His second paragraph continues the doublet of nature—the endlessness of time and beauty amenable to shaping by humans—and the social and political lives of people and the emotions they create. He invokes the ancient belief that poetry is the expression of a moral or aesthetic reaction, stimulated by the conditions that one encounters in relationships with others, with nature, or with time as historical process. Leaving his poetic drama behind for others, he claims to have made them understandable to all and, in a wry poke at his own inability to conceal his feelings, realizes that he cannot avoid an excess of emotion that will lay bare his inner thoughts for those who follow.

In the earliest texts, there is a short preface for each play listed in sequence. For the benefit of modern readers, these small prefaces have been moved to the front of each play, a custom we follow below. After these thirty-two short introductions to the plays, the collection then follows with a "dedication" (*tici* 題詞). The term "dedication" is used to introduce several forms of literature, including drama, where it is the written equivalent to the "curtain raisers" of later drama.

Dedication

NANGONG: *Manjiang hong*

(MO *enters*:)

Floating clouds in the temporal and physical world,

Illusory towers and people in the air—

For whom the useless scowling and laughter,
And the idle obsessions?
"One should sing when facing wine,"[8] but where is best?
Climb heights to lament those of antiquity, but no one will know.
But here I write out my feelings when heaven and human nature match,
And idly pass judgement.

The affairs of a hundred years,
A pen of a thousand autumns,
The tears of girls and boys,
The blood of heroes—
Count the boundless murky epochs past,
The broken fragments of stelae.
In the flow of time it is hard to grind away the true likeness,
Yet rivers and mountains never exhaust idle pleasures of beauty.
There are morning gongs and evening drums[9] to send to you:
Listen carefully.

ZHONGLÜ: *Qinyuan chun*
Beautiful sights and fine mornings,
A heart of appreciation and happy affairs
How many times do they happen in a human life?
From the new sounds of Zheng and Wei[10]
Licentiousness and sycophancy arose in contestation,
The sorrowing songs of Yan and Zhao
Were deep feelings and all expressions of injury.
"Grand Elegance" now so distant,[11]
"Sunny Springs" are few indeed:[12]
And the filial piety of sons and loyalty of ministers lack enough songs.
Where interests can change
And romantic charm is strongly valued—
Those are set to a separate formulary for strings and reeds.
Strolling here beneath the Studio of Singing on the Wind,
There is a short flute to play and spontaneous singing.
I have availed myself of the vibrant events of old,
And by adding luster brought their features to life.
The idle talk of fishermen and woodcutters
Can evaluate them fairly.
Turn it around to look at it,
And a great bewilderment is brought up:
In the green annals of history, whose name is really fragrant?

Call in the lad,
And we'd better go
To carefully set each proper *gong* and *shang* modal pitch.[13]

Here, Yang attempts to summarize his purpose in writing the plays as a kind of historical reflection that will probe the human qualities of its notables. While he does deal with "filial piety and great ministers," however, he often does so in an exaggerated way, mixing religious and popular traditions with more stolid Confucian accounts to animate his characters. The "dedication" should not be seen as a general summary of the contents of his thirty-two plays but as an expression of the author's motives for creating the collection, of its place in the history of literature, and of the confoundment that serious contemplation of the past brings to any reader or viewer of these historical plays.

A NOTE ON TEXT AND CONVENTIONS

There are three major editions of the collection, the first of which contains twenty-eight plays (1764); the first reprinting of the original edition, in 1766, added two plays to bring the total to thirty; and the second reprinting (1774) resulted in our final text. For this translation, I have used an 1820 edition found in Harvard University East Asian Library rare book collection. The original edition is highlighted at places with the traditional circle and dot additions meant to call attention to important passages. We have been unable to incorporate these in translation.

MA ZHOU DRINKS ALONE AT A XINFENG WINESHOP

Ma Zhou 馬周 (601–648) rose from penury and disappointment to a high position under the reign of Emperor Taizong (Li Shimin 李世民; r. 627–649) of the Tang dynasty (617–906). The story of his ascent from a disaffected student, whose talents were unrecognized and underappreciated, to the most trusted civilian member of the early Tang bureaucracy is well represented in poetry, drama, and classical narratives, as well as in two biographies in the official Tang histories, one compiled in 945 and the other in 1060. Later dramas and vernacular tales embellished the story even further, focusing on the old theme of what, in Chinese, is called *huaicai buyu* 懷才不遇, "full of talent but not destined to meet the proper time for use." The earliest narrative account we have of his career is found in an early Tang work, *Essentials of Governance in the Zhenguan Reign Period* (*Zhenguan zhengyao* 貞觀政要) that was presented to the court sometime in the winter or early spring of 709, by Wu Jing 吳兢 (670–749). The anecdotes in this text focus primarily on the interactions between the court and the bureaucracy, the emperor and his ministers. The short account of Ma Zhou shows him as a quick study of political events, a master rhetorician, and an intimate advisor to Emperor Taizong:

> Ma Zhou was a man of Chiping 茌平 in Bozhou 博州.[14] In the fifth year of *zhenguan* [February 7, 631–January 26, 632] he arrived in the capital and lodged in the household of the Commander of the Prince Regents Compound, Chang He 常何. At that time Taizong had ordered his officials to each send up a document discussing the successes and failures [of his government]. On behalf of Chang He, Ma Zhou discussed in sequence some twenty-odd proposals of convenience and had [Chang] send them up as a memorial. In every instance his proposals matched [the emperor's] mind. Taizong marveled at [Chang He's] capability and questioned him. He replied, "These are not proposals I thought of, but are those of Ma Zhou, a retainer in my household." Taizong immediately summoned [Ma Zhou] and, even before he had arrived, had dispatched a deputy to hasten him along four times. When he finally saw him, he was extremely delighted to talk with him. He assigned him to be Auxiliary to the Chancellery and bestowed on him the rank of Investigating Censor. Ma Zhou subsequently was appointed to be a Drafter in the Central Secretariat.
>
> Zhou had quick-witted disputations and was capable of fully reporting them to the emperor. He had a profound understanding of the causes of political events and therefore was always on the mark when he went into action. Taizong once said, "If I do not see Ma Zhou, even for a minute, I begin to think about him." In the eighteenth year [February 14, 644–February 1, 645] he was promoted to be Director of the Central Secretariat and simultaneously as Secretary to the Heir Apparent. Once Zhou had taken a position simultaneously in the two palaces [of the emperor and the heir apparent], he dealt with affairs in an evenhanded and impartial way. This really garnered him a reputation at that time. And another time he also held the post of Secretary of the Board of Personnel simultaneously with his original basic office. Taizu once remarked to an official-in-waiting, "Zhou sees events clearly and quickly, is serious by nature and cautious in approach. And when it comes to discussing the capacity of personalities, he speaks directly to the point in his assessments. And when I have employed him, he does precisely what I hoped. He has both completely expressed his loyalty and sincerity and he is extremely close to me. In truth I rely on this man to share administering government in an age of peace."[15]

A second work that includes an account of Ma Zhou's career is called *A New Account of the Great Tang* (*Da Tang xinyu* 大唐新語) and bears a preface dated 804. We can see that in the space of less than one hundred years the story was being fleshed out with more detail about Ma's younger life when he was subjected to repeated criticism and physical punishment for his drinking and his lackadaisical attitude about fulfilling his responsibilities. More importantly, we also see the inclusion of direct quotations that show the formation of a story cycle in embryo: a brilliant young man in a position that did not fit his talents, whose frustration led to an incautious attitude toward superiors who were incapable of seeing what he had to offer. Only chance—a retainership in the household of Chang He—put him a position to make his brilliance shine. This passage from 804 becomes the kernel around which both the historical biographies and other fictitious accounts of his life wrap their chaff.

When young, Ma Zhou was very frustrated. He was not respected by his local area, and when he was put into a vacant position as an assistant instructor in [Bo]zhou Prefecture, he was never able to pay proper attention to the job. When the magistrate, a certain Da Xi, became angry and had him bastinadoed, Ma then raised up the hem of his skirt and went off to the area of Cao and Bian. But once there he was humiliated by the Commander of Junyi District and, moved to action, went off west to Chang'an. There he wound up at the household of Chang He, the Commander of the Prince Regents Compound. In the beginning of the Zhenguan era (627–649), Taizong ordered all civil and military officials to lay out the strengths and weaknesses of current policy. Since Chang He (586–653) was a military man, he was not involved with learning, and so he relied on Zhou to draft his document.

Zhou fully prepared forty-odd items that discussed benefits and harm, and when Chang He saw them, he was somewhat alarmed: "Why so many items? I don't dare present these to be heard." Zhou replied: "You, general, have received profound grace from the state and you have personally received the Sage's directive. The benefits and harms that you have laid out have already taken form in writing, so the enterprise cannot be stopped. If you don't make them heard, sir, can the proposals ever eventuate?" Chang He consequently made them known. Taizong was taken aback, and summoned Chang He to question him. Then he hurriedly summoned Ma Zhou for a discussion and Taizong really marveled at him. He put him into the Chancellery, and in an act of favor had him capped as a high official and transferred to the Central Secretariat. What Ma had proposed were items such as to use drums along the major highways to replace a relay of voices [to mark time], to use "flying post horses" to deliver news of urgent and critical events, to gather residence tax, and to set rotational duties for the personal guard.

When Taizong had business that took him to Liaodong,[16] he ordered Zhou to help the heir-apparent [the later Gaozong], who remained in Dingzhou [in modern Hebei] to look after the state. When Taizong returned victoriously, Gaozong sent all of the emperor's favored consorts to welcome him at the temporary capital. Taizong was overjoyed with Gaozong, who said, "Ma Zhou told me to do it." Taizong laughed and said, "That Shandong fellow[17] always has insight into me!" He then rewarded him handsomely. When Ma Zhou died, Taizong felt deep sorrow, and whenever he fondly recalled him, Taizong would avail himself of Daoist techniques to see if he could actually make him appear.[18] This was the kind of grace that Ma Zhou encountered.

In the beginning, Zhou was installed in the Chancellery as a civilian. Taizong ordered him to be a Probationary Censor and then had him suddenly promoted to Investigating Censor. The office "Probationary Censor" began with Zhou.[19]

From this simple story, the narrative went in two directions. In the main, adapting the first paragraph, the two official histories of the Tang detailed Ma's public life: the positions he held, his great aid to Taizong, his skill in presenting well-thought-out memorials, and the rhetorical force of his writing, all the while citing his memorials within their texts. Fictional narratives took a considerably different route, creating fuller imaginative narratives about how Ma Zhou came to appear on earth at the precise time that the Tang needed a powerful civilian minister. In the earliest fictional tale known to us, by a Tang writer of uncertain date, and which appears in the Song dynasty anthology *Broadly Gathered Stories from an Era of Great Peace* (*Taiping guangji* 太平廣記, Ma Zhou is dispatched to aid the Tang by no less than Laozi (Li Dan), who was considered to be an ancestor of the ruling house:

Ma Zhou was a transcendent official in the Palace of Unsullied Noumena located on Mt. Hua. When the house of Tang was about to receive the mandate, the Most-High commanded him to descend to earth to bring aid to the state. But he was deeply addicted to alcohol and indulged himself in worldly pleasures for twenty years. He lived in penury and hunger and was blocked in whatever path he took, almost to the point of being brought to his knees.[20]

He heard that Yuan Tiangang (d. 627–634) was coming to Qin [Shaanxi] from Shu [Sichuan] and that he excelled in the art of physiognomy. So, he went to pay him a visit, in order to get a definitive take on his future prospects. Tiangang eyed him for a long time, then said, "Your five vital spirits have fled and dispersed. Your corporeal body is situated between morning and evening,[21] what is there to physiognomize?" Greatly taken aback, Zhou asked him about the techniques for warding off or controlling disaster through prayers to ghosts and gods. Tiangang said, "You can go directly east from here, there should be an old codger riding a buffalo. You must not pressure him, and he will speak to you. Simply follow his directions."

Zhou followed his words and before he even got out of the gates of the capital there was, indeed, and old codger riding a buffalo on his way out of the capital; Zhou followed silently along behind. Round about village pathways the old man went and then ascended a large mountain. Zhou followed him to the peak. The old man turned around to acknowledge him and then dismounted to sit under a tree. He began to talk to Zhou, saying, "The Most-High has commanded you to aid his sagely descendants to establish their dynasty and rescue the world. What are you doing sodden drunk and bringing penury and hunger on yourself? Your five spirits have already dispersed, and your correct ether has withered to the point of transformation so that you are ready to die at any moment. Yet you neither cultivate nor search your soul."

Zhou was deeply confused and did not yet understand what was being said. The codger said, "You were originally a transcendent in the Palace of Unsullied Noumena. Now the Transcendent King of Mt. Tai Hua has sent people to summon you."[22] He was immediately taken into a palace complex, passed through several palace gates, and arrived before a large hall. The imperial guard was standing sternly at attention—it was just like the place where an emperor resides. He hurried to the front of a curtain where there was someone who upbraided him for his lack of respect for the command he was given. His deputation was annulled, and he was returned to his old office, there to engage in self-reproach and reflect on the error of his ways. The old man and the deputies sent to fetch him accompanied him to a separate compound outside of the eastern corridor, which was composed of magnificent and spacious dwellings. He looked at the door, and his name appeared there. He unlocked the door and went in. The stove, the cooking implements, the bed and couch, mattress and mats were exactly like those where he had been living. He muttered to himself and thought about it, but he was still not able to comprehend.

Suddenly there were five people wearing the colors of the five directions [green, red, white, black, yellow]—tall, large, and impressively extraordinary—standing in front of him. They said, "We are the spirits of your five internal organs. You were taken with alcohol and dissolute, so we were made turbid and shamed in your body. After a long while we have returned. Simply close your eyes, and we will be restored to your spirit houses." Zhou closed his eyes for a bit, then suddenly felt his mind grow sharp and he became clearly conscious of it all. Everything bygone passed before his eyes and it seemed like twenty years were no more than a decade of days.

So, he locked up his residence again, and went out to the Transcendent King's court where he kowtowed and acknowledged his faults. Once again, the command was bestowed on him and he came to visit Chang'an. The next day he went again to visit Yuan Tiangang, who was startled and said, "What happened to you? You have already been cured! You will have nine promotions a day every sixty days and in a hundred days your position will reach to that of prime minister. Avoid being concerned for your own well-being. Act in this manner."

In the Zhenguan era, the emperor ordered every civil and military official to submit proposals for putting the state in order. The ideas that Zhou submitted went far beyond human measure. On that same day he was appointed as the "Probationary Censor" in charge of investigating lapses and mistakes of others. From this point onward he successively occupied important positions, finally becoming Minister of the Secretariat for many years.

One morning a group of immortals descended to his rooms and said, "Your service in aid to the state is finished, and now you can withdraw. Taiyi has ordered that you return and no longer remain."[23] The next day he died despite having no illness. He was granted the posthumous title of the Duke of Loyalty. As for his stellar achievements, his corrective aid to the state government, the history of his posts and ranked positions—these are all in the state histories. They will not be listed in extenso here.[24]

A second story from the *Broadly Gathered Stories from an Era of Great Peace* expands on exactly how Ma Zhou gained entrée into Chang He's household. In this story, an old woman who sells dumplings leads Ma Zhou to Chang He's house.

The Old Crone Who Sold Dumplings

Ma Zhou of the Tang had a style name of Binwang. He was orphaned and poor when young but understood the *Odes* and the *Spring and Autumn Chronicles*. But he was frustrated and did not work at a productive career, so he was not respected by his local area. He was put into a vacant position as a teaching assistant in [Bo]zhou Prefecture. He drank daily and the magistrate, a certain Da Xi 達奚, becoming enraged, frequently criticized him. Ma then raised up the hem of his skirt and went off to the area of Cao and Bian. After drinking he was insubordinate to Cui Xian 崔賢, the magistrate of Junyi 浚儀.[25] So, he was humiliated again and went to Xinfeng where he stayed in an inn. The inn was primarily set up for various kinds of merchants and traders, and the master paid no attention to Zhou. Zhou ordered up a flagon of ale and drank alone. He then removed his shoes and washed his feet with the ale that was left. The innkeeper secretly felt he was rather extraordinary.

As Ma Zhou reached the capital, he stopped at a dumpling shop run by an old woman. After several days he politely asked if she would help find an official residence where he might live as a retainer. The old lady led him to the home of Commander Chang He. Back when the crone had first started selling dumplings, Li Chunfeng 李淳風 and Yuan Tiangang 袁天綱 encountered her and thought her different from others. They both secretly said, "This woman is extremely noble. What is she doing here?" Sire Ma sought her out to take her as a wife.

Later there was a rescript that ordered all civil and military officials above rank five to each send up a secret memorial. Zhou laid out twenty-odd proposals of benefit and sent them to Chang He to send up. These were requests to set up drums along the streets, define sumptuary colors of scarlet, purple, blue, and green for civil and military officials, as well as a proposal that the left and right gates of the gate of the [imperial] city be used for entering and leaving. Each of these matched the aim of the emperor. Taizong marveled at this and questioned Chang He about his opinions. Chang He replied, "These were written up by a retainer at my house, Ma Zhou." Taizong summoned him to an audience and spoke to him, then commanded him to take up a position in the Chancellery, and next ordered Fang Xuanling to examine him on the classics and policy proposals. He was appointed as Esquire of the Forest of Scholars and took the post of Investigating Censor. Because the emperor attained this person through the recommendation of Chang He, Chang was given one hundred bolts of silk.

Later Zhou became Supervisory Secretary and Drafter in the Chancellery. He was quick witted and eloquent in speech and could lay out things clearly in memorials. He

> had a profound understanding of how disturbances begin, and every move he made was right on point.
>
> Cen Wenben 岑文本 (595–645) [a chancellor] saw him and said, "I have seen Sir Ma, and he makes one forget one's weariness. But he has the acutely angled wings of a kite [sharply hunched shoulders] and the appearance of the humor of fire. He will surely be speedy in his ascent, but I just fear it cannot last long." In the space of a few years, Ma's posts reached to prime minister, and that crone became his wife. Later he became Secretary of the Board of Personnel, but he had diabetes, which was chronically incurable. He perished at forty-eight and was given the posthumous title of Director of the Department of State Affairs.[26]

Two characters who appear in the story, Yuan Tiangang[27] and Li Chunfeng (602–670)[28] are known as formidable physiognomists of the early Tang. Li Chunfeng was also a prominent Daoist figure and an able court astronomer. He is most famous for his prediction that the very young concubine of Tang Taizong would one day assume the throne. She did, of course, and ruled as the notorious Wu Zetian.

The movement of the Ma Zhou story into the world of fiction and religion turned him into a figure of the Daoist pantheon as well as a bureaucrat and political figure. One can see behind this change the force of mythmaking in traditional society. Ma Zhou's rise must have seemed a wonder to many, particularly when Ma was ordered into the bureaucracy outside of what the later examination system would hold as a standard. This creation of a story to explain his rise from rags to riches and his early death is already visible in the early ninth century in the *New Words of the Great Tang*, where the observing eye of the narrator recreates subjective feelings of characters and reproduces conversations to which he could not possibly been privy. This may explain the nature of the short drama below, where we are left wondering at the end if those who come to fetch Ma Zhou are transcendent beings, or whether they are court officials who reached a status and privilege in which styling them as "transcendent" is a metaphor of their power and prestige.

MA ZHOU DRINKS ALONE IN A XINFENG WINESHOP

Xinfeng Wine Shop *considers the actions [of Ma Zhou] appropriate. That there was nobody to take command in the world and Ma Zhou was encountered in an alleyway is a salutary tale for the world; here I elaborate on the story to casually comfort all those who "harbor great talent but have not yet been tested."*

(SOUTHERN NANLÜ MODE: *San deng yue*) (SHENG *enters costumed as* Ma Zhou:)
The pylons of Heaven[29] rise high and abrupt,
Lacking only a golden beam[30] to stretch across the oceans.
To dodge this bitter penury, where can I flee?

I want to borrow a pot and flagon
To flood the rocky injustices in my breast,
And let my words flow like a waterfall.
Well, I might as well let my steps sunder the chalcedony luster[31]
And go sit all alone in a market wine loft.

What a fine day of wind and cloud! Since I have arrived at the inn in Chang'an, my journey has been quite lonely, and I have been very frustrated. Yesterday, General Chang He wanted me to write up the draft of a memorial in his name, and he has retained me here for the while. True it is,

If your fate is not matched up with an intelligent lord,
In civilian clothes you will vainly stir up the dust of Luoyang.[32]

Bored all day long, I'll go into Xinfeng and get some wine to relieve my cares. Having to brave the cold today and walking alone along the Imperial Way, I'll just have to get drunk. Well, here I am. Barkeeper, where are you?

(CLOWN enters, costumed as the barkeep:)

This guy is wearing calf-nose pants,
Calf-nose pants,[33]
And just faces the stove to count his wine take!
At the front door everyone takes a fancy to Zhuo Wenjun,
But in the back, we catch Clerk of the Civil Board Bi,
Clerk of the Civil Board Bi.[34]

Sir, your place to sit is not in this section. Look at upstairs and downstairs; all other places are occupied to the full by high officials, important people, the sons of dukes and grandsons of kings. Go on over there to the side.

(MALE LEAD:)

A fat horse braves the wind,
A limping donkey yields the road!

It doesn't matter where I sit, all I care about is you bringing me some warm strained wine.

(CLOWN:) Well, looking at the single layer on your cold body, you are probably going to need a few pitchers from me.

(ZHENGGONG MODE: *Jinchan dao*) (MALE LEAD:)
You say I'm a Yuan An stretched out beside a broken-down kiln,[35]
Freezing for no reason.
Well, just look at how red my drunken face will be after a good bout of drinking!

(CLOWN:) What do you want to accompany the wine?

(MALE LEAD:) The ancients say, "Cloudy wine should be accompanied by the *Documents of the Han*."[36] There's no need for anything else.

(CLOWN:) Books are good snacks? If you scholars had early on swallowed all those books whole, wouldn't they bloat you to death?

(*Backstage summons him, he exits.*)

(MALE LEAD:) I recall that the founding emperor of the Han, Gaozu, in his day freely cursed all Confucian scholars, saying, "I obtained the empire on horseback, what use do I have for the *Odes* and *Documents*?"[37] These were clueless comments.

Considering how tired of war all points of the empire were in those days of the Han,
He simply relied on those of old who followed the imperial dragon,
"Until mountains are like whetstones and rivers like a belt."[38]
But can't we say that in molding the world in the crucible of heaven and earth
Many things leaked out[39]—
He listened only to the songs of fierce warriors.
He wanted no help in ruling from the *Odes* or the *Documents*.
Let those bookish students command as much institutional ritual as they wanted,
The hats of the Confucians were trampled under horses' hooves—
How could this have made the Worthies of Mt. Shang desire to come over?[40]

Barkeep! Wine!

(CLOWN *enters* [*and speaks*:]) Here it is.

(*Exits.*)

(MALE LEAD:) Now when the Tang established its state, it was the same: "A three-foot sword in dust of war, / altars of Earth and Grain, one man in armor."[41] But at present both the civil and military are advanced equally; a scene quite different from the beginning of the Han.

(XIANLÜ GONG MODE: *Zao luo pao*)
Battle ended all contestations in the world,[42]
And all expelled then, either scraped or pared away
Were those insignificant sons who had plotted to seize the throne.[43]
The emperor solemnly asks how to heal the scars of war,
I still worry that the "golden vase of state" might be broken.
Those old generals in the Lingyan Gallery[44]
Surged forward with all their might, calling out in the palace,
And the scholars on the fairy isle of Yingzhou
Assembled in harmony as divine transcendent beings.[45]

(MALE LEAD:) You might ask, what is lacking among the great ministers of court?
Where else can an educated man go to find some enterprise to do?

(MALE LEAD:) I think about what Confucius said about being poor and of low status when a state possesses the proper Way.[46] Isn't someone like me, poor and cold and looking like a beggar, drunk my whole life, turning his back on the times when he lives in such a great age? (*Acts out laughing.*) And how can I explain it away? It's just a case of

Ten thousand horses vie to win,
But Hualiu[47] drops to the rear.

(*To the previous tune*:)
But to soar up on high is impossible!
Let me sit, chanting long and clasping my knees,
Fortunate as I am to be moved by the harmony of wind and cloud's conjunction.
How can it not be the time to reap the brave and eminent?
Now the bice and vermillion [paints out "The Song of] Miraculous Transformation,"[48]
And one eulogizes with a song about how the Yellow River flows clear.[49]
The dragons of the mountain are stitched on the emperor's robes,[50]
And the worthy and good have offered remonstrations in the exams.
How can it compare to having one's portrait of merit painted later in the eastern Unicorn Hall?[51]

Let me put the cup down for the time being; I have to go and inscribe the wall of this inn with a poem on snow, idly scribbling out the feelings of this tired traveler.

Who is it in the void, sprinkling these little gems,
So Su Qin in his marten cloak cannot stand the cold?[52]
Today, a pot of wine in Xinfeng wine shop
Melts the stony cares in my breast along with the snow.

Look at how the light from the snow is shining on the white wall—how bright it is. Bring some more wine!

(CLOWN *enters*:) Here's more wine. (*Acts out looking at the wall.*) Hei! You are an annoying one! My business is thriving, and I keep the seats swept clean, . . .

(MALE LEAD:) Not necessarily so!

(CLOWN:) But I must be visited by a sourpuss scholar who deigns to make his appearance and makes it his habit to scribble and dash ink everywhere!

(MALE LEAD:) Who's going to stop me?

(CLOWN:) The owner will be really disgusted! It will have to be papered over so it's snow white again.

(MALE LEAD:) [A talented hand] so hard to come by!

(CLOWN:) I was just one step too late, unawares that you were already dirtying up my wall!

(MALE LEAD:) It's all to the wall's advantage! My poetry is priceless.

(CLOWN:) Don't say "priceless," I don't think that it's worth half a cent.

(*Act out backstage summoning him.* CLOWN *exits.*)

(MALE LEAD:) Well, that threw a wet blanket on everything! I've been ridiculed by this guy for nothing at all.

(SHANGDIAO MODE: *Ying zao bao*)
Demons and devils delight in the transgressions of men—
I've been derided and ridiculed,
Nothing I can do about that—
I sigh that *Odes* and *Documents* are not commodities stored away until priced right.

So, enjoy a red face from Gaoyang wine,
Embrace the sultry songs of seductive beauties,
Hotly chase along with [the fine young men] who swiftly pass with fine furs and horses.
Today,
It is the chicken and dogs in Xinfeng shop
That got the best of me and left me unhappy and disappointed;
It is the wind and snow of Chang'an
That has ground me down.
I just want to ask the Master of Heaven,
"What have you planned for me, one who puts concern for his fellow men before everything else?"

All the time I've been talking, I have been blind to the fact I've gotten myself drunk all by myself. (*Acts out nodding off.*)

(SECOND COMIC *costumed as an Inner Palace Official enters with a* SECONDARY MALE, *costumed as a general leading a group of followers* [*and speaks*:]) I am presenting an imperial document bearing His instructions, asking for that young scholar from Shandong, Ma Zhou. It's said he is in the Xinfeng Wine Shop, but we couldn't find him anywhere. Turns out he's passed out drunk here. Scholar Ma! Master Ma!

(MALE LEAD *acts out waking up.*) Barkeep! Bring some more wine! What are all of you doing here? What do you want here?

(GROUP:) I'm a Daoist official bearing a tally and who comes as fast as lightning, dispatched from the palace of Tuṣita Heaven.

(MALE LEAD:) Who are you looking for?

(GROUP:)

All the fixed stars arrayed in heaven are counted complete,
Except, that is, for the Star of Examinations and Literary Endeavor.

(MALE LEAD:) Well. If he's not showing up, then keep looking for him.

(GROUP:)

We came to the world of men before we were able to learn
That it's said you are the banished Literary Star.

(MALE LEAD:) Be sure you're not making a mistake.

(GROUP:)

Truly, you have the color of fire and the acutely angled wings of a kite,[53]
And the Jade Emperor sits and awaits you in the Palace of Noumenal Clouds.[54]

(MALE LEAD:) I'll go after paying my tab.

(GROUP:) You can pay it again after you've gone. Go over and take up that formal hat and belt. The Imperial Stableman has picked out a horse for you and is waiting. Now we must go forward and face the Sage.

(ALL TOGETHER:) True it is

When in penury, with only a clay cooking pot in the cold, thin smoke,
Who recognizes a worthy, with his long chanting, rare in any age?
But one morning your time comes, and you understand you will rise high as an official,
Just look, "He goes to audience with the emperor after three tankards."[55]

(*Exit.*)

(CLOWN *acts out bringing the play to an end.*) Wonderful! Fantastic! True it is, "I had eyes but couldn't recognize Mount Tai." Just look at the poem he inscribed on the wall—this is "to keep the ink traces of a famous and noble man." Waiter, hurry and get some blue gauze and cover it over!

(*Backstage calls. Exit.*)

JING DUKE OF WEI SUBSTITUTES FOR A DRAGON AND SPREADS RAIN

Li Jing 李靖 (571–649), courtesy name Yaoshi 藥師, was a famous military strategist and general at the end of the Sui (581–618) and in the early Tang (618–907). He came from an important family who had served as officials in the Northern Zhou (557–81) and Sui dynasties. Most importantly, his maternal uncle Han Qinhu 韓擒虎 (538–592), was a great general under the Sui,[56] and undoubtedly became the greatest influence on Li Jing, who became known in his own prime as a brilliant tactician. Early on, Li had a complicated relationship with the man who would become the first ruler of the Tang, Emperor Gaozu, Li Yuan 李淵 (566–635). Li Jing first served under him as a local official, but fled to the capital, planning to accuse Li Yuan of plotting rebellion against the Sui. He was still in the capital when Li Yuan captured it, was set to be put to death, but was then pardoned because of his courage and ethical stand. Then, he was brought into the fold as one of Li Yuan's finest and most trusted military leaders. His service continued on for the second Tang ruler, Emperor Taizong, Li Shimin 李世民 (598–649), whom he served with remarkable military savvy, defeating aggressive nomadic and Turkic armies in the steppes.[57] Because of his strategic and tactical genius, through time several military works were attributed to him, although not by any source contemporary to him. The two best known of these works are the *Interrogatory Dialogues Between Emperor Taizong and Li, the Duke of Wei* (*Tang Taizong Li Weigong wenda* 唐太宗李衛公問答), which was incorporated into the *Seven Military Classics* of China,[58] and *Gazing South of the River by Li Weigong* (*Li Weigong Wang Jiangnan* 李衛公望江南), a long discourse on military strategy written in the form of *ci* 詞 lyric poetry. This latter work has been thoroughly discussed by the late Jao Tsung-I and shown to be a work done no earlier than the Song dynasty.[59]

Li Jing also appears early on in Chinese fiction, most famously in Du Guangting's 杜光庭 (850–933) *Tale of the Curly-Bearded Guest* (*Qiuran ke* 虯髯客)—and the Ming play based on it, *Story of the Red Dustwhisk* (*Hongfu ji* 紅拂記)—in which the eponymous hero teaches Li Jing all about military strategy.[60] Li also occurs in other stories in the Song anthology of classical fiction *Extensively Gathered Stories from an Era of Peace* (*Taiping guangji* 太平廣記), first compiled in 977; in the early decades of the Qing dynasty, he was featured in the vernacular novel *The Historical Romance of the Sui and Tang Dynasties* (*Sui Tang yanyi* 隋唐演義). Over the ages his reputation as a fictional character has come to rival that of the historical Li Jing.

Our play is woven of two major strands; first, a stated purpose—Li Jing is in search of Wang Tong, whom he desires as a teacher and second, the incidental but main plot, Li Jing being asked to substitute for a rain dragon to spread rain over a drought-stricken area. Dragons in China do not breathe fire but are intimately entwined with rain and with women. There are many variations on the now idiomatic phrase from the *Book of Changes*, "clouds follow the dragon and wind follows the tiger." And, as Schafer has shown,[61] dragon maidens are always associated with watery depths of rivers, lakes, and oceans. This element of the story clearly came from earlier sources unattached to Li Jing. For instance, the source of the story of Li Jing and rain seems to be "The Village Headman at Yingyang," a somewhat earlier and more direct telling of the tale:

The Village Headman at Yingyang[62]

A Village Headman of Yingyang[63] explained to me that someone—I didn't get a name—was riding back to his village drunk when he reached the Temple of the Younger Aunt.[64] He tied off his horse and sprawled by the temple gate. Gradually he began to sober up and, though he could turn his head, he was still unable to get up. He heard someone knocking at the Temple gate whose voice was very stern. In a moment, he heard a voice from inside ask, "Who is there?" The visitor responded, "I was ordered by an official to find a person to spread rain." The person in the temple said, "The whole family went to the Mount [Song] Temple to visit. There's no one here." The visitor said, "Just use the person who is lying by the gate. He'll do." The person in the temple said, "This is a passing traveler. How can we use him?" They argued bitterly, but in the end the visitor had no choice, so he told the guy to get up. That guy followed him to a place where everything was a drizzly, misty cloudy vapor. There was a creature there that looked like a camel. The person lifted the villager up on the back of the camel, gave him a jar, and warned him, "Just carry this jar upright, but don't let it tip over."

The creature began to walk, and the water sloshed out of the jar, falling as drops. At that time, there had been a drought for a long time. When he looked down and saw where he lived, he worried that the rain was insufficient, so he tipped the jar.

After he finished spreading the rain, the official who was in charge released him and allowed him to go home. When he reached the gate of the Temple, he saw his own body in the water. As soon as he went forward and entered his body, he came back to life again, got on his horse and went home. But because he had tipped the jar, his home had been swept away [by the floods] and his whole household had died. Then that fellow went mad, and he also died in a few months.

The short story based on this earlier version, simply called "Li Jing, Duke of Wei," is far more interesting. It begins with Li owing a personal debt of gratitude to villagers who had accommodated him whenever he went hunting. It then narrates the story of the rain episode, in which the rationale for inundating one area is based on repayment or reciprocity: as he spreads the rain, a drop at a time, he feels moved to sprinkle twenty drops over the village that had been so kind to him. Of course, he inundates the village, for which the dragon lady and her sons are beaten with a rod. But the short story ends quite differently. Li makes a rational choice about which of two "lackeys" the dragon lady offers him for his help in making it rain to take. This addition moves the short story in a different direction, as it accounts for Li's success as a military genius, at the expense of a high civil career.

Li Jing, Duke of Wei[65]

When Li Jing, the Duke of Wei, was still an insignificant person, he often hunted on Mount Huo where he lodged and ate in a mountain village. The old men in the village considered him an extraordinary man and often presented large amounts of food to him there. After many years, he had deep feelings for the village. [When he was hunting one day], he suddenly encountered a herd of deer, so he pursued them. Just as it grew dark, he wanted to leave off, but he could not. Unexpectedly, he lost his way because of the gloomy darkness, and everything was confused. He didn't know what to do next, so he kept going in a disheartened way, feeling increasingly exhausted and worried. He gazed as far away as he could and saw the light of lamps. Accordingly, he spurred his horse on to go there. Once he had arrived, he [found out] it to be a mansion with a vermillion gate, the building of which was very grand.

Li Jing then knocked on the door, and after a while, a person came out to ask who it was. The Duke explained that he was lost and asked to stay overnight. The person responded, "The young gentlemen have all left already. Only the Matriarch is at home. Staying overnight cannot be allowed." The Duke asked, "Please try to explain it to her for me." Subsequently, the person entered to report, and then emerged, saying, "At first, the Matriarch did not want to allow it. But because it is dark, and the guest has claimed that he is lost, she feels she must be your host." The Duke was invited into the hall. In a little while, a maid came out, saying, "The Matriarch is coming." The Matriarch was around fifty and wore a black skirt and a plain jacket, had a refined air, and was just like one of those ladies from the families of scholar-gentry. The Duke walked forward and bowed to her. The Matriarch responded in kind and said, "Since both of my sons are not at home, it is not proper for me to let you stay. But it is really dark today, and you have lost your way back. If we do not allow you to stay here, where else could we send you? But this is a residence in the mountains, and my sons are on their way home. If they make a lot of noise when they come in tonight, please do not be frightened." The Duke said, "I don't deserve such consideration." Then, the Matriarch ordered food [for him], all of which was very delicious, but it had too many fish dishes. After the meal was done, the Matriarch went into her rooms, and two maids brought out a couch, mattresses, mats, and quilts. All were fragrant, clean, and really displayed their wealth. Then they closed the door, locked it, and left.

When the Duke was alone, he thought, "What kind of creatures out there in the wild would come home at night and make a lot of noise?" He was so scared that he did not dare to go to bed but sat in a formal pose, listening for them. Around midnight, he heard the sound of urgent knocking at the gate. He also heard someone answer the door, saying, "It is a tally from Heaven. Pass on the message to the Elder Young Master of the House that he should deliver rain for seven hundred *li* around this mountain, and that enough rain should be delivered by the fifth watch. Don't tarry! Don't cause any harm!" The person who answered the door accepted the tally and came in to present it to the Matriarch. The Matriarch said, "My two sons are not back yet, but the tally for delivering rain is here. It is certainly not possible to decline it, but if we miss the time, we will be punished. Even if I sent somebody to tell my sons, it would be already too late. It is impossible to entrust this to a servant or slave. What should I do?" A young maid said, "In the hall I just noticed that our guest is no ordinary man. Why not ask him?" The Matriarch was pleased. So, she personally knocked at the door of the hall and asked, "Are you awake now? Please come out for a bit." The Duke said, "Alright." Subsequently, he went down the stairs to see her.

The Matriarch said, "This is not a human residence, but a dragon's palace. My elder son went to the East Sea to attend a wedding ceremony; my younger son is out accompanying his sister. We just now received a tally from heaven, and it is my sons' turn to deliver rain, but even a cloud-path journey between the two places is over ten thousand *li*. We cannot inform them in time, and it is hard to find a substitute. Might I humbly trouble you for a moment?" The Duke responded, "I am but a traveler in the world, not someone who can ride on the clouds. How can I deliver any rain? If you have a method that you can teach me, however, you have only to give your command." The Matriarch said, "If you follow my words, everything is possible."

Accordingly, she commanded a young male servant, "Harness up the piebald horse." Then she ordered people to bring the instruments for delivering rain, and it turned out to be just a small jar tied to the front of the saddle. She warned him, "When you ride the horse, do not use bit and the bridle. Instead, give him his head. Whenever the horse leaps from the ground and neighs, you just take a drop of water in the jar and drip it on the horse's mane. Be careful, not too much."

At that point, the Duke mounted the horse, and went riding off, as if he was flying and soaring. The horse's feet rose gradually higher and higher from the ground, and

Jing was surprised by its stability and speed, quite unawares that he was already above the clouds. The wind was as quick as arrows, and peals of thunders rose from the hooves of the horse. Then, whenever the horse leapt, he would drip water. Soon, lightning struck, and the clouds opened up, and below him he saw the village where he had been resting. He thought, "I have eaten and drunk many times in this village. I was just thinking about how grateful I was to them and that I had no way to repay them. There is now an extended drought, and the crops are about to wither and die. Now that rain is in my hands, how could I begrudge it?" Thinking that a single drop was not enough to soak the ground, he dripped twenty drops in a row. Suddenly, the rain stopped, and he rode the horse back.

The Matriarch was weeping in the hall. "How could you do so much harm? Originally, we agreed on a single drop. How could you make it twenty on the basis of your private feelings? One drop in heaven is a foot of rain on earth. At midnight, this village's fields were covered by twenty feet of water. How could anyone survive? I have already been condemned and received eighty lashes." She exposed her back to Jing's view, and it was all bloody wounds. "My sons have also been both punished. How do you feel?" The Duke was shamed and terrified and didn't know how to respond.

The Matriarch then said, "You, Sir, are a man of the mortal world, and do not recognize the transformational changes of clouds and rain. I truly dare not hold a grudge against you. However, should the dragon Master come to seek you out, I'm afraid you will be startled and scared. It is best if you leave quickly. However, I still have nothing to repay your trouble. I live in the mountains and have nothing. I only have two lackeys to present as gifts. Choose both or one of them at your own discretion." Then, she ordered the two lackeys to come out. One came out from the east hall: his manner and appearance were pleasant and agreeable; the other came out from the west hall, looking indignant and agitated, and standing with an air of resentment. The Duke thought privately, "I am a hunter, and make my living by fighting the ferocious. If I take the one who looks agreeable, won't people consider me timid?" Accordingly, the Duke said, "I do not dare to take both, but since You, Matriarch, have bestowed on me [this opportunity], I would like to take the angry one." The Matriarch smiled, saying, "Let it be so if that is your choice." The Duke then bowed to her and bid farewell. The retainer also followed him. After he was a few steps out of the gate, he turned to look, but the residence was gone. When he turned to ask the lackey, he had also disappeared. He found his way back by himself. When it turned light, the Duke gazed at the village where the water stretched beyond his vision. The tall trees showed only their tips, and there were no people anymore.

Thereafter, he wound up pacifying many incursions through clever military strategies, and his achievements covered the empire. That he never reached the position of prime minister—was that because he did not also take the pleasant lackey? The world says, "The area to the east of the [Tong 潼] Pass[66] often produces ministers, while the area to the west of the Pass often produces generals." Did not the east and the west

> [halls] symbolize [these areas]? The reason they were called lackeys is to symbolize that they were officials. If he had chosen both lackeys at that time, then he would have surely attained the positions of prime minister and supreme commander.[67]

It is the lesson of the central "rain" narrative upon which Yang Chaoguan chooses to expand his short play: that overreaching, even when well motivated, can have disastrous results. This is a lesson, he implies, that people who are starting out on their bureaucratic careers must learn. The plot implies that genius, untutored by either experience or a brilliant teacher, easily pursues wayward courses leading to endangerment of those in one's charge.

The frame story of the drama is Li Jing's original quest to meet Wang Tong 王通 (584?–617), who was thought to have been a mentor to several early Tang statesmen, including Li Jing, Fang Xuanling 房玄齡 (579–648), Wei Zheng 魏徵 (580–643), and Chen Shuda 陳叔達 (572–635).[68] The frame story concludes with Wang Tong giving solid advice to Li Jing:

> Since you have nothing in your past that you repent, we can probably figure that the local deities here were destined for a flood. But there is one thing: people who wanted to save the world in the past were all too capable of doing something that wronged the world. And that was because they believed too deeply in their own heartfelt sense and then just overdid it. People who are going to do great things cannot have an evil heart, but neither can they have a heart of goodness. The subtleness of the creator of transformations is that he makes all things equally heartless. You should have known this.[69]

In this light, the play appears to be arranged in such a way that Li Jing, as we say, "put the cart before the horse," and did not comprehend that responsibility as an official means keeping "local deities" at arm's length. The avuncular note at the end, we may say, bolsters the reading of this play, as well as the other thirty-one, as a cautionary note to those who held bureaucratic office.

LI, THE DUKE OF WEI, SPREADS RAIN IN PLACE OF THE DRAGON

Authorial Note: Spreads Rain *considers how difficult it is to save the world. One nourishes talent through study, one harnesses talent in service to the Way. Who can accomplish this other than a great worthy?*

(NORTHERN XIANLÜ MODE: *Dian jiangchun*) (YOUNG MALE *costumed as Li Jing enters:*)

Precious sword hung aslant across my waist,

I seek a master to inquire of the Way.
The road far and out of sight,
The sun now hangs from the branch tips—
I ask, where should I halt my three-horse team?

([*Speaks*:]) I am Li Jing, from Sanyuan. I've just reached the capping age[70] and I stem from a family of generals. My uncle, Han Qinhu,[71] is the number-one general these days. After he had quelled Wu, he taught me everything he knew about martial arts and every kind of military strategy. But I have not been able to combine the civil and military arts completely, and I have heard that there is a certain Master Wenzhongzi,[72] whose practice of the Way is at an elevated stage. I want to go and study the Way with him for three years, before I appear upon the scene. Then I naturally will be "a stunning talent to support heaven" and my name "will be renowned on paper and silk." For this reason, I have taken to the road and come forward to seek out my master. Well, while I've been talking, I was oblivious to the day growing late, and I have missed the rest stop. But look, there in the forest is a flicker of firelight, and methinks it must be someone's house. Let me go right ahead and knock on the door.

(OLD FEMALE *costumed as the dragon mother enters*:) I fear it is a traveler burning a rhinoceros horn,[73] and I must prevent anyone who wants to boil up the sea.[74] Who is knocking?

(YOUNG MALE:) Forgive me for startling you, mother, but I wonder if you would permit me to stay overnight in your marvelous estate?

(OLD FEMALE:) Don't take this amiss, young master, but my child has gone out, and there's no one else at home. So that would be impossible. But there is a grass hut outside of the compound where you, young sir, may make do.

(YOUNG MALE:) As long as I don't have to sleep in the open—I have again received your kindness, mother.

(OLD FEMALE:)

It's not because of rain that Heaven has detained this guest here.
(*Closes door and exits.*)

(YOUNG MALE:)

Hard to think that Heaven would keep me here, but she wouldn't.
(*Exits.*)

(YOUNG FEMALE *costumed as the dragon granddaughter runs on stage*:)

When an important sage summons a minor one,
It is as urgent as a command of law!

Mama, open the door! On my way back, I ran smack into a heavenly tally that has been sent down, with an urgent summons for my father, the dragon king, to spread some rain in the area East of the Yellow River.[75] Tomorrow from three to seven in the morning, he should send down exactly one foot of sweet heavy rain, to save those drought-stricken sprouts—I have the edict right here! But my father the king has not returned, so what shall we do?

(OLD FEMALE:) What can we do about this? I've got it! Bring the edict along. (*She acts out knocking on a door.*) Wake up, young master, I have something I need you to do for me. I'll tell you the truth—I am not an ordinary person but actually the mother of the Dragon King. Right now, we have in hand an edict from the High Emperor, dispatching us to spread rain in the area East of the Yellow River. But my son went out, and the youngster here is not old enough. This is really urgent, and I would like to request you, sir, to please take on this responsibility for us.

(YOUNG MALE:) Oh, so that's how it is. But I'm just an ordinary person, how can I replace you?

(OLD FEMALE:) You sir, are no ordinary person. If you are willing to replace my son, I have a white horse that sails through the void, and black flags to guide you on. When you get there, all you have to do is to shake the pure bottle of water, use the willow branch to sprinkle it down and the realm below will naturally begin to rain, right at the right time. But this pure bottle is no little thing: expand its lip and it takes in the whole sea, raise it in your hand and the mountains shake. On earth below, myriads of drops are not too many; in heavens above, a single drop is not too few. I give this to you, but you must heed my instructions.

(YOUNG MALE:) "There's a way to rise up into Heaven"[76] of course: you just look at my rain techniques!

(YOUNG FEMALE:) Mama, I really want to go roaming about in the heavens, you can let me go along with him to carry the pure pitcher.

(OLD FEMALE:) Fine.

Beware that the moment you are utilized to make it rain
Is the moment when the people there will hope for it.

(*Exits.*)

(*Hunjiang long*) (YOUNG MALE:)
Just listen to that single whistle,
As the horse's hooves slowly enter the clouds on high.
True it is, "Traversing the void, driving the cloud ethers before us
We rise straight up on the whirlwind."
What are these commanderies and provinces that pass beneath my feet?
The silver pot drips drop by drop, pushing out the last bit of leakage.
Above my head we have broken apart what is neither mist nor fog,[77]
The strong wind of the highest heaven scours and washes, sprinkling goose down:
Blackness spreads forever.
The morning stars disperse and fall, the golden rooster crows:
Light radiates everywhere,
The sunrise of the ocean is set off like the landmark of the Red City.[78]
Look at the morning brightness of the sky, my body in the infinite sky.
I am not the roaming traveler in Yangzhou,

Riding on a crane with money tied about my waist.[79]
I am not the charming guest at Qin Terrace,
Riding on a phoenix playing the flute.[80]
I want to be close enough to knock on Heaven's gates,
I want to reward the mournful complaints of the lower realm.
Look down there below, everywhere,
Those who can, flee,
Those who can, disperse—
Swirling souls in boiling water and fire,
From five hundred years of hardships.
Look there right in midair,
The one who can, leaps,
The one who can, dances,
The demons of drought in blazing sunlight
Scorch the earth for a thousand miles, withering everything,
Wearing down to nothing the riches and plenty of the era of *kaihuang*,[81]
And beginning to punish the ostentatious extravagance of the *daye* reign.[82]

Today happily the protection of heaven has borrowed a hand from me. Ah, this white horse,

Look how the hooves of this horse leap and stride,
This steed is so well schooled and smooth,
Rushing through the yellow dust that rings the land.

And this black banner,

Look how the tip of the banner summons the whirlwind,
The very image of Chiyou,[83]
Covering from sight the red sun in the empyrean.

And this pure bottle,

Miraculously empty,
A single mouth sucking up all of the Silver River, the Stream of Heaven.[84]

And this sprig of willow,

A little light quiver,
And a few leaves saturate an auspicious gale of sweet dew.
Everything as the heart and mind desire, truly a rare treasure—
Still incompetent in all, still incredulous, I am learning to be in control.

(*Acts out ascending on high*, [*speaks*:])

If you want to use all your thousand-*li* vision,
Then go up one more stratum of clouds.[85]

And here I am!

(TALISMAN GUARD *enters*; MERIT OFFICIAL[86] *enters*; *each do a turn and exit*.)

([YOUNG MALE *continues singing*:])

Now that one is the Heavenly talisman agent,
And that one is the day-duty merit official.

That is the one whose commands the spirits of each mountain and every river alike heed;
That is the one who controls the wind, controls the rain, and controls lightning and thunder, for whom all four directions pull on their bridles to halt their horses.

You look—half in cloud, half in mist, all of the divinities are already here. It's just that, with such a drought in the lower realm, what help will come from following the dragon mother's orders of a single drop from the branch tip?

Shedding silky threads—mane and tail of the divine horse,
Dripping drop by drop—branch tips of the live willow.
Why so miserly, so loath to use it?
For no reason, my hand is unbearably hard to control.

From ancient times on, it's been said, "When the general is in the camp, there are orders from the lord that are not accepted." So, naturally, when the dragon is in the clouds, there are some orders from the emperor that are not honored! True it is, "One day when power lies in your hand, grasp the command and carry it out!" First group! Now heed my command, all you deities in the Office for Creating Wind in the House of the Southeastern Winds:

(*You hulu*)
The Great Clod has no sound, for it is silent and quiet,
But you agitate the vanguard and are the first to strike,
Casually stirring up sounds irritatingly sad from the tips of duckweed.
Just wait until the deities of flying sand and rolling rocks arrive,
To change it into a grand furnace that will agitate all the pores of Yin and Yang.
You have come from formlessness and disappear without a trace,
Used to expelling and uprooting, capable of sweeping all away.
You sound out at unfairness,
Aid the tiger's roar in the empty forests
And make those chaotic thunderclouds float in the heavens.

Be dispatched now to Uncle and Auntie Wind, quickly as by order!

(WIND DEITIES *circle the stage and exit.*)

Second group! You generals from the Upper Cloud Terrace in the House of the Northwest. Now heed my command!

(*Tianxia le*)
Abruptly I see linked mountains, oh, a thousand *li* distant,
High, so high,
Rising, then falling,
And an ether that encompasses all,
Still enshrouding the mountain peak.
Hang down your dragon body
And drag your tail end.
Swirl the "pond of the leviathan"[87]

And follow the rising tide.
You spread stratum by stratum into the void, covering day's morn.

Be dispatched now to Cloud Mother and Cloud Lad, quickly as by order!

(CLOUD DEITIES *circle the stage and go off.*)

Third group! You deities from the Upper Water Office in the House of Enriching Moistness, and you deities from the House of Water who spread rain! Now heed my command!

(*Nezha ling*)

Just regard that misty drizzle, dense and vague,
Spreading over the tips of pine trees and bamboos.
That rich earth saturated and soaked,
Drenching rice sprouts and wheat sprouts.
And more so the water sprites are cavorting in confusion,
Raising the tides of rivers and sea;
Washing all of Heaven and Earth,
Dissolving all that malignant ether from the top down.
At the juncture of wind and cloud,
You turn the basin completely upside down,
And helped me to command as I desire, so to be thought noblest among men!

(*Acts out sprinkling with the willow switch.* [*Speaks*:])

Be dispatched now to the dragon deities in the four seas. Quickly as by order!

(RAIN DEITIES *circle the stage and go off.*)

Fourth group! You deities from the Thunder Section of the House of Quaking, and you several deities, Lightning Mothers from the House of Splitting Open. Now heed my command!

(*Que ta zhi*)

Taking advantage of the flying of lightning bolts,
And the burning of thunder fires,
I want you to illumine in clearest light the hearts of people,
And reveal in their greatness the laws of Heaven.
An inky dark blackness
Locks tight the gloom of every direction.
A soaking, sopping cleavage of the heavens,
Has shot down below ten thousand *qing* of waves.

(*Acts out turning the pure bottle over.*) Be dispatched to the Five Thunder Envoys.

(THUNDER DEITIES *circle the stage and go off.*)

(YOUNG MALE:) The heaven appointed time has come. All you deities of the wind, clouds, thunder, and rain; you now muster for roll call every section, all to descend from heaven and lead these heavenly soldiers. Now heed my command!

(*Acts out pouring out of the pure bottle.*) (YOUNG FEMALE *acts out stopping him and speaks*:) Stop! It's overflowing, you can't pour out anymore!

(ALL OF THE DEITIES *circle the stage and go off.*)

(YOUNG MALE:) Ah, this whole extravaganza was truly handled in a grand way. Come to think of it, all of the drought-stricken sprouts down in the earth down below are all saturated with moisture. All demons currently in use—you can all return to your respective positions. I'll just tug the bridle of my horse here and go on down to the mortal world.

(THE HOST OF DEITIES:) Upon your divine command!

(*Exit.*)

(*Jisheng cao*) (YOUNG MALE:)
I see the heavy darkness disperse,
And the blue sky so high,
That whole stretch of homing clouds still twines about to moisten the dragon's scales,
That whole stretch of angled sunlight already lights up morning's rosy rays,
And that distant arching void sends the swan-goose far, far away.
It turns out to be "it's as lonely as if nothing were there after the divine deeds disappear,"
But look at me return having done what I had to do.

(YOUNG MALE:) In a human life, I think, no one can reach to Heaven, so I will halt my horse at the clouds' edge for a bit, let my eyes open out to the world, and look upon it all.

(*Reprise*)
This is not the phoenix from Cinnabar Hill,
Nor the great turtle from the azure sea,
This is a loan of the wind-chasing skewbald from his stables.
Look at the nine dots of mist covering all the realms,
And look at the Gates of Heaven at night, where no one goes:
True it is that the green dragon has shaken his tail and gone deep into the clouds,
I'm only afraid that this great Peng of mine will not have enough wind below its wings.

(YOUNG MALE:) I have to lower down these high clouds. Dragon granddaughter, you take the horse and go on back.

(YOUNG FEMALE:) Oh, sir, you have done much! I come from the clouds and disappear into the mist.

(*She circles the stage and hurries off.*)

(YOUNG MALE:) Look! The scenery suddenly emerges, and the rivers' flow rises strangely. Let me step out of the saddle on this high slope and go forward to ask. Look, there's a temple over there at mid-mountain, and on its main gate is written "Dragon Gate Mountain." Why, I think my teacher is here. Isn't that too lucky?

(EXTRAS *enter, circling the stage.* [*Speaks*:]) What a flood! The fields are all submerged, run for your life!

(*Exit.*)

(YOUNG MALE:) Look! The monastery gate is opening. I'll just walk into the temple to look for my teacher, Wenzhongzi.

(*Makes false exit.*)

(MALE *enters costumed as* Wenzhongzi *and speaks*)

My three-thousand disciples of the rites and music stand on either side,
My finest years might have left me, but not my august presence;
At the gate of my compound I plant neither peach nor plum,
For there are cedars and cypress like dragons to accompany this hoary one.

I am Wenzhongzi, Wang Tong.

(YOUNG MALE *enters and acts out seeing him.* [*Speaks*:]) It is my teacher indeed! You disciple has come to pay his respects.

(MALE:) And who are you? Where did you come from?

(YOUNG MALE:) I am Li Jing, and I have come from the heavens.

(MALE:) This youngster is trying to put one over one me! What do you want?

(YOUNG MALE:) Don't take it amiss, master, let me explain.

(MALE:) Well, speak!

(*Houting hua*) (YOUNG MALE:)
Ah, your disciple
Is a young brave from Sanyuan,
A friend of the omni-talented Yuanlong,
And by my uncle Han Qinhu
Was personally instructed as a child,
Receiving the strategems of the dragon.
All I lack is a way to "prop up heaven,"
And so, I have come to the dragon's gate.

(MALE:) If that's so, why did you say you came from the heavens?

(YOUNG MALE:) I won't lie, master.

(*Qing ge'er*)
It's all because I barged into the Dragon Palace,
But the dragon had no treasure,
So he begged me to act in his stead.
And when I held a hand above my eyes, I saw down below,
The heatwaves from the oppressive drought.
The Cloud Stream that had been scorched:
All the shrubs and trees had withered,
And there were no sprouts in the field.
But alas, heaven was so high,
That I could not hear the calls of lamentation,
A cartload of fire burned on and on,
And only a cupful of water to lightly sprinkle!
If I didn't spread this bounty of richness evenly,

How could I save those howling with pain?
And based on this
I happily contravened the command and braved the sanction of heaven—
I've almost poured out the whole pure pitcher.

(MALE:) Aiyo! Over here the waters are flooding up to the heavens, and it turned out to be you who committed this sin.

(YOUNG MALE:) I did this out of the goodness of my heart, how can you say it was an act of evil?

(MALE:) It's precisely your good heart which has created the problem. You could have never guessed that what you call good, is in fact not. That pure bottle is formed from the essential ethers from the house of water: a drop from the bottle is a foot on the ground. How can we put up with you scattering it all around as you like? Isn't this killing ten thousand people out of a desire to save a thousand? Moreover, you disobeyed the command of the Jade Emperor, and now it will be hard for that Dragon King mother to avoid heaven's punishment. Is not this a case of accepting a task on behalf of another, but ruining what they asked you to do?

(YOUNG MALE:) Just hearing what you said, master, makes the sweat flow down my back. As it stands, I want with all my might to report to heaven that I alone was responsible, take on that punishment myself, and avoid implicating the Dragon Lord.

(MALE:) What a laugh! Why trouble you to report yourself? Whenever a mortal gets an idea or acts on a whim, heaven and earth both know it. You were snug against the gates of heaven there, committing your stupid acts—you think the Heavenly One doesn't know about it?

(SOUTHERN XIANLÜ MODE: *Basheng ganzhou*)
You so happily joined [what should have been] a meeting of wind and cloud,
But it turned out to be a rare disaster that submerged everything.
Look at the farmers' houses swept away,
So much worse than the breach of the River at Huzi Dike.
You acted on behalf of the people but wound up harming them,
I fear you are no Fu Yue and have not his talent for rescuing the world from drought.[88]
Don't guess—it was probably his bad luck to be on duty.

Since you have nothing in your past that for which you need to repent, we can probably figure that the local deities here were destined for a flood. But there is one thing: people who wanted to save the world in the past were all too capable of doing something that wronged the world. And that was because they believed too deeply in their own heartfelt intentions and then just overdid it. People who are going to do great things cannot have an evil heart, but neither can they have a heart of goodness. The subtleness of the creator of transformations is that he makes all things equally heartless. You should have known this.

(YOUNG MALE:) I know now.

(MALE:) Well, get yourself together [adjust your clothes and headgear], and follow me in. Bear in mind Red Pine of olden days; he was the former rain master for Shen Nong.[89]

(*Exits.*)

(NORTHERN XIANLÜ MODE: *Coda*) (YOUNG MALE:)
The Master of Ghost Valley,[90]
The Hoary Heads of Mt. Shang[91]
I dare say should be recognized as muddleheaded pedants.
The way they put Heaven and Earth in order and saved the world,
Are the same as the foolhardy futile efforts of my youth.
My *qi* assailed the empyrean,
And my hand controlled the dipper bowl.
And I nearly wronged every person within the four seas.
That was just flaunting a little trick of divine intelligence,
And nothing like the whole stuff of being a hero,
So, I'd better bow my head, carry my books, all to be shaped into a better vessel.

NOTES

1. The printed versions of this text all attribute authorship to Yang Chaoguan, as does the preface to this text signed by Hua Ximin 華希閔 (1672–1751) and dated to 1727. See Yang Chaoguan (1729, 1a–2b).
2. Yuan Mei (1884, 5, 36b). Reprinted in Yang Chaoguan (1963, 227).
3. Du Guiping (2008, 102.)
4. Yuan Mei (1884, *j.* 232.35a–37a.)
5. Natural sounds emitted by the resonance of the earth and of the heavens. Allusion to the famous passage in *Zhuangzi*, "The Sorting which Evens Things Out" (*qiwu pian*). See Graham (1981, 48–49).
6. From an anecdote in the *New Tales of the World*, Xie An once said to Wang Xizhi, "In my middle years I'm so affected by grief or joy that whenever I part with a relative or friend I'm always indisposed for several days." Wang replied, "Since our hearts are at the 'mulberry and elm' stage, it's natural we should come to this; it's precisely the time to depend on stringed instruments and pipes to dispel our *feelings*. But the continual fear lest the younger generation will find out about it has spoiled my zest for this pleasure" (Mather 2002, 64; Wade-Giles romanization changed to pinyin, and small changes noted by italics.) This quote was surely a rebuke to Xie An for not becoming more serious and giving up his love for his household troupe of female singers whose music allowed him to freely vent his feelings of old age (i.e., the "mulberry and elm" stage). See Liu Yiqing (1984, 121).
7. Yang Chaoguan (1963, 1).
8. A trope for "making the most out of your time on this earth." From Cao Cao's lament over brevity of life: "Facing ale, one should sing, / Human life, how long can it be?"
9. Originally signals of the watch and markers of the hours, the terms later come to mean to "alert one to" or "to wake one to the realization of." Here, of course, there is a double meaning of the sound of the music in the drama.
10. That is, dissolute music.

11. "Grand Elegance" is also the name of a section of the *Book of Odes*, but it also became a term in poetics to mean the grand classical refinement of ancient poetry.
12. From a fragment of a discourse by the poet Song Yu (300–ca. 250 BCE), "In the ancient capital of Ying there was a traveler who sang. His first song was called 'A Villager from Ba [Sichuan]' and there were thousands of people who could make a match to it. But when he made 'Sunny Springs and Snowy White' there were very few who could do so." Later these two terms are used to differentiate, respectively, colloquial or vulgar songs from those that possess an elegant beauty.
13. Yang Chaoguan (1963, 2–3).
14. Just northeast of modern Liaocheng, Shandong.
15. Wu Jing and Xie Baocheng (2003, *j.* 8.33–34); submitted to Tang Zhongzong in the first month of *jingling* 3, between February 19–March 19, 709.
16. The first Tang-Goguryeo war in 645; Liaodong is east and north of Beijing, from Shenyang to the North Korean border.
17. That is, Ma Zhou.
18. A reference to raising the dead. It refers to a famous story found in the *Search for the Supernatural* (*Soushen ji*), about Emperor Wu of the Han's grief over the death of his favorite concubine Madam Li. A necromancer, Li Shaoweng duped the emperor into believing he could bring her back to life by having a look-alike dance behind curtain screens as the emperor watched. Of course, the dancer disappeared as the emperor approached her. See HS *j.* 25A, 1219–1220, *j.* 97, 3952–3955 and Gan Bao (1957, 15).
19. The Probationary Censor was, in the beginning, an appointed sub-functionary who populated various bureaucratic offices, most often having to do with investigatory functions; other sources say this office began in the *Longshuo* period under the famed empress Wu Zetian. See Wang Bo (1955, 60.1055) and Ye Mengde (1984, 74).
20. The account of this story in the *Saintly Chronicle of Chaotic Origin*, the *Hunyuan shengji* 混元聖紀, a hagiography of Laozi, specifies that it is Laozi (Li Dan) who dispatches Ma to aid the house of his descendants, the Li royal house, "It was ordered by edict that the two sections of Laozi's *The Way and Its Virtue* be translated into Sanskrit to send as gifts to the various nations of India. In the beginning, when the Tang was about to receive the mandate, Lord Lao once commanded that Ma Zhou descend in order to aid the descendants of the Lord [Lao] in establishing the state. The rest of the text then essentially repeats the *Taiping guangji* stories. See Xie Shouhao (1985, *j.* 8.110a, 112a).
21. That is to say, you may die any moment.
22. As one of the Five Marchmounts, Mt. Hua, the holy mountain of the West, was one of the highest deities in the Chinese pantheon. See "The Worshippers of Mount Hua," in Dudbridge (1995, 86).
23. Taiyi (Great Unity) is the highest deity in heaven.
24. *TPGJ j.* 19.128–29.
25. One of the prefectures near Bianliang, modern Kaifeng.
26. This is significant because Taizong himself had served as Director before he ascended the throne. Out of respect for him when he became emperor, this post was never filled. Here, in this story, Taizong gives him a great posthumous honor. See *TPGJ j.* 224.1719.
27. Biography is found in *JTS j.* 191.5092–93 and *XTS j.* 204.5800–5801; he is also well-represented in fictional works from the Tang onward.
28. Biography is found in *JTS j.* 79.2717–19; a much-reduced biography is found in *XTS j.* 204.5798.
29. The imperial palace.
30. Proper eminent officials.
31. Of the snow in the moonlight.
32. You turn out to be nothing.

33. A kind of leather apron, open in the back except for the tie, associated with the legendary Sima Xiangru, a great poet of the Han. According to *A New Account of Tales of the World*, "[Sima Xiangru] later dwelt in poverty. Upon reaching Linqiong, he purchased a wine shop. [Zhuo] Wenjun minded the wine vats and Xiangru, wearing a calf-nose apron, washed the utensils in the marketplace." Translation adapted from Liu Yiqing and Mather (2002, 291). See also SJ *j.* 117, 3000–3003.
34. Bi Zhuo 畢卓 (d. 329) was one of a group of serious drinkers who scandalized Luoyang. Bi Zhuo did so by stripping off his clothes when drunk. In the *Recent Anecdotes from the Talk of the Ages*, he is recorded as saying, "Holding a crab's claw in one hand and a cup of wine in the other, paddling and swimming about in a pool of wine—ah! with that I'd be content to spend my whole life" (Liu Yiqing and Mather 2002, 407). Another anecdote, more salient here, is quoted from the *History of the Jin Mid-Revival*, in the *History of the Jin*, "Bi Zhuo . . . was a clerk in the Board of Civil Office, and he often drank and neglected his duties. His next-door neighbor's brew had matured and, because he was drunk, Zhuo went one night among the vats to filch some to drink. He was bound up by the watchman. The next morning, they looked at him and it turned out he was the Clerk of the Board of Civil Office, Bi, so they released him. Subsequently Bi asked the master of that house to drink with him beside the vats. He got very drunk and then left." From "Biography of Bi Zhuo" (*JS j.* 49.1381).
35. Yuan An 袁安 (d. 92.9.4), a renowned official. According to the *Ru'nan xianxian zhuan* (*Traditions of the Former Worthies of Ru'nan*), incorporated into the *Hou Hanshu* (*History of the Later Han*), "At the time there was a heavy snowfall of more than ten feet. The Magistrate of Luoyang went out personally to investigate and he saw that everyone had removed the snow, and there were beggars out in the street. When he got to Yuan An's doorway, there was no path leading to it. Thinking that An was already dead, [the magistrate] ordered someone to remove the snow and go into the door, where they saw An lying there stiff from the cold. When asked why he did not go out, An replied, 'In a heavy snowfall, everyone is starving; it's not right to bother people.' The magistrate took him to be worthy and recommended him as "filial and honest." See *HHS j.* 80.1517.
36. Refers to a story about the Song poet Su Shunqin 蘇舜欽 (1008–1048) who, while staying at his father-in-law's house would drink a large amount of wine when reading at night. His father-in-law had a servant spy on him, and when Su would read passages from the *Han History*, he would pound the table when upset and stroke the table when pleased by a passage in the text. Upon hearing the report of the scene his father-in-law, he said, "A large measure of wine is indeed necessary when taking it with these 'wine helpers' [snacks, but here also stories]!" See Gong Mingzhi (2008, 201).
37. Paraphrasing a passage from the biography of Lu Jia 陸賈 (240–170 BCE) in the *Shiji* (*Records of the Grand Historian*), "Occasionally, Master Lu would try and persuade him and praise the *Odes* and *Documents* [i.e., the classics]. The Exalted Emperor cursed him and said, 'I obtained [the empire] on horseback, what do I have to do with the *Odes* and *Documents*?' Master Lu said, 'You obtained it on horseback, but how can you rule it on horseback?'" (*SJ j.* 97.2699).
38. "Master Grand Scribe says, 'In ancient times, there were five categories of meritorious merit for ministers. To establish ancestral halls and fix the altars of grain is called *xun*; to do that through words is called *lao*; to do it through power is called *gong*; to be clear about its hierarchy is called *fa*, and that which deepens over the days is called *yue*.' The oath of enfeoffment says, 'Let the Yellow River be but a belt and Mount Tai but a whetstone, but the enfeoffed state will be at eternal peace which will reach to its posterity. There are none who do not desire to make their roots firm at the beginning, but the branches and leaves will gradually wither then sere and decay.'" (*SJ j.* 18.877).
39. The "crucible of heaven and earth" is represented as a round sphere with intricately carved patterns on the outside. It was supposedly used by the sage Nüwa to melt the precious stones with which she patched up the sagging corner of heaven.

40. Han Gaozu had tried to enlist the four worthies who had been prominent men at the end of the Qin, but at first they were hesitant to come to Gaozu's court because of the way he treated men of learning. They were finally persuaded to come to court in an elaborate plan created by the empress and a high court official.
41. From Du Fu's (712–770) poem "Again Passing the Tomb of Taizong of the Tang" (Chong guo Zhaoling 重過昭陵), see translation in Owen (2016, 346).
42. Here, referring to the first Han Emperor and Empress's slaughter of loyal officials who had helped found the dynasty.
43. An anachronistic reference to the killing of loyal ministers in the Han, but also a veiled reference to the brothers of Tang Emperor Li Shimin, who were murdered since they could be potential rivals.
44. The Lingyan Ge (凌煙閣 Beyond the Clouds Tower) is a gallery in which Li Shimin 李世民, the second emperor of the Tang, had portraits painted of twenty-four meritorious officers and officials who helped him found the dynasty. For a study of the imaginative re-creation of the portraits in the gallery and the discursive space that the name implies, see Burkus-Chasson 2010.
45. That is, members of the civil service court bureaucracy who helped Li Shimin.
46. *Analects* 8.13. "In a state that possesses the Way, it is shameful to be poor and of low status in it." The phrase is followed by, "if a state is without the Way, to be wealthy and noble in it is also a cause for shame." The original edition deletes the word "shame," which makes the sentence more of a recollection of key parts of the passage, which I have attempted to reproduce in the translation.
47. A magnificent horse, one of the legendary eight steeds that pulled the chariot of King Mu of Zhou.
48. A song that "spoke of how his Highness [of the state of Wu] cultivated the civil, trained the martial, took his pattern from Heaven in order to act; the fecundity of his benevolence flowed over all, and the world was happy and joyous" 言上修文訓武，則天而行仁澤流洽，天下喜樂也. See Guo Maoqian (1982, 18.274).
49. Which happened only when the world was in perfect order. As the name of the Yellow River makes clear, it is always full of loess silt.
50. To right the emperor's wrongs.
51. To be of actual service at the time is better than being remembered for it.
52. Su Qin 蘇秦 was a Warring State rhetorician who had long tried to have his policies accepted in the state of Qin, but he was unsuccessful. "His black marten cloak was tattered, one-hundred catties of precious metal were gone, and he was completely out of supplies, so he left Qin and returned" (Liu Xiang 1985, 85). Su Qin would later succeed in uniting the other states against Qin.
53. Red-faced from drink, hunched shoulders from the cold.
54. The emperor in his palace.
55. From Du Fu's "Song of Eight Drinking Immortals."
56. Idema (2010).
57. Cf. Graff (2011–2012).
58. Translated as "Questions and Replies Between T'ang T'ai-tsung and Li Wei-gung," in Harvey (1993, 307–61).
59. Jao Tsung-i (1990, iii–viii).
60. See Jing Wang translation; Wang (2010). See also Xu (2014, 46–53).
61. See Schafer (1973, 7–53, 147–86).
62. This translation, by Liu Qian (with some changes), is based on the text in *Taiping guangji*, 304.2413. See Liu (2017, 173–74).
63. Located at the west of modern Dengfeng 登封 county in Henan Province.
64. According to Dudbridge, "婦" should be read as "姨" here and Shaoyi 少姨 Temple is located at Shaoshi 少室 Mount. See Dudbridge (1995, 157).

65. Liu (2017, 269–74).
66. The "Pass" 關 refers to Tongguan 潼關, the eastern portal of North China Plain (Guanzhong 關中 Plain). It is located between the Qin Mountains and the Yellow River. During the Tang dynasty, the safety of the national capital Chang'an was directly connected to the successful defense of Tongguan.
67. Li Fang (1986, *j.* 418.3407–09). Translation by Liu Qian, with some changes.
68. This was a prevalent opinion with scant historical verification, although Warner (2001, 371–76, 384–85), based on an assembly of sources, makes an extremely compelling case that it happened. See also Warner (2004, passim).
69. See note 72 below. Versions of the phrase about people who will do great things can be found in anecdotes 19.3 and 19.5 in the *Shishuo xinyu*.
70. At the [Western] age of nineteen, there was a ceremony for males to mark their entry into manhood as an adult. The formal hairdo and capping ceremony were referred to as "tender capping" (*ruoguan*) since the young man had not reached full physical maturity and strength.
71. Han Qinhu (538–592) was a brilliant general, and he was instrumental in crushing the Chen dynasty and establishing the Sui. On his role in the military battles of the era, see Graff (2002, 134, 177).
72. This is Wang Tong (?584–617), a noted Confucian scholar and teacher of several Tang intellectuals. A full account of his life and his works can be found in Warner (2004).
73. A certain Wen Qiao, upon reaching a deep-water eddy at a dike on his way to Wuchang, heard the sound of music coming from the depths of the water. Rumor had it that there were many strange creatures in the depths, and he lit a rhinoceros horn to illuminate them. "In just a short time the water creatures snuffed the flame, and they were all strange shapes and weird forms, and some were in horse carts, dressed in red clothes. That night he dreamt that someone told him, 'We are separated from you by the Way of light and Way of dark. What was on your mind when you decided to light us up?' [Wen] really detested the dream. He had had a tooth go bad, and he pulled it at this time, consequently getting sick. When he reached the place of appointment, he died in fewer than ten days. He was forty-two at the time." *JS* (vol. 6, 1795).
74. Refers to Li Haogu's play, *Student Zhang Boils the Sea*. In this story a student and candidate in the examinations, Zhang Yu, was traveling along the seashore and lodged at a Buddhist monastery. On a nice evening, he played his zither, and the third daughter of the Dragon King of the Eastern Sea came to listen. They fell in love. She gave him a handkerchief woven by sea maidens as a token at parting and asked him to come see her on the Mid-Autumn Festival for a betrothal. In his search during the festival, Zhang meets a demon who tells him that the dragon king is an irascible creature that cannot be crossed, and that he must be first forced to submit. She gives him a silver wok, a golden coin, and an iron ladle, has him scoop sea water into the wok, toss in the golden coin and boil it. As the water in the wok boils and evaporates so does the sea. The dragon king is finally quelled and submits to taking Yu as a son-in-law. For a translation of the play, see Li (2014, 371–401).
75. This would be the area of modern Shanxi, east of the bend of the Yellow River and west of the Taihang mountain range.
76. *Shangtian you lu* 上天有路, a play on the common phrase *shangtian wu lu ru di wu men* 上天無路, 入地無門, "no road to ascend to heaven, no door through which to enter earth, i.e. 'there is no way out.'"
77. That is, clouds.
78. A mountain in the Tiantai area of Zhejiang that is red and has a shape like the crenellations on a city wall.
79. Several people were traveling together and they each voiced their desire. One wanted to be the magistrate of Yangzhou, another wanted to be rich, and a third wanted to ascend to the heavens riding a

crane. One said, "I want to combine the three: ride a crane to Yangzhou with ten-thousand strings of cash tied to my belt."

80. Refers to the Xiaoshi, a famous player of pipes who could imitate the sounds of the phoenix. Duke Mu of Qin gave his daughter Nongyu to him in marriage, and he taught her to imitate the call of the phoenix, and the fabulous bird came to roost on their dwelling. Xiaoshi then constructed the Phoenix Terrace where they stayed. One morning, they were seen ascending to heaven with Xiaoshi astride a dragon and Nongyu straddling a phoenix.
81. The inaugural reign period of the Sui dynasty (581–600).
82. The reign period of the notoriously extravagant Emperor Yang of the Sui (605–616).
83. Legend claims that a red ether emanated from the grave of Chiyou—who had sowed the earth with soldiers in his fight against the Yellow Emperor—like a long strip of silk, and this was called the "flag of Chiyou."
84. Both the Silver River and the Stream of Heaven are names for the Milky Way.
85. A play on very popular lines from Tang poem, "Climbing Stork Tower," "The white sun reclines upon the mountains and is gone, / The Yellow River flows on into the seas; / Should you desire to use all of your thousand-*li* eyes, / Go up one more floor in the tower."
86. Originally a bureaucratic post, "registrar of merit," that was adopted into Daoism as names of helpers for Daoist priests; used to transmit messages to deities.
87. Home of the huge *kun* fish that would soon turn into the *peng* bird, whose body was thousands of miles long.
88. Fu Yue was a slave in the area of Fuyan (modern Shanxi), where he worked on constructing walls of rammed earth (he is often wrongly credited as the inventor of the form system for these walls:). According to the *Records of the Historian*, the Shang thearch, Wuding, dreamt of obtaining a wise sage named Yue. Based on what he had seen in his dream, he looked at the assembled ministers and hundred clerks of his government, but none of them matched. At that point he sent his hundred officers to seek him in the wilds, and he obtained Yue from the precipices of Fu. At this time, Yue was a slave, forming walls in the precipices of Fu, and when Wuding saw him, he said, "This is he." He got him and conversed with him, and indeed Yue was a sagely man, so he was raised to be minister and the state of Yin was grandly governed. Therefore, he consequently bestowed on him the surname Fu because of the precipices of Fu and called him Fu Yue.
89. Red Pine was a Daoist *xianren*, or transcendent being. He acted as the Master of Rain for Shen Nong, the Divine Agriculturist.
90. Master of Ghost Valley (*guiguzi* 鬼谷子), who is known by a series of different names, was supposedly a hermit who lived in the 4th century BCE. The text is a political treatise based on Yin-Yang cosmology, dating uncertain, and it is claimed Master of the Ghost Valley was the teacher of Su Qin 蘇秦 (d. 284 BCE:) and Zhang Yi 張儀 (373–310 BCE:), the most famous political rhetoricians of the 4th and 3rd centuries BCE. In fact, it is believed this text is probably by several hands, and portions of it stem from a much later era.
91. Four aged hermits who had served as officials of the Qin dynasty but eventually escaped its cruel reign by residing in Mt. Shang, where they existed on a diet of efficacious mushrooms (*lingzhi* 靈芝, glossy Ganoderma, *ganoderma lucidum*). After the fall of the Qin, they were courted by Liu Bang, founder of the Han, but rebuffed him because he did not esteem men of worth in his government.

11

Song of Dragon Well Tea

WANG WENZHI (1730–1802)
TRANSLATED BY TIAN YUAN TAN AND PINGYU SUN

In 1780, the Qianlong emperor (1711–1799, r. 1736–1795) visited Hangzhou during his fifth southern tour. An elite writer and retired official named Wang Wenzhi 王文治 (1730–1802, *jinshi* 1760) was commissioned to compose new plays for the occasion. In *Notes on Songs* (*Quhua*), Liang Tingnan 梁廷枏 (1796–1861) provides an informative account of the context behind the production of these plays in which his uncle Liang Sen (fl. 1770s) was involved:

> During the Qianlong reign, when His Majesty made his fifth visit to the south, my uncle Liang Sen was serving as an official in Central Zhejiang and received an assignment to dutifully undertake the task of organizing theatrical performances and elegant music [for the visit]. An order was issued in advance and a hefty sum was paid to engage the Junior Compiler Wang Wenzhi (*hao* Menglou) in composing nine new plays, all of which were written based on the local landscape and scenery. These nine plays are respectively titled *Sannong deshu* (*The Three Harvests Receive Timely Rain*), *Longjing cha ge* (*Song of Dragon Well Tea*), *Xiangzheng bingjian* (*Auspicious Signs of Icy Silkworm Cocoons*), *Haiyu ge'en* (*Songs of Grace within the Seas*), *Dengran fajie* (*Lantern Lights in the Dharma-world*), *Geling danlu* (*Elixir Furnace at Geling Hill*), *Xianyun yanling* (*Immortal Wine to Extend Life*), *Ruixian Tiantai* (*Lucky Omens at Mount Tiantai*), and *Yingbo qingyan* (*Fairy Waves Clear and Peaceful*). Performers with the best skills were selected to play [the roles] and the plays were offered at the West Lake Traveling Palace. Before each act was performed, a copy was first bound with yellow silk and respectfully presented for consultation by His Majesty. These theatrical productions always received praise and rewards, and such bestowals were frequent. Nowadays when these "dharma tunes" (*faqu*)[1] are once again performed, we can still look up to the old times when the seas were peaceful, people were happy, and products were bountiful.

> The seventy-year-old Son-of-Heaven inspected the region to find out about local customs. Among the mulberry and hemp fields, His Majesty shared His joy with the common people. Such airs of harmony and peace are rarely seen in a thousand years. This was truly a grand ceremony.[2]

The play we are reading in this chapter, *Song of Dragon Well Tea*, was one of the nine short, single-act plays produced on this occasion. It presents an interesting example to explore a form of court drama commissioned and produced locally for imperial entertainment.[3]

Written in the style and tradition of Chinese court drama, *Song of Dragon Well Tea* serves as a functional text to celebrate the occasion, the emperor's visit to Hangzhou, and is filled with panegyrics as well as visual spectacle. In the play, readers are introduced to a hodgepodge of Buddhist arhats, Daoist immortals, Buddhist monks, tea-picking men and women, tea-serving (heavenly) maidens, and the Dragon King of Longjing and his daughters. Such an assembly of multiple characters, especially divine immortals, is not unusual in the court theatrical tradition. But certain specific elements in *Song of Dragon Well Tea* distinguish it from the routine court plays in the imperial palace. For example, Wang Wenzhi creates a link between the characters in the play and the local region of Longjing (Dragon Well), an area well known for its tea plantations. What may appear at first glance to be an assembly of random episodes is indeed part of his consciously constructed local tribute to the Qianlong emperor. Wang's drama not only draws extensively from local folklore and tales, but also engages actively with Qianlong's previous visits to Longjing and Qianlong's own writings on the cultural site.

Court theater may be renowned for its staging effects and visual spectacle,[4] but Wang's play *Song of Dragon Well Tea* also invites us to explore a less studied aspect of these "local" court plays—its literary characteristics, poetic borrowings, and intertextual relations with other genres, all of which call for a more contemplative mode of close reading than is usually accorded court drama. As tempting as it is for many to characterize court literature in general as the epitome of panegyrics and flattery with minuscule literary value, this notion is, to some extent, challenged and subverted in *Song of Dragon Well Tea* by its subtly woven intertextual references and allusions. Apart from quoting two poems written by Qianlong himself during his previous trips to Longjing (one on the scenic view and one on the tea), Wang also quotes from a court poem by the Tang poet Shen Quanqi (656–ca. 716) about a Dragon pool, and another three poems about the Longjing spring by various Song and Ming dynasty writers as recorded in Ming dynasty texts such as *Sightseeing Gazetteer of West Lake* (*Xihu youlan zhi*) and *The Quest for Dreams at West Lake* (*Xihu mengxun*). By borrowing various Longjing-themed works across different historical periods, Wang crafts a semirealistic, semimythical plot that condenses different temporal and spatial dimensions into a singular plane.

Besides depicting locales by borrowing past literary works centered on the same theme and detailing various real-life scenic spots and monuments at Longjing, Wang heightens the sensory experience of the play by using end rhymes and reduplications. One such example is the set of arias under the "Yanguojiang" tune, where reduplicative adjectives such as *su-su* (rustling pines), *di-di* (pattering rain), and *ji-ji* (silent human voices) reinforce nature sounds through words. In our translation we attempt to bring out this important literary feature by first changing the adjectives to reduplicative verbs (to whistle, to patter, to murmur), and second, to include an "-ing" suffix after each word to create a sense that everything was ongoing in real time. The end result is hence "the whistling, whistling sound of pines.... Like the pattering, pattering sound of rain.... Also alike the murmuring, murmuring sound of people...."

Bringing together deities, mythical figures, heavenly maidens, and a long-deceased elderly monk just to make them compliment a certain emperor's rule and his mediocre poems may seem absurd or excessive to many today, especially when much emphasis is usually placed on the expression of self in judging the value and merit of a literary work. But we should not disregard the context—that this is work commissioned by the imperial court, entrusted to a well-known scholar, who was paid ("a hefty sum") to write for the emperor's southern inspection tour, and performed in front of the emperor and his retinue—which means that there were certain themes and directions expected of the play. Before rushing to condemn the "oppressive rulers" of the past, we should bear in mind that this process of commissioning is actually very similar to what we have now, where artists or composers will be paid to create or compose for key festivals or state events, such as national day celebrations or the opening of the Olympic Games.

A court play should not be disregarded simply because it was a product of imperial commission. Nor should it be read only within the confines of the court milieu. Instead, reading *Song of Dragon Well Tea* in its cultural-historical contexts will encourage us to explore it as a site of intersections of various cultural currents among the court, the elites (e.g., tea making, calligraphy, rock collection), and the local villagers (tea pickers). Imperial patronage of various schools of thought also allows Buddhist, Confucian, and Daoist ideals to co-exist in the same play and creates freedom for flexible and direct application of religious references and metaphors in literature.

Dramatis Personae in Order of Appearance

Role Type	*Name, family role, or social role*
ALL UNSPECIFIED	Arhat Aṅgaja
	Arhat Pindola Bharadvaja
	Fourteen arharts
	Yang Xihe
	Cai Shaoxia
	Four heavenly maidens
	Two attendants
	Monk Biancai

Six Male Villagers (tea pickers)
Six Female Villagers (tea pickers)
Four Maidens
Dragon Well's Dragon King
Two Dragon Daughters

SONG OF DRAGON WELL TEA

([Performer, ROLE TYPE UNSPECIFIED] *costumed as* THE VENERABLE ARHAT[5] AŃGAJA, *holding a walking staff, enters:*)

(ZHENGGONG MODE: Northern Tune: *Duanzhenghao*)
The vermilion sun shines on the misty river,
Transformative rain envelops the cloudless peaks.
Across the mountains and streams are auspicious airs and propitious rays.
Look—those clear sounds coming beyond the Rustling Bamboos Ridge,[6]
Are the pines and cypresses being lined up as rows of celestial staffs.

I, the Venerable Ańgaja, among the sixteen arhats[7] was known to be placed the thirteenth. Owing to the title bestowed by His Majesty, I am now redesignated as the first.[8] Today, with Heaven's will, the sky is clear and harmonious. What can stop me from washing my alms bowl by the Dragon Well spring?[9]

([Performer, ROLE TYPE UNSPECIFIED] *costumed as* THE VENERABLE ARHAT PINDOLA BHARADVAJA, *with a khakkhara,*[10] *enters:*)

(*Reprise*)
On my shoulders I carry the palm-leaf scriptures,
In my hands I hold a green-rattan staff.
I roam at will through the eastern lands and the western regions.
What a joy to see this peaceful and orderly world giving rise to the *Dragon Canon*,[11]
Revealing the Arhats' image.

I, the Venerable Pindola Bharadvaja, am ranked twelfth out of the sixteen arhats, but was erroneously transmitted as the First Arhat in Cina. Thanks to the rectification and title bestowed by His Majesty, I have been restored to my original stature. Now I've come to the Alms Pond[12] in Dragon Well. Senior, let's wash our alms bowls together.

(*The other fourteen* ARHATS, *together riding on clouds,*[13] *enter:*) Seniors, the Dragon Well's Dragon King, and his daughters, have prepared a vegetarian meal in their Crystal Palace today to feast the five hundred arhats.[14] We should accept the invitation and go there.

(*The* TWO ARHATS*:*) We were just washing our alms bowls, and now there is the opportunity of a meal. Favorable circumstances have brought forth such coincidence. My seniors, let us go to the Dragon Palace together.

(*Together:*)

The pool reveals the river of stars, following the Yellow Course,
The Dragon heads to Heaven's gates, guarding the *Ziwei* Star.[15]

(*Exit.*)

(\[Performer, ROLE TYPE UNSPECIFIED\] *costumed as* YANG XIHE *and* CAI SHAOXIA *enter dressed as immortals and holding flywhisks, leading four* HEAVENLY MAIDENS. *One carries flowers, one carries an incense burner, one carries a court tablet, and one carries a brush and an ink stone.*)

(ZHENGGONG MODE: *Yanguojiang*)

Barely having passed ten *li*[16] of lush greenery along the resounding Rustling Bamboos,
Already we are at the roaring torrents splattering and crashing against the jade steps.
Look—the whistling, whistling sound of pines, and the still sound of the stream,
Resemble the pattering, pattering sound of rain, echoed by the sound of the wind,
And the murmuring, murmuring sound of people, answered by the sound of orioles.

I, Yang Xihe, and I, Cai Shaoxia, have always loved calligraphy and today roam the Azure Heaven. We both have been appointed as the celestial officials in charge of writing. Since the Heavenly Court is more leisurely, we have specially come to the Dragon Well to have a pure chat with Master Biancai.[17] (*Acts out knocking on the door.*)

(TWO ATTENDANTS *enter:*)

Beneath the cliff lies a deep spring,
Faraway and fathomless beyond sight.
Above it brews a misty cloud,
Imparting mortals with nourishing might.[18]

(*Acts out opening the door.*) It's Deity Yang and Deity Cai! Our Master has gone into meditation at the Fangyuan Hut[19] for quite some time; it is best not to interrupt him. Please wait a little while in the Juan'e Chamber.

(*Exit.*)

(YANG *and* CAI:) Let's take a walk around here.

As we leisurely walk on the verdant moss to pass time,
Flowers and grasses emit a pure scent,
As if following the Master into meditation.

(*Onstage the "Wisp of Cloud" rock*[20] *is installed.* YANG *acts out seeing it:*) Oh, marvelous! This rock is so beautifully pure and sleek, floating like a traveling cloud. The pieces stowed in Mi Fu's sleeves are probably nothing compared to this.[21] (\[YANG\] *acts out looking up and seeing the Imperial script.*) This is a poem composed by the Sagely Son of Heaven.[22] (*Acts out respectfully reciting it:*)

The delicate slice of rock rests by the azure peak,

Resplendently it is always surrounded by thick clouds.
The Hall in the Summer Villa[23] originates from here,
Facing the sight, I once again look up towards the sagely traces.[24]

Look, these heavenly words will remain glorious for ages. How blessed we are to have an opportunity to view the illustrious writings by His Majesty, we should pay our respects. (*Acts out paying respects.*) (*Monk* BIANCAI *enters*:)

On a whim we come to the riverbank and beat the fading moon;[25]
As words fade we face the wind and lean against "Wisp of Cloud."[26]

(*Acts out mutual greetings.*) It's the two Deities of writing! In my meditation just now, I was approaching Prajna wisdom[27] and illuminated true understanding. Then I saw the light of beautiful writings shining upon the heaven and earth, just as the two of you are passing by. (YANG *and* CAI:) Although we do know some characters, how could we bear comparison with such glorious light of beautiful writing? Since, Elder, you have unbounded powers of supernatural knowledge, what you've just seen must be a prophecy of something else. (BIANCAI:) The sky is pure and peaceful, so why don't we take a walk at the mountain's rear? (YANG *and* CAI:) We would love to. (*Acts out walking together.*) Walking out from the monastery gate, we are treated with such a pleasingly pure view.

(*Yujiaozhi*)
The winding peaks and entwined ridges
Are splashed by fresh gusts of wind and ten thousand layers of light.
The hundred streams of the flowing source vie with silver waves,
Showing off even more the mountains so still throughout the day.
Look—the trees hazy and misty, as though there are people passing by,
The waters deep and still, enfolding reflections of graceful blossoms.

(*Together*:)
Beneath our feet, gentle clouds gather gradually,
Under our arms, light breezes form naturally.[28]

(Monk BIANCAI:) Deities, there comes a team of tea-pickers.

([Performers, ROLE TYPES UNSPECIFIED] *costumed as* SIX MALE VILLAGERS, *enter in unison*:)

(Northern Tune: *Chao Tianzi*)
Through mountains high and ridges long,
By clouds deep and flowers sweet,
Facing the wind, the dew-covered new sprouts come forth.
Half opened and half closed:
Each like a single flag, each a single lance,[29]
With the warmth of sun rays, the leaves secretly grow.
The spring days are gradually getting longer,
As the midday mists first rise upward.
Nodding high and low, the dainty branches dip and wave,

In unison, we sing this tea-picking song.

(TRIO:) Here comes another group of female tea-pickers. ([Performers, ROLE TYPES UNSPECIFIED] *costumed as* SIX VILLAGE TEA-PICKING WOMEN, *enter*:)

(*Reprise*)

Adoring the fragrant wind and fragrant dew,
Scooping up the mountain's splendor and water's splendor,
We see green grass growing on narrow paths along the dike.
Amongst the bamboo fences and thatched cottages,
Rise a few lines of smoke from tea roasting—
Set against the red flowers, the more they seem to wave.
Gold threads tender and yellow,
Jade shoots face to face.
Carrying overflowing aprons and filled baskets,
In unison, we sing the tea-picking song.

(*Act out picking tea leaves and exit.*)

(TRIO:) How delightful! This group of tea-picking men and women are in such harmony and contentment, jointly celebrating at the spring terrace.[30] The Sage's rule "transforms where he passes through and influences one in a spiritual way,"[31] and "there is no place it cannot reach."[32] (BIANCAI:) I nearly forgot—it is near the rainy season now, so everyone is picking tea leaves. I've plucked some tender tea leaf buds half a month before the rainy season. May I have the pleasure of you both joining me to taste the tea beside the Dragon Well spring? (YANG *and* CAI:) Trekking through the mountain paths in pure leisure, chatting over tea in the Chan forest: one day this will again be added to history as a splendid anecdote! (BIANCAI:) Please rest by the Imperial Stele Pavilion. (*Onstage,*[33] *the Imperial Poetry Stele Pavilion has been installed first.*) (YANG *and* CAI:[34]) The maidens are simmering tea, let the Senior Monk draw some water. (*The* FOUR MAIDENS *act out arranging the tea stove and accessories and simmering the tea.*)

(*They respond all together*:)

We all know that the Guzhu tea[35] is unparalleled,
We must try the best water from the spring of Mt. Wu.[36]

(*Yujiaozhi*)

Clear spring like a mirror,
On the bamboo brazier [water boils like] "pine sounds" and "crab-eye shapes."[37]
Fresh tea and fresh water all prepared at the Dragon Well,
This taste is truly a class apart.

(*Four* MAIDENS *act out pointing tea*[38] *and delivering tea.*)

With jade-like fingers they hold up the azure-green cup,
Although their narrow shoes are tiny, their small steps are properly poised.

([MAIDEN] *acts out serving* BIANCAI *a cup of tea, but he dares not receive it.*) (YANG *and* CAI:) Elder, the heavenly maiden is serving you tea, why do you refuse it?

(BIANCAI:) I am worried about breaking the religious precepts. (YANG *and* CAI:) Elder, you have already attained unbound powers of supernatural knowledge, why do you still need to be bound by this? (BIANCAI:) I wish to set an example for the future generations. (YANG *and* CAI *laugh.*) (YANG:) If so, then let me serve you instead. (BIANCAI *receives the tea, and* YANG *and* CAI drink the tea together [with BIANCAI]:) Good tea indeed!

(*Together*:)

Under our arms, light breezes gather naturally,
Beneath our feet, light clouds gather gradually.

(YANG *acts out looking up and seeing the Imperial script*:) These are poetic lines written by His Majesty. (*Recites respectfully*:)

Dragon Well tea fresh by the Dragon Well spring,
A truly exquisite taste of its own suited to boiling and roasting.
Inch-long tea buds sprout from pulverized rock[39]
And are ready for drying before the rainy season.
Why praise the royal tea using terms like "Phoenix lumps?"
The delicate "Sparrow-tongue" leaves moisten my lotus heart.
I call out wishing to see Master Biancai by my side,
Who'll laugh at me for still being attached to "literary Zen."[40]

We can see that the mind of the Sage is like the sun that radiates everywhere, like the sea that nourishes all. Shaoxia, the scene of us tasting tea just now was captured in advance by the Sage. (BIANCAI:) His Majesty's poem clearly mentions "Biancai," so I, Biancai, can only prostrate myself in worship with boundless reverence. Since you, the Immortal Master, have long enjoyed a reputation in calligraphy, and your copy of the internal manuscript of the *Yellow Court Classic*[41] has been passed down as a model for generations,[42] would you write me a copy [of His Majesty's poem] for veneration in my Chan chamber? (YANG:) His Majesty's calligraphy is like a soaring Phoenix and a flying Dragon, how can we emulate even a fraction of it? (MAIDENS bring out an ink stone and grind ink) (BIANCAI:) I'll spread the paper. (YANG:) Shaoxia, your inscription of the immortal palace was personally received from a jade order,[43] so today you should also respectfully copy the work. (CAI:) You're the senior, please don't be so modest. (YANG *acts out copying respectfully.*)

(*Chuanbozhao*)

On the lustrous cloud-patterned paper,
The ink spreads and my inner brush is upright.
Do not say that I have long enjoyed a reputation in calligraphy,
Do not say that I have long enjoyed a reputation in calligraphy:
I follow His model, basking in the light of His sagely purity!

(*Auspicious clouds appear on the table. Everyone acts out being joyously surprised*:)

Why do auspicious clouds appear on the paper, not fading for a long time?
Transforming into auspicious clouds, lit by the sun and the stars,

Manifesting as auspicious clouds to assist the sun and the stars.

(YANG:) Elder, just now when you had approached Prajna wisdom and illuminated true understanding through Samadhi, you saw how the lights of beautiful writings shone upon heaven and earth. This must be the evidence of that. (BIANCAI *closes palms in salutation*:) So it is the light from the writings of the Sagely Son of Heaven! It's surely shining down on the heaven and earth! Let me respectfully store this copy away and worship it.

(*Exits stage respectfully holding the scrolls.*)

(YANG *and* CAI:) Oh, look, the Dragon King emerges from the Dragon Well!

([Performer, ROLE TYPE UNSPECIFIED] *costumed as the Dragon Well's* DRAGON KING, *enters leading two* DRAGON DAUGHTERS *holding pearls, while* THE SIXTEEN ARHATS *disperse flowers and act out displaying all auspicious signs*:)

([SHUANGDIAO MODE:] *Gu meijiu* followed by *Taiping ling*)

How envious we are of the fabled mountains harboring the Imperial inscriptions,
How envious we are of the fabled mountains harboring the Imperial inscriptions.
We, the army of *deva*s and *nāga*s[44] are fine guards.
A marvelous copy made by dipping the brush in fragrant ink,
Moving the Heavenly patterns around unfettered,
Scattering Mandārava flowers[45] across ten directions.[46]
And thereby the rustling bamboo forests above the ridge
Are magically transfigured into heavenly writings:
Scroll after scroll adorned and embellished by a hundred jewels,
Each and every character a Dharma Repository of the Blue Lotus.
As for us, the miraculous clouds, the miraculous banners,
The miraculous sounds, and miraculous lights,
Oh, we shall keep them at the Crystal Palace to serve with our most solemn worship.

(*Exit.*)

NOTES

1. The use of the term "dharma tunes" resonates with the court entertainment in the Tang dynasty as this form of music was once performed in the Pear Garden conservatory of Emperor Xuanzong.
2. Liang Tingnan (1959, 265).
3. The full set of nine plays currently survives in at least three different Qing-dynasty editions. The translation here is based on the Daoguang edition printed by Liang Tingnan in his *Tenghuating shiwu zhong* 籐花亭十五種 collection, now readily accessible through a reprint in Wang Wenzhang (2010, vol. 63, 397–412).
4. References to performers "treading the clouds" and the constant calling of attention to "look" at certain objects onstage remind us of the fanciful props and elaborate stage machinery typical of court theater.

5. In Buddhism, an arhat refers to an individual that has gained enlightenment. The term is often reserved for the first generation of disciples of the Buddha.
6. Located in the southwest of Hangzhou in Zhejiang Province, China. The place is famous for the tea plantations at Longjing 龍井 (Dragon Well), made known through visits and poems written by various literati throughout history. It later became one of the "Eight Scenic Sights of Longjing" (*Longjing bajing* 龍井八景) canonized by the poems of the Qianlong emperor.
7. It was believed that sixteen arhats guarded the righteous order of the Buddha's law. Although the number of arhats was a recurring subject of scholarly discourse, early Buddhist scriptures and artworks showed that there were only sixteen arhats. It was only during the Qing dynasty, when the Qianlong emperor issued his imperial approval of eighteen arhats, that the latter number became mainstream.
8. In 1757, during his second southern inspection tour, the Qianlong emperor visited the Shengyin Temple in Hangzhou where he was taken to view a set of portraits of the sixteen arhats. He later renamed and reordered the images according to a system then popular in Tibet, which is reflected in this play. See Weidner (1994, 264).
9. Known as one of the four springs of Hangzhou, once believed to be the residence of dragons.
10. Sanskrit name for a staff with a ringed finial that produces a jingling sound when it is tapped on the ground, commonly carried by monks to warn animals of the bearer's impending approach.
11. The *Qianlong Tripiṭaka* (*Qianlong dazangjing* 乾隆大藏經) is a major Buddhist canon edition of the Qing produced under the sponsorship of the Qianlong Emperor. He worked closely with Tibetan Buddhists, oversaw the publication of Tibetan and Mongolian Buddhist canons, and had a substantial personal stake in Buddhist religiosity, sponsoring the publishing of the *Longzang* 龍藏 (carved 1735–1738) in Beijing.
12. Place name in Longjing: Pond for Washing Alms Bowls (Xibo Chi 洗鉢池).
13. To achieve such effects, the Qing palace troupe was known to have made use of cloud machines not dissimilar to the ones seen in Renaissance theaters across Europe.
14. An expansion from the sixteen (main) arhats.
15. This couplet is quoted from Shen Quanqi's 沈佺期 (656–714) poem titled "Dragon Pool" (龍池篇), but with some minor changes. The original couplet was: "This pool reveals the river of stars, / **discerns** the Yellow Course, / Its dragon heads to Heaven's gates, / **enters** the Tzu-wei" (池開天漢分黃道, 龍向天門入紫薇). Translation quoted from Owen (1977, 342). In this play, Wang changes the characters *fen* (分, "to discern") to *yi* (依, "to follow"), and *ru* (入, "to enter") to *hu* (護, "to guard"). We could simply suppose this to be an instance of variant text, but no well-known Qing editions of Tang poetry collections, including *Quan Tangshi* (the largest collection of Tang poems published in Qing dynasty), appear to have contained the same lines as the ones presented in this play. Hence, this might be a conscious decision by Wang, to adapt the slightly varied couplet and bring it more in line with the nature of the play.
16. A traditional Chinese measuring unit, equivalent to approximately one-third of a mile, or half a kilometer.
17. Biancai 辯才 (1011–1091) was a monk from the Northern Song dynasty, in Hangzhou. His original Dharma name was Yuanjing 元淨, but Emperor Renzong (r. 1022–1063) was impressed by his profound lectures and insights on Buddhism and bestowed on him the title "Biancai" (master of rhetoric). Biancai was known to have played a significant role in the cultivation of Longjing tea and often regarded as the forefather of this famous tea.
18. The poem appears in *Xihu youlan zhi* 西湖遊覽志 (see Tian Rucheng [1773–1781, 4.14b]). It was originally composed by the Northern Song official Yang Jie 楊傑 (*jinshi* 1059), who was also known to be a disciple of the Chan master Tianyi Yihuai 天衣義懷 (993–1064).

19. One of the eight scenic spots in Longjing as inscribed in Qianlong's poems.
20. The "Wisp of Cloud" is a piece of rock that stood tall on Rustling Bamboos Ridge. The renowned late Ming writer Zhang Dai described the rock in his work *Xihu mengxun* 西湖夢尋 as a "green, smooth and exquisite piece, almost as though it had been carved by hand." See Zhang Dai (2007, 204–06).
21. This is a reference to the Song dynasty painter and poet Mi Fu's (1051–1107) admiration for rocks—he would collect precious stones and keep some in his sleeves to show to friends.
22. This title reflects the ancient Chinese belief that each emperor was the son of Heaven, and the succession of each emperor was decided by a mandate of Heaven.
23. A reference to the "Wisp of Cloud" Hall in the Imperial Summer Villa (Bishu shanzhuang 避暑山莊) in Chengde, which was modeled after this scenic spot at West Lake. The Kangxi emperor gave the hall its name.
24. The poem recited is none other than an actual poem written by Qianlong on this site during his previous visit in 1765.
25. Most likely it is the oars of a boat that are beating the reflections of the moon in the water.
26. These lines appear, with minor variants, in Zhang Dai's *Xihu Mengxun* where they are attributed to Sun Long 孫隆 (1525–1594). See Zhang Dai (2007, 205).
27. In Buddhism, Prajna refers to one achieving true insights and transcendent enlightenment.
28. The line describes the effects of drinking Dragon Well (Longjing) Tea and resembles a similar line from a Tang poem by Lu Tong (790–835).
29. Tender tea leaves are said to resemble the shape of flags and lances. This description was first recorded by the Song emperor Huizong (1082–1135) in his book *Treatise on Tea in the Daguan Reign Era* (大觀茶論).
30. Reference to this passage from section 20 of the *Tao Te Ching* 道德經. See translation by D. C. Lau: "The multitude are joyous / As if partaking of the t'ai lao offering / Or going up to a terrace in spring." See Laozi and Lau (2001, 76).
31. Reference to *Mencius* 13.3. See translation by James Legge: "Wherever the superior man passes through, transformation follows; wherever he abides, his influence is of a spiritual nature. It flows abroad, above and beneath, like that of Heaven and Earth. How can it be said that he mends society but in a small way!" Legge (1960b, 445).
32. Reference to *Shujing* (*Book of Documents*). See translation by James Legge, "It is virtue that moves Heaven; there is no distance to which it does not reach." See Book 2, "Counsels of the Great Yu," in Legge (1960a, 65).
33. The original text appears as *Yang shang* (楊上, "Yang enters"), which is mostly likely a mistake of what should have been *chang shang* (場上, "onstage"). *Changshang she X* (場上設 X), indicating that a certain prop is installed onstage, is a formulaic stage direction found in many court plays including those by Wang Wenzhi. Here, we follow the emendation in the later *Fuzhuang jin yuefu xuan* edition.
34. Here, the attribution of the line to Yang and Cai might have resulted from the mistaken understanding of Yang's entrance onstage above. Instead, the line is best read as Biancai's speech: "The maidens are simmering tea, let me draw some water." Throughout the play, the term *laoseng* 老僧 (literally "old monk") is always used as Biancai's self-reference.
35. Guzhu tea leaves are famous for their tender, purplish buds shaped like bamboo shoots. Their clear fragrance and quality made the tea a local tribute item to the court from the Tang onward.
36. This couplet is drawn from a Ming dynasty poem "Thanking the Longjing Monk for sending tea" (謝龍井僧獻秉中寄茶) by Liu Bangyan, recorded in Tian Rucheng's *Supplement* 24.21b.

37. The sound of boiling water resembles that of wind blowing through pine trees; "crab-eye" describes the shape of the desired size of bubbles attained at a certain stage of boiling water suitable for making tea.
38. The term *diancha* 點茶 ("pointing tea") refers to the Song-dynasty method for making tea by "pointing" a thin stream of hot water into powdered tea, which produces a creamy tea mixture. See Benn (2015, chap. 6).
39. According to Lu Yu's 陸羽 (733–804) *Chajing* (*Classic of Tea*), the best tea grows on a type of soil classified as *lanshi* 爛石 ("pulverized rock"). See Fu Shuqin and Ouyang Xun (1983, 3). The most exquisite Longjing tea comes from the Lion Peak (Shifeng 獅峰) region, where the soil has a white sand and quartz mixture that belongs to this category.
40. This is yet another poem written by the Qianlong emperor when he passed by Longjing during his third southern inspection tour. He tasted the tea, loved it, and wrote the poem "Impromptu lines written while brewing tea by the Longjing spring" (坐龍井上烹茶偶成).
The Northern Song period witnessed a rise in "literary Zen" (*wenzi chan* 文字禪) and the close communication between Chan masters and literary elites. The concept is also encountered in a poem by Biancai addressed to Qin Guan, in which he proposed that "words do not deviate from Zen." See Wang Mengjuan (2004, 7.182).
41. The *Yellow Court Classic* is a crucial meditation manuscript for Daoism, believed to have been created during the Period of Division (220–589). It is passed down in two forms, known respectively as the "External" manuscript, which is shorter, and the "Internal" manuscript, which is more comprehensive. The full contents of the "External" can be found in the "Internal," and there are conflicting opinions on which version predates the other.
42. Yang Xihe 楊羲和 (b. 330) was known to have written a copy, according to Dong Qichang 董其昌 (1555–1536) in his engraved model-letters project, *Xihongtang tie* 戲鴻堂帖 (*Model Letters of the Hall of the Frolicking Wild Geese*). See Yan Wenru and Yin Jun (2013, vol. 2, 580). Here, it is also interesting to note Wang Wenzhi's reputation as a major calligrapher and how he regarded Dong very highly and learned from Dong's style.
43. Cai Shaoxia 蔡少霞 (d. 820), a Daoist practitioner, once dreamt that he received a stele inscription composed by Shan Xuanqing, the Realized Person of Ziyang, about a new celestial palace. Once awakened from the dream, Cai transcribed it from memory. In some accounts, Cai copied this inscription in his role as a "Scribe in the Secretariat of the Five-Coloured Clouds" (五雲書閣吏), which explains the reference in this play to Cai as a deity of writing. See *TPGJ* 55.340–41 and Hong Mai (2019, 107).
44. Refers to the Eight Legions Headed by the Heavens and Dragons (*tianlong babu*) in Chinese Buddhism, which eight types of deities (Deva, Nāga, Yakṣa, Gandharva, Asura, Garuḍa, Kiṁnara, and Mahoraga) set to protect the Dharma (the Buddhist cosmic law and order).
45. The Mandārava flower is known as one of the four types of heavenly flowers in Buddhism.
46. A comprehensive Buddhist spatial term that refers to north, south, east, west, northeast, northwest, southeast, southwest, above, and below. Common usage includes "all worlds in the ten directions," or "all Buddha / sentient beings in the ten directions."

APPENDIX

A LIST OF SHORT PLAYS FROM THE PERIOD 1400 TO 1850 ALREADY AVAILABLE IN ENGLISH TRANSLATION

Anonymous, *Shuang douyi* 雙鬥醫

William Dolby, trans. "'The Battling Doctors': *Excerpt from* Cai Shun Shares the Mulberries (*Cai Shun fenshen*). Yuanben play attributed to Liu Tangqing (late thirteenth or early fourteenth century)." In William Dolby, *Eight Chinese Plays from the 13th Century to the Present*, 21–28. London: Paul Elek, 1978.

Stephen H. West, trans. *Two Physicians Raise Cain*. In Stephen H. West, *Vaudeville and Narrative: Aspects of Chin Theater*, 33–43. Wiesbaden: Franz Steiner, 1977.

Stephen H. West and Wilt L. Idema, trans. *A Pair of Battling Quacks*. In Wang Shifu, *The Moon and the Zither: The Story of the Western Wing*, ed. and trans. by Stephen H. West and Wilt L. Idema, 417–28. Berkeley: University of California Press, 1991.

Anonymous, *Wang Po* 王勃

James Crump Jr., trans. *Wang P'o Yüan-pen*. *Dodder* 2 (1970): 31–34.

Wilt L. Idema, trans. *Wang P'o*. *Chinese Literature: Essays, Articles, Reviews* 6 (1984): 73–75.

David Roy, trans. *The Plum in the Golden Vase or Chin P'ing Mei*. Volume Two: *The Rivals*, 234–38. Princeton, NJ: Princeton University Press, 2001.

Li Kaixian 李開先 (1502–1568), *Yuanlin wumeng* 園林午夢

Wilt L. Idema, trans. *A Noontime Dream in a Garden Grove*. *Chinese Literature: Essays, Articles, Reviews* 6 (1984): 70–73.

Stephen H. West and Wilt L. Idema, trans. *A Noontime Dream in a Garden Grove*. In Wang Shifu, *The Moon and the Zither: The Story of the Western Wing*, ed. and trans. Stephen H. West and Wilt L. Idema, 429–36. Berkeley: University of California Press, 1991.

Wang Jide 王驥德 (1540–1623), *Nan wanghou* 男王后

Sophie Volpp, trans. *The Male Queen*. In Sophie Volpp, *Worldly Stage: Theatricality in Seventeenth-Century China*, 263–314. Cambridge, MA: Harvard University Asia Center, 2011.

Wang Jiusi 王九思 (1468–1551), *Zhongshanlang yuanben* 中山狼院本

James Crump Jr., trans. Wang Chiu-ssu: *The Wolf of Chung shan*. *Renditions* 7 (1977): 29–38.

William Dolby, trans. *"Wolf of Mount Zhong (Zhong-shan lang)*: Brief *zaju* play by Wang Jiusi (1468–1551." In William Dolby, *Eight Chinese Plays from the 13th Century to the Present*, 93–102. London: Paul Elek, 1978.

Wang Yinglin 王應遴 (d. 1644), *Xiaoyaoyou* 逍遙遊

Wilt L. Idema, trans. *Free and Easy Roaming*. In Wilt L. Idema, *The Resurrected Skeleton: From Zhuangzi to Lu Xun*, 163–94. New York: Columbia University Press, 2014.

Wu Zao 吳藻 (1799–1863), *Qiao Ying* 喬影

Wilt L. Idema and Beata Grant, trans. *The Fake Image*. In Wilt Idema and Beata Grant, *The Red Brush: Writing Women of Imperial China*, 685–93. Cambridge MA: Harvard University Asia Center, 2004.

Sophie Volpp, trans. *Drinking Wine and Reading "Encountering Sorrow": A Reflection in Disguise* by Wu Zao (1799–1862). In *Under Confucian Eyes: Writing on Gender in Chinese History*, ed. Susan Mann and Yu-Yin Cheng, 239–50. Berkeley: University of California Press, 2001.

Shu-chu Wei, trans. "*Qiaoying* (The Image in Disguise), by Wu Zao." *Chinoperl Papers* 26 (2005–2006): 171–80.

Xu Wei 徐渭 (1521–1593), *Kuanggushi Yuyang sanlong* 狂鼓史漁陽三弄

Jeanette Faurot. "Hsü Wei's Mi Heng: A Sixteenth Century *Tsa-chü*," *Literature East and West* 17 (1977): 282–304.

Shiamin Kwa, trans. *The Mad Drummer Plays the Yuyang Triple Rolls*. In Shiamin Kwa, *Strange Eventful Histories: Identity, Performance, and Xu Wei's* Four Cries of a Gibbon, 117–38. Cambridge MA: Harvard University Asia Center, 2012.

Xu Wei, *Yu chanshi Cuixiang yimeng* 玉禪師翠鄉一夢

Shiamin Kwa, trans. Chan*Master Yu Has a Dream of Cuixiang*. In Shiamin Kwa, *Strange Eventful Histories: Identity, Performance, and Xu Wei's* Four Cries of a Gibbon, 139–68. Cambridge MA: Harvard University Asia Center, 2012.

Xu Wei, *Ci Mulan tifu congjun* 雌木蘭替父從軍

Shiamin Kwa, trans. *The Female Mulan Joins the Army in Place of Her Father*. In *Mulan: Five Versions of a Classic Chinese Legend, with Related Texts*, ed. and trans. Shiamin Kwa and Wilt L. Idema, 9–30. Indianapolis: Hackett, 2010.

Shiamin Kwa, trans. *The Female Mulan Joins the Army in Place of Her Father*. In Shiamin Kwa, *Strange Eventful Histories: Identity, Performance, and Xu Wei's* Four Cries of a Gibbon, 169–88. Cambridge MA: Harvard University Asia Center, 2012.

Ma Qian, trans. *Mulan* (*Ci Mulan*). In Ma Qian, *Women in Traditional Chinese Theater: The Heroine's Play*, 129–51. Lanham, MD: University Press of America, 2005.

Xu Wei, *Nü zhangyuan cihuang defeng* 女狀元辭凰得鳳

Shamin Kwa, trans. *The Girl Graduate Rejects the Female Phoenix and Gains the Male Phoenix*. In Shiamin Kwa, *Strange Eventful Histories: Identity, Performance, and Xu Wei's Four Cries of a Gibbon*, 189–239. Cambridge MA: Harvard University Asia Center, 2012.

Zhu Youdun 朱有燉 (1379–1439), *Changshouxian xianxiang tianshou* 長壽仙獻香添壽

William Dolby, trans. "*Yuanben* from *Meeting of the Immortals* by Zhu Youdun," In William Dolby, *A History of Chinese Drama*, 22–25. London: Paul Elek, 1976).

CONTRIBUTORS

Robert Ashmore is an associate professor at the University of California, Berkeley. He received his MA in medieval Chinese Literature from Peking University, and a PhD in Chinese Literature from Harvard University. His research centers on medieval Chinese literature and culture from the third to eleventh centuries, with a focus on music, ritual, and the interrelations of literary and scholarly cultures, as well as on issues of performance and hermeneutical thought. His publications include *The Transport of Reading: Text and Understanding in the World of Tao Qian* (Harvard Asia Center, 2010), and *The Poetry of Li He* (de Gruyter, 2023), a complete annotated facing-page translation of the works of the Tang dynasty poet Li He (790–816).

Yuming He is an associate professor at the University of California, Davis. She received her BA and MA from Peking University and PhD from UC Berkeley. She taught at Reed College and the University of Chicago before joining the faculty at UC Davis. Her recent work is focused on the history of the book, theater, and epistemological processes in late imperial China. She is the author of *Home and the World: Editing the "Glorious Ming" in Woodblock-Printed Books of the Sixteenth and Seventeenth Centuries* (Harvard University Asia Center, 2013, also published in a revised and expanded Chinese edition titled *Jiayuan yu tianxia: Mingdai shu wenhua yu xunchang yuedu* 家園與天下: 明代書文化與尋常閱讀 [Zhonghua shuju, 2019]).

Wilt L. Idema, professor emeritus of Chinese Literature at Harvard University, has focused most of his research on the vernacular traditions of late imperial Chinese literature, ranging from fiction and drama to popular prosimetric narrative. He has also published on China's women's literature. Some of his recent books include *The Orphan of Zhao and Other Yuan Plays: The Earliest Known Versions* (with Stephen H. West; Columbia University Press, 2015), *Two Centuries of Manchu Women Poets, An Anthology*

(University of Washington Press, 2017), and *The Pitfalls of Piety for Married Women: Two Precious Scrolls of the Ming Dynasty* (Cornell University Press, 2021).

S. E. Kile is an assistant professor in the Department of Asian Languages and Cultures at the University of Michigan. As a specialist in Ming and Qing literature and culture, he brings his research on the operations of gender and performance to the foreground; see, for instance, "Transgender Performance in Early Modern China," in *differences* 24.2 (2013): 130–49 (Chinese version: 邝师华. "Zaoqi jindai Zhongguo de kuaxingbie biaoyan" 早期近代中国的跨性别表演 in *Zhongguo xing/bie: lishi chayi* 中国性／别：历史差异 Shanghai: Sanlian, 2015). He has also addressed contemporary interpretations of premodern same-sex romance in "Sensational Kunqu: The April 2010 Beijing Production of *Lianxiang ban* (*Women in Love*)," *CHINOPERL Papers* (*Chinese Oral and Performing Literatures Papers*) 30.1 (2011): 215–22. *Towers in the Void*, his monograph theorizing early modern mediation and entrepreneurship through Li Yu's (1611–1680) cultural production, was published by Columbia University Press (2023).

Shiamin Kwa is an associate professor of East Asian Languages and Cultures at Bryn Mawr College, where she teaches Chinese fiction, drama, and film. She received her PhD in East Asian Languages and Civilizations from Harvard University. Her study and translation of Xu Wei's *Four Cries of a Gibbon* was published as *Strange Eventful Histories: Identity, Performance, and Xu Wei's* Four Cries of a Gibbon (Harvard University Asia Center, 2012).

Wai-yee Li is the 1879 Professor of Chinese Literature at Harvard University. She has published several books on early China and Ming-Qing literature and culture. Her recent publications include *Women and National Trauma in Late Imperial Chinese Literature* (Harvard University Asia Center, 2014), *The Columbia Anthology of Yuan Drama* (with C. T. Hsia and George Kao; Columbia University Press, 2014), *Zuo Tradition / Zuozhuan: Commentary on the Spring and Autumn Annals* (with Stephen Durrant and David Schaberg; University of Washington Press, 2016), *The Oxford Handbook of Classical Chinese Literature* (with Wiebke Denecke and Xiaofei Tian; Oxford University Press, 2017), *Plum Shadows and Plank Bridge: Two Memoirs about Courtesans* (CUP, 2020), *Keywords in Chinese Culture* (with Yuri Pines; CUP, 2020), *Zuo Tradition / Zuozhuan Reader: Selections from China's Oldest Narrative History* (with Stephen Durrant and David Schaberg; UWP, 2020), and *The Promise and Perils of Things: Literature and Material Culture in Late Imperial China* (CUP, 2022).

Xiaoqiao Ling is an associate professor of Chinese at Arizona State University. Her main field of interest is late imperial Chinese literature with a focus on performance texts, vernacular fiction, and the print culture. She has published in both Chinese and English on fiction and drama commentary, the legal imagination in literature, and memory and trauma in seventeenth-century China. Her first book, *Feeling the Past in Seventeenth-Century China* (Harvard University Asia Center, 2019), explores traumatic memories and their transmission across generations during the Manchu conquest of China. She is currently working on a second book-length project on the romantic play *The Story of the*

Western Wing. By tracing how various social groups across cultural and regional geographies interpreted, adapted, and appropriated the play, this project aims at investigating how *The Story of the Western Wing* has sustained its iconic status in the early modern East Asian cultural sphere.

Casey Schoenberger obtained his PhD from Yale University. His research focuses on cognitive, comparative, musicological, and linguistic approaches to Chinese poetry and performing arts. He has recently completed a monograph on these topics titled *The Voice Extended: Music, Mind, and Language in Chinese Poetry and Performance*, along with a database of traditional vocal melodies titled "Nine Modes Manual Online."

Pingyu Sun is an aspiring translator and writer with a focus on literature and the arts. She graduated from the National University of Singapore in 2019 with a BA (Hon) in Chinese Studies and a minor in translation. She currently works full-time in the financial service industry and provides freelance translation services to local arts institutions. Her writings can also be found in local publications such as *Singapore Chinese Literature* 新华文学 and the bimonthly magazine *Yuan* 源.

Tian Yuan Tan is the Shaw Professor of Chinese at the University of Oxford. His main areas of research include Chinese literary history and historiography, text and performance, and crosscultural literary interactions. He is the author of *Songs of Contentment and Transgression: Discharged Officials and Literati Communities in Sixteenth-Century North China* (Harvard University Asia Series, 2010), *A Critical Edition of the Sanqu Songs by Kang Hai (1475–1541) with Notes and Two Essays* 康海散曲集校箋 (2011), coauthor of *Passion, Romance, and Qing: The World of Emotions and States of Mind in Peony Pavilion* (2014), and coeditor of *Text, Performance, and Gender in Chinese Literature and Music: Essays in Honor of Wilt Idema* (Brill, 2009), *An Anthology of Critical Studies on Tang Xianzu in Western Scholarship* 英語世界的湯顯祖研究論著選譯 (2013), and *1616: Shakespeare and Tang Xianzu's China* (2016).

Stephen H. West works primarily in Song and Yuan literature with a focus on early performance literature, textual representations of urban culture, and late medieval gardens. In collaboration with Wilt L. Idema he has authored several books on Yuan *zaju*. A collaborative work with Ruth Dunnell and Yang Shao-yun, *The Travels of Qiu Chuji: A New Translation of the Record of the* Perfected Changchun's Journey to the West (*Changchun zhenren xiyouji* 長春真人西遊記), will be published by Oxford University Press, and he is currently translating *Master Dong's* Story of the Western Wing*: A Ballad in All Modes* for the Hsu-Tang Library, and *Dreaming of Pleasures Past* (*Meng Hua lu*) for the Library of Chinese Humanities.

REFERENCES

Abbreviations for Common and Canonical Works

CBT Chinese Buddhist Electronic Text Association, comp. 2021. *Dianzi Fodian jicheng* 電子佛典集成. Taipei, Taiwan: CBETA.

DEB Current. In *Digital Dictionary of Buddhism*, ed. Charles Muller. http://www.buddhism-dict.net/ddb: Charles Muller.

DMB L. Carrington Goodrich and Chaoying Fang, eds. 1976. *Dictionary of Ming Biography 1368–1644*. New York: Columbia University Press.

EOT Fabrizio Pregadio, ed. 2008. *Encyclopedia of Taoism*. 2 vols. London: Routledge.

HHS Fan Ye 范曄 (389–445) and Sima Biao 司馬彪 (ob. 306) comps. 1965. *Hou Hanshu* 後漢書. Li Xian 李賢 (655–684), ann. 12 vols. Beijing: Zhonghua shuju.

HNZ Liu An 劉安 (179–122 BCE) et al., comps. 1989. *Huainanzi* 淮南子. Ed. and ann. Liu Wendian 劉文典. Beijing: Zhonghua shuju.

HS Ban Gu 班固 (32–92), comp. 1962. *Hanshu* 漢書. Yan Shigu 顏師古 (581–645) ann. 12 vols. Beijing: Zhonghua shuju.

HFZ Han Feizi 韓非子 (attr., ob. 233 BCE), and ann. Chen Qiyou 陳奇猷. 1958. *Hanfeizi* 韓非子. Beijing: Zhonghua shuju.

JS Fang Xuanling 房玄齡 (578–648) et al., comp. 1974. *Jinshu* 晉書. 10 vols. Beijing: Zhonghua shuju.

JTS Liu Xu 劉昫 et al., comp. 1975. *Jiu Tangshu* 舊唐書. 16 vols. Beijing: Zhonghua shuju.

LJZS *Liji zhushu* 禮記注疏. Zheng Xuan 鄭玄 (127–200), comm. Kong Yingda 孔穎達 (574–648) subcomm. In SSJ.

LZ Liezi 列子 (attr). 1979. *Liezi jishi* 列子集釋. Ed. and ann. Tang Bojun 楊伯峻. Beijing: Zhonghua shuju.

MS Zhang Tingyu 張廷玉 (1672–1755) et al., eds. 1974. *Mingshi* 明史. 28 vols. Beijing: Zhonghua shuju.

MZZS Zhao Qi 趙岐 and Sun Shi 孫奭, comms. 2000. *Mengzi zhushu* 孟子注疏. Ed. Liu Youping 劉佑平, Xun Qian 錢遜, and Liao Mingchun 廖名春. Beijing: Beijing daxue chubanshe.

NS Li Yanshou 李延壽 (570–628), ed. 1981. *Nanshi* 南史. 8 vols. Beijing: Zhonghua shuju.

QQS *Quan Song shi* 全宋詩. 1991–98. Comp. Beijing daxue guwenxian yanjiusuo 北京大學古文獻研究所. Ed. Fu Xuancong 傅璇琮 et al. 72 vols. Beijing: Beijing daxue chubanshe.

QTS Peng Dingqiu 彭定求 (1645–1719) et al., eds. 1985. *Quan Tang shi* 全唐詩. 25 vols. Beijing: Zhonghua shuju.

SGZ Chen Shou 陳壽1980. *Sanguo zhi* 三國志. Comm. Pei Songzhi 裴松之. Taipei: Dingwen shuju.

SHJ Yuan Ke 袁珂 coll. and ann. 2014. *Shanhai jing jiaozhu* 山海經校注. Shanghai: Shanghai guji chubanshe.

SJ Sima Qian 司馬遷 (145–87 BCE). 1985. *Shiji* 史記. Comm. Sima Zhen 司馬貞, Pei Yin 裴駰, and Zhang Shoujie 張守節. 10 vols. Beijing: Zhonghua shuju.

SKQS Ji Yun 紀昀 (1724–1805) et al., eds. 1773–1781. *Wenyuan ge Siku quanshu* 文淵閣四庫全書. 36381 vols.

SS Tuotuo 脫脫 (Toqt'a) (1314–1356) et al. 1980. *Songshi* 宋史. 40 vols. Beijing: Zhonghua shuju.

SSJ Ruan Yuan 阮元 (1764–1849) et al., eds. 1965. *Chongkan Songben Shisan jing zhushu fu jiaokan ji* 重刊宋本十三經注疏附校勘記. 8 vols.

SSJS Qu Wanli 屈萬里 ann. 1980. *Shangshu jishi* 尚書集釋. Taipei: Lianjing chuban shiye.

TPGJ Li Fang 李昉 et al., eds. 1975. *Taiping guangji* 太平廣記. 10 vols. Beijing: Zhonghua shuju.

WS Wei Shou 魏收 (506–572) et al., comps. 1980. *Weishu* 魏書. 4 vols. Beijing: Zhonghua shuju

XTS Ouyang Xiu 歐陽修 (1007–1072) et al., comps. 1991. *Xin Tangshu* 新唐書. 20 vols. Beijing: Zhonghua shuju.

YZCQ Wu Zeyu 吳則虞, comp. and ann. 1962. *Yanzi chunqiu jishi* 晏子春秋集釋. Beijing: Zhonghua shuju.

ZY 2017. Zhou Yi 周易. Beijing: Guojia tushuguan chubanshe.

ZYZS Wang Bi 王弼 (226–249) and Han Kangbo 韓康伯 (332–380), comms, Kong Yingda 孔穎達 (574–648) subcomm. 1976. *Zhouyi zhushu* 周易注疏. In *SSJ* vol. 1.

Zuo Durrant, Stephen, Li Wai-yee, and David Schaberg, trans. 2016. *Zuo Tradition / Zuozhuan: Commentary on the* "Spring and Autumn Annals." 3 vols, vol. 1. Seattle: University of Washington Press.

ZZ Du Yu 杜預 (222–284) and comm., Lu Deming 陸德明 (550–630) ann., and Kong Yingda 孔穎達 (574–648) subcomm. 1976. *Chongkan ben Zuozhuan zhushu fu jiaokan ji* 重刊本左傳注疏附校勘記. In *SSJ* vol. 6.

ZZJS Zhuang Zhou (attr.) and Guo Qingfan 郭慶藩, comm. 1961. *Zhuangzi jishi* 莊子集釋. 4 vols, ed. Wang Xiaoyu 王孝魚. 4 vols. Beijing: Zhonghua shuju.

Modern Editions, Articles, Book Sections

Allan, Sarah. 2015. *Buried Ideas: Legends of Abdication and Ideal Government in Early Chinese Bamboo-Slip Manuscripts.* Albany: State University of New York Press.

Altenburger, Roland. 2009. *The Sword or the Needle: The Female Knight-Errant (Xia) in Traditional Chinese Narrative.* Bern: Peter Lang.

Anon. 1936. *Jianxia zhuan* 劍俠傳. Ed. Wu Guan 吳棺 (16th c.). Vol. 2690, 1–92. *Congshu jicheng.* Shanghai: Shangwu yinshuguan.

Anon. 1997. "Shunzi bian 舜子變." In *Dunhuang bianwen jiaozhu* 敦煌變文校注. Ed. Huang Zheng 黃征 and Zhang Yongquan 張湧泉. Beijing: Zhonghua shuju.

Ashmore, Robert. 2008. "Recent Style *Shi* Poetry: Heptasyllabic Regulated Verse (*Qiyan Lüshi*)." In *How to Read Chinese Poetry*. Ed. Zongqi Cai, 181–96. New York: Columbia University Press.

Bai Juyi 白居易 (772–846). 1999. *Bai Juyi quanji* 白居易全集. Ed. Ding Ruming 丁如明 and Nie Shimei 聶世美. Shanghai: Shanghai guji chubanshe.

Benn, James A. 2015. *Tea in China: A Religious and Cultural History*. Honolulu: University of Hawai'i Press.

Berg, Daria. 2013. *Women and the Literary World in Early Modern China 1588–1700*. London: Routledge.

Besio, Kimberly. 2009. "Singing in Place of Screaming; Subversion as Satire in Late Imperial China." In *Text, Performance, and Gender in Chinese Literature and Music: Essays in Honor of Wilt Idema*, ed. Tian Yuan Tan, Maghiel van Crevel, and Michel Hockx, 153–73. Leiden: E. J. Brill.

Birrell, Anne, trans. 1982. *New Songs from a Jade Terrace*. London: George Allen and Unwin.

Blakely, Barry S. 1999. "Chu Society and State: Image Versus Reality." In *Defining Chu: Image and Reality in Ancient China*, ed. Constance A. Cook and John S. Major, 51–66. Honolulu: University of Hawai'i Press.

Bloom, Irene, and Philip J. Ivanhoe, trans. 2009. Mengzi. *Mencius*. New York: Columbia University Press.

Boretti, Valentina. 2004. "The Quasi-genderless Heresy: The Dhūtaists and Master Jizhao." *Bulletin of the School of Oriental and African Studies* 67 (3): 349–68.

Bu Jian 卜鍵. 1989. *Li Kaixian zhuanlüe* 李開先傳略. Beijing: Zhongguo xiju chubanshe.

Burkus-Chasson, Anne. 2010. *Through a Forest of Chancellors: Fugitive Histories in Liu Yuan's* Lingyan ge, *an Illustrated Book from Seventeenth-Century Suzhou*. Cambridge, MA: Harvard University Asia Center.

Cahill, Suzanne. 1992. "Sublimation in Medieval China: The Case of the Mysterious Woman of the Nine Heavens." *Journal of Chinese Religions* 20 (1): 91–102.

Cai, Zongqi, ed. 2008. *How to Read Chinese Poetry*. New York: Columbia University Press.

Cai, Zongqi, ed. 2018. *How to Read Chinese Poetry in Context: Poetic Culture from Antiquity Through the Tang*. New York: Columbia University Press.

Campany, Robert Ford. 2002. *To Live As Long As Heaven and Earth: A Translation and Study of Ge Hong's Traditions of Divine Transcendents*. Berkeley: University of California Press.

Chang, Kang-i Sun, and Haun Saussy, eds. 1999. *Women Writers of Traditional China: An Anthology of Poetry and Criticism*. Stanford, CA: Stanford University Press.

Chang, Kang-i Sun, and Stephen Owen, eds. 2010. *The Cambridge History of Chinese Literature*. 2 vols, vol. 1. Cambridge: Cambridge University Press.

Chen Shidao 陳師道. 1983. *Houshan shihua* 後山詩話, vol. 1478, *SKQS*. Taipei: Shangwu yinshuguan.

Chen Qiyou 陳奇猷, ed. 1995. Lüshi chunqiu jiaoshi 呂氏春秋校釋. 2 vols. Shanghai: Xuelin chuban she.

Chen Yuanjing 陳元靚 (ca. 1240–1280). 1939. *Suishi guangji* 歲時廣記, ed. Wang Yunwu 王雲五, *Congshu jicheng chubian*. Shanghai: Shangwu yinshuguan.

Cheng Junying 程俊英, Jiang Jianyuan 蔣見元. 2017. *Shijing zhuxi* 詩經注析. Beijing: Zhonghua shuju.

Confucius, and Edward G. Slingerland. 2003. *Analects: With Selections from Traditional Commentaries*. Indianapolis: Hackett.

Cuadrado, Clara Yü. 1986. "You Tong." In *The Indiana Companion to Traditional Chinese Literature, Vol. 1*, ed. William H. Nienhauser, 939–40. Bloomington: Indiana University Press.

Cutter, Robert Joe. 2012. "'Well how'd you become king, then?' Swords in Early Medieval China." *Journal of the American Oriental Society* 132 (4): 523–38.

Daoxuan 道宣. n.d. *Xu Gaoseng zhuan* 續高僧傳. *CBT* 2060.

de Bary, Wm. Theodore. 1999. *Sources of Chinese Tradition*. New York: Columbia University Press.

Dent-Young, Alex, and John Dent-Young, trans. 1994. *The Marshes of Mount Liang: A New Translation of the* Shuihu Zhuan *or* Water Margin *of Shi Nai'an and Luo Guanzhong*.

Ding Yaokang 丁耀亢 (1599–1669). 1999. *Ding Yaokang quanji* 丁耀亢全集. Ed. Li Zengpo 李增坡 and comp. Zhang Qingji 張清吉. Jinan: Zhongzhou guji chubanshe.

Du Guiping 杜桂萍. 2008. "Yang Chaoguan shengping chuangzuo ruogan wenti kaolun 楊潮觀生平創作若干問題考論." *Jinyang xuekan* 晉陽學刊 (3): 101–106.

Du Mu 杜牧 (803–852). 1984. *Fanchuan wenji* 樊川文集. Shanghai: Shanghai guji chubanshe.

Dudbridge, Glen. 1995. "The Worshippers of Mount Hua." In *Religious Experience and Lay Society in T'ang China: A Reading of Tai Fu's Kuang-i chi*. Cambridge: Cambrdge University Press.

Ebrey, Patricia Buckley, ed. 1993. *Chinese Civilization: A Sourcebook*. New York: The Free Press.

Egan, Charles. 2008. "Recent Style *Shi* Poetry: Quatrains (*Jueju*)." In *How to Read Chinese Poetry*, ed. Zongqi Cai, 199–225. New York: Columbia University Press.

Egan, Ronald. 1994. *Word, Image, and Deed in the Life of Su Shi*. Cambridge, MA: Harvard University Press.

Fang Shiming 方詩銘 and Wang Xiuling 王秀齡, comps. 1998. *Guben Zhushu jinian jizheng* 古本竹書紀年輯證. Shanghai: Shanghai guji chubanshe.

Fang Xuanling 房玄齡. 1974. *Jinshu* 晉書. Beijing: Zhonghua shuju.

Fang Xuanling, et al. 1980. *Jinshu*. Taipei: Dingwen shuju.

Feng Yan 封演. 2005. *Fengshi wenjian ji jiaozhu* 封氏聞見集校注. Ann. Zhao Zhenxin 趙貞信. Beijing: Zhonghua shuju.

Feng, Linda. 2017. "The Woman in the Carriage." In *Tales from Tang Dynasty China: Selections from the Taiping Guangji*, ed. Jessey Choo, Alexei Ditter, Sarah M. Allen, 31–36. Indianapolis: Hackett.

Feng Menglong. 2000a. "Abbot Mingwu Redeems Abbot Wujie." In *Stories Old and New: A Ming Dynasty Collection*, 517–36. Seattle: University of Washington Press.

Feng Menglong. 2000b. *Stories Old and New: A Ming Dynasty Collection*, trans. Shuhui Yang and Yunqin Yang. Seattle: University of Washington Press.

Fisher, Carney T. 1990. *The Chosen One: Succession and Adoption in the Court of Ming Shizong*. Sydney: Allen and Unwin.

Fu Shuqin 傅樹勤 and Ouyang Xun 歐陽勛, eds. 1983. *Lu Yu Chajing yizhu* 陸羽茶經譯注. Wuhan: Hubei renmin chubanshe.

Gan Bao 干寶 (286–336) and Hu Huaichen 胡懷琛, coll. 1957. *Xinjiao Soushen ji* 新校搜神記. Shanghai: Shangwu yinshuguan.

Gao Chunming 高春明. 2001. *Zhongguo fushi mingwu kao* 中國服飾名物考. Shanghai: Shanghai wenhua chubanshe.

Gao Lian 高濂 (1573–1620). 1988. *Zunsheng bajian* 遵生八箋. Chengdu: Ba Shu chubanshe.

Gong Mingzhi 龔明之 (1091–1182). 2008. *Zhong Wu jiwen* 中吳紀聞. ed. Zhu Yi'an 朱易安. 10 vols, vol. 3, *Quan Song biji: Disanji* 全宋筆記：第三集. Zhengzhou: Daxiang chubanshe.

Graff, David. 2002. *Medieval Chinese Warfare, 300–900*. New York: Routledge Press.

Graff, David. 2011–2012. "China, Byzantium, and the Shadow of the Steppe." *Dumbarton Oaks Papers* (65–66): 157–68.

Graham, A. C. 1981. *Chuang-tzŭ: The Inner Chapters*. London: Allen & Unwin.

Grant, Beata. 2009. *Eminent Nuns: Women Chan Masters of Seventeenth-Century China*. Honolulu: University of Hawai'i Press.

Guo Maoqian 郭茂倩 (1041–1099), ed. 1989. *Yuefu shiji* 樂府詩集. 4 Vols. Shanghai: Shanghai shudian.

Han Ying 韓嬰 (ca. 200–130 BCE). 1986. *Han Shi waizhuan* 韓詩外傳. Ed. and ann. Lai Yanyuan 賴炎元. Taipei: Shangwu yinshuguan.

Hanan, Patrick. 1973. *The Chinese Short Story: Studies in Dating, Authorship, and Composition*. Cambridge, MA: Harvard University Press.

Handler-Spitz, Rivi, Pauline Lee, and Haun Saussy, eds. 2016. *A Book to Burn and a Book to Keep (Hidden)*. New York: Columbia University Press, 2016.

Hao Yixing 郝懿行 (1757–1825), ed. 1974. *Shanhai jing jianshu* 山海經箋疏. Taipei: Yiwen yinshuguan.

Harvey, Stefan, trans. 1993. "Questions and Replies Between T'ang T'ai-tsung and Li Wei-kung." In *The Seven Military Classics of Ancient China*, ed. Mei-chün and Ralph D. Sawyer, 307–52. Boulder: Westview.

Hawkes, David. 1985. *The Songs of the South*. Rpt. New York: Penguin, 2011.

He, Yuming. 2013. *Home and the World: Editing the "Glorious Ming" in Woodblocks of the Sixteenth and Seventeenth Centuries*. Cambdrige, MA: Harvard University Asia Center.

Hinton, David, trans. 1996. *The Selected Poems of Li Po*. New York: New Directions.

Hinton, David, trans. 2015. *Tao Te Jing*. Berkeley, CA: Counterpoint.

Hong, Jeehee. 2016. *Theater of the Dead: A Social Turn in Chinese Funerary Art*. Honolulu: University of Hawai'i Press.

Hong Mai 洪邁 (1123–1202). 2019. *Rongzhai suibi* 容齋隨筆. Nanjing: Fenghuang chubanshe.

Hong Sheng 洪昇 (1645–1705). 1955. *The Palace of Eternal Youth*, trans. Yang Hsien-yi and Gladys Yang. Peking: Foreign Languages Press.

Hsia, C. T., Wai-yee Li, and George Kao, eds. 2014. *The Columbia Anthology of Yuan Drama*. New York: Columbia University Press.

Huang Wenyang 黃文暘 (b. 1736), comp. 1967. *Quhai zongmu tiyao* 曲海總目. 3 vols. Hong Kong: Hanxue tushu gongyinshe.

Huangfu Mi 皇甫謐. 1983. *Gaoshi zhuan* 高士傳. Taipei: Shangwu yinshu guan.

Hung, Eva, ed. 1994. *Paradoxes of Traditional Chinese Literature*. Hong Kong: Chinese University Press.

Idema, W. L. 1974. "Novels About the Founding of the Song Dynasty." *Song Studies Newsletter* 9 (1974), 2–9.

Idema, W. L. 1984. "Yüan-pen as a Minor Form of Dramatic Literature in the Fifteenth and Sixteenth Centuries." *Chinese Literature: Essays, Articles, Reviews (CLEAR)* 6 (1/2): 53–75.

Idema, W. L. 1985. *The Dramatic Oeuvre of Chu Yu-tun, 1379–1439*. Leiden: E. J. Brill.

Idema, W. L. 2004. "'Blasé Literati:' Lü T'ien-ch'eng and the Lifestyle of the Chiang-nan Elite in the Final Decades of the Wan-li Period." In *Erotic Colour Prints of the Ming Period, with an Essay on Chinese Sex Life from the Han to the Ch'ing Dynasty, BC 206–AD 1644, Volume 1*, ed. R. H Van Gulik. In *Sinica Leidensica*, xxi–xxii. Leiden: E. J. Brill.

Idema, W. L. 2006. "Li Kaixian's *Revised Plays by Yuan Masters* (*Gaiding Yuanxian chuanqi*) and the Textual Transmission of Yuan *Zaju* as Seen in Two Plays by Ma Zhiyuan." *Chinoperl Papers* (26): 47–65.

Idema, Wilt L. 2010. "Emperor and General: Some Comments on the Formal and Thematic Continuities between the Vernacular Stories from Dunhuang and the Vernacular Stories from Later Dynasties." *Beijing Forum 2004*. Accessed March 21, 2023, from https://cyberleninka.org/article/n/1087128.

Idema, Wilt L., and Beata Grant. 2004. *The Red Brush: Writing Women of Imerial China*, Cambridge, MA: Harvard Asia Center.

Idema, Wilt, and Stephen H. West. 1982. *Chinese Theater from 1100–1450: A Source Book*. Wiesbaden: Franz Steiner, 1982.

Jansen, Thomas. 2006. "The Art of Severing Relationships (*juejiao*) in Early Medieval China." *Journal of the American Oriental Society* 126 (3): 347–65.

Jao Tsung-i (Rao Zongyi) 饒宗頤, ed. 1990. *Li Weigong Wang Jiangnan* 李衛公望江南. Taipei: Xinwenfeng chuban gongsi.

Ji Yougong 計有功 (ca. 1120–1135). 2007. *Tang shi jishi jiaojian* 唐詩紀事校箋. Ed. Wang Zhongyong 王仲鏞. Beijing: Zhonghua shuju.

Jin Ping Mei cihua (Mengmei guan jiaoben) 金瓶梅詞話（夢梅館校本）. 2007. Ed. Mei Jie 梅節. 3 vols. Taipei: Liren shuju.

Jing Lihu 景李虎, ed. 1992. *Li Shouqing Di Junhou ji* 李壽卿 狄君厚集. Taiyuan: Shanxi renmin chubanshe.

Jiao Xun 焦循 comp. 2015. *Mengzi zhengyi* 孟子正義. 2 vols. Beijing: Zhonghua shuju

Kao, Karl, ed. 1985. *Classical Chinese Tales of the Supernatural and the Fantastic: Selections from the Third to the Tenth Century*. Bloomington: Indiana University Press.

Knechtges, David R., trans. and ann. [Xiao Tong.] 1982. *Wen Xuan, or Selections of Refined Literature, Volume 1: Rhapsodies on Metropolises and Capitals*. Princeton, NJ: Princeton University Press.

Knechtges, David R., trans. and ann. [Xiao Tong.] 1987. *Wen xuan, or Selections of Refined Literature, Volume 2*. Princeton, NJ: Princeton University Press.

Knechtges, David R., trans. and ann. [Xiao Tong.] 2006.*Wen xuan, or Selections of Refined Literature, Volume 3*. Princeton, NJ: Princeton University Press.

Knickerbocker, Brice J. 2010. "Record from Inside a Pillow." In *Tang Dynasty Tales: A Guided Reader*, ed. William H. Nienhauser, 73–130. Singapore: World Scientific.

Knoblock, John, and Jeffrey Riegel, trans. 2000. *The Annals of Lü Buwei*. Stanford, CA: Stanford University Press.

K'ung Shang-jen [Kong Shangren 孔尚任]. 1976. *The Peach Blossom Fan*, trans. Chen Shih-hsiang and Harold Acton, coll. Cyril Birch. Berkeley: University of California Press.

Kwa, Shiamin. 2010. "The Shape Of Things: Locating The Self In Xu Wei's Chan Master Yu Has A Voluptuous Dream." In *Text, Performance, and Gender in Chinese Literature and Music: Essays in Honor of Wilt Idema*, ed. Tian Yuan Tan, Maghiel van Crevel, and Michel Hockx, 175–92. Leiden: E. J. Brill.

Kwa, Shiamin. 2012. *Strange Eventful Histories: Identity, Performance, and Xu Wei's Four Cries of a Gibbon*. Cambridge, MA: Harvard University Asia Center.

Laozi, and D. C. Lau, trans. 2001. *Tao Te Ching*. Hong Kong: Chinese University Press.

Legge, James (1815–1897), ed. and trans. 1885. *The Li Ki, Sacred Books of the East: Sacred Books of China: Texts of Confucianism*. Oxford: Clarendon Press.

Legge, James, ed. and trans. 1960a. *The Chinese Classics, Vol. 1, part 2, The Shoo King*. Hong Kong: Hong Kong University Press.

Legge, James, ed. and trans. 1960b. *The Chinese Classics, Vol. 2, The Works of Mencius*. Hong Kong: Hong Kong University Press.

Legge, James, trans. 1962. *The Texts of Taoism*. New York: Dover. First published 1891.

Legge, James, ed. and trans. 1991. *The Texts of Taoism*. Oxford: Oxford University Press.

Li Bujia 李步嘉, ed. and coll. 2013. *Yuejue shu jiaoshi* 越絕書校釋. Beijing: Zhonghua shuju.

Li Daoyuan 酈道元. 1999. *Shuijing zhu jiaoshi* 水經注校釋, ann. Chen Qiaoyi 陳橋驛. Hangzhou: Hangzhou daxue chubanshe.

Li Jie 李潔. 2015. "Lü Yinchang, Lü Tiancheng fuzi shengping ziliao xinzheng" 呂胤昌、呂天成父子生平資料新證. *Xiqu yanjiu tongxun* 戲曲研究通訊 10 (December): 229–36.

Li Kaixian. 1995. *A Noontime Dream in the Garden Grove*. In *The Story of the Western Wing*, ed. Stephen H. West and W. L. Idema, 299–304. Berkeley: University of California Press.

Li Kaixian. 2009. *Yuanlin wumeng* 園林午夢. In *Qunyin leixuan* 群音類選, ed. Hu Wenhuan 胡文煥. Beijing Hangzhou: Airusheng Shuzihua jishu yanjiu zhongxin.

Li Kaixian 李開先, and Bu Jian 卜鍵, ed. 2004. *Li Kaixian quan ji* 李開先全集. 1st. edition. 3 vols, vol. 1. Beijing: Wen hua yi shu chubanshe.

Li, Haogu (ob. ca. 1300), and Allen Zimmerman, trans. 2014. "Scholar Zhang Boils the Sea." In *The Columbia Anthology of Yuan Drama*, ed. C. T. Hsia, George Kao, and Li Wai-yee 371–401. New York: Columbia University Press.

Li, Wai-yee. 2014. *Women and National Trauma in Late Imperial Chinese Literature*. Cambridge, MA: Harvard University Asia Center.

Li, Wai-yee, trans. 2020. *Plum Shadows and Plank Bridge: Two Memoirs by Courtesans. By Mao Xiang and Yu Huai*. New York: Columbia University Press.

Li Yanshou 李延壽. 1980. *Nanshi* 南史. Taipei: Dingwen shuju.

Li Zhi 李贄 (1527–1602), and Zhang Jianye 張建業 et al., anns. 2010. *Li Zhi quanji zhu* 李贄全集注. 14 vols. Beijing: Shehui kexue wenxian chubanshe.

Liang Tingnan 梁廷枏. 1959. *Quhua* 曲話, *Zhongguo gudian xiqu lunzhu jicheng* 中國戲曲論著集成. Beijing: Zhongguo xiju chubanshe.

Lin Shirong 林世榮. 2010. "Chanzong gongan yanbian tantao" 禪宗公案演變探討. *Ehu yuekan* 鵝湖月刊 (426): 15–24.

Liu An 劉安, with commentary by Liu Wendian 劉文典. 1989 [1926]. *Huainan honglie ji jie* 淮南鴻烈集解. *Sibu congkan chubian* 73, 425–28. Shanghai: Shanghai shudian.

Liu Jingshu 劉敬叔 (ob. ca. 468). 1996. *Yiyuan* 異苑. Beijing: Zhonghua shuju.

Liu Ming 劉銘. 2016. "Yuanben "Dayachan" de sucai laiyuan yu zhuti xin tan" 院本《打啞禪》的素材來源與主喻新探. *Shandong qingnian zhengzhi sueyuan xuebao* 山東青年政治學院學報 32 (6): 142–47.

Liu Xiang 劉向 (77–6 BCE), ed. 1995. *Shuoyuan* 說苑. Ed. and ann. Lu Yuanjun 盧元駿. Taipei: Shangwu yinshuguan.

Liu Xu. 1975. *Jiu Tang shu* 舊唐書. Beijing: Zhonghua shuju.

Liu Yiqing 劉義慶 (403–444), and Richard Mather, trans. 2002. *Shih-shuo hsin-yü: A New Account of Tales of the World, Michigan Monographs in Chinese Studies*. Ann Arbor: University of Michigan Center for Chinese Studies.

Liu Yiqing, and Xu Zhen'e 徐震堮, comp. and ann. 1984. *Shishuo xinyu jiaojian* 世說新語校箋. Beijing: Zhonghua shuju.

Liu, Qian. 2017. "Reading Resonance in Tang Tales: Allegories and Beyond." PhD dissertaton. School of International Letters and Cultures, Arizona State University.

Liu, Yuan-ju, and Hsiao-yen Peng. 2019. "The Assassin and Heibai Wei: Two Dramatic Adaptations of 'Nie Yinniang.'" In *The Assassin: Hou Hsiao-hsien's World of Tang China*, ed. Hsiao-yen Peng, 59–71. Hong Kong: Hong Kong University Press.

Lu,Tina. 2010. "The Literary Culture of the Late Ming (1573–1644)." In *The Cambridge History of Chinese Literature Volume II: From 1375*, ed. Kang-I Sun Chang, 133. Cambridge: Cambridge University Press.

Lü Buwei 呂不韋 (ca. 290–235 BCE) (attr.), and Chen Qiyou 陳奇猷, ann. 2002. *Lüshi chunqiu xin jiaoshi* 呂氏春秋新校釋. Shanghai: Shanghai guji chubanshe.

Lü Jingbo 呂靖波. 2001. "*Yuanlin wumeng, Da yachan* tizhi bianzheng" 《園林午夢》、《打啞禪》體制辨正. *Wenxue yichan* 文學遺產 (3): 139–41.

Lu Qinli 逯欽立. 1983. *Xian Qin Han Wei Jin Nanbeichao shi* 先秦漢魏晉南北朝詩. Beijing: Zhonghua shuju.

Luo Dajing 羅大經. 1983. *Helin yulu* 鶴林玉露, ed. Wang Duanlai 王端來. Beijing: Zhonghua shuju.

Lynn, Richard, trans. 1994. *The Classic of Changes: A New Translation of the I Ching as Interpreted by Wang Bi*. New York: Columbia University Press.

Mair, Victor H., trans. 2007. *The Art of War: Sun Zi's Military Methods*. New York: Columbia University Press.

Major, John S., et al., trans. 2010. *The Huainanzi: A Guide to the Theory and Practice of Government in Early Han China*. New York: Columbia University Press.

Mallory, J. P., and Victor H. Mair. 2000. *The Tarim Mummies: Ancient China and the Mystery of the Earliest Peoples from the West*. London and New York: Thames and Hudson.

Mansvelt Beck, B. J. 1986. "The Fall of the Han." In *The Cambridge History of China: Volume 1: The Ch'in and Han Empires, 221 BC–AD 220*, ed. Denis Twitchett and Michael Loewe, 317–76. New York: Cambridge University Press.

Maraldo, John C. 2009. "The Alternative Normativity of Zen." In *Frontiers of Japanese Philosophy 6: Confluences and Cross-Currents*, ed. Raquel Bouso and James W. Heisig, 190–214. Nagoya: Nanzan Institute for Religion and Culture.

Milburn, Olivia. 2008. "The Weapons of Kings: A New Perspective on Southern Sword Legends in Early China." *Journal of the American Oriental Society* 128 (3): 423–37.

Milburn, Olivia, trans. 2010. *The Glory of Yue: An Annotated Translation of the Yuejue shu, Sinica Leidensia*. Leiden: E. J. Brill.

Milburn, Olivia, trans. 2015. *The Springs and Autumns of Master Yan, Sinicia Leidensia*. Leiden: E. J. Brill.

Minford, John, and Joseph S. M. Lau. 2000. *Classical Chinese Literature, An Anthology of Translations Volume I: From Antiquity to the Tang Dynasty*. New York and Hong Kong: Columbia University Press, The Chinese University Press.

Mulligan, Jean, trans. 1980. *The Lute: Kao Ming's P'i-p'a chi*. New York: Columbia University Press.

Nienhauser, William H. Jr., ed. 2010. *Tang Dynasty Tales: A Guided Reader*. New Jersey: World Scientific Publishing.

Nienhauser, William H., and Cheng Tsai Fa, eds. 1994. *The Grand Scribe's Records, Volume 1: The Basic Annals of Pre-Han China*, ed. William H. Nienhauser. Bloomington: Indiana University Press.

Ning Xiyuan 寧西元. 1988. *Yuankan zaju sanshizhong xinjiao* 元刊雜劇三十種新校. Lanzhou: Lanzhou daxue chubanshe.

Nylan, Michael. 2001. *The Five "Confucian" Classics*. New Haven, CT: Yale University Press.

Ouyang Xiu 歐陽修 (1007–1072). 1986. *Ouyang Xiu quanji* 歐陽修全集. Facsimile reproduction of the 1936 Shijie shuju edition. 2 vols. Beijing: Zhongguo shudian.

Ouyang Xun 歐陽詢, comp. (557–641), ed. 1999. *Yiwen leiju* 藝文類聚, ed. Wang Shaoying 汪紹楹. Shanghai: Shanghai guji chubanshe.

Owen, Stephen. 2006a. *The Late Tang: Chinese Poetry of the Mid-Ninth Century (827–860)*. Cambridge, MA: Harvard University Asia Center.

Owen, Stephen. 2006b. *The Making of Early Chinese Classical Poetry*. Cambridge, MA: Harvard University Asia Center.

Owen, Stephen. 2016. *The Poetry of Du Fu*, ed. Ding Xiang Warner and Paul Kroll. 6 vols, vol. 2, *Library of Chinese Humanities*. Berlin: De Gruyter.

Owen, Stephen, ed. and trans. 1977. *The Poetry of the Early T'ang*. New Haven, CT: Yale University Press.

Owen, Stephen, ed. and trans. 1996. *An Anthology of Chinese Literature: Beginnings to 1911*. New York: Norton.

Owen, Stephen, and Wendy Swartz, trans. 2017. *The Poetry of Ruan Ji and Xi Kang*. Ed. Paul Kroll, *Library of Chinese Humanities*. Berlin and Boston: De Gruyter.

Pei Zhe 裴喆. 2015. *Qi Biaojia Yuanshan tang qupin jupin kaolun* 祈彪佳與《遠山堂曲品》《劇品》考論. Luoyang: Henan daxue chubanshe.

Peterson, Barbara Bennet, ed. 2016. *Notable Women of China: Shang Dynasty to the Early Twentieth Century*. New York: Routledge.

Peterson, C. A. 1979. "Court and Province in Mid and Late Tang." In *The Cambridge History of China: Volume 3: Sui and T'ang China 589–906 AD, Part One*. Ed. Denis C. Twitchett, 464–560. Cambridge: Cambridge University Press.

Pines, Yuri. 2005. "Disputers of Abdication: Zhanguo Egalitarianism and the Sovereign's Power." *T'oung Pao* 91 (4/5): 243–300.

Pines, Yuri. 2005/2006. "Subversion Unearthed: Criticism of Hereditary Succession in the Newly Discovered Manuscripts." *Oriens Extremus* 45: 159–178.

Qi Biaojia 祁彪佳 (1603–1645). 1959. *Yuanshan tang qupin* 遠山堂曲品. Beijing: Zhongguo xiju chubanshe.

Qi Biaojia. 1959. *Yuanshan tang qupin* 遠山堂曲品 *Yuanshan tang jupin* 遠山堂劇品. In *Zhongguo gudian xiqu lunzhu jicheng* 中國古典戲曲論著集成, vol. 6. Beijing: Zhongguo xiju chubanshe.

Ren Weirong 任偉榕. 2011. "Lü Tiancheng Qupin tanxi" 呂天成《曲品》探析. *Dongwu zhongwen yanjiu jikan* 東吳中文集刊 17: 127–48.

Roberts, Chloe Garcia, ed. and trans. 2018. *Li Shangyin*. New York: NYRB Poets.

Roy, David, trans. 1993–2013. *The Plum in the Golden Vase, or Chin P'ing Mei*. Princeton, NJ: Princeton University Press.

Sanders, Graham. 2006. *Words Well Put: Visions of Poetic Competence in the Chinese Tradition*. Cambridge, MA: Harvard University East Asia Center.

Sanders, Graham. 2014. "I Read They Said He Sang What He Wrote: Orality, Writing, and Gossip in Tang Poetry Anecdotes." In *Idle Talk: Gossip and Anecdote in Traditional China*. Ed. Jack W. Chen and David Schaberg, 88–106. Berkeley: University of California Press.

Schafer, Edward H. 1973. *The Divine Woman: Dragon Ladies and Rain Maidens in T'ang Literature*. Berkeley: University of California Press.

Schipper, Kristopher. 1993. *The Taoist Body*. Berkeley: University of California Press.

Schoenberger, Casey. 2019. "Storytellers, Sermons, Sales Pitches, and other Deceptive Features of City Life: A Cognitive Approach to Point of View in Chinese Plays." *CHINOPERL: Journal of Chinese Oral and Performing Literature* 38 (2): 129–64.

Shang, Wei. 2003. "*Jin Ping Mei* and Late Ming Print Culture." In *Writing and Materiality in China*. Ed. Lydia Liu and Judith T. Zeitlin, 187–238. Cambridge, MA: Harvard University Asia Center.

Shen Defu 沈德符 (1578–1642). 1997. *Wanli yehuo bian* 萬曆野獲編. 3 Vols. Beijing: Zhonghua shuju.

Shen Jing 沈璟. 1985. *Shen Jing ji* 沈璟集. Ed. Xu Shuofang 徐朔方. Shanghai: Shanghai guji chubanshe.

Shao Yong 邵雍. 1983. *Huangji jingshi shu* 皇極經世書. *Yingyin Wenyuange Siku quanshu* 景印文淵閣四庫全書, vol. 803. Taipei: Shangwu yinshu guan.

Ssu-ma Ch'ien (Sima Qian). 2019. "The Witty Courtiers, Memoir 66." In *The Grand Scribe's Records, Volume 11: The Memoirs of Han China Part 4*. Ed. William H. Nienhauser. Bloomington: Indiana University Press.

Strassberg, Richard, trans. and ed. 1994. *Inscribed Landscapes: Travel Writing from Imperial China*. Berkeley: University of California Press, 1994.

Strassberg, Richard, trans. and ed. 2002. *A Chinese Bestiary: Strange Creatures from the Guideways Through Mountains and Seas*. Berkeley and Los Angeles: University of California Press.

Su Shi 蘇軾 (1037–1101). 1968. *Su Shi shi* 蘇軾詩. Ann. Yan Jicheng 嚴既澄. Taipei: Shangwu yinshu guan.

Su Shi. 2001. *Su Shi shiji hezhu* 蘇軾詩集合注. Comp. Feng Yingliu 馮應榴. Ed. Huang Renke 黃任軻 and Zhu Huaichun 朱懷春. 12. vols. Shanghai: Shanghai guji chubanshe.

Su Shi. 2011. *Su Shi wenji biannian jianzhu* 蘇軾文集編年箋注. 12 Vols. Chengdu: Ba Shu shushe.

Sukhu, Gopal, trans. 2017. *The Songs of Chu: An Anthology of Ancient Chinese Poetry by Qu Yuan and Others*. New York: Columbia University Press.

Sun Guangxian 孫光憲 (900–968). 2002. *Beimeng suoyan* 北夢瑣言. Beijing: Zhonghua shuju.

Sun Shulei 孫書磊. 2011. "Gedaixiao jiujing chaoben ji qi zuozhe kaobian" 歌代嘯舊精抄本及其作者考辯. In *Nanjing tushuguan cang guben xiqu congkao* 南京圖書館藏孤本戲曲叢考. Beijing: Zhonghua shuju.

Sunzi 孫子 (ca. 5th c. BCE). 1987. *Sunzi bingfa* 孫子兵法. Beijing: Jiefang jun chubanshe.

Swartz, Wendy, Robert Ford Campany, Yang Lu, and Jessey J. C. Choo, eds. 2014. *Early Medieval China: A Sourcebook*. New York: Columbia University Press.

Tan, Tian Yuan. 2009. "Rethinking Li Kaixian's Editorship of *Revised Plays by Yuan Masters*: A Comparison with His *Banter About Lyrics*." In *Text, Performance, and Gender in Chinese Literature and Music: Essays in Honor of Wilt Idema*. Ed. Tian Yuan Tan, Maghiel van Crevel, and Michel Hockx, 139–52. Leiden: E. J. Brill.

Tan, Tian Yuan. 2010. *Songs of Contentment and Transgression, Harvard-Yenching Institute Monograph Series*. Cambridge, MA: Harvard University East Asia Center.

T'ang, Chün-i. 1973. "The Criticisms of Wang Yang-ming's Teachings as Raised by His Contemporaries." *Philosophy East and West* 23 (1/2): 163–86.

Tang Xianzu 湯顯祖 (1550–1616). 1980. *The Peony Pavilion* [*Mudan ting*], trans. Cyril Birch. Bloomington: Indiana University Press.

Tang Xianzu. 2002. *The Peony Pavilion: Mudan ting*, 2nd edition, trans. Cyril Birch, intro. Catherine Swatek. Bloomington: Indiana University Press.

Tanbo Yasuyori 丹波康賴. 1996. *Ishinpō* 醫心方. Ann. Zhao Mingshan 趙明山 et al. Shenyang: Liaoning kexue jishu chubanshe.

Tao Gu 陶穀 (903–970). 2003. *Qingyi lu* 清異錄. Ed. Zhu Yi'an 朱易安. 1st edition. 10 vols, vol. 2, *Quan Song biji* 全宋筆記. Zhengzhou: Daxiang chubanshe.

Tao Yuanming 陶淵明. 1987. *Tao Yuanming ji* 陶淵明集. Ann. Lu Qinli 逯欽立. Hong Kong: Zhonghua shuju.

Tian, Xiaofei. 2005. *Tao Yuanming & Manuscript Culture: The Record of a Dusty Table.* Seattle: University of Washington Press.

Tian Rucheng 田汝成 (1503–1577). 1773–1781. *Xihu youlan zhi* 西湖遊覽志. *SKQS* vol. 585.

Tsao, Joanne. 2017. "The Creation of the Bronze Bird Terrace-Scape in the Northern and Southern Dynasties Period." *Early Medieval China* (23): 89–104.

Tseng Yong-yih (Zeng Yongyi) 曾永義. 1972. "Wang Heng yu Shen Zizheng de shengping jiqi chuangzuo (shang)" 王衡與沈自徵的生平及其創作 (上). *Xiandai xueyuan* 現代學苑 8: 15–20.

Tseng Yong-yih (Zeng Yongyi). 1983. *Zhongguo gudian xiju xuanzhu* 中國古典戲劇選注. 1st ed. Taibei: Guojia chubanshe.

Van Gulik, R. H. 1967. *The Gibbon in China: An Essay in Chinese Animal Lore.* Leiden: E. J. Brill.

Waltner, Ann. 1987. "T'an-Yang-Tzu and Wang Shih-chen: Visionary and Bureaucrat in the Late Ming." *Late Imperial China* 8 (1): 105–33.

Waltner, Ann. 2011. "Life and Lettres: Reflections on Tanyangzi." In *Beyond Exemplary Tales: Women's Biography in Chinese History*. Ed. Joan Judge and Hu Ying. Berkeley and Los Angeles: University of California Press.

Wang, Jing, trans. 2010. "The Tale of the Curly-Bearded Guest" [Qiuran ke zhuan 虯髯客傳 by Du Guangting 杜光庭]. In *Tang Dynasty Tales: A Guided Reader*, ed. William H. Nienhauser, 189–232. Singapore: World Scientific.

Wang Ayling 王瑷玲. 2005. *Wan Ming Qing chu zhi xiqu shenmei gousi jiqi yishu chengxian* 晚明清初之戲曲審美構思及其藝術呈現. Taipei: Zhongyang yanjiu yuan Wenzhe yanjiu suo.

Wang Bo 王溥 (ob. 905). 1955. *Tang huiyao* 唐會要, *Congshu jicheng xinbian zhengbian* 叢書集成新編正編. Taipei: Xinwenfeng chuban gongsi.

Wang Cheng 王偁. 1795. *Dongdu shilüe* 東都事略. [China]: Saoye shanfang 掃葉山房. https://search.lib.umich.edu/catalog/record/990022577960106381?library=All+libraries&query=%E2%80%9D%E6%9D%B1%E9%83%BD%E4%BA%8B%E7%95%A5%E2%80%9C.

Wang Genlin 王根林, Huang Yiyuan 黃益元, and Cao Guangfu 曹光甫, eds. 1999. *Han Wei Liuchao biji xiaoshou da guan* 漢魏六朝筆記小說大觀. Shanghai: Shanghai guji chubanshe.

Wang Guowei 王國維 (1877–1927). 1996. *Song Yuan xiqu shi* 宋元戲曲史. Beijing: Dongfang chubanshe.

Wang Mengjuan 汪孟鋗 (1721–1770). 2004. *Longjing jianwen lu* 龍井見聞錄. In *Xihu wenxian jicheng* 西湖文獻集成, vol. 21. Ed. Wang Guoping 王國平. Hangzhou: Hangzhou chubanshe.

Wang Pijiang 汪辟疆. 1971. *Tangren chuanqi xiaoshuo* 唐人傳奇小說. Tainan: Cuiwen tang.

Wang Shizhen 王世貞. 1986. *Yanzhou sibu gao 174 juan xugao 207 juan* 弇州四部稿 174 卷續稿207卷. *Yingyin Wenyuange Siku quanshu* 景印文淵閣四庫全書, vols. 1279-81. Taipei: Shangwu yinshu guan.

Wang Shumin 王叔岷 ed. and ann. 1995. *Liexian zhuan jiaojian* 列仙傳校箋. Taipei: Academia Sinica.

Wang Su 王肅 (195–256), comm. 1991. *Kongzi jiayu* 孔子家語. Taipei: Shijie shuju.

Wang Wenzhang 王文章, et al. 2010. *Fu Xihua cang guben xiqu zhenben congkan tiyao* 傅惜華藏古本戲曲珍本叢刊提要. Beijing: Xueyuan chubans

Wang Xun 王遜. 2018. *Zhongguo shuhua lilun* 中國書畫理論. Shanghai: Shanghai shuhua chubanshe.

Wang Zhiyong 汪志勇. 1980. *Du Liu Cui Cuixiang meng yu Honglian zhai sanju de bijiao yanjiu* 度柳翠翠鄉夢與紅蓮債三劇的比較研究. Taipei: Xuesheng shuju.

Warner, Ding Xiang. 2001. "Wang Tong and the Compilation of the Zhongshuo: A New Evaluation of the Source Materials and Points of Controversy." *Journal of the American Oriental Society* 121 (2): 370–91.

Warner, Ding Xiang. 2004. *Transmitting Authority: Wang Tong (ca. 584–617) and the Zhongshuo in Medieval China's Manuscript Culture, Sinica Leidensia*. Leiden: E. J. Brill.

Watson, Burton, trans. 1967. *The Lotus Sutra*. New York: Columbia University Press.

Watson, Burtson, trans. 1968. *The Complete Works of Chuang Tzu*. New York: Columbia University Press.

Watson, Burton, trans. 1969. Ssu-ma Ch'ien (Sima Qian), *Records of the Grand Historian: Chapters from the Shih chi of Ssu-ma Ch'ien*. New York: Columbia University Press.

Watson, Burton, trans. 1971. *Records of the Grand Historian of China, Translated from the Shih chi of Ssu-ma Ch'ien: Volume I: Early Years of the Han Dynasty, 209 to 141 BC*. New York: Columbia University Press.

Watson, Burton, trans. 1993. [Sima Qian]. *Records of the Grand Historian, Han Dynasty II*. Rev. ed. Hong Kong and New York: Renditions and Columbia University Press.

Watson, Burton, trans. 2000. "The Goddess of the Luo." In *Classical Chinese Literature: An Anthology of Translations, Volume 1: From Antiquity to the Tang Dynasty*, ed. John Minford and Joseph S. M. Lau. Hong Kong and New York: Chinese University Press and Columbia University Press.

Watson, Burton, trans. 2013. *The Complete Works of Zhuangzi*. New York: Columbia University Press.

Wei Xuan 韋絢, comp. (796–ca. 850), ed. 1936. *Liu Binke Jiahua lu* 劉賓客嘉話錄. Ed. Wang Yunwu 王雲五, *Congshu jicheng* 叢書集成. Shanghai: Shanghai yinshuguan.

Wei Zheng 魏徵 et al. 1980. *Suishu* 隋書. Taipei: Dingwen shuju.

Weidner, Marsha, ed. 1994. *Latter Days of the Law: Images of Chinese Buddhism 850–1850*. Honolulu: University of Hawai'i Press.

Wen Yiduo 聞一多, comp. 1985. *Tianwen shuzheng* 天問疏證. Shanghai: Shanghai guji chubanshe.

West, Stephen H., and Wilt L. Idema, eds. and trans. 1995. Wang Shifu. *The Story of the Western Wing*. Berkeley: University of California Press.

West, Stephen H., and Wilt L. Idema. 2010. *Monks, Bandits, Lovers, and Immortals: Eleven Early Chinese Plays*. Indianapolis: Hackett.

West, Stephen H., and Wilt L. Idema, trans. 2015. *The Orphan of Zhao and Other Yuan Plays*. New York: Columbia University Press.

Wilhelm, Hellmut. 1959. "Shih Ch'ung and His *Chin-ku-yüan*." *Monumenta Serica* 18: 315–27.

Wu Cheng'en 吳承恩 attr. 1983. *Xiyou ji* 西遊記. Taipei: Guiguan chubanshe.

Wu Jing 吳兢 (670–749), and coll. Xie Baocheng 謝保成. 2003. *Zhenguan zhengyao jijiao* 貞觀政要集校. Beijing: Zhonghua shuju.

Wujiang xianzhi 吳江縣志. 1747. Ni Shimeng 倪師孟 and Shen Tong 沈彤, comps. Ed. Chen Xunxiang 陳葉纕 and Ding Yuanzheng 丁元正. Harvard Yenching Library Rare Book (Online Access).

Wu Shuyin 吳書蔭. 2018. *Tang Xianzu ji Mingdai xiqujia yanjiu* 湯顯祖及明代戲曲家研究. Shanghai: Fudan daxue chubanshe.

Wu Zeng 吳曾. 1985. *Nenggai zhai manlu* 能改齋漫錄. *Congshu jicheng chubian* 叢書集成初編, 289–91. Beijing: Zhonghua shuju.

Xia Tingzhi 夏庭芝 (ca. 1320–1389). 1990. *Qinglou ji jianzhu* 青樓集箋注. Ed. Sun Chongtao 孫崇濤 and Xu Hongtu 徐宏圖. Beijing: Zhongguo xiju chubanshe.

Xiao Tong 蕭統 (501–531). 2008 [1997]. *Wenxuan* 文選. Beijing: Zhonghua shuju. https://searchworks-lb.stanford.edu/view/5815226.

Xie Shouhao 謝守灝 (1134–1212). 1985. *Hunyuan shengji* 混元聖紀. Ed. Zhang Yuchu 張宇初 et al. Original edition, 1191 ed, *Zhengtong Daozang* 正統道藏. Taipei: Xinwenfeng chubanshe.

Xu, Xiaowen. 2014. "Transgression in Texts: Literary Quality of Qi from Tang Tales of Marvels to Wang Xiaobo's Tang Tales." PhD dissertation, East Asian Studies, University of Toronto.

Xu Chunfu 徐春甫, comp. 1991. *Gujin yitong daquan* 古今醫統大全. Beijing: Renmin weisheng chubanshe.

Xu Shuofang 徐朔方. 1993. *Wan Ming qujia nianpu* 晚明曲家年譜. 5 Vols. *Xu Shuofang ji* 徐朔方集. Hangzhou: Zhejiang guji chubanshe.

Xu Wei 徐渭. 1968. "Yu Chanshi cuixiang yi meng" 玉禪師翠鄉一夢. In *Xu Wenchang sanji* 徐文長三集, 1720–1754. Taipei: Guoli zhongyang tushuguan.

Xu Wei and Zhou Zhongming 周中明, ed. 1984. *Si sheng yuan / Ge dai xiao (fu)* 四聲猿 歌代嘯 (附). Shanghai: Shanghai guji chubanshe.

Xu Zheng 徐征 et al., ed. 1998. *Quan Yuanqu* 全元曲. 12 vols, vol. 2. Shijiazhuang: Hebei jiaoyu chubanshe.

Xu Zifang 徐子方. 2005. "Li Kaixian jiqi yuanben chuangzuo" 李開先及其院本創作. *Wenshi zhishi* 文史知識 (3): 78–83.

Yampolsky, Phillip. 1967. *The Platform Sutra of the Sixth Patriarch: the Text of the Tun-huang Manuscript.* New York: Columbia University Press.

Yan Wenru 嚴文儒 and Yin Jun 尹軍, eds. 2013. *Dong Qichang quanji* 董其昌全集 Shanghai: Shanghai shuhua chubanshe.

Yan Kejun 嚴可均 (1762–1843), comp. 1958. "Quan Sanguo wen" 全三國文. In *Quan Shanggu Sandai Qin Han Sanguo Liuchao wen* 全上古三代秦漢三國六朝文, 1051–1460. Beijing: Zhonghua shuju.

Yan Zhitui 顏之推 (531–591). 1980. *Yanshi jiaxun jijie* 顏氏家訓集解. ed. and ann. Wang Liqi 王利器. Shanghai: Shanghai guji chubanshe.

Yan Zhitui (531–591), and Tian Xiaofei, trans. 2021. *Family Instructions for the Yan Clan and Other Works by Yan Zhitui (531–590s).* Ed. Paul Kroll. *Library of Chinese Humanities.* Berlin, Boston: De Gruyter Mouton.

Yang Bojun 楊伯峻 ed. and trans. 1960. *Mengzi yizhu* 孟子譯註. Beijing: Zhonghua shudian.

Yang Chaoguan 楊潮觀 (1710–1788). 1729 (?) Preface dated 1716. *Gujin zhiping huiyao* 古今治平彙要. 4 vols, vol. 1. Unidentified: Hua Ximin 華希閔 (?).

Yang Chaoguan 楊潮觀 (1710–1788). 1963. *Yinfeng ge zaju* 吟風閣雜劇. Beijing: Zhonghua shuju.

Yang, Shuhui, and Yunqin Yang, trans. 2009. [Feng Menglon.] *Stories to Awaken the World: A Ming Dynasty Collection.* Seattle: University of Washington Press.

Ye Mengde 葉夢得 (1077–1148). 1984. *Shilin yan yu* 石林燕語, *Tang Song shiliao biji congkan.* Beijing: Zhonghua shuju.

Ye Shaoyuan 葉紹袁 2015. *Wumeng tang ji* 午夢堂集. Edited by Ji Qin 冀勤. 2 vols. Beijing: Zhonghua shuju.

Ye Xiaoqing. 2012. *Ascendant Peace in the Four Seas: Drama and the Qing Imperial Court.* Hong Kong: The Chinese University Press.

Yee, Cordell D. K., trans. 1985. "Hung-hsien, by Yüan Chiao." In *Classical Chinese Tales of the Supernatural and the Fantastic: Selections from the Third to the Tenth Century*, ed. Karl S. Y. Gao. Bloomington: Indiana University Press.

Yi Lidu. 2011. "'He Wore Flowers in His Hair': Understanding a Late Ming Artist Through His Mid-Ming Subject." *Ming Studies* 64, 33-45.

Yongming Yanshou 永明延壽 (904–976). 961. *Zongjing lu* 宗鏡錄. CBT 2106.

Yuan Haowen 元好問, Di Baoxin 狄寶心, ed. and ann. 2011. *Yuan Haowen shi biannian jiaozhu* 元好問詩編年校注. 4 vols, vol. 3. Beijing: Zhonghua shuju.

Yuan Ke 袁珂, ed. and ann. 1980. *Shanhai jing jiaozhu* 山海經校注. Shanghai: Shanghai guji chubanshe.

Yuan Mei 袁枚 (1716–1797). 1884. "Yang Chaoguan 楊潮觀." In *Guochao qixian leizheng chubian* 國朝耆獻類徵初編. Ed. Li Huan 李桓. Xiangyin 湘陰: Li Family 李氏.

Zeitlin, Judith T. 2019. "From the Natural to the Instrumental: Chinese Theories of the Sounding Voice before the Modern Era." In *The Voice as Something More: Essays Toward Materiality*. Ed. Martha Feldman and Judith T. Zeitlin. Chicago: Chicago University Press.

Zeitlin, Judith T., and Yuhang Li, eds. 2014. *Performing Images: Opera in Chinese Visual Culture*. Chicago: Smart Museum of Art.

Zeng Yingjing 曾影靖. 1995. *Qingren zaju lunlüe* 清人雜劇論略. Taipei: Xuesheng shuju.

Zeng Yongyi 曾永義 (See Tseng Yong-yih).

Zha Jizuo 查繼佐. 1986. *Zui wei lu* 罪惟錄. 4 vols. Hangzhou: Zhejiang guji chubanshe.

Zhang Dai 張岱 (1597–1679). 2007. *Tao'an meng yi Xihu mengxun* 陶庵夢憶 西湖夢尋. Coll. Ma Xingrong 馬興榮. Beijing: Zhonghua shuju.

Zhang Ping 張萍. 2012. *Mingdai Yuyao Lüshi jiazu yanjiu* 明代余姚呂氏家族研究. Hangzhou: Zhejiang daxue chubanshe.

Zhang Shunmin 張舜民 (ca. 1045–1100). 2012. *Huaman lu* 畫墁錄. In *Guitian lu (wai wu zhong)* 歸田錄（外五種）. Shanghai: Shanghai guji chubanshe.

Zhang Xihou 張錫厚, ed. 2006. *Quan Dunhuang shi* 全敦煌詩. Beijing: Zuojia chubanshe.

Zhang Zhengxue 張正學. 2019. "Gedaixiao fanli 'shi' zhe Chonghe jushi fei Xu Wei, Xia Lüxian, Fang Ruhao kaolun" 《歌代嘯·凡例》「識」者沖和居士非徐渭、夏履先、方汝浩考論. *Huaihua xueyuan xuebao* 懷化學院學報 38 (8): 79–82.

Zhang Zhibin 張志斌 et al., ed. 2001. *Bencao gangmu jiaozhu* 本草綱目校注. Shenyang: Liaohai chubanshe.

Zhou Banyan 周邦彥 1985. *Zhou Banyan Qingzhen ji jian* 周邦彥清真集箋. Ann. Luo Kanglie 羅忼烈. Hong Kong: Sanlian shudian.

Zhao Lin 趙璘 (ca. 1600). 1939. *Yinhua lu* 因話錄. Ed. Wang Yunwu 王雲五, *Congshu jicheng chubian*. Changsha: Shangwu yinshuguan.

Zhao Youwen 趙幼文 ed. and ann. 2016. *Cao Zhi ji jiaozhu* 曹植集校注. Beijing: Zhonghua shuju.

Zhao Zhongyi 趙仲邑 ann. 1997. *Xinxu xiangzhu* 新序詳注. Beijing: Zhonghua shuju.

Zhou Mi 周密 (1232–1298/1308). 1997. *Qi dong yeyu* 齊東野語. Ed. Zhang Maopeng 周茂鵬. Beijng: Zhonghua shuju.

Zhou Shengchun 周生春, ed. 1997. [Zhao Ye 趙曄.] *Wu Yue chunqiu jijiao huikao* 吳越春秋輯校彙考. Beijing: Zhonghua shuju.

Zhu Hongzhao 朱紅昭. 2010. "Baichi sao chou zhi sao qianzhang diao shi zhi gou: *Yixiaosan* yuanben tese qiantan" 百尺掃愁之掃 千丈釣詩之鉤—《一笑散》院本特色淺談. *Shangqiu shifan xueyuan xuebao* 商丘師範學院學報 26 (2): 45–49.

Zhu Xi 朱熹 (1130–1200) comp. 1983. *Dianjiao Sishu zhangju jizhu* 點校四書章句集注. Beijing: Zhonghua shuju.

Zhu Xi.1987. *Chuci jizhu* 楚辭集注. Hong Kong: Zhonghua shuju.

Zhu Xi 朱熹 and Li Jingde 黎靖德. 1973. *Zhuzi yulei: fu suoyin* 朱子語類：附索引. Taipei: Zhengzhong shuju.

Zhu Yu 朱彧 (ca.1075–1132). 1989. "Pingzhou ketan" 萍州可談. In *Pingzhou ketan; Houshan tancong* 萍州可談後山談叢. Shanghai: Shanghai guji chubanshe.

www.ingramcontent.com/pod-product-compliance
Lightning Source LLC
Chambersburg PA
CBHW082057090726
47909CB00011B/3066

* 9 7 8 0 2 3 1 2 0 8 9 7 0 *